New Perspectives on

MICROSOFT®
WINDOWS 2000
PROFESSIONAL

Comprehensive

JUNE PARSONS & DAN OJA
MediaTechnics

JOAN & PATRICK CAREY
Carey Associates

COURSE
TECHNOLOGY

Thomson Learning™

ONE MAIN STREET, CAMBRIDGE, MA 02142

Australia • Canada • Denmark • Japan • Mexico • New Zealand • Philippines
Puerto Rico • Singapore • South Africa • Spain • United Kingdom • United States

New Perspectives on Microsoft Windows 2000 Professional—Comprehensive is published by Course Technology.

Managing Editor	Greg Donald
Senior Editor	Donna Gridley
Senior Product Manager	Rachel Crapser
Production Editor	Catherine DiMassa
Developmental Editor	Mary Kemper
Product Managers	Catherine V. Donaldson
	Karen Shortill
Associate Product Manager	Melissa Dezotell
Editorial Assistant	Jill Kirn
Text Designer	Meral Dabcovich
Cover Art Designer	Douglas Goodman

PREFACE

The New Perspectives Series

About New Perspectives

Course Technology's **New Perspectives Series** is an integrated system of instruction that combines text and technology products to teach computer concepts, the Internet, and microcomputer applications. Users consistently praise this series for innovative pedagogy, use of interactive technology, creativity, accuracy, and supportive and engaging style.

How is the New Perspectives Series different from other series?

The **New Perspectives Series** distinguishes itself by **innovative technology**, from the renowned Course Labs to the state-of-the-art multimedia that is integrated with our Concepts texts. Other distinguishing features include **sound instructional design**, **proven pedagogy**, and **consistent quality**. Each tutorial has students learn features in the context of solving a realistic case problem rather than simply learning a laundry list of features. With the **New Perspectives Series**, instructors report that students have a complete, integrative learning experience that stays with them. They credit this high retention and competency to the fact that this series incorporates critical thinking and problem-solving with computer skills mastery. In addition, we work hard to ensure accuracy by using a multi-step quality assurance process during all stages of development. Instructors focus on teaching and students spend more time learning.

Choose the coverage that's right for you

New Perspectives applications books are available in the following categories:

Brief: approximately 150 pages long, two to four "Level I" tutorials, teaches basic application skills.

Introductory: approximately 300 pages long, four to seven tutorials, goes beyond the basic skills. These books often build out of the Brief book, adding two or three additional "Level II" tutorials.

Comprehensive: approximately 600 pages long, eight to twelve tutorials, all tutorials included in the Introductory text plus higher-level "Level III" topics. Also includes two Windows tutorials and three or four fully developed Additional Cases. The book you are holding is a Comprehensive book.

Advanced: approximately 400 pages long, cover topics similar to those in the Comprehensive books, but offer the highest-level coverage in the series. Advanced books assume students already know the basics, and therefore go into more depth at a more accelerated rate than the Comprehensive titles. Advanced books are ideal for a second, more technical course.

Office: approximately 800 pages long, covers all components of the Office suite as well as integrating the individual software packages with one another and the Internet.

Custom Books The New Perspectives Series offers you two ways to customize a New Perspectives text to fit your course exactly: *CourseKits*™ are two or more texts shrink-wrapped together, and offer significant price discounts. *Custom Editions*®, offer you flexibility in designing your concepts, Internet, and applications courses. You can build your own book by ordering a combination of topics bound together to cover only the subjects you want. There is no minimum order, and books are spiral bound. Contact your Course Technology sales representative for more information.

Brief
2-4 tutorials

Introductory
6 or 7 tutorials, or Brief + 2 or 3 more tutorials

Comprehensive
Introductory + 4 or 5 more tutorials. Includes Brief Windows tutorials and Additional Cases

Advanced
Quick Review of basics + in-depth, high-level coverage

Office
Office suite components + integration + Internet

Custom Editions
Choose from any of the above to build your own Custom Editions or CourseKits

What course is this book appropriate for?

New Perspectives on Microsoft Windows 2000 Professional—Comprehensive can be used in any course in which you want students to learn most of the important topics of Windows 2000 Professional, including organizing files with Windows Explorer, personalizing your windows environment, bringing the World Wide Web to the desktop, searching for information, working with Graphics, and Managing Windows 2000. This book assumes that students have had little or no prior computer experience.

Proven Pedagogy

CASE

Tutorial Case   Each tutorial begins with a problem presented in a case that is meaningful to students. The case turns the task of learning how to use an application into a problem-solving process.

45-minute Sessions.   Each tutorial is divided into sessions that can be completed in about 45 minutes to an hour. Sessions allow instructors to more accurately allocate time in their syllabus, and students to better manage their own study time.

1.
2.
3.

Step-by-Step Methodology   We make sure students can differentiate between what they are to do and what they are to read. Through numbered steps – clearly identified by a gray shaded background – students are constantly guided in solving the case problem. In addition, the numerous screen shots with callouts direct students' attention to what they should look at on the screen.

TROUBLE?

TROUBLE? Paragraphs   These paragraphs anticipate the mistakes or problems that students may have and help them continue with the tutorial.

Tutorial Tips ⊢

Tutorial Tips Page   This page, following the Table of Contents, offers students suggestions on how to effectively plan their study and lab time, what to do when they make a mistake, how to use the Reference Windows, MOUS grids, Quick Checks, and other features of the New Perspectives Series.

Read

"Read This Before You Begin" Page   Located opposite the first tutorial's opening page for each level of the text, the Read This Before You Begin Page helps introduce technology into the classroom. Technical considerations and assumptions about software are listed to save time and eliminate unnecessary aggravation. Notes about the Student Disks help instructors and students get the right files in the right places, so students get started on the right foot.

Quick Check Questions   Each session concludes with meaningful, conceptual Quick Check questions that test students' understanding of what they learned in the session. Answers to the Quick Check questions are provided at the end of each tutorial.

RW

Reference Windows   Reference Windows are succinct summaries of the most important tasks covered in a tutorial and they preview actions students will perform in the steps to follow.

TASK REFERENCE

Task Reference   Located as a table at the end of the book, the Task Reference contains a summary of how to perform common tasks using the most efficient method, as well as references to pages where the task is discussed in more detail.

End-of-Tutorial Review Assignments, Case Problems, and Lab Assignments   Review Assignments provide students with additional hands-on practice of the skills they learned in the tutorial using the same case presented in the tutorial. These Assignments are followed by three to four Case Problems that have approximately the same scope as the tutorial case but use a different scenario. In addition, some of the Review Assignments or Case Problems may include Exploration Exercises that challenge students encourage them to explore the capabilities of the program they are using, and/or further extend their knowledge. Finally, if a Course Lab accompanies a tutorial, Lab Assignments are included after the Case Problems.

File Finder Chart

This chart, located in the back of the book, visually explains how a student should set up their data disk, what files should go in what folders, and what they'll be saving the files as in the course of their work.

The Instructor's Resource Kit for this title contains:

- Electronic Instructor's Manual
- Figure Files
- Course Labs
- Sample Syllabus
- Make Data Disk program for Level I, Level II, and Level III tutorials (Tutorials 1–2, 3–6, and 7–11)

- Course Test Manager Testbank
- Course Test Manager Engine
- WebCT

These teaching tools come on CD-ROM. If you don't have access to a CD-ROM drive, contact your Course Technology customer service representative for more information.

The New Perspectives Teaching Tools Package

Electronic Instructor's Manual. Our Instructor's Manuals include tutorial overviews and outlines, technical notes, lecture notes, solutions, and Extra Case Problems. Many instructors use the Extra Case Problems for performance-based exams or extra credit projects. The Instructor's Manual is available as an electronic file, which you can get from the Instructor Resource Kit (IRK) CD-ROM or download it from **www.course.com**.

Data Files Data Files contain all of the data that students will use to complete the tutorials, Review Assignments, and Case Problems. A Readme file includes instructions for using the files. See the "Read This Before You Begin" page/pages for more information on Data Files.

Course Labs: Concepts Come to Life These highly interactive computer-based learning activities bring concepts to life with illustrations, animations, digital images, and simulations. The Labs guide students step-by-step, present them with Quick Check questions, let them explore on their own, test their comprehension, and provide printed feedback. Lab icons at the beginning of the tutorial and in the tutorial margins indicate when a topic has a corresponding Lab. Lab Assignments are included at the end of each relevant tutorial. The Labs available with this book and the tutorials in which they appear are:

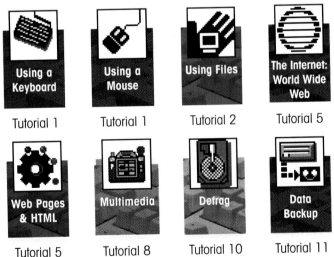

| Using a Keyboard | Using a Mouse | Using Files | The Internet: World Wide Web |
| Tutorial 1 | Tutorial 1 | Tutorial 2 | Tutorial 5 |

| Web Pages & HTML | Multimedia | Defrag | Data Backup |
| Tutorial 5 | Tutorial 8 | Tutorial 10 | Tutorial 11 |

Figure Files Many figures in the text are provided on the IRK CD-ROM to help illustrate key topics or concepts. Instructors can create traditional overhead transparencies by printing the figure files. Or they can create electronic slide shows by using the figures in a presentation program such as PowerPoint.

Course Test Manager: Testing and Practice at the Computer or on Paper Course Test Manager is cutting-edge, Windows-based testing software that helps instructors design and administer practice tests and actual examinations. Course Test Manager can automatically grade the tests students take at the computer and can generate statistical information on individual as well as group performance.

Online Companions: Dedicated to Keeping You and Your Students Up-To-Date Visit our faculty sites and student sites on the World Wide Web at *www.course.com*. Here instructors can browse this text's password-protected Faculty Online Companion to obtain an online Instructor's Manual, Solution Files, Data Files, and more. Students can also access this text's Student Online Companion, which contains Data files and all the links that the students will need to complete their tutorial assignments.

More innovative technology

Course CBT Enhance your students' Office 2000 classroom learning experience with self-paced computer-based training on CD-ROM. Course CBT engages students with interactive multimedia and hands-on simulations that reinforce and complement the concepts and skills covered in the textbook. All the content is aligned with the MOUS (Microsoft Office User Specialist) program, making it a great preparation tool for the certification exams. Course CBT also includes extensive pre- and post-assessments that test students' mastery of skills. These pre- and post-assessments automatically generate a "custom learning path" through the course that highlights only the topics students need help with.

SAM How well do your students really know Microsoft Office? SAM is a performance-based testing program that measures students' proficiency in Microsoft Office 2000. SAM is available for Office 2000 in either a live or simulated environment. You can use Course Assessment to place students into or out of courses, monitor their performance throughout a course, and help prepare them for the MOUS certification exams.

WebCT WebCT is a tool used to create Web-based educational environments and also uses WWW browsers as the interface for the course-building environment. The site is hosted on your school campus, allowing complete control over the information. WebCT has its own internal communication system, offering internal e-mail, a Bulletin Board, and a Chat room.

Course Technology offers pre-existing supplemental information to help in your WebCT class creation, such as a suggested Syllabus, Lecture Notes, Figures in the Book/Course Presenter, Student Downloads, and Test Banks in which you can schedule an exam, create reports, and more.

Acknowledgments

We want to thank all of the New Perspectives Team members for their support, guidance, and advice. Their insights and team spirit were invaluable. Thanks to our reviewers: Jody Baty, Ralph Brasure, Liberty University; and Sally Tiffany, Milwaukee Area Technical College. Our appreciation goes to Catherine DiMassa, Senior Production Editor. Thanks also to Greg Bigelow, John Bosco, Li-Juian Jang, and all the QA testers. We are grateful to Donna Gridley, Rachel Crapser, Christine Guivernau, Catherine Donaldson, Karen Shortill, Melissa Dezotell, and Jill Kirn for their editorial support, and to Karen Seitz for her marketing efforts.

June Parsons, Dan Oja, Joan & Patrick Carey

We would also like to acknowledge and thank our five little sons, Stephen, Michael, Peter, Thomas, and John Paul, for their unfailing love, cheer, and faith in us.

Joan & Patrick Carey

TABLE OF CONTENTS

Tutorial 4   WIN 2000 4.01

Personalizing Your Windows Environment
Changing Desktop Settings at Companions, Inc.

Tutorial 5   WIN 2000 5.01

Bringing the World Wide Web to the Desktop
Using Active Desktop at Highland Travel

Tutorial 6   WIN 2000 6.01

Searching for Information
Using the Search Feature to Locate Files for a Speechwriter

Microsoft Windows 2000 Professional—
Level III Tutorials   **WIN 2000 7.01**

Read This Before You Begin   WIN 2000 7.02

Tutorial 7   WIN 2000 7.03

Working with Graphics
Creating Advertisement Graphics at Kiana Ski Shop

Tutorial 8   WIN 2000 8.01

Object Linking and Embedding
Creating a Multimedia Document for the Jugglers Guild

Reference Window List

Tutorial Tips

These tutorials will help you learn about Microsoft Windows 2000 Professional. Please note that this book is about Windows 2000 Professional, for those who have Windows 2000 Millennium, you might notice some differences. The tutorials are designed to be worked through at a computer. Each tutorial is divided into sessions. Watch for the session headings, such as Session 1.1 and Session 1.2. Each session is designed to be completed in about 45 minutes, but take as much time as you need. It's also a good idea to take a break between sessions.

To use the tutorials effectively you, read the following questions and answers before you begin.

Where do I start?

Each tutorial begins with a case, which sets the scene for the tutorial and gives you background information to help you understand what you will be doing. Read the case before you go to the lab. In the lab, begin with the first session of a tutorial.

How do I know what to do on the computer?

Each session contains steps that you will perform on the computer to learn how to use Microsoft Windows 2000 Professional. Read the text that introduces each series of steps. The steps you need to do at a computer are numbered and are set against a shaded background. Read each step carefully and completely before you try it.

How do I know if I did the step correctly?

As you work, compare your computer screen with the corresponding figure in the tutorial. Don't worry if your screen display is somewhat different from the figure. The important parts of the screen display are labeled in each figure. Check to make sure these parts are on your screen.

What if I make a mistake?

Don't worry about making mistakes—they are part of the learning process. Paragraphs labeled "TROUBLE?" identify common problems and explain how to get back on track. Follow the steps in a TROUBLE? paragraph only if you are having the problem described. If you run into other problems:

- Carefully consider the current state of your system, the position of the pointer, and any messages on the screen.

- Complete the sentence, "Now I want to…" Be specific, because identifying your goal will help you rethink the steps you need to take to reach that goal.

- If you are working on a particular piece of software, consult the Help system.

- If the suggestions above don't solve your problem, consult your technical support person for assistance.

How do I use the Reference Windows?

Reference Windows summarize the procedures you will learn in the tutorial steps. Do not complete the actions in the Reference Windows when you are working through the tutorial. Instead, refer to the Reference Windows while you are working on the assignments at the end of the tutorial.

How can I test my understanding of the material I learned in the tutorial?

At the end of each session, you can answer the Quick Check questions. The answers for the Quick Checks are at the end of that tutorial.

After you have completed the entire tutorial, you should complete the Review Assignments and Case Problems. They are carefully structured so that you will review what you have learned and then apply your knowledge to new situations.

What if I can't remember how to do something?

You should refer to the Task Reference at the end of the book; it summarizes how to accomplish tasks using the most efficient method.

Before you begin the tutorials, you should know the basics about your computer's operating system. You should also know how to use the menus, dialog boxes, Help system, and My Computer.

Now that you've read Tutorial Tips, you are ready to begin.

New Perspectives on

MICROSOFT®

WINDOWS® 2000

PROFESSIONAL

Read This Before You Begin

To the Student

Make Data Disk Program

To complete the Level I tutorials, Review Assignments, and Projects, you need three Data Disks. Your instructor will either provide you with Data Disks or ask you to make your own.

If you are making your own Data Disks you will need three blank, formatted high-density disks and access to the Make Data Disk program. If you want to install the Make Data Disk program to your home computer, you can obtain it from your instructor or from the Web. To download the Make Data Disk program from the Web, go to www.course.com, click Data Disks, and follow the instructions on the screen.

To install the Make Data Disk program, select and click the file you just downloaded from www.course.com, 6548-9.exe. Follow the onscreen instructions to complete the installation. If you have any trouble obtaining or installing the Make Data Disk program, ask your instructor or technical support person for assistance.

Once you have obtained and installed the Make Data Disk program, you can use it to create your Data Disks according to the steps in the tutorials.

Course Labs

The Level I tutorials in this book feature three interactive Course Labs to help you understand Using a Keyboard, Using a Mouse, and Using Files concepts. There are Lab Assignments at the end of Tutorials 1 and 2 that relate to these Labs. To start a Lab, click the **Start** button on the Windows 2000 taskbar, point to **Programs**, point to **Course Labs**, point to **New Perspectives Course Labs**, and click the name of the Lab you want to use.

Using Your Own Computer

If you are going to work through this book using your own computer, you need:

■ **Computer System** Microsoft Windows 2000 Professional must be installed on a local hard drive or on a network drive. This book is about Windows 2000 Professional—for those who have Windows 2000 Millennium, you might notice some differences.

■ **Data Disks** You will not be able to complete the tutorials or exercises in this book using your own computer until you have your Data Disks. See "Make Data Disk Program" above for details on obtaining your Data Disks.

■ **Course Labs** See your instructor or technical support person to obtain the Course Lab software for use on your own computer.

Visit Our World Wide Web Site

Additional materials designed especially for you are available on the World Wide Web. Go to http://www.course.com.

To the Instructor

The Make Data Disk Program and Course Labs for this title are available in the Instructor's Resource Kit for this title. Follow the instructions in the Help file on the CD-ROM to install the programs to your network or standalone computer. For information on using the Make Data Disk Program or the Course Labs, see the "To the Student" section above. Students will be switching the default installation settings to Web style in Tutorial 2. You are granted a license to copy the Data Files and Course Labs to any computer or computer network used by students who have purchased this book.

In this tutorial you will:

- Start and shut down Windows 2000

- Identify the objects on the Windows 2000 desktop

- Practice mouse functions

- Run software programs, switch between them, and close them

- Identify and use the controls in a window

- Use Windows 2000 controls such as menus, toolbars, list boxes, scroll bars, option buttons, tabs, and check boxes

- Explore the Windows 2000 Help system

LABS

Using a Keyboard

Using a Mouse

EXPLORING THE BASICS

Investigating the Windows 2000 Operating System

CASE

Your First Day on the Computer

You walk into the computer lab and sit down at a desk. There's a computer in front of you, and you find yourself staring dubiously at the screen. Where to start? As if in answer to your question, your friend Steve Laslow appears.

"You start with the operating system," says Steve. Noticing your puzzled look, Steve explains that the **operating system** is software that helps the computer carry out operating tasks such as displaying information on the computer screen and saving data on your disks. (Software refers to the **programs**, or **applications**, that a computer uses to perform tasks.) Your computer uses the **Microsoft Windows 2000 Professional** operating system—Windows 2000, for short.

Steve explains that much of the software available for Windows 2000 has a standard graphical user interface. This means that once you have learned how to use one Windows program, such as Microsoft Word word-processing software, you are well on your way to under-standing how to use other Windows software. Windows 2000 lets you use more than one program at a time, so you can easily switch between them—between your word-processing software and your appointment book software, for example. Finally, Windows 2000 makes it very easy to access the **Internet**, the worldwide collection of com-puters connected to one another to enable communication. All in all, Windows 2000 makes your computer effective and easy to use.

Steve recommends that you get started right away by starting Microsoft Windows 2000 and practicing some basic skills.

Starting Windows 2000

Using a Keyboard

Windows 2000 automatically starts when you turn on the computer. Depending on the way your computer is set up, you might be asked to enter your username and password.

To start Windows 2000:

1. Turn on your computer.

TROUBLE? If you are asked to select an operating system, do not take action. Windows 2000 will start automatically after a designated number of seconds. If it does not, ask your technical support person for help.

TROUBLE? If prompted to do so, type your assigned username and press the Tab key. Then type your password and press the Enter key to continue.

TROUBLE? If this is the first time you have started your computer with Windows 2000, messages might appear on your screen informing you that Windows is setting up components of your computer. If the Getting Started with Windows 2000 box appears, press and hold down the Alt key on your keyboard and then, while you hold down the Alt key, press the F4 key. The box closes.

After a moment, Windows 2000 starts. Windows 2000 has a **graphical user interface** (**GUI,** pronounced "gooey"), which uses **icons,** or pictures of familiar objects, such as file folders and documents, to represent items in your computer such as programs or files. Microsoft Windows 2000 gets its name from the rectangular work areas, called "windows," that appear on your screen as you work (although no windows should be open right now).

The Windows 2000 Desktop

In Windows terminology, the area displayed on your screen when Windows 2000 starts represents a **desktop**—a workspace for projects and the tools needed to manipulate those projects. When you first start a computer, it uses **default** settings, those preset by the operating system. The default desktop, for example, has a plain blue background. However, Microsoft designed Windows 2000 so that you can easily change the appearance of the desktop. You can, for example, add color, patterns, images, and text to the desktop background.

Many institutions design customized desktops for their computers. Figure 1-1 shows the default Windows 2000 desktop and two other examples of desktops, one designed for a business, North Pole Novelties, and one designed for a school, the University of Colorado. Although your desktop might not look exactly like any of the examples in Figure 1-1, you should be able to locate objects on your screen similar to those in Figure 1-1. Look at your screen and locate the objects labeled in Figure 1-1. The objects on your screen might appear larger or smaller than those in Figure 1-1, depending on your monitor's settings.

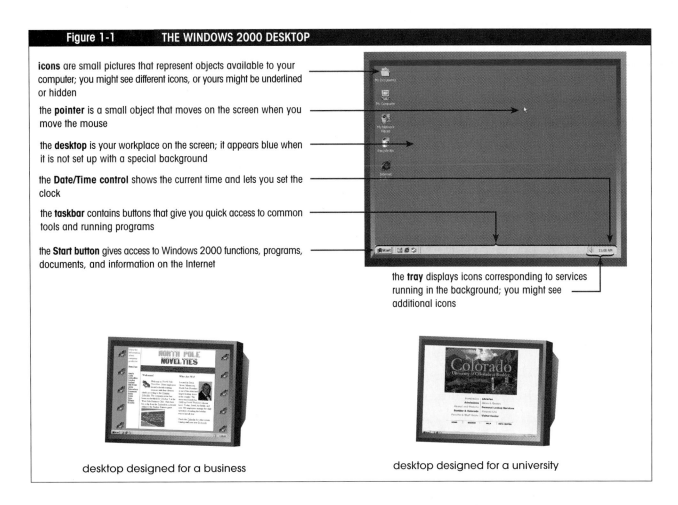

| Figure 1-1 | THE WINDOWS 2000 DESKTOP |

icons are small pictures that represent objects available to your computer; you might see different icons, or yours might be underlined or hidden

the **pointer** is a small object that moves on the screen when you move the mouse

the **desktop** is your workplace on the screen; it appears blue when it is not set up with a special background

the **Date/Time control** shows the current time and lets you set the clock

the **taskbar** contains buttons that give you quick access to common tools and running programs

the **Start button** gives access to Windows 2000 functions, programs, documents, and information on the Internet

the **tray** displays icons corresponding to services running in the background; you might see additional icons

desktop designed for a business

desktop designed for a university

If the screen goes blank or starts to display a moving design, press any key to restore the Windows 2000 desktop.

Using a Pointing Device

Using a Mouse

A **pointing device** helps you interact with objects on the screen. Pointing devices come in many shapes and sizes; some are designed to ensure that your hand won't suffer fatigue while using them. Some are directly attached to your computer via a cable, whereas others function like a TV remote control and allow you to access your computer without being right next to it. Figure 1-2 shows examples of common pointing devices.

The most common pointing device is called a **mouse**, so this book uses that term. If you are using a different pointing device, such as a trackball, substitute that device whenever you see the term "mouse." Because Windows 2000 uses a graphical user interface, you need to know how to use the mouse to manipulate the objects on the screen. In this session you will learn about pointing and clicking. In Session 1.2 you will learn how to use the mouse to drag objects.

You can also interact with objects by using the keyboard; however, the mouse is more convenient for most tasks, so the tutorials in this book assume you are using one.

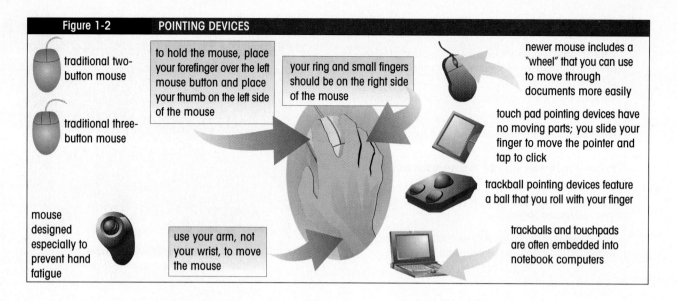

Figure 1-2   POINTING DEVICES

- traditional two-button mouse
- traditional three-button mouse
- mouse designed especially to prevent hand fatigue

to hold the mouse, place your forefinger over the left mouse button and place your thumb on the left side of the mouse

your ring and small fingers should be on the right side of the mouse

use your arm, not your wrist, to move the mouse

newer mouse includes a "wheel" that you can use to move through documents more easily

touch pad pointing devices have no moving parts; you slide your finger to move the pointer and tap to click

trackball pointing devices feature a ball that you roll with your finger

trackballs and touchpads are often embedded into notebook computers

Pointing

You use a pointing device to move the pointer over objects on the desktop. The pointer is usually shaped like an arrow ▸ , although it can change shape depending on where it is on the screen and on what tasks you are performing. Most computer users place the mouse on a **mouse pad**, a flat piece of rubber that helps the mouse move smoothly. As you move the mouse on the mouse pad, the pointer on the screen moves in a corresponding direction.

You begin most Windows operations by positioning the pointer over a specific part of the screen. This is called **pointing**.

To move the pointer:

1. Position your right index finger over the left mouse button, as shown in Figure 1-2, but don't click yet. Lightly grasp the sides of the mouse with your thumb and little fingers.

   TROUBLE? If you want to use the mouse with your left hand, ask your instructor or technical support person to help you use the Control Panel to swap the functions of the left and right mouse buttons. Be sure to find out how to change back to the right-handed mouse setting, so that you can reset the mouse each time you are finished in the lab.

2. Place the mouse on the mouse pad and then move the mouse. Watch the movement of the pointer.

   TROUBLE? If you run out of room to move your mouse, lift the mouse and place it in the middle of the mouse pad. Notice that the pointer does not move when the mouse is not in contact with the mouse pad.

When you position the mouse pointer over certain objects, such as the objects on the taskbar, a "tip" appears. These "tips" are called **ScreenTips**, and they tell you the purpose or function of an object.

To view ScreenTips:

1. Use the mouse to point to the **Start** button ![Start], but don't click it. After a few seconds, you see the tip "Click here to begin," as shown in Figure 1-3.

   TROUBLE? If the Start button and taskbar don't appear, point to the bottom of the screen. They will then appear.

Figure 1-3   **VIEWING SCREENTIPS**

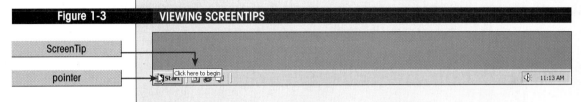

ScreenTip

pointer

2. Point to the time on the right end of the taskbar. Notice that today's date (or the date to which your computer's time clock is set) appears.

Clicking

Clicking is when you press a mouse button and immediately release it. Clicking sends a signal to your computer that you want to perform an action on the object you click. In Windows 2000 most actions are performed using the left mouse button. If you are told to click an object, click it with the left mouse button, unless instructed otherwise.

When you click the Start button, the Start menu appears. A **menu** is a list of options that you use to complete tasks. The **Start menu** provides you with access to programs, documents, and much more. Try clicking the Start button to open the Start menu.

To open the Start menu:

1. Point to the **Start** button ![Start].

2. Click the left mouse button. An arrow ▶ following an option on the Start menu indicates that you can view additional choices by navigating a **submenu**, a menu extending from the main menu. See Figure 1-4.

Figure 1-4   **START MENU**

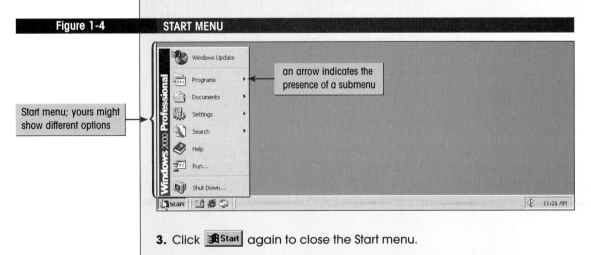

an arrow indicates the presence of a submenu

Start menu; yours might show different options

3. Click ![Start] again to close the Start menu.

Next you'll learn how to select items on a submenu.

Selecting

In Windows 2000, pointing and clicking are often used to **select** an object, in other words, to choose it as the object you want to work with. Windows 2000 shows you which object is selected by highlighting it, usually by changing the object's color, putting a box around it, or making the object appear to be pushed in, as shown in Figure 1-5.

Figure 1-5	SELECTED OBJECTS

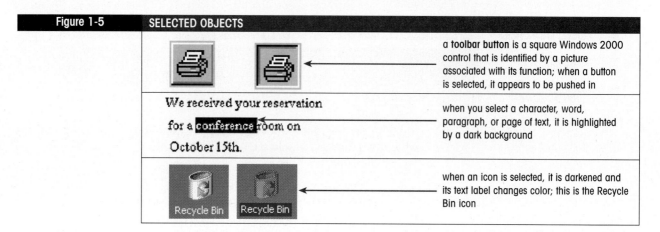

a **toolbar button** is a square Windows 2000 control that is identified by a picture associated with its function; when a button is selected, it appears to be pushed in

when you select a character, word, paragraph, or page of text, it is highlighted by a dark background

when an icon is selected, it is darkened and its text label changes color; this is the Recycle Bin icon

In Windows 2000, depending on your computer's settings, some objects are selected when you simply point to them, others when you click them. Practice selecting the Programs option on the Start menu to open the Programs submenu.

To select an option on a menu:

1. Click the **Start** button and notice how it appears to be pushed in, indicating it is selected.

2. Point to (but don't click) the **Programs** option. After a short pause, the Programs submenu opens, and the Programs option is highlighted to indicate it is selected. See Figure 1-6.

Figure 1-6	PROGRAMS SUBMENU

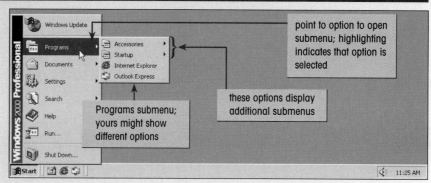

point to option to open submenu; highlighting indicates that option is selected

these options display additional submenus

Programs submenu; yours might show different options

TROUBLE? If a submenu other than the Programs menu opens, you selected the wrong option. Move the mouse so that the pointer points to Programs.

TROUBLE? If the Programs option doesn't appear, your Start menu might have too many options to fit on the screen. If that is the case, a double arrow ⌄ appears at the top or bottom of the Start menu. Click first the top and then the bottom arrow to view additional Start menu options until you locate the Programs menu option, and then point to it.

3. Now close the Start menu by clicking 🞂Start again.

You return to the desktop.

Right-Clicking

Pointing devices were originally designed with a single button, so the term "clicking" had only one meaning: you pressed that button. Innovations in technology, however, led to the addition of a second and even a third button (and more recently, options such as a wheel) that expanded the pointing device's capability. More recent software—especially that designed for Windows 2000—takes advantage of the additional buttons, especially the right button. However, the term "clicking" continues to refer to the left button; clicking an object with the *right* button is called **right-clicking**.

In Windows 2000, right-clicking both selects an object and opens its **shortcut menu**, a list of options directly related to the object you right-clicked. You can right-click practically any object—the Start button, a desktop icon, the taskbar, and even the desktop itself—to view options associated with that object. For example, the first desktop shown in Figure 1-7 illustrates what happens when you click the Start button with the left mouse button to open the Start menu. Clicking the Start button with the right button, however, opens the Start button's shortcut menu, as shown in the second desktop.

Figure 1-7	CLICKING WITH THE LEFT AND RIGHT MOUSE BUTTONS

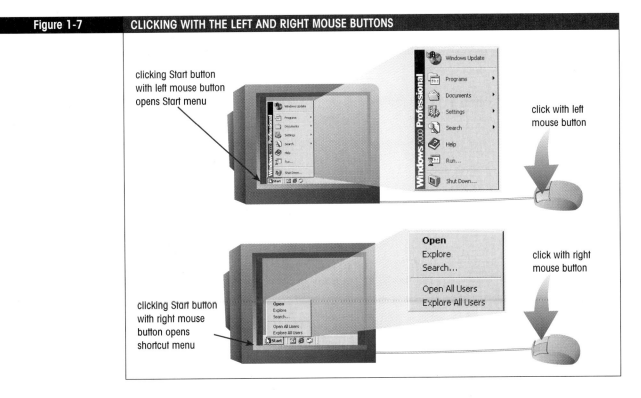

Try using right-clicking to open the shortcut menu for the Start button.

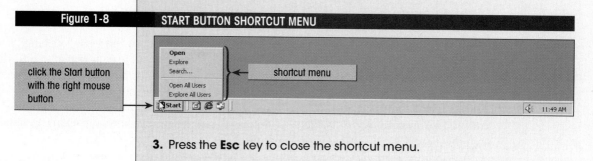

To right-click an object:

1. Position the pointer over the Start button.

2. Right-click the **Start** button [Start]. The shortcut menu that opens offers a list of options available to the Start button.

TROUBLE? If you are using a trackball or a mouse with three buttons or a wheel, make sure you click the button on the far right, not the one in the middle.

TROUBLE? If your menu looks slightly different from the one in Figure 1-8, don't worry. Different systems will have different options.

Figure 1-8	START BUTTON SHORTCUT MENU

click the Start button with the right mouse button

Open
Explore
Search...
Open All Users
Explore All Users
← shortcut menu

Start   11:49 AM

3. Press the **Esc** key to close the shortcut menu.

You again return to the desktop.

Starting and Closing a Program

To use a program, such as a word-processing program, you must first start it. With Windows 2000 you usually start a program by clicking the Start button and then you locate and click the program's name in the submenus.

The Reference Window below explains how to start a program. Don't do the steps in the Reference Windows as you go through the tutorials; they are for your later reference.

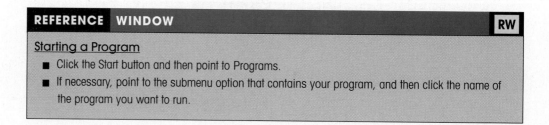

REFERENCE WINDOW   **RW**

Starting a Program
- Click the Start button and then point to Programs.
- If necessary, point to the submenu option that contains your program, and then click the name of the program you want to run.

Windows 2000 includes an easy-to-use word-processing program called WordPad. Suppose you want to start the WordPad program and use it to write a letter or report. You open Windows 2000 programs from the Start menu. Programs are usually located on the Programs submenu or on one of its submenus. To start WordPad, for example, you select the Programs and Accessories submenus.

If you can't locate an item that is supposed to be on a menu, it is most likely temporarily hidden. Windows 2000 menus use a feature called **Personalized Menus** that hides menu options you use infrequently. You can access hidden menu options by pointing to the menu name and then clicking the double arrow ✯ (sometimes called a "chevron") at the bottom of the menu. You can also access the hidden options by holding the pointer over the menu name.

To start the WordPad program from the Start menu:

1. Click the **Start** button [Start] to open the Start menu.

2. Point to **Programs**. The Programs submenu appears.

3. Point to **Accessories**. The Accessories submenu appears. Figure 1-9 shows the open menus.

   TROUBLE? If a different menu opens, you might have moved the mouse diagonally so that a different submenu opened. Move the pointer to the right across the Programs option, and then move it up or down to point to Accessories. Once you're more comfortable moving the mouse, you'll find that you can eliminate this problem by moving the mouse quickly.

   TROUBLE? If WordPad doesn't appear on the Accessories submenu, continue to point to Accessories until WordPad appears.

Figure 1-9 **START MENU**

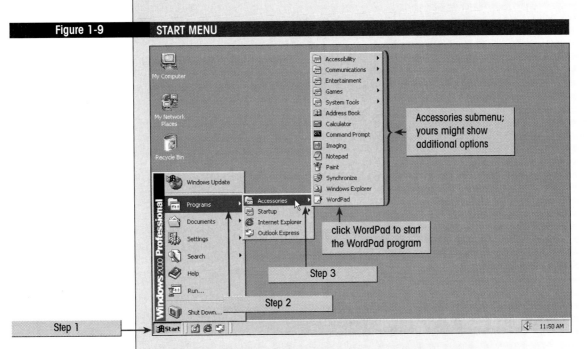

4. Click **WordPad**. The WordPad program opens, as shown in Figure 1-10. If the WordPad window fills the entire screen, don't worry. You will learn how to manipulate windows in Session 1.2.

Figure 1-10   **THE WORDPAD PROGRAM**

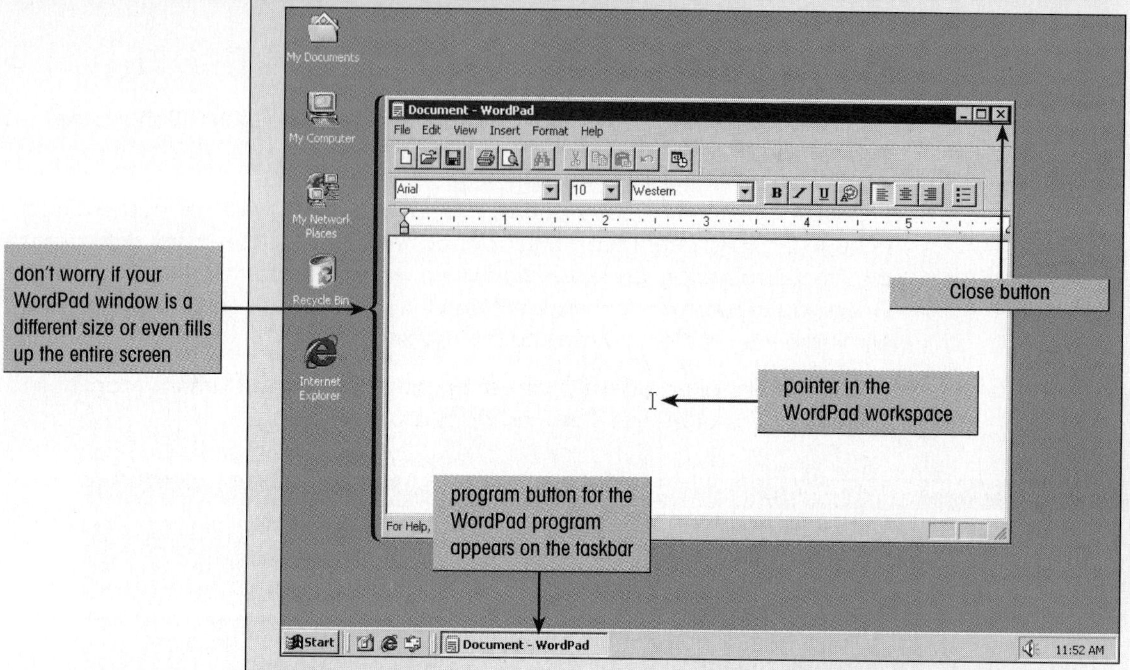

don't worry if your WordPad window is a different size or even fills up the entire screen

Close button

pointer in the WordPad workspace

program button for the WordPad program appears on the taskbar

When a program is started, it is said to be **open** or **running**. A **program button** appears on the taskbar for each open program. You click program buttons to switch between open programs. When you are finished using a program, click the Close button ✕.

To exit the WordPad program:

1. Click the **Close** button ✕ . See Figure 1-10. You return to the Windows 2000 desktop.

Running Multiple Programs

One of the most useful features of Windows 2000 is its ability to run multiple programs at the same time. This feature, known as **multitasking**, allows you to work on more than one project at a time and to switch quickly between projects. For example, you can start WordPad and leave it running while you then start the Paint program.

To run WordPad and Paint at the same time:

1. Start WordPad again and then click the **Start** button 🏁Start again.

2. Point to **Programs** and then point to **Accessories**.

3. Click **Paint**. The Paint program opens, as shown in Figure 1-11. Now two programs are running at the same time.

TROUBLE? If the Paint program fills the entire screen, don't worry. You will learn how to manipulate windows in Session 1.2.

Figure 1-11	THE PAINT PROGRAM

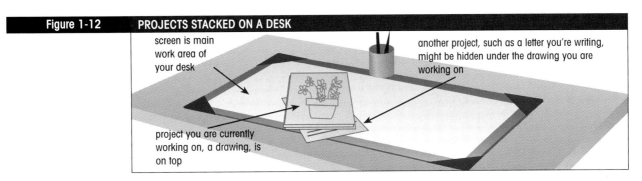

What happened to WordPad? The WordPad program button is still on the taskbar, so even if you can't see it, WordPad is still running. You can imagine that it is stacked behind the Paint program, as shown in Figure 1-12. Paint is the active program because it is the one with which you are currently working.

Figure 1-12	PROJECTS STACKED ON A DESK

screen is main work area of your desk

another project, such as a letter you're writing, might be hidden under the drawing you are working on

project you are currently working on, a drawing, is on top

Switching Between Programs

The easiest way to switch between programs is to use the buttons on the taskbar.

To switch between WordPad and Paint:

1. Click the button labeled **Document - WordPad** on the taskbar. The Document WordPad button now looks as if it has been pushed in, to indicate that it is the active program, and WordPad moves to the front.
2. Next, click the button labeled **untitled - Paint** on the taskbar to switch to the Paint program.

The Paint program is again the active program.

Accessing the Desktop from the Quick Launch Toolbar

The Windows 2000 taskbar, as you've seen, displays buttons for programs currently running. It also can contain **toolbars**, sets of buttons that give single-click access to programs or documents that aren't running or open. In its default state, the Windows 2000 taskbar displays the **Quick Launch toolbar**, which gives quick access to Web programs and to the desktop. Your taskbar might contain additional toolbars, or none at all.

When you are running more than one program but you want to return to the desktop, perhaps to use one of the desktop icons such as My Computer, you can do so by using one of the Quick Launch toolbar buttons. Clicking the Show Desktop button 📄 returns you to the desktop. The open programs are not closed; they are simply made inactive and reduced to buttons on the taskbar.

To return to the desktop:

1. Click the **Show Desktop** button 📄 on the Quick Launch toolbar. The desktop appears, and both the Paint and WordPad programs are temporarily inactive. See Figure 1-13.

   TROUBLE? If the Quick Launch toolbar doesn't appear on your taskbar, right-click the taskbar, point to Toolbars, and then click Quick Launch and try Step 1 again.

| Figure 1-13 | ACCESSING THE DESKTOP |

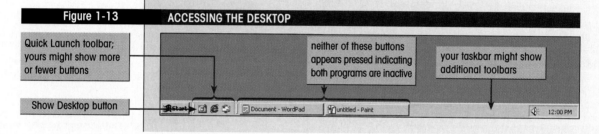

Quick Launch toolbar; yours might show more or fewer buttons

neither of these buttons appears pressed indicating both programs are inactive

your taskbar might show additional toolbars

Show Desktop button

Closing Inactive Programs from the Taskbar

It is good practice to close each program when you are finished using it. Each program uses computer resources, such as memory, so Windows 2000 works more efficiently when only the programs you need are open. You've already seen how to close an open program using the Close button ❌ . You can also close a program, whether active or inactive, by using the shortcut menu associated with the program button on the taskbar.

To close WordPad and Paint using the program button shortcut menus:

1. Right-click the **untitled – Paint** button on the taskbar. To right-click something, remember that you click it with the right mouse button. The shortcut menu for that program button opens. See Figure 1-14.

2. Click **Close**. The button labeled "untitled – Paint" disappears from the taskbar, indicating that the Paint program is closed.

3. Right-click the **Document – WordPad** button on the taskbar, and then click **Close**. The WordPad button disappears from the taskbar.

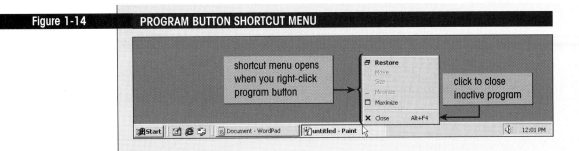

| Figure 1-14 | PROGRAM BUTTON SHORTCUT MENU |

Shutting Down Windows 2000

It is very important to shut down Windows 2000 before you turn off the computer. If you turn off your computer without correctly shutting down, you might lose data and damage your files.

You should typically use the "Shut Down" option when you want to turn off your computer. However, your school might prefer that you select the Log Off option in the Shut Down Windows dialog box. This option logs you out of Windows 2000, leaves the computer turned on, and allows another user to log on without restarting the computer. Check with your instructor or technical support person for the preferred method at your lab.

To shut down Windows 2000:

1. Click the **Start** button ![Start] on the taskbar to display the Start menu.

2. Click the **Shut Down** menu option. A box titled "Shut Down Windows" opens.

   TROUBLE? If you can't see the Shut Down menu option, your Start menu has more options than your screen can display. A double arrow ⅋ appears at the bottom of the Start menu. Click this button until the Shut Down menu option appears, and then click Shut Down.

   TROUBLE? If you are supposed to log off rather than shut down, click the Log Off option instead and follow your school's logoff procedure.

3. Make sure the **Shut Down** option appears in the box shown in Figure 1-15.

   TROUBLE? If "Shut down" does not appear, click the arrow to the right of the box. A list of options appears. Click Shut Down.

| Figure 1-15 | SHUTTING DOWN |

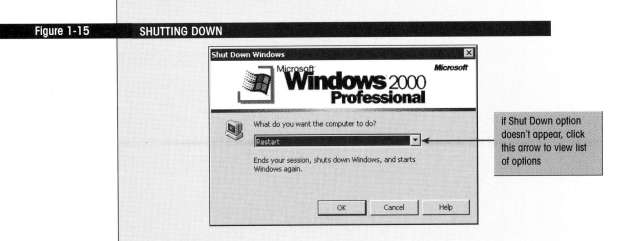

4. Click the **OK** button.

5. Wait until you see a message indicating it is safe to turn off your computer. If your lab staff has requested you to switch off your computer after shutting down, do so now. Otherwise leave the computer running. Some computers turn themselves off automatically.

Session 1.1 QUICK CHECK

1. What is the purpose of the taskbar?

2. The _____ feature of Windows 2000 allows you to run more than one program at a time.

3. The _____ is a list of options that provides you with access to programs, documents, submenus, and more.

4. What should you do if you are trying to move the pointer to the left edge of your screen, but your mouse bumps into the keyboard?

5. Even if you can't see an open program on your desktop, the program might be running. How can you tell if a program is running?

6. Why is it good practice to close each program when you are finished using it?

7. Why should you shut down Windows 2000 before you turn off your computer?

SESSION 1.2

In this session you will learn how to use many of the Windows 2000 controls to manipulate windows and programs. You will also learn how to change the size and shape of a window; how to move a window; and how to use menus, dialog boxes, tabs, buttons, and lists to specify how you want a program to carry out a task.

Anatomy of a Window

When you run a program in Windows 2000, it appears in a window. A **window** is a rectangular area of the screen that contains a program or data. Windows, spelled with an uppercase "W," is the name of the Microsoft operating system. The word "window" with a lowercase "w" refers to one of the rectangular areas on the screen. A window also contains controls for manipulating the window and for using the program. Figure 1-16 describes the controls you are likely to see in most windows.

Figure 1-16	WINDOW CONTROLS
CONTROL	**DESCRIPTION**
Menu bar	Contains the titles of menus, such as File, Edit, and Help
Sizing buttons	Let you enlarge, shrink, or close a window
Status bar	Provides you with messages relevant to the task you are performing
Title bar	Contains the window title and basic window control buttons
Toolbar	Contains buttons that provide you with shortcuts to common menu commands
Window title	Identifies the program and document contained in the window
Workspace	Part of the window you use to enter your work—to enter text, draw pictures, set up calculations, and so on

WordPad is a good example of a typical window, so try starting WordPad and identifying these controls in the WordPad window.

To look at window controls:

1. Make sure Windows 2000 is running and you are at the Windows 2000 desktop.

2. Start WordPad.

TROUBLE? To start WordPad, click the Start button, point to Programs, point to Accessories, and then click WordPad.

3. On your screen, identify the controls labeled in Figure 1-17. Don't worry if your window fills the entire screen or is a different size. You'll learn to change window size shortly.

Figure 1-17	WORDPAD WINDOW CONTROLS

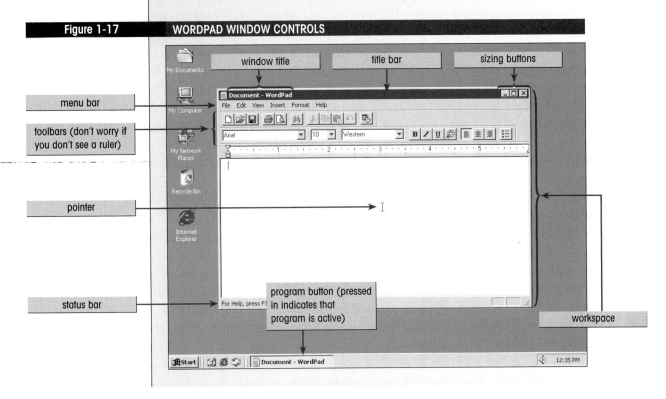

Manipulating a Window

There are three buttons located on the right side of the title bar. You are already familiar with the Close button. The Minimize button ■ hides the window so that only its program button is visible on the taskbar. The other button changes name and function depending on the status of the window (it either maximizes the window or restores it to a predefined size). Figure 1-18 shows how these buttons work.

Minimizing a Window

The Minimize button hides a window so that only the button on the taskbar remains visible. You can use the Minimize button when you want to temporarily hide a window but keep the program running.

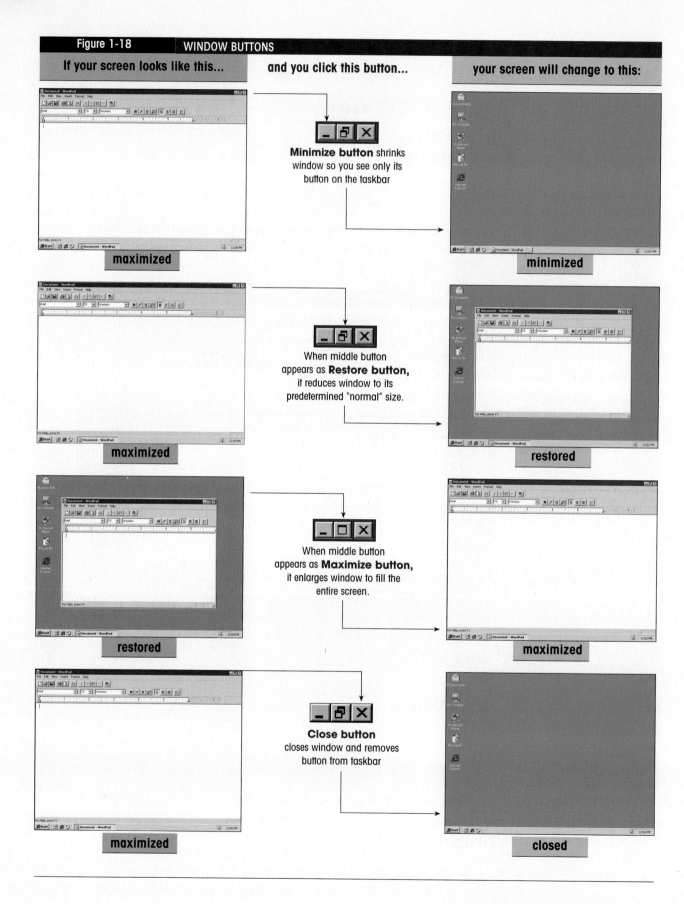

Figure 1-18   **WINDOW BUTTONS**

If your screen looks like this...   **and you click this button...**   **your screen will change to this:**

maximized

Minimize button shrinks window so you see only its button on the taskbar

minimized

maximized

When middle button appears as **Restore button,** it reduces window to its predetermined "normal" size.

restored

restored

When middle button appears as **Maximize button,** it enlarges window to fill the entire screen.

maximized

maximized

Close button closes window and removes button from taskbar

closed

To minimize the WordPad window:

1. Click the **Minimize** button ![minimize]. The WordPad window shrinks so that only the Document - WordPad button on the taskbar is visible.

TROUBLE? If you accidentally clicked the Close button and closed the window, use the Start button to start WordPad again.

Redisplaying a Window

You can redisplay a minimized window by clicking the program's button on the taskbar. When you redisplay a window, it becomes the active window.

To redisplay the WordPad window:

1. Click the **Document - WordPad** button on the taskbar. The WordPad window is restored to its previous size. The Document - WordPad button looks pushed in as a visual clue that WordPad is now the active window.

2. The taskbar button provides another means of switching a window between its minimized and active state: Click the **Document – WordPad** button on the taskbar again to minimize the window.

3. Click the **Document – WordPad** button once more to redisplay the window.

Maximizing a Window

The Maximize button enlarges a window so that it fills the entire screen. You will probably do most of your work using maximized windows because they allow you to see more of your program and data.

To maximize the WordPad window:

1. Click the **Maximize** button ![maximize] on the WordPad title bar.

TROUBLE? If the window is already maximized, it will fill the entire screen, and the Maximize button won't appear. Instead, you'll see the Restore button ![restore]. Skip Step 1.

Restoring a Window

The Restore button ![restore] reduces the window so it is smaller than the entire screen. This is useful if you want to see more than one window at a time. Also, because of its smaller size, you can drag the window to another location on the screen or change its dimensions.

To restore a window:

1. Click the **Restore** button ![restore] on the WordPad title bar. Notice that once a window is restored, ![restore] changes to the Maximize button ![maximize].

Moving a Window

You can use the mouse to move a window to a new position on the screen. When you click an object and hold down the mouse button while moving the mouse, you are said to be **dragging** the object. You can move objects on the screen by dragging them to a new location. If you want to move a window, you drag its title bar. You cannot move a maximized window.

To drag the WordPad window to a new location:

1. Position the mouse pointer on the WordPad window title bar.
2. While you hold down the left mouse button, move the mouse to drag the window. A rectangle representing the window moves as you move the mouse.
3. Position the rectangle anywhere on the screen, then release the left mouse button. The WordPad window appears in the new location.
4. Now drag the WordPad window to the upper-left corner of the screen.

Changing the Size of a Window

You can also use the mouse to change the size of a window. Notice the sizing handle at the lower-right corner of the window. The **sizing handle** provides a visible control for changing the size of a window.

To change the size of the WordPad window:

1. Position the pointer over the sizing handle . The pointer changes to a diagonal arrow .
2. While holding down the mouse button, drag the sizing handle down and to the right.
3. Release the mouse button. Now the window is larger.
4. Practice using the sizing handle to make the WordPad window larger or smaller, and then maximize the WordPad window.

You can also drag the window borders left, right, up, or down to change a window's size.

Using Program Menus

Most Windows programs use menus to organize the program's menu options. The menu bar is typically located at the top of the program window and shows the titles of menus such as File, Edit, and Help.

Windows menus are relatively standardized—most Windows programs include similar menu options. It's easy to learn new programs, because you can make a pretty good guess about which menu contains the option you want.

Selecting Options from a Menu

When you click any menu title, choices for that menu appear below the menu bar. These choices are referred to as **menu options** or **commands**. To select a menu option, you click it. For example, the File menu is a standard feature in most Windows programs and contains the options typically related to working with a file: creating, opening, saving, and printing a file or document.

To select the Print Preview menu option on the File menu:

1. Click **File** on the WordPad menu bar to display the File menu. See Figure 1-19.

   TROUBLE? If you open a menu but decide not to select any of the menu options, you can close the menu by clicking its title again.

Figure 1-19	FILE MENU

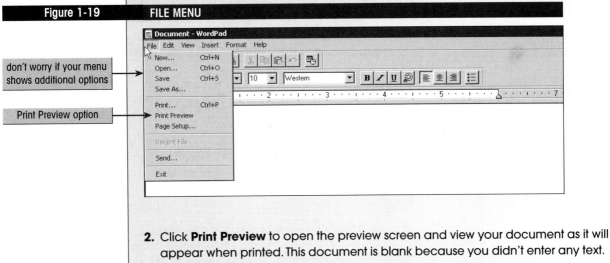

don't worry if your menu shows additional options

Print Preview option

2. Click **Print Preview** to open the preview screen and view your document as it will appear when printed. This document is blank because you didn't enter any text.

   TROUBLE? If your computer is not set up with printer access, you will not be able to open Print Preview. Ask your instructor or technical support person for help.

3. After examining the screen, click the button with the text label "Close" to return to your document.

   TROUBLE? If you close WordPad by mistake, restart it.

Not all menu options immediately carry out an action—some show submenus or ask you for more information about what you want to do. The menu gives you hints about what to expect when you select an option. These hints are sometimes referred to as **menu conventions**. Figure 1-20 describes the Windows 2000 menu conventions.

Figure 1-20	MENU CONVENTIONS
CONVENTION	**DESCRIPTION**
Check mark	Indicates a toggle, or "on-off" switch (like a light switch) that is either checked (turned on) or not checked (turned off)
Ellipsis	Three dots that indicate you must make additional selections after you select that option. Options without dots do not require additional choices—they take effect as soon as you click them. If an option is followed by an ellipsis, a dialog box opens that allows you to enter specifications for how you want a task carried out.
Triangular arrow	Indicates the presence of a submenu. When you point at a menu option that has a triangular arrow, a submenu automatically appears.
Grayed-out option	Option that is not available. For example, a graphics program might display the Text Toolbar option in gray if there is no text in the graphic to work with.
Keyboard shortcut	A key or combination of keys that you can press to activate the menu option without actually opening the menu
Double arrow	Indicates that additional menu options are available; click the double arrow to access them

Figure 1-21 shows examples of these menu conventions.

Figure 1-21   **EXAMPLES OF MENU CONVENTIONS**

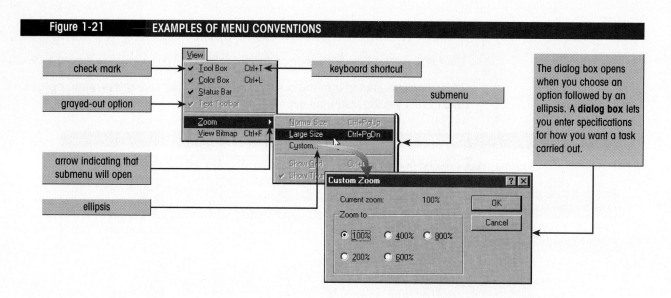

Using **Toolbars**

Although you can usually perform all program commands using menus, toolbar buttons provide convenient one-click access to frequently used commands. For most Windows 2000 functions, there is usually more than one way to accomplish a task. To simplify your introduction to Windows 2000 in this tutorial, we will usually show you only one method for performing a task. As you become more accomplished at using Windows 2000, you can explore alternate methods.

In Session 1.1 you learned that Windows 2000 programs include ScreenTips, which indicate the purpose and function of a tool. Now is a good time to explore the WordPad toolbar buttons by looking at their ScreenTips.

To find out a toolbar button's function:

1. Position the pointer over any button on the toolbar, such as the Print Preview button 🔍. After a short pause, the name of the button appears in a box near the button, and a description of the button appears in the status bar just above the Start button. See Figure 1-22.

Figure 1-22   **TOOLBAR BUTTON AIDS**

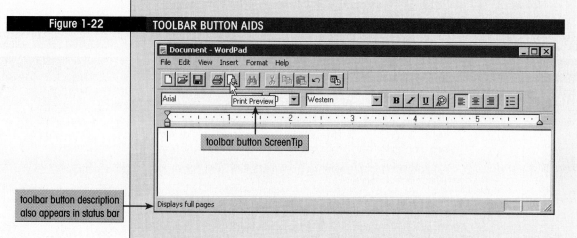

2. Move the pointer over each button on the toolbar to see its name and purpose.

You select a toolbar button by clicking it.

To select the Print Preview toolbar button:

1. Click the **Print Preview** button. The Print Preview screen appears. This is the same screen that appeared when you selected Print Preview from the File menu.

2. After examining the screen, click the button with the text label "Close" to return to your document.

Using **List Boxes and Scroll Bars**

As you might guess from the name, a **list box** displays a list of choices. In WordPad, date and time formats are shown in the Date/Time list box. List box controls usually include arrow buttons, a scroll bar, and a scroll box, as shown in Figure 1-23.

To use the Date/Time list box:

1. Click the **Date/Time** button to display the Date and Time dialog box. See Figure 1-23.

| Figure 1-23 | LIST BOX |

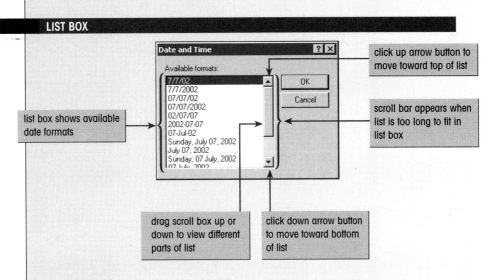

list box shows available date formats

click up arrow button to move toward top of list

scroll bar appears when list is too long to fit in list box

drag scroll box up or down to view different parts of list

click down arrow button to move toward bottom of list

2. To scroll down the list, click the **down arrow** button. See Figure 1-23.

3. Find the scroll box on your screen. See Figure 1-23.

4. Drag the **scroll box** to the top of the scroll bar. Notice how the list scrolls back to the beginning.

   TROUBLE? You learned how to drag when you learned to move a window. To drag the scroll box up, point to the scroll box, press and hold down the mouse button, and then move the mouse up.

5. Find a date in the format "July 07, 2002." Click that date format to select it.

6. Click the **OK** button to close the Date and Time dialog box. This inserts the current date in your document.

You can access some list boxes directly from the toolbar. When a list box is on the tool-bar, only the current option appears in the list box. A **list arrow** appears on the right of the box and you can click it to view additional options.

To use the Font Size list box:

1. Click the **Font Size** list arrow, as shown in Figure 1-24.

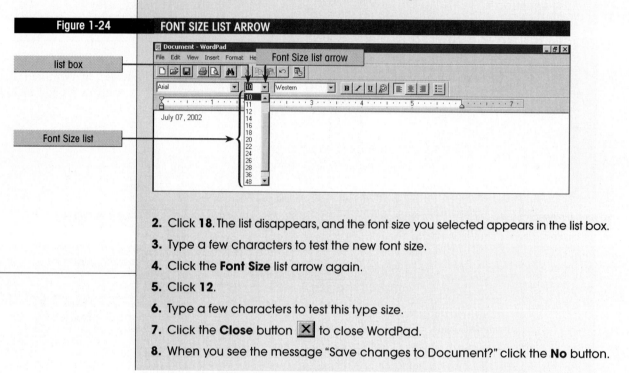

Figure 1-24	FONT SIZE LIST ARROW

list box

Font Size list arrow

Font Size list

July 07, 2002

2. Click **18**. The list disappears, and the font size you selected appears in the list box.

3. Type a few characters to test the new font size.

4. Click the **Font Size** list arrow again.

5. Click **12**.

6. Type a few characters to test this type size.

7. Click the **Close** button ☒ to close WordPad.

8. When you see the message "Save changes to Document?" click the **No** button.

Using Dialog Box Controls

Recall that when you select a menu option or button followed by an ellipsis, a dialog box opens that allows you to provide more information about how a program should carry out a task. Some dialog boxes group different kinds of information into bordered rectangular areas called **panes**. Within these panes, you will usually find tabs, option buttons, check boxes, and other controls that the program uses to collect information about how you want it to perform a task. Figure 1-25 describes common dialog box controls.

Figure 1-25	DIALOG BOX CONTROLS
CONTROL	**DESCRIPTION**
Tabs	Modeled after the tabs on file folders, tab controls are often used as containers for other Windows 2000 controls such as list boxes, radio buttons, and check boxes. Click the appropriate tabs to view different pages of information or choices.
Option buttons	Also called **radio buttons**, option buttons allow you to select a single option from among one or more options.
Check boxes	Click a check box to select or deselect it; when it is selected, a check mark appears, indicating that the option is turned on; when deselected, the check box is blank and the option is off. When check boxes appear in groups, you can select or deselect as many as you want; they are not mutually exclusive, as option buttons are.
Spin boxes	Allow you to scroll easily through a set of numbers to choose the setting you want
Text boxes	Boxes into which you type additional information

Figure 1-26 displays examples of these controls.

Figure 1-26	EXAMPLES OF DIALOG BOX CONTROLS

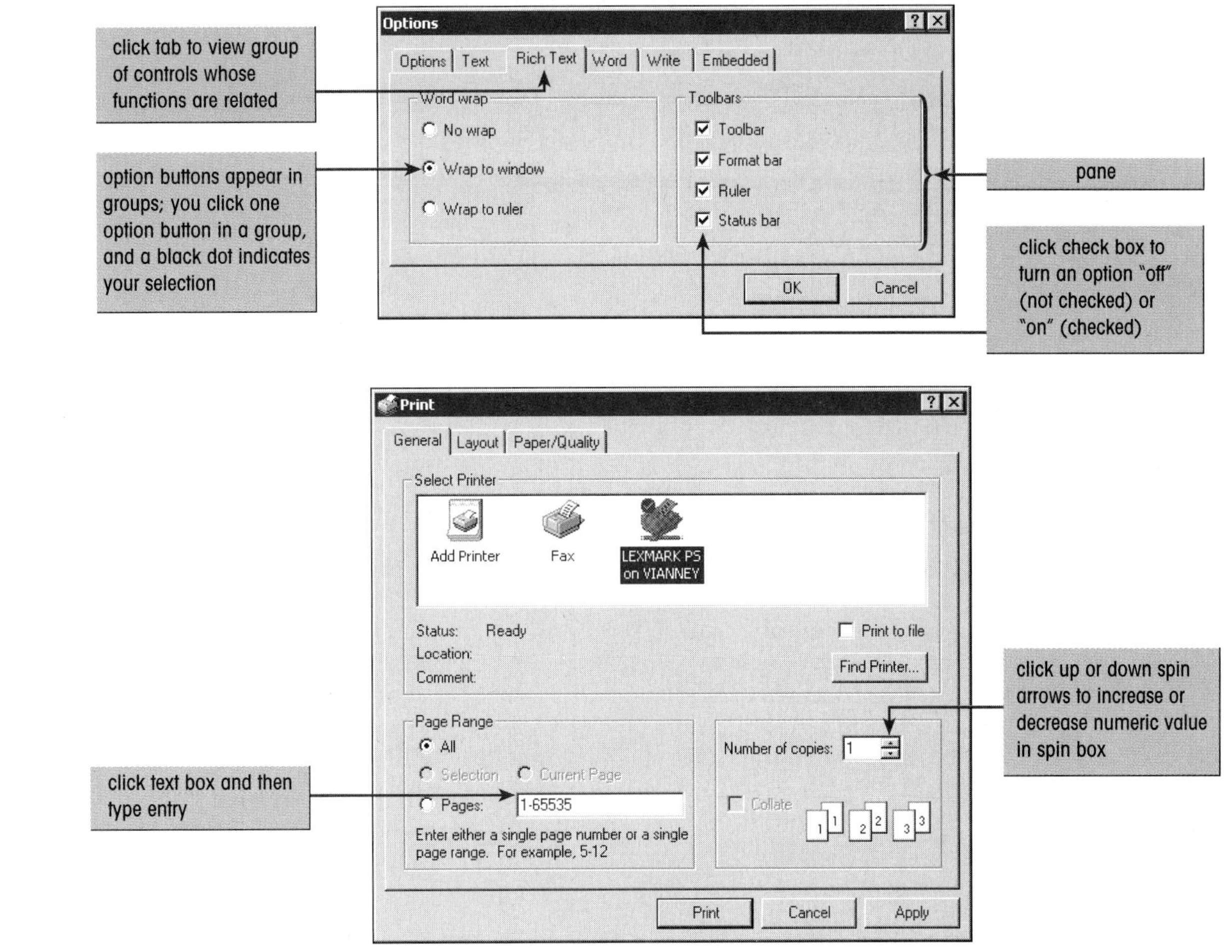

click tab to view group of controls whose functions are related

option buttons appear in groups; you click one option button in a group, and a black dot indicates your selection

pane

click check box to turn an option "off" (not checked) or "on" (checked)

click up or down spin arrows to increase or decrease numeric value in spin box

click text box and then type entry

Using **Help**

Windows 2000 **Help** provides on-screen information about the program you are using. Help for the Windows 2000 operating system is available by clicking the Start button on the taskbar, then selecting Help from the Start menu. If you want Help for a program, such as WordPad, you must first start the program, then click Help on the menu bar.

When you start Help, a Windows Help window opens, which gives you access to help files stored on your computer as well as help information stored on Microsoft's Web site. If you are not connected to the Web, you have access only to the help files stored on your computer.

To start Windows 2000 Help:

1. Click the **Start** button.

2. Click **Help**. The Windows 2000 window opens to the Contents tab. See Figure 1-27.

TROUBLE? If the Contents tab is not in front, click the Contents tab to view the table of contents.

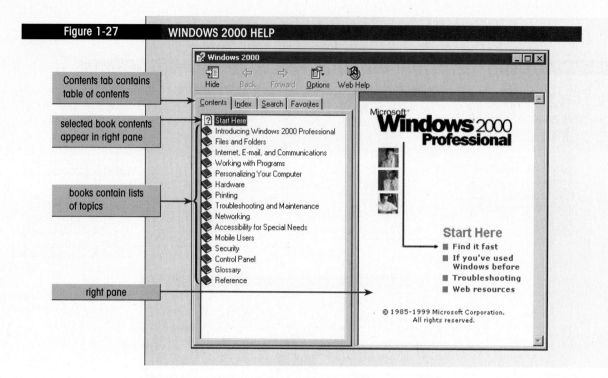

Figure 1-27 WINDOWS 2000 HELP

Contents tab contains table of contents

selected book contents appear in right pane

books contain lists of topics

right pane

Help uses tabs for the four sections of Help: Contents, Index, Search, and Favorites. The **Contents tab** groups Help topics into a series of books. You select a book 📖 by clicking it. The book opens, and a list of related topics appears from which you can choose. Individual topics are designated with the ❓ icon. Overview topics are designated with the 📄 icon.

The **Index tab** displays an alphabetical list of all the Help topics from which you can choose. The **Search tab** allows you to search the entire set of Help topics for all topics that contain a word or words you specify. The **Favorites tab** allows you to save your favorite Help topics for quick reference.

Viewing Topics from the Contents Tab

You know that Windows 2000 gives you easy access to the Internet. Suppose you're wondering how to connect to the Internet from your computer. You can use the Contents tab to find more information on a specific topic.

To use the Contents tab:

1. Click the **Internet, E-mail, and Communications** book icon 📖. A list of topics and an overview appear below the book title.

2. Click the **Connect to the Internet** topic icon ❓. Information about connecting to the Internet appears in the right pane. See Figure 1-28.

| Figure 1-28 | LOCATING INFORMATION ABOUT HOW TO CONNECT TO THE INTERNET |

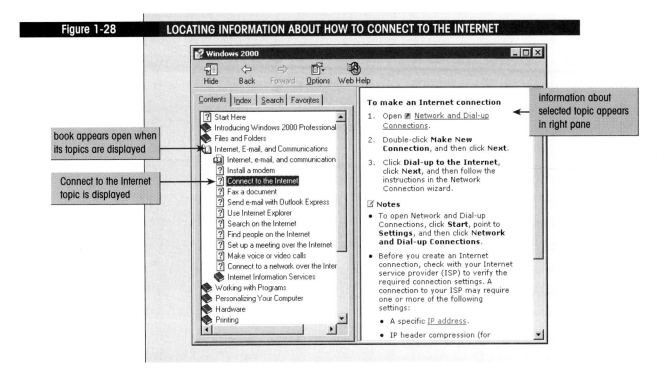

book appears open when
its topics are displayed

Connect to the Internet
topic is displayed

information about
selected topic appears
in right pane

Selecting a Topic from the Index

The Index tab allows you to jump to a Help topic by selecting a topic from an indexed list. For example, you can use the Index tab to learn more about the Internet.

To find a Help topic using the Index tab:

1. Click the **Index** tab. A long list of indexed Help topics appears.

   TROUBLE? If this is the first time you've used Help on your computer, Windows 2000 needs to set up the Index. This takes just a few moments. Wait until you see the list of index entries in the left pane, and then proceed to Step 2.

2. Drag the scroll box down to view additional topics.

3. You can quickly jump to any part of the list by typing the first few characters of a word or phrase in the box above the Index list. Click the box and then type **Internet**.

4. Click the topic **searching the Internet** (you might have to scroll to see it) and then click the **Display** button. When there is just one topic, it appears immediately in the right pane; otherwise, the Topics Found window opens, listing all topics indexed under the entry you're interested in. In this case, there are four choices.

5. Click **Using Internet Explorer** and then click the **Display** button. The information you requested appears in the right pane. See Figure 1-29. Notice in this topic that there are a few underlined words. You can click underlined words to view definitions or additional information.

Figure 1-29   USING THE INDEX TO LOCATE INFORMATION

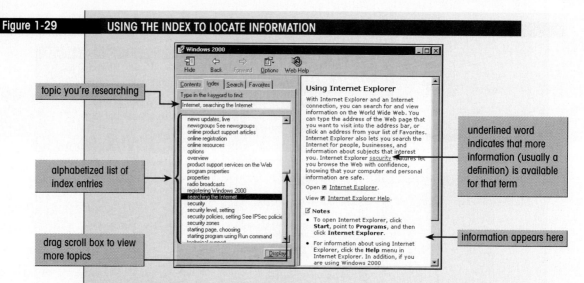

6. Click **security**. A small box appears that defines the term "security." See Figure 1-30.

Figure 1-30   VIEWING ADDITIONAL INFORMATION

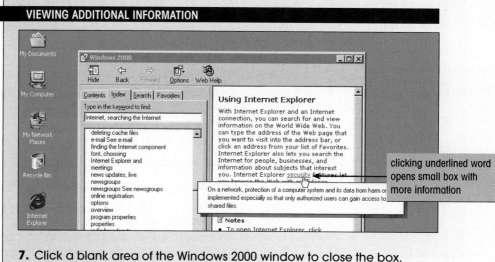

7. Click a blank area of the Windows 2000 window to close the box.

The third tab, the Search tab, works similarly to the Index tab, except that you type a word, and then the Help system searches for topics containing that word. You'll get a chance to experiment with the Search and Favorites tabs in the Review Assignments.

Returning to a Previous Help Topic

You've looked at a few topics now. Suppose you want to return to the one you just saw. The Help window includes a toolbar of buttons that help you navigate the Help system. One of these buttons is the **Back** button, which returns you to topics you've already viewed. Try returning to the help topic on connecting to the Internet.

To return to a Help topic:

1. Click the **Back** button. The Internet topic appears.

2. Click the **Close** button ⊠ to close the Windows 2000 window.

3. Log off or shut down Windows 2000, depending on your lab's requirements.

Now that you know how Windows 2000 Help works, don't forget to use it! Use Help when you need to perform a new task or when you forget how to complete a procedure.

You've finished the tutorial, and as you shut down Windows 2000, Steve Laslow returns from class. You take a moment to tell him all you've learned: you know how to start and close programs and how to use multiple programs at the same time. You have learned how to work with windows and the controls they employ. Finally, you've learned how to get help when you need it. Steve is pleased that you are well on your way to mastering the fundamentals of using the Windows 2000 operating system.

Session 1.2 QUICK | CHECK

1. What is the difference between the title bar and a toolbar?

2. Provide the name and purpose of each button:
   a. 🗕   b. 🗖   c. 🗗   d. ❎

3. Describe what is indicated by each of the following menu conventions:
   a. Ellipsis...   b. Grayed-out   c. ▶   d. ✔

4. A(n) _____ consists of a group of buttons, each of which provides one-click access to important program functions.

5. What is the purpose of the scroll bar? What is the purpose of the scroll box?

6. Option buttons allow you to select _____ option(s) at a time.

7. It is a good idea to use _____ when you need to learn how to perform new tasks.

REVIEW ASSIGNMENTS

1. **Running Two Programs and Switching Between Them** In this tutorial you learned how to run more than one program at a time, using WordPad and Paint. You can run other programs at the same time, too. Complete the following steps and write out your answers to questions b through f:
   a. Start the computer. Enter your username and password if prompted to do so.
   b. Click the Start button. How many menu options are on the Start menu?
   c. Run the Calculator program located on the Accessories menu. How many program buttons are now on the taskbar (don't count toolbar buttons or items in the tray)?
   d. Run the Paint program and maximize the Paint window. How many programs are running now?
   e. Switch to Calculator. What are two visual clues that tell you that Calculator is the active program?
   f. Multiply 576 by 1457 using the Calculator accessory. What is the result?
   g. Close Calculator, then close Paint.

Explore ▶ 2. **WordPad Help** In Tutorial 1 you learned how to use Windows 2000 Help. Almost every Windows 2000 program has a Help feature. Many users can learn to use a program just by using Help. To use Help, start the program, then click the Help menu at the top of the screen. Try using WordPad Help:
   a. Start WordPad.
   b. Click Help on the WordPad menu bar, and then click Help Topics.
   c. Using WordPad Help, write out your answers to questions 1 through 4.
      1. How do you create a bulleted list?
      2. How do you set the margins in a document?
      3. How do you undo a mistake?
      4. How do you change the font style of a block of text?
   d. Close WordPad.

Explore

3. **The Search Tab** In addition to the Contents and Index tabs you worked with in this tutorial, Windows 2000 Help also includes a Search tab. Windows 2000 makes it possible to use a microphone to record sound on your computer. You could browse through the Contents tab, although you might not know where to find information about microphones. You could also use the Index tab to search through the indexed entry. Or you could use the Search tab to find all Help topics that mention microphones.

   a. Start Windows 2000 Help and use the Index tab to find information about microphones. How many topics are listed?
   b. Now use the Search tab to find information about microphones. Type "microphone" in the box on the Search tab, and then click the List Topics button.
   c. Write a paragraph comparing the two lists of topics. You don't have to view them all, but indicate which tab seems to yield more information, and why. Close Help.

4. **Getting Started** Windows 2000 includes Getting Started, an online "book" that helps you discover more about your computer and the Windows 2000 operating system. You can use this book to review what you learned in this tutorial and pick up some tips for using Windows 2000. Complete the following steps and write out your answers to questions d–j.

   a. Start Help, click the Contents tab, click Introducing Windows 2000 Professional, and then click Getting Started online book. Read the information and then click Windows 2000 Professional Getting Started.
   b. In the right pane, click New to Windows? Notice the book icons in the upper-right and upper-left corners of the right pane.
   c. Read each screen, and then click the right book icon to proceed through the Help topics. Alternately, you can view specific Getting Started Help topics by clicking them on the Contents tab. To answer the following questions, locate the information on the relevant Help topic. All the information for these questions is located in Chapter 4—"Windows Basics." When you are done, close Help.
   d. If your computer's desktop style uses the single-click option, how do you select a file? How do you open a file?
   e. What features are almost always available on your desktop, regardless of how many windows you have open?
   f. How can you get information about a dialog box or an area of the dialog box?
   g. How does the Getting Started online book define the word "disk"?
   h. If your computer is connected to a network, what Windows 2000 feature can you use to browse network resources?
   i. Why shouldn't you turn off your computer without shutting it down properly?

5. **Favorite Help Topics** You learned in this tutorial that you can save a list of your favorite Help topics on the Favorites tab. Try adding a topic to your list of favorites.

   a. Open a Help topic in the Help system. For this assignment, click the Contents tab, click Personalizing Your Computer, and then click Personalizing your workspace overview.
   b. Click the Favorites tab. The topic you selected appears on the right, and the topic name appears in the lower-left corner.
   c. Click the Add button. The topic appears in the box on the Favorites tab. This provides you an easy way to return to this topic.
   d. Click the Remove button to remove the topic from the Favorites list.

PROJECTS

1. There are many types of pointing devices on the market today. Go to the library and research the types of devices available. Consider what devices are appropriate for these situations: desktop or laptop computers, connected or remote devices, and ergonomic or standard designs (look up the word "ergonomic").

Use up-to-date computer books, trade computer magazines such as *PC Computing* and *PC Magazine*, or the Internet (if you know how) to locate information. Your instructor might suggest specific resources you can use. Write a one-page report describing the types of devices available, the differing needs of users, special features that make pointing devices more useful, price comparisons, and what you would choose if you needed to buy a pointing device.

2. Using the resources available to you, either through your library or the Internet (if you know how), locate information about the release of Windows 2000. Computing trade magazines are an excellent source of information about software. Read several articles about Windows 2000 and then write a one-page essay that discusses the features that are most important to the people who evaluated the software. If you find reviews of the software, mention the features that reviewers had the strongest reaction to, pro or con.

3. Upgrading is the process of placing a more recent version of a product onto your computer. When Windows 2000 first came out, people had to decide whether or not they wanted to upgrade to Windows 2000. Interview several people you know who are well-informed Windows computer users. Ask them whether they are using Windows 2000 or an older version of Windows. If they are using an older version, ask why they have chosen not to upgrade. If they are using Windows 2000, ask them why they chose to upgrade. Ask such questions as:
   a. What features convinced you to upgrade or made you decide to wait?
   b. What role did the price of the upgrade play?
   c. Would you have had (or did you have) to purchase new hardware to make the upgrade? How did this affect your decision?
   d. If you did upgrade, are you happy with that decision? If you didn't, do you intend to upgrade in the near future? Why, or why not?

   Write a single-page essay summarizing what you learned from these interviews.

4. Choose a topic to research using the Windows 2000 online Help system. Look for information on your topic using three tabs: the Contents tab, the Index tab, and the Search tab. Once you've found all the information you can, compare the three methods (Contents, Index, Search) of looking for information. Write a paragraph that discusses which tab proved the most useful. Did you reach the same information topics using all three methods? In a second paragraph, summarize what you learned about your topic. Finally, in a third paragraph, indicate under what circumstances you'd use which tab.

LAB ASSIGNMENTS

Using a Keyboard

Using a Keyboard To become an effective computer user, you must be familiar with your primary input device—the keyboard. See the Read This Before You Begin page for information on installing and starting the lab.

1. The Steps for the Using a Keyboard Lab provide you with a structured introduction to the keyboard layout and the function of special computer keys. Click the Steps button and begin the Steps. As you work through the Steps, answer all of the Quick Check questions that appear. When you complete the Steps, you will see a Summary Report that summarizes your performance on the Quick Checks. Follow the directions on the screen to print the Summary Report.

2. In Explore, start the typing tutor. You can develop your typing skills using the typing tutor in Explore. Take the typing test and print out your results.

3. In Explore, try to improve your typing speed by 10 words per minute. For example, if you currently type 20 words per minute, your goal will be 30 words per minute. Practice each typing lesson until you see a message that indicates that you can proceed to the next lesson.

Create a Practice Record, as shown here, to keep track of how much you practice. When you have reached your goal, print out the results of a typing test to verify your results.

Practice Record
Name:
Section:
Start Date: Start Typing Speed: wpm
End Date: End Typing Speed: wpm
Lesson #:   Date Practiced/Time Practiced

Using a Mouse

Using a Mouse A mouse is a standard input device on most of today's computers. You need to know how to use a mouse to manipulate graphical user interfaces and to use the rest of the Labs. See the Read This Before You Begin page for information on installing and starting the lab.

1. The Steps for the Using a Mouse Lab show you how to click, double-click, and drag objects using the mouse. Click the Steps button and begin the Steps. As you work through the Steps, answer all of the Quick Check questions that appear. When you complete the Steps, you will see a Summary Report that summarizes your performance on the Quick Checks. Follow the directions on the screen to print the Summary Report.

2. In Explore, create a poster to demonstrate your ability to use a mouse and to control a Windows program. To create a poster for an upcoming sports event, select a graphic, type the caption for the poster, then select a font, font styles, and a border. Print your completed poster.

QUICK CHECK ANSWERS

Session 1.1
1. The taskbar contains buttons that give you access to tools and programs.
2. multitasking
3. Start menu
4. Lift the mouse up and move it to the right.
5. Its button appears on the taskbar.
6. To conserve computer resources such as memory.
7. To ensure you don't lose data and damage your files.

Session 1.2
1. The title bar identifies the window and contains window controls; toolbars contain buttons that provide you with shortcuts to common menu commands.
2. a. Minimize button shrinks window so you see button on taskbar
   b. Maximize button enlarges window to fill entire screen
   c. Restore button reduces window to predetermined size
   d. Close button closes window and removes button from taskbar
3. a. ellipsis indicates a dialog box will open
   b. grayed-out indicates option is not currently available
   c. arrow indicates a submenu will open
   d. check mark indicates a toggle option
4. toolbar
5. Scroll bars appear when the contents of a box or window are too long to fit; you drag the scroll box to view different parts of the contents.
6. one
7. online Help

In this tutorial you will:

- Format a disk

- Enter, select, insert, and delete text

- Create and save a file

- Open, edit, and print a file

- Create and make a copy of your Data Disk

- View the list of files on your disk and change view options

- Move, copy, delete, and rename a file

- Navigate a hierarchy of folders

LABS

Using Files

WORKING WITH FILES

Creating, Saving, and Managing Files

CASE

Distance Education

You recently purchased a computer in order to gain new skills so you can stay competitive in the job market. You hope to use the computer to enroll in a few distance education courses. **Distance education** is formalized learning that typically takes place using a computer and the Internet, replacing normal classroom interaction with modern communications technology. Distance education teachers often make their course material available on the **World Wide Web**, a popular service on the Internet that makes information readily accessible.

Your computer came loaded with Windows 2000. Your friend Shannon suggests that before you enroll in any online courses, you should get more comfortable with your computer and with Windows 2000. Knowing how to save, locate, and organize your files will make your time spent at the computer much more productive. A **file**, often referred to as a **document**, is a collection of data that has a name and is stored in a computer. Once you create a file, you can open it, edit its contents, print it, and save it again—usually using the same program you used to create it.

Shannon suggests that you become familiar with how to perform these tasks in Windows 2000 programs. Then she'll show you how to choose different ways of viewing information on your computer. Finally, you'll spend time learning how to organize your files.

SESSION 2.1

In Session 2.1, you will learn how to format a disk so it can store files. You will create, save, open, and print a file. You will find out how the insertion point differs from the mouse pointer, and you will learn the basic skills for Windows 2000 text entry, such as entering, selecting, inserting, and deleting. For the steps of this tutorial you will need two blank 3½-inch disks.

Formatting a Disk

Before you can save files on a floppy disk, the disk must be formatted. When the computer **formats** a disk, the magnetic particles on the disk surface are arranged so that data can be stored on the disk. Today, many disks are sold preformatted and can be used right out of the box. However, if you purchase an unformatted disk, or if you have an old disk you want to completely erase and reuse, you can format the disk using the Windows 2000 Format command. This command is available through the **My Computer window**, a feature of Windows 2000 that you use to view, organize, and access the programs, files, drives and folders on your computer. You open My Computer by using its icon on the desktop. You'll learn more about the My Computer window later in this tutorial.

The following steps tell you how to format a 3½-inch high-density disk, using drive A. Your instructor will tell you how to revise the instructions given in these steps if the procedure is different for your lab.

Make sure you are using a blank disk (or one that contains data you no longer need) before you perform these steps.

To format a disk:

1. Start Windows 2000, if necessary.

2. Write your name on the label of a 3½-inch disk and insert your disk in drive A. See Figure 2-1.

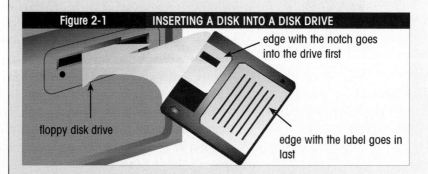

Figure 2-1   INSERTING A DISK INTO A DISK DRIVE

edge with the notch goes into the drive first

floppy disk drive

edge with the label goes in last

TROUBLE? If your disk does not fit in drive A, put it in drive B and substitute drive B for drive A in all of the steps for the rest of the tutorial.

3. Click the **My Computer** icon on the desktop. The icon is selected. Figure 2-2 shows this icon on your desktop.

TROUBLE? If the My Computer window opens, skip Step 4. Your computer is using different settings, which you'll learn to change in Session 2.2.

4. Press the **Enter** key to open the My Computer window. See Figure 2-2 (don't worry if your window opens maximized).

TROUBLE? If you see a list of items instead of icons like those in Figure 2-2, click View, and then click Large Icons. Don't worry if your toolbars don't exactly match those in Figure 2-2.

TROUBLE? If you see additional information or a graphic image on the left side of the My Computer window, Web view is enabled on your computer. Don't worry. You will learn how to return to the default Windows 2000 settings in Session 2.2.

Figure 2-2	MY COMPUTER WINDOW

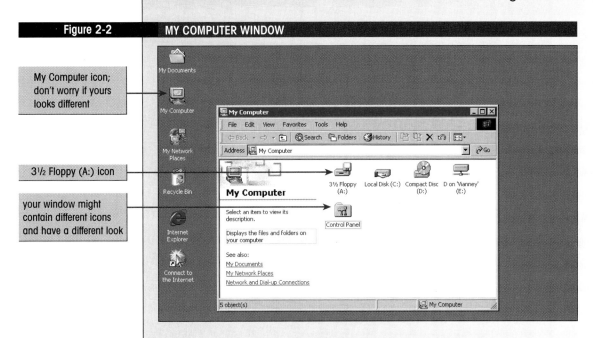

My Computer icon; don't worry if yours looks different

3½ Floppy (A:) icon

your window might contain different icons and have a different look

5. Right-click the **3½ Floppy (A:)** icon to open its shortcut menu, and then click **Format**. The Format dialog box opens.

6. Make sure the dialog box settings on your screen match those in Figure 2-3.

Figure 2-3	FORMATTING A FLOPPY DISK

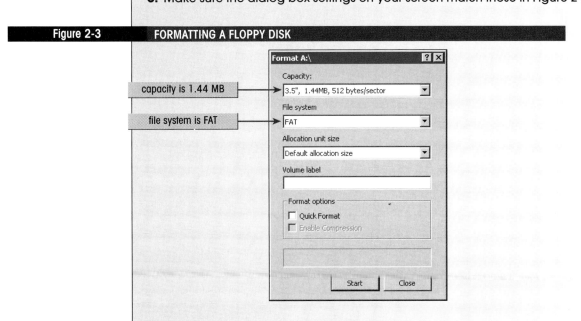

capacity is 1.44 MB

file system is FAT

By default, Windows 2000 uses the FAT (File Allocation Table) file system for floppy disks. A **file system** is the way files are organized on the disk. Windows 2000 supports other file systems such as FAT32 and NTFS, but this is a more advanced topic.

7. Click the **Start** button to start formatting the disk.

8. Click the **OK** button to confirm that you want to format the disk (the actual formatting will take a minute to perform). Click the **OK** button again when the formatting is complete.

9. Click the **Close** button.

10. Click the **Close** button ❌ to close the My Computer window.

Now that you have a formatted disk, you can create a document and save it on your disk. First you need to learn how to enter text into a document.

Working with Text

To accomplish many computing tasks, you need to enter text in documents and text boxes. This involves learning how to move the pointer so the text will appear where you want it, how to insert new text between existing words or sentences, how to select text, and how to delete text. When you type sentences of text, do not press the Enter key when you reach the right margin of the page. Most software contains a feature called **word wrap**, which automatically continues your text on the next line. Therefore, you should press Enter only when you have completed a paragraph.

If you type the wrong character, press the Backspace key to back up and delete the character. You can also use the Delete key. What's the difference between the Backspace and Delete keys? The **Backspace** key deletes the character to the left, while the **Delete** key deletes the character to the right. If you want to delete text that is not next to where you are currently typing, you need to use the mouse to select the text; then you can use either the Delete key or the Backspace key.

Now you will type some text, using WordPad, to practice text entry. When you first start WordPad, notice the flashing vertical bar, called the **insertion point**, in the upper-left corner of the document window. The insertion point indicates where the characters you type will appear.

To type text in WordPad:

1. Start WordPad and locate the insertion point.

TROUBLE? If the WordPad window does not fill the screen, click the Maximize button ▢.

TROUBLE? If you can't find the insertion point, click in the WordPad **document window**, the white area below the toolbars and ruler.

2. Type your name, pressing the Shift key at the same time as the appropriate letter to type uppercase letters and using the Spacebar to type spaces, just as on a typewriter.

3. Press the **Enter** key to move the insertion point down to the next line.

4. As you type the following sentences, watch what happens when the insertion point reaches the right edge of the page:

This is a sample typed in WordPad. See what happens when the insertion point reaches the right edge of the page. Note how the text wraps automatically to the next line.

TROUBLE? If you make a mistake, delete the incorrect character(s) by pressing the Backspace key on your keyboard. Then type the correct character(s).

TROUBLE? If your text doesn't wrap, your screen might be set up to display more information than the screen used for the figures in this tutorial, or your WordPad program might not be set to use Word Wrap. Click View, click Options, make sure the Rich Text tab is selected, click the Wrap to window option button, and then click the OK button.

The Insertion Point Versus the Pointer

The insertion point is not the same as the mouse pointer. When the mouse pointer is in the text-entry area, it is called the **I-beam pointer** and looks like ⊺. Figure 2-4 explains the difference between the insertion point and the I-beam pointer.

| Figure 2-4 | THE INSERTION POINT VS. THE POINTER |

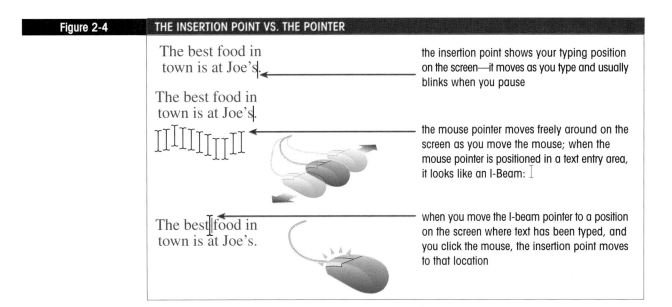

When you enter text, the insertion point moves as you type. If you want to enter text in a location other than where the mouse pointer is currently positioned, you move the I-beam pointer to the location where you want to type, and then click. The insertion point jumps to the location you clicked. In most programs, the insertion point blinks, making it easier for you to locate it on a screen filled with text.

To move the insertion point:

1. Check the locations of the insertion point and the I-beam pointer. The insertion point should be at the end of the sentence you typed in the last set of steps. The easiest way to locate the I-beam pointer is to move your mouse gently until you see the pointer. Remember that it will look like ⟋ until you move the pointer into the document window.

2. Use the mouse to move the I-beam pointer just to the left of the word "sample" and then click the mouse button. The insertion point should be just to the left of the "s."

   TROUBLE? If you have trouble clicking just to the left of the "s," try clicking in the word and then using the arrow keys to move the insertion point one character at a time.

3. Move the I-beam pointer to a blank area near the bottom of the workspace and then click. Notice the insertion point does not jump to the location of the I-beam pointer. Instead the insertion point jumps to the end of the last sentence or to the point in the bottom line directly above where you clicked. The insertion point can move only within existing text. It cannot be moved out of the existing text area.

Selecting Text

Many text operations are performed on a **block** of text, which is one or more consecutive characters, words, sentences, or paragraphs. Once you select a block of text, you can delete it, move it, replace it, underline it, and so on. To deselect a block of text, click anywhere outside the selected block.

If you want to delete the phrase "See what happens" in the text you just typed and replace it with the phrase "You can watch word wrap in action," you do not have to delete the first phrase one character at a time. Instead, you can select the entire phrase and then type the replacement phrase.

To select and replace a block of text:

1. Move the I-beam pointer just to the left of the word "See."

2. While holding down the mouse button, drag the I-beam pointer over the text to the end of the word "happens." The phrase "See what happens" should now be highlighted. See Figure 2-5.

TROUBLE? If the space to the right of the word "happens" is also selected, don't worry. Your computer is set up to select spaces in addition to words. After completing Step 4, simply press the Spacebar to type an extra space if required.

Figure 2-5	SELECTING TEXT

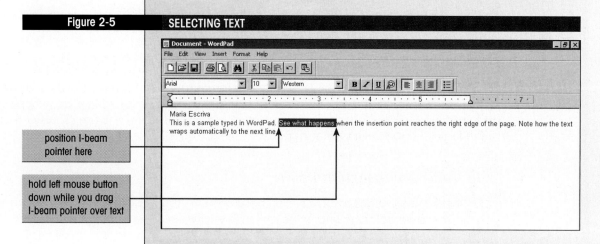

position I-beam pointer here

hold left mouse button down while you drag I-beam pointer over text

3. Release the mouse button.

TROUBLE? If the phrase is not highlighted correctly, repeat Steps 1 through 3.

4. Type **You can watch word wrap in action**

The text you typed replaces the highlighted text. Notice that you did not need to delete the selected text before you typed the replacement text.

Inserting a Character

Windows 2000 programs usually operate in **insert mode**—when you type a new character, all characters to the right of the insertion point are pushed over to make room.

Suppose you want to insert the word "page" before the word "typed" in your practice sentences.

To insert text:

1. Move the I-beam pointer just before the word "typed" and then click to position the insertion point.

2. Type **page**

3. Press the **Spacebar**.

Notice how the letters in the first line are pushed to the right to make room for the new characters. When a word gets pushed past the right margin, the word-wrap feature moves it down to the beginning of the next line.

Saving a File

As you type text, it is held temporarily in the computer's memory, which is erased when you turn off the computer. For permanent storage, you need to save your work on a disk. In the computer lab, you will probably save your work on a floppy disk in drive A.

When you save a file, you must give it a name, called a **filename**. Windows 2000 allows you to use up to 255 characters in a filename—this gives you plenty of room to name your file accurately enough so that you'll know the contents of the file by just looking at the filename. You may use spaces and certain punctuation symbols in your filenames. You cannot use the symbols \ / ? : * " < > | in a filename, because Windows uses those for designating the location and type of the file, but other symbols such as & ; - and $ are allowed.

Another thing to consider is whether you might use your files on a computer running older programs. Programs designed for the Windows 3.1 and DOS operating systems (which were created before 1995) require that files be eight characters or less with no spaces. Thus when you save a file with a long filename in Windows 2000, Windows 2000 also creates an eight-character filename that can be used by older programs. The eight-character filename is created from the first six nonspace characters in the long filename, with the addition of a tilde (~) and a number. For example, the filename Car Sales for 1999 would be converted to Carsal~1.

Most filenames have an extension. An **extension** (a set of no more than three characters at the end of a filename, separated from the filename by a period) is used by the operating system to identify and categorize the file. In the filename Car Sales for 1999.doc, for example, the file extension "doc" identifies the file as one created with Microsoft Word. You might also have a file called Car Sales for 1999.xls—"xls" identifies the file as one created with Microsoft Excel, a spreadsheet program. When pronouncing filenames with extensions, say "dot" for the period, so that the file Resume.doc is pronounced "Resume dot doc."

You usually do not need to add extensions to your filenames because the program you use to create the file does this automatically. Also, Windows 2000 keeps track of file extensions, but not all computers are set to display them. The steps in these tutorials refer to files by using the filename without its extension. So if you see the filename Practice Text in the steps, but "Practice Text.doc" appears on your screen, don't worry—these refer to the same file. Also don't worry if you don't use consistent lowercase and uppercase letters when saving files. Usually the operating system doesn't distinguish between them. Be aware, however, that some programs are "case-sensitive"—they check for case in filenames.

Now you can save the WordPad document you typed.

To start saving a document:

1. Click the **Save** button 🖫 on the toolbar. The Save As dialog box opens, as shown in Figure 2-6.

| Figure 2-6 | SAVING A FILE |

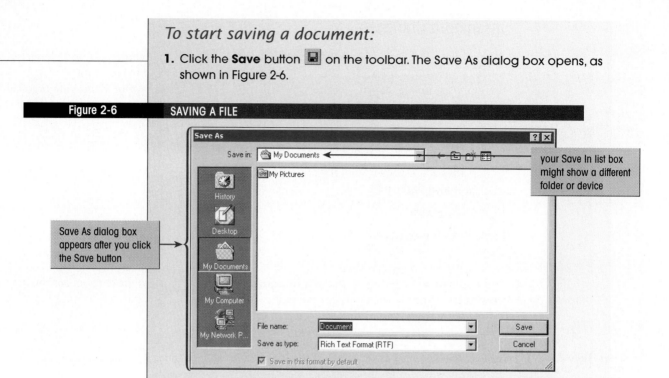

Save As dialog box appears after you click the Save button

your Save In list box might show a different folder or device

You use the Save As dialog box to specify where you want to save your file (on the hard drive or on a floppy disk, in a folder or not, and so on). Before going further with the process of saving a file, let's examine some of the features of the Save As dialog box so that you learn to save your files exactly where you want them.

Specifying the File Location

In the Save As dialog box, Windows 2000 provides the **Places Bar**, a list of important locations on your computer. When you click the different icons in the Places Bar, the contents of those locations will be displayed in the white area of the Save As dialog box. You can then save your document directly to those locations. Figure 2-7 displays the icons in the Places Bar and gives their function.

| Figure 2-7 | ICONS IN THE PLACES BAR |

ICON	DESCRIPTION
History	Displays a list of recently opened files, folders, and objects
Desktop	Displays a list of files, folders, and objects on the Windows 2000 desktop
My Documents	Displays a list of files, folders, and objects in the My Documents folder
My Computer	Displays a list of files, folders, and objects in the My Computer window
My Network P...	Displays a list of computers and folders available on the network

To see this in action, try displaying different locations in the dialog box.

To use the Places Bar:

1. Click the **Desktop** icon in the Places Bar.

2. The Save As dialog box now displays the contents of the Windows 2000 desktop. See Figure 2-8.

| Figure 2-8 | USING THE PLACES BAR |

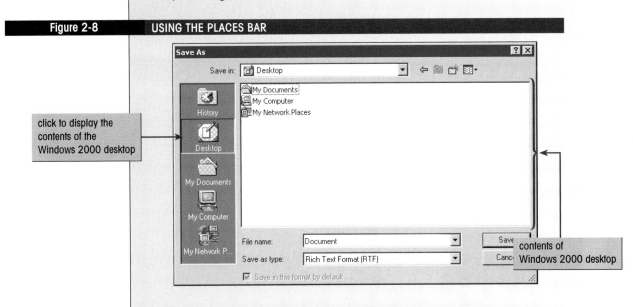

click to display the contents of the Windows 2000 desktop

contents of Windows 2000 desktop

3. Click the **My Documents** icon to display the contents of the My Documents folder.

Once you've clicked an icon in the Places Bar, you can open any file displayed in that location, and you can save a file into that location. The Places Bar doesn't have an icon for every location on your computer, however. The **Save in** list box (located at the top of the dialog box) does. Use the Save in list box now to save your document to your floppy disk.

To use the Save in list box:

1. Click the **Save in** list arrow to display a list of drives.

2. Click **3½ Floppy (A:)**.

   Now that you've specified where you want to save your file, you can specify a name and type for the file.

Specifying the File Name and Type

After choosing the location for your document, you have to specify the name of the file. You should also specify (or at least check) the file's format. A file's **format** determines what type of information you can place in the document, the document's appearance, and what kind of programs can work with the document. There are five file formats available in WordPad: Word for Windows 6.0, Rich Text Format (RTF), Text, Text for MS-DOS, and Unicode Text. The Word and RTF formats allow you to create documents with text that can use bold-faced or italicized fonts as well as documents containing graphic images and scanned photos. However, only word-processing programs like WordPad or Microsoft Word can work with those files. The three text formats allow only simple text with no graphics or special formatting, but such documents are readable by a wider range of programs. The default format for WordPad documents is RTF, but you can change that, as you'll see shortly.

Continue saving the document, using the name "Practice Text" and the file type Word 6.0.

To finish saving your document:

1. Select the text **Document** in the File name text box and then type **Practice Text** in the File name text box. The new text replaces "Document."

2. Click the **Save as type** list arrow and then click **Word for Windows 6.0** in the list. See Figure 2-9.

Figure 2-9	COMPLETED SAVE AS DIALOG BOX

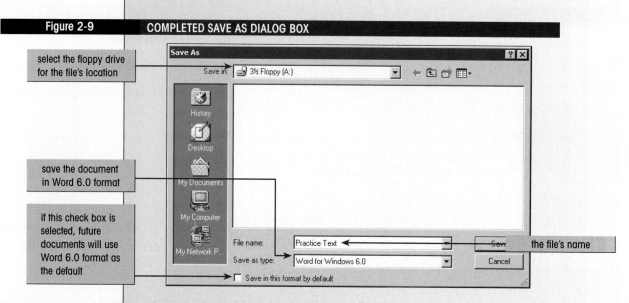

select the floppy drive for the file's location

save the document in Word 6.0 format

if this check box is selected, future documents will use Word 6.0 format as the default

the file's name

Note that if you want all future documents saved by WordPad to use the Word 6.0 format as the default format rather than RTF, you can select the Save in this format by default check box. If you select it, the next time you save a document in WordPad, this format will be the initial choice, so you won't have to specify it.

3. Click the **Save** button in the lower-right corner of the dialog box.

4. If you are asked whether you are sure that you want to save the document in this format, click the **Yes** button.

Your file is saved on your Data Disk, and the document title, "Practice Text," appears on the WordPad title bar.

Note that after you save the file the document appears a little different. What has changed? By saving the document in Word 6.0 format rather than RTF, you've changed the format of the document slightly. One change is that the text is wrapped differently in Word 6.0 format. A Word 6.0 file will use the right margin and, in this case, limit the length of a single line of text to 6 inches.

What if you try to close WordPad before you save your file? Windows 2000 will display a message—"Save changes to Document?" If you answer "Yes," Windows will display the Save As dialog box so you can give the document a name. If you answer "No," Windows 2000 will close WordPad without saving the document. Any changes you made to the document will be lost, so when you are asked if you want to save a file, answer "Yes," unless you are absolutely sure you don't need to keep the work you just did.

After you save a file, you can work on another document or close WordPad. Since you have already saved your Practice Text document, you'll continue this tutorial by closing WordPad.

To close WordPad:

1. Click the **Close** button ⊠ to close the WordPad window.

Opening a File

Suppose you save and close the Practice Text file, then later you want to revise it. To revise a file you must first open it. When you open a file, its contents are copied into the computer's memory. If you revise the file, you need to save the changes before you close the program. If you close a revised file without saving your changes, you will lose them.

There are several methods to open a file. You can select the file from the Documents list (available through the Start menu) if you have opened the file recently, since the Documents list contains the 15 most recently opened documents. This list is very handy to use on your own computer, but in a lab, other student's files quickly replace your own. You can also locate the file in the My Computer window (or in **Windows Explorer**, another file management tool) and then open it. And finally, you can start a program and then use the Open button within that program to locate and open the file. Each method has advantages and disadvantages.

The first two methods for opening the Practice Text file simply require you to select the file from the Documents list or locate and select it from My Computer or Windows Explorer. With these methods the document, not the program, is central to the task; hence, this method is sometimes referred to as **document-centric**. You need only to remember the name of your file—you do not need to remember which program you used to create it.

Opening a File from the My Computer Window

If your file is not in the Documents list, you can open the file by selecting it from the My Computer window. Either way, Windows 2000 uses the file extension (whether it is displayed or not) to determine which program to start so you can manipulate the file. It starts the program, and then automatically opens the file. The advantage of both methods is simplicity. The disadvantage is that Windows 2000 might not start the program you expect. For example, when you select Practice Text, you might expect Windows 2000 to start WordPad because you used WordPad to create it. Depending on the programs installed on your computer system, however, Windows 2000 might start Microsoft Word instead. Usually this is not a problem. Although the program might not be the one you expect, you can still use it to revise your file.

To open the Practice Text file by selecting it from My Computer:

1. Open the **My Computer** window, located on the desktop.

2. Click the **3½ Floppy (A:)** icon in the My Computer window.

   TROUBLE? If the 3½ Floppy (A:) window opens, skip Step 3.

3. Press the **Enter** key. The 3½ Floppy (A:) window opens.

4. Click the **Practice Text** file icon.

   TROUBLE? If the Practice Text document opens, skip Step 5.

5. Press the **Enter** key. Windows 2000 starts a program, and then automatically opens the Practice Text file. You could make revisions to the document at this point, but instead, you'll close all the windows on your desktop so you can try the other method for opening files.

   TROUBLE? If Windows 2000 starts Microsoft Word or another word-processing program instead of WordPad, don't worry. You can use Microsoft Word to revise the Practice Text document.

6. Close all open windows on the desktop.

Opening a File from Within a Program

The third method for opening the Practice Text file requires you to open WordPad, and then use the Open button to select the Practice Text file. The advantage of this method is that you can specify the program you want to use—WordPad, in this case. This method, however, involves more steps than the method you tried previously.

You can take advantage of the Places Bar to reduce the number of steps it takes to open a file from within a program. Recall that one of the icons in the Places Bar is the History icon, which displays a list of recently opened files or objects. One of the most recently opened files was the Practice Text file, so it should appear in the list.

To start WordPad and open the Practice Text file:

1. Start **WordPad** and, if necessary, maximize the WordPad window.

2. Click the **Open** button 📂 on the toolbar.

3. Click **History** in the Places Bar.

The Practice Text file doesn't appear in the list. Why not? Look at the Files of Type list box. The selected entry is "Rich Text Format (*.rtf)". What this means is that the Open dialog box will display only RTF files (as well as drives). This frees you from having to deal with the clutter of unwanted or irrelevant files. The downside is that unless you're aware of how the Open dialog box will filter the list of files, you may mistakenly think that the file you're looking for doesn't exist. You can change how the Open dialog box filters this file list. Try this now by changing the filter to show only Word documents.

To change the types of files displayed:

1. Click the **Files of type** list arrow and then click **Word for Windows (*.doc)**

   The Practice Text file now appears in the list.

2. Click **Practice Text** in the list of files. See Figure 2-10.

| Figure 2-10 | THE OPEN DIALOG BOX |

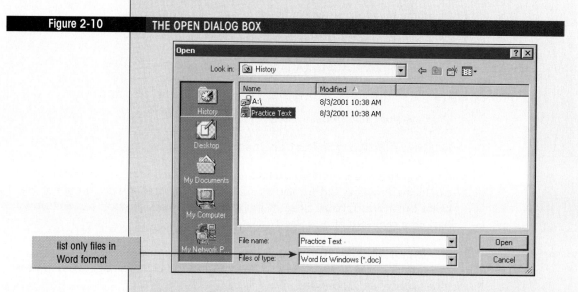

list only files in Word format

3. Click the **Open** button. The document should once again appear in the WordPad window.

Now that the Practice Text file is open, you can print it.

Printing a File

Windows 2000 provides easy access to your printer or printers. You can choose which printer to use, you can control how the document is printed, and you can control the order in which documents will be printed.

Previewing your Document Before Printing

It is a good idea to use Print Preview before you send your document to the printer. **Print Preview** shows on the screen exactly how your document will appear on paper. You can check your page layout so that you don't waste time and paper printing a document that is not quite the way you want it. Your instructor might supply you with additional instructions for printing in your school's computer lab.

To preview, then print, the Practice Text file:

1. Click the **Print Preview** button 🔍 on the toolbar.

   TROUBLE? If an error message appears, printing capabilities might not be set up on your computer. Ask your instructor or technical support person for help, or skip this set of steps.

2. Look at your document in the Print Preview window. Before you print the document, you should make sure the font, margins, and other document features look the way you want them to.

   TROUBLE? If you can't read the document text on screen, click the Zoom In button as many times as needed to view the text.

3. Click the **Close** button to close Print Preview and return to the document.

Now that you've verified that the document looks the way you want, you can print it.

Sending the Document to the Printer

There are three ways to send your document to the printer. The first approach is to print the document directly from the Print Preview window by clicking the Print button. Thus once you are satisfied with the document's appearance, you can quickly move to printing it.

Another way is to click the Print button 🖨 on your program's toolbar. This method will send the document directly to your printer without any further action on your part. It's the quickest and easiest way to print a document, but it does not allow you to change settings such as margins and layout. What if you have access to more than one printer? In that case, Windows 2000 sends the document to the default printer, the printer that has been set up to handle most print jobs.

If you want to select a different printer, or if you want to control how the printer prints your document, you can opt for a third method—selecting the Print command from the File menu. Using this approach, your program will open the Print dialog box, allowing you to choose which printer to use and how that printer will operate. Note that clicking the Print button from within the Print Preview window will also open the Print dialog box so you can verify or change settings.

To open the Print dialog box:

1. Click **File** on the WordPad menu bar and then click **Print**.

2. The Print dialog box opens, as displayed in Figure 2-11. Familiarize yourself with the controls in the Print dialog box.

Figure 2-11 **THE PRINT DIALOG BOX**

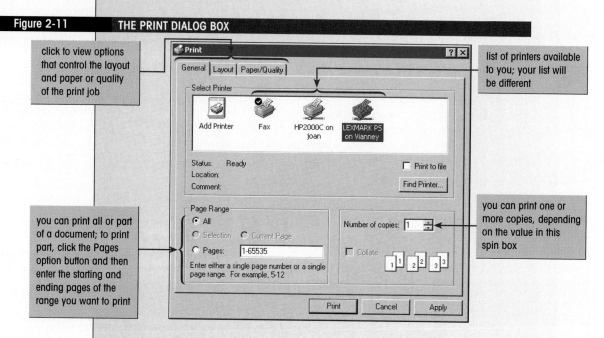

click to view options that control the layout and paper or quality of the print job

list of printers available to you; your list will be different

you can print all or part of a document; to print part, click the Pages option button and then enter the starting and ending pages of the range you want to print

you can print one or more copies, depending on the value in this spin box

3. Make sure your Print dialog box shows the Print range set to "All" and the Number of copies set to "1."

4. Select one of the printers in the list (your instructor may indicate which one you should select) and then click the **Print** button. The document is printed.

5. Close WordPad.

TROUBLE? If you see the message "Save changes to Document?" click the No button.

You've now learned how to create, save, open, and print word-processed files—essential skills for students in distance education courses that rely on word-processed reports transmitted across the Internet. Shannon assures you that the techniques you've just learned apply to most Windows 2000 programs.

Session 2.1 QUICK CHECK

1. A(n) _____ is a collection of data that has a name and is stored on a disk or other storage medium.

2. _____ erases all the data on a disk and arranges the magnetic particles on the disk surface so that the disk can store data.

3. True or False: When you move the mouse pointer over a text entry area, the pointer shape changes to an I-beam.

4. What indicates where each character you type will appear?

5. What does the History icon in the Places Bar display?

6. A file that you saved does not appear in the Open dialog box. Assuming that the file is still in the same location, what could be the reason that the Open dialog box doesn't display it?

7. What are the three ways to print from within a Windows 2000 application? If you want to print multiple copies of your document, which method(s) should you use and why?

SESSION 2.2

In this session, you will learn how to change settings in the My Computer window to control its appearance and the appearance of desktop objects. You will then learn how to use My Computer to manage the files on your disk; view information about the files on your disk; organize the files into folders; and move, delete, copy, and rename files. For this session you will use a second blank 3½-inch disk.

Creating Your Data Disk

Starting with this session, you must create a Data Disk that contains some practice files. You can use the disk you formatted in the previous session.

If you are using your own computer, the NP on Microsoft Windows 2000 menu option will not be available. Before you proceed, you must go to your school's computer lab and find a computer that has the NP on Microsoft Windows 2000 program installed. If you cannot get the files from the lab, ask your instructor or technical support person for help. Once you have made your own Data Disk, you can use it to complete this tutorial on any computer running Windows 2000.

To add the practice files to your Data Disk:

1. Write "Disk 1 - Windows 2000 Tutorial 2 Data Disk" on the label of your formatted disk (the same disk you used to save your Practice Text file).

2. Place the disk in drive A.

3. Click the **Start** button Start .

4. Point to **Programs**.

5. Point to **NP on Microsoft Windows 2000 – Level I**.

   TROUBLE? If NP on Microsoft Windows 2000 - Level I is not listed, ask your instructor or technical support person for help.

6. Click **Disk 1 (Tutorial 2)**. A message box opens, asking you to place your disk in drive A (which you already did, in Step 2).

7. Click the **OK** button. Wait while the program copies the practice files to your formatted disk. When all the files have been copied, the program closes.

Your Data Disk now contains practice files you'll use throughout the rest of this tutorial.

My Computer

The My Computer icon, as you have seen, represents your computer, with its storage devices, printers, and other objects. The My Computer icon opens into the My Computer window, which contains an icon for each of the storage devices on your computer. My Computer also gives you access to the **Control Panel**, a feature of Windows 2000 that controls the behavior of other devices and programs installed on your computer. Figure 2-12 shows how the My Computer window relates to your computer's hardware.

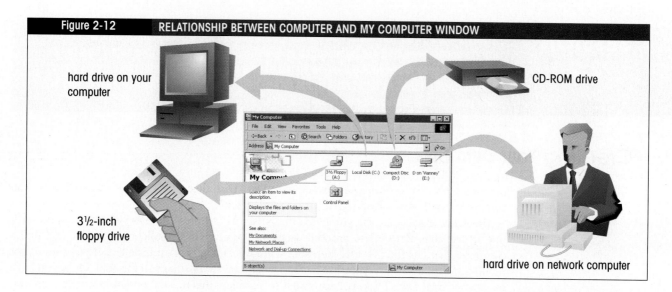

Figure 2-12   RELATIONSHIP BETWEEN COMPUTER AND MY COMPUTER WINDOW

hard drive on your computer

CD-ROM drive

3½-inch floppy drive

hard drive on network computer

Each storage device that you have access to has a letter associated with it. The first floppy drive on a computer is usually designated as drive A (if you add a second floppy drive, it is usually designated as drive B), and the first hard drive is usually designated drive C. Additional hard drives will have letters D, E, F and so forth. If you have a CD-ROM drive, it will usually have the next letter in the alphabetic sequence. If you have access to hard drives located on other computers on a network, those drives will sometimes (though not always) have letters associated with them. In the example shown in Figure 2-12, the network drive has the drive letter E.

You can use the My Computer window to organize your files. In this section of the tutorial, you'll use the My Computer window to move and delete files on your Data Disk, which is assumed to be in drive A. If you use your own computer at home or work, you will probably store your files on drive C instead of drive A. In a school lab environment, you can't always save your files to drive C, so you need to carry your files with you on a floppy disk. Most of what you learn about working on the floppy drive will also work on your home or work computer when you use drive C (or other hard drives).

Now you'll open the My Computer window.

To open the My Computer window and explore the contents of your Data Disk:

1. Open the My Computer window.

2. Click the **3½ Floppy (A:)** icon and then press the **Enter** key. A window appears showing the contents of drive A; maximize this window if necessary. See Figure 2-13.

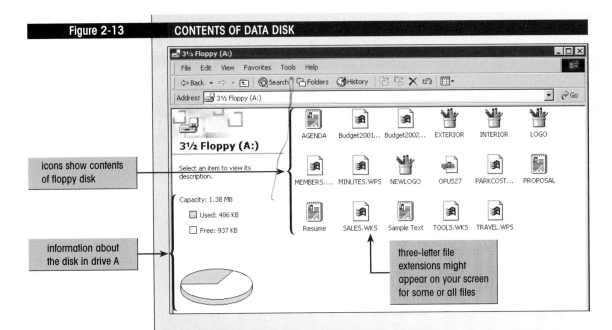

| Figure 2-13 | CONTENTS OF DATA DISK |

icons show contents of floppy disk

information about the disk in drive A

three-letter file extensions might appear on your screen for some or all files

TROUBLE? If the window appears before you press the Enter key, don't worry. Windows 2000 can be configured to use different keyboard and mouse combinations to open windows. You'll learn about these configuration issues shortly.

TROUBLE? If you see a list of filenames instead of icons, click View on the menu bar and then click Large Icons on the menu.

Changing the Appearance of the My Computer Window

Windows 2000 offers several different options that control how toolbars, icons, and buttons appear in the My Computer window. To make the My Computer window look the same as it does in the figures in this book, you need to ensure three things: that only the Address and Standard toolbars are visible, that files and other objects are displayed using large icons, and that the configuration of Windows 2000 uses the default setting. Setting your computer to match the figures will make it easier for you to follow the steps.

Controlling the Toolbar Display

The My Computer window, in addition to displaying a Standard toolbar, allows you to display the same toolbars that can appear on the Windows 2000 taskbar, such as the Address toolbar or the Links toolbar. These toolbars make it easy to access the Web from the My Computer window. In this tutorial, however, you need to see only the Address and Standard toolbars.

To display only the Address and Standard toolbars:

1. Click **View**, point to **Toolbars**, and then examine the Toolbars submenu. The Standard Buttons and Address Bar options should be preceded by a check mark. The Links and Radio options should not be checked. Follow the steps below to ensure that you have check marks next to the correct options.

2. If the Standard Buttons and Address Bar options *are not checked*, then click them to select them (you will have to repeat Step 1 to view the Toolbars submenu to do this for each option).

3. If the Links or Radio options *are checked*, then click them to deselect them (you will have to repeat Step 1 to view the Toolbars submenu to do this for each option).

4. Click **View** and then point to **Toolbars** one last time and verify that your Toolbars submenu and the toolbar display look like Figure 2-14.

Figure 2-14	CHECKING VIEW OPTIONS

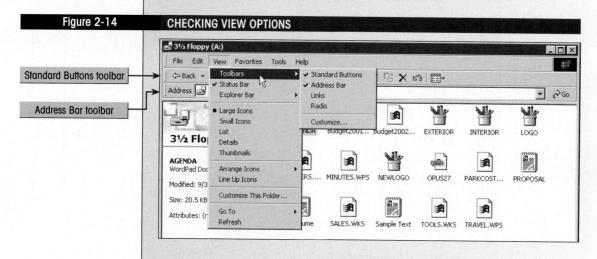

Standard Buttons toolbar

Address Bar toolbar

TROUBLE? If the check marks are distributed differently than in Figure 2-14, repeat Steps 1–4 until the correct options are checked.

TROUBLE? If your toolbars are not displayed as shown in Figure 2-14 (for example, both the Standard and Address toolbars might be on the same line, or the Standard toolbar might be above the Address toolbar), you can easily rearrange them. To move a toolbar, drag the vertical bar at the far left of the toolbar. By dragging that vertical bar, you can drag the toolbar left, right, up, or down.

Changing the Icon Display

Windows 2000 provides five ways to view the contents of a disk—Large Icons, Small Icons, List, Details, and Thumbnails. Figure 2-15 shows examples of these five styles.

Figure 2-15	VIEWING STYLES

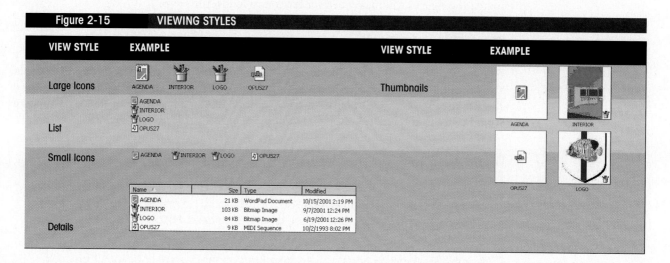

The default view, **Large Icons view**, displays a large icon and title for each file. The icon provides a visual cue to the type of the file, as Figure 2-16 illustrates. You can also get this same information with the smaller icons displayed in the **Small Icons** and **List** views, but in less screen space. In Small Icons and List views, you can see more files and folders at one time, which is helpful when you have many files in one location.

Figure 2-16	TYPICAL ICONS IN WINDOWS 2000

FILE AND FOLDER ICONS	
	Text documents that you can open using the Notepad accessory are represented by notepad icons.
	Graphic image documents that you can open using the Paint accessory are represented by drawing instruments.
	Word-processed documents that you can open using the WordPad accessory are represented by a formatted notepad icon, unless your computer designates a different word-processing program to open files created with WordPad.
	Word-processed documents that you can open using a program such as Microsoft Word are represented by formatted document icons.
	Files created by programs that Windows does not recognize are represented by the Windows logo.
	A folder icon represents folders.
	Certain folders created by Windows 2000 have a special icon design related to the folder's purpose.

PROGRAM ICONS	
	Icons for programs usually depict an object related to the function of the program. For example, an icon that looks like a calculator represents the Calculator accessory.
	Non-Windows programs are represented by the icon of a blank window.

All of the three icon views (Large Icons, Small Icons, and List) help you quickly identify a file and its type, but what if you want more information about a set of files? **Details view** shows more information than the Large Icon, Small Icon, and List views. Details view shows the file icon, the filename, the file size, the program you used to create the file, and the date and time the file was created or last modified.

Finally, if you have graphic files, you may want to use **Thumbnails view**, which displays a small "preview" image of the graphic, so that you can quickly see not only the filename, but also which picture or drawing the file contains. Thumbnails view is great for browsing a large collection of graphic files, but switching to this view can be time-consuming, since Windows 2000 has to create all of the preview images.

To see how easy it is to switch from one view to another, try displaying the contents of drive A in Details view.

To view a detailed list of files:

1. Click **View** and then click **Details** to display details for the files on your disk, as shown in Figure 2-17. Your files might be listed in a different order.

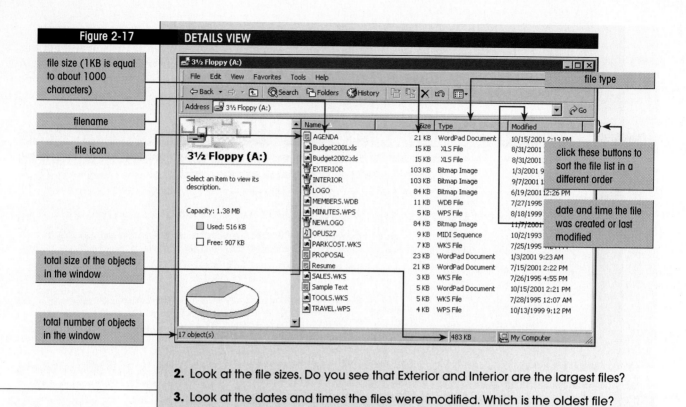

Figure 2-17 DETAILS VIEW

file size (1KB is equal to about 1000 characters)

filename

file icon

total size of the objects in the window

total number of objects in the window

file type

click these buttons to sort the file list in a different order

date and time the file was created or last modified

2. Look at the file sizes. Do you see that Exterior and Interior are the largest files?

3. Look at the dates and times the files were modified. Which is the oldest file?

One of the advantages that Details view has over other views is that you can sort the file list by filename, size, type, or the date the file was last modified. This helps if you're working with a large file list and you're trying to locate a specific file.

To sort the file list by type:

1. Click the **Type** button at the top of the list of files.

The files are now sorted in alphabetical order by type, starting with the "Bitmap Image" files and ending with the "XLS File" files. This would be useful if, for example, you were looking for all the .doc files (those created with Microsoft Word), because they would all be grouped together under "M" for "Microsoft Word."

2. Click the **Type** button again.

The sort order is reversed with the "XLS File" files now at the top of the list.

3. Click the **Name** button at the top of the file list.

The files are now sorted in alphabetical order by filename.

Now that you have looked at the file details, switch back to Large Icon view.

To switch to Large Icon view:

1. Click **View** and then click **Large Icons** to return to the large icon display.

Restoring the My Computer Default Settings

Windows 2000 provides other options in working with your files and windows. These options fall into two general categories: Classic style and Web style. **Classic style** is a mode of working with windows and files that resembles earlier versions of the Windows operating system. **Web style** allows you to work with your windows and files in the same way you work with Web pages on the World Wide Web. For example, to open a file in Classic style, you can double-click the file icon (a **double-click** is clicking the left mouse button twice quickly) or click the file icon once and press the Enter key. To open a file in Web style, you would simply click the file icon once, and the file would open. You could also create your own style, choosing elements of both the Classic and Web styles, and add in a few customized features of your own.

In order to simplify matters, this book will assume that you're working in the Default style, that is the configuration that Windows 2000 uses when it is initially installed. No matter what changes you make to the configuration of Windows 2000, you can always revert back to the Default style. Try switching back to Default style now.

To switch to the Default style:

1. Click **Tools** and then click **Folder Options** on the menu.

2. If it is not already selected, click the **General** tab.

   The General sheet displays general options for working with files and windows. Take some time to look over the list of options available.

3. Click the **Restore Defaults** button.

4. Click the **View** tab.

   The View sheet displays options that control the appearance of files and other objects. You should set these options to their default values as well.

5. Click the **Restore Defaults** button.

6. Click the **OK** button to close the Folder Options dialog box.

Working **with Folders and Directories**

Up to now, you've done a little work with files and windows, but before going further you should look at some of the terminology used to describe these tasks. Any location where you can store files on a computer is referred to as a **directory**. The main directory of a disk is sometimes called the **root directory**, or the **top-level directory**. All of the files on your Data Disk are currently in the root directory of your floppy disk.

If too many files are stored in a directory, the list of files becomes very long and difficult to manage. You can divide a directory into **subdirectories,** also called **folders**. The number of files for each folder then becomes much fewer and easier to manage. A folder within a folder is called a **subfolder**. The folder that contains another folder is called the **parent folder**.

All of these objects exist in a **hierarchy**, which begins with your desktop and extends down to each subfolder. Figure 2-18 shows part of a typical hierarchy of Windows 2000 objects.

Figure 2-18 | PART OF A TYPICAL HIERARCHY OF WINDOWS 2000 OBJECTS

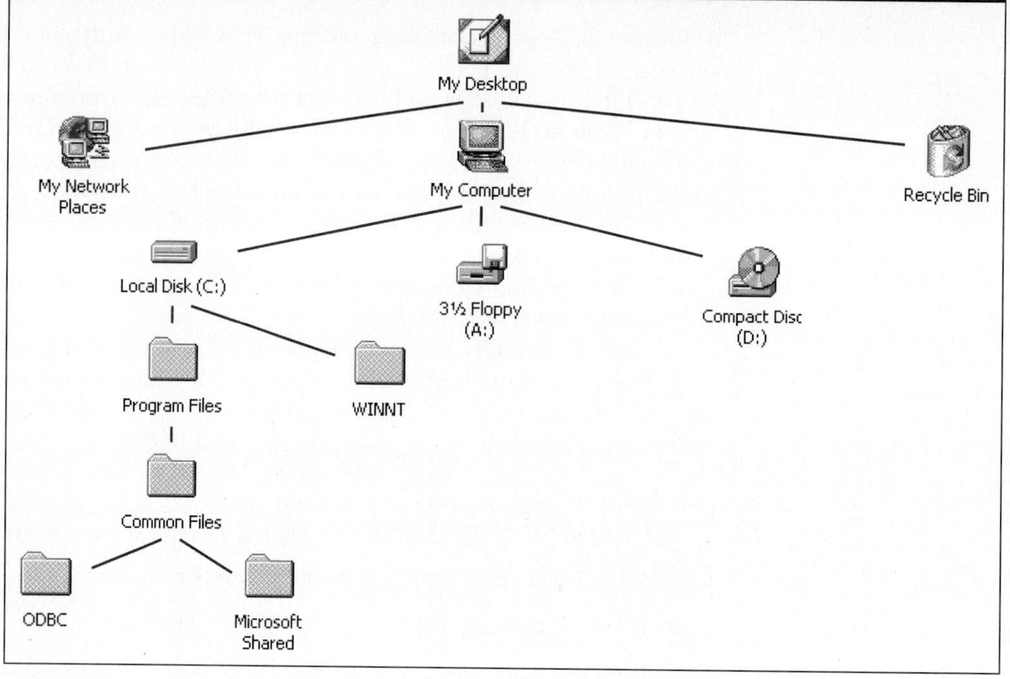

Creating a Folder

You've already seen folder icons in the various windows you've previously opened. Now, you'll create your own folder called Practice to hold your documents.

To create a Practice folder:

1. Click **File** and then point to **New** to display the submenu.

2. Click **Folder**. A folder icon with the label "New Folder" appears.

3. Type **Practice** as the name of the folder.

   TROUBLE? If nothing happens when you type the folder name, it's possible that the folder name is no longer selected. Right-click the Practice folder, click Rename, and then repeat Step 3.

4. Press the **Enter** key.

   The folder is now named "Practice" and is the selected item on your Data Disk.

5. Click a blank area next to the Practice folder to deselect it.

Navigating Through the Windows 2000 Hierarchy

Now that you've created a subfolder, how do you move into it? You've seen that to view the contents of a file, you open it. To move into a subfolder, you open it in the same way.

To view the contents of the Practice folder:

1. Click the **Practice** folder and press the **Enter** key.

2. The Practice folder opens. Because there are no files in the folder, there are no items to display. You'll change that shortly.

You've seen that to navigate through the devices and folders on your computer, you open My Computer and then click the icons representing the objects you want to explore. But what if you want to move back to the root directory? The Standard toolbar, which stays the same regardless of which folder or object is open, includes buttons that help you navigate through the hierarchy of drives, directories, folders, subfolders and other objects in your computer. Figure 2-19 summarizes the navigation buttons on the Standard toolbar.

Figure 2-19		NAVIGATION BUTTONS
BUTTON	**ICON**	**DESCRIPTION**
Back	⇐	Returns you to the folder, drive, directory, or object you were most recently viewing. The button is active only when you have viewed more than one window in the current session.
Forward	⇒	Reverses the effect of the Back button.
Up	⬆	Moves you up one level in the hierarchy of directories, drives, folders, and other objects on your computer.

You can return to your floppy's root directory by using the Back or the Up button. Try both of these techniques now.

To move up to the root directory:

1. Click the **Back** button ⇐.

Windows 2000 moves you back to the previous window, in this case the root directory of your Data Disk.

2. Click the **Forward** button ⇒.

The Forward button reverses the effect of the Back button and takes you to the Practice folder.

3. Click the **Up** button ⬆.

You move up one level in hierarchy of Windows 2000 objects, going to the root directory of the Data Disk.

Another way of moving around in the Windows 2000 hierarchy is through the Address toolbar. By clicking the Address list arrow, you can view a list of the objects in the top part of the Windows 2000 hierarchy (see Figure 2-20). This gives you a quick way of moving to the top without having to navigate through the intermediate levels.

Figure 2-20 | A HIERARCHY OF OBJECTS DISPLAYED IN THE ADDRESS LIST BOX

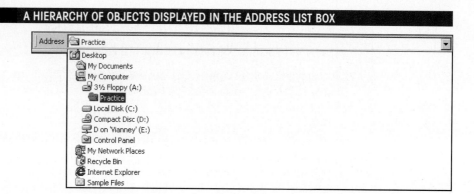

Now that you know how to move among the folders and devices on your computer, you can practice manipulating files. The better you are at working with the hierarchy of files and folders on your computer, the more organized the hierarchy will be, and the easier it will be to find the files you need.

Working with Files

As you've seen, the Practice folder doesn't contain any files. In the next set of steps, you will place a file from the root directory into it.

Moving and Copying a File

If you want to place a file into a folder from another location, you can either move the file or copy it. **Moving** a file takes it out of its current location and places it in the new location. **Copying** places the file in both locations. Windows 2000 provides several different techniques for moving and copying files. One way is to make sure that both the current and the new location are visible on your screen and then hold down the right mouse button and drag the file from the old location to the new location. A menu will then appear, and you can then select whether you want to move the file to the new location or make a copy in the new location. The advantage of this technique is that you are never confused as to whether you copied the file or merely moved it. Try this technique now by placing a copy of the Agenda file in the Practice folder.

To copy the Agenda file:

1. Point to the **Agenda** file in the root directory of your Data Disk and press the *right* mouse button.

2. With the right mouse button still pressed down, drag the **Agenda** file icon to the **Practice** folder icon; when the Practice folder icon turns blue, release the button.

3. A menu appears, as shown in Figure 2-21. Click **Copy Here**.

Figure 2-21 | **COPYING A FILE**

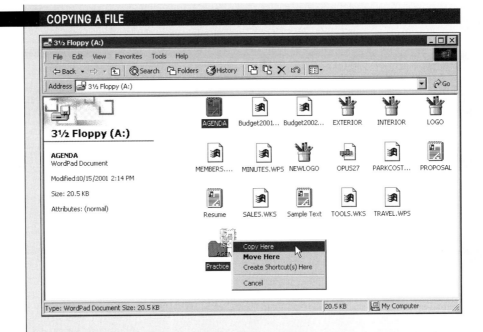

TROUBLE? If you release the mouse button by mistake before dragging the Agenda icon to the Practice folder, the Agenda shortcut menu opens. Press the Esc key and then repeat Steps 1 and 2.

4. Double-click the **Practice** folder.

The Agenda file should now appear in the Practice folder.

Note that the "Move Here" command was also part of the menu. In fact, the command was in boldface, indicating that it is the default command whenever you drag a document from one location to another on the same drive. This means that if you were to drag a file from one location to another on the same drive using the left mouse button (instead of the right), the file would be moved and not copied.

Renaming a File

You will often find that you want to change the name of files as you change their content or as you create other files. You can easily rename a file by using the Rename option on the file's shortcut menu or by using the file's label.

Practice using this feature by renaming the Agenda file "Practice Agenda," since it is now in the Practice folder.

To rename the Agenda file:

1. Right-click the **Agenda** icon.

2. Click **Rename**. After a moment the filename is highlighted and a box appears around it.

3. Type **Practice Agenda** and press the **Enter** key.

TROUBLE? If you make a mistake while typing and you haven't pressed the Enter key yet, you can press the Backspace key until you delete the mistake, then complete Step 3. If you've already pressed the Enter key, repeat Steps 1-3 to rename the file a second time.

The file appears with a new name.

Deleting a File

You should periodically delete files you no longer need so that your folders and disks don't get cluttered. You delete a file or folder by deleting its icon. Be careful when you delete a folder, because you also delete all the files it contains! When you delete a file from a hard drive on your computer, the filename is deleted from the directory but the file contents are held in the Recycle Bin. The Recycle Bin is an area on your hard drive that holds deleted files until you remove them permanently; an icon on the desktop allows you easy access to the Recycle Bin. If you change your mind and want to retrieve a file deleted from your hard drive, you can recover it by using the Recycle Bin. However, once you've emptied the Recycle Bin, you can no longer recover the files that were in it.

When you delete a file from a floppy disk or a disk that exists on another computer on your network, it does not go into the Recycle Bin. Instead, it is deleted as soon as its icon disappears—and you can't recover it.

Try deleting the Practice Agenda file from your Data Disk. Because this file is on a floppy disk and not on the hard disk, it will not go into the Recycle Bin, and if you change your mind you won't be able to get it back.

To delete the Practice Agenda file:

1. Right-click the icon for the Practice Agenda file.

2. Click **Delete** on the menu that appears.

3. Windows 2000 asks if you're sure that you want to delete this file. Click the **Yes** button.

4. Click the **Close** button ☒ to close the My Computer window.

If you like using your mouse, another way of deleting a file is to drag its icon to the Recycle Bin on the desktop. Be aware that if you're dragging a file from your floppy disk or a network disk, the file will *not* be placed in the Recycle Bin—it will still be permanently deleted.

Other Copying and Moving Techniques

As was noted earlier, there are several ways of moving and copying. As you become more familiar with Windows 2000, you will no doubt settle on the technique you like best. Figure 2-22 describes some of the other ways of moving and copying files.

Figure 2-22	METHODS FOR MOVING AND COPYING FILES	
METHOD	**TO MOVE**	**TO COPY**
Cut, copy, and paste	Select the file icon. Click **Edit** on the menu bar and **Cut** on the menu bar. Move to the new location. Click **Edit** and **Paste**.	Select the file icon. Click **Edit** on the menu bar and **Copy** on the menu bar. Move to the new location. Click **Edit** and **Paste**.
Drag and drop	Click the file icon. Drag and drop the icon in the new location.	Click the file icon. Hold down the Ctrl key and drag and drop the icon in the new location.
Right-click, drag and drop	With the right mouse button pressed down, drag the file icon to the new location. Release the mouse button and click **Move Here** on the menu.	With the right mouse button pressed down, drag the file icon to the new location. Release the mouse button and click **Copy Here** on the menu.
Move to folder and copy to folder	Click the file icon. Click **Edit** on the menu bar and **Move to Folder** on the menu bar. Select the new location in the Browse for Folder dialog box.	Click the file icon. Click **Edit** on the menu bar and **Copy to Folder** on the menu bar. Select the new location in the Browse for Folder dialog box.

The techniques shown in Figure 2-22 are primarily for document files. Because a program might not work correctly if moved into a new location, the techniques for moving program files are slightly different. See the Windows 2000 online Help for more information on moving or copying a program file.

Copying **an Entire Floppy Disk**

You can have trouble accessing the data on your floppy disk if the disk is damaged, is exposed to magnetic fields, or picks up a computer virus. To avoid losing all your data, it is a good idea to make a copy of your floppy disk.

If you wanted to make a copy of an audiocassette, your cassette player would need two cassette drives. You might wonder, therefore, how your computer can make a copy of your disk if you have only one floppy disk drive. Figure 2-23 illustrates how the computer uses only one disk drive to make a copy of a disk.

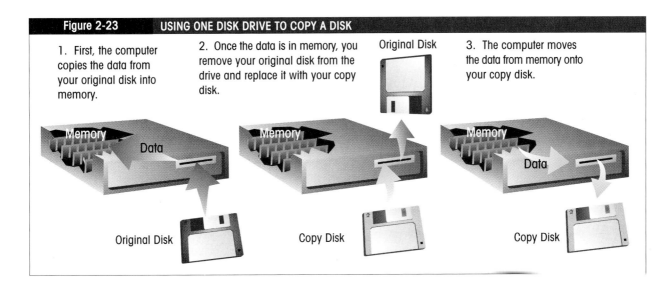

| Figure 2-23 | USING ONE DISK DRIVE TO COPY A DISK |

1. First, the computer copies the data from your original disk into memory.

2. Once the data is in memory, you remove your original disk from the drive and replace it with your copy disk.

3. The computer moves the data from memory onto your copy disk.

REFERENCE WINDOW RW

Copying a Disk
- Insert the disk you want to copy in drive A.
- In My Computer, right-click the 3½ Floppy (A:) icon, and then click Copy Disk.
- Click Start to begin the copy process.
- When prompted, remove the disk you want to copy, place your second disk in drive A, and then click OK.

If you have an extra floppy disk, you can make a copy of your Data Disk now. Make sure you copy the disk regularly so that as you work through the tutorials in this book it will stay updated.

To copy your Data Disk:

1. Write your name and "Windows 2000 Disk 1 Data Disk Copy" on the label of your second disk. Make sure the disk is blank and formatted.

   TROUBLE? If you aren't sure if the disk is blank, place it in the disk drive and open the 3½ Floppy (A:) window to view its contents. If the disk contains files you need, get a different disk. If it contains files you don't need, you could format the disk now, using the steps you learned at the beginning of this tutorial.

2. Make sure your original Data Disk is in drive A and the My Computer window is open.

3. Right-click the **3½ Floppy (A:)** icon, and then click **Copy Disk**. The Copy Disk dialog box opens.

4. Click the **Start** button and then the **OK** button to begin the copy process.

5. When the message "Insert the disk you want to copy to (destination disk)..." appears, remove your Data Disk and insert your Windows 2000 Disk 1 Data Disk Copy in drive A.

6. Click the **OK** button. When the copy is complete, you will see the message "Copy completed successfully." Click the **Close** button.

7. Close the My Computer window.

8. Remove your disk from the drive.

As you finish copying your disk, Shannon emphasizes the importance of making copies of your files frequently, so you won't risk losing important documents for your distance learning course. If your original Data Disk were damaged, you could use the copy you just made to access the files.

Keeping copies of your files is so important that Windows 2000 includes a program called Backup that automates the process of duplicating and storing data. In the Projects at the end of the tutorial you'll have an opportunity to explore the difference between what you just did in copying a disk and the way in which a program such as the Windows 2000 Backup program helps you safeguard data.

Session 2.2 QUICK CHECK

1. If you want to find out about the storage devices and printers connected to your computer, what window could you open?

2. If you have only one floppy disk drive on your computer, it is usually identified by the letter _____.

3. The letter C is typically used for the _____ drive of a computer.

4. What information does Details view supply about a list of folders and files?

5. The main directory of a disk is referred to as the _____ directory.

6. What is the topmost object in the hierarchy of Windows 2000 objects?

7. If you have one floppy disk drive, but you have two disks, can you copy the files on one floppy disk to the other?

REVIEW ASSIGNMENTS

1. **Opening, Editing, and Printing a Document** In this tutorial you learned how to create a document using WordPad. You also learned how to save, open, and print a document. Practice these skills by copying the document called **Resume** into the Practice folder on your Data Disk. Rename the file **Woods Resume**. This document is a resume for Jamie Woods. Make the changes shown in Figure 2-24. Save your revisions in Word for Windows 6.0 format, preview, and then print the document. Close WordPad.

Figure 2-24

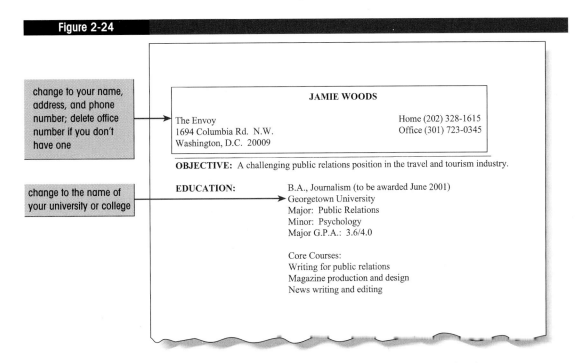

change to your name, address, and phone number; delete office number if you don't have one

change to the name of your university or college

JAMIE WOODS

The Envoy
1694 Columbia Rd. N.W.
Washington, D.C. 20009

Home (202) 328-1615
Office (301) 723-0345

OBJECTIVE: A challenging public relations position in the travel and tourism industry.

EDUCATION:
B.A., Journalism (to be awarded June 2001)
Georgetown University
Major: Public Relations
Minor: Psychology
Major G.P.A.: 3.6/4.0

Core Courses:
Writing for public relations
Magazine production and design
News writing and editing

2. **Creating, Saving, and Printing a Letter** Use WordPad to write a one-page letter to a relative or a friend. Save the document in the Practice folder on your Data Disk with the name **Letter**. Use the Print Preview feature to look at the format of your finished letter, then print it, and be sure to sign it. Close WordPad.

3. **Managing Files and Folders** Using the copy of the disk you made at the end of the tutorial, complete steps a through f below to practice your file-management skills, and then answer the questions below.

  a. Create a folder called Spreadsheets on your Data Disk.
  b. Move the files **Parkcost**, **Budget2001**, **Budget2002**, and **Sales** into the Spreadsheets folder.
  c. Create a folder called Park Project.
  d. Move the files **Proposal**, **Members**, **Tools**, **Logo**, and **Newlogo** into the Park Project folder.
  e. Delete the file called **Travel**.
  f. Switch to the Details view and write out your answers to Questions 1 through 5:
   1. What is the largest file or files in the Park Project folder?
   2. What is the newest file or files in the Spreadsheets folder?
   3. How many files (don't include folders) are in the root directory of your Data Disk?
   4. How are the Opus and Exterior icons different? Judging from the appearance of the icons, what would you guess these two files contain?
   5. Which file in the root directory has the most recent date?

4. **More Practice with Files and Folders** For this assignment, you need a third blank disk. Complete steps a through g below to practice your file-management skills.

  a. Write "Windows 2000 Tutorial 2 Assignment 4" on the label of the blank disk, and then format the disk if necessary.
  b. Create another copy of your original Data Disk, using the Assignment 4 disk. Refer to the section "Creating Your Data Disk" in Session 2.2.
  c. Create three folders on the Assignment 4 Data Disk you just created: Documents, Budgets, and Graphics.
  d. Move the files **Interior**, **Exterior**, **Logo**, and **Newlogo** to the Graphics folder.
  e. Move the files **Travel**, **Members**, and **Minutes** to the Documents folder.
  f. Move **Budget2001** and **Budget2002** to the Budgets folder.
  g. Switch to Details view and write out your answers to Questions 1 through 6:
   1. What is the largest file or files in the Graphics folder?
   2. How many word-processed documents are in the root directory? *Hint*: These documents will appear with the WordPad, Microsoft Word, or some other word-processing icon, depending on what software you have installed.
   3. What is the newest file or files in the root directory (don't include folders)?
   4. How many files in all folders are 5 KB in size?
   5. How many files in the root directory are WKS files? *Hint*: Look in the Type column to identify WKS files.
   6. Do all the files in the Graphics folder have the same icon? What type are they?

5. **Searching for a File** Windows 2000 Help includes a topic that discusses how to search for files on a disk without looking through all the folders. Start Windows Help, then locate this topic, and answer Questions a through c:

  a. To display the Search dialog box, you must click the _____ button, then point to _____ on the menu, and finally click _____ on the submenu.
  b. Do you need to type in the entire filename to find the file?
  c. How do you perform a case-sensitive search?

6. **Help with Files and Folders** In Tutorial 2 you learned how to work with Windows 2000 files and folders. What additional information on this topic does Windows 2000 Help provide? Use the Start button to access Help. Use the Index tab to locate topics related to files and folders. Find at least two tips or procedures for working with files and folders that were not covered in the tutorial. Write out the tip in your own words and include the title of the Help screen that contains the information.

7. **Formatting Text** You can use a word processor such as WordPad to format text, that is, to give it a specific look and feel by using bold, italics, and different fonts, and by applying other features. Using WordPad, type the title and words to one of your favorite songs and

then save the document on your Data Disk (make sure you use your original Data Disk) with the filename Song.

a. Select the title, and then click the Center ≣ , Bold **B** , and Italic *I* buttons on the toolbar.

b. Click the Font list arrow and select a different font. Repeat this step several times with different fonts until you locate a font that is appropriate for the song.

c. Experiment with other formatting options until you find a look you like for your document. Save and print the final version.

PROJECTS

1. Formatting a floppy disk removes all the data on a disk. Answer the following questions using full sentences:

   a. What other method did you learn in this tutorial for removing data from a disk?

   b. If you wanted to remove all data from a disk, which method would you use? Why?

   c. What method would you use if you wanted to remove only one file? Why?

2. A friend who is new to computers is trying to learn how to enter text into WordPad. She has just finished typing her first paragraph when she notices a mistake in the first sentence. She can't remember how to fix a mistake, so she asks you for help. Write the set of steps she should try.

3. Computer users usually develop habits about how they access their files and programs. Follow the steps below to practice methods of opening a file, and then evaluate which method you would be likely to use and why.

   a. Using WordPad, create a document containing the words to a favorite poem, and save it on your Data Disk with the name Poem.

   b. Close WordPad and return to the desktop.

   c. Open the document using a document-centric approach.

   d. After a successful completion of step c, close the program and reopen the same document using another approach.

   e. Write the steps you used to complete steps c and d of this assignment. Then write a paragraph discussing which approach is most convenient when you are starting from the desktop, and indicate what habits you would develop if you owned your own computer and used it regularly.

Explore 4. The My Computer window gives you access to the objects on your computer. In this tutorial you used My Computer to access your floppy drive so you could view the contents of your Data Disk. The My Computer window gives you access to other objects too. Open My Computer and write a list of the objects you see, including folders. Then open each icon and write a two-sentence description of the contents of each window that opens.

Explore 5. In this tutorial you learned how to copy a disk to protect yourself in the event of data loss. If you had your own computer with an 80 MB hard drive that was being used to capacity, it would take many 1.44 MB floppy disks to copy the contents of the entire hard drive. Is copying to floppy disks a reasonable method to use for protecting the data on your hard disk? Why, or why not?

   a. As mentioned at the end of the tutorial, Windows 2000 also includes an accessory called Backup that helps you safeguard your data. Backup doesn't just copy the data—it organizes it so that it takes up much less space than if you simply copied it. This program might not be installed on your computer, but if it is, try starting it (click the Start button, point to Programs, point to Accessories, point to System Tools, and then click Backup) and opening the Help files to learn what you can about how it functions. If it is not installed, skip Part a.

   b. Look up the topic of backups in a computer concepts textbook or in computer trade magazines. You could also interview experienced computer owners to find out which method they use to protect their data. When you have finished researching the concept of the backup, write a single-page essay that explains the difference between copying and backing up files, and evaluates which method is preferable for backing up large amounts of data, and why.

Using Files

LAB ASSIGNMENTS

Using Files In this Lab you manipulate a simulated computer to view what happens in memory and on disk when you create, save, open, revise, and delete files. Understanding what goes on "inside the box" will help you quickly grasp how to perform basic file operations with most application software. See the Read This Before You Begin page for instructions on starting the Using Files Course Lab.

1. Click the Steps button to learn how to use the simulated computer to view the contents of memory and disk when you perform basic file operations. As you proceed through the Steps, answer all of the Quick Check questions that appear. After you complete the Steps, you will see a Quick Check Summary Report. Follow the instructions on the screen to print this report.

2. Click the Explore button and use the simulated computer to perform the following tasks:

   a. Create a document containing your name and the city in which you were born. Save this document as NAME.
   b. Create another document containing two of your favorite foods. Save this document as FOODS.
   c. Create another file containing your two favorite classes. Call this file CLASSES.
   d. Open the FOOD file and add another one of your favorite foods. Save this file without changing its name.
   e. Open the NAME file. Change this document so that it contains your name and the name of your school. Save this as a new document called SCHOOL.
   f. Write down how many files are on the simulated disk and the exact contents of each file.
   g. Delete all the files.

3. In Explore, use the simulated computer to perform the following tasks.

   a. Create a file called MUSIC that contains the name of your favorite CD.
   b. Create another document that contains eight numbers and call this file LOTTERY.
   c. You didn't win the lottery this week. Revise the contents of the LOTTERY file, but save the revision as LOTTERY2.
   d. Revise the MUSIC file so that it also contains the name of your favorite musician or composer, and save this file as MUSIC2.
   e. Delete the MUSIC file.
   f. Write down how many files are on the simulated disk and the exact contents of each file.

QUICK CHECK ANSWERS

Session 2.1
1. file
2. Formatting
3. True
4. insertion point
5. a list of recently opened files and objects
6. The Files of Type list box could be set to display files of a different type than the one you're looking for.
7. From the Print Preview window, using the Print button on the toolbar, and using the Print command from the File menu. If you want to print multiple copies of a file, use either the Print button from the Print Preview window or the Print command from the File menu—both of these techniques will display the Print dialog box containing the options you need to set.

Session 2.2
1. My Computer
2. A
3. hard
4. filename, size, type, and date modified
5. root or top-level
6. the Desktop
7. yes

New Perspectives on

MICROSOFT®
WINDOWS® 2000
PROFESSIONAL

Read This Before You Begin

To the Student

Make Data Disk Program

To complete the Level II tutorials, Review Assignments, and Projects, you need three Data Disks. Your instructor will either provide you with Data Disks or ask you to make your own.

If you are making your own Data Disks you will need three blank, formatted high-density disks and access to the Make Data Disk program. If you want to install the Make Data Disk program to your home computer, you can obtain it from your instructor or from the Web. To download the Make Data Disk program from the Web, go to www.course.com, click Data Disks, and follow the instructions on the screen.

To install the Make Data Disk program, select and click the file you just downloaded from www.course.com, 7093-8.exe. Follow the onscreen instructions to complete the installation. If you have any trouble obtaining or installing the Make Data Disk program, ask your instructor or technical support person for assistance.

Once you have obtained and installed the Make Data Disk program, you can use it to create your Data Disks according to the steps in the tutorials.

Course Labs

The Level II tutorials in this book feature two interactive Course Labs to help you understand Internet: World Wide Web and Web Pages & HTML concepts. There are Lab Assignments at the end of Tutorial 5 that relate to these Labs. To start a Lab, click the **Start** button on the Windows 2000 taskbar, point to **Programs**, point to **Course Labs**, point to **New Perspectives Course Labs**, and click the name of the Lab you want to use.

Using Your Own Computer

If you are going to work through this book using your own computer, you need:

- **Computer System** Microsoft Windows 2000 Professional must be installed on a local hard drive or on a network drive. This book is about Windows 2000 Professional—for those who have Windows 2000 Millennium, you might notice some differences.

- **Data Disks** You will not be able to complete the tutorials or exercises in this book using your own computer until you have your Data Disks. See "Make Data Disk Program" above for details on obtaining your Data Disks.

- **Course Labs** See your instructor or technical support person to obtain the Course Lab software for use on your own computer.

Visit Our World Wide Web Site

Additional materials designed especially for you are available on the World Wide Web. Go to http://www.course.com

To the Instructor

The Make Data Disk Program and Course Labs for this title are available in the Instructor's Resource Kit for this title. Follow the instructions in the Help file on the CD-ROM to install the programs to your network or standalone computer. For information on using the Make Data Disk Program or the Course Labs, see the "To the Student" section above. You are granted a license to copy the Data Files and Course Labs to any computer or computer network used by students who have purchased this book.

OBJECTIVES

In this tutorial you will:

- "Quick" format a floppy disk

- View the structure of folders and files in Windows Explorer

- Select, create, and rename folders in Windows Explorer

- Navigate through devices and folders using navigation buttons

- Select a single file, a group of files, all files, or all files but one

- Create a printout showing the structure of folders and files

- Move and copy one or more files from one disk to another

- Display lists of recently opened files

ORGANIZING FILES WITH WINDOWS EXPLORER

Structuring Information on a Disk at Kolbe Climbing School

CASE

Kolbe Climbing School

Bernard Kolbe knew how to climb before he could ride a bike. In college he started what is now one of the most popular guide services in the Front Range, the Kolbe Climbing School, known to locals as "KCS." KCS offers guided climbs in the Front Range area, especially in Rocky Mountain National Park and nearby climbing areas such as Lumpy Ridge. While most clients simply want to learn rock and sport climbing, a few want guides for longer alpine climbs and ice climbing.

Since he started his business, Bernard has handled the paperwork using yellow pads, clipboards, and manila folders. Recent conversations with his insurance agent and accountant, though, convinced him that he needs to keep better records on his employees, clients, and the use and condition of his equipment. The KCS offices adjoin a business services office, so Bernard rented some computer time and began creating the files he needs, storing them on a floppy disk.

Not too long ago, Bernard asked if you could help him out with KCS recordkeeping. You agreed (in exchange for some free climbing lessons) and got to work updating the client files on his floppy disk. When Bernard first gave you the disk he warned you that it could use a little organization, so you began by creating a folder structure on the disk.

This morning, you walked into the office to find that Bernard had spent yesterday evening at the rented computer adding new files to his disk. You realize you need to show him the folder structure you created so he can learn to use it. You point out that an important part of computerized recordkeeping is creating and using a system that makes it easy to find important information. Bernard is willing to learn more (it's too cold to climb anyway), so the two of you head over to the business services office to spend some time looking over Bernard's files.

SESSION 3.1

In this session, you will learn how Windows Explorer displays the devices and folders your computer can access. Understanding how to manipulate this display is the first step in using Windows Explorer to organize files, which will make you a more productive Windows user. In this tutorial you will work with files and folders on a floppy disk. If you have your own computer or are in a business environment, you will more likely work with files and folders on a hard drive. You will discover that file management techniques are practically the same for floppy disks and hard drives. For this tutorial, you will need two blank 3½-inch disks.

Creating Your Data Disk with Quick Format

Before you begin, you need to prepare a new Data Disk that contains the sample files you will work with in Tutorials 3 and 4. You can make your Data Disk using the NP on Microsoft Windows 2000 menu.

If you are using your own computer, the NP on Microsoft Windows 2000 menu will not be available. Before you proceed, bring a blank disk to your school's computer lab and use the NP on Microsoft Windows 2000 menu to make your new Data Disk. Once you have made the disk, you can use it to complete this tutorial on any computer that runs Windows 2000.

When you want to erase the contents of a floppy disk, you can use the Quick format option rather than the Full format that you use on a new disk. A Quick format takes less time than a Full format because, instead of preparing the entire disk surface, a Quick format erases something called the file allocation table. The **file allocation table (FAT)** contains information that your operating system uses to track the locations of all the files on the disk. By erasing the FAT, you erase all the information that tells the computer about the files on the disk, and so the disk appears empty to the computer. Note that to merely delete a few files from a floppy disk, you don't need to format the disk; you can just select the files (as you'll learn in this tutorial) and delete them.

To Quick format your Data Disk:

1. Write "Disk 2—Windows 2000 Tutorials 3 & 4 Data Disk" on the label of your disk.

2. Place your disk in drive A.

   TROUBLE? If your 3½-inch disk drive is B, place your disk in that drive instead, and for the rest of this tutorial substitute drive B wherever you see drive A.

3. Open the My Computer window.

4. Right-click the **3½ Floppy (A:)** icon.

5. Click **Format** to display the Format dialog box.

6. Click the **Quick Format** check box, as shown in Figure 3-1.

Figure 3-1	FORMAT DIALOG BOX

click to Quick
format a disk

7. Click the **Start** button and then click the **OK** button.

TROUBLE? If an error message appears, it is possible your disk capacity is double-density instead of high-density. Make sure you are using a high-density disk.

8. Wait a few moments. When the formatting is complete, click the **OK** button and then click the **Close** button.

9. Close the My Computer window.

Now that you have formatted your disk, you can make a Data Disk for Tutorials 3 and 4.

To create your Data Disk:

1. Click the **Start** button, point to **Programs**, point to **NP on Microsoft Windows 2000-Level II**, and then click **Disk 2 (Tutorials 3 & 4)**.

2. When a message box opens, click the **OK** button. Wait while the program copies the practice files to your formatted disk. When all the files have been copied, the program closes.

Windows Explorer

The root directory of Bernard's disk contains three folders—Clients, Gear, and Guides—plus the files he hasn't yet organized.

One tool for file organization tasks, you tell Bernard, is Windows Explorer. **Windows Explorer** is a program included with Windows 2000 that is designed to simplify file management tasks. Through an easy-to-navigate representation of the resources on your computer, Windows Explorer makes it easy to view, move, copy, or delete your files and folders.

Many of the techniques you used in Tutorial 2 with the My Computer window apply to Windows Explorer—and vice-versa. A window like the My Computer window can be modified to appear like Windows Explorer. So as you learn about Windows Explorer, keep in mind that you can apply these tools to almost any Windows 2000 window that displays the contents of a folder or drive.

Starting Windows Explorer

As with other Windows 2000 applications, you start Windows Explorer using the Start menu. It is possible that on your desktop is a Windows Explorer icon, which you can click to start Windows Explorer easily.

To start Windows Explorer:

1. Make sure your Data Disk is in drive A, click the **Start** button [Start], point to **Programs**, point to **Accessories**, and then click **Windows Explorer**.

   TROUBLE? If you can't see Windows Explorer on the Accessories menu, the menu item has been temporarily hidden. Click the two arrows pointing down to display the complete menu, and then click Windows Explorer.

2. If the Exploring window is not maximized, click the **Maximize** button [□].

Like the My Computer window, the Exploring window can display the Standard, Address, Links, and Radio toolbars and a status bar. For this tutorial, you need to make sure you can see the Standard toolbar, the Address bar, and the status bar. These are the default settings for Windows 2000. To match the figures in this tutorial, you should also display the files in Large Icons view rather than the other views offered by Windows 2000.

To set up the appearance of Windows Explorer:

1. Click **View** and then point to **Toolbars**. Make the necessary changes so that the Standard Buttons toolbar and the Address Bar are the only toolbars displayed.

2. If necessary, reopen the View menu. Make sure that Status Bar is checked and the Large Icons option is selected. If Status Bar is not checked, click Status Bar. If Large Icons is not selected, open the menu again if necessary and then select Large Icons.

Displaying the Explorer Bar

Windows Explorer is divided into two sections called **panes**. The left pane, also called the **Explorer bar**, shows different ways of locating specific files or folders on your computer. The pane on the right displays lists of these files and folders (similar to the view of files and folders you had in examining the contents of the floppy disk in Tutorial 2).

The Explorer bar can be displayed in one of four ways: as a Search pane, a Favorites pane, a History pane, or a Folders pane. The **Search** pane includes tools to help you search for a particular file or folder on your computer. The **Favorites** pane displays a list of your favorite files and folders on your computer and sites on the World Wide Web. The **History** pane organizes the files and folders on your computer by the date you last worked with them. The **Folders** pane organizes your files and folders based on their location in the hierarchy of objects on your computer. To move between these different panes, you click the appropriate button on the Standard Buttons toolbar or choose the appropriate option from the View menu. Note that the Explorer bar is available in any Windows 2000 window that displays files and folders. You can, for example, use the Explorer bar in the My Computer window.

You'll start working with Windows Explorer by making sure that the Folders pane is displayed.

> ### To view the Folders pane:
>
> 1. Click **View** and then point to **Explorer Bar**.
>
> 2. Make sure that the Folders option has a check mark next to it. If it does not, click Folders; otherwise click a blank area of the screen to close the View menu. Your Exploring window should now resemble Figure 3-2.

Figure 3-2	WINDOWS EXPLORER OVERVIEW

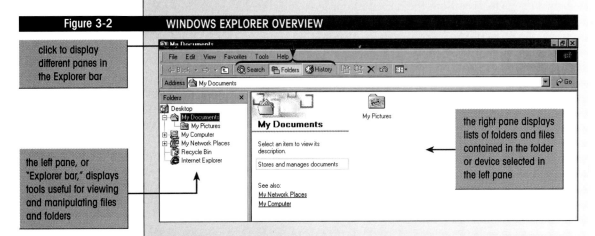

click to display different panes in the Explorer bar

the left pane, or "Explorer bar," displays tools useful for viewing and manipulating files and folders

the right pane displays lists of folders and files contained in the folder or device selected in the left pane

TROUBLE? Depending on the configuration of your computer, your Windows Explorer window may look slightly different from the one displayed in Figure 3-2.

The Folders pane initially displays a list of the objects on your desktop: the My Documents folder, the My Computer window, the My Network Places window, the Recycle Bin, and Internet Explorer. If your desktop contains other folders or objects, those will be displayed as well. The right pane of the Exploring window displays the contents of the object selected in the Folders pane. In this case, the My Documents folder is the selected object, and it contains only one item—the My Pictures folder. An icon for this object is therefore displayed in the right pane.

Working with the Folders Pane

To see the devices and resources available to your computer, you can scroll through the list of objects in the Folders pane. Each object in the list has a small icon next to it. In this session you will use the Folders pane to explore your computer's contents. Explorer uses the icons shown in Figure 3-3, among others, to represent different types of storage objects.

Figure 3-3	STORAGE DEVICE ICONS

ICON	REPRESENTS	ICON	REPRESENTS
	Floppy disk drive		Network disk drive
	Hard disk drive on your computer		CD ROM drive
	Shared disk drive		Zip drive

Opening an Object in the Folders Pane

Like a file cabinet, a typical storage device on your computer contains files and folders. These folders can contain additional files and one or more levels of subfolders. If Windows Explorer displayed all the storage devices, folders, and files on your computer at once, it could be a very long list. Instead, Windows Explorer allows you to open devices and folders only when you want to see what they contain. Otherwise, you can keep them closed.

The small icon next to each object in the list, called the **device icon** or **folder icon**, represents the device or folder on your computer. Many of these icons also have a plus box or minus box next to them, which indicates whether the device or folder contains additional folders. Both the device/folder icon and the plus/minus box are controls that you can click to change the display in the Exploring window. You click the plus box to display folders or subfolders, and you click the minus box to hide them. (You can also refer to clicking the plus box as "expanding" the view of the file hierarchy, and clicking the minus box as "collapsing" the view of the file hierarchy.) You click the device/folder icon to control the display of object contents in the right pane.

You begin assisting Bernard by showing him how you've structured the folders on drive A, which is located in the Windows 2000 hierarchy beneath the My Computer icon. You explain to him how the plus/minus boxes can be used to open the My Computer icon and then the drive icon for his floppy disk.

REFERENCE WINDOW **RW**

Displaying or Hiding Objects in the Folders Pane
- Click the plus box ⊞ next to a device or folder to display its next level of folders.
- Click the minus box ⊟ next to a device or folder to hide all its subfolders.

To display or hide the levels of folders on drive A:

1. Click ⊞ to the left of the My Computer icon in the Folders pane.

2. Click the ⊞ to the left of the 3½ Floppy (A:) device icon. The folders in the root directory of drive A appear in the left pane, and the plus box in front of drive A changes to a minus box ⊟. See Figure 3-4.

| Figure 3-4 | FOLDERS ON DRIVE A, DISPLAYED IN THE FOLDERS PANE |

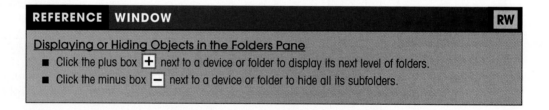
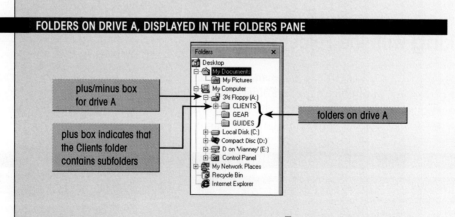

plus/minus box
for drive A

plus box indicates that
the Clients folder
contains subfolders

folders on drive A

TROUBLE? The 3½ Floppy (A:) device icon 🖫 might appear with a different name on your computer. This is the icon representing the device that contains your Data Disk. In the steps in this tutorial, this icon is called simply drive A.

TROUBLE? If you initially see a minus box in front of the device icon for drive A, your drive A folders are already visible in the left pane. You don't need to click the icon in Step 1.

3. Click ⊟ in front of 3½ Floppy (A:). Now the Folders pane shows only drive A, without the folders it contains.

4. Click ⊞ in front of 3½ Floppy (A:) one more time to redisplay the folders on the drive.

When you click the plus box ⊞ next to drive A, you do not necessarily see all the folders on the drive. You only see the first level of folders. If one of these folders contains subfolders, a plus box appears next to it. The Clients folder on drive A has a plus box next to it, indicating that it contains subfolders. When you originally created the structure for Bernard's disk, you grouped his clients into Advanced and Basic, and then grouped the Advanced clients by their primary interests—Alpine, Ice, and Sport.

To view the subfolders for Clients:

1. Click ⊞ next to the Clients folder. You see that Clients contains two subfolders: Advanced and Basic. Because there is a ⊞ box next to the Advanced folder, you know it contains subfolders as well.

2. Click ⊞ next to the Advanced folder. Now you see three additional subfolders: Alpine, Ice, and Sport. See Figure 3-5.

| Figure 3-5 | ENTIRE FOLDER AND SUBFOLDER STRUCTURE ON DRIVE A |

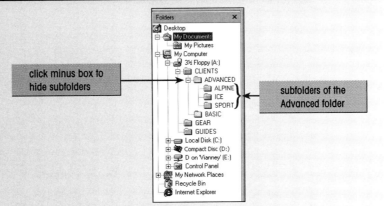

click minus box to hide subfolders

subfolders of the Advanced folder

3. Click ⊟ next to the Clients folder to hide its folders. Notice that you were able to "collapse" the entire Clients folder hierarchy by clicking the Clients minus box; you didn't have to click each level.

4. Click ⊞ next to the Clients folder again. Note that the entire folder structure is displayed again—including the subfolders—because the last time you collapsed the Clients folder, you had all its subfolders displayed.

Selecting an Object in the Folders Pane

To work with a device or folder in the Folders pane, you first click it to select it, and Windows highlights it. It is important to understand that using the plus/minus box does not select a device or folder. Notice that as you were clicking the plus/minus boxes in front of the folders in drive A, the right pane still displayed the contents of the My Documents folder.

To select a device or folder, you must click its icon, not its plus/minus box. When you select a device or folder, it becomes active. The **active** device or folder is the one the computer uses when you take an action. For example, if you want to create a new folder on drive A, you first need to select drive A in the Folders Explorer bar. It then becomes the active drive. If you don't first activate drive A, the new folder you create will be placed in whatever device or folder is currently active—it could be a folder on the hard drive or network drive. How do you know which device or folder is active? You can know in three ways. First, it is selected. Second, its name appears in the Address bar and finally, its contents appear in the right pane.

You can experiment with changing the active device and folder by selecting drive A and then selecting the Clients folder.

To select devices and folders:

1. Click 🖫 **3½ Floppy (A:)** if necessary. To show that drive A is selected, the computer highlights the label and displays it in the Address Bar.

2. Click 🗀 **Clients** in the Folders pane. The computer highlights the label "Clients" and displays it in the Address bar. Its contents appear in the right pane. See Figure 3-6.

Figure 3-6	THE ACTIVE DEVICE OR FOLDER IN THE FOLDERS PANE

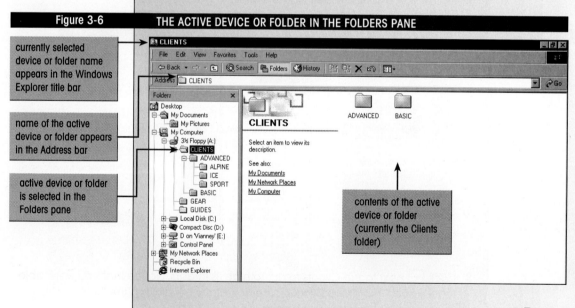

currently selected device or folder name appears in the Windows Explorer title bar

name of the active device or folder appears in the Address bar

active device or folder is selected in the Folders pane

contents of the active device or folder (currently the Clients folder)

Note that as you click the Clients folder icon, it changes from a 🗀 to a 🗁 indicating that the folder is "open," that is it's become active, and its contents are displayed in the right pane of the Explorer window.

Creating a New Folder

You can create a new folder using the same techniques you used to create new folders in Tutorial 2. You just have to make sure that you've selected the correct object in the Folders pane before inserting the new folder.

Bernard tracks gear usage for ropes and other types of equipment such as carabiners, belay plates, and so on. His disk already contains a folder named "Gear" that contains files for each of the KCS ropes. You decide to create two new subfolders within the Gear folder: one for all files having to do with ropes and the other for files having to do with hardware equipment.

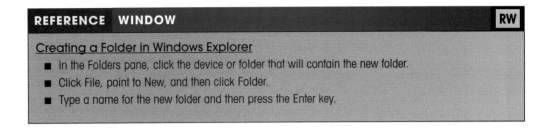

REFERENCE WINDOW RW

Creating a Folder in Windows Explorer
- In the Folders pane, click the device or folder that will contain the new folder.
- Click File, point to New, and then click Folder.
- Type a name for the new folder and then press the Enter key.

The Clients folder is currently active. If you create a new folder now, it will become a subfolder of Clients. Because you want to create the two subfolders in the Gear folder, you must make the Gear folder active.

To create the new subfolders within the Gear folder:

1. Click 📁 **Gear** in the Folders pane to activate the Gear folder.

2. Click **File** on the menu bar, point to **New**, and then click **Folder**. A folder icon labeled "New Folder" appears in the right pane. The folder name is selected, and anything you type will replace the current name.

3. Type **Hardware** as the title of the new folder, and then press the **Enter** key. Now create the second subfolder of the Gear folder for all the rope files.

   TROUBLE? If you pressed Enter twice by mistake, Hardware becomes the active folder. Be sure Gear is still the active folder; click the Gear folder icon in the left pane, if necessary.

4. Click **File**, point to **New**, click **Folder**, type **Ropes** as the name of the second folder, and then press the **Enter** key.

5. Click ➕ next to the Gear folder in the left pane to see the new folders in the left pane. See Figure 3-7.

| Figure 3-7 | CREATING NEW FOLDERS |

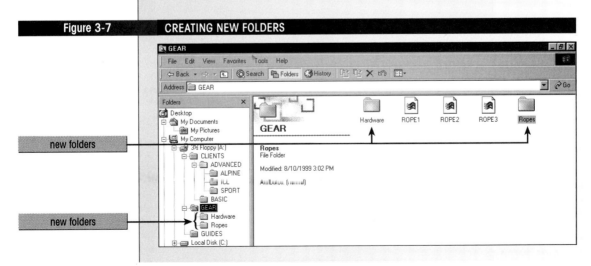

As you and Bernard go over the current folder structure, you realize that a complete inventory of the KCS gear also includes the harnesses climbers wear to attach themselves to the rope for protection in case they fall. Because harnesses aren't considered hardware, you decide that the harness inventory files should go in the same folder with the ropes. Thus, you need to rename the Ropes folder "Ropes and Harnesses." You rename a folder by right-clicking the folder icon in either the Folders pane or the right pane and then clicking the Rename command.

To change the name of the Ropes folder:

1. Right-click **Ropes** in the Folders pane.

2. Click **Rename**. The folder name is selected, and anything you type will replace the current name.

3. Type **Ropes and Harnesses** as the new folder name, and then press the **Enter** key.

The new name now appears in both the left and right panes, although it might be truncated if the panes are too narrow to display it.

Adjusting the Width of the Folders Pane

As you create or view more and more levels of folders, the Explorer bar might not be wide enough to display all the levels of folders. As a result, you might not be able to see all the device and folder icons. Whether or not this occurs depends on how long your folder names are and how wide the All Folders Explorer bar was in the first place. You can change the width of the Exploring window panes by dragging the dividing bar that separates the two panes.

REFERENCE WINDOW   RW

Adjusting the Width of the Explorer bar
- Move the mouse pointer to the dividing bar between the left and right panes.
- When the arrow-shaped pointer ⌖ changes to a double-ended arrow ←→, hold down the left mouse button and drag the dividing line right or left, as necessary.
- When the dividing bar is in the desired position, release the mouse button.

To increase the width of the Explorer bar:

1. Move the mouse pointer to the dividing bar between the two panes. The ⌖ pointer changes to a ←→ pointer.

2. Hold down the left mouse button while you drag the dividing bar about one-half inch to the right, as shown in Figure 3-8.

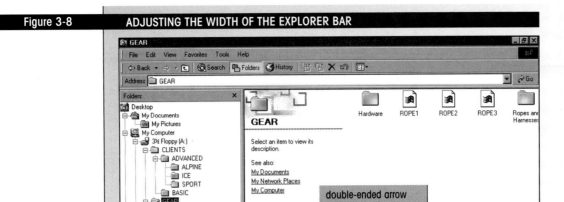

| Figure 3-8 | ADJUSTING THE WIDTH OF THE EXPLORER BAR |

3. Release the mouse button. Use this method as necessary when you work with the Explorer Bar.

4. Click the **Close** button [X] to close the Exploring window. You return to the Windows 2000 desktop.

Session 3.1 QUICK CHECK

1. _____ is an alternative to using My Computer for file management tasks.

2. The Exploring window is divided into two panes. Describe each pane, using one sentence for each pane.

3. True or False: If you see folders with the same names in both the right and left panes of the Exploring window, the folders are duplicates and you should erase those in the right pane.

4. True or False: The Folders pane displays all the files in a folder.

5. A folder that is contained in another folder is referred to as a(n) _____.

6. You click the _____ to expand the display of folders in the Folders pane.

7. If you want to create a new folder on drive A, what should you first click in the Folders pane?

8. True or False: The Explorer Bar exists *only* in Windows Explorer. You cannot use the Explorer Bar in the My Computer window.

SESSION 3.2

In Session 3.2 you will work with the right pane of the Exploring window, which displays folders and files. You'll learn how to select multiple files from the right pane. You'll work with different methods of moving and copying files from one location to another. You'll also see how to print a copy of the Explorer window to use as a reference later on.

Working with Files in Windows Explorer

Now that you've worked with the Explorer bar, it's time to put the right pane of Windows Explorer to use. You've already created a folder structure for Bernard's files. Now you have to work on putting the right files into the proper folders. To do this you have to learn how to select and work with multiple files in the Explorer window. Before getting started, you should reopen the Data Disk.

To open the Data Disk:

1. Make sure your Data Disk is in drive A, and then start Windows Explorer. Set up Windows Explorer so that the Standard Buttons toolbar, Address Bar, and Folders pane are all visible.

2. Locate and click the 🖥 **3½ Floppy (A)** in the Folders pane to display the contents of the root directory of drive A.

3. Click **View** on the menu bar and then click **Details** to display the file icons in Details view.

Working with files displayed in the right pane is exactly like working with files displayed in the My Computer window or any Windows 2000 window that displays a list of files. You can use the View command, switching from Large Icons view to Details or Thumbnails view. You can click the Back ⬅, Forward ➡ and Up buttons 🗁 buttons to navigate through the hierarchy of objects in your computer. You can open a file by clicking its icon and pressing the Enter key. You can rename a file by right-clicking its icon and choosing the Rename command from the menu. Selecting which files to work with is the same as well.

Selecting Multiple Files

You select files by clicking the file's icon in the right pane of the Explorer window. If you want to select multiple files, Windows 2000 provides several different ways of accomplishing this. The first technique you'll explore is how to select all of the files in a folder. You can do this by using one of the commands in the Windows Explorer menu.

To select all of the files in the root directory:

1. Click **Edit** on the menu bar and then click **Select All**. Explorer highlights the files and folders to show that they are selected. Note that the status bar indicates that 19 objects are selected and that the total size of the selection is 158 kilobytes. See Figure 3-9.

Figure 3-9	SELECTING ALL FILES IN A FOLDER

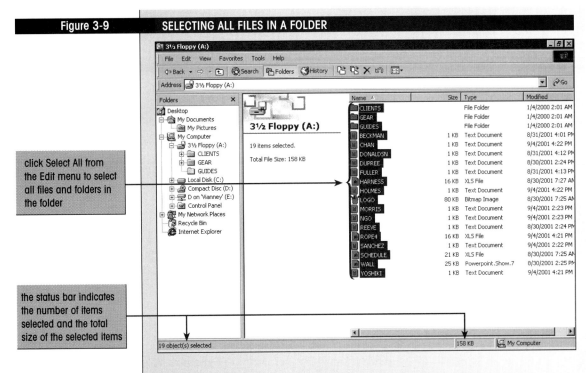

click Select All from the Edit menu to select all files and folders in the folder

the status bar indicates the number of items selected and the total size of the selected items

2. Deselect the files by clicking any blank area. The highlighting is removed to indicate that no files are currently selected.

What if you want to work with more than one file, but not with all the files in a folder? For example, suppose Bernard wants to delete three of the files in a folder. In Explorer there are two ways to select a group of files. You can select files listed consecutively using the Shift key, or you can select files scattered throughout the right pane using the Ctrl key. Figure 3-10 shows the two different ways to select a group of files.

Figure 3-10	TWO WAYS TO SELECT A GROUP OF FILES

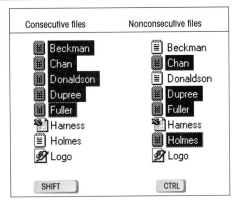

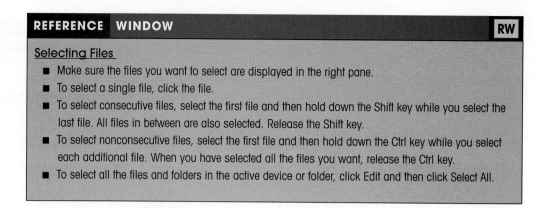

REFERENCE WINDOW   RW

Selecting Files

- Make sure the files you want to select are displayed in the right pane.
- To select a single file, click the file.
- To select consecutive files, select the first file and then hold down the Shift key while you select the last file. All files in between are also selected. Release the Shift key.
- To select nonconsecutive files, select the first file and then hold down the Ctrl key while you select each additional file. When you have selected all the files you want, release the Ctrl key.
- To select all the files and folders in the active device or folder, click Edit and then click Select All.

First try selecting a set of consecutive files, and then a set of nonconsecutive files scattered within a folder.

To select groups of files:

1. Make sure the right pane displays the root directory of drive A and then click the **Beckman** file icon.

2. Hold down the **Shift** key while you click the **Fuller** file. Release the **Shift** key. The Beckman and Fuller files and all files in between are selected. See Figure 3-11.

Figure 3-11   SELECTING CONSECUTIVE FILES

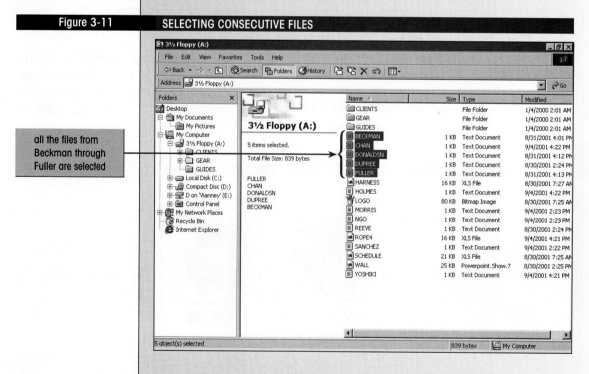

all the files from
Beckman through
Fuller are selected

3. Now select a set of nonconsecutive files. First click the **Reeve** file. Notice that selecting this file automatically deselects any selected files.

4. Hold down the **Ctrl** key and select the **Morris** file and then the **Sanchez** file. All three files should be selected. Release the **Ctrl** key. See Figure 3-12.

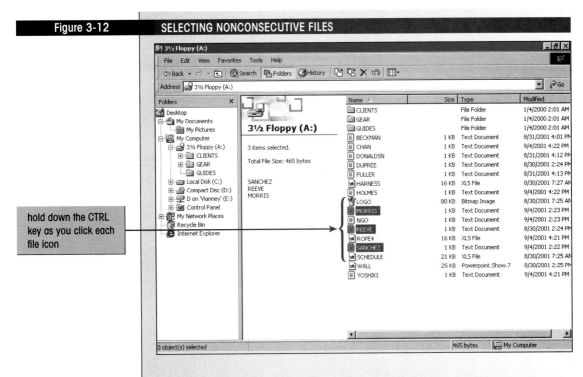

| Figure 3-12 | SELECTING NONCONSECUTIVE FILES |

hold down the CTRL key as you click each file icon

TROUBLE? If you release the Ctrl key by mistake while selecting a set of nonconsecutive files, press it again and select the files you want.

While selecting multiple files with the Ctrl key, you can deselect any file by clicking it again while holding down the Ctrl key. You can also select more files by holding down the Ctrl key again, then selecting the additional files. The files do not need to be in consecutive order for you to select them as a group.

To select and deselect additional files:

1. Hold down the **Ctrl** key and click the **Chan** file to select it. Four files are now selected.

2. Keep holding down the **Ctrl** key and click the **Sanchez** file to deselect it. Now three files are selected: Chan, Morris, and Reeve.

Suppose you want to select all the files in a folder except one. You can use the Invert Selection menu option to select all the files that are not selected.

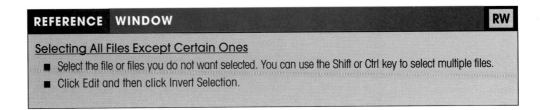

| REFERENCE | WINDOW | | RW |

Selecting All Files Except Certain Ones
- Select the file or files you do not want selected. You can use the Shift or Ctrl key to select multiple files.
- Click Edit and then click Invert Selection.

To use Invert Selection to select all files except Dupree:

1. Click the **Dupree** file icon.

2. Click **Edit** and then click **Invert Selection**. All the folders and files except Dupree are now selected.

3. Click a blank area to remove the highlighting for all the files on drive A.

Selecting Files in Web Style

Up to now, you've been selecting files using the Windows 2000 default method. You may be more comfortable using a "Web-style" method, in which files are selected and deselected by simply pointing to the file icon with the mouse pointer. To select consecutive files, you point to the first file in the list, hold down the Shift key and then point to the last file in the list. To select a group of individual files, you hold down the Ctrl key as you point to each file in the list. The advantage of this method is that there are fewer mouse-clicks involved for each action, something people with computer-related hand and wrist problems would need.

To turn on the Web-style file selection:

1. Click **Tools** and then click **Folder Options**.

2. Click the **General** dialog sheet tab, if necessary, to display the General dialog sheet.

3. Click the **Single-click to open an item (point to select)** option button. See Figure 3-13.

Figure 3-13	TURNING ON WEB-STYLE FILE SELECTION

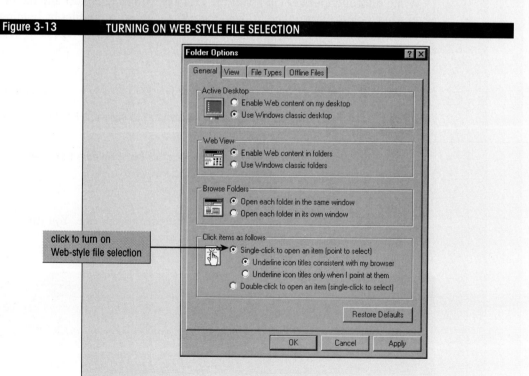

click to turn on Web-style file selection

At this point, if you click the OK or Apply buttons, you can start selecting files by pointing at them, rather than clicking. However, since this book assumes that you'll use the Default option, you'll close this dialog box *without* enacting any changes.

4. Click the **Cancel** button to close the Folder Options dialog box without making any changes.

You may find that this method of file selection works best for you. Try experimenting on your own later.

Printing the Exploring Window

You are almost ready to start moving Bernard's files into the appropriate folders. Bernard would like to identify the files that need to be moved. He wonders if there's a quick way to get a hard copy (that is, a paper copy) of the Exploring window so he can write on it. You tell him you can temporarily store an image of your computer screen in memory using the Print Screen key. Then, you can start the WordPad program and paste the image into a blank WordPad document. Finally, you can print the document, which will contain an image of your screen—in this case, the Exploring window. It can be handy to have a printout of the structures of certain important devices for reference, so this is a good procedure to learn.

To print the Exploring window:

1. Make sure the right pane still displays the contents of drive A; if not, click **3½ Floppy (A:)** in the left pane.

2. Click ➕ next to 3½ Floppy (A:), FlooClients, Advanced, and Gear as necessary so that all the folders and subfolders on Bernard's disk are visible.

3. Press the **Print Screen** key. Although it seems as if nothing happens, an image of the Exploring window is stored in memory.

   TROUBLE? If you cannot locate the Print Screen key, it might be accessible through another key on your keyboard or it might be labeled with an abbreviation such as "PrtScn." Ask your instructor or technical support person for help.

4. Start WordPad.

5. Maximize the WordPad window if necessary, type your name and the date at the top of the WordPad window, and then press the **Enter** key twice.

6. Click the **Paste** button 📋 and then scroll to the top of the document (also scroll left, if necessary). The picture of the Exploring window appears in the WordPad document. See Figure 3-14.

Figure 3-14 | **WINDOWS EXPLORER SCREEN IMAGE IN WORDPAD**

picture of Exploring window within WordPad →

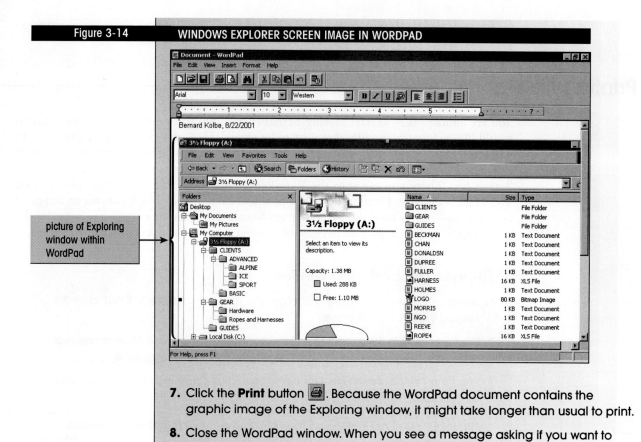

7. Click the **Print** button 🖨. Because the WordPad document contains the graphic image of the Exploring window, it might take longer than usual to print.

8. Close the WordPad window. When you see a message asking if you want to save changes to the document, click the **No** button.

9. Return to Windows Explorer.

Bernard annotates the printout as shown in Figure 3-15. His notes show you where to move the files in the root directory.

Figure 3-15 | **BERNARD'S PRINTOUT**

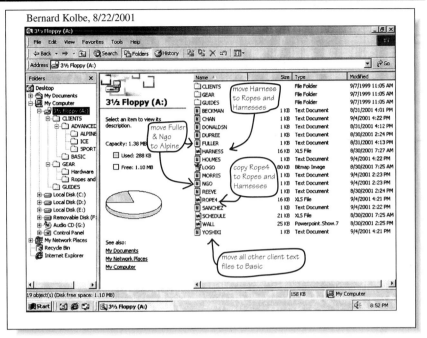

Moving Files in the Explorer Window

You've already had some experience in moving files. You saw in Tutorial 2 how you could right-click an object and drag it into a folder on a floppy disk, choosing whether to copy or move the file. Moving files in Windows Explorer is exactly the same, except that you have the added benefit of using the Folders pane to navigate the hierarchy of Windows 2000 objects. Because the Folders pane can display a detailed tree of folders and devices, you can easily move a file to almost any location on your computer.

Bernard has already marked the printout you created to show which files you need to move. You begin by moving the Harness file from the root directory to the Equipment folder.

To move the Harness file:

1. Make sure that the active device in the Folders pane is the 3½ Floppy (A:) drive and that in the Folders pane you can see both the Hardware and the Ropes and Harnesses subfolders of the Gears folder.

2. Hold down the right mouse button while you drag the Harness file icon from the right pane to the Ropes and Harnesses folder, as shown in Figure 3-16.

| Figure 3-16 | MOVING A SINGLE FILE USING THE FOLDERS PANE |

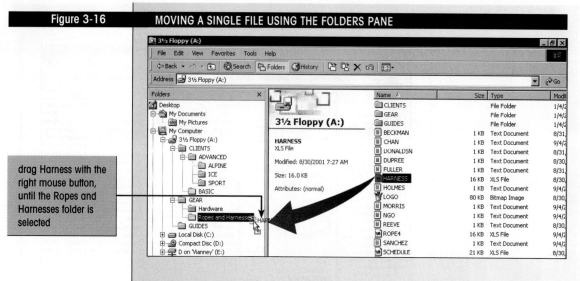

drag Harness with the right mouse button, until the Ropes and Harnesses folder is selected

3. Make sure the Ropes and Harnesses folder is selected, and then release the right mouse button. Click **Move Here** from the shortcut menu that appears.

TROUBLE? If you selected the wrong folder, click Cancel on the shortcut menu and repeat Steps 1 through 3.

TROUBLE? If you moved the file to a different folder by mistake, click Undo Move from the Edit menu and then repeat Steps 1 through 3.

The Harness file is moved to the new folder, and it disappears from the right pane.

4. Click 🗀 **Ropes and Harnesses** in the Folders pane. The Harness file should appear in the right pane.

If you use other Windows programs, you know that in most programs you drag objects with the left mouse button. Although you can drag files in Windows Explorer with the left mouse button, be careful. When you use the left mouse button, Windows Explorer will not open the shortcut menu. Instead, it will simply move or copy the file to the folder you selected, depending on the circumstances. When you drag a file from one folder to another on the same drive, Explorer moves the file. However, when you drag a file from a folder on one drive to a folder on a different drive, Explorer copies the file; it does not move it. Therefore, to prevent mistakes and lost files, most beginners should use the right mouse button to drag files.

Bernard recently purchased a fourth rope, and he is tracking its use in the file Rope4. He wants a copy of the Rope4 file in the Ropes and Harnesses folder.

To copy the Rope4 file into the Ropes folder:

1. Click 💾 **3½ Floppy (A:)** in the Folders pane to view the files in the root directory once again.

2. Hold down the right mouse button while you drag the **Rope4** icon from the root directory to the Ropes and Harnesses folder.

3. Make sure the Ropes and Harnesses folder is selected, and then release the right mouse button.

4. Click **Copy Here** from the shortcut menu. Rope4 is copied from the root directory to the Ropes and Harnesses folder. Notice that Rope4 is still displayed in the right pane for drive A, because you copied the file rather than moved it.

> **5.** Click 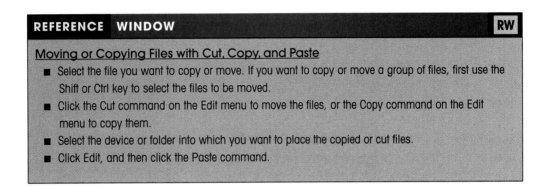 **Ropes and Harnesses** in the Folders pane and notice that Rope4 now appears in this folder along with the Harness file.

Moving Files with Cut and Paste

Although dragging works well when you can see the file in the right pane and its destination folder in the Folders pane, this will not always be the case. Instead of dragging, you can use the Cut, Copy, and Paste buttons on the Standard Buttons toolbar to move or copy objects. The Cut, Copy, and Paste commands are also available on the selected objects' shortcut menus.

REFERENCE WINDOW   **RW**

<u>Moving or Copying Files with Cut, Copy, and Paste</u>
- Select the file you want to copy or move. If you want to copy or move a group of files, first use the Shift or Ctrl key to select the files to be moved.
- Click the Cut command on the Edit menu to move the files, or the Copy command on the Edit menu to copy them.
- Select the device or folder into which you want to place the copied or cut files.
- Click Edit, and then click the Paste command.

Bernard wants to move the three rope files from the Gear folder to the Ropes and Harnesses folder. The rope files are listed consecutively, so you should use the Shift key to select these three files and then you move them as a group. Then use the Cut and Paste commands to move the files.

To move the rope files to the Ropes and Harnesses folder:

1. Click the 🗀 **Gear** folder in the left pane to activate the Gear folder and view the other rope files, which also need to be moved into the Ropes and Harnesses folder.

2. Select the three rope files, **Rope1**, **Rope2**, and **Rope3** using the usual techniques to select multiple files.

3. Click **Edit** on the menu bar and then click **Cut**.

4. Click the **Ropes and Harnesses** folder in the Folders pane.

5. Click **Edit** and then click **Paste** to move the files to the Ropes and Harnesses folder. The Ropes and Harnesses folder now contains Harness, Rope1, Rope2, Rope3, and Rope4.

If you cut or copy a file or set of files but then neglect to paste them into a destination folder, don't worry. Windows Explorer doesn't actually carry out the cut or copy until you paste. It simply flags the file until it actually performs the action desired. Thus, if you close Windows Explorer without having pasted a file, the file remains in its original position.

Using the Move To Folder and Copy To Folder Commands

You've got Bernard's gear files organized, so now it's time to look at the new client files he added. Mark Fuller and George Ngo are interested exclusively in alpine climbing, so you'll move the Fuller and Ngo client files into the Alpine folder. If you want to move these folders without having to work with the Folders pane, you can do so with the Move To Folder and Copy To Folder commands. These commands display a dialog box from which you can navigate the hierarchy of objects on your computer, explicitly choosing the folder that you want to move or copy the file selection to.

REFERENCE WINDOW   **RW**

<u>Moving or Copying Files with the Move To Folder and Copy To Folder commands</u>
- Select the file you want to copy or move. If you want to copy or move a group of files, first use the Shift or Ctrl key to select the files to be moved.
- Click Edit and Move To Folder to move the file(s).
- Click Edit and Copy To Folder to copy the file(s).
- Locate the folder you want to move or copy the files to in the Browse For Folder dialog box.

Try this technique now by moving the Fuller and Ngo files into the Alpine folder.

To move files using the Move To command:

1. Click 🖴 **3½ Floppy (A:)** in the Folders pane to display the files on the floppy disk's root directory.

2. Select the **Fuller** and **Ngo** files.

3. Click **Edit** on the menu bar and then click **Move To Folder**.

   The Browse For Folder dialog box opens and displays the hierarchy of objects and folders on your computer.

4. Click ⊞ in front of the My Computer icon to display the contents of that object.

5. Move through the rest of the hierarchy of objects by clicking ⊞ in front of the 3½ Floppy (A:) icon and then clicking the ⊞ boxes in front of the Clients and then the Advanced folders.

6. Click the 📁 **Alpine** folder icon to select this folder. The Browse For Folder dialog box should appear as shown in Figure 3-17.

Figure 3-17	MOVING FILES USING THE MOVE TO FOLDER COMMAND

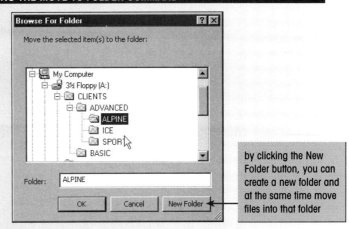

by clicking the New Folder button, you can create a new folder and at the same time move files into that folder

7. Click the **OK** button to move the files into the Alpine folder.

8. Click the **Alpine** folder in the Folders pane to confirm that the Ngo and Fuller files have been moved to that location (there should now be 5 files).

Moving Files of Similar Type

You need to move the remaining client files from the root directory into the Basic folder. You can combine some of the methods you have already learned to complete this task most efficiently. If you are in Details view, you'll see that the client files (the ones with people's names) are all text files. If you arrange these files by type, they'll all be next to each other, so you can select them as a group and move them together to the Basic folder. You'll use the technique of cutting and pasting to accomplish this task.

To move a group of related files to a new folder:

1. Click 🖴 **3½ Floppy (A:)** to display the files of the floppy drive's root directory.

2. If necessary, click **View** and then **Details** on the Explorer menu to display the files in the root directory in Details view.

3. Click the **Type** button. The client text files are now grouped together.

   TROUBLE? The Type button is at the top of the third column under the Address Bar in the right pane.

4. Use the Shift key to select the **Beckman** and **Yoshiki** text files and all the files in between.

5. Right-click the selection, click **Cut**, right-click the **Basic** folder icon in the Folders pane, and then click **Paste**. The files move from the root directory into the Basic folder.

Bernard's disk is now reorganized, with the appropriate files in the gear and client folders.

Moving or Copying Files Between Drives

So far all the moving and copying you've done has been within a single drive—the floppy drive. Often you will want to move or copy files between drives, for example between your floppy drive and your hard drive, or between one floppy drive and another. You can do this using the same techniques you've learned so far: dragging and dropping with the right mouse button, using cut and paste, and so forth.

Moving Files from the Floppy to the Hard Drive

In your computer lab you will rarely need to copy a file from your floppy drive to the hard drive of a lab computer. However, if you have a computer at home, you might frequently want to move or copy files from your floppy disk to your hard drive, to take advantage of its speed and large storage capacity. To practice this task, copy the Excel spreadsheet file named Schedule to the hard drive.

> ### To copy a file from a floppy disk to the hard drive:
>
> **1.** If necessary, scroll through the left pane so you can see the icon for drive C.
>
> **2.** Click ▭ **(C:)** in the Folders pane. Your drive C icon might appear slightly different if it is a network or shared drive.
>
> **3.** Click **File**, point to **New**, and then click **Folder** to create a new folder on drive C.
>
> TROUBLE? If a message warns you that you can't create a folder on drive C, you might be on a computer that restricts hard drive access. Ask your instructor or technical support person about other options for working on a hard drive, and read through the rest of this section to learn how you would work on a hard drive if you had the opportunity.
>
> **4.** Type **Climbing** as the name of the new folder and then press the **Enter** key.
>
> TROUBLE? If there is already a Climbing folder on the hard drive, you must specify a different name. Use the name "Climb" with your initials, such as "ClimbJP." Substitute this folder name for the Climbing folder for the rest of this tutorial.
>
> **5.** Click ▱ **3½ Floppy (A:)** in the Folders pane (you might have to scroll to see it) to display its contents in the right pane.
>
> **6.** Right-click the **Schedule** file in the right pane of the Explorer window.
>
> **7.** Click **Copy**. Locate and then right-click the **Climbing** folder on drive C in the Folders pane (you might have to scroll to see it).
>
> **8.** Click **Paste**. The original Schedule file remains in the root directory of drive A. A copy of the file now appears in the Climbing folder on drive C.
>
> **9.** Click ▨ **Climbing** on drive C if necessary to ensure that the Schedule file was copied onto the hard drive.

The Schedule file is now in the Climbing folder on your hard drive.

Copying Between Floppy Drives with the Send To Command

You notice that Bernard has a file on his disk called Wall; you ask him about it. He explains that it is a PowerPoint file that contains a slide presentation for the local Parks and Recreation Department, proposing the construction of an indoor climbing wall. You tell Bernard you would love to help him develop the slide show; if he gave you a copy of the file on a new disk, you could work on it on your computer at home. Although you could use the Copy Disk command you used in Tutorial 2 to copy the entire disk, you want only the Wall file on the new disk.

If your computer has only one floppy disk drive, you can't just drag a file from one floppy disk to another, because you can't put both floppy disks in the drive at the same time. So how do you copy the file from one floppy to another? You first copy the file from the first floppy disk—the source disk—to a temporary location on the hard drive, then you insert the second floppy disk—the destination disk—into drive A; finally, you move the file from the hard drive to the second floppy disk. Figure 3-18 shows this procedure.

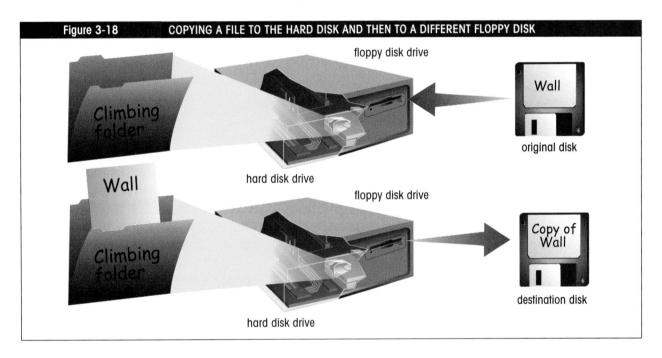

| Figure 3-18 | COPYING A FILE TO THE HARD DISK AND THEN TO A DIFFERENT FLOPPY DISK |

REFERENCE WINDOW   **RW**

Copying a File from One Floppy Disk to Another
- Make sure you have a folder on the hard drive to which you can copy a file. If necessary, create a new folder on the hard drive.
- Copy the file to the hard drive.
- Take your Data Disk out of the floppy drive and insert the floppy disk to which you want the file copied.
- Click View and then click Refresh to view the contents of the second disk.
- Move the file from the hard drive to the floppy disk that is now in the floppy disk drive.

To move a file from the hard drive to the destination disk, you use another Windows 2000 feature: the Send To command. The Send To command provides a simple one-click method of sending any file on your computer's hard drive to your floppy drive (you can also use the Send To command to send files to other locations on your computer, such as the Desktop.) Be aware however, that the Send To command can only send files to the root directory of the floppy drive; you can't direct a file to a specific folder within the floppy drive.

To carry out this procedure, you need two disks: your Data Disk and another blank, formatted floppy disk.

To copy a file from one floppy disk to another:

1. Click  **3½ Floppy (A:)** in the Folders pane (you might have to scroll to see it) to display its contents in the right pane.

2. Right-click the **Wall** file to select it and then click **Copy**.

3. Right-click the **Climbing** folder on drive C and then click **Paste** to copy the file into the folder.

4. After the copy is complete (the drive A light goes out), remove your Data Disk (the source disk).

5. Write "Wall disk" on the label of your second disk, the destination disk. Insert the Wall disk (the destination disk) into drive A.

6. Open the Climbing folder on drive C.

7. Right-click the **Wall** file, click **Send To**, and then click **3½ Floppy (A)** (see Figure 3-19).

Figure 3-19 COPYING A FILE TO THE FLOPPY DISK WITH THE SEND TO COMMAND

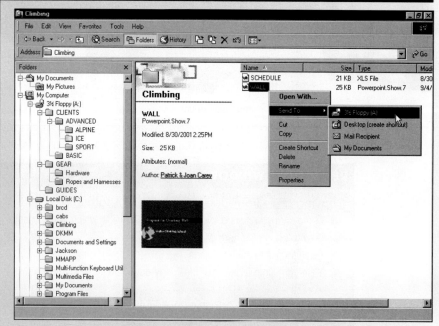

The file should now be copied into the destination disk.

8. Click  **3½ Floppy (A:)** and make sure the Wall file is safely on the disk, then remove the destination disk from drive A.

9. Place your Data Disk back in drive A, click **View**, and then click **Refresh** to view the files on the Data Disk.

This example shows how you can quickly copy a file to your floppy disk by using the Send To command. The Send To command saves you the trouble of navigating through the hierarchy of Windows 2000 objects. The Send To command can also be used to send files as faxes or e-mail messages.

Since this exercise was an example to give you experience in copying from the floppy to the hard drive, and since you don't want to clutter up your hard drive with unneeded files, you should delete the Climbing folder before continuing on.

You can do so easily by simply removing the Climbing folder from drive C. If you weren't able to move any files to drive C, you can skip these steps.

To delete the Climbing folder from drive C:

1. Right-click the **Climbing** folder icon in the Folders pane.

2. Click **Delete** to display the Confirm Folder Delete dialog box.

   TROUBLE? If a message appears telling you that you can't perform this operation, your system administrator might have restricted the deletion privileges from the hard drive. Continue reading the rest of the instructions to understand the process.

3. Make sure the Confirm Folder Delete message indicates that the Climbing folder will be moved to the Recycle Bin.

   TROUBLE? If a different filename appears in the Confirm Folder Delete dialog box, click the No button and go back to Step 1.

4. Click the **Yes** button to delete the folder from drive C.

5. Click the **Close** button [X] to close the Exploring window. You return to the Windows 2000 desktop.

You look over the structure of folders and files on Bernard's disk and realize that, as his business increases, this structure will become increasingly useful. You've used the power of Windows Explorer to simplify tasks such as locating, moving, copying, and deleting files. You can apply these skills to larger file management challenges when you are using a computer of your own and need to organize and work with the files on your hard drive.

Session 3.2 QUICK CHECK

1. You hold down the _____ key when you select files, to select consecutive files, whereas you hold down the _____ key to select nonconsecutive files.

2. How do you set up Windows 2000 to select files by simply pointing at them (rather than by pointing and clicking)?

3. What view must you be in, and what button do you click, to view files organized by date?

4. How can you make a printout of your computer screen?

5. Why is it a good habit to use the right mouse button, rather than the left, to drag files in Windows Explorer?

6. True or False: You can copy a file from one floppy disk to another even if you only have one floppy disk drive in your computer, if you have access to a hard drive.

7. True or False: When you delete files or folders from the floppy disk, they go into the Recycle Bin.

8. If you want to copy a file from your hard drive directly to the root directory of your floppy disk (without having to navigate through the hierarchy of Windows 2000 objects), what command can you use?

SESSION 3.3

In this session you'll learn how to view a list of recently opened files with the History pane. You'll learn how to search through the History list based on date, number of times accessed, and most recently accessed, and by site. You'll learn how to search in the History pane to locate a specific file you've recently used.

Viewing Your File History

Now that you've finished working with the Folders pane in Windows Explorer to organize your files, Bernard is interested in the other organizational tools that Explorer offers. You decide to introduce him to the History pane, which displays a history of the files and objects that Bernard has opened recently (within the last week). For example, if Bernard remembers opening a particular file last Tuesday, but can't remember the file's location, he might still be able to locate it with the History pane by viewing a list of files opened on that date.

Displaying the History Pane

Like the Folders pane, the History pane is displayed in the Explorer Bar. You open the History pane using the View command on the menu bar.

To open the History pane:

1. Open Windows Explorer.

2. Click **View**, point to **Explorer Bar**, and then click **History**.

Explorer displays the History pane as shown in Figure 3-20.

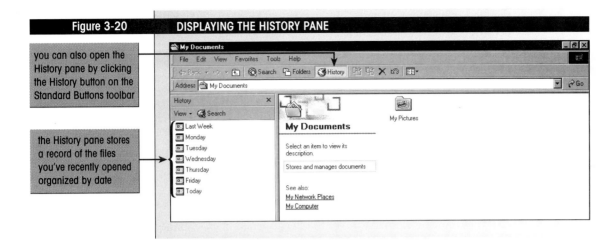

Figure 3-20   **DISPLAYING THE HISTORY PANE**

you can also open the History pane by clicking the History button on the Standard Buttons toolbar

the History pane stores a record of the files you've recently opened organized by date

The history pane shows an icon for each of the last few days you've worked with the computer as well as an icon for the entire previous week. Each icon displays a list of the files, folders, Web pages, and other objects, that were opened during those times. Thus, if Bernard needs to locate the file that he worked on last Tuesday, he can do so by opening the Tuesday icon in the History pane. Try this now.

To view objects opened on Tuesday:

1. Click 🔲 **Tuesday** in the History pane.

2. Within the Tuesday icon are the various files and sites Bernard has opened recently (yours will be different). For example, if he's used this computer to access the Web, those Web sites will be listed along with local sites, such as the My Computer window. Bernard is interested only in the files he's accessed on his computer.

3. Click the **My Computer** icon listed under Tuesday in the left pane.

   Depending on what files you've opened during that time, you'll see a variety of icons at this point. Figure 3-21 displays the list of files accessed by Bernard on Tuesday. Your list of files will be different.

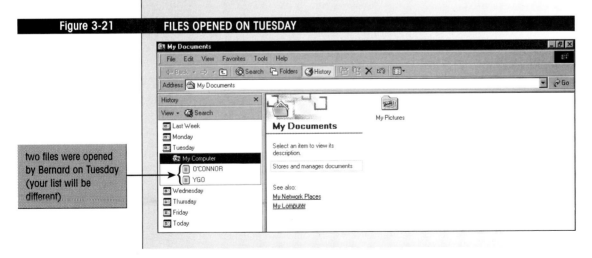

Figure 3-21   **FILES OPENED ON TUESDAY**

two files were opened by Bernard on Tuesday (your list will be different)

If Bernard wanted to open one of these files (the O'Connor file for instance) he could do so by clicking the file icon, and Windows 2000 would open the file. One important point: if the file has been moved since Tuesday, then Windows 2000 will not be able to open the file because it will be looking for it in its previous location.

Other Views in the History Pane

You have several choices of how to view the list of recently opened files. You can view the recent file list:

- By the date that the files were opened (the default)
- By the site where the files reside
- By the number of times you've opened each file
- By the order in which you've opened the files on the current day

For example, if Bernard knows that he's opened the O'Connor file a lot recently, he may decide that it's quicker to view the History pane organized by the number of times each file has been opened. The O'Connor file would probably be near or at the top of that list. Bernard asks to see how to show such a list.

To view the list of files ordered by most visits:

1. Click **View** in the History pane.

2. Click the **By Most Visited** option.

3. Windows Explorer displays a list of recent files organized by the number of times you've visited or opened the files. The files you've visited most often are displayed at the top of the list. See Figure 3-22.

| Figure 3-22 | THE HISTORY LIST ORDERED BY THE MOST VISITED FILES |

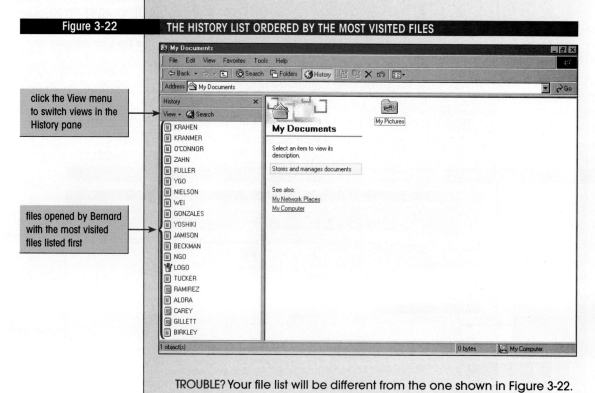

click the View menu to switch views in the History pane

files opened by Bernard with the most visited files listed first

TROUBLE? Your file list will be different from the one shown in Figure 3-22.

Once again, Bernard could click the O'Connor file icon to open that file directly without having to know where the file is located within the Windows 2000 hierarchy of objects. The only limitation is that if the file is located on a CD-ROM or floppy disk, that disk must be in place before the file can be accessed.

In this case, Bernard is doing a lot of work with a floppy disk, so that disk is most likely to be in place. If he wants to quickly move back and forth between the files he's opened recently, he might find it most useful to have the History pane organized in order of the files he's visited in the current day.

To view the list of recently opened files:

1. Click **View** in the History pane and then click **By Order Visited Today**.

Figure 3-23 shows the files that Bernard has opened in the current day, with the most recent files listed first.

Figure 3-23	DISPLAYING FILES OPENED IN THE CURRENT DAY

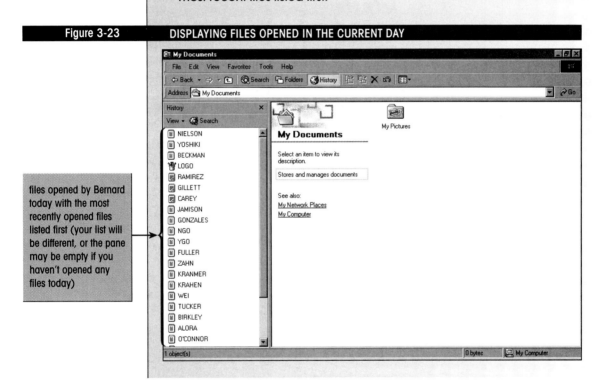

files opened by Bernard today with the most recently opened files listed first (your list will be different, or the pane may be empty if you haven't opened any files today)

The final view option, By Site, becomes useful when you use your computer to tour the World Wide Web. Those Web pages that you visit will then be organized by the different Web sites in the By Site view. Since Bernard is working *only* with files on his own computer—the My Computer site if you will—there's no value in viewing the History list by site.

Searching the History Pane

Bernard finds the History pane a useful tool for locating the files he's recently worked with. But he wonders what he would do if he didn't know where the file was located, wasn't sure when he last accessed the file, and was a bit unclear on the file's name. For example, Bernard knows that he's opened a client's file sometime in the last week, but he's not sure of the filename. He can't remember if it's spelled "Kranmmer," "Kranmar," "Kranmere," or "Kranmer," he just knows that it starts with a "Kran." Could the History pane still help him locate the file?

He could, by trial and error, work through the various views of the History pane to locate the file, but it would be quicker and more instructive to use the Search command. With the Search command you can specify the name or part of a name of a recently opened file, and Windows Explorer will then locate the file for you (assuming that you've worked with the file within the last week). You show Bernard how to do this with the "Kran" file.

To locate the "Kran" file:

1. Click the **Search** button in the History pane.

2. Type **Kran** in the Search For text box.

3. By typing "Kran" you are limiting your search only to files with the text "kran" in their filenames, such as "Kranmer" or "Ckrank".

4. Click the **Search Now** button.

   The Kranmer file is listed in the History pane, as shown in Figure 3-24. This is the file that Bernard is looking for. However, since you haven't actually opened the Kranmer file recently, it won't show up in your History pane.

Figure 3-24	LOCATING THE KRANMER FILE

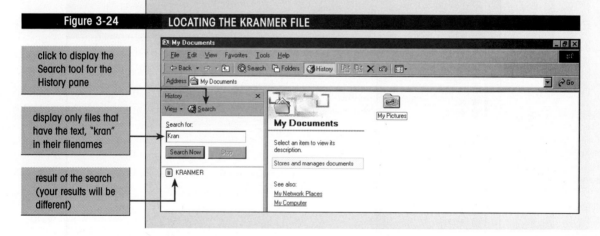

click to display the Search tool for the History pane

display only files that have the text, "kran" in their filenames

result of the search (your results will be different)

The Search tool in the History pane is limited to searching through the list of files you've opened within the last week. If you want to perform a more general search for *any* file located on your computer (whether you've opened it or not), you can do so with the Search pane. The Search pane is a rich tool containing many features for complex and detailed searches. You'll get a chance to explore some of the features in a later tutorial.

You've completed your work with Windows Explorer. You remind Bernard that each of the tools and techniques you've shown him can be used with most of the windows in Windows 2000. For example, if he wants to use the History or Search panes in the My Computer window, he can do so.

To finish your work:

1. Close Windows Explorer.

2. Remove your floppy disk from the floppy drive.

Session 3.3   QUICK | CHECK

1. True or False: This History pane contains a list of all of the files you've ever opened on your computer.

2. True or False: If a file is moved from its original location, the History pane will display the new file location.

3. To display a list of files you've most often visited, click _____ from the History pane view menu.

4. The By Site view option in the History pane is useful if you are using your computer to access the _____ .

5. True or False: The Search tool in the History pane can be used to locate any file on your computer.

REVIEW ASSIGNMENTS

1. **Copying Files to the Hard Drive** Bernard wants to place his sport-climbing client files (those in the Sport folder) on the hard drive to work with them on an advertisement campaign. The Sport folder is a subfolder of Advanced, which is itself a subfolder of Clients.

   a. Using the Wall disk you used in Session 3.2, Quick format the disk, then make a new Data Disk, using the Level II Disk 2 option.
   b. Start Windows Explorer and then create a new folder on drive C called Advertise.
   c. Copy the files in the Sport folder on your Data Disk to the Advertise folder on the hard drive.
   d. Open the Advertise folder on the hard drive to display the files it contains.
   e. Print the Exploring screen from WordPad (using the steps in this tutorial), including your name and the date on the printout.
   f. Delete the Advertise folder from the hard drive when your printout is complete.

2. **Creating a New Folder and Copying Files** Bernard now wants a folder that contains all the clients he has, because he'd like to do a general mailing to everyone, advertising an expedition to the Tetons. (*Hint*: The client files are all text files, so consider viewing the files in the root directory by type. Don't forget that there are also client files in the Clients folder and its subfolders.)

   a. Create a folder called All Clients on the drive A root directory, and then copy all the text files from the root directory into the All Clients folder.
   b. Open the Clients folder and then all its subfolders one at a time, and copy the text files from each of those folders into the new All Clients folder.
   c. Print out the Exploring screen from WordPad (using the steps in this tutorial), showing the contents of the All Clients folder arranged by name. Be sure to include your name and the date on your printout.
   d. Delete the All Clients folder from the floppy disk when your printout is complete.

3. **Copying Between Floppy Disks** Suppose someone who doesn't know how to use Windows Explorer (she missed class) wants to copy the Guides folder from her Data Disk to another floppy disk—but she doesn't want the entire contents of the Data Disk. Try this yourself, and as you go through the procedure, write down each step so that this student will be able to follow the steps and make a copy of Guides. Keep in mind that she doesn't know how to use Explorer.

4. **Restructuring a Disk** Use Quick Format to format the second disk you used in Session 3.3 (the "Wall" disk). Now make a new Data Disk, using the Level I Disk 1 menu option rather than the Level II Disk 2 option. (Disk 1 contains the files you used in Tutorial 2.) Rearrange the files on the disk so they correspond to Figure 3-27. Delete any files or folders not shown in

the figure. Print out the Explorer screen from WordPad (using the steps from this tutorial) that shows your new organization and the files in the Yellowstone Park folder arranged by size.

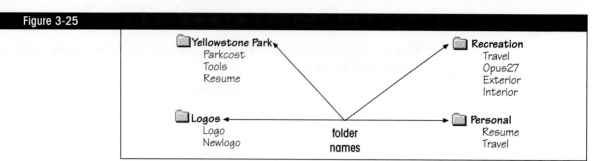

Figure 3-25

5. **Creating a Folder Structure** When you complete your computer class, you are likely to use a computer for other courses in your major and for general education requirements such as English and Math. Think about how you would organize the floppy disk that would hold the files for your courses, and then prepare a disk to contain your files. If you're not a student, prepare a disk using fictitious data.

    a. Make a sketch of this organization.

    b. Use Quick Format to erase the contents of the second disk you used in Session 3.3 (the Wall disk).

    c. Create the folder structure on your Data Disk (even though you don't have any files to place in the folders right now). Use subfolders to help sort files for class projects (your composition course, for example, might have a midterm and a final paper).

    d. Make sure all folders and subfolders are displayed in the left pane, and then paste an image of the Exploring screen into WordPad (using the steps in this tutorial). Be sure to include your name and the date, but don't print anything yet.

    e. Use WordPad to write one or two paragraphs after your name explaining your plan. Your explanation should include information about your major, the courses you plan to take, and how you might use computers in those courses. Print the document when it is finished.

6. **Exploring Your Computer's Devices, Folders, and Files** Answer each of the following questions about the devices, folders, and files on your lab computers. You can find all the answers using the Exploring window. Note that your answers will vary from those of other students because different computers have different devices, folder hierarchies, and files.

    a. How many folders (not subfolders) are on drive C?

    b. How many of these folders on drive C have subfolders? What is the easiest way to find the answer to this question?

    c. Do you have a Windows folder on drive C? If so, how many objects does it contain? What is the easiest way to answer this question?

    d. Do you have a folder named My Documents on drive C? If so, what is the size of the largest file in this folder?

    e. Does your computer have a CD-ROM drive? If so, what drive letter is assigned to the CD-ROM drive?

    f. Does your computer have access to a network storage device? If so, indicate the letter(s) of the network storage device(s).

    g. How much space do the files in the root directory of drive C occupy? How much free space is left on drive C?

    h. What file has been most recently opened?

    i. Of the files most recently opened, which file has been opened most often?

7. **Separating Program and Data Files** Hard drive management differs from floppy disk management because a hard drive contains programs and data, whereas a floppy disk (unless it is an installation disk that you got from a software company) generally only contains data files. On a hard drive, a good management practice is to keep programs in folders separate from data files. Keeping this in mind, read the following description, draw a sketch of the folder structure described, and then make a sketch of how the current structure could be improved.

The Marquette Chamber of Commerce uses a computer to maintain its membership list and track dues. It also uses the computer for correspondence. All the programs and data used by the Chamber of Commerce are on drive C. The program for the membership database is in a folder called Members. The data file for the membership database is in a subfolder of Members called Member Data. The accounting program used to track income and expenditures is in a folder called Accounting Programs. The data for the current year is in a folder directly under the drive C icon called Accounting Data 2001. The accounting data from 1999 and 2000 is stored in two subfolders of the folder called Accounting Programs. The word-processing program is in a folder called Word. The documents created with Word are stored in the Member Data folder. Finally, Windows 2000 is stored in a folder called Windows, which has 10 subfolders.

8. **Using the Send To Command** The Send To command provides an efficient way to send files to the root directory of the floppy disk. Use the Windows Explorer Help system to learn about the Send To command. Then write the steps you would take to use this command to send a file on your floppy disk to your computer's desktop. How would you add other options to the Send To command (for example, to send files directly to the My Documents folder)?

PROJECTS

1. Shortly after graduation, you start working for your aunt and uncle, who own a thriving antique store. They hope to store data about their inventory and business on the computer they recently purchased. They have hired you to accomplish this task. Your Aunt Susan asks you to organize her client files and to prepare some financial statements. Your Uncle Gabe wants you to create customized forms for invoicing and inventory. Two part-time employees, Julia and Abigail, have asked you to help develop documents for advertising. You realize that a folder structure would be helpful to keep things straight.

   a. Create a folder on your Data Disk named Antiques.
   b. Create the following subfolders: Customers, Finances, Invoices, Inventory, and Advertising.
   c. Create each of the documents listed below in WordPad and save them to the correct folders on your Data Disk:

Customers subfolder:	Inventory subfolder:
Harrington	Furniture
Searls	Art
Finances subfolder:	Advertising subfolder:
Budget	Anniversary Sale
Profit and Loss	Winter Clearance
Balance Sheet	
Invoices subfolder:	
Sales	
Vendors	

   d. In Windows Explorer, display the entire Antiques folder hierarchy in the left pane, and display the contents of the Finances subfolder in the right pane. Press the Print Screen key. Then open a new WordPad document, type your name and the date at the top, and paste an image of the Exploring window into the document. Print the document. Close WordPad, but don't save the changes.

2. Uncle Gabe decided to have his financial statements prepared by an accountant, so you need to copy the files in the Finances subfolder onto a different disk that you can give to the accountant. Use the folders and files you created in Project 1. You will need a blank floppy disk and the ability to access your computer's hard drive to complete this project. Uncle Gabe wants to know how to copy files to a new disk, so as you copy the files, write down in detail what you are doing so he can repeat this procedure by following your directions.

   a. Create a folder on your hard drive called Accountant.
   b. Copy the three files in the Finances folder on your Data Disk to the Accountant folder on your hard drive, using the drag technique.

    c. Copy the contents of the Accountant folder to the blank disk, using the cut-and-paste technique.

    d. Delete the Accountant folder from your hard drive.

3. Two of the methods you've learned for moving files between folders are the drag-and-drop method and the cut-and-paste method. Answer the following questions:

    a. Can you think of any situations in which you could not use drag and drop to move a file in Windows Explorer?

    b. In such a situation, what should you do instead?

    c. Which method do you prefer? Why?

4. Windows 2000 enables users to extensively customize their working environment. For each item, first write the steps you take to make the change, and then comment on the benefits or disadvantages of using the following options in the Exploring window:

    a. Details view or List view

    b. Displaying or hiding the status bar

    c. Displaying or hiding the Folders pane

    d. Switching from the Folders pane to the History pane

    e. Displaying or hiding the Standard Buttons option (for this option, also address how you accomplish your work without the Standard buttons visible)

QUICK CHECK ANSWERS

Session 3.1

1. Windows Explorer
2. The left pane, displays tools, such as the Folders pane, History pane, and Search pane, used to organize the files on your computer; the right pane displays the contents of the object selected in the right pane.
3. False
4. False
5. subfolder
6. plus box
7. the drive A device icon
8. False

Session 3.2

1. Shift, Ctrl
2. Click Folder options from the Tools menu and then choose the Single-click to Open option button from the General dialog sheet.
3. Details
4. Press the Print Screen key, paste the image into WordPad, and print the WordPad document.
5. Using the right mouse button opens a shortcut menu that gives you the choice to move or copy.
6. True
7. False
8. the Send To command

Session 3.3

1. False
2. False
3. By Most Visited
4. World Wide Web
5. False

In this tutorial you will:

- Place a document icon on the desktop and use Notepad's time-date stamp

- Create and delete shortcuts to a drive, a document, and a printer

- Change desktop appearance

- Configure your taskbar

- Create and modify taskbar toolbars

- Edit your Start menu

- Use the Control Panel to access system settings

PERSONALIZING
YOUR WINDOWS ENVIRONMENT

Changing Desktop Settings at Companions, Inc.

Companions, Inc.

Bow Falls, Arizona, is a popular Sun Belt retirement mecca that is also a college town with several distinguished universities. Beth Yuan, a graduate of Bow Falls University, realized that the unusual mix of ages in her town might be perfectly suited to a service business. She formed Companions, Inc. to provide older residents with trained personal care assistants who help with housecleaning, home maintenance, and errands. Many of Beth's employees are students at local colleges who like the flexible hours and enjoy spending time with the elderly residents. In addition to employees who work directly with clients, Beth has hired office staff people who help manage the day-to-day tasks of running a business.

The offices of Companions, Inc. are equipped with computers that are used to maintain client records, schedule employees, manage company finances, develop training materials, and create informational documents about Beth's business. Beth recently upgraded her computers to Windows 2000. She has heard that it's easy to change Windows 2000 settings to reflect the needs of her office staff. She asks you to find a way to make it easier to access documents and computer resources. She would also like you to give the desktop a corporate look and feel.

SESSION 4.1

In this session, you will learn how to place a Notepad document icon on the desktop and how to "stamp" the document with the time and date. You will create shortcuts to the objects you use most often, including your computer's floppy drive, a document, and a printer. You will learn how to use the icons you create and how to restore your desktop to its original state.

Document-centric **Desktops**

Windows 2000 automatically places several icons on your desktop, such as the My Computer and the Recycle Bin icons. You can place additional icons on the desktop that represent objects such as printers, disk drives, programs, and documents, making it easier for you to access them. For example, you can create an icon on your desktop that represents your resume. To open this document, you would use its icon. You would no longer have to navigate menus or windows or even locate the program you used to create the document. A desktop that gives this kind of immediate access to documents is called **document-centric**.

Creating a Document Icon on the Desktop

Employees in the Companions, Inc. offices keep a log of their telephone calls, using the Notepad accessory. Notepad, like WordPad, allows you to edit simple text documents, but because it does not include the formatting options provided by WordPad, it is used only for text documents with no formatting. Notepad includes a time-date stamp that automatically inserts the time and date whenever you open the document. Figure 4-1 shows you a Notepad document with automatic time-date stamps.

Figure 4-1	NOTEPAD DOCUMENT WITH TIME-DATE STAMP

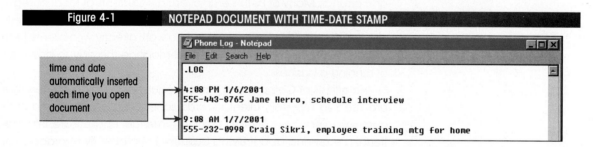

time and date automatically inserted each time you open document

You create a new document on the desktop by right-clicking the desktop and then selecting the type of document you want from a list. A **document icon** appears on the desktop to represent your document. The appearance of the document icon depends on the type of document you create. For example, a Notepad document icon appears as ▤, whereas a WordPad document icon appears as ▥. When you open the document represented by the icon, the operating system checks the file's extension to determine which program it should start.

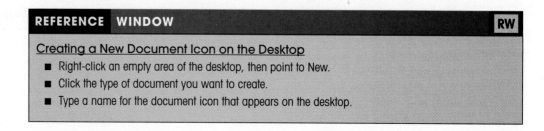

REFERENCE WINDOW   **RW**

Creating a New Document Icon on the Desktop
- Right-click an empty area of the desktop, then point to New.
- Click the type of document you want to create.
- Type a name for the document icon that appears on the desktop.

The phone log is a perfect candidate for a document icon because employees use it so frequently. When you use the document icon to open the document, Windows 2000 locates and starts the appropriate program for you (in this case, Notepad).

To create a Notepad document icon on the desktop:

1. Right-click a blank area of the desktop and then point to **New**. The menu shown in Figure 4-2 opens.

TROUBLE? If no menu appears, you might have clicked with the left mouse button instead of the right. Repeat Step 1.

TROUBLE? If your list of options on the New menu looks different from the one in Figure 4-2, don't worry. The document types that appear on the New menu depend on the programs installed on your computer.

TROUBLE? If the objects on your screen take up more or less space than those shown in the figures, don't worry. Your monitor settings are different.

Figure 4-2	CREATING A NEW TEXT DOCUMENT

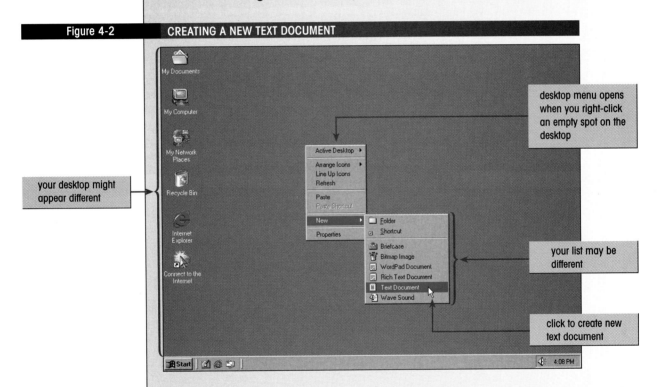

desktop menu opens when you right-click an empty spot on the desktop

your desktop might appear different

your list may be different

click to create new text document

2. Click **Text Document**. A document icon for your new text document appears on the desktop. See Figure 4-3. Its default filename, "New Text Document," is selected so you can assign it an appropriate name.

TROUBLE? If you receive an error message when you try to create a new document on the desktop, your lab might not allow you to make any changes to the desktop. Ask your instructor which sections of this tutorial your lab allows you to complete.

Figure 4-3	DOCUMENT ICON

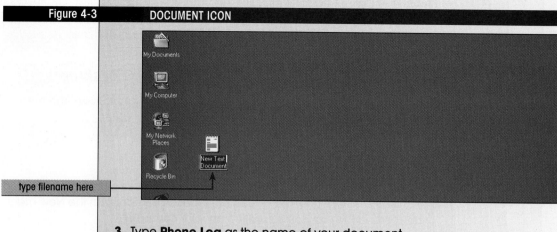

type filename here

3. Type **Phone Log** as the name of your document.

TROUBLE? If nothing happens when you type the document name, you might have inadvertently pressed a key or mouse button that deactivated the document icon. Right-click the New Text Document icon, click Rename, and then type Phone Log.

4. Press the **Enter** key. See Figure 4-4.

TROUBLE? If you see a message about changing the filename extension, click No, type Phone Log.txt, and then press Enter. Your computer is set to display file extensions, and because you didn't supply one with the title, the operating system deletes the extension unless you click No and supply an extension.

Figure 4-4	PHONE LOG DOCUMENT ICON

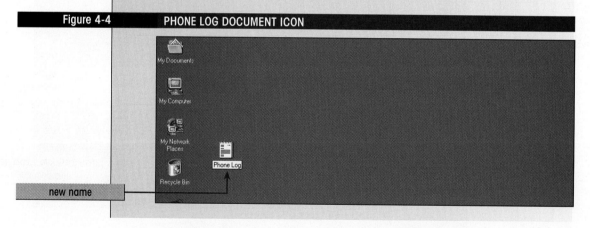

new name

You can often identify an object's type by the appearance of its icon. The Phone Log document icon ⬚ identifies a Notepad text document. Later in this tutorial you'll identify other icons that represent other object types.

Opening a Document on the Desktop

When you use a desktop document icon to open a document, Windows 2000 starts the appropriate program, which in this case is Notepad, so you can edit the document.

To open the Phone Log:

1. Double-click the **Phone Log** icon. Windows 2000 starts Notepad. See Figure 4-5.

Figure 4-5	PHONE LOG DOCUMENT OPENS IN NOTEPAD

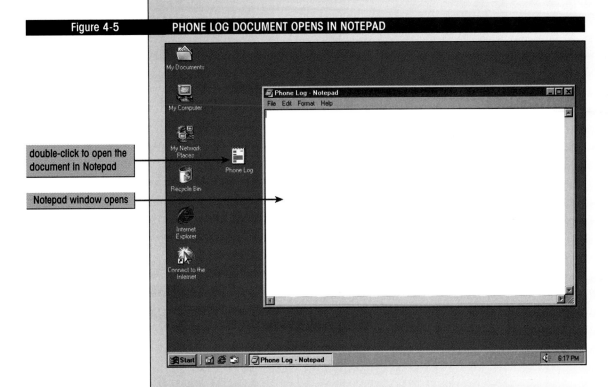

double-click to open the document in Notepad

Notepad window opens

TROUBLE? If the Notepad window hides the Phone Log document icon, drag and resize the window as necessary to view both the icon and the window. If the window is maximized, you'll first need to restore it.

Creating a LOG File

Notepad automatically inserts the date when you open a document only if the document begins with .LOG, in uppercase letters. Your next step is to create a document with .LOG at the beginning and to enter some text. Then you will save the document and close it, so that next time you open it, the time and date will be entered automatically.

To set up the Phone Log document:

1. Type **.LOG**. Be sure to first type the period and to use uppercase letters.

2. Press the **Enter** key to move to the next line.

3. Type **Phone Log for** and then type your name.

4. Press the **Enter** key.

5. Click the **Close** button ⊠ to close Notepad.

6. Click **Yes** to save the changes.

Now you will test the Phone Log document to see if an automatic time-date stamp appears when you open it.

To test the .LOG feature:

1. Open the Phone Log document.

2. Make sure your document contains a time and date stamp. See Figure 4-6.

Figure 4-6	TIME-DATE STAMP

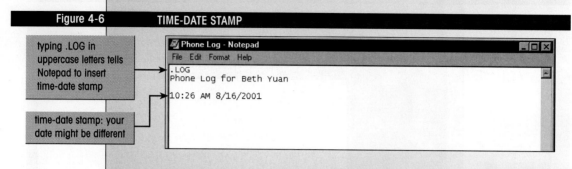

typing .LOG in uppercase letters tells Notepad to insert time-date stamp

time-date stamp: your date might be different

3. Now enter your first phone log entry: type **941-555-0876 Charlene Maples, prospective client needs household help 5 hrs/week.**

4. Press the **Enter** key. See Figure 4-7.

Figure 4-7	FIRST PHONE LOG ENTRY - NOTEPAD

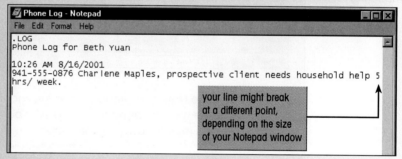

your line might break at a different point, depending on the size of your Notepad window

TROUBLE? If your text doesn't automatically move to a new line when it reaches the window border, as shown in Figure 4-7, click Format and then click Word Wrap.

5. Click the **Close** button ✕ to close Notepad.

6. Click **Yes** to save the changes.

Using Shortcuts
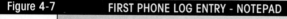

Beth uses her floppy drive regularly and would like an easier way to access it. One way is to create a shortcut on the desktop to her floppy drive. A **shortcut** is an icon that "points" to an object on your computer. You can create shortcuts to access drives, documents, files, Web pages, programs, or other computer resources such as a printer.

A shortcut icon is identified by the arrow in the lower-left corner. For example, a document icon might appear as 📄, while the shortcut icon for the same document would appear as 📄. One advantage of shortcuts is that you can store your documents in one location, but place shortcuts to those documents in several different locations (such as on your desktop), making it easier to access those files or objects directly without having to navigate through the Windows 2000 hierarchy.

Creating Shortcuts

Windows 2000 provides several different ways of creating shortcuts. For example, you can right-click an object and choose "Create Shortcut(s) Here." Figure 4-8 summarizes the various techniques you can use to create shortcuts. Which one you choose is a matter of personal preference.

Figure 4-8	METHODS FOR CREATING SHORTCUTS
METHOD	**DESCRIPTION**
Copy and Paste Shortcut	Use Windows Explorer or My Computer to locate and select the file icon. Click **Edit** and **Copy** from the menu bar. Move to the new location. Click **Edit** and **Paste Shortcut**.
Drag and Drop	Use Windows Explorer or My Computer to locate and select the file icon. Click the file icon. Drag and drop the icon in the new location, holding down the **Alt** key.
Right-click Drag and Drop	Use Windows Explorer or My Computer to locate and select the file icon. With the right mouse button pressed down, drag the file icon to the new location. Release the mouse button and click **Create Shortcut(s) Here** in the menu.

Be aware that the technique of dragging and dropping with your left mouse button does not work the same way for all objects. For example, if you drag and drop a document icon from one folder to another on the same drive, the document is moved to the new location. However, if you drag and drop a program or drive icon, a shortcut is created at the new location. This is because a program might not work correctly if moved into a new location (Windows 2000 expects to find it in the folder in which it was installed), and so the default is to create a shortcut rather than move the file. Similarly, Windows 2000 cannot move a drive or disk, so it creates a shortcut instead. Finally, if you drag and drop a document between one drive and another, the document is copied and *not* moved.

If this seems confusing, remember you can always tell which task Windows 2000 is performing by observing the icon as you drag it into the new location. If the icon has a shortcut arrow , a shortcut is being created. If no shortcut arrow is present , the file is being moved to the new location. If a plus box appears , the file is being copied to the new location.

REFERENCE	WINDOW	RW

Creating a Shortcut on the Desktop
- Use Windows Explorer or My Computer to locate the icon that represents the program, document, or resource for which you want to create a shortcut.
- Make sure you can see a blank area of the Windows 2000 desktop, and that none of the windows is maximized.
- Hold down the right mouse button and drag the icon for the shortcut to the desktop, and then release the mouse button to display the menu.
- Click Create Shortcut(s) Here.

Creating a Shortcut to a Drive

Now you will create a shortcut to your floppy drive. Once this shortcut is on the desktop, you can open it to view the contents of your Data Disk, or you can move or copy documents to it without having to start Windows Explorer. You'll begin by making a new Data Disk, since the one you used in Tutorial 3 no longer contains the necessary files. You can use your original Data Disk if you don't need it anymore, or you can use a new, blank disk.

To make a new Data Disk and then create a shortcut to your floppy drive:

1. Format your disk so that it contains no files.

   TROUBLE? If you don't remember how to format a disk, refer to Tutorial 3.

2. Click the **Start** button ![Start], point to **Programs**, point to **NP on Microsoft Windows 2000-Level II**, and then click **Disk 2 (Tutorials 3 & 4)**.

   TROUBLE? Don't worry if your menu items appear abbreviated.

3. When a message box opens, click the **OK** button. Wait while the program copies the practice files to your formatted disk. When all the files have been copied, the program closes. If necessary, close any open windows.

4. Start the Windows Explorer program.

   TROUBLE? To start Windows Explorer, click the Start button, point to Programs, point to Accessories, and then click Windows Explorer.

5. Make sure the Exploring window is open, but not maximized.

   TROUBLE? If the Exploring window is maximized, click ![icon]. If necessary, resize the Exploring window further so you can see an empty part of the desktop.

6. Locate the device icon ![icon] for **3½ Floppy (A:)** in the Folders pane of the Exploring window.

   TROUBLE? If the Folders pane does not appear, click View, point to Explorer Bar, and then click Folders.

7. Hold down the right mouse button while you drag the device icon ![icon] for 3½ Floppy (A:) from the Folders pane into an empty area of the desktop.

   TROUBLE? If you dragged with the left mouse button instead of the right, you'll get a message saying you can't move or copy the item and asking if you want to create a shortcut instead. Click the No button and then repeat Step 7 so you learn the correct method.

8. Release the mouse button. Notice the menu that appears, as shown in Figure 4-9.

Figure 4-9	CREATING A SHORTCUT TO DRIVE A

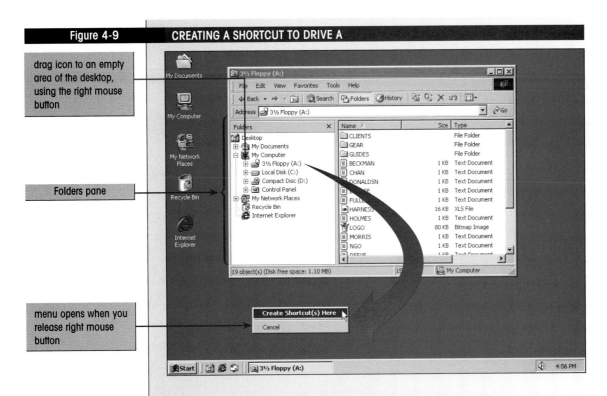

drag icon to an empty area of the desktop, using the right mouse button

Folders pane

menu opens when you release right mouse button

9. Click **Create Shortcut(s) Here**.

10. Click the **Close** button ⊠ to close Windows Explorer. A shortcut labeled "Shortcut to 3½ Floppy (A:)" now appears on the desktop (yours may be in a different location). See Figure 4-10.

Figure 4-10	SHORTCUT TO DRIVE A

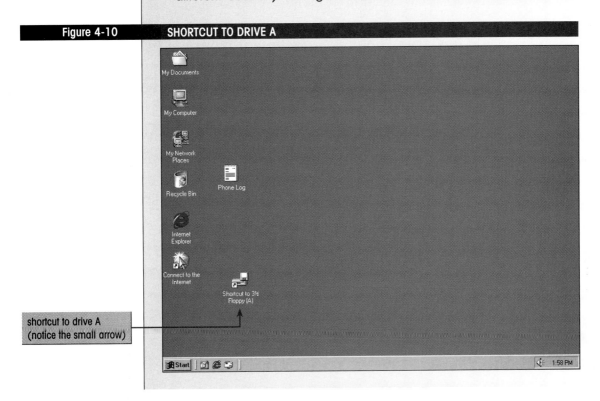

shortcut to drive A (notice the small arrow)

Now you can test the shortcut to see how it gives you immediate access to the contents of the disk in drive A.

To test the 3½ Floppy (A:) shortcut:

1. Double-click the **3½ Floppy (A:)** shortcut icon. A window opens, showing the contents of the disk in your 3½ Floppy (A:) drive.

2. Click the **Close** button ☒ to close the 3½ Floppy (A:) window.

Beth often works at her home office, and she'd like to store the log on a disk that she carries back and forth. To move the log to a floppy disk, all she has to do is drag the Phone Log icon to the 3½ Floppy (A:) shortcut icon. You'll do this using the Cut and Paste method of moving a document.

To move the document from the desktop to a floppy disk:

1. Right-click the **Phone Log** icon on your desktop and then click **Cut** on the menu.

2. Right-click the **3½ Floppy (A:)** icon and then click **Paste** on the menu. The Phone Log icon disappears from the desktop.

When you moved the document icon to the drive A shortcut, the file itself was moved to the disk in drive A and off your desktop. Beth can now take the disk home with her and use a shortcut to drive A on her desktop there to open the file. Practice this now, using the shortcut you just created. (You could also open drive A from My Computer or Windows Explorer, but it is handier to use the drive A shortcut.)

To open the Phone Log document from the new 3½ Floppy (A:) window and add a new entry:

1. Use the 3½ Floppy (A:) shortcut icon to open the drive A window. Scroll through the window, if necessary, to verify that the Phone Log document is on your Data Disk.

   TROUBLE? If you don't see the Phone Log document on your Data Disk, click the Undo button (or click Edit, then click Undo Move), and then repeat the previous set of steps for moving a document to a floppy disk.

2. Open the **Phone Log** document from the 3½ Floppy (A:) window.

   Notice that another time-date stamp is entered.

3. If necessary, click the last line of the phone log so you can type a new entry.

4. Type **941-555-1248 Frank Meyers, next week's home care schedule**.

5. Press the **Enter** key.

6. Click the **Close** button ☒ to close Notepad.

7. Click **Yes** to save the changes.

Creating a Shortcut to a Document

The Phone Log document is now on a floppy disk, as Beth requested; however, it no longer has an icon on the desktop. If you want to access the Phone Log document (now saved on your Data Disk) directly from the desktop, you can create a shortcut that automatically starts Notepad and opens the Phone Log from your Data Disk.

To create a shortcut to the Phone Log document on your Data Disk:

1. Resize the 3½ Floppy (A:) window as necessary to see both the Phone Log icon in the window and a blank area of the desktop.

2. Hold down the right mouse button while you drag the **Phone Log** icon from the 3½ Floppy (A:) window onto the desktop, and then release the mouse button.

3. Click **Create Shortcut(s) Here** on the menu.

   An icon labeled "Shortcut to Phone Log" now appears on the desktop.

4. Click the **Close** button ☒ to close the 3½ Floppy (A:) window.

5. Hold your mouse pointer over the icon for the new shortcut and note the ScreenTip that appears next to the icon, indicating the location of the source document (in this case, on the root directory of drive A). See Figure 4-11.

Figure 4-11	CREATING A SHORTCUT TO THE PHONE LOG DOCUMENT ON DRIVE A

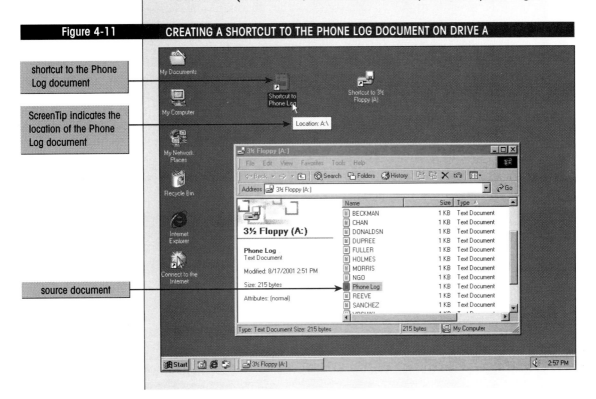

Now you can test the shortcut to see if it automatically opens the Phone Log.

To test the Phone Log shortcut:

1. Click the **Shortcut to Phone Log** icon and press the **Enter** key. Windows 2000 starts the Notepad program and then opens the Phone Log document on your Data Disk.

2. Type: **941-555-7766 Trinity River Accounting** below the new time-date stamp, and then press the **Enter** key.

3. Click the **Close** button ☒ to close Notepad.

4. Click **Yes** to save the changes.

The shortcut icon you just created and tested is different from the Phone Log icon you created at the beginning of this tutorial. That icon was not a shortcut icon. It was a document icon representing a document that was actually located on the desktop. The shortcut icon currently on your desktop represents a document located on your Data Disk.

If you delete a document icon, you also delete the document. If you delete a shortcut icon you don't delete the document itself, because it is stored elsewhere; you are just deleting the shortcut that points to the document. If you were to remove your Data Disk from drive A, the shortcut to the Phone Log would no longer work because the source document would no longer be available.

You might notice that some of the icons on your desktop, such as My Computer and the Recycle Bin, don't have arrows and are therefore not shortcut icons. These icons are installed by the operating system and cannot be removed (although they can be hidden).

Creating a Shortcut to a Printer

You now have an efficient way to open the Phone Log and to access your floppy drive. Now you want to add a printer shortcut to the desktop so that employees can easily print their phone logs and other documents.

You create a printer shortcut in much the same way as you created a shortcut for the floppy drive: by locating the printer icon and then dragging the icon onto your desktop. You can locate your printer's icon by opening the Printers window located on your computer's Start menu.

To create a printer shortcut:

1. Click the **Start** button 🔲 Start , point to **Settings**, and then click **Printers**.

2. Position the pointer over the icon of the printer for which you want to create a shortcut.

   TROUBLE? If you are using a computer that is not connected to a network or printer, read through the following steps for later reference.

   TROUBLE? If more than one printer is listed and you do not know which printer you usually use, use the default printer, identified with the ● icon.

3. Hold down the right mouse button while you drag the printer icon to the desktop.

4. Release the right mouse button to drop the printer icon on the desktop.

5. Click **Create Shortcut(s) Here** on the menu. The printer shortcut appears. See Figure 4-12.

TUTORIAL 4   PERSONALIZING YOUR WINDOWS ENVIRONMENT **WIN 2000** | **4.13**

WINDOWS

| Figure 4-12 | CREATING A SHORTCUT TO A PRINTER |

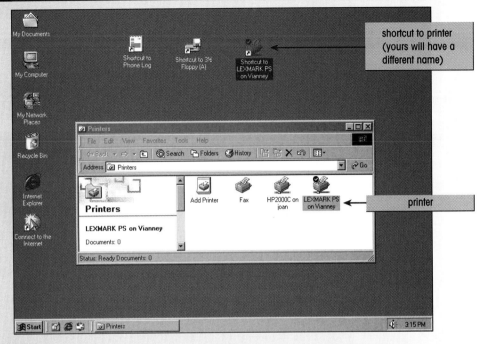

6. Click the **Close** button ☒ to close the Printers window.

Once a printer shortcut icon is on the desktop, you can print a document by dragging its icon to the printer shortcut icon. Think of the steps you save by printing this way: you don't have to open any programs or search through menus to locate and open the document and then locate the Print dialog box. Practice printing using the Phone Log document icon on your Data Disk.

To print the Phone Log document using the printer shortcut icon:

1. Drag the **Shortcut to Phone Log** icon with the left mouse button and drop it on the **Shortcut to Printer** icon that you just created.

2. When you release the mouse button, watch as Windows 2000 starts the Notepad program, opens the Phone Log, and then prints the Phone Log. (Normally Windows 2000 would simply close the program, but because your document has an automatic time-date stamp, the document is changed every time you open it. Thus, Windows 2000 asks if you want to save changes to the document before closing it. You don't need to save it because you don't have any new phone entries to log.)

3. Click **No**. Windows 2000 closes Notepad without saving the new time-date stamp.

Identifying Shortcut Icons on the Desktop

Your desktop now has three new shortcut icons. Although the names of the shortcut icons help you identify what the shortcuts are for, the icons themselves help you identify the shortcut type. Figure 4-13 shows the types of icons you might see on a desktop and the objects they represent.

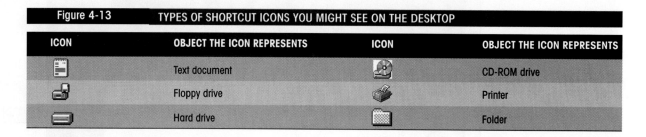

Figure 4-13	TYPES OF SHORTCUT ICONS YOU MIGHT SEE ON THE DESKTOP		
ICON	**OBJECT THE ICON REPRESENTS**	**ICON**	**OBJECT THE ICON REPRESENTS**
	Text document		CD-ROM drive
	Floppy drive		Printer
	Hard drive		Folder

When you are opening a document represented by a desktop icon, you can usually identify which program Windows 2000 will start by looking at the icon representing the document.

Deleting Shortcut Icons

If you are working on your own computer, you can leave the printer and drive icons in place, if you think you'll find them useful. Otherwise, you should delete all the shortcuts you created so that the desktop is restored to its original condition for the next user. You can delete them all at once.

> ### To delete your shortcuts:
>
> **1.** Click the printer shortcut icon to select it.
>
> **2.** Press and hold down the **Ctrl** key, then click the floppy drive shortcut icon, the printer shortcut icon, and the Phone Log shortcut icon, so that all three icons are highlighted. Make sure no other icons are highlighted. If they are, deselect them.
>
> **3.** Press the **Delete** key.
>
> **4.** Click **Yes** if you are asked if you are sure you want to send these items to the Recycle Bin.

Your desktop is restored to its original appearance.

QUICK | CHECK

1. True or False: On a document-centric desktop, the quickest way to open a document is by locating the program that created the document, starting the program, and then using the Open command to locate and open the document.

2. True or False: You can create a document with an automatic time-date stamp in Notepad by typing "log" at the beginning of the document.

3. What happens if you delete a document icon that does not have an arrow on it?

4. What happens if you delete a shortcut icon?

5. What happens if you drag and drop a document icon from one drive to another, using the left mouse button? What happens if you drag and drop the document icon within the same drive?

SESSION 4.2

In this session, you'll change the appearance of your desktop by working with the desktop's property sheets. You'll experiment with your desktop's background and appearance, enable a screen saver, try different colors to see how they look, and modify desktop settings to explore your monitor's capabilities. As you proceed through this session, check with your instructor or technical support person before you change settings on a school lab computer, and make sure you change them back before you leave.

Changing Desktop Properties

In Windows 2000, you can think of all the parts of your computer—the operating system, the programs, and the documents—as individual objects. For example, the desktop is an object, the taskbar is an object, a drive is an object, a program is an object, and a document is an object. Each object has **properties**, or characteristics, that you can examine and sometimes change. The desktop itself has many properties, including its color, its size, and the font it uses. Most objects in Windows 2000 have property sheets associated with them. A **property sheet** is a dialog box that you open to see or change an object's properties. To open an object's property sheet, you right-click the object and then click Properties on the shortcut menu that appears.

To view desktop properties:

1. Right-click an empty area of the desktop to open the shortcut menu.

2. Click **Properties** to open the Display Properties dialog box. See Figure 4-14.

Figure 4-14   DISPLAY PROPERTIES DIALOG BOX

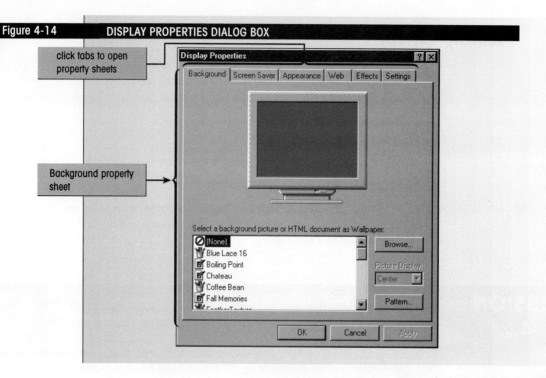

click tabs to open property sheets

Background property sheet

The Display Properties dialog box has several tabs along the top. Each tab corresponds to a property sheet. Some objects require only one property sheet, but the desktop has many properties associated with it, so there are more tabs for it. The Background tab appears first. To view a different property sheet, you click its tab.

Changing Your Desktop's Background

Beth wants the staff computers in the Companions, Inc. offices to have a corporate look. You can change the desktop background color, or you can select a **wallpaper**—a graphic or other type of file that you designate to give your desktop a different appearance—using the Wallpaper list on the Background property sheet. The image of a monitor at the top of the Background property sheet lets you preview the wallpaper. You can also choose a **pattern**, a design or shape that uses the current background color and is repeated over the entire desktop. When you change the background, you are not placing a new object on the desktop; you are simply changing its appearance. If you choose a wallpaper that doesn't occupy the entire background, you can choose a pattern that "fills in" the area around the wallpaper. When a pattern is in effect and you choose a wallpaper that occupies the entire background, the wallpaper covers up the pattern, and not the other way around. Either way, you can continue to work with the desktop just as you always have.

You'll first experiment by choosing a pattern, and then by choosing a wallpaper and a graphic.

To select a pattern:

1. Look at the Wallpaper list and check if a wallpaper is already selected. If one is, write the name down, because you will restore this setting later. Then scroll to the top of the Wallpaper list, click **(None)**, and then click the **Apply** button.

2. Click the **Pattern** button. The Pattern dialog box opens.

3. Click the **Boxes** pattern in the Pattern list. The preview changes to show the Boxes pattern. See Figure 4-15.

TROUBLE? If the Boxes pattern isn't available, choose a different one.

TROUBLE? If you have installed desktop themes, a feature that changes the look of your desktop and desktop icons, you need to turn this feature off before you can work with patterns. Click the Start button, point to Settings, and then click Control Panel. Locate and open Desktop Themes, and note the theme your computer is using. To temporarily disable desktop themes, click the Theme list arrow, and then click Windows Default. Click the OK button, close any open windows, and repeat Steps 1–3. When you are finished with this section, restore your themes setting to its original state.

| Figure 4-15 | SELECTING A DESKTOP PATTERN |

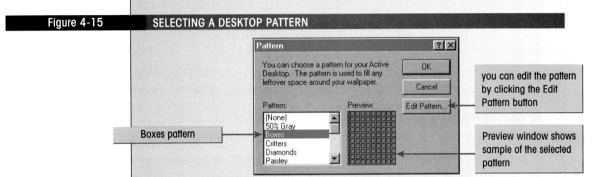

Boxes pattern

you can edit the pattern by clicking the Edit Pattern button

Preview window shows sample of the selected pattern

4. Scroll toward the bottom of the Pattern list and then click **Weave**. The preview now shows the Weave pattern.

5. Click the **OK** button to close the Pattern dialog box and then click the **Apply** button in the Display Properties dialog box to see how this pattern appears on the entire desktop. See Figure 4-16.

| Figure 4-16 | WEAVE PATTERN APPLIED TO THE DESKTOP |

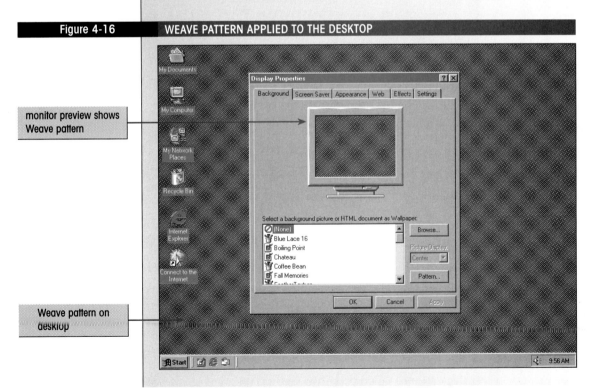

monitor preview shows Weave pattern

Weave pattern on desktop

Beth doesn't think this pattern fits her company very well. You decide to experiment with the Windows 2000 wallpapers. Perhaps you can find one that matches the Companions, Inc. corporate look. When you choose a wallpaper, you can display a single image in the middle of the desktop, stretch the image across the width and length of the desktop, or repeat—or **tile**—the image across the desktop.

To select a wallpaper:

1. Click **Prairie Wind** in the Wallpaper list.

   TROUBLE? If the Prairie Wind wallpaper isn't available, choose a different one.

2. If necessary, click the **Picture Display** list arrow and then click **Tile** to display multiple copies of the wallpaper image repeated across the entire desktop.

3. Click the **Apply** button. See Figure 4-17. The resulting wallpaper is a little overwhelming. You know Beth wouldn't want this look, so you return to the Background property sheet to make a different selection.

Figure 4-17	PRAIRIE WIND IMAGE APPLIED TO THE DESKTOP

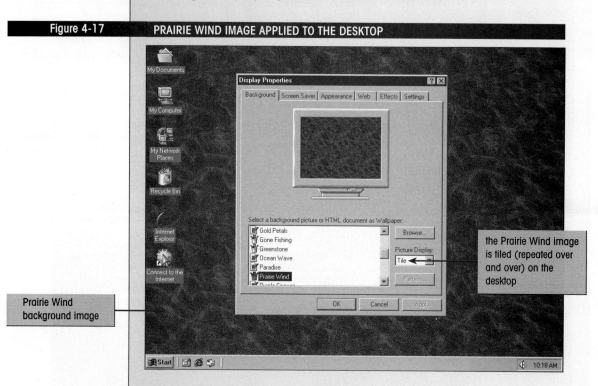

Prairie Wind background image

the Prairie Wind image is tiled (repeated over and over) on the desktop

4. Experiment with the other wallpapers available on your computer by clicking them in the Wallpaper list and previewing them. Click the **Apply** button to see each wallpaper on your desktop rather than just in the preview monitor.

   TROUBLE? Some wallpapers will require you to have Active Desktop installed. **Active Desktop** is a feature of Windows 2000 that allows you to place Web components such as Web pages directly on your desktop. If you receive this prompt, click No (so as not to change the configuration of your computer) and try a different wallpaper.

5. Click **(None)** when you have finished examining the wallpaper styles.

6. Click the **Pattern** button, scroll to the top of the Pattern list, click **(None)**, click the **OK** button in the Pattern dialog box, and then click the **Apply** button on the Background property sheet. Your desktop is restored to the default position, and the Display Properties dialog box remains open.

None of the wallpapers that come with Windows 2000 suits Beth's corporate image, so you ask her if she would like to use a graphic of her company logo. She is enthusiastic; it would be great if clients who come to the offices could see the company logo on the office computers.

To use a graphic image as custom wallpaper:

1. If necessary, place your Data Disk in drive A.

2. Click the **Browse** button on the Background property sheet.

3. Click the **Look in** list arrow, and then click **3½ Floppy (A:)**.

4. Click the file **Logo**.

   TROUBLE? If Logo appears as Logo.bmp, click Logo.bmp. Your computer is set to display file extensions.

5. Click the **Open** button.

6. Click the **Display** list arrow, and then click **Center** to center the image on the screen.

7. Click the **OK** button to close the Display Properties dialog box. See Figure 4-18. The logo for Companions, Inc. appears in the middle of the desktop.

Figure 4-18	COMPANIONS LOGO APPLIED AS WALLPAPER

Changing Your Desktop's Appearance

Beth looks over your shoulder and comments that the red of the logo doesn't go very well with the blue of the screen background. She asks if you can try other background colors. The Appearance property sheet gives you control over the color not only of the desktop background but also of all the items on the screen: icons, title bars, borders, menus, scroll bars, and so on.

To view the Appearance property sheet:

1. Right-click an empty area of the desktop, and then click **Properties**.

2. Click the **Appearance** tab. The Appearance property sheet is shown in Figure 4-19.

Figure 4-19   APPEARANCE PROPERTY SHEET

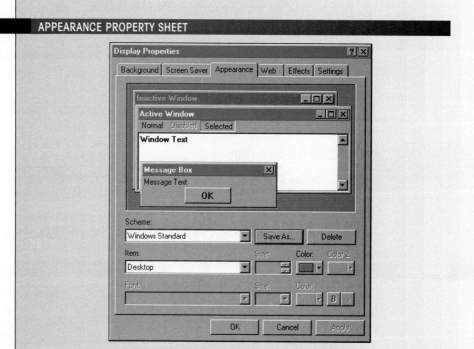

The Appearance property sheet includes several list boxes from which you choose options to change the desktop's appearance. Notice the Scheme list box. A **scheme** is a desktop design. Windows 2000 includes a collection of schemes. You can create your own by working with the Appearance property sheet until you arrive at a look you like, and then using the Save As button to save all the changes as one scheme. The default scheme is Windows Standard. However, if your computer is in a lab, your technical support person might have designed and selected a different scheme. Before you experiment with the appearance of your desktop, you should write down the current scheme so you can restore it later.

The preview in the Appearance property sheet displays many of the elements you are likely to see when working with Windows 2000. You can click an item in the preview to change its color, and sometimes its font or size. You want to change the desktop itself to white. The Item list box currently displays "Desktop," so any changes you make in the Color list affect the desktop.

To change the color of your desktop to white:

1. Write down the name of the current scheme, which is displayed in the Scheme list box.

TROUBLE? If your Scheme list box is empty, your technical support person might have changed scheme settings without saving the scheme. Each time you change an object's color, write down the original color so you can restore that object's color when you are finished.

2. Make sure the Item list box displays Desktop.

TROUBLE? If the Item list box does not display Desktop, click the Item list arrow, scroll until you see Desktop, and then click Desktop.

3. Click the **Color** list arrow and then click **white**, the first box in the first row. See Figure 4-20.

Figure 4-20	CHANGING THE COLOR OF THE DESKTOP

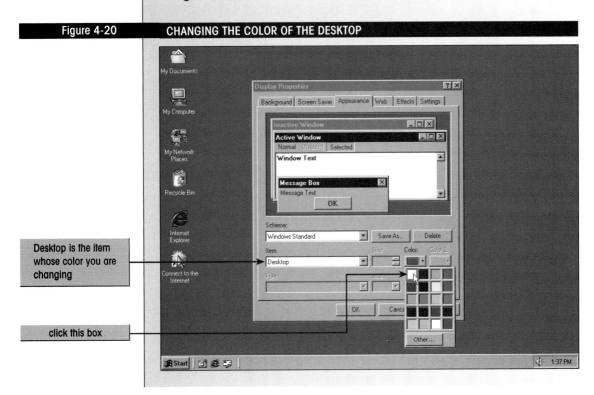

Desktop is the item whose color you are changing

click this box

The desktop color in the preview changes to white. Notice that the Scheme list box is now empty because you are no longer using the default scheme. You realize that blue title bars might look strange in contrast to the red and white desktop. You decide to change the title bars to red. To change an element, you either click it in the preview or select it from the Item list.

To change the title bars to red:

1. Click the **Active Window** title bar in the preview window. See Figure 4-21 for the location of this title bar. Note that the Item list box now displays "Active Title Bar."

2. Click the **Color** list arrow (in the same row as the Item box) and then click **red**, the first box in the second row. See Figure 4-21.

TROUBLE? If your Color 2 box displays a color, change it to red too. In Figure 4-21 the Color 2 box is gray because in this color scheme, active title bars use only one color.

Figure 4-21   **CHANGING THE COLOR OF THE ACTIVE TITLE BARS**

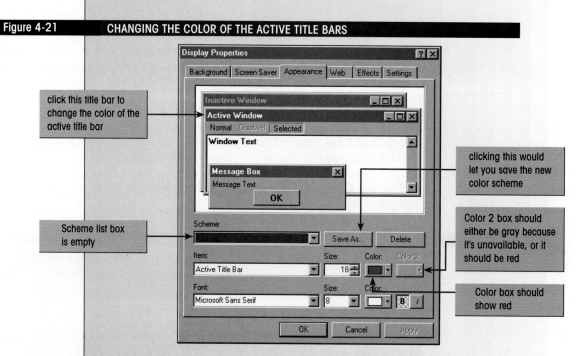

click this title bar to change the color of the active title bar

clicking this would let you save the new color scheme

Scheme list box is empty

Color 2 box should either be gray because it's unavailable, or it should be red

Color box should show red

3. Click the **OK** button to see how the desktop looks. See Figure 4-22.

Figure 4-22   **APPEARANCE OF MODIFIED DESKTOP**

The next time you open a dialog box, you'll see a red title bar. First you'll open My Computer to view the changed title bar, and then you'll restore the desktop to its original settings. You can do this by simply selecting the scheme you wrote down earlier. You could save the colors that match Beth's logo as a scheme if you wanted to. To do this, you would open the Display Properties dialog box, click the Save As button, type a name for your scheme, and then click the OK button.

To restore the desktop colors and wallpaper to their original settings:

1. Open **My Computer** and observe its red title bar. Then close **My Computer**.

2. Right-click an empty area of the desktop, and then click **Properties**.

3. Click the **Appearance** tab.

4. Click the **Scheme** list arrow, and then locate and click the scheme you wrote down earlier. Most likely this is Windows Standard, which you will find at the bottom of the list.

   TROUBLE? If your Scheme list box was blank when you began working with the Appearance property sheet, skip Step 3 and instead restore each setting you changed to the original color you wrote down in the beginning of this section. Then proceed to Step 5.

5. Click the **Background** tab to open the Background property sheet.

6. Scroll to the top of the **Wallpaper** list and then click **(None)**.

7. Click the **Apply** button. The original desktop is restored, and the Display Properties dialog box remains open.

Activating a Screen Saver

A **screen saver** blanks the screen or displays a moving design whenever you haven't worked with the computer for a specified period of time. In older monitors, a screen saver can help prevent "burn-in," or the permanent etching of an image into the screen, which occurs when the same image is displayed for long periods of time. This is not a concern with newer monitors. Screen savers are still handy for hiding your data from the eyes of passers-by if you step away from your computer. When a screen saver is on, you restore your screen by moving your mouse or pressing a key.

You can select how long you want the computer to sit idle before the screen saver activates. Most users find settings between 3 and 10 minutes to be the most convenient. You can change the setting by clicking the up or down arrow on the Wait box, as you'll see in the next set of steps.

Windows 2000 provides a wide variety of screen savers. Beth would like a screen saver that displays the name of the company. One of the Windows 2000 screen savers accomplishes this. You decide to show her how to set up this screen saver.

To activate a screen saver:

1. Click the **Screen Saver** tab in the Display Properties dialog box.

2. Select **3D Text (OpenGL)** from the Screen Saver list box.

TROUBLE? If 3D Text (Open GL) is not displayed in the Screen Saver list box, do not select a different screen saver, but review the rest of the steps in this example.

3. Click the **Settings** button.

4. Note the text that has been entered into the Text box located in the upper-left corner of the 3D Text Setup dialog box. You'll need to reenter this text later, so write it down now.

5. Select the text in the Text box and then type **Companions, Inc.**. See Figure 4-23.

Figure 4-23   THE 3D TEXT SETUP DIALOG BOX

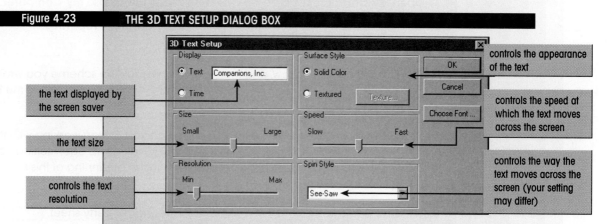

the text displayed by the screen saver

the text size

controls the text resolution

controls the appearance of the text

controls the speed at which the text moves across the screen

controls the way the text moves across the screen (your setting may differ)

The 3D Text Setup dialog box contains several options you can set to control the screen saver. You can control the speed at which the text appears on the screen, the size of the text, the texture or color of the text, and also the way the text moves across the screen. You'll keep the defaults for all of these options.

6. Click the **OK** button.

The Preview window in the Screen Saver property sheet shows a preview of the screen saver. See Figure 4-24. You can also get a full-screen preview of the screen saver.

7. Click the **Preview** button.

The screen saver fills the screen.

TROUBLE? If you move the mouse after clicking the Preview button, the screen saver will disappear, sometimes so quickly that you can't even see it. Repeat Step 7, but make sure you don't move the mouse after you click the Preview button.

8. When you're done previewing the screen saver, click the **Settings** button again and enter the text that was initially displayed in the Text box. Click the **OK** button to close the 3D Text Setup dialog box.

9. Click the **Cancel** button to cancel your screen saver changes and close the Display Properties dialog box. If you were working on your own computer and wanted to save the changes, you would click the Apply button to save the changes or the OK button to save the changes and close the Display Properties dialog box.

Figure 4-24   **THE SCREEN SAVER PROPERTY SHEET**

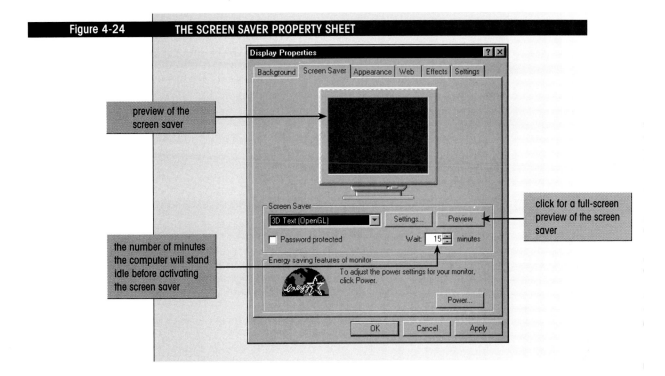

preview of the screen saver

click for a full-screen preview of the screen saver

the number of minutes the computer will stand idle before activating the screen saver

Changing Display Settings

The Settings property sheet allows you to control additional settings that you might never need to consider. However, if you want to take full advantage of your monitor type, you should be aware of the options you have on the Settings property sheet. The settings you can change depend on your monitor type and on the **video card** inside your computer that controls visual information you see on the screen. Windows 2000 allows you to use more than one monitor, so you might be able to change settings for multiple monitors.

Changing the Size of the Desktop Area

The Screen area slider bar on the Settings property sheet lets you display less or more of the screen on your monitor. If you display less, objects will look bigger, while if you display more, objects will look smaller. You can drag the slider bar between these two extremes. You are actually increasing or decreasing the **resolution**, or sharpness, of the image. Resolution is measured by the number of individual dots, called **pixels**, short for "picture elements," that run across and down your monitor. The more pixels, the more you see on the screen at one time, and the smaller the objects look.

The 640 x 480 (640 pixels across and 480 pixels down) resolution shows the least information, but uses the largest text and is preferred by most users with 14-inch monitors. The 800 x 600 resolution shows more information, but uses smaller text. Many users with 15-inch monitors prefer the 800 x 600 resolution. This is the setting that Beth's computers use. The 1024 x 768 resolution shows the most information, but uses the smallest text. Most users find the 1024 x 768 resolution too small for comfortable use unless they are using a 17-inch or larger monitor. Users with limited vision might prefer the 640 x 480 setting even on larger monitors, because objects and text are bigger and easier to see. You might also want to change your monitor's resolution, depending on what software you are using.

To change the size of the desktop area:

1. Right-click an empty area of the desktop and then click **Properties**.

2. Click the **Settings** tab to display the Settings properties.

3. Write down the original setting in the Screen area so you can restore it after experimenting with it.

4. To select the 640 by 480 resolution, if it is not already selected, drag the Screen area slider to the left. The preview monitor shows the relative size of the 640 x 480 display. See Figure 4-25.

| Figure 4-25 | 640 BY 480 RESOLUTION |

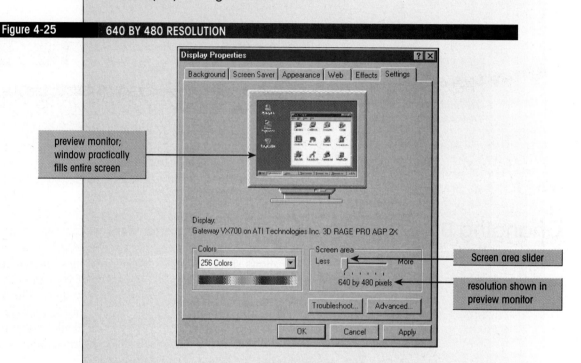

5. To select the 800 x 600 resolution, drag the **Screen area** slider to the right. The preview monitor shows the relative size of the 800 by 600 display.

6. Return the slider to the setting you wrote down in Step 3. Leave the Display Properties dialog box open.

Changing the Color Palette

You can also use the Settings property sheet to change the color palette, which specifies the number of colors available to your computer. Beth's computers have a 256-color palette. Figure 4-26 provides additional information on common palettes.

Figure 4-26	COLOR PALETTES
PALETTE	**DESCRIPTION**
16 colors	Very fast, requires the least video memory, sufficient for use with most programs but not adequate for most graphics
256 colors	Relatively fast, requires a moderate amount of video memory, sufficient for most programs and adequate for the graphics in most games and educational programs. This is a good setting for general use.
High color	Requires higher-quality video card and additional video memory. This setting is useful for sophisticated painting, drawing, and graphics manipulation tasks.
True color	Requires the most video memory and runs most slowly. This setting is useful for professional graphics tasks, but might not be available or might be too slow on some computer systems.

Once you change the color palette, you are prompted to reboot Windows 2000. In the next set of steps, you will see how to change the color palette—but to avoid rebooting, you won't actually do so.

To view the color palette options:

1. Click the **Colors** list arrow to display the list of color palettes. See Figure 4-27.

Figure 4-27	COLOR PALETTES

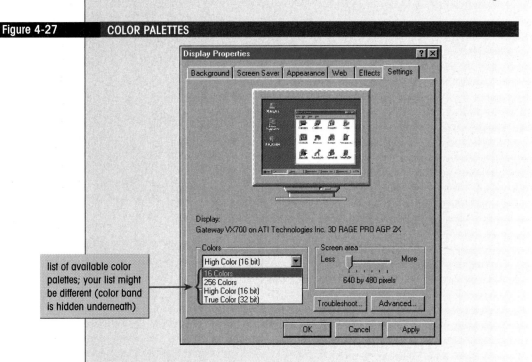

list of available color palettes; your list might be different (color band is hidden underneath)

2. Click **16 Colors** and observe that the color band below the Colors list box displays only 16 colors.

TROUBLE? If 16 Colors doesn't appear in your Colors list, skip Step 2.

3. Click the **Colors** list arrow again, and then click **256 Colors**. Now the color band displays a greater range of colors.

4. Click the **Cancel** button to close the Display Properties dialog box without accepting any changes you might have inadvertently made.

5. If you are working in a school lab, make sure you have changed all settings back to their original state before moving on to Session 4.3.

QUICK CHECK

1. True or False: Although a document is an object, and so is a drive, the desktop is not an object.

2. How do you open an object's property sheet?

3. Name three desktop properties you can change from the Display Properties dialog box.

4. If you have an older monitor and you want to protect it from damage caused by displaying the same image for a long time, what can you do?

5. What does it mean to say that a monitor's resolution is 640 x 480?

6. Users with limited vision might want to use which resolution: 640 x 480, 800 x 600, or 1024 x 768? Why?

7. What is the disadvantage of using a color palette with many colors, such as True Color?

SESSION 4.3

In this session you'll work with your taskbar and Start menu. You'll learn how to modify the appearance and location of the taskbar. You'll see how to add items to the taskbar. You'll work with the properties of the Start menu: how to add items to the menu and how to modify the existing menu items. Finally, you'll learn about the Control Panel, another Windows 2000 tool that makes it easy for you to change the properties of different objects on your computer.

Modifying the Taskbar

So far you've shown Beth how to work with the properties of the Windows 2000 desktop. There are two other parts of the Windows 2000 screen that you haven't worked with yet: the taskbar and the Start menu. You'll start by showing her how to work with the taskbar.

Moving and Resizing the Taskbar

Beth's previous computer was a Macintosh, and she's used to seeing a menu bar at the top of the desktop. She wants to know how to revise the position of the taskbar to create this familiar appearance.

To move the taskbar:

1. Click any blank spot on the taskbar and, with the left mouse button pressed down, drag the pointer to the top of the desktop.

2. Release the left mouse button when the taskbar appears at the top of the desktop. See Figure 4-28. Notice that the icons moved down slightly to make room for the taskbar.

| Figure 4-28 | MOVING THE WINDOWS 2000 TASKBAR TO THE TOP OF THE SCREEN |

taskbar at top of screen

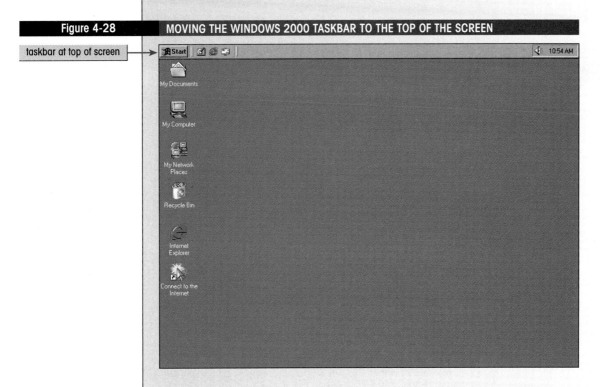

3. Click a blank spot on the taskbar and, with the left mouse button pressed, move the taskbar back down to the bottom of the screen.

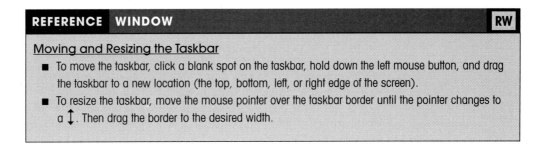

REFERENCE WINDOW   **RW**

Moving and Resizing the Taskbar

■ To move the taskbar, click a blank spot on the taskbar, hold down the left mouse button, and drag the taskbar to a new location (the top, bottom, left, or right edge of the screen).

■ To resize the taskbar, move the mouse pointer over the taskbar border until the pointer changes to a ↕. Then drag the border to the desired width.

Beth has also noticed that when she has several programs running simultaneously, the icons for those programs fill up the taskbar, sometimes to such an extent that the individual icons are compressed beyond recognition. You tell her that one way of dealing with that problem is to increase the size of the taskbar. This is easily accomplished by dragging the taskbar border to a new location. Try this now.

To increase the size of the taskbar:

1. Move the mouse pointer over the upper edge of the taskbar until the pointer changes to ↗.

2. Click and drag the upper border upwards, releasing the left mouse button when the taskbar has increased in height. See Figure 4-29.

Figure 4-29   RESIZING THE TASKBAR

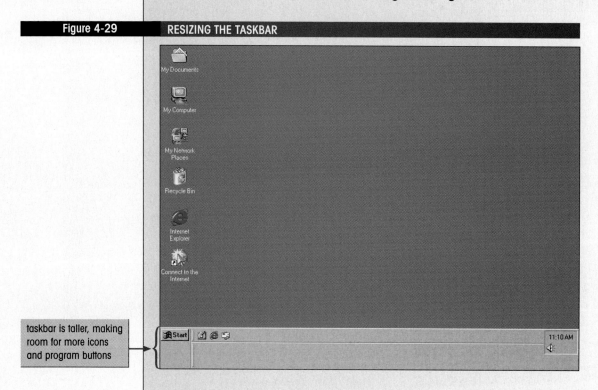

taskbar is taller, making room for more icons and program buttons

3. Click the upper taskbar border again and drag it back to its original height.

Setting Taskbar Properties

There are other properties you can set for the taskbar besides its size and position. For example, you can increase the amount of screen space available for your program windows by hiding the taskbar. Or you can allow your program windows to cover the taskbar rather than letting the taskbar take up space. Try changing these properties now.

To set other taskbar properties:

1. Right-click a blank spot in the taskbar and click **Properties** on the menu.

   The Taskbar and Start Menu Properties dialog box appears, as shown in Figure 4-30.

Figure 4-30 | **THE TASKBAR AND START MENU PROPERTIES DIALOG BOX**

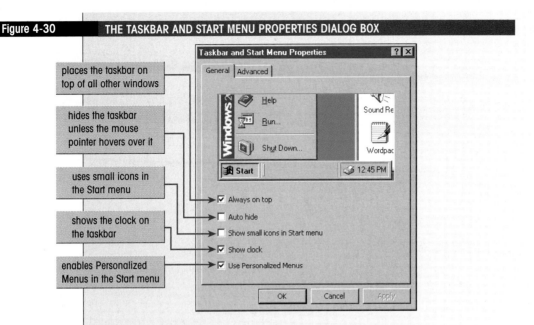

places the taskbar on top of all other windows

hides the taskbar unless the mouse pointer hovers over it

uses small icons in the Start menu

shows the clock on the taskbar

enables Personalized Menus in the Start menu

2. Write down which check boxes are currently selected in this dialog box.

3. Click to select the **Auto hide** check box, and then click the **Apply** button.

TROUBLE? If the Auto hide check box is already selected, skip Step 3.

The taskbar disappears.

4. Move the mouse pointer over the location where the taskbar previously appeared and note that the taskbar is visible as long as the mouse pointer is over it.

5. Deselect the **Auto hide** check box, and then click the **Apply** button.

6. Click to deselect the **Always on top** check box, and then click the **Apply** button.

TROUBLE? If the Always on top check box is already deselected, skip Step 6.

7. Move the Taskbar and Start Menu Properties dialog box over your taskbar. Note that the dialog box now appears over the taskbar.

8. Return the check boxes to their original state, and then click the **OK** button to close the dialog box.

Working **with Taskbar Toolbars**

One of the features of the taskbar is the ability to display toolbars. By default, the Windows 2000 taskbar will display the Quick Launch toolbar, containing icons for running your Web browser and accessing your mail. You can select other toolbars to display, or you can create your own customized toolbar.

Displaying a Toolbar on the Taskbar

Beth often has several programs running at once, filling up the screen and hiding the desktop. She has seen the benefit of placing icons on the desktop, but she wonders if they're going to be as useful for her. Is there a way that she can access those desktop icons without having to minimize all of her programs? She can do so, if she places a Desktop toolbar on her taskbar. The Desktop toolbar will display all of the icons that appear on her desktop.

To display the Desktop toolbar:

1. Right-click a blank area of the taskbar.

2. On the menu that appears, point to **Toolbars** and then click **Desktop**. See Figure 4-31.

Figure 4-31	DISPLAYING THE DESKTOP TOOLBAR

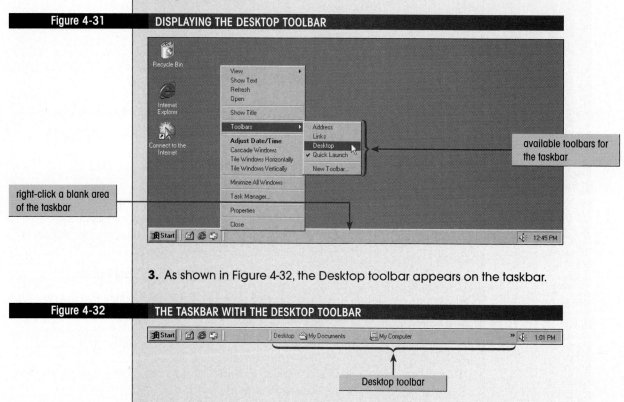

right-click a blank area of the taskbar

available toolbars for the taskbar

3. As shown in Figure 4-32, the Desktop toolbar appears on the taskbar.

Figure 4-32	THE TASKBAR WITH THE DESKTOP TOOLBAR

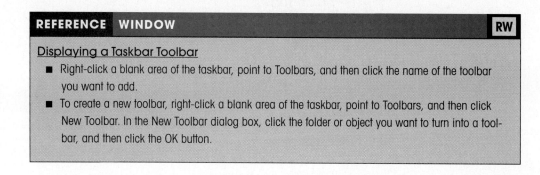

Desktop toolbar

REFERENCE WINDOW RW

Displaying a Taskbar Toolbar

- Right-click a blank area of the taskbar, point to Toolbars, and then click the name of the toolbar you want to add.
- To create a new toolbar, right-click a blank area of the taskbar, point to Toolbars, and then click New Toolbar. In the New Toolbar dialog box, click the folder or object you want to turn into a toolbar, and then click the OK button.

Modifying the Appearance of a Taskbar Toolbar

Beth likes the fact that you can place the desktop icons on a toolbar, but wishes she could see more of them. She would like the toolbar to look more like the Quick Launch toolbar, with no names next to the icon and no title displayed for the toolbar. You explain that you can modify the toolbar's appearance by changing its properties.

To modify the appearance of the Desktop toolbar:

1. Right-click a blank area in the newly created Desktop toolbar.

2. On the menu, deselect **Show Text** so that no check mark appears next to the menu entry.

   TROUBLE? If you don't see the Show Text entry on the menu, you may have right-clicked one of the buttons on the Desktop toolbar. Be sure to select a blank area on the toolbar.

3. Right-click a blank area in the Desktop toolbar again and deselect **Show Title** from the menu.

   Figure 4-33 displays the final appearance of the toolbar. Note that each item on the desktop is matched by an item in the toolbar and that the icons are small, like those in the Quick Launch toolbar.

Figure 4-33	THE MODIFIED DESKTOP TOOLBAR

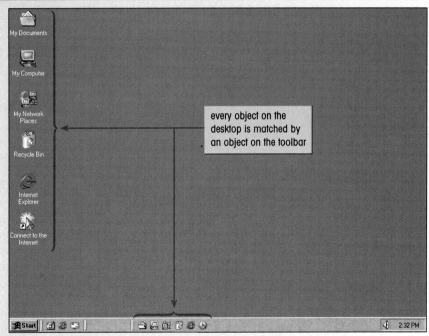

every object on the desktop is matched by an object on the toolbar

Now Beth can access all the items on her desktop without minimizing open windows

Creating a Custom Toolbar

Beth is happy with the new appearance of the taskbar. She notices that when she clicks the My Computer icon on the Desktop toolbar it opens the My Computer window. Beth finds the My Computer window useful and wonders if you could create a toolbar on the taskbar displaying all of the icons in the My Computer window. This would give her even quicker access to all of the drives on her computer.

To create a toolbar for the My Computer window:

1. Right-click a blank area on the taskbar, point to **Toolbars**, and then click **New Toolbar**.

   A dialog box opens from which you can select a drive, folder, or object whose contents you want to display in a toolbar. You want to display the contents of the My Computer window, which lies at the top of the Windows 2000 hierarchy of objects.

2. Click **My Computer** in the New Toolbar dialog box and then click the **OK** button.

3. The My Computer toolbar appears on the taskbar.

4. Right-click a blank spot on the My Computer toolbar and deselect **Show Text** on the menu.

5. Right-click a blank spot on the My Computer toolbar again and deselect **Show Title** on the menu.

   Figure 4-34 displays the new My Computer toolbar on your taskbar.

| Figure 4-34 | THE MY COMPUTER TOOLBAR |

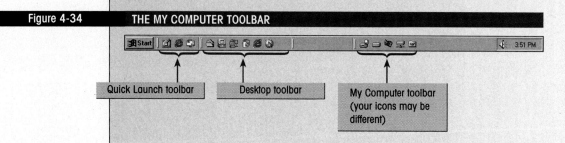

Removing a Taskbar Toolbar

Having seen how to create and modify toolbars on the taskbar, you should now restore the taskbar to its original state, deleting the Desktop and My Computer toolbars. Note that this will not affect the desktop or the My Computer window. These toolbars contain shortcuts to those objects, not the objects themselves.

To remove a toolbar from the taskbar:

1. Right-click a blank spot on the taskbar and then point to **Toolbars**.

2. Click **Desktop** in the list of toolbars displayed in the submenu to deselect it.

   The menu closes and the Desktop toolbar is removed.

3. Right-click a blank spot on the taskbar again and then point to **Toolbars**.

> **4.** Deselect **My Computer** in the list of toolbars.
>
> Both the Desktop and My Computer toolbars should now be removed from your taskbar.

Editing **the Start Menu**

The final component on your Windows 2000 screen that you can customize is the Start menu. Most of the items in the Start menu are created for you by Windows 2000 or by the various programs you install. However, you also can determine the content and appearance of your Start menu, removing items you don't use and adding those you do.

Controlling the Appearance of the Start Menu

The first aspect of the Start menu's appearance that you can control is whether the menu uses small or large icons. The default is to use large icons, but you can save screen space by changing this to the smaller icon style.

The second customizable aspect of the Start menu is whether or not personalized menus are used. **Personalized menus** are menus that change depending on your work habits, showing those items in the Start menu you use most often and temporarily hiding items you seldom use. You still have easy access to "hidden" items: you may have noticed a set of double arrows pointing down on some of the menus in the Start menu. If you click those double arrows, you'll display those items that Windows 2000 has chosen to hide. Figure 4-35 shows the Start menu with and without the personalized menu option enabled.

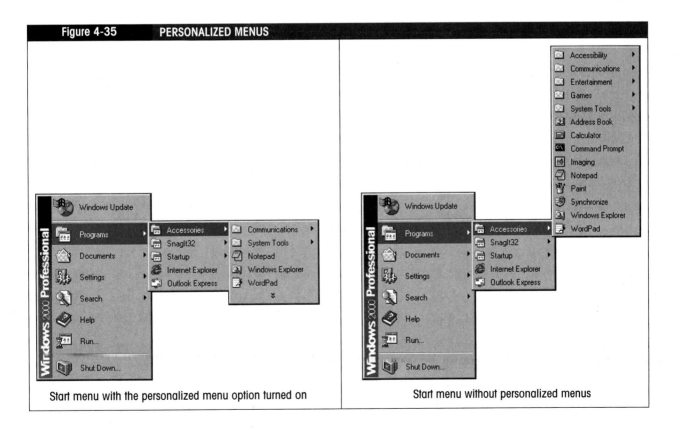

Figure 4-35   **PERSONALIZED MENUS**

Start menu with the personalized menu option turned on

Start menu without personalized menus

Personalized menus are an effective way to reduce the clutter of the Start menu, a feature you'll appreciate as you add more and more items to the menu. However, at first you may find personalized menus confusing as you try to locate a specific menu item that does not appear right away.

Because the Start button is considered part of the taskbar, you change settings for the Start menu using the same dialog box you used earlier to control the appearance of the taskbar. As shown earlier in Figure 4-30, you can select and deselect the check boxes that turn features on and off.

Adding an Item to the Start Menu

Most of the work you'll do in modifying the Start menu will be to modify its content, adding and deleting items. Like the desktop and the taskbar, the Start menu can contain shortcut icons to give you one-click access to your most important programs, folders, and files.

REFERENCE WINDOW   RW

Adding an Item to the Start Menu
- Right-click a blank area of the taskbar, and then click Properties.
- Click the Advanced tab in the dialog box, and then click the Add button.
- In the Create Shortcut Wizard, locate the file, folder, or object that you want to add to the Start menu, and then specify a name and icon for the item. Finish the Create Shortcut Wizard.

Beth wants to see how she could use the Start menu to get quick access to her floppy drive.

To create a floppy drive icon on the Start menu:

1. Right-click an empty area on the taskbar and then click **Properties** on the menu.

2. Click the **Advanced** tab.

3. Click the **Add** button.

   The Create Shortcut Wizard starts (a **wizard** is a series of dialog boxes that help you complete tasks). From this dialog box you specify the location of the object, folder, or file to which you want to create a shortcut.

4. Click the **Browse** button.

5. Click the 🖴 **3½ Floppy (A:)** icon and then click the **OK** button.

6. Click the **Next** button.

   Now you'll specify where on the Start menu you want to place the shortcut to the floppy drive. In this case, you'll specify the main menu of the Start menu. Note that you could also add an item to any one of the submenus or create a new folder (or submenu) of your own.

7. Click **Start Menu** in the Select Program Folder window, as shown in Figure 4-36, and then click the **Next** button.

| Figure 4-36 | SELECTING THE LOCATION FOR THE NEW START MENU ITEM |

the folders in the dialog box match the submenus in the Start menu

The final part of the Create Shortcut Wizard asks you to specify a name for the shortcut icon. A default name is offered.

8. Keep the default name, "3½ Floppy (A)," offered by the Shortcut Wizard, and then click the **Finish** button.

9. Leave the Taskbar and Start Menu Properties dialog box open.

Now test your new Start menu entry to verify that it will open your floppy drive for you.

To test the new Start menu entry:

1. Click the **Start** button.

2. Click **3½ Floppy (A)** on the Start menu. See Figure 4-37.

| Figure 4-37 | NEW ITEM ON THE START MENU |

new item on the Start menu to access the floppy drive

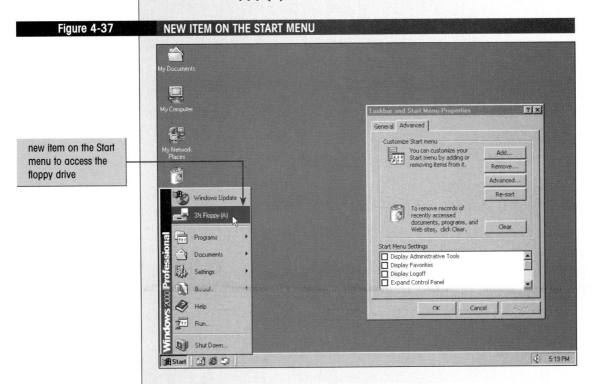

> The contents of the floppy drive are displayed in a window.
>
> **3.** Click the **Close** button ⊠ to close the window.

Removing an Item from the Start Menu

Now that you've seen how to create a Start menu item by yourself, you should remove it so that the Start menu returns to its default position. To remove a Start menu item, you use the same dialog box you opened to create one.

REFERENCE WINDOW **RW**

Removing a Start Menu Item
- Right-click a blank area of the taskbar, and then click Properties.
- Click the Advanced tab in the dialog box that appears, and then click the Remove button.
- Select the item in the Remove Shortcuts/Folders dialog box that you want to remove, and then click the OK button.

To remove the floppy drive item from the Start menu:

1. Click the **Remove** button in the Advanced dialog sheet in the Taskbar and Start Menu Properties dialog box.

2. Click **3½ Floppy (A)** in the list of Start menu items and then click the **Remove** button.

Note that you are only removing the floppy drive shortcut from your Start menu; other methods of opening the floppy drive will remain unchanged.

3. Click the **Yes** button to confirm that you want to remove 3½ Floppy (A) from the Start menu.

4. Click the **Close** button to close the Remove Shortcuts/Folders dialog box.

5. Click the 🏁 Start **Start** button again to confirm that the floppy disk item has been removed from the Start menu, and then click outside the menus to close them.

6. Leave the Taskbar and Start menu Properties dialog box open.

Choosing Start Menu Settings

Windows 2000 also includes a list of options or settings for your Start menu. These settings include the ability to display the contents of your My Documents folder, a list of available printers, or a list of favorite Web pages and files. Figure 4-38 describes the settings that you can turn on or off on your Start menu.

Figure 4-38	START MENU SETTINGS

SETTING	DESCRIPTION
Display Administrative Tools	Display a menu of tools used to administer Windows 2000 and your computer
Display Favorites	Display a list of your favorite Web sites, files, and folders
Display Logoff	Display the Logoff command for use on computers with multiple users
Expand Control Panel	Display individual applets in the Control Panel
Expand My Documents	Display the contents of the My Documents folder
Expand Network and Dial-up Connections	Display individual computers on your network
Expand Printers	Display individual printers attached to your computer
Scroll the Programs Menu	Add scrolling to the Programs Menu (used for very long lists of programs and program groups)

By default, all of these settings are turned off. Beth is interested in adding the printer list to the Start menu so she can have quick access to the printers in her office. You'll show her how this could be done.

To display the printer list in the Start menu:

1. In the Start Menu Settings list box at the bottom of the Advanced tab, scroll to and click the **Expand Printers** check box to select it.

   TROUBLE? If the Expand Printers check box is already selected, skip Step 1.

2. Click the **Apply** button.

3. Click the 🏁 Start **Start** button, point to **Settings**, and then point to **Printers** to display the list of printers available on your computer. See Figure 4-39.

Figure 4-39	DISPLAYING THE PRINTER LIST IN THE START MENU

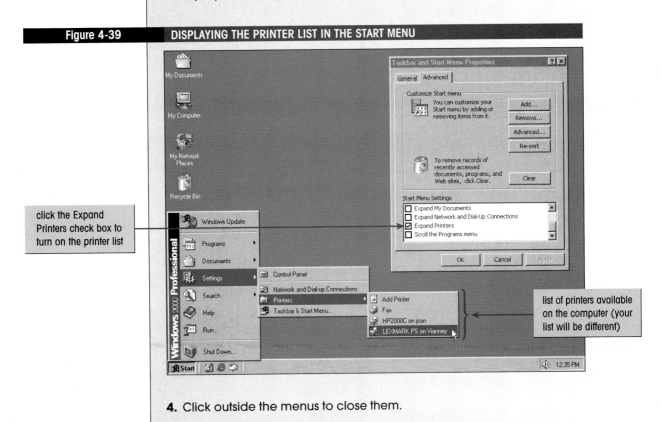

click the Expand Printers check box to turn on the printer list

list of printers available on the computer (your list will be different)

4. Click outside the menus to close them.

As she allows the mouse pointer to hover over each printer icon in the list, a box appears telling Beth the status of the printer (whether it's ready to print or not) and the number of documents queued up (waiting to be printed). This is valuable information for Beth as she works with the variety of printers installed at the company's offices.

To remove the printer list from the Start menu:

1. If the Expand Printers check box was *not* selected before you started this exercise, click the **Expand Printers** check box to deselect it.

2. Click the **OK** button to close the Taskbar and Start Menu Properties dialog box.

Using the Control Panel

You've worked with a variety of objects and properties in this tutorial: the desktop, your display, the Start menu, and the taskbar. There are even more objects and properties on your computer that you haven't examined yet. Windows 2000 organizes some of these objects into the **Control Panel**.

To open the Control Panel:

1. Click the **Start** button, point to **Settings**, and then click **Control Panel**.

   TROUBLE? If a message appears indicating that the Control Panel is not available, you might be in a computer lab with limited customization access. Ask your instructor or technical support person for options.

2. Click **View** and then click **List** to display the icons in a list, as shown in Figure 4-40.

   TROUBLE? Because some tools are optional, your Control Panel might display different tools than the ones shown in Figure 4-40.

Figure 4-40	CONTROL PANEL

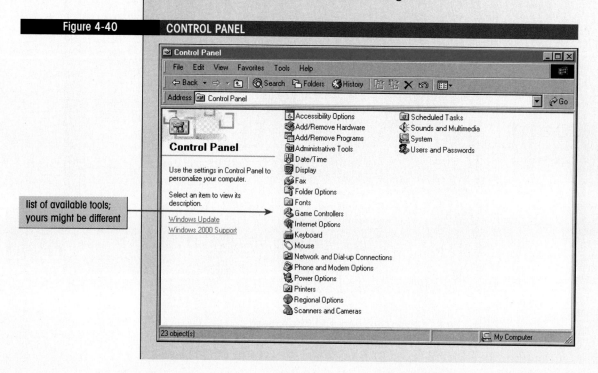

list of available tools; yours might be different

As you look through the icons in the Control Panel, you'll see some familiar objects. The Display icon opens the Display Properties dialog box, which you've used for controlling the properties of your display (the wallpaper, background, screen saver, etc.). You'll also see many unfamiliar objects. The Folder Options icon allows you to customize how you interact with files on your computer; for example, whether you open files by a single mouse click or a double-click. Other icons allow you to control the workings of your mouse, keyboard, and modem. For more information on working with the Control Panel, see Appendix B.

Beth is impressed with the degree of customization possible with Windows 2000. One of the most exciting features of Windows 2000 is the way it lends itself to the needs of its users. Your ability to customize Windows 2000 in a lab setting is limited, and the settings are likely to be changed by the next user. But if you are running Windows 2000 on your own computer, you will find that designing a desktop that reflects your needs is time well spent. In creating a document-centric desktop you should keep one thing in mind: having too many icons on the desktop defeats the purpose of giving quick access to your documents. If you have icons crowded all over the desktop, it is difficult to locate the one you want quickly.

If you are working in a lab setting, make sure you return all settings to their original state before leaving the lab.

QUICK CHECK

1. How do you move the taskbar to the left side of your computer screen?

2. To hide the taskbar, select _____ from the Taskbar and Start Menu Properties dialog box.

3. By default, Windows 2000 displays the _____ toolbar on the taskbar.

4. True or False: To create your own customized Start menu, the Use Personalized Menus check box must be selected.

5. To modify the collection of objects and properties on your computer, you can open the _____ _____.

REVIEW ASSIGNMENTS

1. **Creating Shortcuts** Practice placing a document on the desktop and printing it, using a printer shortcut icon.
   a. Create a shortcut on the desktop to the printer you use regularly.
   b. Open Notepad and create a new text document on your desktop, typing your name and the list of classes you are taking. Name this document **Classes**. Close Notepad.
   c. Drag the Classes document icon to the printer shortcut. Your document prints.
   d. Now use the techniques you learned in the previous tutorial to print an image of your desktop. (Use the Print Screen key to save an image of the desktop, open WordPad, type your name and the date at the top of the document, paste the image into WordPad, and then print the image from WordPad.)
   e. When you are finished, delete both icons from your desktop.

2. **Create a Shortcut to a Folder** Beth recently assigned Sally Hanson, an undergraduate at one of the local colleges, to provide housekeeping for three clients. Sally plans to be out of the area over spring break, so Beth needs to write a memo to each client, asking if they need replacement help. Beth would like to be able to get at the correspondence concerning Sally Hanson more easily.

   a. Start Windows Explorer, and then create a new folder called Sally on your Data Disk.
   b. Start Notepad, and then compose the three memos, typing in your own text. Save the memos in the Sally folder on your Data Disk with the names **Smith**, **Arruga**, and **Kosta** (the names of the three clients). Close Notepad when you are finished.
   c. Drag the Sally folder from Windows Explorer to the desktop, using the right mouse button, and then click Create Shortcut(s) Here.
   d. Name the shortcut icon Sally.
   e. Test the shortcut icon by opening the Sally folder, and then open one of the memos. Use two different methods to open these two objects, and write down which methods you used.
   f. Arrange your desktop so you can see the open memo in Notepad, the open folder window, and the shortcut icon. You might need to resize the windows to make them smaller. Then print an image of the desktop (see step 1d, above).
   g. Remove the desktop shortcut to the folder when you are done.

3. **Create a New Bitmap on the Desktop** In this tutorial, you created a new text document directly on the desktop. In this tutorial assignment, you'll create a new bitmap image document on your Data Disk. You'll use the mouse to write your signature. Then you'll use this bitmap image as the wallpaper on your desktop.

   a. Use My Computer to open drive A and display the contents of your Data Disk.
   b. Right-click an empty area of the drive A window, point to New, and then click Bitmap Image.
   c. Name the new file **My Signature**.
   d. Open **My Signature**. What program does Windows 2000 use to open this file?
   e. Drag the mouse over the empty canvas to write your signature (this will be awkward for even experienced mouse users).
   f. Exit the program, and save your changes. Close the drive A window.
   g. Right-click an empty area of the desktop, click Properties, and then make sure the Background property sheet is visible.
   h. Click the Browse button, and then use the Look in list arrow at the top of the dialog box to select the 3½ floppy drive. Select the **My Signature** bitmap image on your Data Disk, and then click the Open button. Your signature appears as the wallpaper in the preview monitor.
   i. Print an image of the screen (see step 1d, above).
   j. Click the Cancel button to preserve the desktop's original appearance.

4. **Explore Your Computer's Desktop Properties** Answer each of the following questions about the desktop properties on your lab computers.

   a. Open the Display Properties dialog box. What resolution is your monitor using? What other resolution settings are available for your monitor? Drag the slider to find out. If it's an older monitor, it might not have higher resolutions available.

b. What color palette are you using?

c. Is Windows 2000 using a screen saver on your machine? Which one? After how many minutes of idle time does it engage?

d. What is your desktop's default color scheme?

e. Does your desktop display a pattern or wallpaper? Which one?

 f. Open the Power Management Properties dialog box from the Screen Saver tab. What power scheme is your computer using, if any? What settings are in effect for that power scheme?

 g. In the Power Management Properties dialog box, click the Advanced tab. Turn on the option to show the power meter on the taskbar. A power icon, like a plug, appears in the tray. Point at the power icon. What ScreenTip appears? Go back to the Power Management Properties dialog box, turn this option off, and then close the Power Management Properties dialog box.

5. **Customizing Your Desktop** The ability to place icons directly on the desktop gives you the opportunity to create a truly document-centric desktop. Figure 4-41 shows Beth's desktop after she's had a chance to create all the shortcuts you recommended and to add additional shortcuts for programs, folders, files, and other resources she uses regularly.

Figure 4-41

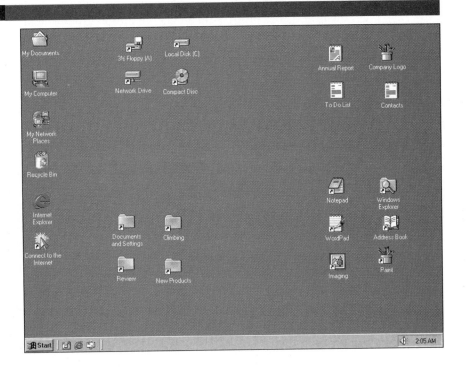

Notice that this desktop has shortcuts not just for drives and documents, but also for programs, utilities, and other Windows 2000 objects. Also notice that the icons are arranged logically and that there aren't so many as to make them hard to find. The amount of time you save by arranging your desktop in this manner cannot be overestimated, if you spend a lot of time at the computer. If you have your own computer, create a desktop that meets your needs.

Use the following strategy:

a. Use Windows Explorer to locate the drives on your computer, and then create a shortcut on the desktop to each of the local or network drives you use regularly.

b. If you haven't done so already, use Windows Explorer to create folders for the work you usually do on your computer. You might want a folder for each class you're taking, letters you write, projects, or hobbies. Then create a shortcut on the desktop to each folder you use regularly.

c. Create shortcuts for each document you use repeatedly. Remember not to overcrowd your desktop.

d. If you know how to locate program and utility files, create shortcuts on the desktop to the programs and utilities you use most often.

e. Group the icons on your desktop so that similar objects are in the same location.

f. Print a copy of your desktop in its final form (see step 1d, above).

6. **Customizing Your Start Menu** A simple way of adding icons to your Start menu is to use drag and drop. For example, you can click a file icon and drag it onto a submenu of the Start menu, and Windows 2000 will automatically create a shortcut to the file for you. Similarly, you can remove any item from the Start menu by clicking the item and dragging it off the Start menu. For example, dragging a Start menu item off the Start menu and onto the desktop moves the shortcut to the desktop. Dragging the same item off the Start menu and onto the Recycle Bin deletes the shortcut.

Figure 4-42 shows a Start menu containing shortcuts to the My Computer and the My Network Places windows. While most Start menu items can be created using either the drag-and-drop technique or the Add method in the Taskbar and Start Menu Properties dialog box, these two new items can be created *only* by dragging and dropping. Try this technique by performing steps a–e below.

Figure 4-42

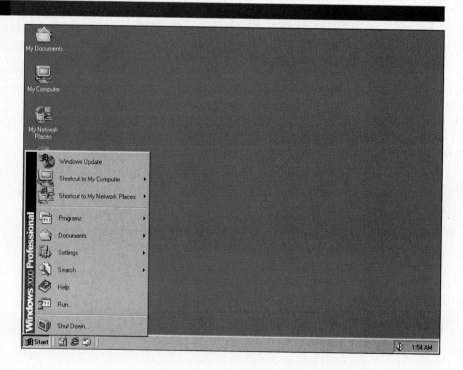

Explore

a. Drag the My Computer icon to the Start button (you will have to hover over the Start button for a few seconds to allow it to open) and drop the icon at the top of the menu.

b. Add the My Network Places icon to the top of the Start menu in the same way.

c. Print a copy of the Start menu you created, showing the two new entries (see step 1d, above).

d. When you view the contents of the My Computer icon and the My Network Places icon in the Start menu, what you do you see? Discuss how the My Computer icon in the Start menu could replace Windows Explorer as a tool to navigate the contents of your computer's drives and folders. What are the advantages and disadvantages of using the Start menu and My Computer this way? Does this approach work better for floppy drives or for your hard drive—and why?

e. Remove the My Computer and Network Places icons from the Start menu by dragging them to the Recycle Bin, one at a time.

7. **Customizing a Taskbar Toolbar** You can also use the drag-and-drop technique to customize a taskbar toolbar. By dragging an icon from a folder or the desktop onto one of the toolbars on the taskbar, you can create additional buttons for quick one-click access to your favorite files and programs.

Figure 4-43 shows a modified Quick Launch toolbar with icons for Notepad, WordPad, and Windows Explorer added. Make similar changes to your Quick Launch toolbar by performing steps a–g below.

Figure 4-43

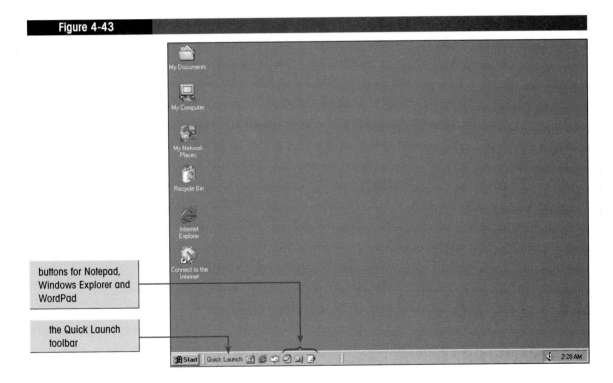

buttons for Notepad, Windows Explorer and WordPad

the Quick Launch toolbar

Explore

a. Open the Start menu so you can see the Accessories submenu, hold down the Ctrl key, and drag icons for Notepad, WordPad, and Windows Explorer from the Accessories submenu on your Start menu to the Quick Launch toolbar on your taskbar. Be sure to hold down the Ctrl key while dragging and dropping these icons, or you'll move the icons off the Start menu.

b. Modify the properties of the Quick Launch toolbar so that it shows the toolbar's title.

c. Print a copy of your screen showing the revised Quick Launch toolbar (see step 1d, above).

d. Test each new button on the toolbar to verify that it opens the appropriate program.

e. Summarize what you've done and discuss the advantages of using the Quick Launch toolbar to launch your favorite programs. Which is easier, the Quick Launch toolbar or the Start menu, and why? What is the most effective use of the Quick Launch toolbar? Would you place all of your programs on the toolbar? Why or why not?

f. Delete the Notepad, WordPad, and Windows Explorer buttons from the Quick Launch toolbar by dragging and dropping them into your Recycle Bin.

g. Remove the title from the Quick Launch toolbar.

PROJECTS

1. Knowing that you have two years left in your college degree program, your parents decide to splurge and give you a computer, complete with Windows 2000, for your birthday. Your parents spent hours getting everything loaded and configured for you, so when you pick it up this weekend you can get right to work on that major project due on Monday. You have about half an hour before your roommate returns with your car, so take out an 8½ by 11 piece of paper, and draw the desktop that will give you the quickest access to all documents, devices, and/or programs needed to carry out the tasks listed below. Indicate shortcut icons with an arrow. Also draw a window showing your 3½-inch disk contents, using the information provided in the "To Do List."

To Do List

a. Finish typing paper for American History project, using WordPad.

___ currently saved on disk

___ will need to print

b. Finish lab report for Organic Chemistry, using WordPad.

___ currently saved on disk

___ will need to print

c. Insert bitmap image saved on disk into Organic Chemistry lab report.

d. Review outline for Office Procedures class test, created in WordPad.

___ currently saved on disk

___ will need to print

2. You provide computer support at Highland Yearbooks, a company that publishes high school and college yearbooks. Highland has just upgraded to Windows 2000, and you'd like to get right to work customizing the desktops of Highland employees for optimal performance. You start with the computer belonging to John McPhee, one of the sales representatives. Create a desktop for John that takes the following circumstances into account. When you are done, print an image of the desktop (see step 1d, above). Then make sure you remove any shortcuts you created and restore the desktop to its original settings. On the back of your printout, write down which options you changed to meet John's needs.

a. John keeps a Notepad file with a time-date stamp of long-distance phone calls stored on the desktop with a shortcut to that file on his Start menu.

b. John wants to be able to print the phone log file quickly, without having to open it first.

c. The company colors at Highland Yearbooks are blue and gold. John would like a blue desktop with gold title bars.

3. In this tutorial you learned ways to work more efficiently. The shortcut menu is another Windows feature that helps you work efficiently. You've learned that a shortcut menu appears when you right-click an object. The operating system, however, changes the shortcut menu, depending on the object you right-click and what you are doing with that object. Using WordPad, create a chart that summarizes the features available when you right-click:

a. an object on the desktop
b. the taskbar
c. selected text in a WordPad document
d. nonselected text in a WordPad document

Write a paragraph that explains why these shortcut menus are all different from one another.

4. You recently took a part-time job at the local high school, assisting the computer lab manager. After your first day on the job, you notice how often the lab manager uses property sheets. You decide to spend the evening exploring property sheets so you can be more useful on the job. For future reference, make a chart in WordPad that describes the information you can glean when you look at the property sheets for:

a. programs
b. devices
c. drives
d. documents (create your own document on the desktop, if there is none available)

After your chart, list which tools you used to locate the property sheets for each of these objects.

5. Your cousin, Joey, has Windows 2000 on his new computer, but has not taken much time to learn about all of the customizable and timesaving features it offers him. In WordPad, type a letter to Joey, explaining three main features covered in this tutorial. Because you know that he is more likely to try to use these features if he has directions in front of him, include basic instructions on how to access them.

6. You just printed your letter to Joey in Project 5, and then remembered the concept of document-centric desktops you learned in this tutorial. You think that if Joey can conceptualize this, it will really expand his Windows 2000 horizons. You decide to add a note explaining the difference between the document- and program-centric desktop. Write a paragraph about this difference.

Explore

7. You are trying to save money on your electric bill and are wondering if you can take advantage of the Windows 2000 power management features. Open the Power Options Properties dialog box in the Control Panel and print the screen you see, using the techniques you learned earlier in this book. On the printout, write a paragraph describing the power management features available specifically to your computer and how they can help save money.

Explore

8. You have been asked to give a presentation at a *Computer Users with Special Needs* seminar on campus. You have a half hour to present participants with information on Windows 2000 Accessibility Options in the Control Panel. Using the online Help as a guide, write a handout describing the ways one can configure Windows 2000 for computer users with special needs. Include in your handout instructions for turning these features on and off.

Explore

9. You would like to learn how to create your own pattern to use as a desktop background.

   a. Open the Pattern dialog box, click any pattern, and then click the Edit Pattern button. The Pattern Editor dialog box opens.

   b. Type your name in the Name box and then click anywhere in the Pattern box and observe what happens.

   c. Continue to click until you have the design you want, and then print the screen that shows the pattern you designed. Click the Close button to close the Pattern Editor dialog box, and click No so your changes aren't saved.

   d. Use online Help to learn how you would save your pattern, apply it, and then remove it from the Pattern list.

QUICK CHECK ANSWERS

Session 4.1

1. False

2. False

3. You delete not only the icon but also the document.

4. You delete only the icon but not the document.

5. Dragging and dropping the document icon from one drive to another creates a copy of the document. Dragging and dropping within the same drive moves the document.

Session 4.2

1. False

2. Right-click the object and then click Properties.

3. Here are four: Background, Screen Saver, Appearance, Settings. You could also mention the properties on each of these sheets, such as color palette, resolution, and so on.

4. Activate a screen saver

5. There are 640 pixels across and 480 down.

6. 640 x 480, because it displays the largest objects

7. It requires extra video memory and runs more slowly.

Session 4.3

1. Click a blank area on the taskbar and, with the left mouse button pressed down, drag the taskbar to the left side of the computer screen.

2. Auto Hide

3. Quick Launch

4. False

5. Control Panel

5. Control Panel

OBJECTIVES

In this tutorial you will:

- Explore the structure of the Internet and the World Wide Web

- View, open, navigate, and print Web pages in Internet Explorer

- Download a file

- Enable Active Desktop in order to add, move, resize, close, and remove Active Desktop items

- Schedule the automatic retrieval of data from the Web

- Use an HTML file as a background

- Send and receive e-mail using Outlook Express

LABS

The Internet: World Wide Web

Web Pages & HTML

BRINGING
THE WORLD WIDE WEB
TO THE DESKTOP

Using Active Desktop at Highland Travel

CASE

Highland Travel

Highland Travel, a touring company that offers guided tour packages to Scotland, recently hired you as an advertising manager. During your first day at work, you meet with the company's technical support person, Scott Campbell. After describing the training you'll receive, Scott explains that Highland Travel uses the Internet and the World Wide Web to promote the company, to provide services to clients, and to improve communication among employees. The company recently upgraded its computers to Windows 2000, and management wants all employees to be able to use its features to the fullest.

You tell Scott you've heard that one popular feature of Windows 2000 is its integration of the operating system with the Web. Scott nods, and tells you that during your first week on the job, you'll go through a training program to familiarize yourself with Windows 2000, and particularly with its Web features. He explains that Windows 2000 brings the richness of the Web to your desktop with Active Desktop. **Active Desktop** is technology that transforms the Windows desktop into your own personal "communications central"—not only for launching programs and accessing files, but also for obtaining and displaying any type of Web-based information. The Windows 2000 desktop is called "active" because it allows you to access the Internet.

Active Desktop manifests itself in several ways on your computer. For example, you can place updatable Web content, such as weather maps, sports news, and stock tickers, on your desktop so it functions as a personalized newspaper. Scott assures you that the training program will familiarize you with these and more features—and will introduce you to Highland Travel's Web site.

SESSION 5.1

In this session, you will learn how Windows 2000 brings the Internet and the World Wide Web to your desktop. You will learn to use Internet Explorer to view Web sites. You will activate a link, navigate a Web page with frames, print a Web page, and download a file. Finally you'll learn how to quickly access your favorite pages using the History pane and the Favorites folder. For this tutorial you will need a blank 3½-inch disk.

The Internet

Scott begins your training by explaining the basic concepts that make the Internet possible. When two or more computers are connected together so that they can exchange information and resources, they create a structure known as a **network**. Networks facilitate the sharing of data and resources among multiple users. Networks can also be connected to each other to allow computers on different networks to share information; when two or more networks are connected, they create an **internetwork**, or **internet**. "The Internet" (capital "I") has come to refer to the "network of networks" that is made up of millions of computers linked to networks all over the world. Computers and networks on the Internet are connected by fiber-optic cables, satellites, phone lines, and other communications systems, as shown in Figure 5-1. Data travels across these communication systems using whatever route is most efficient.

Figure 5-1	STRUCTURE OF THE INTERNET

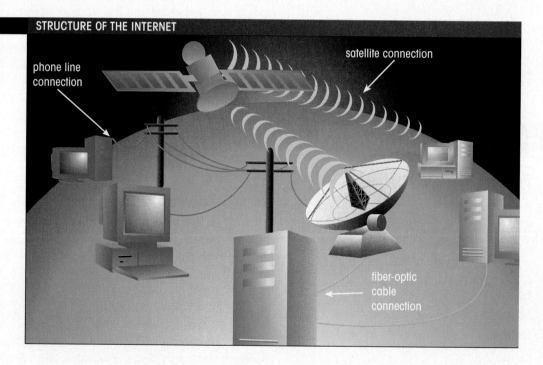

The Internet, by design, is a decentralized structure. There is no Internet "company." Instead, the Internet is a collection of different organizations, such as universities and businesses, each organizing its own information. There are no rules about where information is stored, and no one regulates the quality of information available on the Internet. Even though the lack of central control can make it hard for beginners to find their way through the resources on the Internet, decentralization has some advantages. The Internet is open to innovation and rapid growth, as different organizations and individuals have the freedom to test new products and services and make them quickly available to a global audience. One such service is the World Wide Web.

The World Wide Web makes it easy to share and access data stored on computers around the world with minimal training and support, and for this reason, Microsoft designed Windows 2000 to offer easy Web access. The Web is a system of **hypertext documents**— electronic files that contain elements known as **links**, which target other parts of a document or other documents altogether. A link can be a word or phrase or a graphic image. Figure 5-2 shows a Colorado touring company hypertext document with several links. Each link targets a separate document that offers more information about the company. You can also connect to other file types, including scanned photographs, graphic images, film clips, sounds, online discussion groups, and computer programs.

| Figure 5-2 | WEB PAGE WITH LINKS TO WEB PAGES CONTAINING ADDITIONAL INFORMATION |

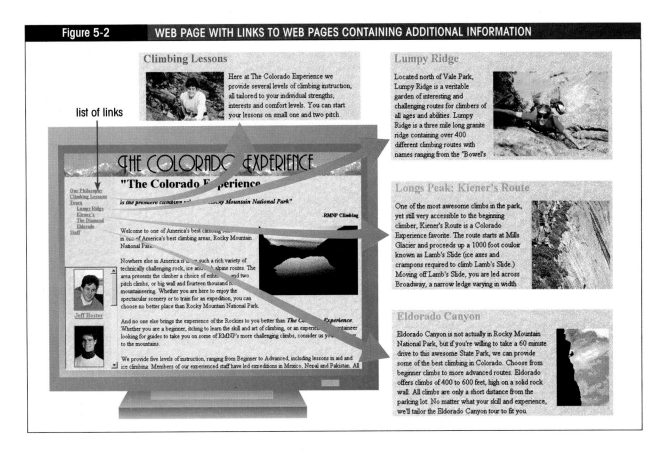

Each hypertext document on the Web is called a **Web page** and is stored on a computer on the Internet called a **Web server**. A Web page can contain links to other Web pages located anywhere on the Internet—on the same computer as the original Web page or on an entirely different computer halfway across the world. The ability to cross-reference other Web pages with links is one of the most important features of the Web.

Navigating Web pages using hypertext is an efficient way to access information. When you read a book you follow a linear progression, reading one page after another. With hypertext, you progress through the pages in whatever order you want. Hypertext allows you to skip from one topic to another, following the information path that interests you, as shown in Figure 5-3.

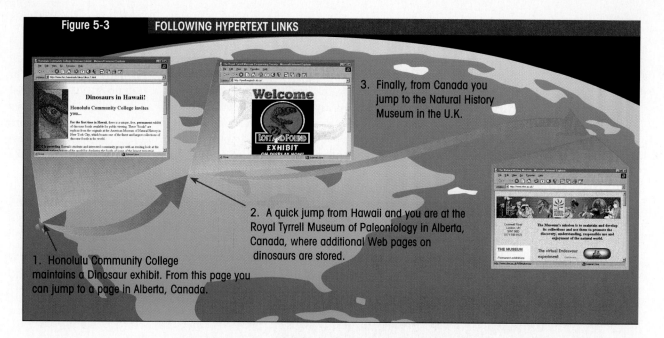

Figure 5-3   FOLLOWING HYPERTEXT LINKS

3. Finally, from Canada you jump to the Natural History Museum in the U.K.

2. A quick jump from Hawaii and you are at the Royal Tyrrell Museum of Paleontology in Alberta, Canada, where additional Web pages on dinosaurs are stored.

1. Honolulu Community College maintains a Dinosaur exhibit. From this page you can jump to a page in Alberta, Canada.

Microsoft has taken advantage of this fact by designing its Windows 2000 operating system to incorporate your experience on the Internet. The techniques you'll learn in this tutorial to navigate Web pages are identical to those you learned in previous tutorials to navigate the objects on your computer. Microsoft's goal with Windows 2000 is to make the user's experience with local files, network files, and files on computers around the world as uniform as possible.

Browsers

To access documents on the Web, you need a **browser**—a program that locates, retrieves, displays, and organizes documents stored on Web servers. Your browser allows you to visit Web sites around the world; view multimedia documents; transfer files, images, and sounds to your computer; conduct searches for specific topics; and run programs on other computers. In Figure 5-3, the dinosaur Web documents that you see appear in a browser window. Windows 2000 includes a set of communications software tools called **Internet Explorer**, which includes the Internet Explorer browser, as well as tools for other Internet functions such as electronic mail, or **e-mail**, electronic messages sent between users over the Internet. Another popular communications software package is **Netscape Communicator**, which includes the Netscape Navigator browser. This tutorial assumes that you'll do your browsing with Internet Explorer. If you're using Netscape Communicator or another browser, talk to your instructor to resolve any difficulties.

Microsoft has integrated the Internet Explorer browser into the Windows 2000 operating system to make its functions available to many Windows 2000 components. For example, the Windows Explorer utility that you used in Tutorial 3 to navigate files on your Data Disk uses Internet Explorer features so that it can function as a browser. The My Computer window works similarly.

There are many advantages to using the same tools to access information regardless of its location. Computer users in the past had to use one tool to access local files, another to access network files, and many additional products to access information on the Internet, such as e-mail, files, and other computers. The Windows 2000 operating system allows you to view information anywhere with a single set of techniques.

When you try to view a Web page, your browser locates and retrieves the document from the Web server and displays its contents on your computer. As shown in Figure 5-4, the server stores the Web page in one location, and browsers anywhere in the world can view it.

Figure 5-4	USING A BROWSER TO VIEW A WEB DOCUMENT ON A SERVER

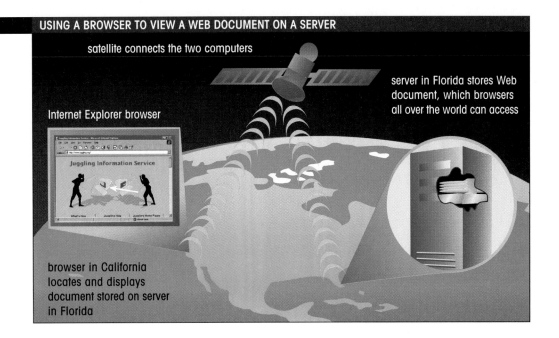

satellite connects the two computers

Internet Explorer browser

server in Florida stores Web document, which browsers all over the world can access

browser in California locates and displays document stored on server in Florida

For your browser to connect to the World Wide Web, you must have an Internet connection. In a university setting, your connection might come from the campus network on which you have an account. If you are working on a home computer and gaining Internet access from your modem over a phone line, your connection is called a **dial-up connection** and is maintained via an account with an **Internet service provider (ISP)**, a company that sells Internet access. See Appendix A, "Connecting Computers over a Phone Line," for more information. With a dial-up connection, you are connected to the Internet only as long as your modem "stays on the line," whereas on most institutional networks, you are always connected to the Internet because the network is actually a part of the Internet. If you are using a dial-up connection to connect to your institution's network, you have probably received instructions that help you establish this connection. Use these instructions any time you need to be connected to the Internet during this tutorial. If you are working from home, connect to the Internet using the instructions provided by your ISP.

Starting **Internet Explorer**

You've already used Windows 2000 to view the files and folders on your disks, and now Scott wants to show you that you can also use it to browse sites on the Web. Scott suggests you start exploring the Web by connecting to the Highland Travel page. When you connect to the Internet without specifying a particular Web page, Windows 2000 automatically loads your **home page**—the Web page designated by the operating system as your starting point. Windows 2000 designates Microsoft Corporation's company page as the default home page, but you can easily designate a different home page. If you are at an institution such as a university, a home page has probably already been designated for you. Note that "home page" can also refer to a personal Web page or to the Web page that an organization or business has created to give information about itself.

Scott suggests that you use Internet Explorer, the browser that comes with Windows 2000, to view a Web page. You'll notice a lot of similarities between Internet Explorer (designed to locate information on the Internet) and Windows Explorer (designed to locate information on your computer or network).

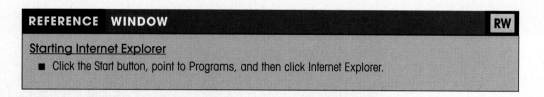

REFERENCE WINDOW   **RW**

Starting Internet Explorer

■ Click the Start button, point to Programs, and then click Internet Explorer.

To view your home page in Internet Explorer:

1. Click the **Start** button [Start], point to **Programs**, and then click **Internet Explorer**.

2. If necessary, click the **Maximize** button ☐ to maximize the Internet Explorer window.

   TROUBLE? If you are in a university setting, you are probably already connected to the Internet, and your home page will appear immediately. If you are working from a computer with a dial-up connection already set up and are not currently connected to the Internet, Windows 2000 will attempt to connect you. Wait and follow the prompts that appear. If you can't establish a connection, check with your technical support person in the lab, or if you are using your own computer, use Dial-Up Networking as instructed by your ISP, or call your ISP's technical support line for assistance. If an error message appears, it's possible that the server on which your home page is stored is temporarily busy or unavailable.

3. Maximize the Internet Explorer window, click **View** on the menu bar, point to **Toolbars**, and then make sure the **Standard Buttons**, **Address Bar**, and **Links** options are checked. The Radio option should *not* be checked.

4. Open the **View** menu again. Make sure **Status Bar** is checked. Your Internet Explorer window should appear similar in form to that shown in Figure 5-5.

   TROUBLE? If your Internet Explorer window shows a different Web page and the Address bar shows a different address, don't worry. Your home page is just different.

Figure 5-5	HOME PAGE DISPLAYED IN INTERNET EXPLORER

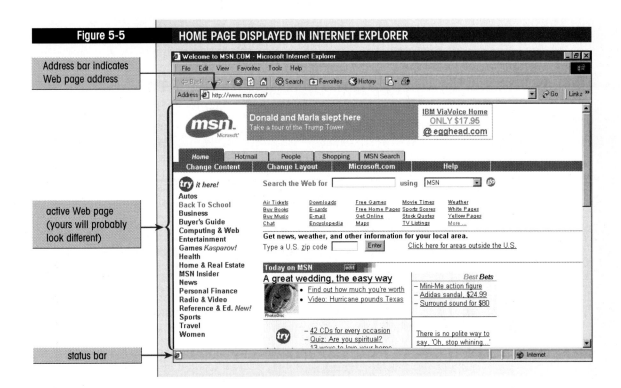

Address bar indicates Web page address

active Web page (yours will probably look different)

status bar

Opening a Page on the Web

Each page on the Web is uniquely identified by an address called a **URL**, or **Uniform Resource Locator**. A company may advertise its Web page by publishing the page's URL, such as "http://www.microsoft.com". A URL consists of three things: a protocol type, a server address, and a file pathname. Let's examine each of these items more closely.

A **protocol** is a standardized procedure used by computers to exchange information. Web documents travel between sites using **HyperText Transfer Protocol**, or **HTTP**. A Web page whose URL begins with the letters "http://" tells the Web browser to use the HTTP protocol when retrieving the page.

The **server address** gives the name of the Web server that is storing the Web page. You can usually learn a great deal about the Web server by examining the server address. For example, in the server address "www.northern.edu" the "www" indicates that the server is on the World Wide Web, "northern" indicates the name of the organization that owns the server (Northern University), and "edu" indicates that it's an educational site. Other common site types include "com" for commercial sites, "gov" for government agencies, and "org" for nonprofit organizations.

Finally, each file stored on a network server must have a unique pathname, just as files on a disk do. The **pathname** includes the folder or folders the file is stored in, plus the filename and its extension. The filename extension for Web pages is usually html, or just htm.

Try deciphering the following URL:

　　http://www.northern.edu/education/programs.html

The protocol is HTTP, the server address is www.northern.edu, the pathname is education/programs.html, and programs.html is the filename. So the Web browser knows it must retrieve the programs.html file from the /education folder located on the Web server at www.northern.edu, using the HTTP protocol.

Scott has given you the URL for the Highland Travel Web page, which is:

　　http://www.course.com/newperspectives/windows2000/highland

REFERENCE WINDOW   **RW**

Opening a Page Using a URL
- Select the contents of the Address box.
- Type the URL in the Address box, and then press the Enter key.

To open a page on the Web with a URL:

1. Click the **Address** box on the Address bar. The contents of the Address box, which should be the URL for your home page, are selected. Anything you type will replace the selected URL.

   TROUBLE? If the contents of the Address box are not selected, select the address manually by dragging the mouse from the far left to the far right of the URL. Be sure to select the entire URL.

2. Type **http://www.course.com/newperspectives/Windows2000/Highland** in the Address box. Make sure you type the URL exactly as shown.

3. Press the **Enter** key. Highland Travel's Welcome page opens in the Internet Explorer window. See Figure 5-6.

   TROUBLE? If you receive a Not Found error message, the URL might not be typed correctly. Repeat Steps 1 through 3, making sure that the URL in the Address box matches the URL in Step 2. If you still receive an error message, ask your instructor or technical support person for help. If you see a different Web page from the one shown in Figure 5-6, click View on the menu bar and then click Refresh.

| Figure 5-6 | CONNECTING TO THE HIGHLAND TRAVEL SITE |

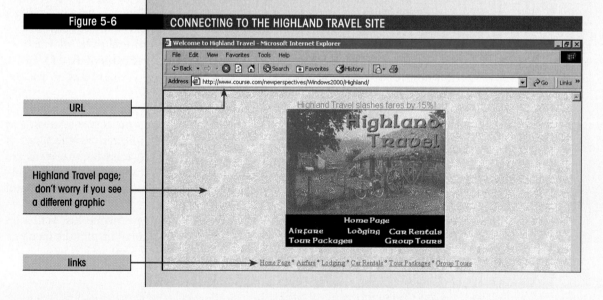

URL

Highland Travel page; don't worry if you see a different graphic

links

You can access information about the Highland Travel company by navigating through its Web pages. Spend some time doing that now.

Navigating the Web

The Highland Travel Web page contains links to other Web pages, so you decide to learn more about the company by activating one of the links on the Welcome page.

Activating a Link

A hypertext link on the Web, like a link in a chain, is a connector between two points. Links can appear in two ways: as text that you click or as a graphic that you click. A **text link** is a word or phrase that is usually underlined and often boldfaced or colored differently from the words around it. A **graphic link** is a graphic image that you click to jump to another location (note that graphic images can be or include text). When you aren't sure whether a graphic image is a link, point to it with the mouse pointer. When you move the mouse pointer over a link—text or graphic—the pointer changes shape from ▸ to 🖑. The 🖑 pointer indicates that when you click, you will activate that link and jump to the new location. The destination of the link appears in the status bar, and, for some graphic links, a small identification box appears next to your pointer.

The Highland Travel page contains both text and graphic links. The text links are at the bottom of the page, underlined, and in color. The graphic links are the words in a fancy font at the bottom of the Highland Travel photo, although graphic links are often images or photos. The links give your browser the information it needs to locate the page. When you activate a link, you jump to a new location. The target of the link can be another location on the current page (for example, you can jump from the bottom of the page to the top), a different page on the current Web server, or a different page located on an entirely different Web server. When you activate a link, there are three possible outcomes:

- You successfully reach the target of the link. The browser contacts the site you want, connects to the site, transfers the data from the site to your computer, and displays the data on your screen.

- The link's target is busy, perhaps because the server storing the link's target is overwhelmed with too many requests. You can click the Stop button 🛑 to prevent your browser from further attempting to make the connection. You'll have to try a different link, or try this link later.

- The link points to a target that doesn't exist. Documents are often removed from Web servers as they become obsolete, or moved to new locations, and links that point to those documents are not always updated. If you click an obsolete link, a message box appears. If an error message box appears, click the OK button and try a different link. Otherwise click the Back button ⬅ to return to the page you were previously viewing.

The amount of time it takes to complete a link, called the **response time**, can vary, depending upon the number of people trying to connect to the same site, the number of people on the Internet at that time, the site design, and the speed of your Internet connection. In fact, one of the differences you might notice between clicking links on your desktop (which target local objects, such as My Computer or a desktop document) and clicking those that target Web pages on the Internet is the difference in response time. Linking to local objects is usually instantaneous, whereas linking to pages on the Web can take many seconds, because of the time required for the data to be transferred over your Internet connection.

As you can see in Figure 5-7, activating a link starts a multistep process. When you point to a link, the status bar displays a message that the browser is connecting to the address of the link's target, its URL. When you click the link, the activity indicator animates. The status bar displays a series of messages indicating that your browser is connecting to the site, is waiting for a reply, is transferring data, and finally, is done.

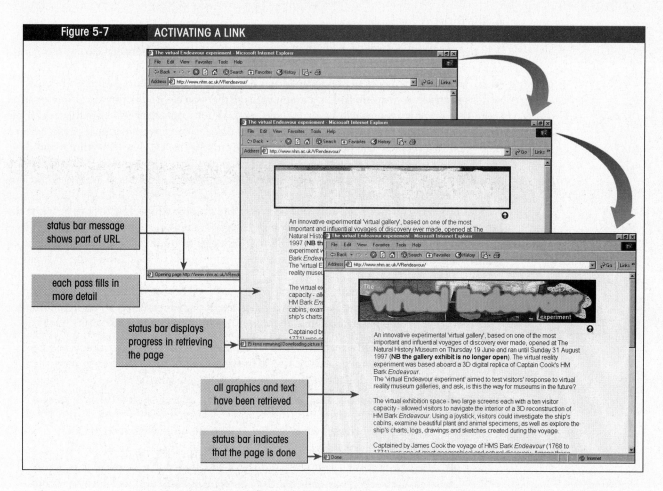

Figure 5-7   ACTIVATING A LINK

- status bar message shows part of URL
- each pass fills in more detail
- status bar displays progress in retrieving the page
- all graphics and text have been retrieved
- status bar indicates that the page is done

You can see the Web page build as your browser transfers information to the screen in multiple passes. The first wave brings a few pieces to the page, and with each subsequent pass, the browser fills in more detail, until the material is complete. Try activating one of the Highland Travel links to access the company's home page.

To activate a link:

1. Point to the text link **Home Page**—the one at the bottom of the page. (You could also point to the graphic link, the one with the fancy font; both links target the same page.) Notice that the pointer changes shape from ⌖ to ⤵, indicating that you are pointing to a hypertext link. The status bar shows the URL for that link. See Figure 5-8.

Figure 5-8	CLICKING A TEXT LINK

graphic links

text links

link's target appears
in the status bar

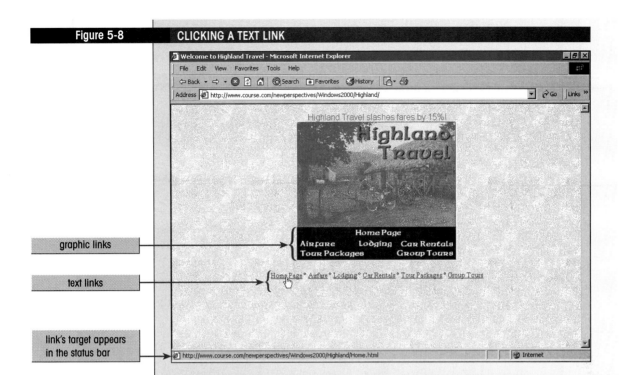

2. Click the **Home Page** text link to activate the link. The status bar notes the progress of the link. When the status bar displays "Done," the link is complete, and the Web page that is the target of the link appears. See Figure 5-9.

Figure 5-9	COMPLETED LINK

Navigating with Frames

Scott mentions that if you spend time using Windows 2000 to explore the Web, you'll probably encounter Web pages with frames. A **frame** is a section of the browser's display area, capable of displaying the contents of a different Web page. Each frame can have its own set of scroll bars, as shown in Figure 5-10. The NEC Products page is made up of two pages: the one on the left lists graphic links to other pages, and the one on the right displays the list of product categories.

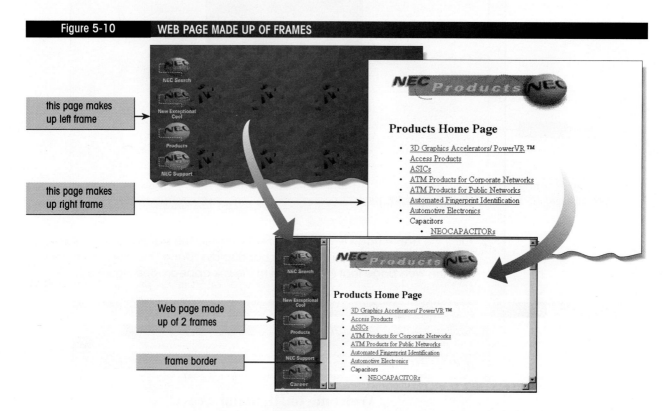

Figure 5-10   WEB PAGE MADE UP OF FRAMES

Many Web sites today use frames because they allow the user to see different areas of information simultaneously. When you scroll through the contents of one frame, you do not affect the other frame or frames. Scott suggests you view the Tour Packages page, which employs frames, to learn about this season's Highland Travel tours.

To view a page with frames:

1. Click the **Tour Packages** text link, located in the yellow box on the left of the home page. The Tour Packages page opens. This page consists of four frames that contain (1) the Tour Packages heading at the top, (2) information on the left about the specified tour, (3) a scroll box on the right, listing the tour itinerary for each tour, and (4) graphic links to four different tours, on the bottom. See Figure 5-11.

   TROUBLE? If no scroll bars appear in the right frame, your screen resolution is so high that it is capable of displaying the entire itinerary. Skip Step 2, and note that in the rest of the steps you might not find it necessary to scroll.

| Figure 5-11 | VIEWING A WEB PAGE WITH FRAMES |

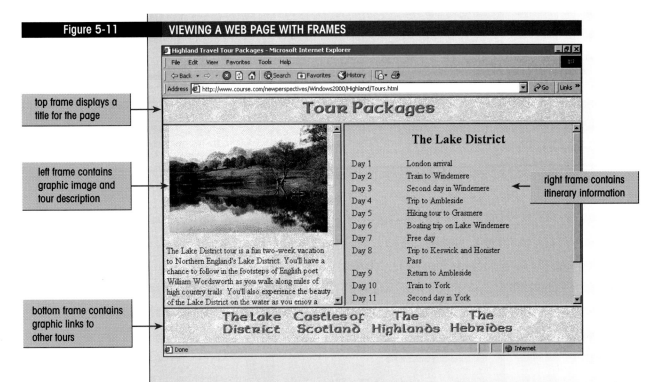

top frame displays a title for the page

left frame contains graphic image and tour description

right frame contains itinerary information

bottom frame contains graphic links to other tours

2. Scroll through the information in the right frame. The other three frames remain static while the right frame changes.

3. To change the display, click the **Castles of Scotland** graphic link in the bottom frame. The information in the left frame changes, and the itinerary in the right frame changes. Scroll through the information in the right frame and again notice that the other frames are static.

4. Click **The Highlands** graphic link to view its itinerary and then click **The Hebrides** graphic link. You have now viewed information on all four tours.

By using frames, the designer of this Web page made it possible for you to view only the information you choose to view.

Returning to a Previously Viewed Page

You've already seen in earlier tutorials how Windows 2000 allows you to navigate the devices and folders on your local and network drives, using the Back ⬅ and Forward ➡ buttons. These buttons are also found in most browsers. The Back button returns you to the Web page you were most recently viewing, and the Forward button reverses the effect of the Back button. Both the Back and Forward buttons contain lists of visited sites; you can return to those sites by clicking the list arrow to the right of either button and clicking the site.

To return to a previously viewed Web page:

1. Click the **Back** button ⬅ repeatedly, to navigate back through the tour itineraries you viewed. You return to the Highland Travel home page, the page you were visiting before you viewed the Tours framed page.

TROUBLE? If you click the small down arrow (not the Forward button) to the right of the Back button, a list opens. Click the arrow again to close the list and then repeat Step 1. This time make sure you click ⬅.

2. Click ⬅ until the Back button dims, indicating that you have reached your starting point, usually your home page. Now try moving forward again to return to the Tours page.

3. Click the **Forward** button ➡ repeatedly until the Forward button dims, indicating that you are looking at the last page you visited.

4. Click the **Home** button 🏠 to return to your home page.

5. Now, you'll use the Back list to see how you can return to a page you've visited without having to navigate through all the pages you've seen in a given session. Click the small down arrow to the right of the Back button. The Back list opens. See Figure 5-12.

Figure 5-12	ACCESSING A PAGE VIA THE BACK LIST

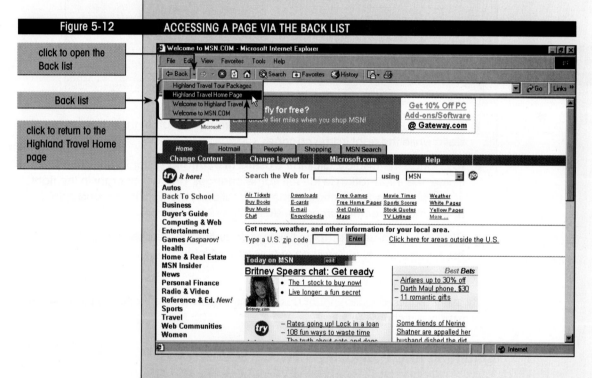

click to open the Back list

Back list

click to return to the Highland Travel Home page

6. Click **Highland Travel Home Page** to return to the Highland Travel home page.

Navigating with the History Pane

Internet Explorer has a lot in common with Windows Explorer. Many of the menu commands and buttons are the same. Internet Explorer also has the same Explorer Bar that Windows Explorer has, and you can always use the Explorer Bar to display a list of the pages you've visited recently (just as you used the History pane to view a list of recently opened files in Windows Explorer).

Scott explains that one limitation of the Back and Forward buttons is that they apply only to your current session on the browser. If you exit Internet Explorer and restart it, the Back list starts afresh. However, you can always use the History pane to quickly access those pages. Scott wants you to try this technique now.

To use the History pane:

1. Click **View**, point to **Explorer Bar**, and then click **History**. Internet Explorer displays the History pane, as shown in Figure 5-13.

Figure 5-13	DISPLAYING THE HISTORY PANE

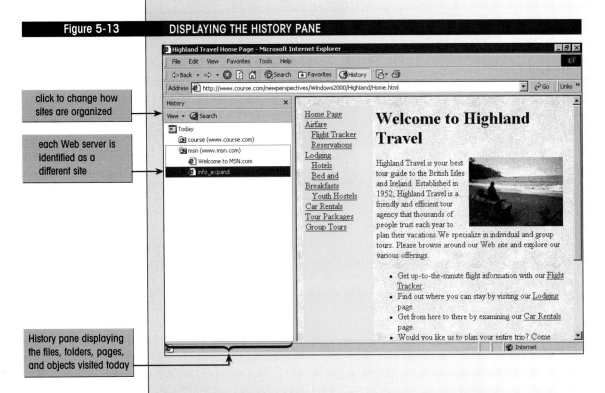

click to change how sites are organized

each Web server is identified as a different site

History pane displaying the files, folders, pages, and objects visited today

2. To make your History pane match the figures, click the **View** button in the History pane (see Figure 5-13) and then click **By Date**.

   In your earlier use of the History pane, you had only one site to examine—the My Computer site for files available on your computer. Now each Web server is identified as a separate site within the History pane.

3. Click the **course (www.course.com)** icon in the History pane. Internet Explorer expands the Course site to display a list of all of the Web pages from the Course Web server that you visited today.

4. Click **Highland Travel Tour Packages** in the list of Web pages. Internet Explorer reopens the tour package page you visited earlier. See Figure 5-14.

Figure 5-14   **RETRIEVING A WEB PAGE FROM THE HISTORY PANE**

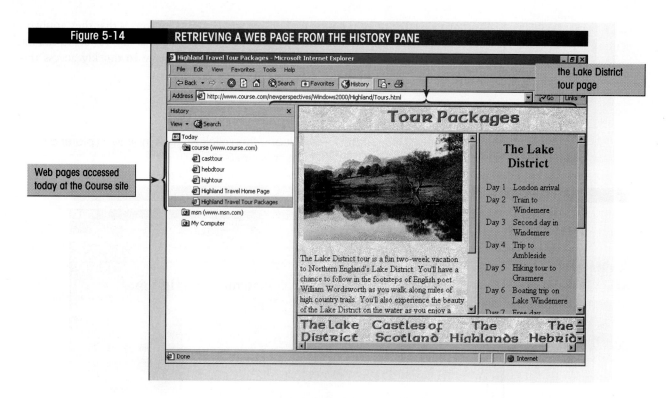

All of the tools you used in Tutorial 3 with the Windows Explorer History pane apply to the History pane in Internet Explorer. You can change the setup, to view the pages in the History pane by date, by site, by the number of times visited, and in the order visited on the current day. You can also search the pages in the History pane to locate a specific Web site you've recently visited.

Using the Favorites Folder

As you explore the Web you'll find pages that are your favorites. Rather than retyping the URL of a page every time you want to visit it, you can save the location of your favorite pages in a list. In Windows 2000, this is your **Favorites folder**, and it contains shortcuts to the files, folders, objects, and Web pages that you visit most often. With a single click of an icon in the Favorites folder, you can retrieve the Web page and display it on your browser. The Favorites folder is a great tool for organizing your files and Web pages.

Viewing the Favorites Folder

Your Favorites list can be displayed in a variety of ways. You've no doubt seen the Favorites menu available on the Internet Explorer menu bar and the Standard Buttons toolbar. You can also display the contents of your Favorites folder in the Explorer Bar for both Internet Explorer and Windows Explorer. The Favorites folder can even be displayed in your Start menu. The method you use to access your favorites depends on your personal preference. You decide to display the Favorites folder in the Explorer bar.

To display the Favorites folder:

1. Click **View**, point to **Explorer Bar**, and then click **Favorites**. Internet Explorer displays the Favorites pane, as shown in Figure 5-15.

Figure 5-15	DISPLAYING THE FAVORITES FOLDER

you can also click here to add to or organize your Favorites folder

Favorites pane, displaying the contents of the Favorites folder

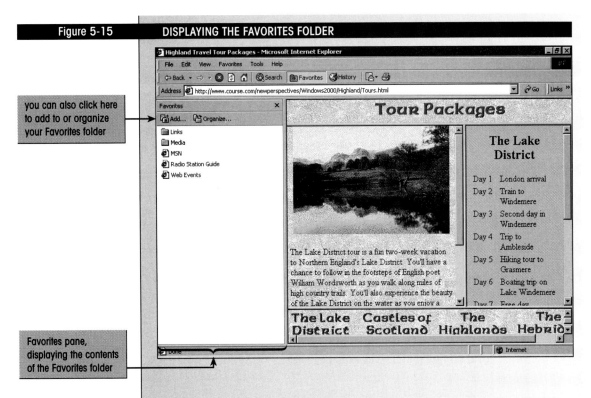

TROUBLE? Your Favorites folder may be different from the one shown in Figure 5-15.

The Favorites folder shown in Figure 5-15 contains shortcuts to a Web page containing a radio station guide, events on the Web, and a page for the Microsoft Network (MSN). It also contains subfolders with additional links. Creating and using subfolders is one way of effectively organizing a long Favorites list.

Adding an Item to the Favorites Folder

Scott suggests that you add the home page for Highland Travel to your Favorites folder. To add a Web page, you must first access the page in Internet Explorer, and then you can use the Add to Favorites command.

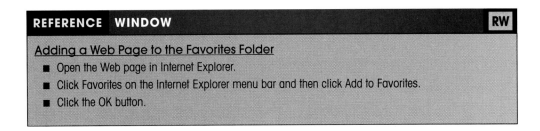

REFERENCE WINDOW   **RW**

__Adding a Web Page to the Favorites Folder__
- Open the Web page in Internet Explorer.
- Click Favorites on the Internet Explorer menu bar and then click Add to Favorites.
- Click the OK button.

To add the Highland Travel home page to the Favorites folder:

1. Click the **Back** button ⬅ to return to the Highland Travel home page.

2. Click **Favorites** on the menu bar and then click **Add to Favorites**.

   Note that you can also click the Add button in the Favorites pane.

3. Click the **OK** button.

   An icon for the Highland Travel home page is added to the Favorites folder.

   TROUBLE? If you are working on a network, you might not have the ability to change the content of the Favorites folder. If that's the case, you should review this material and the material that follows, but you should not attempt to recreate the steps.

Organizing the Favorites Folder

As you add more and more items to the Favorites folder, you will find that you need to organize its contents: deleting some items and moving others to new folders. Using subfolders is an excellent way to organize your favorite files and pages. You decide to create a subfolder for the Highland Travel Web pages.

To organize your Favorites folder:

1. Click **Favorites** on the Internet Explorer menu bar and then click **Organize Favorites**.

   The Organize Favorites dialog box opens. You can also click the Organize button in the Favorites pane to open this dialog box.

2. Click the **Create Folder** button, type **Highland Travel** for the new folder name, and then press the **Enter** key.

   Now you'll move the Highland Travel home page into the new subfolder you created.

3. Click the **Highland Travel Home Page** icon to select it.

4. Click the **Move to Folder** button. The Browse for Folder dialog box opens.

5. Click the **Highland Travel** folder and then click the **OK** button.

6. Click the **Close** button to close the Organize Folders dialog box.

   A folder for Highland Travel should now appear in the Favorites pane.

7. Click the **Highland Travel** folder.

   The contents of the folder appear as shown in Figure 5-16.

Figure 5-16	THE HIGHLAND TRAVEL SUBFOLDER OF THE FAVORITES FOLDER

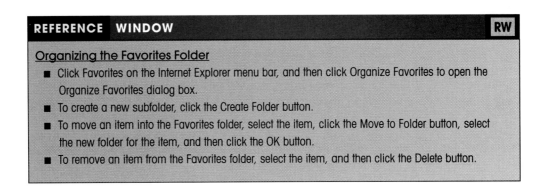

Highland Travel subfolder

the Highland Travel home page has been moved to the subfolder

---

REFERENCE WINDOW   **RW**

Organizing the Favorites Folder
- Click Favorites on the Internet Explorer menu bar, and then click Organize Favorites to open the Organize Favorites dialog box.
- To create a new subfolder, click the Create Folder button.
- To move an item into the Favorites folder, select the item, click the Move to Folder button, select the new folder for the item, and then click the OK button.
- To remove an item from the Favorites folder, select the item, and then click the Delete button.

Before completing your work with the Favorites folder, you should remove the folder you created, and you should close the Favorites pane.

To delete an item from the Favorites folder:

1. Click **Favorites** and then click **Organize Favorites**.
2. Click the **Highland Travel** folder in the Organize Favorites dialog box.
3. Click the **Delete** button.
4. Click the **Yes** button to confirm that you want to remove the folder and its contents.
5. Click the **Close** button to close the Organize Favorites dialog box.
6. Click the **Close** button [X] in the Favorites pane to close the Favorites folder.

Printing a Web Page

Although reducing paper consumption is an advantage of browsing information online, sometimes you'll find it useful to print a Web page. For example, you might want to refer to the information later when you don't have computer access. Although Web pages can be any size, printers tend to use 8½ × 11 sheets of paper. When you print, your browser automatically reformats the text of the Web page to fit the paper dimensions. Because lines might break at different places or text size might be altered, the printed Web page might be longer than you expect. You can specify the number of pages you want to print in the Print dialog box. You decide to print the first page of the Highland Travel Web page.

To print a Web page:

1. Click **File** and then click **Print**.

2. In the Page Range section, click the **Current Page** option button.

3. Click the **Print** button to print the current page of the Highland Travel home page.

Some printers are set up to print headers and footers in addition to the Web page itself, so when you retrieve the page from your printer, you might find the page's title, its URL, the date, and other similar information at the top and bottom of the page.

Downloading a File

Scott explains that Windows 2000 also makes it easy to transfer files stored on the Internet to your computer. **Downloading** is the process of saving a file located on a remote computer (a computer located elsewhere on the Internet) to your own computer. The method you use to download information you find on the Web depends on how the file appears on the Web page. If you want to save the Web page itself, you use the Save As command on the File menu. If you want to save a graphic image located directly on the Web page, you save it by right-clicking the object you want and then using the Save Picture As command that appears in the shortcut menu.

You liked the Lake District graphic on the Tours page, so you decide to download it so you can use it as a background image on your desktop.

To download a file:

1. Click the **Forward** button ⇨ to return to the Lake District tour page.

2. Write "Disk 3—Windows 2000 Tutorial 5 Data Disk" on the label of a blank, formatted 3½-inch disk. Insert your Data Disk into drive A.

3. Return to the Tour Packages page and make sure the Lake District itinerary is visible.

4. Right-click the **Lake District** graphic to open its shortcut menu. See Figure 5-17.

Figure 5-17	SAVING A WEB GRAPHIC

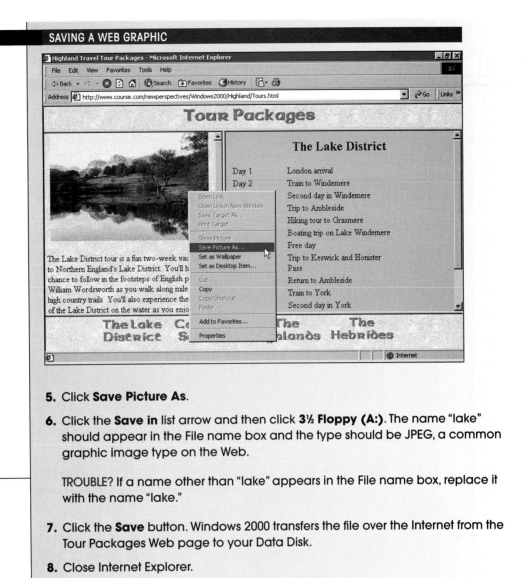

5. Click **Save Picture As**.

6. Click the **Save in** list arrow and then click **3½ Floppy (A:)**. The name "lake" should appear in the File name box and the type should be JPEG, a common graphic image type on the Web.

   TROUBLE? If a name other than "lake" appears in the File name box, replace it with the name "lake."

7. Click the **Save** button. Windows 2000 transfers the file over the Internet from the Tour Packages Web page to your Data Disk.

8. Close Internet Explorer.

The file is now on your Data Disk, and you could open it in a graphics program (such as Paint) and work with it there. Note that content appearing on Web pages is often copyrighted, and you should always make sure you have permission to use it before doing so. Since Highland Travel owns this graphic, Scott tells you that you can use it.

Session 5.1   QUICK CHECK

1. What is a home page?
2. The address of a Web page is called a(n) _____.
3. If someone gives you the URL of an interesting Web page, how can you view it?
4. What does a URL with "edu" in it tell you about that site's Web server?
5. Each Web server you visit is displayed as a different _____ in the History pane.
6. Describe how you could quickly locate a Web page that you viewed a few days earlier.
7. True or False: Only Web pages and folders can be stored in the Favorites folder.
8. How can you download a graphic image that you find on the Web?

SESSION 5.2

In this session, you will learn how to set up your computer so that it delivers Web page content to your desktop without your having to go look for it. You'll add an Active Desktop item to your Windows 2000 desktop. You'll update the Active Desktop item using the Synchronize command, and you'll set up a schedule for automatic updates. Finally, you'll use a Web page as the new background for your Windows 2000 desktop.

Bringing the Web to Your Desktop

Scott now wants to show you how you can receive content from the Web without having to go look for it. When you connected to the Highland Travel Web page in Session 5.1, you had to go looking for it. You were told where to find the information (that is, you were given a URL), and then you went to that location and "pulled" information from the Web server onto your own computer.

Another way of retrieving data, called **push technology**, brings information to your computer without your having to go get it. True push technology occurs when the author of a Web site modifies the site so that it sends information to users on its own, without requiring the user to manually access the site and retrieve the data. Once the data has been retrieved, the user can view it without being connected to the Internet or any network. This is a technique known as **offline viewing** because the user is not "online" with the Web server.

Scott explains that you're going to begin your exploration of push technology and offline viewing by adding live content to the desktop—Active Desktop items. An **Active Desktop** item is an object that you place on your desktop that receives updates from content providers, who push the updates to users on a schedule. For example, you could place a selection of Active Desktop items on your desktop, as in Figure 5-18.

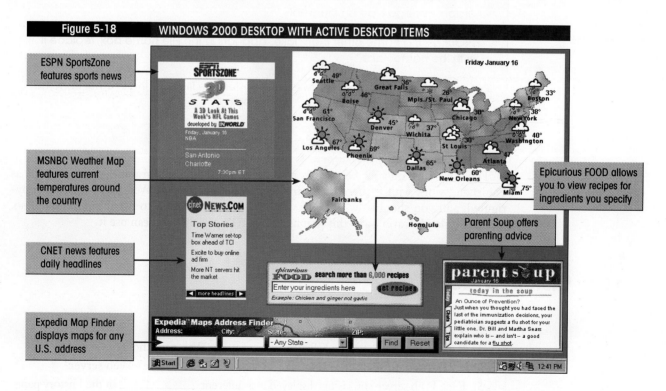

Figure 5-18   WINDOWS 2000 DESKTOP WITH ACTIVE DESKTOP ITEMS

ESPN SportsZone features sports news

MSNBC Weather Map features current temperatures around the country

CNET news features daily headlines

Expedia Map Finder displays maps for any U.S. address

Epicurious FOOD allows you to view recipes for ingredients you specify

Parent Soup offers parenting advice

You can set Active Desktop items to be updated each day, each hour, or on any schedule you choose. Every morning when the user of the computer shown in Figure 5-18 checks her desktop, for example, each component will have been automatically updated. The weather map will show the morning's weather instead of weather from the night before, the news service will display the most recent news, and other Active Desktop items will update in a similar fashion. This user has created her own "mini-newspaper," made up of only the information she's interested in.

Some Active Desktop items are interactive, allowing you to enter information and receive a response. The Epicurious FOOD Active Desktop item, for example, allows you to enter ingredients, such as beans and rice, and when you click the Get Recipes button, Internet Explorer starts (and connects to the Internet if you're not already connected) and displays recipes from the Epicurious site containing those ingredients. Likewise, if you enter a location in the Expedia Maps Address Finder Active Desktop item and then click the Find button, a map will appear showing the location you specified. Microsoft maintains a collection of Active Desktop items at its Active Desktop Gallery Web site, which you'll access in a moment.

Enabling Active Desktop

To add Active Desktop items to your desktop, you must first enable the Active Desktop feature, which allows the desktop to receive pushed information.

To enable Active Desktop:

1. Right-click a blank area of the desktop and then point to **Active Desktop**.

2. Make sure the Show Web Content option is checked; if not, click it to select it.

3. If the My Current Current Home Page option is selected, click it to deselect it.

It might seem that nothing has changed, but your desktop is now poised to receive whatever information you request, on a schedule you set.

Adding an Active Desktop Gallery Item to the Desktop

By enabling Active Desktop, you've added a new list of commands to the menu that appears when you right-click the desktop. You'll use a new command, "New Desktop Item," to add Web content to your desktop.

To add a weather map from the Active Desktop Gallery to your desktop:

1. Right-click a blank area of the desktop.

2. Point to **Active Desktop** and then click **New Desktop Item**.

3. Click the **Visit Gallery** button.

   Windows 2000 opens the Active Desktop Gallery Web page in Internet Explorer.

   TROUBLE? If you are prompted to download a Stock Ticker from Microsoft, talk to your network manager or instructor to decide whether this program can be retrieved and loaded on your computer.

4. Scroll down the icon list if necessary and then click the **Weather** icon, shown in Figure 5-19.

5. Click **MSNBC Weather Map**. After a moment, the weather map appears, along with a button entitled "Add to Active Desktop." See Figure 5-19.

TROUBLE? If the MSNBC Weather Map doesn't appear, choose a different Active Desktop item.

Figure 5-19	ADDING AN ACTIVE DESKTOP ITEM

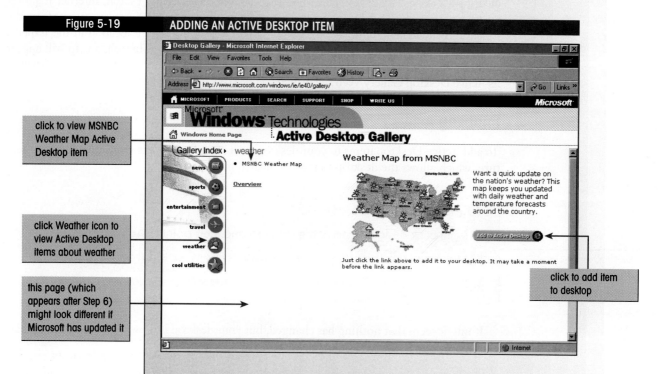

click to view MSNBC Weather Map Active Desktop item

click Weather icon to view Active Desktop items about weather

this page (which appears after Step 6) might look different if Microsoft has updated it

click to add item to desktop

6. Click the **Add to Active Desktop** button. Then click the **Yes** button if a Security Alert dialog box asks if you want to add this item to your active desktop. A dialog box appears that asks you to confirm the procedure. You could click the Customize button to change the default schedule; you'll customize the schedule later.

7. Click the **OK** button to add the item to your desktop.

8. The download process might take one or several minutes, depending on the speed of your Internet connection. Once the download is complete, close your browser. The item you added appears on your desktop. See Figure 5-20.

TROUBLE? If the Active Desktop item appears but doesn't look like a weather map, the MSNBC site might be busy. A desktop item will still appear, but it won't include the map. Continue with the steps, using the Active Desktop item.

TROUBLE? If scroll bars appear around your Active Desktop item or the item is off-center, don't worry. You'll learn momentarily how to resize and move it.

Figure 5-20	ADDING AN ACTIVE DESKTOP ITEM

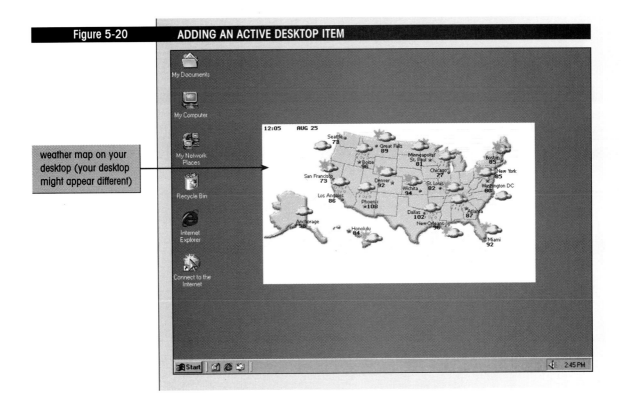

weather map on your desktop (your desktop might appear different)

Resizing and Moving Active Desktop Items

When an Active Desktop item is on your desktop, it occupies a rectangular block that appears as part of the background. To move or resize an Active Desktop item, you must first point to it to select it. When an Active Desktop item is selected, a title bar and border appear, which you can manipulate to move and resize the item as you would any other Windows 2000 window (such as the My Computer window). Practice moving Active Desktop items by moving the weather map.

To move the weather map:

1. Point to the top of the weather map. A gray border appears around the entire Active Desktop item, and a gray bar, similar to a window's title bar, appears at the top. This bar includes a Close button ☒ and a list arrow on the left that opens a menu for that item. See Figure 5-21.

   TROUBLE? If the title bar doesn't appear, move the pointer closer to the top of the Active Desktop item. The title bar should appear just before the pointer reaches the top of the item.

Figure 5-21   **ACTIVATING AN ACTIVE DESKTOP ITEM**

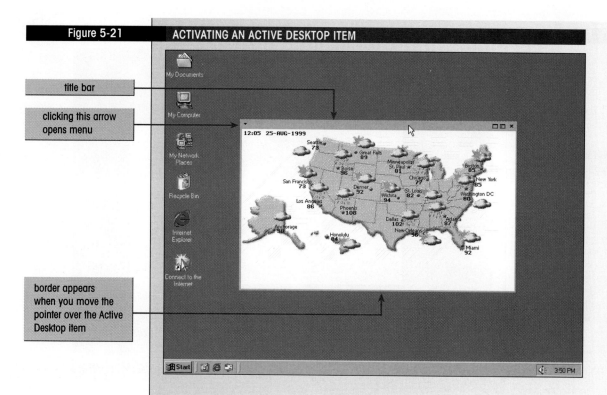

title bar

clicking this arrow opens menu

border appears when you move the pointer over the Active Desktop item

2. Drag the title bar to the center of the screen, if yours was previously off-center. The entire weather map moves.

You can also use the border to resize the item. For example, you drag the left and right borders to widen the item or make it narrower, you drag the top and bottom borders to lengthen or shorten the item, and you drag any corner out to enlarge or reduce both dimensions simultaneously.

To resize the weather map:

1. Point to the lower-right corner of the weather map. The gray border appears, and the mouse pointer changes from ⬚ to ⬚.

2. Drag the corner border to the lower right. The Active Desktop item expands in size. If your map has scroll bars, drag down and to the right until the scroll bars disappear.

You can also change the size of a desktop item by clicking one of the buttons on the upper-right corner of the item border. Figure 5-22 describes the four buttons available on the border and the effect each has on the size of a desktop item.

Figure 5-22   **RESIZE BUTTONS FOR THE ACTIVE DESKTOP ITEM**

BUTTON	NAME	DESCRIPTION
⬚	Cover Desktop	Extend the item across the entire desktop
⬚	Split Desktop with Icons	Move all desktop icons to the far left and fill the remaining desktop with the item
⬚	Reset to Original Size	Reset the item to a window on the desktop
✖	Close	Close the item

To see how these buttons work, you'll try resizing the image: first to fill the whole desktop, then to split the desktop between the icons and the item, and finally to restore the item to its original size and position. Note that you see only three of these buttons at a time. The middle button changes depending on what size the item is currently.

To use the sizing buttons:

1. Move your mouse pointer over the top border of the image to redisplay the title bar (if necessary), and click the **Cover Desktop** button 🔲.

   The weather map fills the entire desktop.

2. Move the mouse pointer to the top of the screen, and then click the **Split Desktop with Icons** button 🔳.

   The weather map is reduced in size, moving to the right of the icons on the desktop.

3. Move the mouse pointer to the top of the screen again and click the **Reset to Original Size** button 🔲.

   The weather map is restored to a window on the desktop.

   Figure 5-23 shows the weather map in each of the three sizes.

Figure 5-23	THE WEATHER MAP IN THREE SIZES

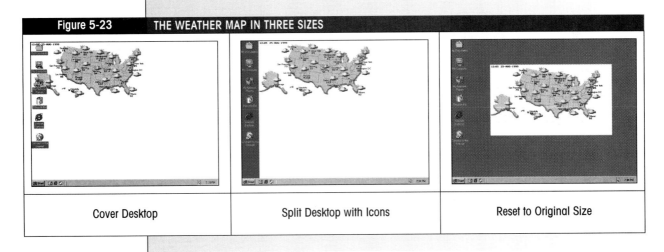

Cover Desktop	Split Desktop with Icons	Reset to Original Size

Updating Web Content

You may be wondering how you update the weather map to reflect current conditions. The process of retrieving current information is called **synchronization**, and Windows 2000 allows you to synchronize not just Web content, but any information available over your network. For example, if you are working on a corporate network and are leaving on a trip, you can retrieve a file for offline viewing on your laptop. Windows 2000 will make a copy of that file available to you, but it might not be current with the network file when you return. You can change this by synchronizing your copy with the network version. Similarly, you can synchronize the weather map on your desktop with the map available on the Web server.

Updating Content Manually

Files and Web pages can be synchronized on a fixed schedule or manually. To see how synchronization works, you'll manually update the weather map now.

To synchronize the weather map:

1. Move the mouse pointer over the upper border of the weather map to display the title bar.

2. Click the down arrow located on the left edge of the title bar and then click **Synchronize** on the menu. See Figure 5-24.

Figure 5-24	SYNCHRONIZING THE WEATHER MAP

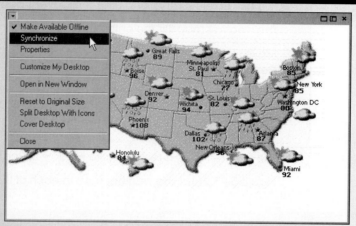

3. Windows 2000 connects to the Web server and updates the weather map with the latest weather information.

REFERENCE WINDOW   RW

Synchronizing an Active Desktop Item
- Move the mouse pointer over the upper border of the Active Desktop item to display the title bar.
- Click the down arrow on the left edge of the title bar to display the menu.
- Click Synchronize.

Viewing an Update Schedule

If you had to manually update the weather map all of the time, having it on your desktop would not be much of an improvement over simply visiting the page on the Web. The advantage of synchronization is the ability of Windows 2000 to access the page for you on a schedule. For example, you could have an Active Desktop item that downloads the latest stock market information every 5 minutes. By glancing at your desktop, you can view data that is no more than 5 minutes old.

Most Active Desktop items retrieved from the Active Desktop gallery have a schedule already set, which you can change. The schedule is one of the properties of the Active Desktop item.

To view the schedule for the weather map:

1. Redisplay the title bar for the weather map, click the down arrow, and then click **Properties** on the menu.

The MSNBC Weather Properties dialog box opens.

2. Click the **Schedule** tab.

As shown in Figure 5-25, the weather map uses the MSNBC Weather Recommended Schedule.

| Figure 5-25 | THE MSNBC WEATHER PROPERTIES DIALOG BOX |

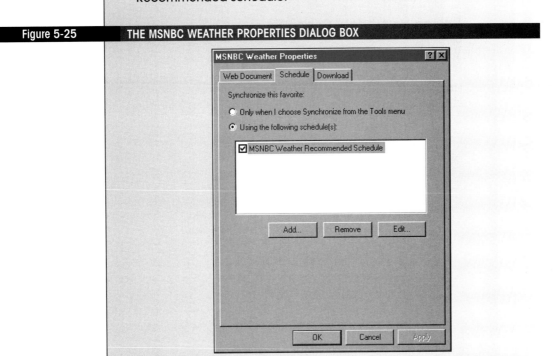

3. To see when the MSNBC Weather schedule downloads updated weather maps, click the **Edit** button.

As shown in Figure 5-26, under the recommended schedule the map is updated every night at 12:00 AM.

| Figure 5-26 | THE MSNBC WEATHER RECOMMENDED SCHEDULE |

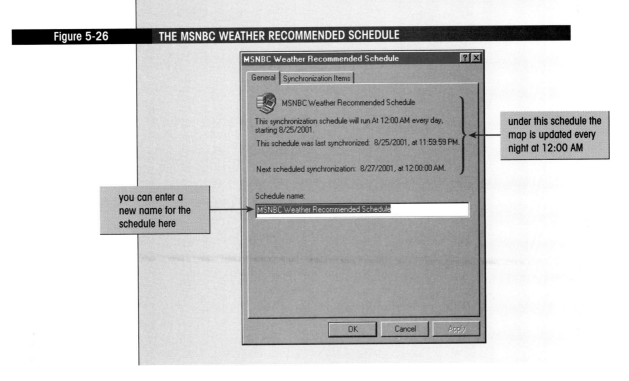

you can enter a new name for the schedule here

under this schedule the map is updated every night at 12:00 AM

4. Click the **OK** button and leave the MSNBC Weather Properties dialog box open.

Editing an Update Schedule

You realize as you examine the current schedule that most of the time your computer will not be turned on at midnight to run the synchronization. A much better time would be 9:00 AM, shortly after you arrive at the office, and 3:00 PM, shortly before you leave. To make this change you have to create two schedules: one for the morning and one for the afternoon.

To create an update schedule:

1. Click the **Add** button.

2. Set the time value to **9:00 AM** (you can set the time value the same way you set the digital clock in Tutorial 4, by selecting each time value and clicking the up and down arrows next to the digital clock).

3. Type **Morning Update** in the Name box.

4. Click the check box to allow Windows 2000 to connect to the Internet automatically to begin synchronization.

Figure 5-27 shows the completed dialog box.

| Figure 5-27 | SCHEDULING THE MORNING UPDATE |

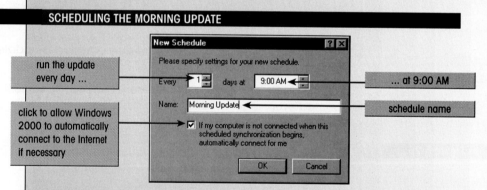

5. Click the **OK** button.

6. Click the **Add** button again and add a new schedule named "Afternoon Update," which will update the map at 3:00 PM every day (automatically connecting to the Internet if needed).

Figure 5-28 shows the new list of scheduled updates. Leave the MSNBC Weather Properties dialog box open.

Figure 5-28	LIST OF UPDATE SCHEDULES

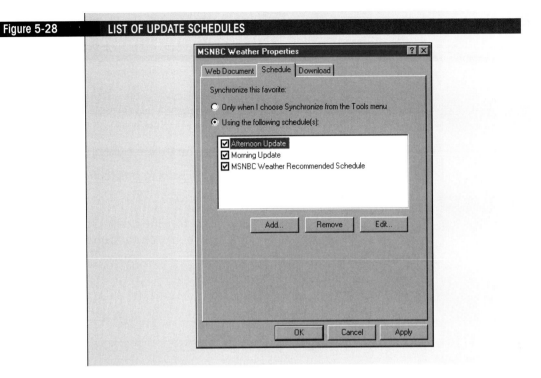

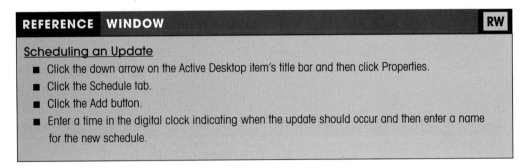

REFERENCE WINDOW   **RW**

Scheduling an Update
- Click the down arrow on the Active Desktop item's title bar and then click Properties.
- Click the Schedule tab.
- Click the Add button.
- Enter a time in the digital clock indicating when the update should occur and then enter a name for the new schedule.

Removing an Active Desktop Item

Now that you've seen how to work with Active Desktop items and update schedules, you should remove the weather map from your desktop. When you remove an Active Desktop item you can either close the item (by clicking the ☒ button on the title bar) or delete it. Closing the item keeps the information about the item and its update schedule available for future use. You can restore the item later by opening the Display Properties dialog box and selecting the item on the Web property sheet. Deleting the item removes the file and all information about it from your computer. When you delete the item, you have to go back to the Web site and download the item again to reinstall it. Now that you know how to use Active Desktop items, Scott suggests that you delete the item and the update schedules you created.

To delete the update schedules and weather map:

1. Click **Morning Update** and then click the **Remove** button. Click the **Yes** button to confirm the deletion.

2. Remove the Afternoon Update schedule in the same way.

3. Click the **OK** button to close the MSNBC Weather Properties dialog box.

4. Right-click an empty spot on the desktop and then click **Properties** on the menu.

5. Click the **Web** tab in the Display Properties dialog box.

The Web property sheet shows a list of all of the Active Desktop objects available for your desktop. Those currently displayed on the desktop have their check-boxes selected.

6. Click **MSNBC Weather** and then click the **Delete** button.

7. Click the **Yes** button to confirm that you want to delete the file.

8. Click the **OK** button.

9. If you had to deselect your home page from the desktop earlier, right-click the desktop, point to **Active Desktop**, and then click **My Current Home Page** on the popup menu.

The map is removed from the desktop.

Using an HTML File as a Background

In Tutorial 4 you worked with the Desktop Properties dialog box to change your desktop's color and pattern, and then to display a graphic image on your desktop. Active Desktop technology extends your control over your desktop's background by allowing you to use Web pages as wall-paper. To create Web pages, you use a language called **HTML**, which stands for **Hypertext Markup Language**. HTML uses special codes to describe how the page should appear on the screen. Figure 5-29 shows a Web page as it appears on your computer screen, and behind it, the underlying HTML code. It is this code that the browser interprets when a Web page is viewed.

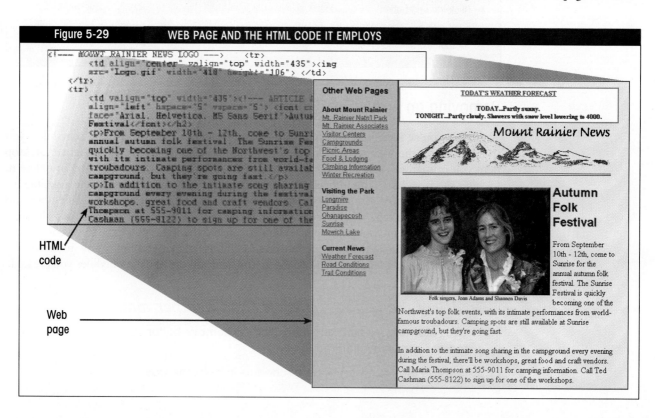

Figure 5-29   WEB PAGE AND THE HTML CODE IT EMPLOYS

A document created using the HTML language is called an **HTML file** and is saved with the .htm or .html extension. Most Web pages are HTML files.

Because Windows 2000 enables you to use an HTML file as your background wallpaper, your Windows 2000 desktop background can feature text, clip art, photos, animated graphics, links, and multimedia objects such as sound and video. Your desktop can also include **applets**, programs attached to a Web page that extend its capabilities. Some applets add movement and interesting visual effects to your page, whereas others are capable of asking you questions, responding to your questions, checking your computer settings, and calculating data. There are even applets that allow you to play interactive games against the computer or against another person logged on to the Web.

You can use a word-processing program such as Microsoft Word to save a document as an HTML file, or you can create a new one using the Web page editor included with Windows 2000, FrontPage Express. If you learn the HTML language, you can use a simple text editor (such as Notepad) to create a more complex and sophisticated HTML file. Alternately, you can use the Internet Explorer browser to save an existing Web page as an HTML file that you can then use as your wallpaper.

The added control Windows 2000 gives you over background wallpaper makes it possible to make the desktop a launch pad for your most important projects. A corporation, for example, might create an HTML file that contains important company information, an updatable company calendar, links to company documents, a company directory, and so on. Scott wants to show you a Web page he's designing to be used as a background for all Highland Travel computers. He has created an HTML file in his Web page editor and has placed it on a disk for you to examine.

To use a Web page as a background:

1. To view the Highland Travel desktop background Web page, you need to place the files on your Data Disk. Place the Data Disk you worked with in Session 5.1 in drive A. Click the **Start** button ⊞**Start**, point to **Programs**, point to **NP on Microsoft Windows 2000 – Level II**, and then click **Disk 3 (Tutorial 5)**. When you are prompted to insert your disk in the drive, click the **OK** button and then wait as the files you need are copied to your Data Disk.

2. Right-click a blank area of the desktop and then click **Properties**.

3. Click the **Background** tab if necessary, click the **Browse** button, click the **Look in** list arrow, click **3½ Floppy (A:)**, and then click the **highland** file icon.

4. Click the **Open** button. The filename appears in the Wallpaper list and a preview appears in the preview monitor.

5. Click the **OK** button. The HTML file appears on your desktop background. Figure 5-30 points out some of the features an HTML file allows you to employ on a desktop background.

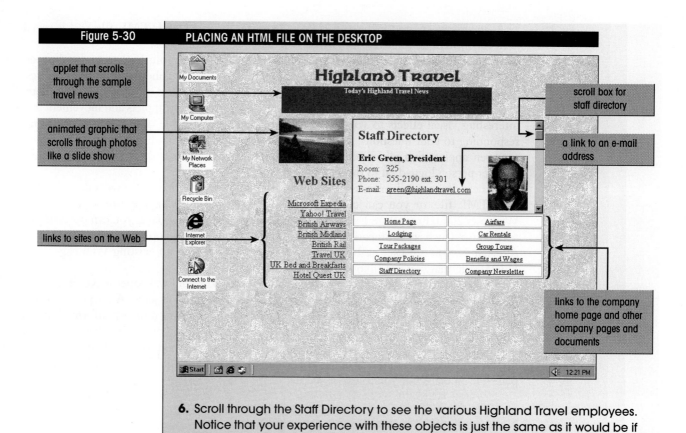

Figure 5-30 PLACING AN HTML FILE ON THE DESKTOP

applet that scrolls through the sample travel news

animated graphic that scrolls through photos like a slide show

links to sites on the Web

scroll box for staff directory

a link to an e-mail address

links to the company home page and other company pages and documents

6. Scroll through the Staff Directory to see the various Highland Travel employees. Notice that your experience with these objects is just the same as it would be if you were working with this page in your Web browser.

The difference between using an HTML file as your wallpaper and using a graphic file, as you did in Tutorial 4, is that a graphic is simply a picture that adds interest to your desktop background, whereas an HTML file allows you to interact with the information on your background. If the HTML file contains links, you can click those links to connect to the sites they target. Try clicking one of the links on the page.

To activate a desktop link:

1. Click the **Home Page** link in the first row of the table below the Staff Directory. Your browser starts, and after a moment the link's target appears in the browser window—the familiar Highland Travel page.

2. Close your browser. You return to the desktop.

Scott explains that once he finishes developing his page, the company will place it on all company desktops, so all employees have access to the information it contains. Since it isn't finished, he recommends that you remove it from your desktop.

To restore the desktop to its original appearance:

1. Right-click a blank area of the desktop and then click **Properties**.

> TROUBLE? If you right-click an area of the Web page that has Web content, properties for that object appear, instead of desktop properties. Make sure the dialog box that opens is the Display Properties dialog box. If it isn't, try right-clicking a different area, and make sure it is blank.
>
> 2. Click the **Background** tab, if necessary.
>
> 3. Scroll up the Wallpaper list and then click **(None)**.
>
> 4. Click the **OK** button.

You've completed your work with bringing Web content directly to your desktop. As you've seen, Windows 2000 provides a rich variety of tools to connect your computer with the Internet.

Session 5.2 QUICK CHECK

1. What is offline viewing?
2. What is push technology?
3. An object on the desktop that receives pushed content is called a(n) _____ .
4. What is synchronization?
5. How would you schedule an object to be synchronized 24 times a day, once each hour?
6. What is HTML?
7. What are some advantages of using an HTML file for your desktop background?

SESSION 5.3

In this session, you'll learn how to start Outlook Express—the Windows 2000 e-mail program. You'll see how to customize Outlook Express, and you'll examine the properties of your mail account. You'll send and receive e-mail messages and reply to an e-mail message.

Getting Started with Outlook Express

Outlook Express, one of the tools that comes with Windows 2000, allows you to send, receive, and manage **electronic mail** or **e-mail**—electronic messages transferred between users on a network. As more people connect to the Internet, communicating by e-mail is becoming more common. When you need to send information to someone else, an e-mail message saves time and money, because you don't need to wait for postal delivery nor make expensive long-distance phone calls. You can send e-mail to and receive e-mail from anyone in the world who has an e-mail address, regardless of the operating system or type of computer the person is using.

Just as you need an Internet account to browse the World Wide Web, you likewise need an account on a **mail server**, a computer that handles the storage and delivery of e-mail. Most Internet service providers also provide access to mail servers.

Scott informs you that the company's systems administrator has just finished a mail server on the company network to handle all e-mail messages. He hands you a slip of paper with your account information, including your user ID, password, and e-mail address. A **user ID**, also called a **username**, is the name that identifies you on the mail server. A **password** is a personal code that verifies that you have the right to read incoming mail. An **e-mail address** consists of the user ID, the @ symbol, and a host name. For example, Scott's e-mail address is:

SCampbell@HighlandTravel.com

Thus Scott's username is Scampbell, and the address of the company's mail server is HighlandTravel.com. Like URLs, every e-mail address is unique. Many people might use the same host, but user IDs distinguish one e-mail address from another.

Customizing the Outlook Express Window

The Outlook Express window offers a number of components that you can choose to display or hide, depending on your needs. These components include:

- **Contacts list**: lists people whose e-mail addresses or other contact information you have saved
- **Folder bar**: identifies the current mail folder
- **Folders list**: displays the hierarchy of mail folders that you can use to store and organize messages
- **Outlook bar**: contains icons for the folders in the Folders list (since this repeats the information in the Folders list, you don't really need to view it unless you find it easier to use than the Folders list)
- **Status bar**: displays messages about the current folder
- **Toolbar**: displays the toolbar buttons used to accomplish most tasks
- **Views bar**: provides you with a quick way to change the message list view so you can switch between showing all messages or hiding read or ignored messages
- **Info pane**: an informational window at the bottom of the Outlook Express window, which may not be an available option, depending on how Outlook Express is installed on your computer

Before you start using Outlook Express, first ensure that your Outlook Express window matches the one shown in the figures. You start Outlook Express by clicking the Outlook Express button 🔄 from the Quick Launch toolbar, clicking the Outlook Express icon on the desktop, or using the Start menu.

To control the Outlook Express display:

1. To open Outlook Express, click the **Start** button 🔣Start, point to **Programs**, and then click **Outlook Express**.

TROUBLE? If more than one e-mail program is installed on your computer, and Outlook Express is not your current default mail program, a dialog box appears asking if you want Outlook Express to be your default mail program. If you are using your own computer and want to use Outlook Express as your mail program, click the Yes button. If you are using a school or institutional computer, click the No button or ask your technical support person for assistance.

TROUBLE? If the Identity Logon dialog box opens, you are using a version of Outlook Express that is configured for multiple users. If your name appears, click it and then enter the password as requested. Otherwise, ask your technical support person for assistance.

TROUBLE? If a connection dialog box appears, you are probably not connected to the Internet. Click the Connect button and follow the directions that appear on your screen. If you are prompted to enter your username and password and you do not know them, consult your technical support person.

TROUBLE? If the Internet Connection Wizard starts, click the Cancel button and the Yes button twice to exit the wizard. Contact your instructor or technical support person about setting up an Internet account on your computer.

2. If necessary, click the **Maximize** button ⬜ . Figure 5-31 shows the maximized Outlook Express window.

| Figure 5-31 | OUTLOOK EXPRESS WINDOW |

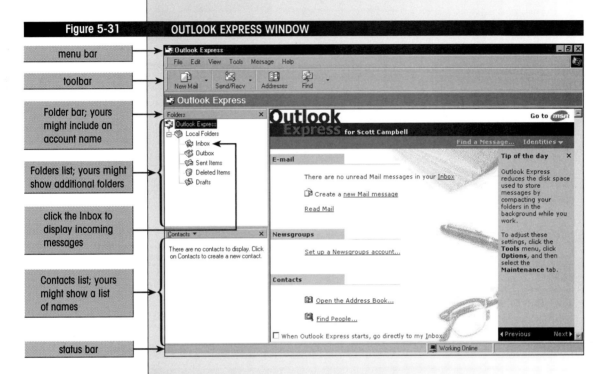

menu bar

toolbar

Folder bar; yours might include an account name

Folders list; yours might show additional folders

click the Inbox to display incoming messages

Contacts list; yours might show a list of names

status bar

3. Click **Inbox** in the Folders list.

TROUBLE? If you see more than one Inbox on the Folders list, you might have more than one mail account. Click Inbox under Local Folders.

4. Click **View** on the menu bar, point to **Current View**, and then click **Show All Messages** so you can view all messages.

5. Click **View**, point to **Sort By**, click **Received**, and then click **View** again, point to **Sort By**, and click **Sort Ascending**. You want to sort your messages in the order they were received, in ascending order (newest first).

TROUBLE? If the Received and Sort Ascending options are already bulleted in the Sort By list, don't worry. Clicking a bulleted menu option does *not* deselect it. Clicking a checked menu option, however, *does* deselect the option.

6. To work with the Outlook Express components layout, click **View** and then click **Layout**.

7. In the Basic area, make sure all check boxes *except* the Outlook Bar, Views Bar, and Info Pane are checked.

TROUBLE? If the Info Pane check box doesn't appear in your Layout dialog box, don't worry. Some installations of Outlook Express do not include this option. Just make sure that the check boxes for Outlook Bar and Views Bar are *not* checked.

8. In the Preview Pane area, make sure the **Show preview pane** and **Show preview pane header** check boxes are both selected and that the **Below messages** option button is selected. See Figure 5-32.

Figure 5-32	CHECKING OUTLOOK EXPRESS LAYOUT

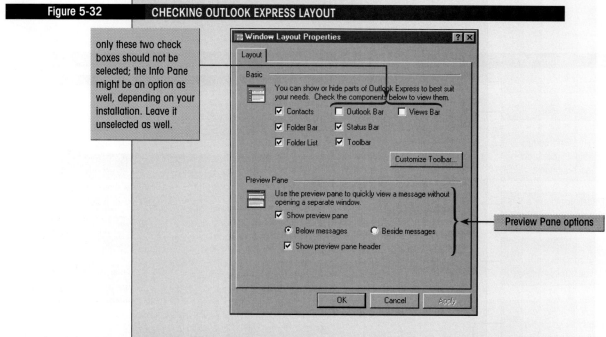

only these two check boxes should not be selected; the Info Pane might be an option as well, depending on your installation. Leave it unselected as well.

Preview Pane options

9. Click the **OK** button. Your screen should resemble Figure 5-33.

Figure 5-33	DEFAULT OUTLOOK EXPRESS WINDOW

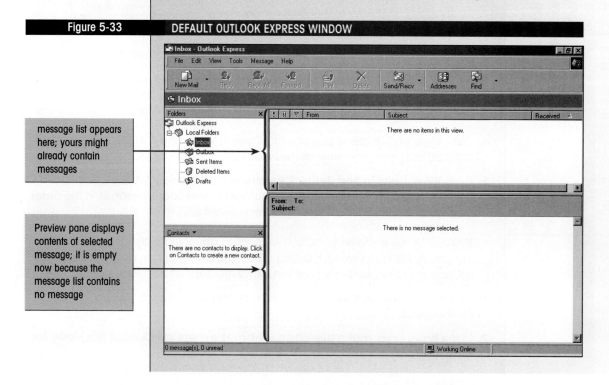

message list appears here; yours might already contain messages

Preview pane displays contents of selected message; it is empty now because the message list contains no message

Now that you have ensured that your display will match the one shown in the figures, you are ready to check the status of your Outlook Express account, using the information Scott Campbell gave you.

Setting Up an Outlook Express Account

Once you have an account with a mail service provider (usually this is your ISP), you add your account to Outlook Express. If you are in a university or other institution, this has probably been done for you, but if you are using your own computer, you will probably have to add it yourself.

Most Internet service providers include mail service as part of their Internet services package. What type of mail account you choose depends on how you plan to access your mail. Outlook Express supports POP, IMAP, and HTTP account types.

- With a **POP**, or **Post Office Protocol**, account, your mail server receives incoming mail and delivers it to your computer. Once messages are delivered, they are usually deleted from the mail server. POP accounts work best when you have only a single computer, since POP is designed for offline mail access. To receive POP mail if you are away from your computer, you must be able to set up a POP mail account on a different computer—an impossibility in many places.

- With an **IMAP**, or **Internet Message Access Protocol**, account, mail is stored on a mail server, not on your computer. Thus you can access your mail from any computer on which you have an account, without having to transfer files back and forth between computers.

- With an HTTP account, known as **Web-based e-mail**, you use the same HTTP protocol used on the Web. You set up an account with a Web-based e-mail provider, and your mail is stored on that provider's mail server. You can access your messages from any Web browser. Libraries, hotels, airports, and banks are increasingly making computers with Web access available to the public, so you don't need to own a computer to use Web-based e-mail. Moreover, Web-based e-mail accounts are often free. However, because messages are stored on a server and not on your local computer, mail retrieval is limited by the speed of your Internet connection. Web-based accounts currently don't offer the same breadth of features you find with a traditional e-mail program. The largest provider of free Web-based e-mail is **Hotmail**, a Microsoft service that is made available from Internet Explorer via the Links toolbar or from Outlook Express when you set up a new mail account. Outlook Express allows you to add a Hotmail account to your Folders list, and it treats incoming mail just as it would in a POP account. Hotmail even also allows you to check POP mail.

REFERENCE WINDOW   **RW**

<u>Setting Up an E-Mail Account</u>
- In the Outlook Express window, click Tools and then click Accounts.
- Click the Add button.
- Click Mail. Follow the steps in the Internet Connection Wizard.

The following steps will help you determine whether or not you already have a mail account. If you don't, you will need to set one up before you can continue with this tutorial. Outlook Express can help you with this task. You can set up a Hotmail account almost instantaneously, but to set up a POP or IMAP account, you will need to provide the account information, such as your incoming and outgoing mail server address and type, your username and password, and your e-mail address.

To examine your mail account:

1. Click **Tools** and then click **Accounts** to open the Internet Accounts dialog box.

2. Click the **Mail** tab, if necessary. See Figure 5-34, which shows one mail account already set up.

| Figure 5-34 | MAIL ACCOUNTS |

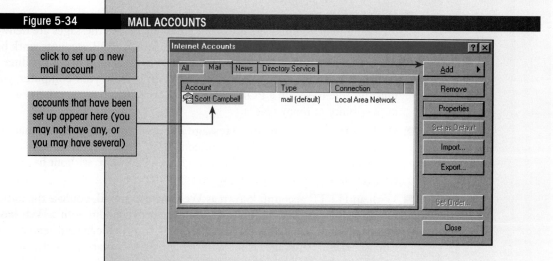

click to set up a new mail account

accounts that have been set up appear here (you may not have any, or you may have several)

3. Click the account you want to use.

    TROUBLE? If no account appears with your name, no account has been set up for you. You can set up an account yourself by clicking the Add button and then clicking Mail. The Internet Connection Wizard starts. This Wizard walks you through the steps of setting up a mail account. If you don't know the answers to all the questions the Wizard asks, you will need to get further assistance from your technical support person or your Internet service provider.

4. Click the **Properties** button. Your name and e-mail address should appear in the account Properties dialog box; Outlook Express uses this information when you send and receive e-mail. See Figure 5-35.

    TROUBLE? If your new mail account doesn't appear in the list of accounts, click the Close button in the Internet Accounts dialog box, click No to the question about downloading services and then repeat Steps 1 through 4. Your account should appear. If the name and e-mail address boxes are blank, ask your instructor or technical support person what to enter in them.

| Figure 5-35 | CONFIGURING E-MAIL PROPERTIES |

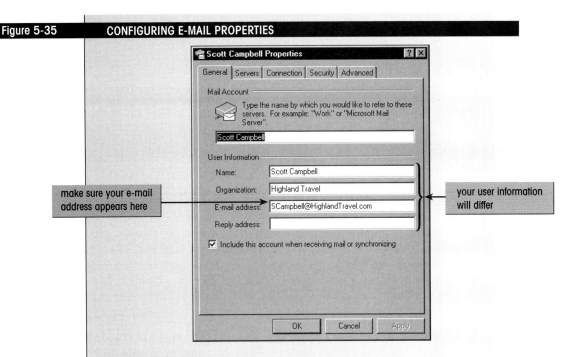

make sure your e-mail address appears here

your user information will differ

5. Click the **Server** tab to check your mail server information. Your account name (user ID) and password should appear, along with information about your mail server (your password will appear as a series of asterisks so that passers-by cannot see it). For an HTTP account such as Hotmail, you would see the URL of the mail provider's Web page, but Highland Travel uses POP accounts, so each account must identify the incoming and outgoing mail server address, as shown in Figure 5-36.

TROUBLE? If any of these boxes is blank, ask your instructor or technical support person what to enter in them.

| Figure 5-36 | CHECKING MAIL SERVER INFORMATION |

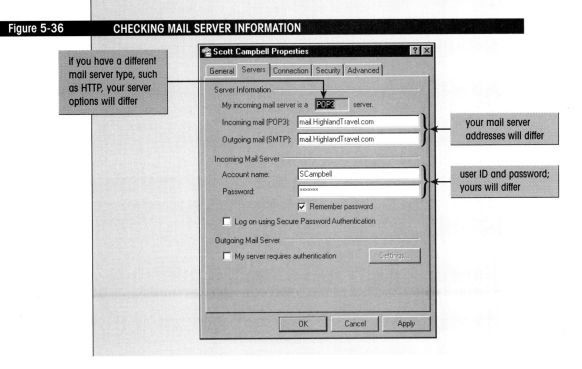

if you have a different mail server type, such as HTTP, your server options will differ

your mail server addresses will differ

user ID and password; yours will differ

6. Click the **OK** button to close the account Properties dialog box and then click the **Close** button in the Internet Accounts dialog box.

Now that you have ensured that Outlook Express can handle your e-mail, you're ready to send e-mail messages.

Sending E-mail

An e-mail message uses the same format as a standard memo: it typically includes From, Date, To, and Subject lines, followed by the content of the message. The **To line** indicates who will receive the message. Outlook Express automatically supplies your name or e-mail address in the **From line** and the date you send the message in the **Date line** (as set in your computer's clock). The **Subject line**, although optional, alerts the recipient to the topic of the message. Finally, the **message area** contains the content of your message. You can also include additional information, such as a **Cc line**, which indicates who will receive a copy of the message, or a Priority setting, which indicates the importance of the message.

When you prepare an e-mail message, you should remember some commonsense guidelines:

- Think before you type; read before you send. Your name and your institution's name are attached to everything you send.
- Type in both uppercase and lowercase letters. Using all uppercase letters in e-mail messages is considered shouting, and messages in all lowercase letters are difficult to read and decipher.
- Edit your message. Keep your messages concise so the reader can understand your meaning quickly and clearly.
- Send appropriate amounts of useful information. Like junk mail, e-mail messages can pile up quickly. If you must send a longer message, attach it as a file.
- Find out if personal e-mail messages are allowed on a work account. E-mail is not free. (Businesses pay to subscribe to a server.)
- E-mail at your workplace or school is not necessarily confidential. Your employer, for example, might be able to access your e-mail.

Viewing Outlook Express Folders

Outlook Express organizes all the messages it handles, outgoing and incoming, into **folders**, or compartments that allow you to sort your messages, located on the Folders list in the Outlook Express window. Figure 5-37 describes the Outlook Express folders that you can use to store mail.

Figure 5-37	OUTLOOK EXPRESS FOLDERS
FOLDER	**DESCRIPTION**
Inbox	Stores messages that have just been delivered and messages that you've read but haven't discarded or filed
Outbox	Stores messages that you've finished composing and plan to send as soon as you connect to your mail server
Sent Items	Stores a copy of every message you've sent until you discard or file them
Deleted Items	Stores the messages you've discarded. They remain in this folder until you delete them from here, and then they are irretrievable.
Drafts	Stores messages that you have written but not finished

When a folder contains one or more messages that you have not sent or read, the folder name appears in boldface and Outlook Express places the number of new or pending messages in that folder within parentheses.

Any folder that contains subfolders is preceded by a plus box ⊞ or minus box ⊟ in the Folders list. When ⊞ appears in front of a folder, its subfolders are hidden. When ⊟ appears, its subfolders are visible. Outlook Express automatically starts with Local Folders open. To see the contents of a folder, you click it in the Folders list.

To work with Outlook Express folders:

1. Click **Outbox** in the Local Folders list. It will probably be empty, unless you have other outgoing mail. See Figure 5-38.

Figure 5-38	VIEWING THE OUTBOX FOLDER

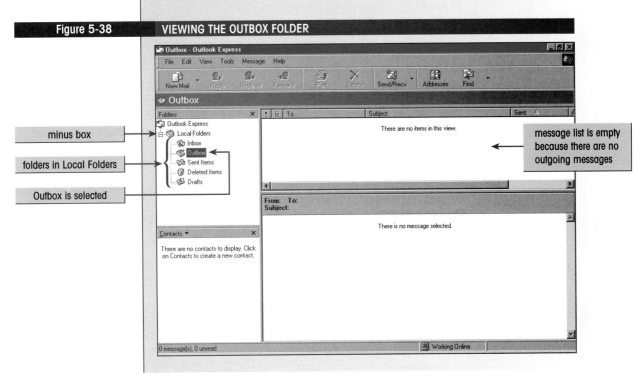

Now you're ready to compose and send your first message.

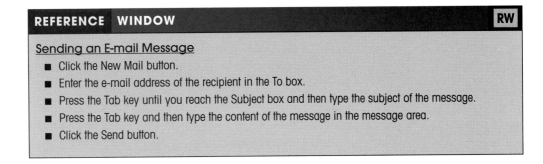

REFERENCE   WINDOW   **RW**

Sending an E-mail Message

- Click the New Mail button.
- Enter the e-mail address of the recipient in the To box.
- Press the Tab key until you reach the Subject box and then type the subject of the message.
- Press the Tab key and then type the content of the message in the message area.
- Click the Send button.

When you click the Send button, Outlook Express places the message in the Outbox and then sends it immediately if you're connected to your mail server and if you haven't changed Outlook's default settings. Because you've opened the Outbox, you'll be able to watch this happen. Remembering that Scott wanted you to contact Katie Herrera about a Highland Travel golf tour as soon as you got settled, you decide to compose your first message to her. Her e-mail address is KHerrera@HighlandTravel.com.

To send an e-mail message:

1. Click the **New Mail** button. The New Message window opens, which allows you to compose a new message.

   TROUBLE? If you receive an error message at any point during these steps, check your mail server properties using the procedure you learned in the previous section. Write down your settings and then ask your instructor or technical support person for help.

   TROUBLE? If you have more than one account, be aware that in the outgoing message, Outlook Express identifies the sender for the currently selected account. If, for example, you want to send a message from your Hotmail account, click Hotmail in the Folders list before you click the New Mail button.

2. Type **KHerrera@HighlandTravel.com**, and then press **Tab**.

3. Type your own e-mail address in the Cc box, and then press **Tab**. Note that normally you would not copy yourself on an e-mail sent to another person. You are sending a copy to yourself only to ensure that you will receive mail later for practice in other sections of this tutorial.

4. Type **Golf Tour** in the Subject box, and then press the **Tab** key.

5. Type the following message in the content area:

   Scott Campbell suggested I contact you regarding the new St. Andrews Golf Tour we're starting next summer.

   Thank you,

   (your name)

6. Before you send the message, make sure you are watching the Outbox. Read all of Step 7 before you perform it, so you know what to watch for.

7. Click the **Send** button. Outlook Express moves your message into the Outbox; the Outbox is briefly boldfaced and followed by a (1) in the Local Folders list, indicating there is one outgoing message. Then, Outlook Express sends the message on its way. The message and the (1) disappear, the Outbox is empty, and the Outbox is no longer boldfaced in the list. See Figure 5-39.

Figure 5-39	SENDING A MESSAGE

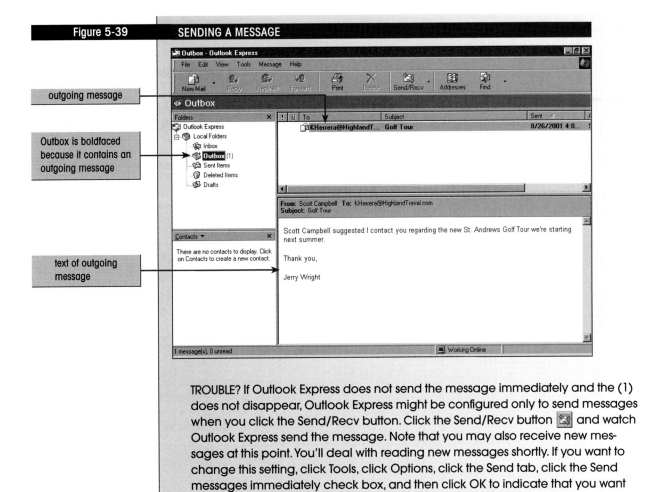

outgoing message

Outbox is boldfaced because it contains an outgoing message

text of outgoing message

TROUBLE? If Outlook Express does not send the message immediately and the (1) does not disappear, Outlook Express might be configured only to send messages when you click the Send/Recv button. Click the Send/Recv button 🖳 and watch Outlook Express send the message. Note that you may also receive new messages at this point. You'll deal with reading new messages shortly. If you want to change this setting, click Tools, click Options, click the Send tab, click the Send messages immediately check box, and then click OK to indicate that you want outgoing mail sent immediately.

TROUBLE? If Outlook Express requests a password, you might need to enter a password before you can send and receive your mail messages.

The time it takes to send an e-mail message depends on the size of the message, the speed of your Internet connection, and the quantity of Internet traffic at that time. When you send an e-mail, your outgoing mail server examines the host name in the e-mail address, locates the host, and delivers the message to that host. Because your mail server is not connected to every other host, e-mail is rarely sent along a direct path to the recipient. Instead, the message is handed from one host to another until the e-mail reaches its destination. Figure 5-40 shows how the Internet routes a message from a student at the University of Alaska to a student at the University of the Virgin Islands.

Figure 5-40   INTERNET E-MAIL ROUTES

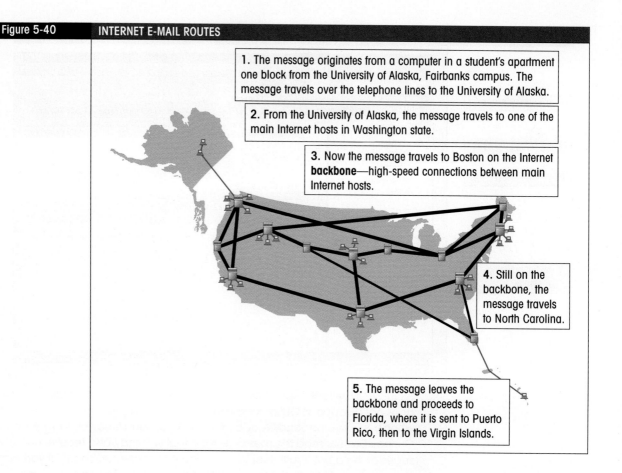

1. The message originates from a computer in a student's apartment one block from the University of Alaska, Fairbanks campus. The message travels over the telephone lines to the University of Alaska.

2. From the University of Alaska, the message travels to one of the main Internet hosts in Washington state.

3. Now the message travels to Boston on the Internet **backbone**—high-speed connections between main Internet hosts.

4. Still on the backbone, the message travels to North Carolina.

5. The message leaves the backbone and proceeds to Florida, where it is sent to Puerto Rico, then to the Virgin Islands.

Receiving E-mail

How you receive e-mail depends on your account. For example, if you are using a Web-based account, you connect to your provider's Web page and view your messages there. If you are using a POP account, your mail server collects your mail and holds it until your mail program contacts the mail server and requests any mail addressed to your user ID. Your mail program then downloads any waiting messages to your computer. (Remember that the Outlook Express mail program allows you to set up a Hotmail account so that it too can receive local mail delivery.)

You can check your e-mail at any time by clicking the Send/Recv button ⊠. Your mail server delivers any e-mail messages that have arrived since you last checked (and sends any messages currently in the Outbox). Some people check for new e-mail messages sporadically during the day, while others check at regular intervals, such as every hour or every morning and evening. If you are always connected to the Internet, Outlook Express automatically checks for messages at a specified interval. You can set this interval on the General tab of the Options dialog box, available on the Tools menu, but you won't do that now.

Remember that you sent a copy of your e-mail to yourself for the purpose of completing this tutorial. You'll now check to see whether the copy arrived.

To check for incoming mail:

1. Click the **Send/Recv** button ▣. If a dialog box opens requesting your password, enter your password and follow the instructions in the dialog box.

2. Click **Inbox** in the Folders list. New messages appear in the message list, and a number in parentheses appears, indicating the number of new messages you've received. See Figure 5-41. Your Inbox folder might contain additional e-mail messages from other people.

Figure 5-41	RECEIVING MESSAGES

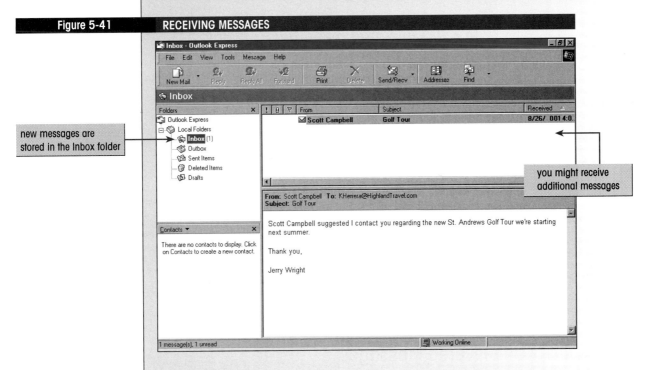

new messages are stored in the Inbox folder

you might receive additional messages

TROUBLE? If you receive a returned mail message in addition to the copy of your message to Katie, don't worry. This happens because the e-mail address you are using for Katie Herrera is fictional. You'll learn more about returned mail shortly.

TROUBLE? If enough time has elapsed since you sent the message, Outlook Express might have checked for incoming mail already. If that's the case, the copy should already appear. If no messages appear, your mail server might not have received or sent the messages yet. Occasionally, some mail servers cause mail to be delayed. Check later to see if your mail has arrived, or consult your technical support person.

Unread messages appear in boldface, preceded by the unread mail icon ✉. The message list displays a **message header** for each message, which identifies the sender, subject (truncated if it's too long), and date received. Your window might list additional columns. You can change the width of the columns in the message list by dragging the column header border in the appropriate direction. You can also click a column button to sort columns by that button. For example, if you click the From button, Outlook Express sorts messages in the current folder alphabetically by name. The default sort order is by date and time received, with newest messages on top.

The message list displays a variety of icons that help you determine the status of the message. For example, ✉ tells you the message has been read; ✉ tells you the message has not been read; ✉ tells you the message is in progress in the Drafts folder.

You can view a message in its own window or in the preview pane. If you click to select an e-mail message from the message list, the contents of that message appear in the preview pane. If you double-click a message from the message list, a separate message window opens. Either way, after a predetermined number of seconds, the message header no longer appears in boldface, indicating that you've displayed the message. You already saw how you can hide the preview pane if you want to view only the message list. You can also resize the preview pane by dragging its upper border up or down. For example, to enlarge the preview so you can see more of a message, drag the top border of the pane up.

Your Inbox should contain the copy of the message you sent yourself. Try reading it now.

To read an e-mail message:

1. If necessary, click the message you sent yourself, which has the subject "Golf Tour" in the message list. The contents of that message appear in the preview pane. After a few seconds (5 is the default), the Unread icon ✉ changes to Read ✉, and the message no longer appears in boldface.

2. Now try adjusting the column widths. Point at the vertical line that forms one of the column borders until your pointer changes to ↔.

3. Drag the pointer slightly to the right to see more of the column, or to the left to see less.

   TROUBLE? If your window shows additional columns, don't worry. You can determine what information to display by clicking View, clicking Columns, and then removing the check from the box of the column display you wish to suppress.

By successfully viewing the copy of the message you sent to yourself, you've verified that Outlook Express is configured properly on your computer.

Handling Undelivered Messages

Sometimes you send an e-mail message to an Internet address that is no longer active, for example when a person switches to a different ISP. When an outgoing mail server cannot locate a recipient's address, it sends an undeliverable mail message to the sender. This is similar to the postal service returning a letter because the street address is incorrect.

Because Katie's e-mail address is fictional, you will probably receive a returned mail message from the mail delivery subsystem of your outgoing mail server, telling you that the host was not found. Check for this message now.

To read a returned mail message:

1. Click the **Send/Recv** button 🖳.

2. Click a message with "Returned mail" or something similar in the Subject column.

   TROUBLE? If no such message appears, don't worry. It might appear later.

3. Read the message. It should inform you that the e-mail address had an unknown host.

If e-mail messages you send are returned undelivered, you should verify the e-mail addresses that you used. Make sure that everything is typed correctly and that the person is still using that e-mail address.

Replying to a Message

Often, you'll want to respond to an e-mail message. Although you could create and send a new message, it's easier to use the Reply feature, which automatically inserts the e-mail address of the sender and the subject into the proper lines in the message window. The Reply feature also "quotes" the sender's text to remind the sender of the message to which you are responding. When you reply to an e-mail message, you can respond to the original sender of the message, or to the sender and everyone else who received the message.

You're first going to view the message you sent yourself, this time in its own window, and then you're going to practice replying to it. To open a message in its own window, double-click the message in the message list. This allows you to display more of the message at once.

Note that this is a *practice* reply. Normally, you would not reply to yourself! Rather, you would reply to someone who sent you a real message.

To open a message in its own window and then reply to it:

1. Double-click the **Golf Tour** message in the message list. The message opens in its own window. Maximize this window if necessary.

2. Click the **Reply** button [icon]. The message window opens, with your name in the To box (because you're replying to your own message) and the original message's subject in the Subject box, preceded by "Re:", which means "regarding." The message quotes your original message.

3. Type the following reply in the message area (the cursor automatically blinks at the beginning of a blank line):

    Thanks for the information.
    (your name)

4. If necessary, scroll down to see how the original text of the message is quoted after the reply you just typed. See Figure 5-42.

Figure 5-42	REPLYING TO A MESSAGE

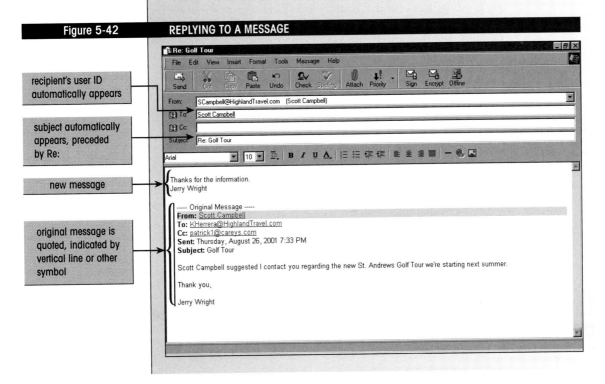

recipient's user ID automatically appears

subject automatically appears, preceded by Re:

new message

original message is quoted, indicated by vertical line or other symbol

> **5.** Click the **Send** button . Outlook Express sends the message. (You can tell that the message has been sent when there is no longer a number next to the Outbox icon in the Folders list.)

Deciding whether or not to quote the sender's original message when you reply to a message depends on several factors. If the recipient might need to be reminded of the message content, it's appropriate to quote. However, long messages take longer to download, so whenever possible you should delete quoted material from your messages.

Printing a Message

You can print an e-mail message using the File menu's Print command. You decide to print the message you received from yourself.

> *To print an e-mail message:*
>
> **1.** Make sure the message you received is either open in its own window or selected in the message list.
>
> **2.** Click **File** and then click **Print**.
>
> **3.** Check the print settings in the Print dialog box and then click the **Print** button.
>
> **4.** If necessary, click the **Close** button to close the message.
>
> **5.** Close Outlook Express.

By default, Outlook Express formats messages using HTML. When you print a message formatted in HTML, it includes lines and boldface headings. However, if the message you are printing uses plaintext instead of HTML, the printout will not contain formatting, and some of the lines might be uneven. You can change this setting by clicking Tools, clicking Options, and then specifying HTML on the Send tab. Your messages will then be sent formatted. If you need a high-quality printout of a plaintext message, you can save the message as a text file, open it in a word processor, and edit it there so that it looks professional.

Scott has now finished your training on e-mail. As you continue to work with Outlook Express, you'll see other ways in which e-mail can be integrated with the workings of Windows 2000 and the Web.

Session 5.3 QUICK CHECK

1. What is a mail server?
2. Identify the user ID portion and the host name portion of the following e-mail address: pcsmith@icom.net.
3. How can you view your mail account properties in Outlook Express?
4. Where can you find a copy of a message you sent?
5. Why shouldn't you type your messages in all uppercase letters?
6. Name two advantages the Reply feature has over the New Mail feature when you are responding to an e-mail.

REVIEW ASSIGNMENTS

1. **History of the Internet and the World Wide Web** Computers have been around for several decades now, but how did the Internet and the World Wide Web get started? Microsoft considered the Internet an important enough development to incorporate many of its features into the Windows 2000 operating system. Go to the library and locate books or articles on the Internet, and write a single-page essay on the history of the Internet. Answer questions such as:
    a. What role did the ARPANET play in the development of the Internet?
    b. What role did CERN play in the development of the World Wide Web?
    c. Over what period of time did the Internet grow? What about the World Wide Web?
    d. When did browsers first become available?

2. **Connecting to the Internet over a Modem** This tutorial mentioned that home computer users can connect to the Internet using a dial-up connection via an account with an ISP. Assume you have your own computer, and you want to connect to the Internet from home. Contact at least three ISPs in your area, ask for their rates and services, and then write a single-page essay describing your findings. Which ISP would you choose, and why?

3. **Exploring Your Home Page** In this tutorial the figures showed Microsoft Corporation's home page as the home page. Your home page might be different—take some time to explore.
    a. Start the Internet Explorer browser and print your home page.
    b. Click one of the links on your home page, and continue to click any interesting links that you encounter. Clicking whatever links interest you is often called "surfing." On your printout, circle the link you followed. Write in the margin where it took you.
    c. Use the Home button to return to your home page, and then click another link and go where it leads you. Again, circle the link on your printout, indicate where you ended up, and write what you saw along the way.

4. **Connecting to Specific Web Sites** You learned in this tutorial that you can enter a URL into the Address box of your browser to connect to a specific Web site. Using the Internet Explorer browser, enter the following URLs, and print the first page of each URL.
    a. http://www.usps.gov
    b. http://www.nps.gov
    c. http://www.cnn.com
    d. Using any one of these pages as a starting point, follow links until you locate a page with frames. Record the URL of the page you found.

5. **Web Page Desktop Background** Because he will be placing the Highland Web page on your desktop soon, Scott wants you to practice using a Web page as a desktop background.
    a. Apply the Highland Web page (not the folder), located in the root directory of your Data Disk, as your desktop background.
    b. Observe the background carefully and work with the objects that are incorporated into this Web page.
    c. Connect to the Active Desktop Gallery and add a desktop item that would add to the usefulness of this desktop.
    d. Using the Highland desktop you just created as an example, write two paragraphs describing what a Web page background offers that a graphic image file, such as you used in Tutorial 4, does not. Give detailed information about the purpose of each element on the desktop.
    e. Restore your computer's background to its original state.

Explore

6. **E-mailing a Web Page and a Link** Scott wants you to share the Highland Travel Home page with some potential clients. Internet Explorer provides tools to easily e-mail either the entire Web page or a link to the page.

    a. Connect to the Internet and open the Highland Travel home page in Internet Explorer.

    b. Click the Mail button ☒ on the Standard Buttons toolbar, and click Send a Link to send a link to the home page to your instructor.

    c. Click the Mail button ☒ again, and send the entire Web page to your instructor.

    d. What problems might there be in sending a Web page to a user? What should you know about the user's e-mail program before attempting to send the page?

Explore

7. **Editing the Links Toolbar** Scott tells you that the Links toolbar is another place, besides the Favorites folder, where you can place shortcuts to your favorite Web sites. The Links toolbar is one of the toolbars displayed by Internet Explorer that displays icons for specific Web sites. Scott wants you to learn how to use it.

    a. Start Internet Explorer and display the Links toolbar in the Web browser (click View on the menu bar, click Toolbars, and then click—if necessary—to place a check mark next to Links).

    b. Click the double arrow on the right side of the Links toolbar, and then click the Customize Links icon (if the Customize Links button is missing, go to the Web page at: http://www.microsoft.com/windows98/usingwindows/internet/tips/advanced/Customize LinksBar.asp).

    c. Print the Web page.

    d. Using the information on this Web page, add a link to the Highland Travel home page to the Links toolbar.

    e. Display the Links toolbar on the Windows 2000 taskbar, making sure that the icon for the Highland Travel home page is visible.

    f. Using the techniques from Tutorial 2, print a copy of your screen with the revised Links toolbar.

    g. Remove the icon for the Highland Travel home page from the Links toolbar.

Explore

8. **Using Rich Text Formatting in E-mail** Scott tells you that with Outlook Express you can use special fonts and formats to liven up your e-mail messages. You decide to test this by sending an e-mail message to Katie Herrera, telling her of your interest in working on the St. Andrews project.

    a. Start Outlook Express and compose an e-mail message to your instructor with the subject line "St. Andrews Project".

    b. In the message area, enter (in your own words) your interest in the project and willingness to participate.

    c. Turn on formatting for the message by clicking Format on the menu bar of the mail message window and then clicking Rich Text. In the message area, boldface at least one word and italicize at least one word. To boldface a word, you select it and then click the Bold button ☒. To italicize it, you select it and then click the Italic button ☒.

    d. Now color one word red: select the word, click the Font Color button ☒, and then click the color red.

    e. Send the message to your instructor.

PROJECTS

1. Internet Explorer and Windows Explorer share many of the same menus, commands, and toolbars. In fact, you can modify Windows Explorer to look and operate exactly like Internet Explorer.

   a. Open Windows Explorer.
   b. In the Address bar, enter the URL of your Home page (or use www.msn.com if you don't know the URL of your home page), and then press the Enter key. Connect to the Internet if you are not already connected.
   c. Modify the Explorer Bar so that it displays the Favorites pane.
   d. Using techniques shown in Tutorial 2, print a copy of your screen. Include the taskbar.
   e. Open the same Web page in Internet Explorer and display the Favorites pane in that program. Compare the displays of Internet Explorer and Windows Explorer. Can you see any difference between the two?
   f. Microsoft's goal with Windows 2000 was to create a "single Explorer." Why do you think Microsoft set this goal? What advantages or disadvantages does the single Explorer have?

2. You have a friend who has used Windows Explorer extensively for managing his own files and folders, and you mention to him that he can also use Windows Explorer as a browser. Write him a note, which you'll e-mail to him, that describes how this is possible. Make sure you describe what happens to elements such as the left and right panes, the Address bar, the activity indicator, and the status bar.

3. In this tutorial you learned how to access information on the Web when you either knew the URL or used a link to jump there. Internet Explorer also includes the Search pane (like Windows Explorer), that helps you find the Web pages you need. Use Internet Explorer's online Help to learn about the Search pane and about the general topic of searching the Web.

   a. How would you search for information on a given topic?
   b. Once the Search feature displays a list of search results, what should you do to display the Web page containing the information?
   c. Follow the directions you studied in the Help file to search for information on one of your hobbies, such as snowboarding. While you are using the Search Explorer bar, write down the exact steps you take. Was your search successful? Write down the URL of the page you connected to.

4. You just went to California for a three-week vacation with some friends. On returning, you decide to "capture the moment" by downloading a graphic image that will remind you of your vacation activities.

   a. Use what you learned in Project 3 to locate a graphic image of surfing, rock climbing, wine tasting, or some other vacation activity, and download it to your Data Disk. (If you skipped Project 3, connect to the Highland site or your home page and download a graphic from there.)
   b. Send an e-mail to your instructor containing the image (you can paste the image into the e-mail document by clicking Insert on the New Message window's title bar—then click Picture, click Browse, locate and click the file, and then click OK.

5. Because most labs can't accommodate subscriptions, you probably will need your own computer to complete this project. Your dream is to plan your investments so you can retire by age 55. To keep yourself posted on the stock market:

   a. Locate a Web site that contains stock market information. You could try http://www.nasdaq.com or http://www.djia.com.
   b. Place this Web page on your desktop as an Active Desktop item (you can add in the Web dialog sheet of the Display Properties dialog box).
   c. Set up a synchronization schedule for the Web page so that it is automatically updated every morning at 8 AM.

   d. Create a log in Notepad (perhaps using the LOG feature you learned about in Tutorial 4) to record information such as the closing value of an index such as NASDAQ or the Dow on a given day.

   e. When you have recorded three days' worth of information in the log, open the log window and your synchronization schedule, and print your screen so your instructor can see which Web page you subscribed to and what information you gained. Make sure you unsubscribe from the Web page once the three days are over.

LAB ASSIGNMENTS

The Internet:
World Wide
Web

The Internet: World Wide Web

One of the most popular services on the Internet is the World Wide Web. This lab is a Web simulator that teaches you how to use Web browser software to find information. You can use this lab whether or not your school provides you with Internet access. See the Read This Before You Begin page for information on starting the lab.

1. Click the Steps button to learn how to use Web browser software. As you proceed through the steps, answer all of the Quick Check questions that appear. After you complete the steps, you will see a Quick Check Summary Report. Follow the instructions on the screen to print this report.

2. Click the Explore button on the Welcome screen. Use the Web browser to locate a weather map of the Caribbean Virgin Islands. What is its URL?

3. A scuba diver named Wadson Lachouffe has been searching for the fabled treasure of Greybeard the pirate. A link from the Adventure Travel Web site www.atour.com leads to Wadson's Web page called "Hidden Treasure." In Explore, locate the Hidden Treasure page and answer the following questions:

   a. What was the name of Greybeard's ship?

   b. What was Greybeard's favorite food?

   c. What does Wadson think happened to Greybeard's ship?

4. In the steps, you found a graphic of Jupiter from the photo archives of the Jet Propulsion Laboratory. In the Explore section of the lab, you can also find a graphic of Saturn. Suppose one of your friends wanted a picture of Saturn for an astronomy report. Make a list of the blue, underlined links your friend must click, in the correct order, to find the Saturn graphic. Assume that your friend will begin at the Web Trainer home page.

5. Enter the URL http://www.atour.com to jump to the Adventure Travel Web site. Write a one-page description of this site. In your paper include a description of the information at the site, the number of pages the site contains, and a diagram of the links it contains.

6. Chris Thomson is a student at UVI and has his own Web pages. In Explore, look at the information Chris has included on his pages. Suppose you could create your own Web page. What would you include? Use word-processing software to design your own Web page. Make sure you indicate the graphics and links you would use.

Web Pages
& HTML

Web Pages & HTML

It's easy to create your own Web pages. There are many software tools to help you become a Web author. In this lab you'll experiment with a Web-authoring Wizard that automates the process of creating a Web page. You'll also try your hand at working directly with HTML code. See the Read This Before You Begin page for information on starting the lab.

1. Click the Steps button to activate the Web-authoring Wizard and learn how to create a basic Web page. As you proceed through the steps, answer all of the Quick Check questions. After you complete the steps, you will see a Quick Check Summary Report. Follow the instructions on the screen to print this report.

2. In Explore, click the File menu, then click New to start working on a new Web page. Use the Wizard to create a home page for a veterinarian who offers dog day-care and boarding services. After you create the page, save it on drive A or C, and print the HTML code. Your site must have the following characteristics:

    a. Title: Dr. Dave's Dog Domain

    b. Background color: Gold

    c. Graphic: Dog.jpg

    d. Body text: Your dog will have the best care day and night at Dr. Dave's Dog Domain. Fine accommodations, good food, playtime, and snacks are all provided. You can board your pet by the day or week. Grooming services also available.

    e. Text link: "Reasonable rates" links to www.cciw.com/np3/rates.htm

    f. E-mail link: "For more information:" links to daveassist@drdave.com

3. In Explore, use the File menu to open the HTML document called Politics.htm. After you use the HTML window (not the Wizard) to make the following changes, save the revised page on drive A or C, and print the HTML code. Refer to Figure 5-43 for a list of HTML tags you can use:

Figure 5-43

HTML TAGS	MEANING AND LOCATION
\<HTML>\</HTML>	States that the file is an HTML document; Opening tag begins the page; closing tag ends the page (required)
\<HEAD>\</HEAD>	States that the enclosed text is the header of the page; Appears immediately after the opening HTML tag (required)
\<TITLE>\</TITLE>	States that the enclosed text is the title of the page; Must appear within the opening and closing HEAD tags (required)
\<BODY>\</BODY>	States that the enclosed material (all the text, images, and tags in the rest of the document) is the body of the document (required)
\<H1>\</H1>	States that the enclosed text is a heading
\ 	Inserts a line break; Can be used to control line spacing and breaks in lines
\<UL>\</UL> \<OL>\</OL>	Indicates an unordered list (list items are preceded by bullets) or an ordered list (list items are preceded by numbers or letters)
\<LI>	Indicates a list item; Precedes all items in unordered or ordered lists
\<CENTER>\</CENTER>	Indicates that the enclosed text should be centered on the width of the page
\<B>\</B>	Indicates that the enclosed text should appear in boldface
\<I>\</I>	Indicates that the enclosed text should appear in italics
\<A HREF="*URL*">\</A>	Indicates that the enclosed text is a hypertext link; The URL of the linked material must appear within the quotation marks after the equal sign
\<IMG SRC="*filename*">	Inserts an inline image into the document where *filename* is the name of the image
\<HR>	Inserts a horizontal rule

    a. Change the title to Politics 2000.

    b. Center the page heading.

    c. Change the background color to FFE7C6 and the text color to 000000.

    d. Add a line break before the sentence "What's next?"

    e. Add a bold tag to "Additional links on this topic"

    f. Add one more link to the "Additional links" list. The link should go to the site http://www.elections.ca, and the clickable link should read "Elections Canada".

    g. Change the last graphic to display the image "next.gif".

4. In Explore, use the Web-authoring Wizard and the HTML window to create a home page about yourself. You should include at least a screenful of text, a graphic, an external link, and an e-mail link. Save the page on drive A, then print the HTML code. Turn in your disk and printout.

QUICK | CHECK ANSWERS

Session 5.1

1. A home page is the Web page designated by the operating system as your starting point, the Web page that an organization or business has created to give information about itself, or a personal Web page with information about an individual.
2. URL
3. Type the URL in the Address box, then press Enter.
4. It is an educational site.
5. site
6. Open the History pane in Internet Explorer. You can then try to locate the page by viewing the list of pages you accessed on a particular day, or you can search the contents of the History pane to locate it.
7. False
8. Right-click the image, click Save Picture As, enter a filename and destination folder, and then click Save.

Session 5.2

1. With offline viewing, your computer can access a Web page or file off of a network so that you can view it later without being connected to the network.
2. Push technology allows both Web site authors and subscribers to gain more control over content delivery and schedule.
3. Active Desktop item
4. Synchronization is a process by which an offline file is updated with the most recent version of the network file.
5. Right-click the object and open its Properties dialog box. On the Schedule dialog sheet, add 24 new schedules, one for each hour of the day.
6. Hypertext Markup Language, the underlying language of Web documents
7. You can add special items such as animated graphics, links to files and Web pages, and applets to run programs for you from the desktop.

Session 5.3

1. A mail server is a computer on a network that manages the storage and delivery of electronic mail.
2. User ID: pcsmith, host name: icom.net
3. Click Tools, click Accounts, click the Mail tab, click the account with your name, and then click the Properties button.
4. the Sent Items folder
5. The recipient might interpret the uppercase letters as shouting—considered rude in most e-mail exchanges.
6. The recipient's e-mail address is automatically inserted, the subject is automatically inserted, and the original message is automatically quoted.

OBJECTIVES

In this tutorial you will:

- Find files by name, contents, and location using several methods, including wildcards

- Open and work with files from the Search window

- Limit a search to a specific folder

- Locate files by date, type, and size

- Open documents with the Documents menu

- Search for information on the Internet using query and subject searches

- Search for people and maps on the Internet

SEARCHING FOR INFORMATION

Using the Search Feature to Locate Files for a Speechwriter

CASE

Speechwriter's Aide

Like thousands of other college students who are graduating soon, you've been dropping in at the campus job center regularly. Today, you notice that Senator Susannah Bernstein's speechwriter has posted an advertisement for an aide. When you call to inquire, Carolyn King, the Senator's speechwriter, asks you to come by the next morning. Your interview goes very well. You learn that the job would primarily entail locating information that Carolyn could use in writing the Senator's speeches. Carolyn explains that her previous aide collected and organized information in a filing cabinet. In addition to the paper archive, the previous aide started an electronic quotations archive that includes over a hundred files on a 3½-inch disk. These files contain anecdotes, jokes, and commentary on a variety of subjects.

You explain to Carolyn that you could maximize the efficiency of the information retrieval process if you had a computer running Windows 2000 with an Internet connection. Carolyn doesn't think that should be a problem, but she hasn't used Windows 2000 before and asks you to update her on the features that make information retrieval easier.

You explain that Windows 2000 includes a powerful search tool called **Search** that helps you find files on the local or network drives to which you have access and helps you search for information on the Internet. The Internet contains a vast number of computers and networks that store information, much of which can be accessed and retrieved by the search tools that Windows 2000 makes available. With Windows 2000 and an Internet connection, information from around the world is accessible from your office computer. Carolyn is intrigued, and by the end of the interview she offers you the job.

After a week of training and orientation, Carolyn assigns you office space that includes a computer running Windows 2000 and an Internet connection. She promises that your first assignment will come soon, and in the meantime asks that you familiarize yourself with the information available locally.

SESSION 6.1

In this session, you will learn techniques for searching for files by their filenames, by the text they contain, and by file date, type, and size. Finally, you'll examine the Documents menu to explore another way of locating a file.

Preparing Your Data Disk

Before you can begin working, you need to bring a blank 3½-inch disk to the computer lab and use the NP on Microsoft Windows 2000 menu to create a Data Disk containing the files you will work with in this tutorial. If you are using your own computer, the NP on Microsoft Windows 2000 menu may not be available. Once you have made the disk at the computer lab, however, you can use the disk to complete this tutorial on any computer that runs Windows 2000.

To make your Data Disk:

1. Write "Disk 4—Windows 2000 Tutorial 6 Data Disk" on the label of a blank, formatted 3½-inch disk. Insert your Data Disk into drive A.

   TROUBLE? If your 3½-inch disk drive is B, place your formatted disk in that drive instead, and for the rest of this tutorial substitute drive B wherever you see drive A.

2. Point to the **Start** button [Start], point to **Programs**, point to **NP on Microsoft Windows 2000-Level II**, and then click **Disk 4 (Tutorial 6)**. When you are prompted to insert your disk in the drive, click the **OK** button, and wait as the files you need are copied to your Data Disk.

3. Close all the open windows on your screen.

Search Strategies

Windows 2000 offers a useful set of search tools, available on the Search submenu of the Start menu, which help you find several types of information. See Figure 6-1.

Figure 6-1	SEARCH TOOLS
SEARCH OPTION	**DESCRIPTION**
For Files or Folders	Locates files or folders on local or network drives; also gives you access to additional options, including searching for a computer or searching for people and searching on the Internet
On the Internet	Locates information on the Internet
For People	Locates people, using directory services available on your computer and on the Internet

On your own computer, the best way to make sure you can find your files quickly and easily is to start with a well-organized folder structure. But even on your own computer, you might forget the names or locations of certain files. One of the options on the Search menu—For Files or Folders—opens the Search window, which helps you locate files and folders on the devices available to your computer. Search can help you avoid looking manually through the hundreds of files your hard drive contains. It is also useful when you are working on someone else's computer, a network computer, or a computer with multiple users who share documents, or when you have a disk with someone else's data, as is the case with the quotations archive disk that Carolyn gave you.

To search for a file, you provide Search with **search criteria**, one or more conditions you want Search to meet as it searches. For example, you could provide search criteria specifying all or part of a filename and the drive you think the file might be on. Search then locates and displays every file that matches those criteria. You can specify the criteria shown in Figure 6-2.

Figure 6-2	SEARCH CRITERIA AVAILABLE IN THE SEARCH RESULTS DIALOG BOX
OPTION	**DESCRIPTION**
Search for files or folders named	All or part of a filename
Containing text	Any words or phrases contained within the text of the file (not the filename)
Look in	The location (computer, drive, or folder) in which you want Windows 2000 to search
Date	The date or range of dates on which the file was created, last modified, or last accessed
Type	File type
Size	File size
Advanced Options	Allows you to specify search settings, such as whether or not to search subfolders or to perform a case-sensitive search

You start browsing through the quotations archive disk. You discover that the disk is organized into several folders. You open a few files and find quotes from a wide variety of people—historical figures such as Eleanor Roosevelt and Gandhi, as well as more modern personalities such as Jay Leno and Alice Walker. As you are reading through one of the files, Carolyn stops by and asks if you could look for appropriate material for a speech the Senator will deliver next week at Stanton College on successful leadership. You see there are so many files on the disk that opening and reading through every one of them would be time-consuming, so you decide to use the Search feature to locate information on the topic of leadership.

Starting Search

You didn't create the quotations files, and you know very little about them, so Search is just the tool to help you locate quotations for Senator Bernstein's speech. You can start Search from the Start menu, or from within Windows Explorer. When you use Windows Explorer, you click the Search icon 🔍 on the toolbar, or you can right-click the folder or device you want to search, and then click Search. You'll use the Start menu method.

To start Search and specify that you want to search for files or folders:

1. Click the **Start** button 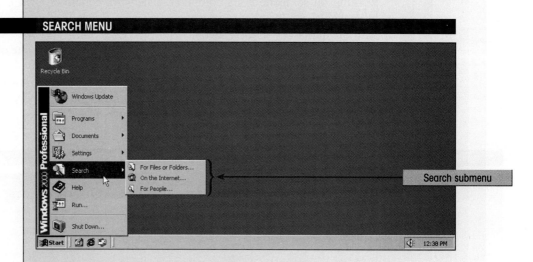 and then point to **Search**. The Search menu opens. Because you are looking for files, choose the first option, **For Files or Folders**, shown in Figure 6-3.

Figure 6-3	SEARCH MENU

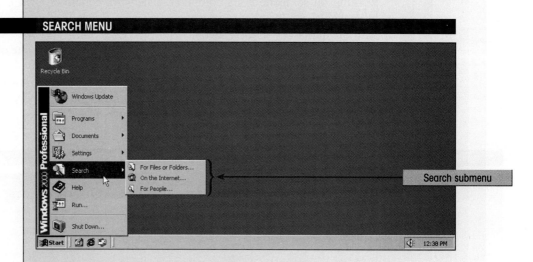

2. Click **For Files or Folders** on the Search menu. A window opens that lets you specify criteria for the file you are looking for. See Figure 6-4.

Figure 6-4	SEARCH RESULTS WINDOW

your Look in box might show a different device or folder

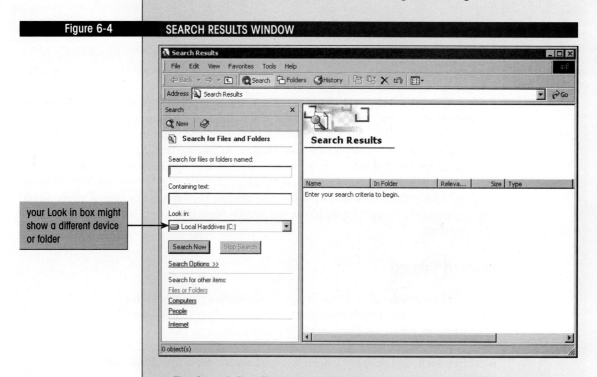

The Search Results window is divided into two parts: on the left is the Search Explorer bar, where you enter search criteria, and on the right is the Search Results pane, where Windows 2000 lists any files it found that matched your criteria.

Searching by Name and Location

To find a specific file, enter as much of the filename as you know. The letters you type to define the search are called a **search string**. By default, Search is not case-sensitive when searching for filenames, so you can type the search string in either uppercase or lowercase letters.

REFERENCE WINDOW   **RW**

Searching for a File by Name
- Click the Start button, point to Search, and then click For Files or Folders.
- Type a search string in the Search for files or folders named box.
- Click the Look in list arrow, and then click the drive you want to search, or click My Computer to select all the drives on your computer.
- Click the Search Now button.

What search string should you enter when you don't know the filename? You can guess, based on the file contents. You decide to start by looking for files named "leadership." Later you can try other search strings.

To search for files containing "leadership" in the filename:

1. Type **leadership** in the Search for files or folders named box.

You've entered a criterion for the filename. Now you need to specify a file location. When you start Search, a folder or drive name, such as Local Harddrives (C:), appears in the Look in box, which specifies where Search will search. If your computer has multiple drives and you aren't sure which drive contains the file, you can search your entire computer by clicking My Computer on the Look in list. However, if you know which drive contains the file, you can speed up your search by limiting the search to that drive. All the files you are looking for are located on your Data Disk, so specify your floppy drive as your search location.

To specify drive A as the file location and then perform the search:

1. Click the **Look in** list arrow and then click **3½ Floppy (A:)** so that Windows 2000 searches only the files on your Data Disk.

2. Click the **Search Now** button. Search searches for all files on drive A whose names contain the search string you entered. Then it displays any matching files in the Search Results pane.

3. Click **View** and then click **Details** to ensure that you are viewing file details. See Figure 6-5.

   TROUBLE? If nothing appeared, Windows 2000 might not be including subfolders in its search. Click Search Options, click the Advanced Options check box, and then make sure the Search Subfolders check box is selected. This ensures that Search will search all folders on the Data Disk, not just the files contained in the root directory. Click Search Options again to close the menu.

TROUBLE? If your results show "txt" extensions after the filenames, your computer is set to show file extensions. Either way is fine. If you want to hide file extensions, open My Computer, click Tools, click Folder Options, click the View tab, select the Hide file extensions for known file types check box, and then click the OK button and close My Computer.

Figure 6-5   **SEARCH RESULTS PANE**

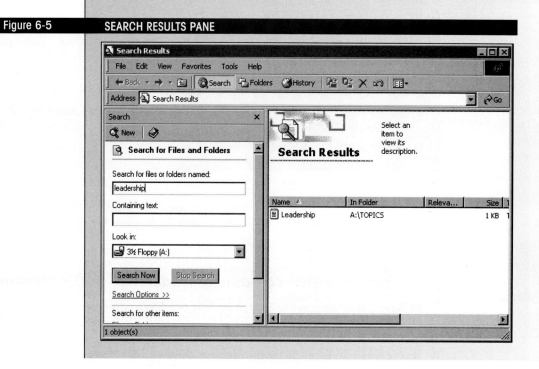

The Search Results list shows one file, Leadership. The In Folder column shows the file location, A:\Topics. The location begins with the drive—in this case, A. If the file is in a folder, a backslash (\) separates the drive from the folder name. Therefore, files in A:\Topics are in the Topics folder on drive A. If there are subfolders, additional backslashes separate the folders from one another. Figure 6-6 shows how this notation works on a drive A that contains two folders, Politics and Speeches, both of which have subfolders.

Figure 6-6   **FILE LOCATIONS**

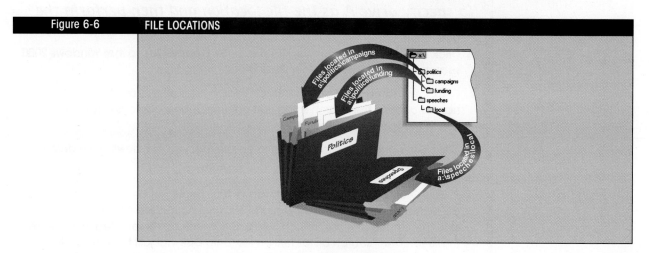

Experimenting with Search Strings

You wonder if you would find more files using a different search string. One rule of thumb is to use the root of your search word as your criterion. For example, if you decide to search for files on political topics for Senator Bernstein's speech, should you enter "politics" as your search string? Probably not, because a file named Politician (for example) will not appear in the Search Results pane. However, the root "politic," without the added "s," would yield files named Politician, Political Quotations, or Politics. Figure 6-7 shows several examples of search strings that use the root of a word (you don't need to try any of these now).

Figure 6-7	CHOOSING EFFECTIVE SEARCH STRINGS	
TOPIC	**USE THIS SEARCH STRING:**	**FINDS THESE FILENAMES:**
politics	politic	Politics, Politicians, Political Quotations
education	educ	Education, Educational Issues, Educators
computers	comput	Computers, Computing, Computerization

Of course, if the root of the word is very general, it might let in unwanted files. Searching for "lead" instead of "leader" would display a file such as "Lead Corrosion." Fortunately, it's easy to adjust your search string until you find only those files you want.

Now that you know there is a file containing quotations specifically about leadership, you look for files on leaders, using "leader" as your search string. To perform a new search, you can change the existing criteria, add a new criterion, or click the New button, which returns all Search settings to their defaults. You change the search string "leadership" to "leader" in the Search for files or folders named box. Drive A is still specified in the Look in box.

To search for files containing the search string "leader" on drive A:

1. Change the entry in the Search for files or folders named box from leadership to **leader**.

   TROUBLE? To change an entry in a text box, often you can simply double-click the text box to select the contents, and whatever you type replaces the existing entry. Or you can click once and then edit the text box contents.

2. Click the **Search Now** button. The Search Results pane now lists three files that might contain information on leadership. See Figure 6-8.

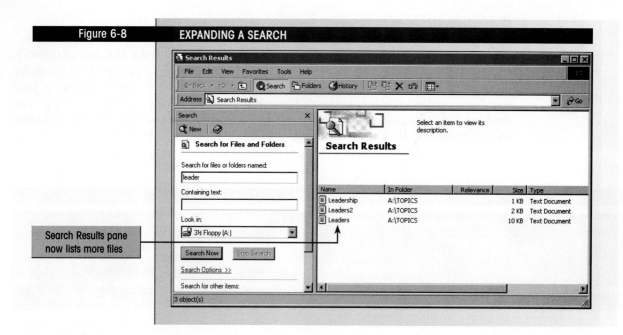

Figure 6-8   EXPANDING A SEARCH

Search Results pane now lists more files

Opening a File from Scratch

Once you locate a file using the Search feature, you can open it directly, as you would from My Computer, Windows Explorer, or any similar window that lists files. You can right-click it and then click Open, click it and then press Enter, or double-click it. Windows 2000 locates and starts the program that created the file, and then it opens the file. If Windows 2000 cannot open your file, it is possible that you don't have the necessary program for that file type installed on your computer. If this is the case, Windows 2000 prompts you to specify the program you want to use to display the file.

You decide to open the Leadership file to see if it contains any quotes the Senator might find useful.

To open a file from the Search Results pane:

1. Right-click the **Leadership** file in the Search Results pane and then click **Open**. The file opens in Notepad.

   TROUBLE? If the text of the quotations extends beyond the right border of the Notepad window, click Format and then click Word Wrap.

2. Browse through the contents of the file and note that it contains several quotations on leadership. When you are finished, click the Notepad **Close** button ✕ to close Notepad. Click **No** if you are prompted to save your changes.

You show Carolyn the files you found for the speech at Stanton College.

Using **Wildcards**

Carolyn is pleased that you found helpful material for her. She mentions that Senator Bernstein will be participating in an atomic energy symposium next month, so anything you can find on that topic would be useful. You decide to check if there are any files on Albert Einstein, but you can't remember how to spell his name. If you make a spelling error, Search won't locate the files you want. You can, however, use wildcards to approximate a filename. **Wildcards** are characters that you can substitute for all or part of a filename in a search string. Search recognizes two wildcards: the asterisk and the question mark. To locate a group of files whose names follow certain specific patterns, such as all files that begin and end with certain characters, or all files with a specified string in a specified location, you can use wildcards.

The * (asterisk) wildcard stands in place of any number of consecutive characters in a filename. With the search string "m*n" for example, Search locates files with names such as Men, Magician, or Modern, but not Male or Women. Here, the files that Search locates have a common characteristic: they all begin with "m" and end with "n." When Search encounters the asterisk wildcard in a search string, it allows additional characters only in those places indicated by the wildcard. Search does not include filenames with characters before the "m" or after the "n." If this is not what you wanted, you can use additional wildcards. If you specify the search string "*m*n*" then Search includes Men, Magician, Modern, Women, and Mention, but not Male. These files have the letter "m" in common, which appears somewhere in the name, followed at a later point by the letter "n."

You can also control the Search Results pane with the ? (question mark) wildcard, which lets you select files when one character in the filename varies. For example, the search string "m?n" locates Men or Man but not Mistaken or Moon.

Files that match the "m?n" criteria must have the letters "m" and "n" in their filenames, separated by a single character. Unlike the asterisk wildcard, however, the question mark wildcard does not cause Search to exclude files with characters before or after the "m" or "n." So although "m*n" excludes Women and Mental, "m?n" does not, because both of these files contain "m" and "n" separated by a single character.

The question mark wildcard is often used to locate files whose names include version numbers or dates, such as Sales1, Sales2, and Sales3, or Tax1997, Tax1998, and Tax1999.

You decide to search for only those files beginning with "e" and ending with "n" because you know those are the first and last letters of Einstein's name, although you aren't sure what's in between. To perform this search, you use "e*n" as your search string. Try this search now.

To locate files using the asterisk wildcard:

1. Select the contents of the **Search for files or folders named** box.

2. Type **e*n** and then click the **Search Now** button. Search locates files on your Data Disk whose names start with "e" followed by any number of characters and then the letter "n." See Figure 6-9.

Figure 6-9	SEARCHING WITH THE ASTERISK WILDCARD

asterisk wildcard

Search Results pane shows files matching your wildcard criteria

this file might appear as a Microsoft Word document if you have Word on your computer

two files on Einstein

You make a mental note that there are files on Einstein that might be appropriate for the atomic energy symposium.

Finding a Text String in a File

You've found a file on Einstein, and you wonder if there are files specifically on atomic energy. You search for files named "atomic" or "energy" but don't find any. You know, however, that this doesn't necessarily mean there are no quotes on atomic energy within the files. A useful feature of the Windows 2000 Search utility is its ability to search for a word or phrase in the contents of a file, not just in the filename. To use this feature, you enter a text string in the Containing text box. A **text string** is any series of characters, such as a word or a phrase. Search searches through the entire text of every file to find the specified text string.

When you use the text string feature of the Search feature, you can specify whether your search is case-sensitive. For example, if you wanted to find a letter you wrote to Brenda Wolf, you could enter "Wolf" as your text string, and then select a case-sensitive search to locate only files containing Wolf with an initial capital letter. The Case sensitive option affects only the case of letters in the Containing text box—not those in the Search for files or folders named box. The Case sensitive option is available, along with other options, in the Search Options list, which you can view by clicking Search Options and then selecting the appropriate check box.

You decide to search for the text string "atomic energy" in hopes of finding files containing quotations Carolyn could use in writing her speech for the atomic energy symposium.

To look for the text string "atomic energy" within a file:

1. Delete the contents of the Search for files or folders named box.

2. Click the **Containing text** box.

3. Type **atomic energy**, but don't click Search Now yet. Because you aren't sure what case the quote might be in, you want to make sure Search isn't set to perform case-sensitive searches.

4. Click **Search Options** to display a list of options with check boxes, scroll down the Search pane if necessary, and then click **Advanced Options**. Another list of options appears.

   TROUBLE? If search options already appear, you don't have to click Search Options.

5. Make sure the **Case sensitive** check box is not checked. If it is, click it to remove the check mark. Otherwise Search might not locate the file if the case of the search string is not all lowercase. See Figure 6-10.

| Figure 6-10 | **SEARCHING FOR TEXT IN A FILE** |

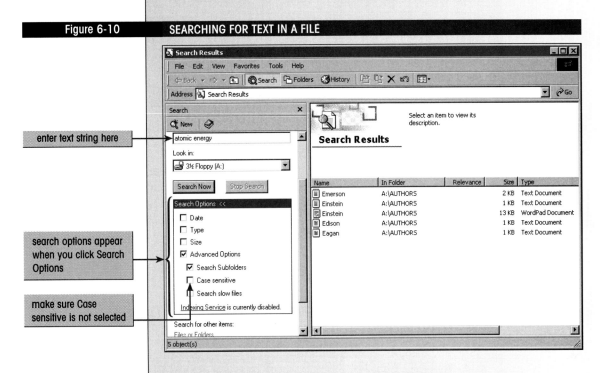

enter text string here

search options appear when you click Search Options

make sure Case sensitive is not selected

6. Click **Search Options** again to hide the search options.

7. Click the **Search Now** button. Search locates one file, Technology, located in the TOPICS folder.

   TROUBLE? Don't worry if Search takes longer than usual. Searching for file contents, even on a 3½-inch disk, is time-consuming.

   TROUBLE? If Search did not locate any file, check to make sure you typed the text string "atomic energy" correctly and that drive A is selected.

8. Delete the entry in the **Containing text** box to clear that search criterion.

If you use the Containing text option on a hard disk, be prepared to wait, because searching file contents one file at a time is time-consuming. If you can narrow the search range using other criteria so that Search searches fewer files—for example, by specifying a folder rather than an entire drive—you will speed things up.

Searching for Files in a Specific Folder

Search can search all drives and folders available to your computer or, as you saw when you selected the drive containing your Data Disk, it can search only a single drive. You can also narrow your search by specifying a specific folder, on your own computer or on a shared network computer.

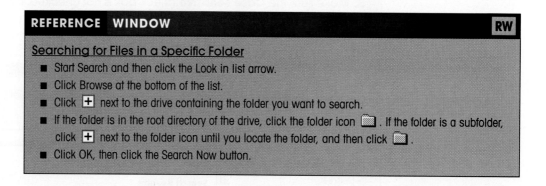

You report to Carolyn that you've found files containing quotations on atomic energy and on Albert Einstein. She suggests that you spend time looking for material you want, to get a better feel for the disk's contents. You noticed there was a Comedy folder, and you wonder whether it contains any quotes by Woody Allen, one of the Senator's favorite celebrities. You decide to tell Search to look only in the Comedy folder.

To specify the Comedy folder, you navigate a folder tree similar to the one in Windows Explorer.

To search the Comedy folder on drive A for files that contain the string "woody allen":

1. Click the **Look in** list arrow and then click **Browse** at the bottom of the list. The Browse For Folder dialog box opens, displaying a list of devices, drives, and folders.

2. Click ➕ next to My Computer. Now click ➕ next to 3½ Floppy (A:). The folders on drive A appear. See Figure 6-11.

   TROUBLE? Your list of devices, drives, and folders might look different, depending on your computer's drives and network.

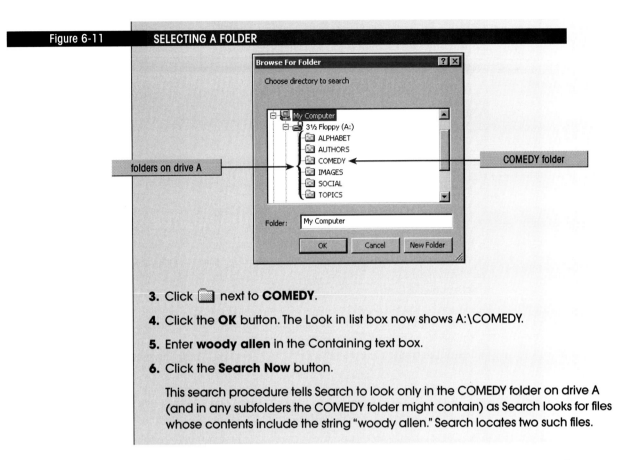

Figure 6-11   SELECTING A FOLDER

3. Click 📁 next to **COMEDY**.

4. Click the **OK** button. The Look in list box now shows A:\COMEDY.

5. Enter **woody allen** in the Containing text box.

6. Click the **Search Now** button.

This search procedure tells Search to look only in the COMEDY folder on drive A (and in any subfolders the COMEDY folder might contain) as Search looks for files whose contents include the string "woody allen." Search locates two such files.

So far, you've been deleting your criteria whenever you enter new criteria, but you can also clear all search criteria at once.

Clearing a Search

When you've completed a search, you need to remember to clear the criterion so it won't affect your next search (unless you want to use it as one of several criteria in a subsequent search). You don't want to limit subsequent searches to just the COMEDY folder, so you will use the New button to clear it and any other criteria.

To clear all criteria:

1. Click the **New** button near the top of the left pane.

The Search Results dialog box now displays the default settings. Note, however, that the Look in box still displays A:\COMEDY. Clicking the New button does not change the Search location.

Working with Search Results

Up until now, the Search Results panes that you've examined have been short and manageable. When your search yields a large number of files, you can adjust the Search Results pane to display the information in a more suitable and organized format.

You wonder whether there is a way to find quotations by author. You decide to search the disk for any files or folders whose filenames contain the term "author."

To search for files and folders named "author" on drive A:

1. Click the **Look in** list arrow and then click **3½ Floppy (A:)** to search all folders, not just the COMEDY folder.

2. Type **author** in the Search for files or folders named box.

3. Click the **Search Now** button. The Search Results pane displays all files and folders that have the word "author" located in their filenames. There are 28 such files.

You can view the files in the results list by Large Icons, Small Icons, List, or Details, and you can resize columns by dragging their borders. These options are the same as in My Computer and Windows Explorer. Details view, the default view, is probably the most useful view because it gives you all the information you need (name, location, relevance, size, type, and date modified of each file) to verify that you've found the file you want. Just as in My Computer and Windows Explorer, you can sort the files in the Search Results pane by any of these criteria.

You see files whose names suggest that they contain quotations from authors, labeled by last name. Is there a file for every letter of the alphabet? You can sort the files by name to find out.

To sort the files by name:

1. Click the **Name** button, as shown in Figure 6-12, to arrange the files in ascending alphabetical order by name.

Figure 6-12	SORTING THE SEARCH RESULTS LIST

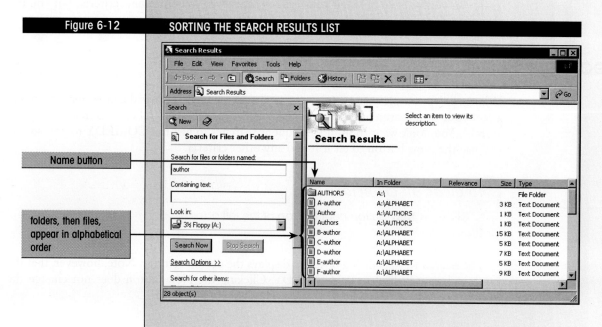

Name button

folders, then files, appear in alphabetical order

2. Scroll down the Search Results list and observe that there are files for most letters of the alphabet.

If you wanted to find quotations by a given author, you could try the file for the author's last name, located in the Alphabet folder. What else can you learn from the Search Results pane? The Type column shows that the first item on the list is a folder and that the rest of the files are text documents. All the files are small (under 16 KB), and you could sort the files by date modified (scroll to the right to see this option), to observe that these files were developed in the years 1996–2001.

Refining a Search

So far you've searched for files with particular filenames or text strings. You can also locate a file using criteria other than the filename or exact contents, including size, date, and type. These options appear when you click Search Options on the Search pane. With these criteria, you can answer questions such as: Are any files more than a few years old? What files were created using a certain program? What files are larger or smaller than a specified size? You enter the characteristic you want to study, and then Search lists all files that share that characteristic, such as all files created after 1998, all Microsoft Word files, or all files larger than 50 KB.

You can use these criteria on their own or in combination with filenames and text strings.

Finding a File by Date

As research assistant, you want to know when the previous aide collected the files. Searching for files by date is also useful when you want a file that you know you were working with on a given date, but you can't remember where you stored it.

You decide to see how many files were created in the years 1994–1996, because you've been told that the aide devoted a lot of time in those years to developing the quotations archive. You'd like to see whether there are any files that haven't changed since then.

To search for files created between 1994 and 1996:

1. Click the **New** button to clear previous search criteria.

2. Click **Search Options** in the Search pane to view additional criteria.

3. Click the **Date** check box. Date options appear; you might need to scroll to see them.

4. Click the **between** option button if necessary.

5. Enter **1/1/1994** as the start date and **12/31/1996** as the end date.

6. Click the **Search Now** button. There are 16 files in that range of dates. Apparently most of the files created in 1994 and 1996 have since been updated. See Figure 6-13.

Figure 6-13   **SELECTING A START AND END DATE**

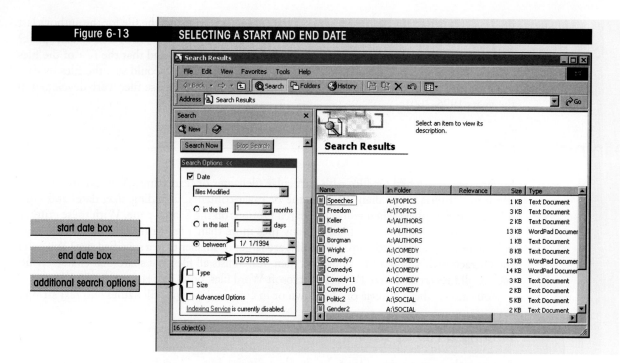

It might have occurred to you that you could get information about file dates more quickly by opening Explorer or My Computer and sorting the files by date. You'd be right, if the files were all in one folder. However, when the files are scattered among multiple folders, Search can display files from any of those folders that meet your date criteria, whereas Explorer and My Computer can display the contents of only one folder at a time.

Finding a File by Type

You'd like to get an overview of the types of files on the quotations archive disk, to see whether you have the software on your computer to open them. You can look for files by their general file type or by the program that created them. The list of file types from which you can choose includes text files, sound files, bitmaps, Word documents, Web documents, and so on, depending on the resources on your computer.

You already know there are lots of text files, but you'd like to know how many. You also wonder whether there are any sound files that the Senator might be able to use in a multimedia presentation. You decide to use file type criteria to answer these questions.

To view files by type:

1. Click the **New** button to clear previous search criteria.

2. Click the **Type** check box (it's located under Search Options in the Search pane).

3. Click the list arrow below the Type check box and then scroll down the alphabetical list to locate "Text Document."

4. Click **Text Document** and then click the **Search Now** button. The status bar reports that there are 92 text files on your disk.

TROUBLE? If your list is much shorter, you might have forgotten to click the New button to reset the Date setting. Forgetting to reset criteria to their original settings can confuse your search efforts.

5. Next you want to look for sound files. Click the list arrow below the Type check box again. Scroll to and then click **Sound Clip**. Click the **Search Now** button. There are two such files.

Finding a File by Size

In searching for files by type, you found two sound files. You know these files are usually bigger than text files or word-processed documents. If you are short on disk space, you'll want to identify the largest files so you can move them to free up space. You can find this information by looking for a file by its size. You specify either "at least" or "at most" and then pick the number of kilobytes you want. If disk space is a problem, you might want to look for all files that are at least 25 KB in size. Try that search now.

To search for files by size:

1. Click the **New** button to clear previous search criteria.

2. Click the **Size** check box under Search Options, and make sure the **at least** option is selected. If it isn't, click the **Size** list arrow and then click **at least**.

3. Enter **25** in the KB box.

4. Click the **Search Now** button. The Search Results pane shows six such files. You can sort these files to more easily identify the largest.

5. Click the **Size** button twice to sort the files by size, with the largest files first. Not surprisingly, the largest files are the two sound files. See Figure 6-14.

| Figure 6-14 | SEARCHING FOR FILES BY SIZE |

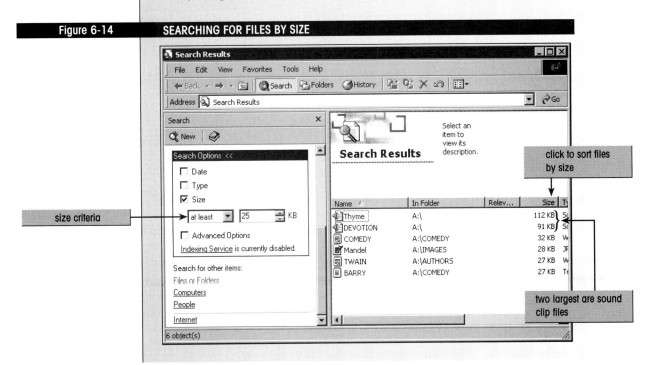

Finding a File Using Multiple Criteria

Carolyn informs you that, because Stanton College is a women's college, Senator Bernstein is interested in having a quote on leadership by a woman. If you specify multiple criteria, such as a likely filename and a likely text string, you might be able to pinpoint such a quote.

You remember that there are files on the archive disk whose filenames contain the search string "women." You guess that the file probably contains the word "leader," so you could specify the root "leader" as your text string. Search uses all the criteria you enter to perform the search.

To find a file with multiple criteria:

1. Click the **New** button to clear previous search criteria.

2. Scroll up to the top of the Search pane, click the **Search for files or folders named** box, and then type **women**.

3. Click the **Containing text** box, type **leader**, and then click the **Search Now** button. One file matches your criteria. See Figure 6-15.

| Figure 6-15 | USING MULTIPLE CRITERIA TO FIND A FILE |

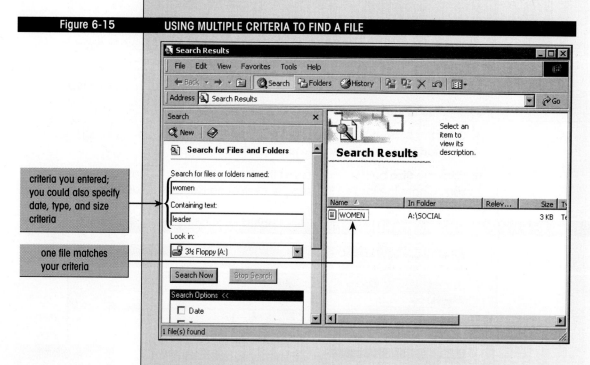

criteria you entered; you could also specify date, type, and size criteria

one file matches your criteria

4. Right-click the **Women** file in the Search Results pane, and then click **Open**. It opens in Notepad. You see a quotation on leaders by Mother Teresa.

5. Close Notepad and the Search Results window.

Opening Recent Documents

You have used Search to locate files. There is another way to locate a file you've worked on recently. You can view a list of recently opened documents, using the Documents command on the Start menu. If you click one of the document names on the Documents menu,

Windows 2000 locates and starts the program that created the document, then opens the document. You decide to use the Documents menu to show Carolyn the file you opened that contains a quote on leadership written by a woman.

To view the most recent documents list:

1. Click the **Start** button 🏁**Start**.

2. Point to **Documents**. The Documents menu opens. See Figure 6-16.

Figure 6-16	OPENING A FILE FROM THE DOCUMENTS LIST

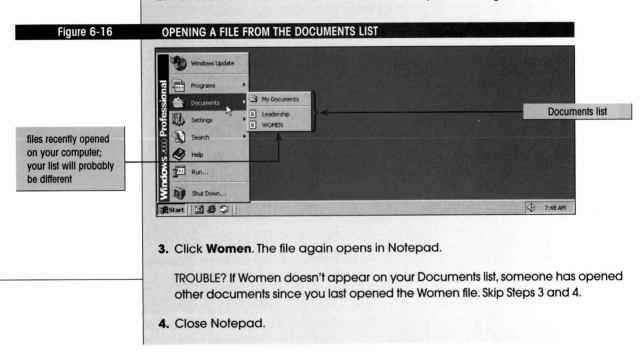

files recently opened on your computer; your list will probably be different

Documents list

3. Click **Women**. The file again opens in Notepad.

TROUBLE? If Women doesn't appear on your Documents list, someone has opened other documents since you last opened the Women file. Skip Steps 3 and 4.

4. Close Notepad.

The Documents command is useful only when you have recently worked on a file on your own computer. When this is the case, it can be the quickest way to find and open a file.

The Search utility has helped you locate files on your disks that meet one or more criteria. In the next session, you'll expand your search to locate more quotation files on the Internet.

Session 6.1   QUICK | CHECK

1. To search for a file only on drive A, what do you do?

2. True or False: The Search Results pane displays only the files whose names exactly match the search string you entered.

3. What is a wildcard? What is the difference between the asterisk wildcard and the question mark wildcard?

4. How do you display the files in the Search Results pane in alphabetical order?

5. If you want the Search utility to display only the bitmapped images on your floppy disk, what should you do?

6. If the Search Results pane displays the file you were looking for, how do you open the file for editing?

7. Something seems to be wrong with Notepad. You can see only the first 10 words or so of each paragraph. What should you do?

SESSION 6.2

In this session, you will learn about searching on the Internet, including searching by query and by subject. You'll learn to search using Autosearch and the Search Explorer bar. Finally, you'll learn to search for maps and people on the Internet.

Searching on the Internet

The Internet has vast resources, and to locate the information you want, you need to search for it. You can search for information on the Internet with the On the Internet option on the Search menu, which starts the Internet Explorer browser and displays the Search Explorer bar. You can perform a quick search by typing the word *find* in the Internet Explorer Address bar, followed by a search word. When you press Enter, the Microsoft Network **Autosearch** feature displays a list of links you might try.

Searching with Autosearch

You would like to expand the set of quotations on the quotation archives disk, so you decide to search the Internet for sites that make quotation collections available.

To search for a Web page using Autosearch:

1. Make sure you are connected to the Internet.

2. Click the **Start** button ![Start], point to **Search**, and then click **On the Internet**. Microsoft starts Internet Explorer and displays the Search Explorer bar.

3. Maximize the Internet Explorer window if necessary.

4. Click the **Address** box on the Address bar, type **find quotations**, and then press the **Enter** key. Internet Explorer connects to the www.quotations.com Web page. See Figure 6-17.

Figure 6-17	PERFORMING AN AUTOSEARCH

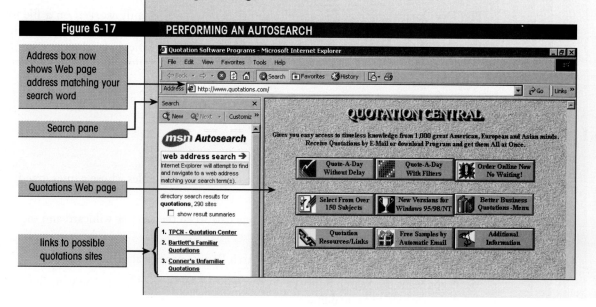

Address box now shows Web page address matching your search word

Search pane

Quotations Web page

links to possible quotations sites

Viewing the Search Explorer Bar

You could look through the links on the quotations.com site, or click any of the links in the Search pane, but for now you'll use the Search Explorer bar to perform a more controlled search.

To view the Search Explorer bar options:

1. Click the **New** button to start a new search.

2. Make sure the **Find a Web page** option button is selected.

3. Click the **More** link below the five option buttons in the Search pane to view all search options. See Figure 6-18.

   TROUBLE? If you are using a different version of Internet Explorer, the search options might look different.

Figure 6-18	SEARCH EXPLORER BAR

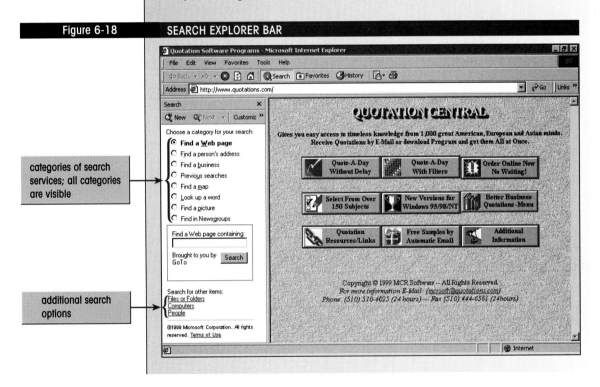

categories of search services; all categories are visible

additional search options

The Search Explorer bar makes available many popular **search services**, software that helps you find information on the Internet. Figure 6-19 describes the categories of search services as they appear on the Search pane shown in Figure 6-18.

Figure 6-19	SEARCH SERVICE CATEGORIES
SEARCH SERVICE CATEGORY	**DESCRIPTION**
Find a Web page	These services help you to search for Web pages, both by subject and by keyword. They include MSN Web Search, InfoSeek, AltaVista, Lycos, GoTo, Excite, Yahoo!, Euroseek, and Northern Light.
Find a person's address	Similar to a telephone book, these services help you locate people's names, e-mail and mailing addresses, phone numbers, and so on. These services include InfoSpace, Bigfoot, and WorldPages.
Find a business	These services provide information about businesses. They include InfoSpace, WorldPages, and Sidewalk YP.
Find a map	These services help you locate maps, addresses, and place names. They include ExpediaMaps and MapQuest.
Look up a word	These services include encyclopedia, dictionary, and thesaurus services, including Encarta, Merriam-Webster, Dictionary.com, and Thesaurus.com.
Find a picture	These services help you locate graphic images. Corbis is the only default service.
Find in Newsgroups	These services help you search newsgroup archives. **Newsgroups**, also called **discussion groups**, bring people with common interests together to exchange e-mail messages on a given topic. Dejanews is the only default service.

Customizing Search Settings

When you use the Search Explorer bar, you first select the category you want to use. The Search Explorer bar displays options appropriate to that category. You then enter a subject and click a button such as Search, Find, Go, or "?". The appearance of the button that starts the search depends on the search service Internet Explorer is using.

You can control the categories and the services that appear on the Search Explorer bar, using the **Search Assistant**. The Search Assistant displays the list of services for each category. When you perform a search, Internet Explorer automatically starts with the first service in that list. If you don't find the information you want with the first search service, you can continue to search, using the next service on the list. You can also control the order in which the services in a category are used, so that Internet Explorer uses your favorite services first.

To customize your search settings:

1. Click the **Customize** button at the top of the Search Explorer pane.

2. Make sure the **Use the Search Assistant** option button is selected at the top of the Customize Search Settings dialog box.

3. Make sure that the **Find a Web page**, **Find a person's address**, and **Find a map** check boxes are all selected. You'll need to scroll through the Customize Search Settings dialog box to see these options. If additional check boxes are selected, leave them selected. Now you'll check the order of services that find Web pages.

4. If necessary, scroll to the top of the Customize Search Settings dialog box. Make sure that at least the **GoTo**, **AltaVista**, and **Yahoo!** check boxes are selected.

5. If GoTo doesn't appear *first* on the list, click **GoTo** in the list of Web page providers on the left, and then click the **Move Up** button ▲ repeatedly to move it to the top of the list. If AltaVista doesn't appear next, click it and then click ▲ until Alta Vista is in second place. Finally, move Yahoo! so it is third in the list. See Figure 6-20. If other services appear in addition to these, you can leave them there.

Figure 6-20	CUSTOMIZING SEARCH SETTINGS

check indicates this search category is selected

GoTo, AltaVista, and Yahoo! are first, second, and third

Move Up button

each search category has a list of providers

6. Click the **OK** button.

Now any searches you perform will use the same settings as those in this tutorial.

Searching for Web Pages

Most Web page search services employ software that regularly searches through Internet documents and compiles a list of Web pages. It organizes and indexes this list by topic. When you use the search service to find Web pages on a specific topic, the service's **search engine** checks the service's index and provides you with links to all the pages it finds on that topic. Because the Internet is changing so quickly, the indexes change regularly too. If you don't find information one day, it might be available the next. Moreover, because different search services use different software to compile their Web page indexes, you might get different results for the same search when using two different search services. If you can't find what you want with one search service, such as Yahoo!, you can try another, such as InfoSeek.

Most search services allow you to perform two types of searches: searches by query and searches by subject. You'll try both kinds of searches.

Searching by Query

A **query** is a request for information. You enter a specific word or phrase, called a **keyword**, into a box, and then click a button, such as Search or Find, that sends your request to the search service. Some search engines allow you to refine your query to get the results you want. For example, if you are looking for information on population statistics, some search engines assume you mean "population" or "statistics" and return pages that contain either word. Other search engines assume you mean "population" and "statistics" and return only pages with both words. These searches take longer and return fewer pages, but the pages are likely to be more useful. Other search engines assume you mean "population" and/or "statistics."

Most search engines allow you to refine your query with symbols called search operators, such as plus (which requires a term or phrase), minus (which excludes a term or phrase), and quotation marks (which identify words that must appear together). Figure 6-21 provides examples of how these operators work in the InfoSeek search engine; other search engines might work differently. You can check a search engine's online Help to learn how to structure your search query using that search engine.

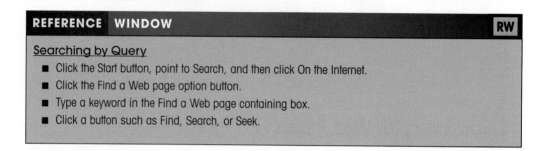

Figure 6-21	HOW KEYWORD OPERATORS WORK IN INFOSEEK
KEYWORD WITH OPERATORS	**RETURNED PAGES**
population statistics	*population* and/or *statistics*
"population statistics"	the word *population* next to the word *statistics*
+population +statistics	*population* and *statistics* but not necessarily next to each other
+population statistics	*population* but not necessarily *statistics*
+statistics –population	*statistics* but not *population*

Using capital letters for proper names can exclude, for example, pages on the color green when you search for information on Greenpeace.

REFERENCE WINDOW — **RW**

Searching by Query
- Click the Start button, point to Search, and then click On the Internet.
- Click the Find a Web page option button.
- Type a keyword in the Find a Web page containing box.
- Click a button such as Find, Search, or Seek.

You want to find information on quotation collections. The Find a Web page option button is already selected, and the "Brought to you by GoTo" line tells you that Internet Explorer will use GoTo as the first search service.

To use the GoTo search service to search for quotation collections:

1. In the Find a Web page containing box, type **quotations**. See Figure 6-22.

Figure 6-22	USING GOTO TO SEARCH FOR A KEYWORD

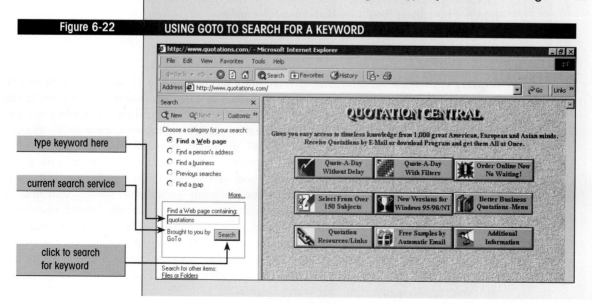

type keyword here

current search service

click to search for keyword

2. Click the **Search** button. After a moment, the Search Explorer bar options are replaced with the GoTo logo and a list of links that GoTo found to match your keyword. See Figure 6-23.

| Figure 6-23 | GOTO'S SEARCH RESULTS |

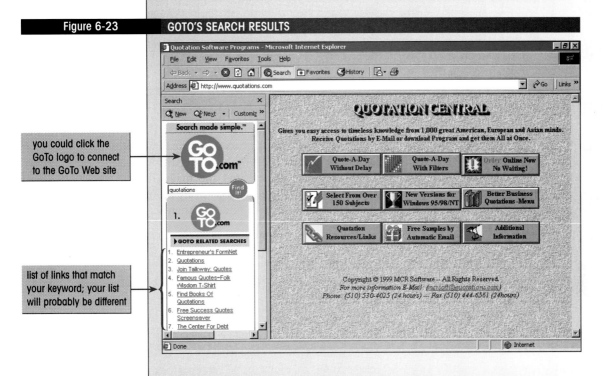

you could click the GoTo logo to connect to the GoTo Web site

list of links that match your keyword; your list will probably be different

Note that since you have not clicked any links in the search results yet, the previous Web page remains in the Internet Explorer window.

3. Scroll down the Search pane to view the list of links.

4. In the Search pane, click the quotation link that looks most promising. In Figure 6-23, there is a link to an entrepreneur's form service, which is probably not what you want, but there are other links that look as if they target quotation collections.

5. Try different links until you locate a collection of quotations.

The search pane usually lists only the first 10 or 20 links; to see the next set of links you need to scroll to locate a link such as More Results, Next, Next 10, or Next 20. Some services rate pages by usefulness according to the keywords you entered, scoring on a 100-point scale and listing the highest scorers first. You can learn about a search service's features by connecting directly to the search service's Web page (for example, www.GoTo.com).

Once you've viewed the links provided by the first search service, you can click the Next button on the Search pane to view results from the next search service. When you customized your search settings, you ensured that AltaVista would be next. Try the same search with AltaVista.

To view the links returned by the next search service:

1. Click the **Next** list arrow at the top of the Search pane. The list of search services appears. You could click any of these services to bypass the predesignated search service order.

2. Press the **Esc** key to close the Next list, and then click the **Next** button. The AltaVista logo now appears in the Search pane, and a list of links returned by the AltaVista service appears in the Search pane.

3. Click the links that look as if they provide promising collections of quotations.

Now you decide to try searching by subject for quotations.

Searching by Subject

Most search services allow you to search by query or subject. When you search by query, you are asking the search engine to locate information on the topic you specify. In a **subject search**, however, you search for information by browsing through a hierarchy of topics, called a **subject guide**. Subject guides are created and maintained by the search service. They are organized first by general and then by successively more specific subjects. Using a subject guide is often more efficient and more effective than searching the entire Web to find pages that contain a few select keywords.

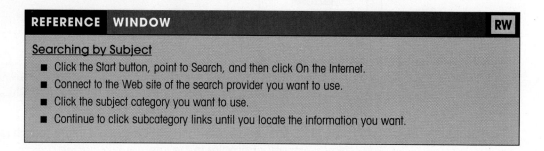

REFERENCE WINDOW   RW

Searching by Subject
- Click the Start button, point to Search, and then click On the Internet.
- Connect to the Web site of the search provider you want to use.
- Click the subject category you want to use.
- Continue to click subcategory links until you locate the information you want.

The Yahoo! search engine offers one of the most popular subject guides; you decide to use it to locate additional information on quotations.

To search the Yahoo! subject guide for quotation collections:

1. Click the **Next** list arrow at the top of the Search pane, and then click **Yahoo!**.

2. Click the **Yahoo!** logo at the top of the Search pane. You connect to Yahoo!'s Web site. See Figure 6-24.

Figure 6-24	SUBJECT GUIDE

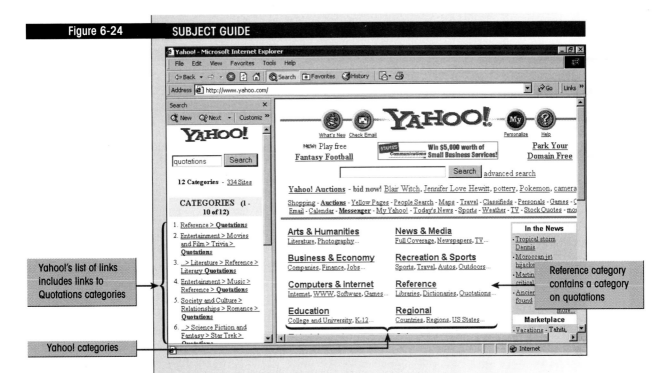

Yahoo!'s list of links includes links to Quotations categories

Yahoo! categories

Reference category contains a category on quotations

3. Click the **Quotations** subcategory on the Yahoo! Web page (it's located below the Reference category). The Quotations category appears, displaying its subcategories. See Figure 6-25.

Figure 6-25	YAHOO! QUOTATIONS CATEGORIES

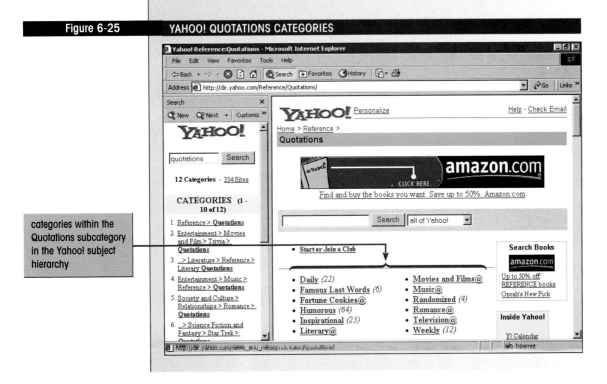

categories within the Quotations subcategory in the Yahoo! subject hierarchy

4. In the category list that appears, click one of the Quotations categories that interests you, and continue clicking relevant links until you locate a quotation collection.

There are many quotation collections on the Web—some have search engines built into them that make it even easier to locate a specific quote. You tell Carolyn that if she isn't satisfied with what you've found on the quotations archive disk, you can easily expand your search to include quotation collections on the Web.

Searching for People

Windows 2000 also includes an option on the Search Explorer bar, Find a person's address, that helps you search for information about specific people. Similar to a telephone book, the Find a person's address option locates information such as a person's mailing address, e-mail address, or phone number from Internet "people search" services such as Bigfoot and SwitchBoard. You enter a name, and the search service returns a list of people with that name. For common names the list is very long; for some names no information is available.

Carolyn has asked you to find contact information for sources she's using to prepare Senator Bernstein's speech. You've managed to do so by searching through journal articles written by the sources, but you wonder if the Internet might give you an alternate method of finding information about people. You decide to test the service by attempting to locate information on yourself.

To find information about a person:

1. Click the **New** button in the Search pane. The Search Explorer bar appears.

2. Click the **Find a person's address** option button. The Search Explorer bar now displays options for a person's address. See Figure 6-26.

Figure 6-26 | SEARCHING FOR A PERSON'S ADDRESS

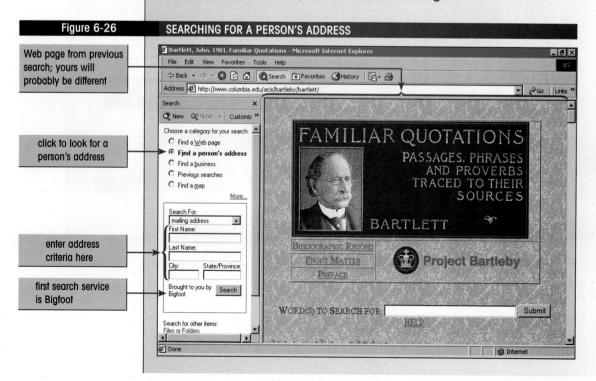

Web page from previous search; yours will probably be different

click to look for a person's address

enter address criteria here

first search service is Bigfoot

3. Type your first name in the First Name box and your last name in the Last Name box. Then enter your city and state.

4. Click the **Search** button. If Bigfoot has any address or phone number information on people with your name, it appears in a list. If Bigfoot wasn't able to find the information you requested, click the New button, then repeat Step 3 using a friend's name, your instructor's name, or a more common name. You could also click **Next** to view results from the next search service.

Searching for a Map

Map services on the Internet provide street maps for addresses you enter. Try searching for your own address. Once the map is located, you can "zoom in" or "zoom out" on the map to view more local detail or more of the surrounding area. Try finding a map of your home or other location.

To locate a map:

1. Click the **New** button on the Search Explorer bar.

2. Click the **Find a map** option button.

3. Enter your address, city, state, and zip code in the appropriate boxes.

4. Click the **Search** button. The map appears in the Internet Explorer window. See Figure 6-27.

   TROUBLE? If the address you tried does not yield a map, try a different address, or try the one shown in Figure 6-27.

Figure 6-27	LOCATING A MAP

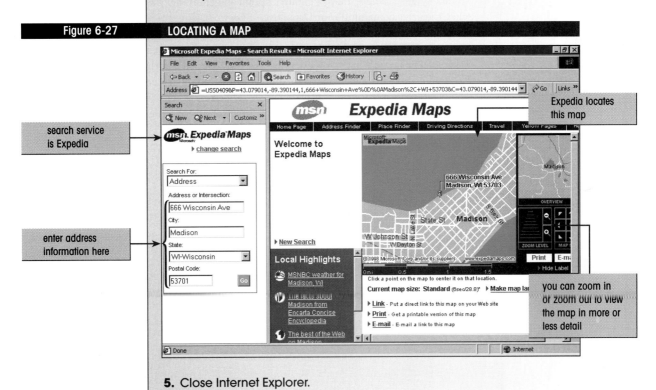

search service is Expedia

enter address information here

Expedia locates this map

you can zoom in or zoom out to view the map in more or less detail

5. Close Internet Explorer.

You're confident that you can use Windows 2000 and the search services it makes available to find just about any information Carolyn needs.

Session 6.2 QUICK CHECK

1. What kind of software searches through Internet documents and compiles a list of Web pages it locates on the Internet?

2. True or False: If you don't find the information you want using Yahoo!, you probably won't find the same information using InfoSeek.

3. What is the difference between a query search and a subject search?

4. If you are using Infoseek and you want information on the dog Toto in *The Wizard of Oz*, but you don't want any pages on the rock band Toto, what search operators can you use?

5. How can you use Windows 2000 to find an e-mail address for your state's governor?

REVIEW ASSIGNMENTS

1. **Using a Search String to Find a File** The governor has asked Senator Bernstein to represent the state in meetings with representatives of Taiwan, to set up a student exchange program. In any international exchange, language is an issue. You remember a funny story about the translation of an ad for Coca-Cola into another language. Might that anecdote be on the quotations archive disk?

   a. To find out, use the For Files or Folders option and enter likely search strings. Make sure you select the drive containing your Data Disk. If you're having trouble locating a file, try using just part of the search string or a different search string.

   b. Once you find a file you think looks promising, open it from the Search Results window.

   c. When you've found what you want, select the text, copy it, and then paste it into a new Notepad document. Type your name in the document you just created. At the end of the document, write a few sentences listing the search string you used and the name of the file(s) you located. Print the document, and then close Notepad and the Search Results window. Don't save the Notepad document.

2. **Learning More About Files** On a sheet of paper, write the answers to the following questions about the files on the Data Disk. You can answer all the questions by examining the filenames.

    a. How many files are there with the search string "comedy" in the filename?

    b. How many files and folders in total are on the disk? What did you do to find the answer? (*Hint*: You can find the answer to this question with a single search.)

    c. Which letters of the alphabet are missing in the filenames of the alphabetically organized Author files?

    d. How many files are there on friendship? What search string did you use to find this answer?

3. **Using Wildcards** What search strings could you use to produce the following results? Write the search strings on a piece of paper. Use a wildcard for each one. For example, a results list of Budget2000.xls, Budget2001.xls, and Budget2002.xls could come from the search string "Budget200?.xls".

    a. Comedy1.doc, Comedy2.doc, Comedy3.doc

    b. Social.txt, Society.txt, Socratic Method.txt

    c. PhotoWorks, Network, Files for Work

4. **Searching for Files by Date** You can answer these questions about the Data Disk by using the Date option. Write the answers on a sheet of paper. Return all settings to their defaults when you are done.

    a. How many files did Carolyn's previous aide modify in 1999?

    b. How many files did the aide modify in August, 1999?

    c. Which file(s) did the aide modify on August 31, 1999?

5. **Locating Files by Size** How many files of 1 KB or less are on the Data Disk? How many files of 15 KB or more? Return this setting to its default when you are done.

6. **Locating Files by Contents** You enjoy Dave Barry's columns. Search the contents of the files on the Data Disk to see how many of them contain the text string "barry", and then record that number. Write down the name of the file that seems to contain the most Dave Barry quotations. Open the file from Search. When you are done, delete the criteria you entered.

7. **Experimenting with Search Criteria** You decide to search for appropriate quotations for Senator Bernstein's upcoming speech topics. For each speech topic, write down the criteria you used to locate a file, and then write down the file location as displayed in the In Folder column of the results list. If you find more than one file, write down the first one in the list.

    a. Senator Bernstein has been invited to give the toast at a football brunch hosted by the president of Riverside College.

    b. The family of a deceased friend has asked Senator Bernstein if she'd like to contribute any thoughts to a written memorial.

    c. Senator Bernstein is cochairing this year's Renaissance Festival downtown. The Festival will feature outdoor performances of three of Shakespeare's plays, including a performance by the Young Shakespearians Guild, a troupe of children under age 18. She's promised to give the opening remarks at the Festival.

8. **Opening Files from Search** You learned how to open a text document from Search in this tutorial. You can open other types of files the same way, as long as your computer contains the program that created the file.

   a. Search for Sound Clip files on your Data Disk. Right-click one of them and then click Play. What did you hear? Click the Close button when the sound file is done playing. If you don't hear anything, your computer might not have speakers, or they might be off.

   b. Search for Video Clip files on your computer's hard drive. If you find any, right-click one of them, and then click the Play button. Describe what you see. Click the Close button when the video clip is done playing.

Explore 9. **Searching and Viewing File Contents** Find the answers to the questions below. You will probably need to search for a text string in the file's contents. For each answer, write the name of the file you used to find the answer. (*Hint*: Once you've located and opened the file, you can either scroll through it to find the answer, or open it in Notepad, click Edit on the Notepad menu bar, and then click Find. Type the text string in the Find what box, and then click the Find Next button.)

   a. What did Elsa Einstein think about her husband Albert's theory of relativity?
   b. Do you think cartoonist Jim Borgman is an optimist or a pessimist? Why?
   c. What was Helen Keller's opinion of college?
   d. How many children did Erma Bombeck recommend that one have? (Look carefully at the filenames in the results list so you don't open more files than necessary.)
   e. What did Elbert Hubbard have to say about books? (Look carefully at the filenames in the results list so you don't open more files than necessary.)

Explore 10. **Locating Information on the Internet** Carolyn asks that you help locate information on Taiwan for Senator Bernstein's upcoming participation in establishing a student exchange program.

   a. Use the Yahoo! search service subject guide to locate information on transportation in Taiwan. Write down the subject guide links you navigated to locate information. (*Hint*: Start with Regional.)
   b. Write down the URL of a page on transportation in Taiwan.
   c. Locate a Web page for one of Taiwan's universities. Write down the name of the university and the URL of its Web page.

11. **Locating People** Use three different people search services to locate the e-mail address of the president of your university. Were you able to find it in any of them? Did the search services have e-mail addresses for other people with the same name?

12. **Locating a Map** Locate and then print a map of your home address.

PROJECTS

1. On which drive is your Windows folder? Open the Search window, specify My Computer in the Look in list, and then search for "Windows." Write the answer on a piece of paper. If there are too many files in the results list, sort the files by name so that folders named "Windows" appear near the top.

2. Can you locate the e-mail address of the president of the United States? (*Hint*: The e-mail address will end with ".gov" because the president works for the government.)

3. Specify the following search strings, and, searching your Data Disk, examine the results list for each search string very carefully. What generalizations about wildcards can you make from your observations?

   men

   men.*

   men.

   men*.*

   men?

   men?.*

4. You can use Search to learn about the files on your hard drive. Record how many files of each of the following types exist on your hard drive.
   a. Application. Write down the names of five application files in the Windows folder of your hard drive.
   b. Bitmap Image. Which folders on your hard drive seem to store the most bitmapped images?
   c. Screen Saver. Write down the locations of some of the screen savers on your hard drive.
   d. Text Document. Once the results list shows all the text documents on your hard drive, order them by Name. Are there any files named README? Write down the locations of two of them. Software programs often come with a README text file that lists known software problems and answers to common questions.

5. Write down the names of 10 documents recently accessed on the hard disk.

Explore

6. You can use the Search Explorer bar to locate computers on a network. If you are on a network, open the Search Explorer bar and scroll to the bottom. Click Computers. Your instructor will give you the name of a computer for which to search on your network. Enter this name in the Computer Name box, and then click the Search Now button. Once Search has located the computer, open it from the results list. Make a hard copy of the window that opens and submit it to your instructor (use the PrintScreen key as shown in Tutorial 3 to create the hard copy).

7. Use the Internet search tools to find information on the city where you live, such as a Chamber of Commerce page or a local news service page. Print the first page of the information you located, and write the URL on the page.

QUICK CHECK ANSWERS

Session 6.1

1. Click the Look in list arrow, and then click 3½ Floppy (A:).
2. False
3. A wildcard is a symbol that stands in place of one or more characters. The asterisk wildcard substitutes for any number of characters; the question mark substitutes for only one.
4. Click the Name button in Details view.
5. Click Search Options (if necessary), select the Type check box, click the Type list arrow, click Bitmap Image, and then click Search Now.
6. Right-click it, and then click Open.
7. Click Format, and then click Word Wrap.

Session 6.2

1. search engine
2. False
3. A query search allows you to search by keyword. In a subject search, you search through predefined categories of information.
4. +Toto+Oz
5. Use the Find a person's address option.

New Perspectives on

MICROSOFT®

WINDOWS® 2000

PROFESSIONAL

Read This Before You Begin

To the Student

Data Disks

To complete the Level III Tutorials, Review Assignments, and Case Problems in this book, you need three Data Disks. Your instructor will either provide you with the Data Disks or ask you to make your own.

If you are making your own Data Disks, you will need three blank, formatted high-density disks. You will need to copy a set of folders from a file server or standalone computer or the Web onto your disks. Your instructor will tell you which computer, drive letter, and folders contain the files you need. You could also download the files by going to www.course.com, clicking Data Disk Files, and following the instructions on the screen.

The following list shows you which folders go on your disks, so that you will have enough disk space to complete all the Tutorials, Review Assignments, and Case Problems:

Data Disk 1

Write this on the disk label:
Data Disk 1: Level I Tutorial 1

No Data Files needed to begin.

Data Disk 2

Write this on the disk label:
Data Disk 2: Level I Tutorial 2

Put these folders on the disk:
The final contents of Data Disk 1

Data Disk 3

Write this on the disk label:
Data Disk 3: Level I Review Assignments and Case Problems

Put these folders on the disk:
No Data Files needed to begin.

When you begin each tutorial, be sure you are using the correct Data Disk. See the inside front or inside back cover of this book for more information on Data Disk files, or ask your instructor or technical support person for assistance.

Using Your Own Computer

If you are going to work through this book using your own computer, you need:

■ **Computer System** Microsoft Windows 2000 must be installed on a local hard drive or on a network drive.

■ **Data Disk** You will not be able to complete the tutorials or exercises in this book using your own computer until you have a Data Disk.

■ **Course Lab** See your instructor or technical support person to obtain the Course Lab software for use on your own computer.

Course Lab

The Level I tutorials in this book feature three interactive Course Labs to help you understand Using a Keyboard, Using a Mouse, and Using Files. There are Lab Assignments at the end of Tutorials 1 and 2 that relate to these Labs.

To start a Lab, click the **Start** button on the Windows taskbar, point to **Programs**, point to **Course Labs**, point to **New Perspectives Applications**, and click the appropriate lab.

Visit Our World Wide Web Site

Additional materials designed especially for you are available on the World Wide Web. Go to http://www.course.com.

To the Instructor

The Data Files and labs are available in the Instructor's Resource Kit for this title. Follow the instructions in the Help file on the CD-ROM to install the programs to your network or standalone computer. For information on creating the Data Disk, see the "To the Student" section above.

You are granted a license to copy the Data Files and labs to any computer or computer network used by students who have purchased this book.

In this tutorial you will:

- Start Paint and explore the Paint window

- Open a graphic in Paint

- Crop and edit a graphic

- Save a graphic in a different bitmapped graphic format

- Draw with a variety of drawing tools, including the Pencil, Brush, Airbrush, Line, and Ellipse tools

- Magnify and edit a graphic, viewing the grid and a thumbnail

- Copy and paste portions of a graphic

- Flip and stretch a graphic

- Add color to an existing graphic, and draw portions of a graphic in color

- Add and format text in a graphic

WORKING WITH GRAPHICS

Creating Advertisement Graphics at Kiana Ski Shop

CASE

Kiana Ski Shop

Cross-country ski enthusiast Joe Nitka owns Kiana Ski Shop in the heart of the northern Wisconsin Chequamegon National Forest, near the site of the world-class Birkebeiner cross-country ski race. Joe is one of the local promoters of the race. He gathers and releases information on lodging and transportation for competitors, the media, and spectators. So far Joe has simply been typing this information in a word processor, without adding graphics or color. An avid cross-country skier yourself, you volunteer to help Joe create his Birkebeiner promotions, to make them look more professional. You tell him his promotions would capture more attention if they included a few graphics, such as a skier or a picture of the race logo.

Joe agrees and says he could photocopy some drawings from a clip-art collection of images and pictures at the library. You tell him there are advantages to using a computer instead: computer graphics can be resized more easily, pasted seamlessly into a word-processed document, and edited. You think you can find some eye-catching graphic images on the Internet that you can customize, or you could even create a graphic or two from scratch. Joe is interested, and explains that his first priority is the announcement that he'll send to local motel and hotel owners, asking if they'd like to advertise their services in his promotions.

You spend a little time on the Internet before Joe arrives, and you find a graphic file called Sports, which includes several sports-related images. When Joe arrives, you explain that if you decide to use computer graphics, you'll need to make sure they are not copyrighted. Only graphics that are in the public domain may be downloaded and used freely.

SESSION 7.1

In this session, you will open a graphic in the Windows 2000 graphics program, Paint. You will crop a portion of the graphic and save it in a new file, then edit the graphic to meet your needs and save it in monochrome and color bitmapped graphic formats. For this tutorial you will need a blank 3½-inch disk.

Preparing Your Data Disks

Before you can begin working, you need to bring a blank 3½-inch disk to the computer lab and use the NP on Microsoft Windows 2000 menu to create a Data Disk containing the files you will work with in this tutorial. If you are using your own computer, the NP on Microsoft Windows 2000 menu will not be available. Once you have made the disk at the computer lab, however, you can use the disk to complete this tutorial on any computer that runs Windows 2000. Before you proceed, refer to the Read This Before You Begin page for instructions on obtaining the necessary files for your Data Disk.

To make your Data Disk:

1. Write "Disk 5—Windows 2000 Tutorial 7 Data Disk" on the label of a blank, formatted 3½-inch floppy disk. Insert your Data Disk into drive A.

   TROUBLE? If your 3½-inch disk drive is B, place your formatted disk in that drive instead, and for the rest of this tutorial substitute drive B wherever you see drive A.

2. Point to the **Start** button ⊞Start , point to **Programs**, point to **NP on Microsoft Windows 2000-Level III**, and then click **Disk 5 (Tutorial 7)**. When you are prompted to insert your disk in the drive, click the **OK** button, and wait as the files you need are copied to your Data Disk.

3. Close all the open windows on your screen.

Working with Paint

Drawings and pictures on a computer are called **graphic images** or **graphics**. Some graphics are created using a **scanner**, which converts an existing paper image into an electronic file that you can open and work with on your computer. You can also use a digital camera to create graphics from pictures you take. You can also create a graphic from scratch by using a **graphics program**, software that includes drawing and graphic editing tools. Windows 2000 includes a basic graphics program called **Paint**, which lets you create, edit, and manipulate graphics. Graphics come in two fundamental types: bitmapped and vector. A **bitmapped graphic** is made up of small dots that form an image, whereas a **vector graphic** is created by mathematical formulas that define the shapes used in the image. Computer graphics can come in either graphic type, although vector graphics are more precise because of their mathematical nature. Many software packages come with collections of graphics called **clip art**. Clip-art images are usually in vector format because this allows them to be more easily manipulated. Paint, however, does not handle vector graphic formats. Because the Sports graphic you found is a bitmapped graphic, for Joe's purpose Paint will work fine. In this session you'll work with an existing graphic, and in Session 7.2 you'll create one from scratch.

You decide to start Paint and introduce Joe to the Windows 2000 graphics tools.

To start Paint:

1. Click the **Start** button [Start].

2. Point to **Programs** and then point to **Accessories**. The Accessories menu opens.

3. Click **Paint**. The Paint window opens. See Figure 7-1.

TROUBLE? If you can't see the entire window, resize it until you can, or maximize it.

Figure 7-1	PAINT WINDOW

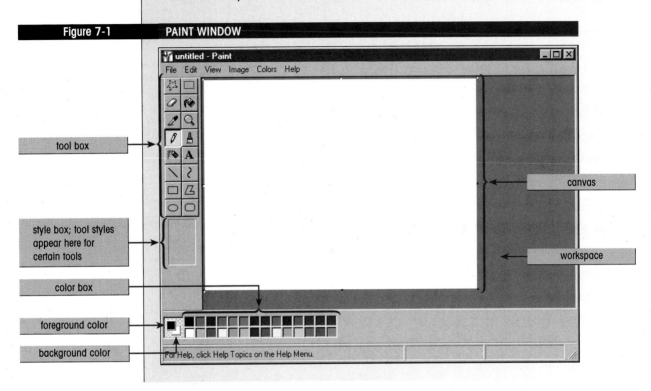

Within the Paint window is a blank white area like an artist's canvas, where you work with your graphic. At the bottom of the window is the color box, which displays available colors or shades for the foreground and background of your graphic. To the left of the color box are two additional overlapping boxes, the top for the foreground color and the bottom for the background color of any object you might draw. The status bar at the bottom of the window provides information about the tools you select and about the location of the pointer when it's in the canvas.

To the left of the canvas is the **tool box**, a collection of tools that you use to draw and edit graphics. The tools all work the same way: you click a tool, the pointer changes to a shape representing the tool, and then you either click or drag on the canvas to draw with the tool. Some of the tools offer different widths or shapes, which are depicted in a style box that appears below the tool box, as you'll see in Session 7.2.

Figure 7-2 shows the available tools, along with the pointer shape that appears when you use the tool.

You'll work with some of the editing tools in this session, with the drawing tools in Session 7.2, and with the color and text tools in Session 7.3.

Figure 7-2	PAINT TOOLS		
TOOL	**BUTTON**	**DESCRIPTION**	**POINTER**
Free-Form Select		Select a free-form portion of a graphic	
Select		Select a rectangular portion of a graphic	
Eraser/Color Eraser		Erase a portion of a graphic	
Fill With Color		Fill an enclosed area with the current color	
Pick Color		Pick up an existing color in the graphic	
Magnifier		Change the magnification	
Pencil		Draw a free-form line or draw one pixel at a time	
Brush		Draw using a brush in a variety of widths	
Airbrush		Draw using an airbrush in a variety of widths	
Text		Insert text into a graphic	
Line		Draw a line	
Curve		Draw a curve	
Rectangle		Draw a rectangle or square	
Polygon		Draw a polygon	
Ellipse		Draw an ellipse or circle	
Rounded Rectangle		Draw a rectangle or square with rounded corners	

Opening a Graphic in Paint

Joe wants to take a look at the Sports graphic to see if there is anything that might work for his announcement. To open an existing graphic in Paint, you use the Open command on the File menu. The Sports graphic is located on your Data Disk.

To open the Sports graphic:

1. Click **File** and then click **Open**.

2. Click the **Look in** list arrow and then click the drive containing your Data Disk.

3. Click **Sports** and then click the **Open** button.

   TROUBLE? If Sports appears as Sports.bmp, your computer is set to display file extensions as part of the filename (this is fine). Click Sports.bmp, click Open, and then continue with Step 4.

4. If necessary, scroll to the bottom of the graphic and to the right side. See Figure 7-3. The Sports graphic contains a number of sporting figures.

   TROUBLE? If you can't see the entire graphic image, resize the Paint window as necessary.

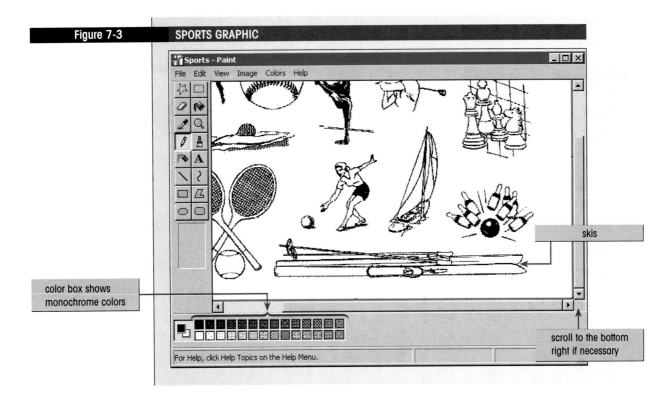

Figure 7-3 **SPORTS GRAPHIC**

color box shows monochrome colors

skis

scroll to the bottom right if necessary

Note the color box at the bottom of the Paint window. It no longer offers the array of colors shown in Figure 7-1. You tell Joe that the Sports graphic is a monochrome graphic, that is, a graphic with only two colors—black and white—available to it. Notice that the color box includes only black, white, and patterns of black and white that give the illusion of gray shading.

Cropping a Portion of a Graphic

Looking over the graphic, Joe notices the pair of skis at the bottom. He thinks that the skis alone would look great at the bottom of the announcement. You tell Joe you can capture just that portion of the graphic by **cropping**, or cutting out, everything around it. To crop a graphic, you use either the Select tool or the Free-Form Select tool. With the **Select tool**, you draw a rectangle, called a selection box, around the area you want to crop. With the **Free-Form Select tool**, you draw any shaped line around the area. Once you have selected the portion of the graphic you need, you can manipulate it. In this case, you want to save the selection to a separate file. The separate file will contain only the cropped area—in Joe's case, the pair of skis.

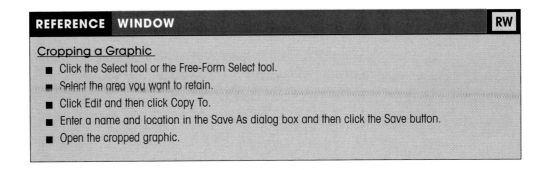

REFERENCE WINDOW   **RW**

Cropping a Graphic
- Click the Select tool or the Free-Form Select tool.
- Select the area you want to retain.
- Click Edit and then click Copy To.
- Enter a name and location in the Save As dialog box and then click the Save button.
- Open the cropped graphic.

In this section, you'll use the Select tool because it's easier to manipulate than the Free-Form Select tool. However, because the sailboat and the bowling ball images are so close to the skis, when you crop you will inadvertently include portions of those graphics. Don't worry; in the next section you'll learn how to erase parts of a graphic that you don't want. In the Tutorial Assignments, you'll have an opportunity to use the Free-Form Select tool to avoid the extra step of erasing. You're ready to select the skis.

To select the skis:

1. Locate and click the **Select** button ▭ in the tool box.

2. Move the pointer over the canvas. The pointer looks like ┼.

3. Next, you need to drag a selection box around the pair of skis. To do this, point to the white space to the upper left of the skis. Press the left mouse button and hold it down while you drag to the lower-right corner of the skis. As you drag, a selection box appears. See Figure 7-4. You'll probably also select part of the sail boat and bowling ball; this is okay.

   TROUBLE? If you release the mouse button too early, or if your selection box doesn't include the entire pair of skis, click an area of the canvas outside the selection box and repeat Step 3.

| Figure 7-4 | SELECTING AN AREA TO CROP |

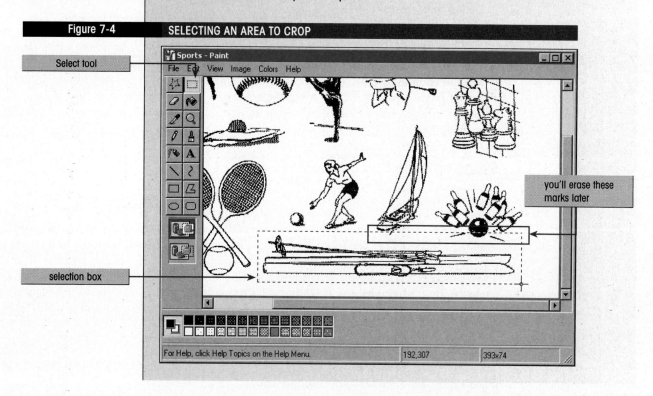

Select tool

you'll erase these marks later

selection box

Now that the skis are selected, you can use the Copy To command to save the selected area to a new file.

To save the selected area to a new file:

1. Click **Edit** and then click **Copy To**.

The Copy To dialog box opens.

TROUBLE? If the Copy To dialog box doesn't open, you probably clicked the Copy command instead of the Copy To command. Repeat Step 1.

2. Type **Skis** in the File name text box. Make sure that the Save in text box shows your Data Disk.

3. Click the **Save** button. The file is saved on your Data Disk with the filename "Skis".

The Sports graphic is still open in Paint, and the Skis graphic is in a separate file. In Paint, you can work with only one graphic file at a time. If you try to open another graphic or create a new graphic, Paint closes the current one, prompting you to save it if necessary. If you want two Paint graphics open at the same time, you must start a separate Paint session, so that there are actually two Paint windows open with one graphic in each. You don't need the Sports graphic for now, so you'll simply open the Skis graphic and let Paint close the Sports graphic.

To open the Skis graphic:

1. Click **File** and then click **Open**.

2. Click **Skis** and then click the **Open** button. If Paint asks if you want to save the changes to Sports, click the **No** button. The Skis graphic opens. See Figure 7-5.

| Figure 7-5 | SKIS IMAGE, CROPPED FROM THE SPORTS GRAPHIC FILE |

these marks need to be erased

canvas

canvas sizing handles

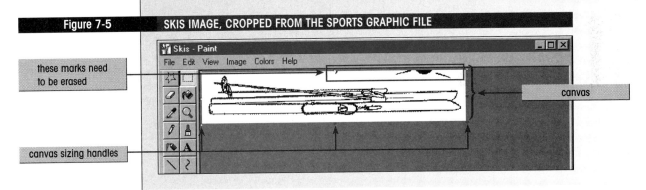

Notice that the canvas now takes up only a small portion of the Paint document window. The canvas sizing handles, the small boxes shown in Figure 7-5, allow you to resize the graphic if necessary.

Erasing Parts of a Graphic

Joe notices the portions of the sailboat and bowling ball graphics at the top of the Skis graphic. You tell him it's easy to erase unneeded portions of a graphic. You use the **Eraser/Color Eraser tool**, which erases the area over which you drag the pointer. If you erase more than you intended, you can use the **Undo** command on the Edit menu, which reverses one or more of your last three actions, depending on how many times you click Undo (up to three times).

To erase the portions of the graphic that you don't want:

1. Click the **Eraser/Color Eraser** tool ⬚. When you move the pointer over the graphic, it changes to a ☐ shape.

2. Drag the ☐ pointer over the areas at the top of the Skis graphic to erase them. As you drag, the unwanted black marks disappear. See Figure 7-6.

   TROUBLE? If the black marks aren't disappearing, make sure you press and hold the mouse button while you move the Eraser pointer over the black marks.

   TROUBLE? If you erase a portion of the graphic that you wanted to keep, click Edit, and then click Undo.

Figure 7-6   **ERASING UNWANTED MARKS**

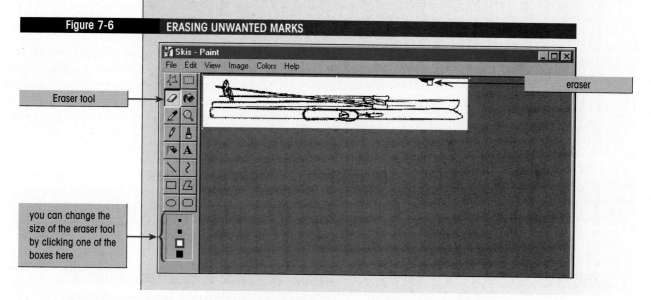

Eraser tool

eraser

you can change the size of the eraser tool by clicking one of the boxes here

Now the graphic looks just the way you want. You tell Joe that he can use a word processor to create his announcement and insert the graphic directly into the word-processed document. But that's a project for another day. You decide to save the Skis graphic.

To save the Skis graphic:

1. Click **File** and then click **Save**.

Joe would like to add color to the Skis graphic. You'll do this next.

Bitmapped Graphics

A computer screen is a gridwork of small dots of light called **pixels,** which is short for "picture elements." The pixels form images on the screen by displaying different colors (including black and white), much as a television set does. Buttons on the taskbar, for example, are formed by the pixels shown in Figure 7-7.

Figure 7-7	PIXELS

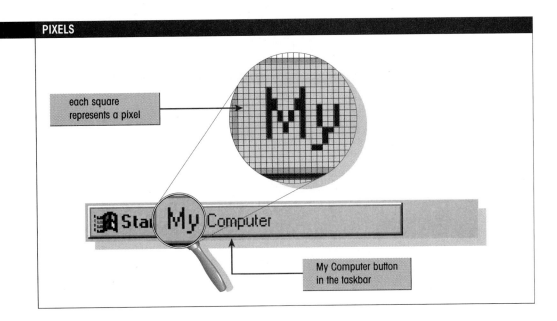

each square
represents a pixel

My Computer button
in the taskbar

Each pixel has a color, and the individual colored pixels form the graphics you see on
your screen. To understand how a graphic can be created from pixels, imagine a piece of
graph paper on which each square represents a pixel. To draw a straight line, you color in a
row of squares, or, to draw a circle you fill in the squares as best you can to approximate the
curve, as shown in Figure 7-8. In this drawing, every pixel within the circle's border is black,
and every pixel not in the circle is white. Your computer uses 0's and 1's as a code for the
color of each pixel. Each 0 or 1 is called a **bit**. To determine the color of each pixel in a
drawing that is only black and white, you need only one bit, because a bit can "take on" a
value of either 0 or 1—that is, it can be either off or on, either black or white.

Figure 7-8	BITS DETERMINE PIXEL COLOR

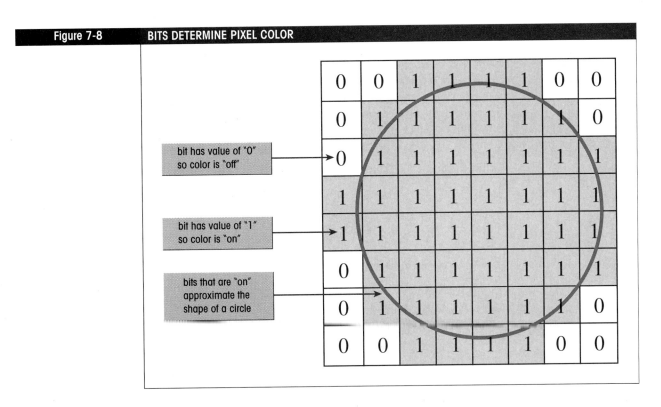

bit has value of "0"
so color is "off"

bit has value of "1"
so color is "on"

bits that are "on"
approximate the
shape of a circle

A 1-bit graphic, in which each pixel is described by a single bit, is also known as a **monochrome bitmap**. The Skis image is such a graphic. If your graphic contains more colors, the computer needs to use more bits for the code. For example, to code the colors black, white, blue, and red, you would need two bits—00 for black, 01 for white, 10 for red, and 11 for blue. There are four bitmap types available in Paint: 1-bit, 4-bit, 8-bit, and 24-bit. The more bits you use, the more colors that are available.

Your computer maps, or assigns, a color to each code, hence the term "bitmap." A sequence of four zeros, 0000, might mean "black"; a sequence of four ones, 1111, might mean "white." The sequence 1000 might mean "blue." With 4 bits there are 16 available colors, so in Paint a graphic that uses 4 bits is saved in the **16 Color Bitmap** file type. The other file types are Monochrome Bitmap, **256 Color Bitmap**, and **24-bit Bitmap**. The 256 Color Bitmap type uses sequences of 8 bits to represent 256 colors. Similarly, the 24-bit Bitmap type uses sequences of 24 bits to represent 16.7 million colors—useful for working with color photos. Figure 7-9 summarizes the bitmap file types that Paint allows, the number of bits per pixel, the number of distinct colors each type can display, and the size of a file that starts out as a 4-KB monochrome bitmap and then is saved in each type.

Figure 7-9	PAINT FILE FORMATS		
FILE TYPE	**NUMBER OF BITS**	**NUMBER OF COLORS**	**SAMPLE FILE SIZE**
Monochrome	1	2	4 KB
16 Color Bitmap	4	16	13 KB
256 Color Bitmap	8	256	27 KB
24-bit Bitmap	24	16.7 million	77 KB

Note that as the number of bits increases, so does the number of available colors. This increases the size of the file. Therefore, you might not want to select a bitmap type with more colors than you need. For a simple black-and-white graphic, monochrome is the best choice.

By default, Paint stores its graphics with the .bmp file extension—the standard Windows 2000 file format for bitmapped graphics. However, if you have Microsoft Office installed, you can also choose to save your file as GIF or JPEG images. These two image types are often used for graphics placed on Web pages. If you want Paint to work with graphics that have other file extensions, or if you do not have Microsoft Office, you need to use a software program called a graphics converter to change the file to a format that Paint can work with.

Resizing Bitmapped Graphics

Joe comments that he's heard people complain about how bitmapped graphics can look rough around the edges. You agree. If the bitmapped graphic is sized correctly it looks fine, but if you try to resize it you might have problems. A bitmapped graphic is defined by pixels, but you can't change the size of an individual pixel. When you try to enlarge a bitmapped graphic, Paint duplicates the pixels to approximate the original shape as best it can—often resulting in jagged edges. On the other hand, when you shrink a bitmapped graphic, Paint removes pixels, and the drawing loses detail. In either case, you distort the original graphic. Sometimes the resized bitmapped graphic will look fine, as when there are many straight lines, but just as often the resized graphic's image quality suffers. For example, if you were to enlarge the Skis graphic, the result might look like Figure 7-10.

How do you get around this problem? In Paint, there is no easy solution to resizing graphics, because they are all bitmapped. If your work with graphics requires resizing—for example, if you want a graphic that will look good on a small business card and a large poster—vector graphics are a better choice. Because vector graphics are mathematically based, you can resize them as necessary without sacrificing image quality. You will need to buy a graphics program that allows you to work with vector graphics, however.

| Figure 7-10 | SKIS GRAPHIC AS IT LOOKS WHEN ENLARGED |

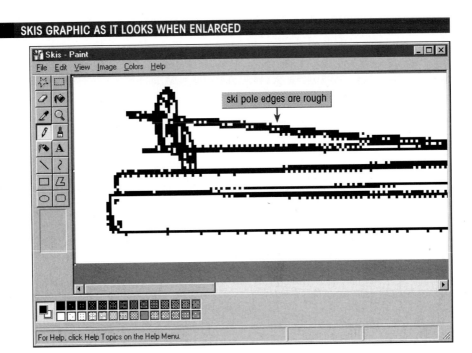

Saving a Bitmapped Graphic

Joe decides he would like you to save the Skis graphic in a color file type so he can experiment later with adding color.

When you save a graphic in a different file type in Paint, the graphic's appearance doesn't change. The pixels that were black stay black, and those that were white stay white. However, the number of bits that defines each color changes, and so the file changes in size. When you are ready to color the graphic, you'll find a new set of colors available to you. Instead of the black, white, and pattern boxes that you see now in the color box, you will see colors. You decide to save the Skis graphic as a 256 Color Bitmap, because this format provides a wide array of colors but doesn't take up as much space as the 24-bit Bitmap format.

To save the graphic file as a 256 Color Bitmap:

1. Click **File** and then click **Save As**.

2. Click the **Save as type** list arrow, and then click **256 Color Bitmap**.

3. Type **Skis256** in the File name box.

4. Make sure the Save in list box specifies your Data Disk.

5. Click the **Save** button.

The monochrome graphic closes. Paint now offers an array of colors in the color box. You decide to show Joe how the 256-color format affects the size of the graphics file.

To view the size of the graphics files:

1. Minimize the Paint window.

2. Open **My Computer**, open the **3½ Floppy (A:)** window, and then maximize the window.

3. Click **View** and then click **Details** to view file sizes and compare the relative sizes of the Skis graphic and the Skis256 graphic. The Skis256 graphic is much larger.

You tell Joe that if he wants to come back another time and add color to the Skis graphic, he can.

To finish the session:

1. Click the **Close** button ☒ to close the floppy drive window.

2. Right-click the **Skis256 - Paint** button on the taskbar, and then click **Close**.

3. Close any other open windows on the desktop.

Session 7.1 QUICK CHECK

1. Describe how you save a portion of a graphic to a separate file.

2. How do you resize the canvas?

3. True or False: You can open only one graphic in Paint at a time.

4. The small dots on your screen are called _____.

5. Why do color graphics use more file space than monochrome graphics?

6. If you have a graphic in a file format that Paint doesn't support, what can you do to open the file in Paint?

SESSION 7.2

In this session, you will learn to edit an existing graphic and draw new graphics with the collection of drawing tools in Paint. You'll use the Pencil, Line, Brush, and Ellipse tools, and you'll look at options for flipping, rotating, sizing, and stretching your graphics. You'll learn techniques that make drawing easier, such as controlling the magnification, editing one pixel at a time, using the grid and a thumbnail, and copying and pasting parts of a graphic.

Drawing with the Pencil Tool

Joe drops by a few days after your initial computer session with a problem: the Skis graphic isn't right for the Birkebeiner announcement because it shows a downhill ski, not a cross-country ski. The bindings for the two ski types are different, as shown in Figure 7-11.

Figure 7-11   PROBLEM WITH THE SKIS GRAPHIC

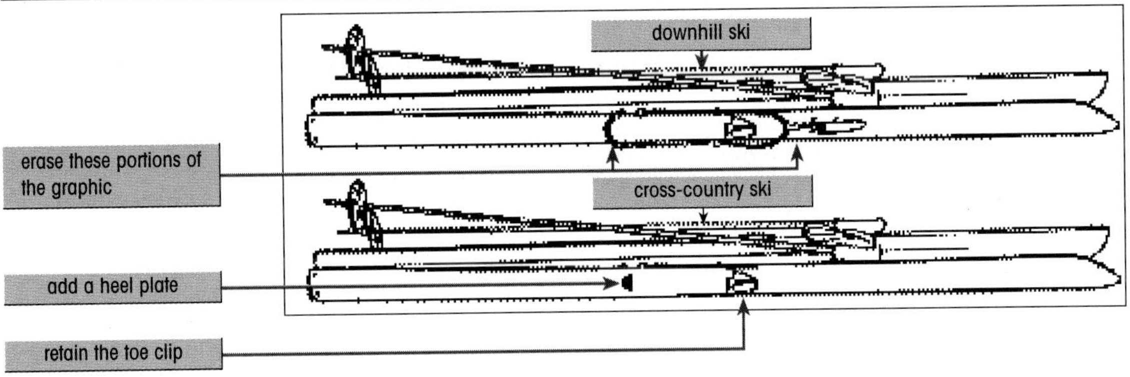

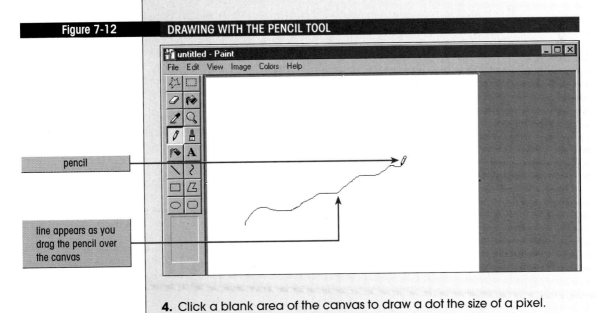

downhill ski

erase these portions of the graphic

cross-country ski

add a heel plate

retain the toe clip

You tell Joe you can fix this problem by erasing unwanted portions of the graphic and then using the Pencil tool to draw free-form dots or lines. Once you have selected the **Pencil tool**, you can click the canvas to draw pixel-size dots, or you can drag over the canvas to draw a line that is one pixel wide. You decide to show Joe these two methods of drawing with the Pencil tool before you fix the Skis graphic.

To experiment with the Pencil tool:

1. Make sure your Data Disk is in drive A, start Paint, and then maximize the Paint window. Paint opens to an empty canvas.

2. If necessary, click the **Pencil** tool 🖊, and then move the pointer onto the canvas. The pointer looks like a 🖊 shape.

3. Hold the mouse button down and drag 🖊 over the canvas. Your pointer draws a line as you drag it. See Figure 7-12. Practice drawing straight and curved lines with the Pencil tool until you feel comfortable with its operation.

Figure 7-12   DRAWING WITH THE PENCIL TOOL

untitled - Paint

File Edit View Image Colors Help

pencil

line appears as you drag the pencil over the canvas

4. Click a blank area of the canvas to draw a dot the size of a pixel.

Now that you've shown Joe how easy it is to draw lines or dots with the Pencil tool, you are ready to edit the Skis graphic. You first must erase the parts of the binding that are for downhill skis, and then you must add a heel plate for the cross-country ski binding.

Magnifying a Drawing

The changes you need to make to the Skis graphic require careful erasing and redrawing—a task made easier when the view is magnified. The **Magnifier tool** allows you to view a graphic at a number of different magnification levels. The default magnification is 100%, also called **Normal view**. If you click the Magnifier tool and then click the graphic, Paint displays it at 400%. You can select a different magnification using the box that appears below the tool box when you click : 1x (Normal view), 2x (200% magnification), 6x (600% magnification), and 8x (800% magnification). The **Custom Zoom dialog box** (which you open by clicking View, then Zoom, and then Custom) adds the 400% zoom option. Increasing the magnification is called **zooming in**.

If you are magnifying the view to edit a few pixels at a time, you can use the grid to help you navigate. The **grid** is a checkerboard background similar to a piece of graph paper, on which each square represents a pixel. The grid guides your drawing so your lines are straight and your shapes are precise.

REFERENCE WINDOW   **RW**

Magnifying a Graphic

- To zoom in, click the Magnifier tool, and then click the graphic to zoom to the default magnification of 400%, or click one of the magnifications in the box below the tool box.
- To view gridlines, switch to a magnified view, click View, point to Zoom, and then click Show Grid.
- To view a portion of the magnified graphic in Normal view, switch to a magnified view, click View, point to Zoom, and then click Show Thumbnail.

You decide to work with the monochrome Skis graphic because Joe's Birkebeiner announcement will be in black and white, not color. You need to open the Skis graphic, zoom in to the highest magnification, and then show the grid so you can more easily edit the graphic. So that your Skis graphic will match the one shown in the figures, you'll open a copy of the graphic, stored on your Data Disk as Skis2, and save it with the name Skis, replacing the original graphic.

To change the view for editing:

1. Click **File**, click **Open**, and then locate and open the **Skis2** file on your Data Disk. Click **No** when you are prompted to save changes to the untitled graphic you were just working with.

2. Click **File** and then click **Save As**. Make sure the Save in box displays the drive containing your Data Disk and that the Save as type box shows Monochrome Bitmap. Enter **Skis** in the File name box, and then click the **Save** button. Click **Yes** when you are asked whether you want to replace the existing file.

3. Click the **Magnifier** tool and move the pointer over the canvas. The pointer changes to , and a box appears that shows the portion of the graphic Paint will magnify.

4. Click the far-left side of the graphic to zoom in on that portion of the picture. The default 400% magnification is used.

5. Click **View**, point to **Zoom**, and then click **Show Grid**. You can see the individual pixels. See Figure 7-13. The boxes are too small to work with easily, so you decide to use the Custom dialog box to zoom in even more.

TROUBLE? If your graphic shows a different portion of the skis, scroll all the way to the left. Resize your paint window as necessary to view the same portion as in Figure 7-13.

| Figure 7-13 | MAGNIFIED VIEW WITH GRID SHOWING |

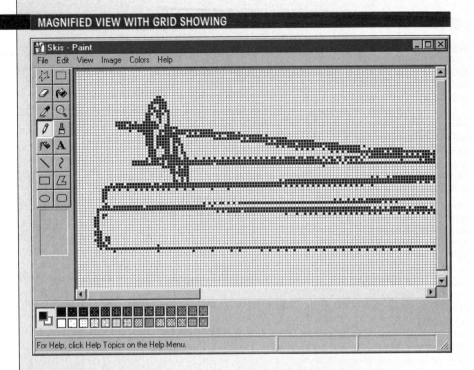

6. Click **View**, point to **Zoom**, and then click **Custom**. The Custom Zoom dialog box opens. See Figure 7-14.

| Figure 7-14 | CHOOSING A DIFFERENT MAGNIFICATION |

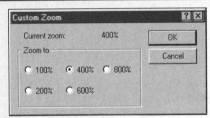

7. Click the **800%** option button and then click the **OK** button. Now the boxes are larger and you'll have no problem editing individual pixels.

When you're zoomed in this closely, you sometimes lose sight of the picture's appearance. You can view a thumbnail, a small box that shows in Normal view the area you're zooming in on. Thumbnails are especially handy for editing. You decide to view a thumbnail of the area you're working on.

To view a thumbnail:

1. Click **View** and then point to **Zoom**.

TROUBLE? If the thumbnail already appears, skip Steps 1 and 2.

2. Click **Show Thumbnail**. A thumbnail of the area you're examining appears on the Paint window. See Figure 7-15.

TROUBLE? If the thumbnail appears in a different area of the Paint window and it obscures an area you want to examine, drag it out of the way.

Figure 7-15	VIEWING A THUMBNAIL OF THE MAGNIFIED AREA

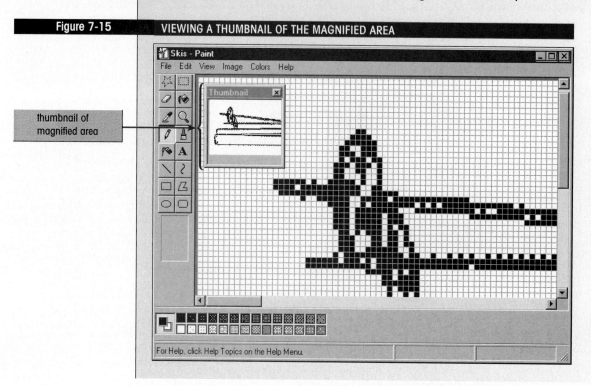

thumbnail of magnified area

With the grid on, you can see each pixel, and you are viewing a thumbnail so you can see how your changes affect the larger picture. You're ready to start editing.

Erasing in a Magnified View

Once you are zoomed in, you can erase unwanted portions of the graphic a few pixels at a time. You need to erase the portions of the binding that are for downhill skis. To erase, you drag the Eraser tool over the appropriate pixels. The Eraser tool comes in several different sizes; select the size according to the number of pixels you need to erase. The largest size lets you erase large sections of a graphic in 10 x 10 boxes (100 pixels at a time). The smallest size lets you erase in 4 x 4 boxes (16 pixels at a time). There is no way to erase one pixel at a time using the Eraser tool. You can, however, use the Pencil tool to accomplish the same purpose: choose white as your drawing color, and then any pixel you click will turn white.

To erase the parts of the ski binding you don't need:

1. Scroll until you see the binding. Watch the thumbnail to see where the binding is located and then click the **Eraser** tool.

TROUBLE? If the thumbnail is in the way, drag it to the lower-right corner of the screen. Resize the window as necessary.

2. Click the **smallest box** in the Eraser tool styles box. See Figure 7-16.

Figure 7-16   **SELECTING THE SMALLEST SIZE OF THE ERASER TOOL**

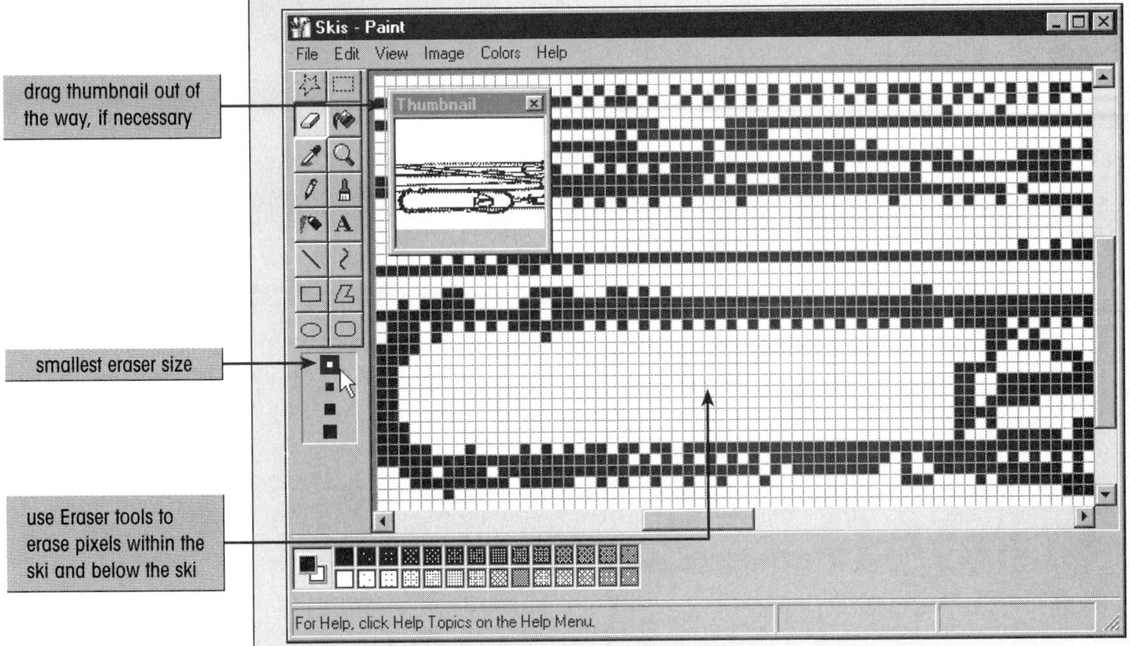

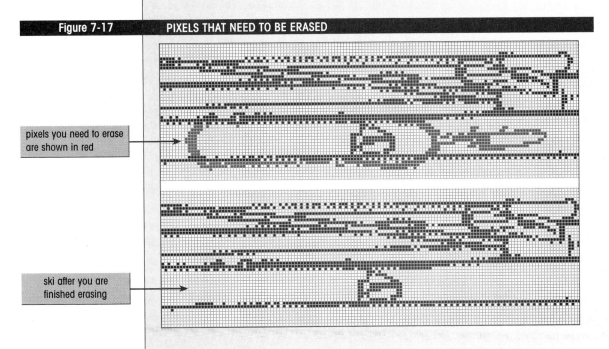

drag thumbnail out of
the way, if necessary

smallest eraser size

use Eraser tools to
erase pixels within the
ski and below the ski

3. Drag the **Eraser** tool 🖉 over the pixels inside the ski and below the ski, as shown in Figure 7-17. Scroll as necessary to complete the erasures. The pixels that you should erase are shown in red in Figure 7-17.

   TROUBLE? If you erased an area you didn't want to erase, click Edit, and then click Undo. If you need to start over, do so without saving your changes.

Figure 7-17   **PIXELS THAT NEED TO BE ERASED**

pixels you need to erase
are shown in red

ski after you are
finished erasing

4. Click the **Magnifier** tool 🔍 and then click 1x to return to Normal view. The grid and thumbnail are both hidden.

In Normal view you can see how your erasures have changed the look of the ski. It looks good.

Drawing in a Magnified View

You are now ready to draw the heel plate, which has a trapezoidal shape. You'll use the Pencil tool to draw it a few pixels at a time.

You've already seen how to use the thumbnail to "locate" yourself in the Paint window. Paint offers one other feature to help you control your location as you draw. The **pixel coordinates** in the status bar specify the exact location of the pointer on the canvas relative to the pixels on your screen. Paint displays the pixel coordinates in an (x,y) format (x representing the horizontal location and y the vertical location). Pixel coordinates of 138,25, for example, indicate that the pointer is 138 pixels from the left edge of the screen and 25 pixels from the top. The next set of steps uses pixel coordinates to help you add the heel plate in just the right location.

You'll use the Magnifier tool to zoom back in, this time to only 600%, because the work isn't as meticulous. A lower magnification lets you view a little more of your graphic.

To create the heel plate:

1. Click 🔍, and then click the **6x** magnification option in the box below the tool box.

2. Scroll to the binding area of the ski.

3. Click the **Pencil** tool ✏, and then position the pointer at pixel coordinate **155,57**. See Figure 7-18 for the location of this pixel.

4. Click both the **155,57** pixel and the **155,58** pixel. Then drag to fill in the rest of the pixels shown in Figure 7-18. When your screen looks like Figure 7-18, view the skis in Normal view.

   TROUBLE? If you draw in an area you didn't intend to, click Edit, and then click Undo.

Figure 7-18	USING PIXEL COORDINATES TO DRAW THE HEEL PLATE

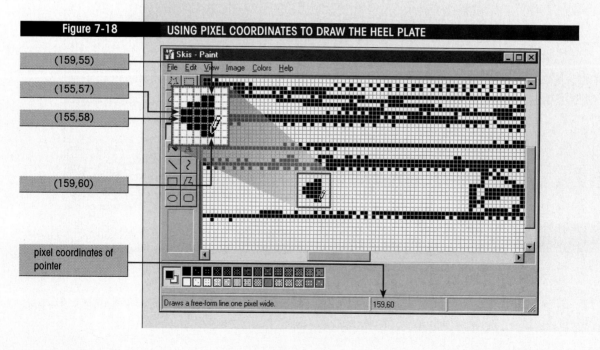

(159,55)

(155,57)

(155,58)

(159,60)

pixel coordinates of pointer

5. Click 🔍, and then click the **1x** magnification option in the style box. See Figure 7-19. Joe is satisfied with the skis, so you decide to save the file.

| Figure 7-19 | FINISHED SKI |

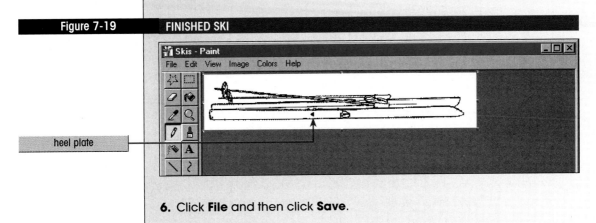

heel plate

6. Click **File** and then click **Save**.

Drawing with the Brush Tool

Joe asks about creating some new graphics that he could use for advertising Kiana Ski Shop. You have three choices for creating a new graphic. You can erase the contents of the canvas using the Eraser tool, and then save the file under a different filename; you can choose Clear Image from the Image menu to clear the canvas and then save the file under a different filename; or you can choose New from the File menu to open a new file. Since you've already saved the Skis graphic, each option will leave that file unchanged. You decide to use the third option.

To create a new file:

1. Click **File** and then click **New**. An empty canvas opens.

Joe sketches a few ideas, and you decide to draw the sketch in Figure 7-20.

| Figure 7-20 | IDEA FOR A KIANA GRAPHIC |

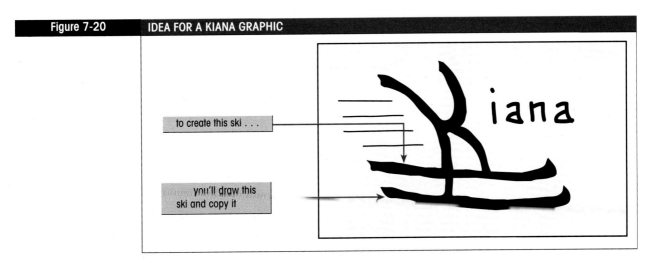

to create this ski . . .

you'll draw this ski and copy it

To create this graphic, you can use the **Brush tool**. Unlike the Pencil tool, the Brush tool offers a variety of widths and different brush styles to draw with. To create the skis, you can use an angular style brush. To create the letter "K" you can use a rounded brush. (You can add letters by typing rather than drawing by using the Text tool, which you'll learn to use in Session 7.3.) First you're going to show Joe how to use the Brush tool.

To draw with the Brush tool:

1. Click the **Brush** tool 🖌. Notice the brush styles in the style box. The current brush style is highlighted.

2. Drag the brush pointer over the canvas. A thick rounded line appears.

3. Now try a different brush style. Click the leftmost **angular line** brush style in the third row, as shown in Figure 7-21, and then drag the brush pointer over the screen. You create a line like the one in Figure 7-21.

| Figure 7-21 | BRUSH STYLES |

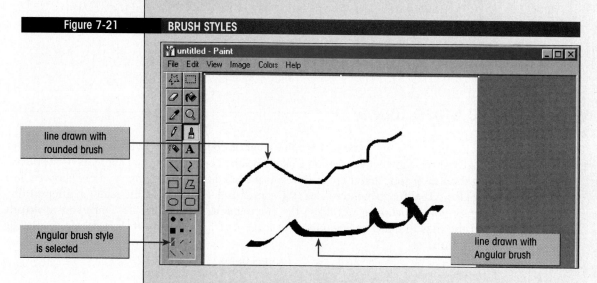

line drawn with rounded brush

Angular brush style is selected

line drawn with Angular brush

4. Drag the brush pointer around a little corner and then draw a straight horizontal line, as in Figure 7-22. Don't worry about being too accurate with this drawing because you're going to erase it shortly anyway.

| Figure 7-22 | DRAWING A SKI, USING THE ANGULAR BRUSH |

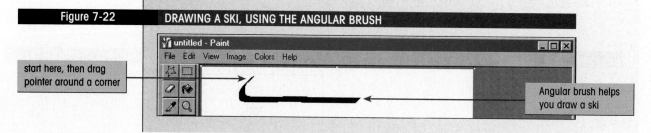

start here, then drag pointer around a corner

Angular brush helps you draw a ski

Now that you have an idea of how the brush tools work, you can clear the screen and try drawing the real ski. This time, rather than using the New command, you'll use the Image menu's Clear Image command, which erases the entire image all at once and lets you start over with an empty canvas.

To clear the graphic and then draw the ski:

1. Click **Image** and then click **Clear Image**. Your drawings disappear as the canvas is cleared.

2. Now try drawing the ski near the bottom of the canvas. This time try to make it look like the ski in Figure 7-22. Click **Undo** if you aren't satisfied, and try again.

TROUBLE? If you have a difficult time holding the mouse steady to draw the straight line, you could try controlling the pointer with the arrow keys rather than the mouse. Use the MouseKeys option available through the Accessibility Options dialog box in the Windows 2000 Control Panel. See Appendix B on the Control Panel for more information. You could also try drawing just one section of the ski at a time. Don't worry if it's not perfectly straight. You won't be saving this file and you'll be learning another technique for drawing straight lines later in this session.

Copying, Pasting, and Moving a Portion of a Graphic

Once you have drawn a satisfactory ski, you want to draw a second ski that has the same size and shape as the first ski. To ensure a consistent look, you can make a copy of the first ski and then paste it on the graphic as the second ski. To copy a portion of a graphic, you select it, and then you choose the Copy command on the Edit menu. Your selection is copied to the Clipboard. You can then use the Edit menu's Paste command to paste the copy into the graphic, where it "floats" in the upper-left corner of the canvas until you drag it to the desired location.

REFERENCE WINDOW **RW**

Copying, Cutting, and Pasting Graphics
- Click the Select or Free-Form Select tool.
- Drag a selection box around the area you want to copy or cut.
- Click Edit, and then click Copy or Cut.
- Click Paste. The selection appears in the upper-left corner of the canvas.
- Drag the selection to the new location, and then click outside the selection box to anchor the selection into place.

You are ready to copy the first ski, paste it, and then move it just above the existing ski. So that your drawing will match the one shown in the figures, you'll open a copy of the drawing of the ski, which is stored on your Data Disk in the Brush file. You'll then save this file with the name "Kiana."

To copy and paste the first ski and then position it:

1. Click **File**, click **Open**, and then locate and open the **Brush** file on your Data Disk. Click **No** if you are prompted to save changes to the untitled graphic you were just working with.

2. Click **File** and then click **Save As**. Make sure the Save in box displays the drive containing your Data Disk and that the Save as type box shows 256 Color Bitmap. Type **Kiana** in the File name box and then click the **Save** button.

3. Click the **Select** tool ▢.

4. Draw a selection box around the ski.

5. Click **Edit** and then click **Copy**. The ski is copied to the Clipboard.

6. Click **Edit** and then click **Paste**. The ski appears in the upper-left corner of the Paint window.

7. Place the pointer over the pasted ski. Make sure the pointer looks like ✛.

8. Drag the ski so that it is above and slightly to the right of the first ski. See Figure 7-23.

TROUBLE? If you want to reposition the second ski after you release the mouse button, repeat Steps 7 and 8.

TROUBLE? If the ski does not move when you drag it, but the selection box changes size, you might have pointed at a sizing handle. Click Edit, and then click Undo. Make sure that the pointer looks like ✛ before you start to drag. Then repeat Steps 7 and 8.

| Figure 7-23 | MOVING THE PASTED SKI |

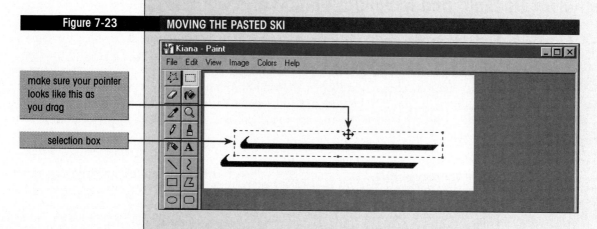

make sure your pointer looks like this as you drag

selection box

9. Once the pasted ski is positioned correctly, click a blank area of the canvas outside the selection box. The ski is anchored into place.

Flipping a Graphic

When you and Joe look at the skis, you decide you want them to point in the other direction. You can flip a graphic using the Flip/Rotate option on the Image menu. This option lets you reverse a graphic or rotate it by a specified number of degrees.

To flip the skis so they point in the other direction:

1. Click **Image** and then click **Flip/Rotate**. The Flip and Rotate dialog box opens. See Figure 7-24.

| Figure 7-24 | FLIP AND ROTATE DIALOG BOX |

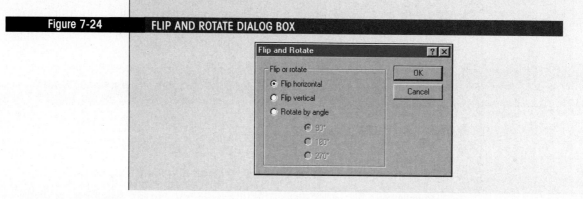

2. Click the **Flip horizontal** option button, if it isn't already selected. This tells Paint to flip the graphic horizontally.

3. Click the **OK** button. The skis now point in the other direction.

4. Click **File** and then click **Save** to save the graphic.

Now you're ready to create the letter "K." You think you can create the look you want by using the rounded brush style, which is in the first row of brush styles.

To create the letter K:

1. Click the **Brush** tool, and then click the **largest circle** in the top row of brush styles.

2. Draw the letter K so it looks like a skier. Follow the steps shown in Figure 7-25.

TROUBLE? If you make a mistake, use the Undo command or erase what you've drawn and start over.

| Figure 7-25 | DRAWING THE LETTER K |

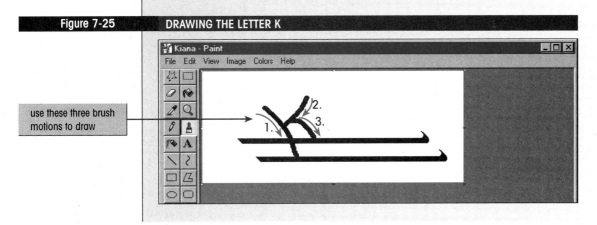

use these three brush motions to draw

Drawing a Straight Line

Now you want to make the K look as if it's moving. The Line option lets you draw straight lines, which you can place in your graphic to give the illusion of movement. You can create a horizontal, vertical, or diagonal line by pressing Shift while you drag the Line pointer in one of those directions. You can, of course, draw a line using the Pencil tool, but it's difficult to keep the line straight. You are going to draw a single line behind the K, and then you'll copy it and paste it a few times to add several "movement" lines.

To add straight lines to your drawing:

1. Click the **Line** tool. Notice that you can draw lines in several different line widths. You want the narrowest line (the default).

2. Press the **Shift** key and hold it down while you draw a horizontal line behind the K, as shown in Figure 7-26.

| Figure 7-26 | DRAWING A STRAIGHT LINE WITH THE LINE TOOL |

draw a line like this

line tool

line widths

3. Release the mouse button and then release the **Shift** key. The line is perfectly straight. You can copy and paste this line several times to create several speed lines that are all the same size.

4. Click the **Select** tool , and then draw a selection box around the line you just drew. Keep the selection box as close to the line as possible to avoid copying the surrounding white space.

5. Click **Edit**, click **Copy**, click **Edit**, and then click **Paste**.

6. Move the line you just pasted so that it is below and slightly to the right of the original line.

7. Click **Edit** and then click **Paste** twice more to add two more straight lines, moving both pasted lines until they match the positions of those shown in Figure 7-27.

8. Click a blank area of the canvas to anchor the last line into place.

Stretching a Graphic

As a final touch, you decide to stretch the graphic to see if that effect enhances the illusion of movement. You can stretch a graphic either horizontally or vertically using the **Stretch/Skew** option on the Image menu. You specify a percentage, and Paint expands or contracts the graphic by that percentage in the direction (horizontal or vertical) that you specify.

To stretch the Skis graphic:

1. Click **Image** and then click **Stretch/Skew**.

2. If necessary, click the **Horizontal** percentage box in the Stretch pane.

3. Replace the default value of 100% with **140%**.

4. Click the **OK** button. The graphic is stretched in the horizontal direction. Your graphic now looks like Figure 7-27.

Figure 7-27   STRETCHED KIANA GRAPHIC WITH ACTION LINES

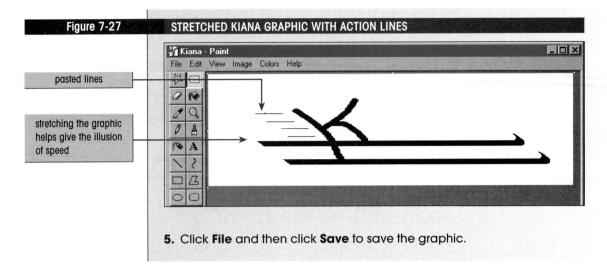

pasted lines

stretching the graphic helps give the illusion of speed

5. Click **File** and then click **Save** to save the graphic.

You'll add the text to the Kiana graphic in the Tutorial Assignments at the end of this tutorial.

Creating Shapes

Joe suggests that you create another image for use in his promotions, such as a few mountains on a sunny day. You tell him that's a job for one or more of the shape tools—Line, Curve, Rectangle, Polygon, Ellipse, and Rounded Rectangle. These tools let you draw predetermined shapes. When you click one of the shape tools, a collection of options appears below the tool box. You can choose the shape as an outline, a filled shape with a border, or a filled shape without a border. See Figure 7-28.

Figure 7-28   FILLS AND BORDERS

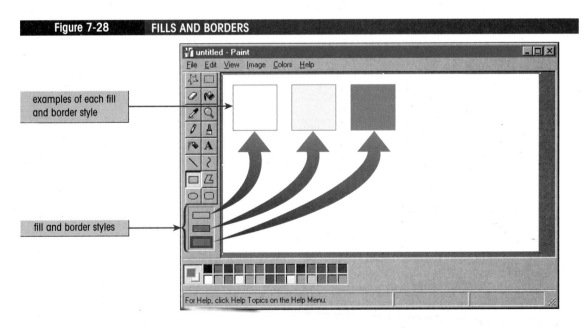

examples of each fill and border style

fill and border styles

You'll learn later how to control the colors of the border and the fill for these shapes.

Joe quickly sketches what he'd like to see, as shown in Figure 7-29, and asks if you can draw it.

Figure 7-29	IDEA FOR A SCENIC GRAPHIC

It's Ski Time!

To create the mountains, you can use the Line tool, which you've already used, and to create the sun you can use the Ellipse tool. Once you have drawn the shapes, you will color them and add text in Session 7.3.

You want to start by giving Joe a quick overview of the shapes you can draw.

To draw with a variety of the Paint shapes:

1. Click **File** and then click **New** to open a new canvas. Click **Yes** if prompted to save changes.

2. Click the **Rectangle** tool ▢ and then drag a rectangle.

3. Click the **Ellipse** tool ◯ and then drag an ellipse.

4. Click the **Rounded Rectangle** tool ▢ and then drag a rounded rectangle. Compare your screen to Figure 7-30.

   TROUBLE? If your screen doesn't look like Figure 7-30, don't worry. These shapes are just for experimenting.

Figure 7-30	SHAPE TOOLS

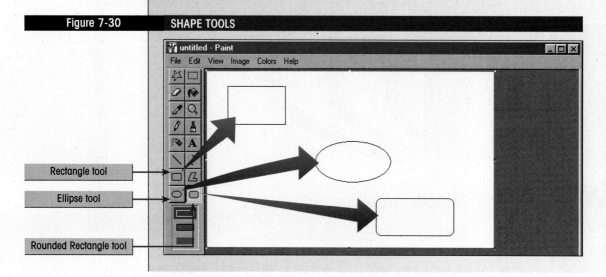

Rectangle tool

Ellipse tool

Rounded Rectangle tool

Now you're ready to create the new graphic. To save you time in this session, the mountains have already been drawn for you. They are stored in a file named Mountain. All you need to do is add the sun.

In the same way the Shift key helped you draw a straight horizontal line, it also helps you draw a perfect circle when the Ellipse tool is selected. Likewise, if you use Shift with the Rectangle tool, you can draw a perfect square. When you draw a shape, you can use the **sizing coordinates**, immediately to the right of the pixel coordinates, to control the size of the shape you are dragging. For example, when you draw a circle, you might start at pixel coordinates 15,15 and drag with sizing coordinates of 30 x 30—so your circle has a 30-pixel diameter.

To open the Mountain file and add the sun:

1. Click **File**, click **Open**, and then locate and open the **Mountain** file on your Data Disk. Click the **No** button if you are prompted to save changes.

2. Click **File**, click **Save As**, and then change the name to **Mountain and Sun**, so your changes won't affect the original file. Click the Save button.

3. Click the **Ellipse** tool 🔘.

4. Press the **Shift** key and then drag a circle starting at pixel coordinates 15,15. Drag to sizing coordinates of 30 x 30 (look to the right of the pixel coordinates on the far-right side of the status bar), and then release the mouse button and the **Shift** key. See Figure 7-31.

| Figure 7-31 | DRAWING A CIRCLE |

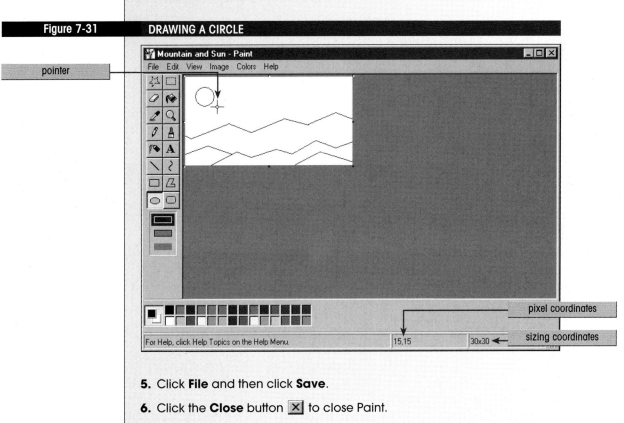

pointer

pixel coordinates

sizing coordinates

5. Click **File** and then click **Save**.

6. Click the **Close** button ❌ to close Paint.

Joe now has three graphics to choose from: the Skis graphic, the Kiana graphic, and the Mountain and Sun graphic. You remind him that you still plan to add text and color to two of these graphics. You'll work with text and color in Session 7.3.

Session 7.2 QUICK CHECK

1. How wide a line do you draw with the Pencil tool, in pixels?

2. When you view the grid, what does each box represent?

3. What option can you use to view the magnified portion of your graphic in Normal view while retaining the magnification on the canvas?

4. Name three ways to clear a canvas.

5. How do you draw a perfect circle?

6. What is the diameter of a circle drawn to 50 x 50 sizing coordinates?

SESSION 7.3

In this session, you will work with color and text. You'll begin by filling enclosed areas with color, using the Fill With Color tool, and then you'll paint with the Airbrush tool and work with background and foreground colors. Finally, you'll add text with the Text tool and format it using the Fonts toolbar. After you finish your graphic, you learn how to display thumbnail preview images of the graphic file.

Filling an Area with Color

Joe is interested to see what effect color has on his graphics. You can add color to a graphic in one of two ways: choosing colors as you draw, or coloring in shapes after you have finished drawing them. You decide to color the Mountain and Sun graphic, whose shapes are already in place. You'll learn to choose colors as you draw later in this session.

REFERENCE WINDOW | **RW**

Filling an Area with Color
- Click the Fill With Color tool.
- Click the color box color you want.
- Make sure the tip of the paint pouring out of the bucket is within the border and then click inside the border of the area you want to color.

To add color to the Mountain and Sun graphic, you click a color in the color box, and then click an enclosed area in the graphic with the Fill With Color pointer 🖌. The area within the borders of the enclosure fills with color. When you use the Fill With Color tool, make sure the area you click is a fully enclosed space. If there are any openings, color "spills out" of the boundaries you are trying to color.

You want to color each mountain range a different color to give the impression of distance and shadow. You decide to use a mix of blues and purples.

To fill the Mountain and Sun graphic with color:

1. Start Paint and then make sure your Data Disk is in drive A.

2. Click **File**, click **Open**, and then locate and open the **Mountain and Sun** file on your Data Disk.

3. Click the **Fill With Color** tool. The pointer changes to. You'll color each layer of mountains a different color.

4. In the color palette at the bottom of the screen, click the **dark blue** color in the top row, seventh from the left.

   TROUBLE? This color might appear purple on your monitor. Make sure it is the seventh from the left in the top row.

5. Click inside the border of the **top mountain range** with the **Fill With Color** pointer. The mountain range turns blue. See Figure 7-32.

   TROUBLE? If the sky turns blue instead of the mountain range, you clicked the sky instead of the mountain range. You must click the area to be colored with the active part of the Fill With Color pointer, which is the tip of the paint pouring out of the can. Click Edit, click Undo, and then repeat Step 5, making sure the tip of the paint is within the border of the mountain range.

Figure 7-32	FILLING FIRST MOUNTAIN RANGE WITH COLOR

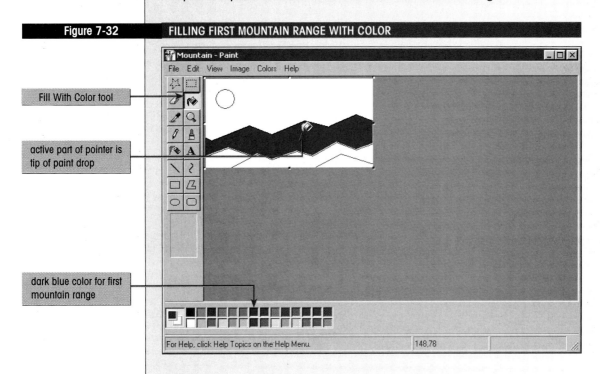

Fill With Color tool

active part of pointer is tip of paint drop

dark blue color for first mountain range

6. Click the **purple** color in the top row, eighth from the left, and then click the **front-left single mountain** to color it purple.

7. Click the **bright blue** color in the bottom row, seventh from the left, and then click the **front-middle mountain range**.

8. Click the **periwinkle** color in the bottom row, third from the right, and then click the **right mountain range**.

9. Finally, click the **yellow** color in the bottom row, fourth from the left, and then click the **sun**.

Joe likes the graphic with the colors you chose.

Coloring with the Airbrush Tool

You have one more idea to enhance the Mountain graphic. You can sprinkle "snow" on the top range of mountains using the **Airbrush tool**, which scatters color a few pixels at a time over the area you "brush." The Airbrush tool has three different sizes. The small size scatters color most thickly, whereas the largest size sprinkles it more sparingly. You'll use the largest size to sprinkle the top mountain range with snow.

To use the Airbrush tool:

1. Click the **white** color in the leftmost box of the bottom row of the color palette.

2. Click the **Airbrush** tool 🖌.

3. Click the **largest Airbrush** style (on the bottom).

4. Drag the **Airbrush** pointer 🖌 over the top range of mountains. See Figure 7-33.

Figure 7-33   USING THE AIRBRUSH TOOL

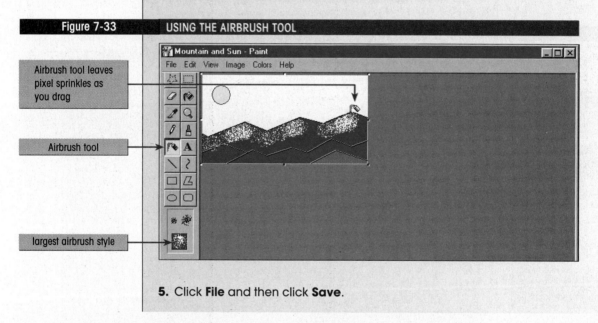

Airbrush tool leaves pixel sprinkles as you drag

Airbrush tool

largest airbrush style

5. Click **File** and then click **Save**.

Using Foreground and Background Colors

In looking over the graphic, you decide you don't like the stark contrast between the sun's black border and yellow color. You think a different border and fill will look more aesthetically pleasing. You've already seen how to color as you draw, when you sprinkled the mountains with white snow using the Airbrush tool. When you draw a shape, Paint can use two colors instead of one. The **foreground color** is used for lines, borders of shapes, and text. The **background color** determines the fill of the inside of enclosed shapes and the background of text frames. It also appears when you use the eraser. To set the foreground color, you click a color with the *left* mouse button. The foreground color box changes to that color. To set the background color, you click a color with the *right* mouse button. The background color box changes to that color. You can draw your shape using one of the three options located below the tool box: only a border using the foreground color, a border using the foreground color and a fill using the background color, or only the fill using the foreground color. (You can reverse the colors by using the right mouse button instead of the left to draw the shape.) Figure 7-34 shows examples of each of these options.

You decide to draw the sun with a foreground color of brown and a background color of orange. First, you'll need to erase the sun you've already drawn and colored. You could use the Eraser tool, but when the area you want to erase is off by itself, where no other parts of the drawing interfere, it can be quicker to select the area and then delete it using the Delete key.

Figure 7-34	EXAMPLES OF FOREGROUND AND BACKGROUND COLORS

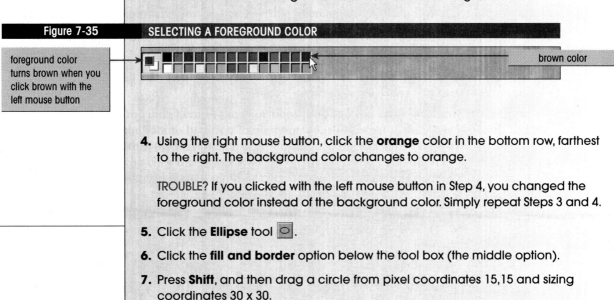

To draw a sun with different foreground and background colors:

1. Click the **Select** tool 🔲, and then drag a selection box around the sun.

2. Press the **Delete** key.

3. Click the **brown** color in the top row, farthest to the right, with the left mouse button. Notice that the foreground box turns brown. See Figure 7-35.

Figure 7-35	SELECTING A FOREGROUND COLOR

foreground color turns brown when you click brown with the left mouse button

brown color

4. Using the right mouse button, click the **orange** color in the bottom row, farthest to the right. The background color changes to orange.

   TROUBLE? If you clicked with the left mouse button in Step 4, you changed the foreground color instead of the background color. Simply repeat Steps 3 and 4.

5. Click the **Ellipse** tool 🔘.

6. Click the **fill and border** option below the tool box (the middle option).

7. Press **Shift**, and then drag a circle from pixel coordinates 15,15 and sizing coordinates 30 x 30.

The new sun has a brown border and an orange fill. However, the orange looks too dark; you decide that the original yellow color looked better.

As you've already seen, you can color an enclosed area using the Fill With Color tool. When you filled in the mountain ranges earlier with this tool, you clicked an area with the *left* mouse button, and Paint then applied the foreground color to the area. You can apply the background color by clicking the area with the *right* mouse button. Notice that this is different from drawing a shape from scratch—in that case, the foreground color determines the border, and the background color determines the fill. When you use the Fill With Color tool on an already existing shape, you are working only with the fill, and you can switch between foreground and background colors using the left or right mouse button. You decide to change the fill color back to yellow.

To select a new background color and use it to fill a shape:

1. Right-click the **yellow** color in the bottom row, fourth from the left, to set the background color to yellow.

2. Click the **Fill With Color** tool and then right-click the sun. The fill color of the sun changes to yellow, the background color you just set. This sun, yellow with a brown border, looks good.

It can be confusing that foreground and background colors take on different roles, depending on whether you're drawing an object from scratch, using a shape tool, or coloring in an object using the Fill With Color tool. Just remember that when you draw an object from scratch, the foreground color is the border, and the background color is the fill. When you are coloring an object with the Fill With Color tool, Paint uses the foreground color if you left-click and the background color if you right-click.

You and Joe are satisfied with the coloring of the Mountain and Sun graphic. Now you're ready to add the text.

Using the Text Tool

Joe had written the phrase "It's Ski Time!" on his sketch. To add words to the graphic, you can draw letters as you did for the "K" earlier, or you can use the **Text tool**. You first use the text tool to create a text box, and then you type your text in this box. If your text exceeds the length and width of the selection box, you can drag the sizing handles to enlarge the selection box.

REFERENCE WINDOW RW

Adding Text to a Graphic
- Click the Text tool and then drag a text box on the canvas.
- Click View and then click Text Toolbar if the Fonts toolbar does not appear.
- Use the Fonts toolbar to select a font, font size, or attributes (bold, italic, or underline).
- Type the text in the selection box, resizing the selection box if necessary, using the sizing handles.
- Adjust the font, font size, or attributes (bold, italic, or underline), and resize the selection box as necessary.
- Click outside the selection box.

You decide to type "It's Ski Time!" just to the right of the sun in the Mountain and Sun graphic, and you decide that the text should appear in the same shade of dark blue you used in the first range of mountains.

To select the text color and create the selection box:

1. With the left mouse button, click the **dark blue** color in the top row, seventh from the left.

2. With the right mouse button, click the **white** color in the bottom row, farthest to the left, to restore the background for the text box to white.

3. Click the **Text** tool A.

4. Create a selection box by dragging from pixel coordinates 54,15 to a size of 185 x 30. Make sure you don't make the box any larger than this or it will obscure the mountains. After you've created the selection box, the Fonts toolbar appears.

   TROUBLE? If the Fonts toolbar does not appear, click View and then click Text Toolbar. (Notice that the Fonts toolbar appears as "Text Toolbar" on the View menu.)

Any letters you type into the selection box will appear with the **font**—or typeface—style, size, attributes, and language shown in the Fonts toolbar. The font size of the letters is measured in **points**, where a single point is ½ inch. Thus a 1-inch tall character would be 72 points, and a ½-inch tall character would be 36 points. Attributes are characteristics of the font, including bold, italic, and underline. You can change the font, font size, font attributes, and language using the Fonts toolbar before you type, after you type, or as you edit the text. Once you are satisfied with the text and its appearance, you click outside the selection box. The selection box disappears, and the text is "anchored" into place, becoming a part of the bitmapped graphic. Once text is anchored in a graphic, you can change the font or its attributes only by deleting the text and starting over with the Text tool.

You decide to use an Arial 12-point font. **Arial** is the name of a common font that comes with Windows 2000.

To choose the Arial 12-point font and insert the text:

1. Click the left-most **Font** list arrow. The list of fonts available on your computer opens. See Figure 7-36. Your list will probably be different.

| Figure 7-36 | FONT LIST |

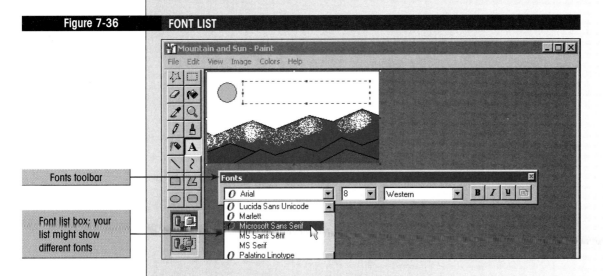

Fonts toolbar

Font list box; your list might show different fonts

2. Scroll the Fonts list until you locate Arial and then click **Arial**.

3. Click the **Font Size** list arrow and then click **12**. Make sure the Bold and Italic buttons are *not* selected; if they are, click them to deselect them.

4. Click inside the selection box.

5. Type **It's Ski Time!** Your text appears in the selection box in the Arial 12-point font. See Figure 7-37.

TROUBLE? If nothing appears when you type, it's possible that you clicked the color white with the left mouse button instead of the right mouse button in the previous set of steps. White text will not appear against a white background. Make sure the foreground color is dark blue and the background color is white.

Figure 7-37   ADDING TEXT USING THE TEXT TOOL

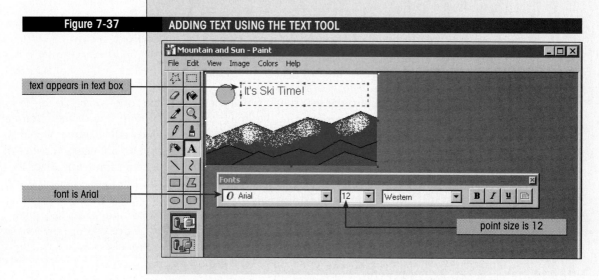

Joe would like to use a more interesting font. You decide to experiment with several fonts, sizes, and attributes to find the look you want. Windows 2000 comes with a standard set of fonts, including Arial and Times New Roman, but most users add fonts so they can format text in a variety of styles. The fonts that appear on your computer will most likely differ from those shown in the figures.

To experiment with the font:

1. Click the **Font** list arrow on the Fonts toolbar.

2. Scroll the Font list until you locate Times New Roman, and then click **Times New Roman**.

The text in your text box changes to the new font.

TROUBLE? If your Times New Roman font appears multiple times with a number of different styles, click any one of the Times New Roman fonts, such as Times New Roman (Baltic).

3. Click the **Bold** button **B** to see how the text looks in bold format.

4. Click the **Italic** button **I**. You like the look of both bold and italic, though you'd like to keep looking at other font styles.

5. Continue to select different fonts and attributes, as shown in Figure 7-38.

TROUBLE? If you can't find the fonts shown in Figure 7-38, experiment with fonts available on your computer. Although Windows 2000 comes with a few fonts, your computer lab technical support person might have added more fonts to your computer.

Figure 7-38	EXPERIMENTING WITH DIFFERENT FONTS

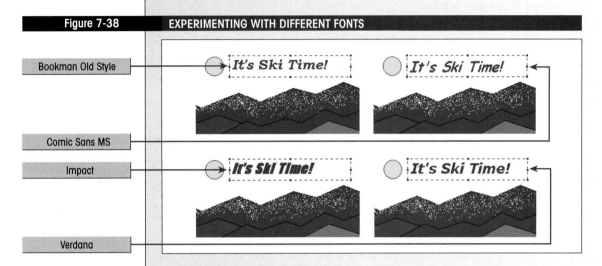

Bookman Old Style

Comic Sans MS

Impact

Verdana

6. Joe likes bold and italic Verdana Baltic best. Click **Verdana** if you have it, using both the Bold and Italic attributes. Otherwise click one of your favorites. (You can also leave it as Times New Roman, which is a font that is installed with Windows 2000, so every computer should have it.)

7. Now enlarge the font to make the text more visible. Click the **Font Size** list arrow and then click **16**.

TROUBLE? If you are using a font that is especially large, 16 points might cause some of the letters to disappear. Repeat Step 7, but this time pick a smaller point size.

8. Click a blank area of the canvas outside the selection box to accept this style of text. The selection box and Fonts toolbar disappear, and the text is anchored into place. See Figure 7-39.

Figure 7-39	COMPLETING GRAPHIC WITH TEXT

9. Click **File** and then click **Save** to save the Mountain and Sun graphic.

10. Click the Paint **Close** button .

Viewing Your Pictures in Thumbnail View

As you create more and more graphic files, you'll want to have the ability to browse quickly through them to locate the file you want. Windows 2000 includes the ability to view file lists in **Thumbnail view**, in which smaller "preview" images of the graphic file appear in the My Computer or Explorer window. You decide to show Joe how to use Thumbnail view to browse his files.

To use Thumbnail view:

1. Open the **My Computer** icon on your Windows 2000 desktop.

2. Open the **3½ Floppy (A:)** icon for your Data Disk.

3. Click **View** on the menu bar and then click **Thumbnails**. Resize or maximize the window as necessary to see the images.

   Windows 2000 displays thumbnail images of the files on the Data Disk (this may take a moment). See Figure 7-40.

Figure 7-40	VIEWING GRAPHIC FILES IN THUMBNAILS VIEW

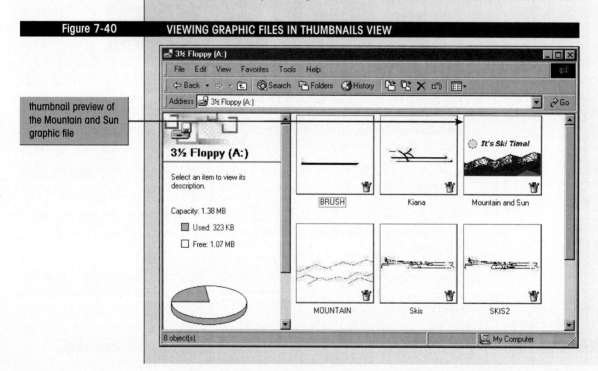

thumbnail preview of the Mountain and Sun graphic file

Joe appreciates the ability to preview images that Windows 2000 provides for him. If Joe wants to better organize his graphic files, he can use the **My Pictures folder**, a subfolder of the My Documents folder that Windows 2000 provides for graphic files. The My Pictures folder is the default location for files created by Paint and also for files created by digital cameras connected to your computer.

Joe has enjoyed watching you work with the Paint program. Although he recognizes that these graphics do not match the quality of those you could create with a full-featured graphics program such as CorelDraw, he is, nevertheless, impressed with Paint's versatility and ease of use. Now that he has a few usable graphics, he looks forward to creating more announcements and promotional materials for the Birkebeiner ski race.

Session 7.3 QUICK | CHECK

1. To change a shape's fill color, you use the _____ tool.
2. What does it mean to say that a font is "10 points"?
3. What font attributes can you work with in Paint?
4. You just opened a graphic containing text, and you'd like to change the font of the text. Describe your options.
5. When you draw an object from scratch, the foreground color controls an object's _____, whereas the background color controls its _____.
6. If you select the Fill With Color tool and then right-click an enclosed area, which color is applied, the foreground or the background?

REVIEW ASSIGNMENTS

1. **Cropping a Graphic**   Joe is the coordinator for a university students' bowling league, and he asks you to help create a graphic for an informational promotion he is preparing.
   a. Open the **Sports** graphic in Paint.
   b. Use the Select tool to select the bowling ball hitting the bowling pins in the lower-right corner of the Sports graphic.
   c. Use the Copy To command to save the cropped graphic to your Data Disk as a monochrome graphic with the name **Bowling Ball**.
   d. Open the **Bowling Ball** graphic and, if necessary, erase any portions of it that aren't part of the graphic.
   e. Save and print the graphic, and then close Paint.

Explore

2. **Cropping a Graphic with the Free-Form Select Tool**   You're designing league jackets for the Community Tennis League. You want to crop the tennis rackets in the lower-left corner of the Sports graphic. In Session 7.1, you used the Select tool to crop part of a graphic, but the selection box included portions of other images that you had to erase. To avoid this extra step, use the Free-Form Select tool to draw a line of any shape around the area you want to crop.
   a. Open the **Sports** graphic.
   b. Use the Free-Form Select tool to draw around the tennis rackets and ball in the lower-left corner of the Sports graphic. When you are done drawing around the rackets, a selection box appears, similar to the one you used with the Select tool. However, when you save the selection to another file, Paint will not include any areas in the box that were not included when you used the Free-Form Select tool.
   c. Use the Copy To command to save the cropped graphic to your Data Disk as a monochrome graphic with the name **Tennis Rackets**.
   d. Open the **Tennis Rackets** graphic and ensure that you didn't include any unwanted portions of the Sports graphic.
   e. Save and print the **Tennis Rackets** graphic, and then close Paint.

3. **Drawing in Color**   One of the Birkebeiner participants was in the most recent Winter Olympics, and Joe's promotion highlights the fact that the Birkebeiner attracts top-notch competitors. Joe asks you to create a graphic of the Olympic rings. The top three rings are blue, black, and red. The bottom two rings are yellow and green. Save the file on your Data Disk as a 256 Color Bitmap graphic with the name **Rings** and print the file. Here are techniques to use to make this assignment easier:
   - Use the Shift key with the Ellipse tool to draw perfect circles.
   - Use the sizing coordinates to ensure that each circle is the same size.
   - Draw each new circle in a blank area of the canvas, and then use the Select tool to select the circle and drag it into place.

■ Use the pixel coordinates to ensure that you place all rings in each row on the same level.

Figure 7-41 shows such a drawing.

Figure 7-41

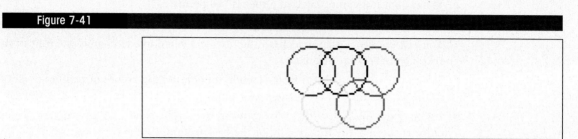

4. **Adding Text to the Kiana Graphic** You and Joe decide to finish the Kiana graphic. You need to add the rest of the word "Kiana." First open the **Kiana** file that you created earlier in this tutorial and saved on your Data Disk. Save the file as **Kiana2**.

a. Use the Text tool to insert a text box, type the letters "iana," and then select a font and font size that you like.

b. Use the Fill With Color tool to fill each letter with a different color.

c. Make the graphic take up less room on your disk by selecting the entire drawing and dragging it up to the corner of the canvas. Then resize the canvas to fit the drawing.

d. Give the graphic a background color that complements the letter colors. Compare your figure to Figure 7-42.

e. Save and print your graphic, and then close Paint.

Figure 7-42

5. **Editing Graphic Images** Joe wants his promotions to look more professional. He wants you to connect to the Internet and locate another ski graphic. He'd like the graphic to have the word "Birkebeiner" on it.

a. Connect to the Internet and use Yahoo's subject guide to search for Web pages that make graphic images available. (*Hint*: Try the Computers and Internet category and the Graphics subcategory.)

b. Once you have located a graphics page, search for a Sports category and locate a skier graphic. The file you choose must have a format that Paint supports: bmp, or, if you have Microsoft Office, gif, or jpeg. If you can't find a graphic image on the Internet, use the Skis graphic you used in this tutorial, and save it as **Skier**.

c. Download the skier graphic you located on the Web to your Data Disk and save it with the name **Skier**.

d. Open the Skier graphic in Paint and add the word "Birkebeiner" to the graphic. (*Hint*: If there is no blank area in which to add this word, resize the canvas as necessary.)

e. Save and print the graphic, and then close Paint.

PROJECTS

1. You work for Jensen Telecommunications, which is hosting an engineering conference to share ideas on making high-speed fiber-optic data lines available to homes. You're helping host the conference banquet, and you'd like to create a classy design to imprint on the cocktail napkins and coasters. Use the Brush tool to draw the graphic, as shown in Steps a through f, and then save it as a Monochrome Bitmap graphic.

   a. Create a vertical line as shown, using the largest angular brush style in the third row.

   b. Copy the vertical line and paste it as shown.

   c. Draw the horizontal line to hook up with the vertical line.

   d. Copy the horizontal line and paste it on top.

   e. Copy a short section of the horizontal line and paste it in the middle.

   f. Save the image as **Letter J** on your Data Disk, print it, and then close Paint.

2. You work for a commercial graphics design company, Ace Design Group (ADG). ADG has just landed a contract to create a new font style for the materials of the American Statistical Association's annual conference. Your boss has asked you to start drafting possible designs. You use Paint to create a few sample letters, specifically, an uppercase and lowercase "a" and "f." You'll probably want to use a combination of drawing tools for this assignment. You'll need to zoom in and edit, using the grid, to ensure consistency from letter to letter. The previous project showed you how to draw a letter. When you are finished drafting a few ideas, save your file as **Fonts** using the monochrome Bitmap file type, print it, and then close Paint.

3. You're preparing a flyer for a Sailing Club, and you need a graphic that shows a sailboat. You plan to print your flyer in color, so you need a graphic with color.

   a. Open the **Sports** graphic and copy the sailboat image to a new file named **Sailboat** on your Data Disk. Save the file as a 24-bit Bitmap image. (If you use the regular Select tool, make sure you erase any parts of the Sports graphic that aren't part of the sailboat.)

   b. Use the Fill With Color tool to color the sails of the sailboat red.

   c. Add the words "Time to Sail!" on the sailboat graphic.

   d. Save the graphic on your Data Disk, print it, and then close Paint.

4. You coordinate the Chess Club at Stanton Junior High. You want to create a simple graphic for a tournament brochure. Use the Rectangle tool and your copy and pasting skills to create the chessboard in the following steps a through f.

   a. Use the Rectangle tool with the Shift key to create a perfect square with sizing coordinates of 35 x 35. Don't forget to use the Shift key.

   b. Copy the square, and then paste it and drag it so that the edges overlap. Do this three times to create the first four squares.

   c. Copy the four squares and then paste that image and drag it to the right of the first four squares.

   d. Copy those eight squares, and then paste that image and drag it to the right of the existing eight squares.

   e. Copy those 16 squares, and paste and drag them three times to create the rest of the chessboard.

   f. Save the image as **Chess** on your Data Disk using the 256 Color Bitmap file type, print it, and then close Paint.

5. You just completed the Chess graphic in Project 4. You now want to add text and color.

a. Color in every other square, using the Fill With Color tool and colors you choose, to create a chessboard.

b. Add the words "Stanton Chess Club" to the top of the chessboard. Choose a font style and size that complement the colors and board you drew.

c. Add the word "Tournament" below the chessboard.

d. Now use the Select tool to select just the word "Tournament." Then rotate the word and drag it to the right side of the chessboard, as shown in Figure 7-43. Using the Flip/Rotate command on the Image menu, click Rotate by angle, and then click 270. Your graphic should look like Figure 7-43, but will vary depending on the font you chose.

e. Save the graphic on your Data Disk as **Chess with Text**, print it, and then close Paint.

Figure 7-43

QUICK | CHECK ANSWERS

Session 7.1

1. Select the portion you want to save, click Edit, then click Copy To, enter a name and location in the Save As dialog box, then click the Save button.
2. Drag the sizing handle.
3. True
4. pixels
5. Color graphics require more bits to define the colors.
6. Convert it to a format Paint does support, using a graphics converter.

Session 7.2

1. a single pixel
2. a single pixel
3. thumbnail
4. the Eraser tool, the Clear Image command on the Image menu, or the New command on the File menu
5. Press Shift and use the Ellipse tool.
6. 50 pixels

Session 7.3

1. Fill With Color
2. Its size is 10 x ½ inch.
3. bold, italic, and underline
4. You must erase or cut the text, then click the Text tool and enter new text with the font you want.
5. border, fill
6. background

OBJECT LINKING AND EMBEDDING

Creating a Multimedia Document for the Jugglers Guild

CASE

Preparing for the Jugglers Guild Convention

The Tenth Annual Jugglers Guild Convention is scheduled for this summer in New Orleans. Maria Arruda, secretary of the Jugglers Guild, is chairing the convention, aided by a committee of which you are a member. Maria has assigned tasks to each committee member—yours is to work on gathering materials that will promote the event. Maria would like you to hire a designer to design a graphics file that can serve as a logo for informational flyers, posters, and convention T-shirts. Maria asks you also to look for an eye-catching video clip that will run on the computer screens used at the convention. A video clip is a file that contains a very short movie, either real-life or animated.

You hire a graphic designer to design the logo and a computer animation company to create an animated video clip. Once you receive the disks containing the graphics file and video clip, you give them to Maria so she can evaluate them. The next day she returns the disks and says she likes the logo and the animation, but she'd like feedback from the rest of the committee. She asks you to create a single WordPad document that will contain the graphics file and the video clip, and into which the committee members can add their comments. A document that includes a variety of media, such as text, graphics, and video, is called a multimedia document.

Windows 2000 provides three ways to combine data from a variety of sources into a single multimedia document: pasting, embedding, and linking. You'll learn about pasting in Session 8.1, embedding in Session 8.2, and linking in Session 8.3. How do you decide which method to use in a given situation? It depends on what you need to do with the information after you've inserted it into the multimedia document—whether you need to use the tools in the program that originally created the data, and whether you are likely to change the data once you've inserted it. As you proceed through these three sessions, notice how the pasting, embedding, and linking techniques offer you different options to meet these needs.

SESSION 8.1

In this session, you will learn how to use the Windows 2000 Clipboard to make data from one source available to another document or program, using the Edit commands. To perform the steps of this tutorial, you will need one blank 3½-inch disk. To complete the Review Assignments and Projects, you will need a second blank 3½-inch disk.

Creating a WordPad Document

You'll start by creating the WordPad document that will contain the data you want other members of the committee to view. You'll format the document as a memo, beginning with a standard memo heading that includes To, Date, and Subject headings.

Before you can begin working, you need to bring a blank 3½-inch disk to the computer lab and use the NP on Microsoft Windows 2000 menu to create a Data Disk containing the files you will work with in this tutorial. If you are using your own computer, the NP on Microsoft Windows 2000 menu will not be available. Once you have made the disk at the computer lab, however, you can use the disk to complete this tutorial on any computer that runs Windows 2000. Before you proceed, refer to the Read This Before You Begin page for instructions on obtaining the files necessary for your Data Disk.

To make your Data Disk:

1. Write "Disk 6—Windows 2000 Tutorials 8 & 9 Data Disk" on the label of a blank, formatted 3½-inch disk. Insert your Data Disk into drive A.

   TROUBLE? If your 3½-inch disk drive is B, place your formatted disk in that drive instead, and for the rest of this tutorial substitute drive B wherever you see drive A.

2. Point to the **Start** button [Start], point to **Programs**, point to **NP on Microsoft Windows 2000-Level III**, and then click **Disk 6 (Tutorial 8)**. When you are prompted to insert your disk in the drive, click the **OK** button, and wait as the files you need are copied to your Data Disk.

3. Close all the open windows on your screen.

To start a new WordPad document:

1. Click the **Start** button [Start], point to **Programs**, point to **Accessories**, and then click **WordPad**.

2. Type the following memo heading into the WordPad document. Press the **Enter** key twice after each line, and the **Tab** key twice after the first two colons (just press the **Tab** key once after the SUBJECT colon).
   MEMO
   TO: **Jugglers Guild Convention Committee**
   DATE: **3/18/2001**
   SUBJECT: **Tenth Annual Jugglers Guild Convention**

3. If you haven't already done so, press the **Enter** key twice after typing the SUBJECT line.

4. Click **File** and then click **Save As** to save the work you've done so far. Type **Feedback** in the File name box and select the Rich Text Format in the Save as Type box.

5. Click the **Save in** list arrow, and then click the drive containing your Data Disk.

6. Click the **Save** button.

The Clipboard

Maria has decided that she wants the committee members to give their feedback on the graphics and video files in a specific way. She drafts a document that outlines the feedback procedure and includes her own feedback. She suggests you insert her document into your Feedback document.

Windows 2000 offers several ways to transfer data from one document to another; the most basic technique is **Paste**, whereby you cut or copy data from one document and then place it into another. This procedure uses the **Clipboard**, an area in your computer's active memory that temporarily stores the data you cut or copy. For example, suppose you had an e-mail message that contained information you wanted to paste into a WordPad document. Figure 8-1 illustrates how you copy the message to the Clipboard and then paste it into your document.

Figure 8-1	USING THE CLIPBOARD

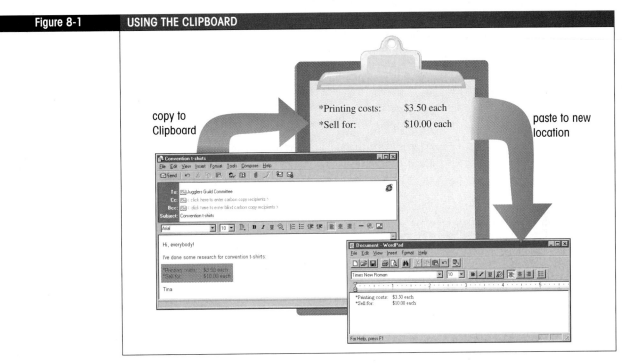

REFERENCE	WINDOW	RW

Using Paste to Transfer Data from One Document to Another
- Select the data you want to transfer, and then click Edit.
- Click Cut to remove the data from the document to the Clipboard, or click Copy to place a replica of the data on the Clipboard while leaving the original document intact.
- Switch to the second document and then place the insertion point where you want to paste the data.
- Click Edit and then click Paste.

The Clipboard is part of the operating system and is available in most Windows programs through standard Cut, Copy, and Paste commands. Figure 8-2 shows the equivalent keyboard methods you can use to cut, copy, and paste data within a document or from one document to another.

Figure 8-2	CUT AND PASTE OPTIONS

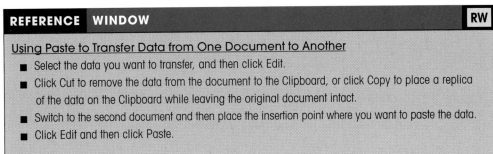

OPERATION	MENU COMMAND	TOOLBAR BUTTON	KEYBOARD SHORTCUT
Cut	Edit, then Cut		Ctrl+x
Copy	Edit, then Copy		Ctrl+c
Paste	Edit, then Paste		Ctrl+v

When you paste data from the Clipboard into a document, you do not remove the data from the Clipboard; you can continue to paste the data as many times as you want, into as many documents as you want. The Clipboard stores the data until you cut or copy new data, since the Clipboard can hold only one piece of data at a time.

If the Clipboard contains a large amount of data when you close a program, Windows 2000 might prompt you to clear the Clipboard contents to free your system's memory. The Clipboard's contents are also cleared when you shut down your computer.

Copying and Pasting from the Calculator Accessory

You decide to open Maria's document to see what it contains.

To open Maria's document:

1. Open the document named **Maria** on your Data Disk in WordPad. Because you can open only one document at a time in WordPad, the Feedback document closes. Figure 8-3 shows Maria's document.

   TROUBLE? If you are asked if you want to save changes, click Yes only if you are sure the document contains the memo heading as typed in the previous set of steps. Otherwise click No.

   TROUBLE? If the Maria document does not appear, select "Word for Windows (*.doc)" in the Files of type list box in the Open dialog box.

| Figure 8-3 | MARIA'S DOCUMENT |

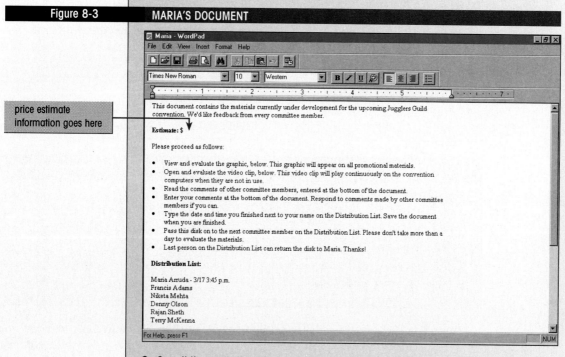

price estimate information goes here

2. Scroll through the document to view its contents.

You see that Maria has left room to insert both the graphic and the video clip. Then you notice she left room for a price estimate at the top. You've received quotes from the two vendors: $235 for the graphic and $390 for the video clip. The graphic design vendor is also offering a 12% discount if you print your convention materials there. You want to inform the committee members of these quotes, so you decide to use the Windows 2000 Calculator to calculate the total. The **Calculator** is a Windows 2000 accessory that looks and functions just like a hand-held calculator. It can appear in two views: **Standard** view, which provides basic arithmetic operations, or **Scientific** view, which includes a variety of algebraic, trigonometric, and statistical functions.

You are less likely to make a mistake entering the total into your document if you use the Clipboard to copy the data from the Calculator to your document, instead of typing it. The Calculator includes a Copy command that copies the current entry to the Clipboard. You can transfer the answer to any program that offers Clipboard access.

To calculate the total, you multiply 235 by .88 to calculate the price of the graphic discounted by 12%, and then add 390.

To open the Calculator and copy the total to Maria's document:

1. Click the **Start** button, point to **Programs**, point to **Accessories**, and then click **Calculator**. See Figure 8-4.

   TROUBLE? If your Calculator window appears twice this size, your Calculator opened in Scientific view. You can perform the calculations in Scientific or Standard view.

Figure 8-4	CALCULATOR ACCESSORY

2. Type (or click the appropriate buttons in the Calculator window) **0.88*235+390=** to calculate to a total value of 596.8.

   TROUBLE? If you are using the numeric keypad on your keyboard and it doesn't work, press the NumLock key and then try again.

3. Click **Edit** on the Calculator menu bar and then click **Copy**. With the Calculator, you don't have to highlight the data you want to copy. Even though the text does not appear highlighted, the Calculator automatically copies whatever entry is currently in the results box. Notice that when you copy, the information is not removed from the program. You have simply placed a copy of it on the Clipboard.

4. Click the **Close** button ☒ to close the Calculator. The information remains on the Clipboard.

The Clipboard now contains the value 596.8. You need to paste this value into Maria's document.

To paste the total into Maria's document:

1. Click and then scroll to the top of Maria's document, and then click to the right of the $ next to the boldface **Estimate:** heading.

2. Click the **Paste** button 📋. See Figure 8-5.

   TROUBLE? If the Paste button doesn't appear, click View on the menu bar and then click Toolbar.

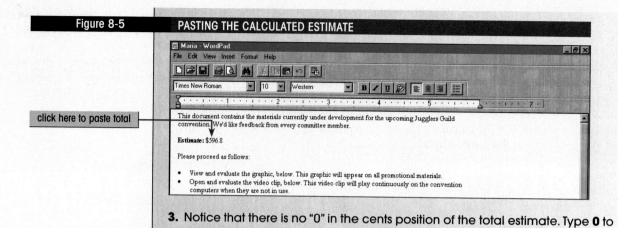

Figure 8-5 — PASTING THE CALCULATED ESTIMATE

click here to paste total

3. Notice that there is no "0" in the cents position of the total estimate. Type **0** to complete the currency format.

Cutting and Pasting Between Two WordPad Documents

The next step in your project is to move the information from Maria's document to your document. This time, rather than copying the information over, you decide to cut it from Maria's document and paste it into yours. When you copied, the information remained in the source program, as you saw with the Calculator accessory. However, when you cut, you permanently remove the information from the original program.

To cut the contents from Maria's document and move it to the Clipboard:

1. Click **Edit** and then click **Select All**. The entire document is selected.

2. Click the **Cut** button ✂. Windows 2000 removes the selected material from Maria's document and places it on the Clipboard.

The Clipboard now contains the data from Maria's document. It will stay there until you copy or cut something else (since the Clipboard can contain only one cut or copied selection at a time), until you manually clear the Clipboard, or until you shut down your computer (which clears the memory, including the Clipboard). You can now open your Feedback document and insert the contents of the Clipboard.

To insert the contents of the Clipboard into your Feedback document:

1. Click **File** and then click **A:\Feedback**, which appears near the bottom of the File menu.

TROUBLE? If A:\Feedback does not appear, and you have left the computer since you were working with the Feedback document in the WordPad window, other files opened more recently might appear at the bottom of the File menu. If this is the case, open the Feedback file using the Open dialog box.

2. Click **No** when WordPad prompts you to save changes to Maria's document; this leaves the document intact in case you want to repeat this tutorial.

3. Click at the end of your Feedback document (below the Subject line). Any text you type or paste will appear at the insertion point.

TROUBLE? If the insertion point appears at the end of the last line, press the Enter key so the text doesn't appear on the same line as the existing text.

4. Click the **Paste** button 📋 to paste the information from Maria's document into your Feedback document.

5. Scroll back to the top of the document. See Figure 8-6.

| Figure 8-6 | FEEDBACK DOCUMENT WITH PASTED INFORMATION |

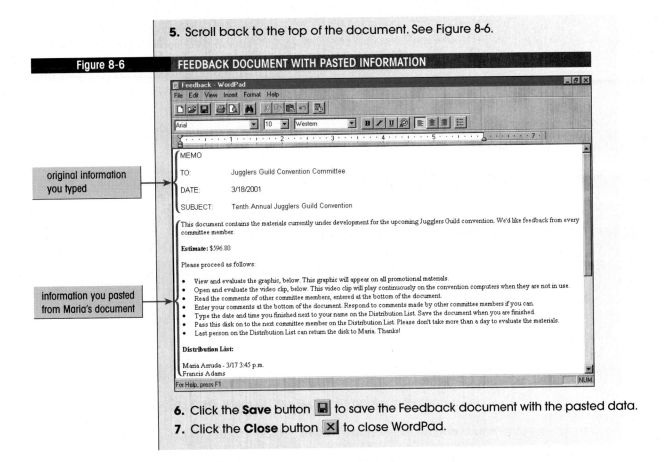

original information you typed

information you pasted from Maria's document

6. Click the **Save** button to save the Feedback document with the pasted data.

7. Click the **Close** button to close WordPad.

Session 8.1 QUICK CHECK

1. What is the Clipboard?
2. What happens to the selected text in the original document when you cut it? When you copy it?
3. What keyboard shortcuts can you use to cut, copy, and paste?
4. True or False: Once you paste the contents of the Clipboard into a document, it is no longer available to be pasted into other documents.
5. Why would you use the Copy and Paste commands to transfer answers from the Calculator or similar programs into other documents?

SESSION 8.2

In this session, you'll learn how object linking and embedding (OLE) extends your ability to transfer data between files. You'll focus on embedding: you'll learn to embed a graphic object, change its size, and edit the embedded object. Then you'll display the embedded object as an icon, change its name, and change the icon that represents it.

Object Linking and Embedding (OLE)

So far you have pasted text into your WordPad document, first from the Calculator accessory and then from another WordPad document. The text you pasted actually became part of the Feedback document, and you can work with it in the same way you work with text you typed in—using the tools provided with WordPad. However, a multimedia document like the one you're creating can contain data from many different sources—graphics from Paint, charts from a spreadsheet, sounds from an audio file—as well as text. This data is often referred to as **objects**.

In your multimedia document, how can you work with objects that come from programs with different tools? For example, your WordPad document offers only text-editing tools. If you place a Paint graphic in this document, you can't use the WordPad tools to edit that object. Windows 2000 provides the tools you need through a process called **object linking and embedding**, or **OLE** (pronounced "oh LAY"). OLE lets you insert an object into a document and access tools to manipulate the object (usually the tools of the program that was used to create the object).

With OLE, you place objects into documents using either of two methods: you embed them or you link them. In this session, you'll learn how to embed objects, and in Session 8.3 you'll learn how to link objects.

To understand both embedding and linking, you need to know the terms listed in Figure 8-7.

Figure 8-7	OLE TERMS
TERM	**DEFINITION**
Source program	The program that created the original object
Source file	The file that contains the original object
Destination program	The program that created the document into which you are inserting the OLE object
Destination file	The file into which you are inserting the OLE object

Figure 8-8 applies the terms in Figure 8-7 to the document Maria wants you to create. Paint and Media Player are the source programs, and the Pins graphic and Video video clip are the source files. WordPad is the destination program, and Feedback is the destination file.

Figure 8-8	MULTIMEDIA DOCUMENT MARIA WANTS YOU TO CREATE

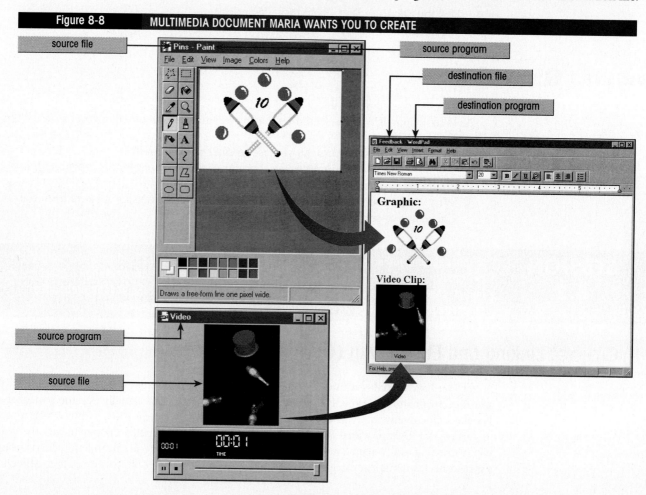

Embedding an Object Using Paste

You are ready to place the graphic into the Feedback document, but you want to retain the ability to work with the graphic with tools from the program that originally created it—in this case, Paint. When you want to be able to use the tools from the source program within the destination file, you should embed the object into the destination file. **Embedding** places a copy of an object into a document and "remembers" which program created the object, although it doesn't remember the name of the source file. Compare this technique to copying, which simply places the copy of the data in the new program with no reference to its source. There are several ways to embed an object. If both the source and destination programs feature OLE technology, you can simply paste the object from one to the other. Many of the programs designed for Windows feature OLE.

The graphic provided by the graphic design company is called Pins. You want to embed a copy of this graphic into the Feedback document.

To copy the Pins graphic to the Clipboard:

1. Click the **Start** button, point to **Programs**, point to **Accessories**, and then click **Paint**.
2. Open the **Pins** graphic on your Data Disk.
3. Click **Edit** and then click **Select All**. A selection box appears around the graphic.
4. Click **Edit** and then click **Copy**. Windows 2000 copies the graphic to the Clipboard.
5. Click the **Close** button ⊠ to close Paint.

The graphic is now copied to the Clipboard. To embed it, you open the Feedback document in WordPad and then use WordPad's Paste command.

To embed the Pins graphic into the Feedback document:

1. Start WordPad and open the **Feedback** document on your Data Disk.
2. Scroll the Feedback document until you locate the boldface **Graphic:** heading.
3. Click the blank line two lines below the Graphic: heading.
4. Click the **Paste** button 📋. The Pins graphic is embedded in the Feedback document, and it appears in a selection box. See Figure 8-9.

Figure 8-9   EMBEDDED OBJECT

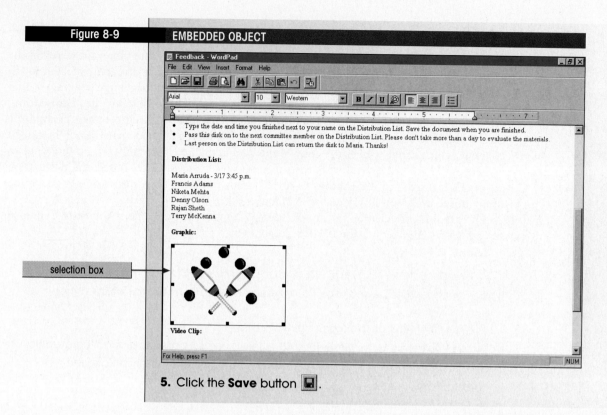

selection box

5. Click the **Save** button 🖫.

It can be confusing that the Paste command seems to function differently with different objects. In Session 8.1, Paste simply pasted text, but here Paste embeds an object. How can you tell what Paste is doing? There are no hard and fast rules for how each program takes advantage of the OLE technology, although the following generalization can be helpful: When you use Paste to transfer data from one document to another that contains data of the same type (as it did when you transferred text into WordPad), Paste inserts the data without embedding. However, when you are transferring data from one document to another that contains no data of that type, and both the source and destination programs use OLE, Paste usually, but not always, embeds the data. When you copy and paste between Windows 2000 programs, it's a good idea to examine what you've pasted so you can see how the program uses the Paste command. One clue is that if a selection box appears when you click the pasted data, it is embedded, and you can edit the data with the tools from the source program.

Changing the Size of an Embedded Object

As you examine the embedded graphic, you wonder if it might be easier to evaluate the image if it were a little bigger.

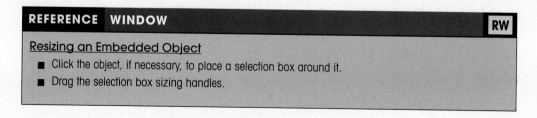

REFERENCE   WINDOW   RW

Resizing an Embedded Object
■ Click the object, if necessary, to place a selection box around it.
■ Drag the selection box sizing handles.

To enlarge the embedded graphic:

1. Drag the lower-right sizing handle down and to the right. The pointer changes to ↘ when you point at the sizing handle. The embedded object is enlarged. See Figure 8-10.

Figure 8-10	ENLARGED EMBEDDED OBJECT

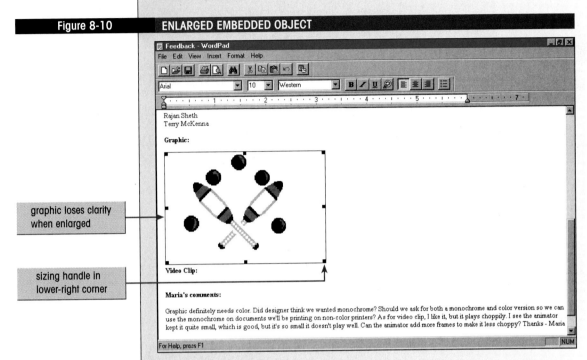

graphic loses clarity when enlarged

sizing handle in lower-right corner

2. You realize that the enlarged graphic is less sharp, so you decide to leave it in its original size. Click **Edit** and then click **Undo** to undo your last action.

Editing an Embedded Object

The graphic is in place, but you decide that before the other committee members see it, you want to enhance it by adding color, since you noticed Maria's comment about the lack of color. You can edit an embedded object using the source program's editing tools. The ability to edit an object that has been embedded into a different program's document is called **in-place editing**—it gives you access to the source program's tools without making you leave the destination program. In-place editing is a valuable Windows 2000 data-transfer feature, because it brings the tools you need to work with your document right to you, rather than making you get them.

When you use in-place editing, you sometimes might momentarily forget which program you are using. In that case, remember that the title bar identifies the program that contains your destination document, whereas the menus and toolbars identify the program you're using to edit the OLE object.

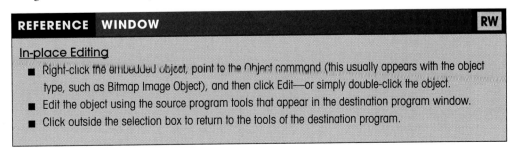

REFERENCE WINDOW **RW**

In-place Editing

- Right-click the embedded object, point to the Object command (this usually appears with the object type, such as Bitmap Image Object), and then click Edit—or simply double-click the object.
- Edit the object using the source program tools that appear in the destination program window.
- Click outside the selection box to return to the tools of the destination program.

To edit the Pins graphic within the WordPad document:

1. Right-click the **Pins** graphic to open its menu, point to **Bitmap Image Object**, and then click **Edit**.

   The graphic appears inside a selection box, the Paint tools appear, and the menu bar changes to the Paint menus—but the title bar identifies that you are still in WordPad. See Figure 8-11.

Figure 8-11	USING IN-PLACE EDITING

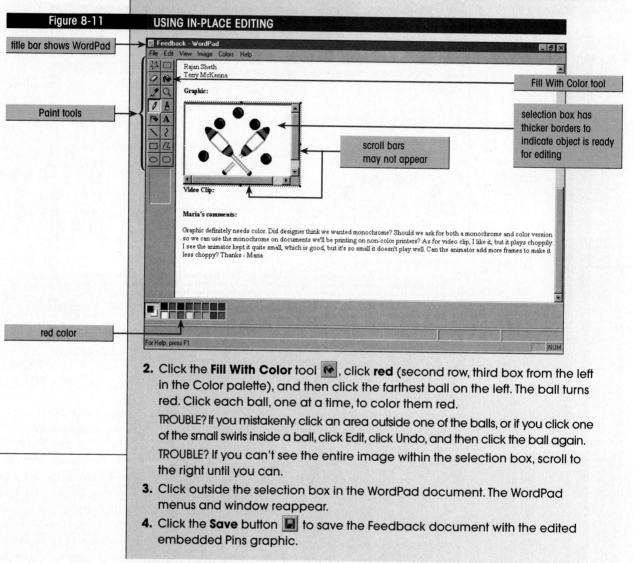

title bar shows WordPad

Paint tools

red color

Fill With Color tool

selection box has thicker borders to indicate object is ready for editing

scroll bars may not appear

2. Click the **Fill With Color** tool [icon], click **red** (second row, third box from the left in the Color palette), and then click the farthest ball on the left. The ball turns red. Click each ball, one at a time, to color them red.

   TROUBLE? If you mistakenly click an area outside one of the balls, or if you click one of the small swirls inside a ball, click Edit, click Undo, and then click the ball again.

   TROUBLE? If you can't see the entire image within the selection box, scroll to the right until you can.

3. Click outside the selection box in the WordPad document. The WordPad menus and window reappear.

4. Click the **Save** button [icon] to save the Feedback document with the edited embedded Pins graphic.

As you'll see in Session 8.3, one of the important features that distinguish embedding from linking is that when you edit an embedded object, the source file is not affected. You are accessing the tools that created the object, not the original file. You can verify that the original graphic remains unchanged by opening the original Pins graphic in Paint.

To see that the original Pins graphic has not changed:

1. Click the **Start** button, point to **Programs**, point to **Accessories**, and then click **Paint**.

2. Click **File**, and then click **A:\Pins** near the bottom of the **File** menu. Notice that the original Pins graphic has not changed.

3. Click the **Close** button [X] to close Paint.

Embedding an Object Using Insert Object

To cut or copy an object in order to paste it into a different document, the object must be open and displayed on the screen. However, most Windows programs that offer OLE technology also offer the Insert Object command, which lets you embed an object without having to open it and copy it to the Clipboard.

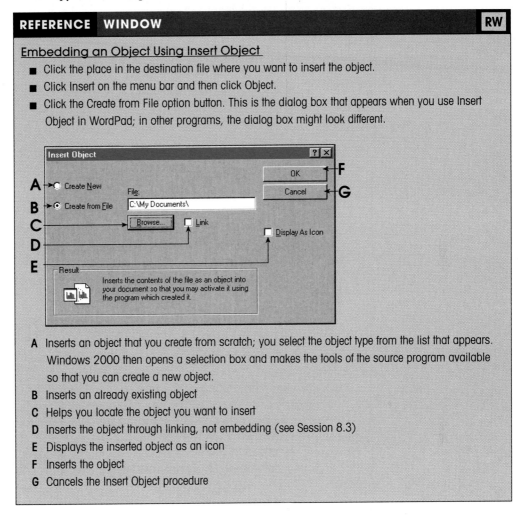

REFERENCE WINDOW   **RW**

Embedding an Object Using Insert Object
- Click the place in the destination file where you want to insert the object.
- Click Insert on the menu bar and then click Object.
- Click the Create from File option button. This is the dialog box that appears when you use Insert Object in WordPad; in other programs, the dialog box might look different.

A Inserts an object that you create from scratch; you select the object type from the list that appears. Windows 2000 then opens a selection box and makes the tools of the source program available so that you can create a new object.
B Inserts an already existing object
C Helps you locate the object you want to insert
D Inserts the object through linking, not embedding (see Session 8.3)
E Displays the inserted object as an icon
F Inserts the object
G Cancels the Insert Object procedure

Insert Object embeds the entire file, without giving you the option to embed just a part of it, such as a single paragraph of text or a single table or chart. To embed a part of a file, you must use Paste Special or open the file, select the data you want, cut or copy it, and then paste it into the new document.

When you talked to the graphic designer on the phone the other day, you mentioned that it might be nice to include the number "10" in the graphic, for 10th anniversary. The designer has just delivered a new disk with the revised file, called Pins10. You decide to embed Pins10 into the Feedback document, using the Insert Object command.

To embed an object using the Insert Object command:

1. Scroll down the Feedback document until you see the boldface **Video Clip:** heading.
2. Click to the left of the **Video Clip:** heading.
3. Press the **Enter** key twice to add two new lines, and then press the **Up Arrow** twice.

4. Click **Insert** on the menu bar and then click **Object**.

5. Click the **Create from File** option button.

6. Click the **Browse** button and then locate and click the **Pins10** file on your Data Disk.

7. Click the **Open** button. The filename is inserted into the File box.

8. Verify that the Link and Display As Icon check boxes are not selected. See Figure 8-12.

Figure 8-12	INSERT OBJECT DIALOG BOX

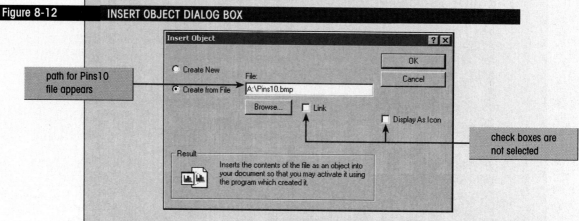

9. Click the **OK** button in the Insert Object dialog box. The object appears in the Feedback document.

Controlling an OLE Object's Appearance

When you place a graphic image in a document, your computer might take longer to display the document than if it contained only text. For example, when you scroll up and down the Feedback document, depending on the speed of your computer and the size of the graphics, it may take significantly longer to "redraw" the graphics as you scroll. For this reason, some users prefer to use the ability of Windows 2000 to display OLE objects as icons, especially during the draft phases of creating a multimedia document. Like most Windows 2000 objects, your embedded object has a property sheet that lets you work with the object. You decide to display the first graphic you embedded, the red Pins graphic, as an icon.

To display the embedded Pins graphic as an icon:

1. Scroll up the Feedback document so you can see the first graphic you embedded, the Pins graphic with the red balls.

2. Right-click the **Pins** graphic and then click **Object Properties**.

3. Click the **View** tab.

4. Click the **Display As Icon** option button and then click the **OK** button. An icon appears that represents the graphic. See Figure 8-13.

Figure 8-13   DISPLAYING AN OBJECT AS AN ICON

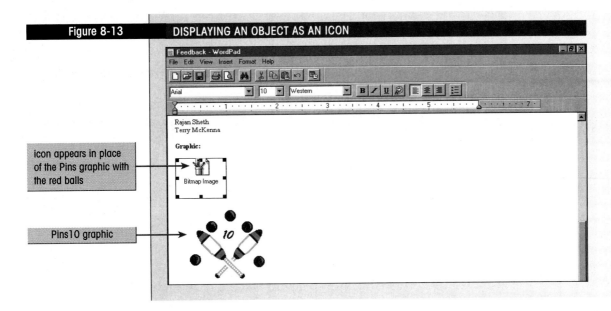

icon appears in place of the Pins graphic with the red balls

Pins10 graphic

Changing the Display Icon

Because you changed the graphic to an icon, and so can no longer identify the contents of the embedded object, you decide to change the label of the icon to make it more descriptive. You can change the icon label using the embedded object's property sheet.

To change the label of the icon:

1. Right-click the icon representing the embedded Pins graphic.
2. Click **Object Properties**.
3. Click the **View** tab.
4. Click the **Change Icon** button.
5. Delete the contents of the Label box at the bottom of the dialog box and then type **Pins Graphic**. See Figure 8-14.

Figure 8-14   CHANGE ICON DIALOG BOX

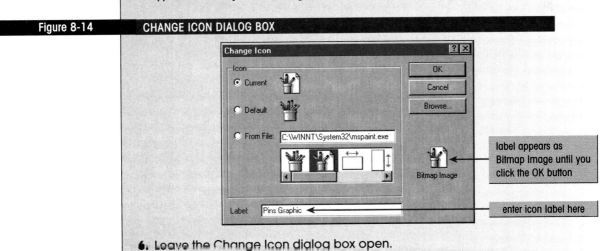

label appears as Bitmap Image until you click the OK button

enter icon label here

6. Leave the Change Icon dialog box open.

If your multimedia document includes icons in its final form, you can change the icon representing the embedded object, using the property sheet, if you don't like the look of the icons Windows 2000 chooses. Incidentally, you can use this method to change the appearance of many icons, including some icons on the desktop.

REFERENCE WINDOW   RW

<u>Changing an Icon</u>
- Open the icon's property sheet. You usually do this by right-clicking the existing icon to open its object menu, and then clicking Properties, although for embedded objects the command appears as Object Properties.
- If necessary, click the tab in the Properties dialog box that contains the Change Icon button.
- Click the Change Icon button.
- Click one of the icons that appears in the Change Icon dialog box. You could also click Create From File, click the Browse button, and then locate and select the file containing the icon (switch the Files of type list to All Files if you are looking for a file with an extension other than .ICO, the default type that appears).
- Click the OK button in the Change Icon dialog box and in the Properties dialog box.

You decide to change the icon representing the Pins graphic to a more descriptive icon. Your Data Disk contains a bitmap graphics file called Icon that you will use as the icon.

To change the appearance of the icon:

1. In the Change Icon dialog box, which should still be open, click the **From File** option button and then click the **Browse** button.
2. Click the **Look in** list arrow and then click the drive containing your Data Disk.
3. Click the **Files of type** list arrow and then click **All Files**.
4. Click **Icon** (the name of the file you'll use to represent the icon) and then click the **Open** button.
5. Click the **OK** button in the Change Icon dialog box and then click the **OK** button in the Bitmap Image Properties dialog box. The new icon appears. Click outside the selection box. See Figure 8-15.

TROUBLE? Windows 2000 can be a little unpredictable when you change an icon in a document. If the new icon doesn't appear, wait a few seconds, then scroll up the document until the original icon is no longer visible on the screen. Then scroll back down. This should make the correct icon appear.

Figure 8-15	NEW ICON FOR EMBEDDED OBJECT

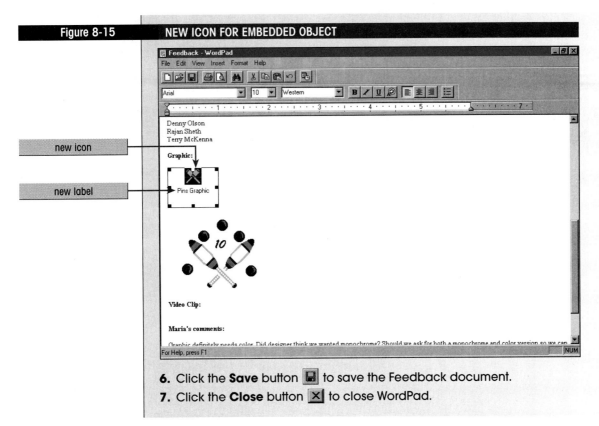

6. Click the **Save** button ⊞ to save the Feedback document.
7. Click the **Close** button ☒ to close WordPad.

You could reduce the size of the icon image, to take up even less space; in this example, it's not much smaller than the original graphic. However, displaying objects as icons is a good skill to remember if your computer is low on memory and you are working with a document with multiple embedded objects.

Paste Special

When you want to embed only a portion of a file, such as a Microsoft Excel chart without the corresponding worksheet, you can't use Insert Object, because Insert Object inserts an entire file. Although you can use Paste in some circumstances, you have more control over the embedding process when you use **Paste Special**, a command on the Edit menu of programs that support OLE. Figure 8-16 shows the Paste Special dialog box as it appears when you embed an Excel chart into a Word document. This dialog box appears when you select a chart in Excel, copy it, switch to Word, and then choose Paste Special on the Edit menu.

Paste Special sometimes gives you more than one embedding option. In this example, you can embed the object either as a chart or as a bitmap image. If you choose the latter, the Excel tools are no longer available to you, and the chart is inserted as a graphic image.

Figure 8-16   PASTE SPECIAL DIALOG BOX

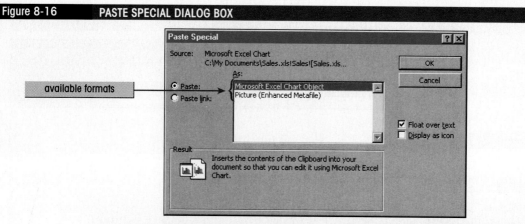

available formats

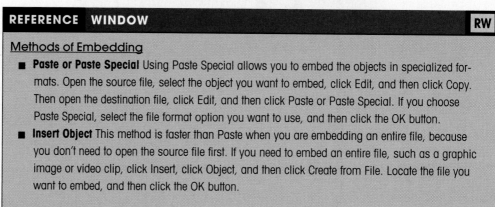

REFERENCE WINDOW   RW

Methods of Embedding

- **Paste or Paste Special** Using Paste Special allows you to embed the objects in specialized formats. Open the source file, select the object you want to embed, click Edit, and then click Copy. Then open the destination file, click Edit, and then click Paste or Paste Special. If you choose Paste Special, select the file format option you want to use, and then click the OK button.
- **Insert Object** This method is faster than Paste when you are embedding an entire file, because you don't need to open the source file first. If you need to embed an entire file, such as a graphic image or video clip, click Insert, click Object, and then click Create from File. Locate the file you want to embed, and then click the OK button.

Be aware that there are programs that feature neither OLE nor Clipboard. When using such programs, you must depend on the data transfer commands that they provide—commands that often appear on the File menu as Import or Export. When you attempt to transfer data from other programs and it doesn't seem to be working as you expect, the first thing you should suspect is that the program doesn't support OLE.

Session 8.2 QUICK CHECK

1. What is OLE?
2. You just embedded text from a WordPad document into a PowerPoint presentation. Which is the source program, and which is the destination program?
3. Name two ways to embed an object with OLE. Under what circumstances might you use these different methods?
4. What is in-place editing?
5. True or False: You can use the Clipboard to transfer data between any two programs.

SESSION 8.3

In this session, you will link a new version of the Pins graphic into your Feedback document. Then you'll work with the original file to see how linking lets you update the linked information in the source document. You'll learn how to delete OLE objects from your document. Then you'll link a video clip into the Feedback document and work with the Windows 2000 Media Player.

Linking

The graphic designer you have been working with has supplied you with another new version of the Pins graphic, called Pins2, that makes better use of color. You want the committee members to see this new version. But what if the graphic designer calls again with an even newer version? You don't want to have to re-embed the graphic every time you receive a new version. Therefore, you decide to link the Pins2 graphic into your Feedback document rather than embed it.

Linking is another way to insert information into a document, but with linking you insert a *representation* of the object. When you edit a linked object, you are editing the original object, the source file itself, whether you are in the source or destination file. For example, if you change the color of the balls in a linked object, you are changing the color of the balls in the source file itself. Notice how this differs from embedding. With embedding you place a copy of the object into the destination file; it does not connect to the source file, so any changes you make to the embedded object are not reflected in the source file. With linking, however, you maintain a connection between the source file and the destination file, and a change to one object changes the other object. See Figure 8-17.

| Figure 8-17 | LINKING VS. EMBEDDING |

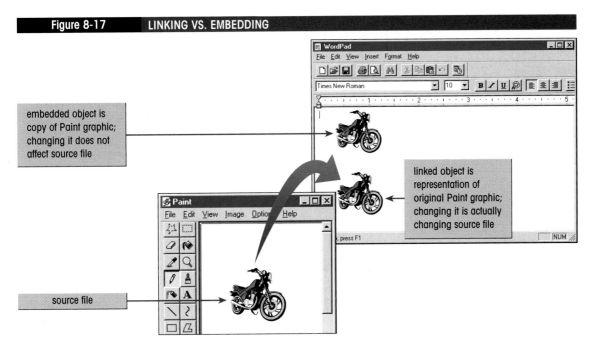

You link an object when you want only one copy of the object to exist. For example, you might want to use an object in several documents. When you update the object, all the documents use the updated version. When you give someone a document that contains links, make sure to include the source files. Note also that links target specific locations on a disk, so if you move the linked object source, the destination document will no longer be able to display it (although you can update a link by right-clicking it, clicking Object Properties, clicking Link, and then clicking Change Source).

Linking a Graphic File to a WordPad Document

You want only one version of the Pins graphic to be in use, so you decide to link Pins2 to the Feedback document. As with embedding, you can use Insert Object, Paste, or Paste Special to link objects. Insert Object allows you to insert an entire file, while Paste Special allows you to insert a portion of a file.

REFERENCE WINDOW **RW**

Linking an Object
- To use Insert Object, click the location in the destination file where you want to insert the object. Then click Insert, click Object, and then click Create from File. Next click Browse, locate and select the file, click the Link check box, and then click the OK button twice.
- To use Paste Special, first open the source file and highlight the information you want to insert. Click Edit, and then click Copy. Next open the destination file and click the location where you want to insert the object. Click Edit, click Paste Special, click Paste Link, and then click the OK button. Note that Paste Special does not always allow you to paste with a link.

You'll use Insert Object to link the Pins2 graphic because you want to link the entire file, not just a portion of it.

To insert the Pins2 graphic as a linked object:

1. Start **WordPad** and then open the **Feedback** file on your Data Disk.
2. Scroll down the Feedback document below the two embedded objects. Click to the left of the Video Clip: heading, press the **Enter** key twice to insert two new lines, and then press **Up Arrow** twice.
3. Click **Insert** on the menu bar and then click **Object**.
4. Click the **Create from File** option button, click the **Browse** button, click the **Look in** list arrow, click the drive containing your Data Disk, click **Pins2**, and then click the **Open** button.
5. Click the **Link** check box to place a check mark in it, and then click the **OK** button. The multicolored Pins2 graphic appears in the Feedback document.

Arranging Windows Using Tile and Cascade

You like the look of the color graphic, but you think it would look better if all the balls were one color. You decide to edit the source file, Pins2, in Paint, but you want to see the effect on your WordPad document at the same time. You could resize and drag the windows into place, or you could use the Tile or Cascade commands on the taskbar shortcut menu. The **Tile** command arranges all open windows so that they are all visible. You can tile vertically (side by side) or horizontally (one above the other). The **Cascade** command arranges all open windows so that they overlap each other and all their title bars are visible. Figure 8-18 shows these two arrangements.

Figure 8-18   **ARRANGING WINDOWS**

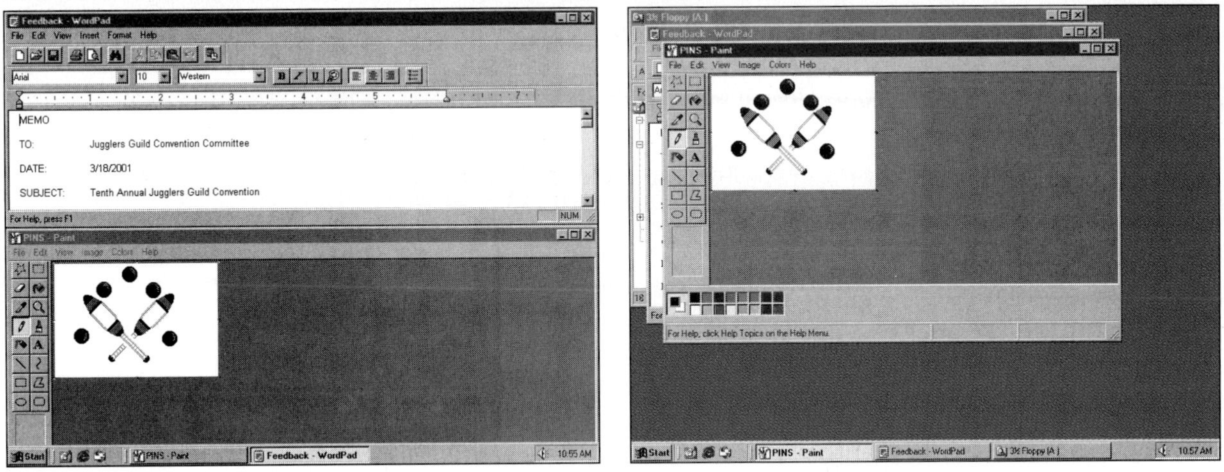

two horizontally tiled windows   three cascaded windows

Tiling is useful when you have just a few open windows, whereas cascading is useful when you have many open windows. Arranging windows can be helpful when you work with data transfer, because you are often working with more than one open program, and you want to see what's happening in the open programs at the same time. You decide to vertically tile the WordPad and Paint windows.

To open and tile the Paint and WordPad windows:

1. Click the **Start** button, point to **Programs**, point to **Accessories**, and then click **Paint**.

2. Open the **Pins2** file on your Data Disk. This is the file you just linked to the Feedback document.

3. Right-click a blank area of the taskbar to open the taskbar menu. See Figure 8-19.

   TROUBLE? If program buttons fill your taskbar, right-click the space between two program buttons until your menu looks like that in Figure 8-19.

Figure 8-19   **OPENING THE TASKBAR MENU**

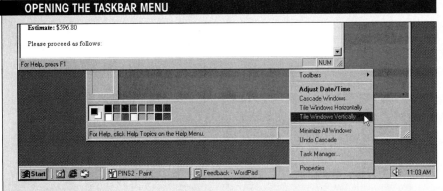

4. Click **Tile Windows Vertically**. The two windows appear side by side.

5. Scroll down the WordPad window, if necessary, so that you can see the multicolored Pins2 graphic.

Editing a Linked Object in the Source Program

The object you just inserted is linked, so you can change it in either the source or destination file, and your changes will be stored in the original file. You decide to color the balls red in the original Pins2 file.

To edit the Pins2 graphic in Paint:

1. In Paint, click the **Fill With Color** tool 🖌.
2. Click the **red** box (in second row, third box from left in Color palette) and then click each of the four balls that aren't already red. All five balls should be red when you finish.
3. In Paint, click **File** and then click **Save**.

Updating a Linked Object

If the destination file is closed when you change the source file, any linked objects will usually update automatically the next time you open the file, or you'll be given the option to update the links when you next open the file. If the destination file is open when you change the source file, you have to update it manually, using the Links command. This opens the Links dialog box, which gives you control over the links in your document.

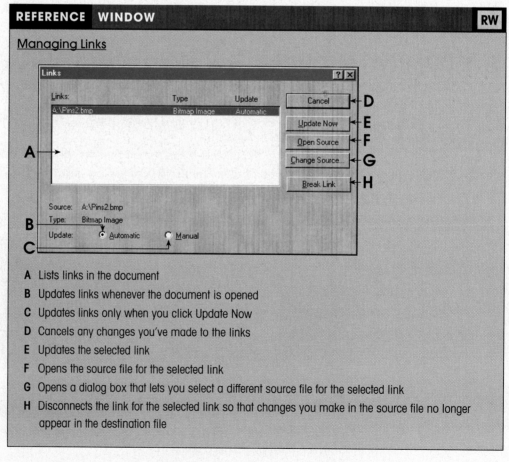

REFERENCE WINDOW | RW

Managing Links

A Lists links in the document
B Updates links whenever the document is opened
C Updates links only when you click Update Now
D Cancels any changes you've made to the links
E Updates the selected link
F Opens the source file for the selected link
G Opens a dialog box that lets you select a different source file for the selected link
H Disconnects the link for the selected link so that changes you make in the source file no longer appear in the destination file

You decide to update the link between the Pins2 source file and the Feedback destination file so you can verify that the changes take place.

To update the link in the WordPad document:

1. Click the multicolored **Pins2** graphic in the WordPad window.
2. Click **Edit** on the WordPad menu bar and then click **Links**. The Links dialog box opens, displaying all links in the current document (in this case, there is only one). See Figure 8-20.

| Figure 8-20 | LINKS DIALOG BOX |

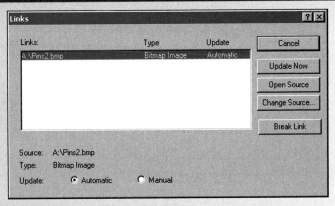

3. Click the **Update Now** button. The graphic is updated. (Move the Links dialog box if you can't see the change.)
4. Click the **Close** button to close the Links dialog box.
5. Click the **Close** button ✕ to close Paint.
6. Maximize the WordPad window.

Deleting **an OLE Object**

As you look over your document, you notice that you have now inserted three graphic objects into the Feedback document. The first two are both older versions of the graphic. You decide you don't need to include them in the Feedback document, so you delete them.

To delete the two old embedded graphics, Pins and Pins10:

1. Scroll up the Feedback document until you see the icon representing the first Pins graphic.
2. Click the icon labeled **Pins Graphic**. A selection box appears.
3. Press the **Delete** key.
4. Click the **Pins10** graphic (the monochrome one). A selection box appears.
5. Press the **Delete** key.
6. Delete two blank lines below the boldface Graphic: heading.

You've completed the graphics portion of your Feedback document.

Linking **and Playing a Video Clip**

Now you turn your attention to the next object you want to show to the committee members: the video clip. You decide to link the video clip to your Feedback document so that if the computer animation vendor sends you an updated file, you won't have to reinsert the file. You can link a video clip in the same way you linked a graphic, using Insert Object, since you are linking an entire file and not just a portion of a file.

To link a video clip to a document:

1. Scroll the Feedback document until you locate the boldface **Video Clip:** heading.
2. Click two lines below the Video Clip: heading (the line above the boldface **Maria's comments:** heading).
3. Click **Insert** on the menu bar and then click **Object**.
4. Click the **Create from File** option button.
5. Click the **Browse** button.
6. If necessary, click the **Look in** list arrow and then click the drive containing your Data Disk.
7. Click **Video**, and then click the **Open** button.
8. Click the **Link** check box to place a check mark in it and then click the **OK** button.

The video clip looks like a graphic object, but of course it isn't. You can play the video clip by double-clicking it or by right-clicking it and using the Play Linked Video Clip Object command. Because it is a linked object using OLE technology, you don't have to leave WordPad or start a separate program to play it.

To play the video clip:

1. Right-click the video clip and then point to **Linked Video Clip Object**.

   TROUBLE? If this appears as "Linked Media Clip Object," point to that instead.

   TROUBLE? If a message appears warning you that Windows 2000 couldn't launch the server application, ask your instructor or lab manager to install the multimedia accessories.

2. Click **Play**. The video clip plays in a small window. It might play once very quickly and then stop, perhaps even before it appears to reach the end, or it might play continuously. You'll learn momentarily how to control the way the video clip plays. See Figure 8-21.

   TROUBLE? If your clip plays very choppily, your computer might not have sufficient memory to play it smoothly.

   TROUBLE? Depending on what programs have been installed on your computer, the video clip might appear in a different window than the one shown in Figure 8-21.

3. If necessary, click the video clip window's **Close** button [X] to close the window.

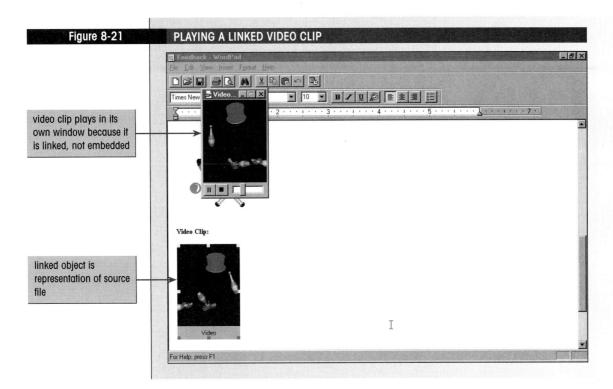

Figure 8-21   PLAYING A LINKED VIDEO CLIP

video clip plays in its own window because it is linked, not embedded

linked object is representation of source file

You've now inserted the video clip into the Feedback document. However, you'd like to refine the way it plays.

Windows 2000 **Multimedia**

The window that opened when you played the video clip was part of Windows 2000 Media Player, one of the accessories Windows 2000 provides that handles multimedia files. The Windows 2000 multimedia accessories, listed in Figure 8-22 and available on the Entertainment and Communication submenus of the Accessories menu, let you create, edit, and play multimedia clips. Some of the accessories, such as DVD Player, won't appear if you don't have the appropriate hardware.

Figure 8-22   MULTIMEDIA ACCESSORIES

ACCESSORY	DESCRIPTION
ActiveMovie Control	An Internet Explorer component that enhances the playing of audio and video files on a Web page
CD Player	Plays music CDs
DVD Player	Plays DVD discs or regular CDs from a DVD drive
Media Player	Plays audio and video clips
NetShow	Plays audio and video across the Internet, playing immediately without having to wait for the entire file to download
Sound Recorder	Records and plays audio files
Multimedia Sound Schemes	Provides different sounds that you can attach to Windows 2000 events (such as exiting a program)
Volume Control	Adjusts your speaker volume

Multimedia clips can use sound, video, or both. To play a clip that uses sound, you need a sound card and speakers. If your computer doesn't have these hardware devices, you can still hear sounds through your computer's internal speaker—such as the "beeps" you hear when the computer alerts you to something. The internal speaker, however, is inadequate for playing most sound files.

The **Sound Recorder** accessory uses the **WAV** (which is short for waveform-audio) file format to store and record sounds as realistically as possible. The **Media Player** accessory, on the other hand, uses the **MIDI** (short for Musical Instrument Digital Interface) format. MIDI files use artificial, synthesized sounds to mimic real sounds and hence are usually much smaller than WAV files. Although you can't use MIDI files to store voices, you can use them very effectively to store the synthesized sounds of special MIDI instruments.

To play a video clip, you don't need a sound card or speakers, but the quality of the video will depend on your computer's video card capabilities and on its speed and memory capacity. You use the Media Player accessory to play ActiveMovie files or video clips in the **AVI** (short for Audio Video Interleaved) format. This format is sometimes called "Video for Windows." AVI files can contain both images and sound (of course, if you want to hear the sound you'll need a sound card and speakers). Media Player lets you scroll back and forth through a video clip, but you cannot use Media Player to edit the clip itself.

ActiveMovie plays many existing file types, including MPEG audio and video, AVI video, WAV audio, MIDI audio, and QuickTime video.

Using Media Player

When you played the juggler video clip, it might have played only once and then stopped, or it might have played continually. You want to control the way it plays. To do this, you need to start Media Player and edit the video's settings. Media Player plays a video one frame at a time, just as a filmstrip is shown. A slider appears that shows you which frame is appearing at any given moment, so you can move forward or backward through individual frames. Media Player also includes a set of buttons that resemble the buttons on a cassette tape player or a VCR, as described in Figure 8-23.

Figure 8-23		MEDIA PLAYER BUTTONS
BUTTON	**NAME**	**DESCRIPTION**
▶	Play	Plays the multimedia clip; turns into the Pause button when multimedia clip is playing
❙❙	Pause	Play button turns into Pause button when multimedia clip is playing; pauses clip
■	Stop	Stops the clip at its current frame or track
⏏	Eject	Appears only when you are playing a clip off a CD-ROM; ejects the CD
⏮	Previous Mark	Moves to the previous mark (like a track on a CD)
◀◀	Rewind	Moves backward in increments as you click
▶▶	Fast Forward	Moves forward in increments as you click
⏭	Next Mark	Moves to the next mark (like a track on a CD)
⤒	Start Selection	Starts the selection (if you select just a few frames to play)
⤓	End Selection	Ends the selection (if you select just a few frames to play)

You decide you want to make sure the video plays continually. You can either start Media Player from the Start menu and then open the video clip source file, or you can start Media Player from within the Feedback document by opening the video clip for editing.

To make changes to the video clip's settings:

1. Right-click the video clip, point to **Linked Video Clip Object**, and then click **Edit**. Media Player opens. See Figure 8-24.

Figure 8-24	MEDIA PLAYER

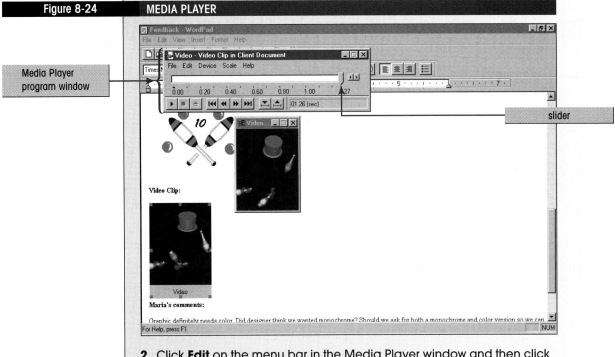

Media Player program window

slider

2. Click **Edit** on the menu bar in the Media Player window and then click **Options**. First see how the video plays when it is not set on Auto Repeat.

3. If necessary, click the **Auto Repeat** check box to deselect it, and then click the **OK** button.

    TROUBLE? If Auto Repeat is already deselected, skip Step 3. See Figure 8-25.

Figure 8-25	MEDIA PLAYER OPTIONS

make sure this check box is not selected for now

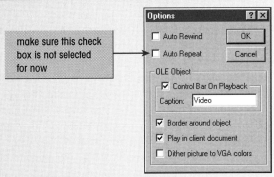

4. Click the **Play** ▶ button. The video clip plays once and then stops.

5. Click **Edit**, click **Options**, click the **Auto Repeat** check box to select it, and then click the **OK** button.

6. Click the **Play** button ▶ . The video clip plays over and over. Notice the slider as it moves through the frames of the video clip.

7. Click the **Close** button ✕ to close Media Player. Click **Yes** to update the Client Document with the new settings.

    TROUBLE? If you close the video clip window instead of the Media Player window, repeat Step 7 to close Media Player.

The Feedback document now contains no embedded objects and two linked objects: the graphic and the video clip. You can send the document, along with the two source files, to the committee members for their feedback. They can easily view both objects and can then add their comments to the bottom of the document.

To save your work and close all open windows:

1. Click the **Save** button 🖫 to save your Feedback document.
2. Click the **Close** button ⊠ to close WordPad.

Your final version of the Feedback document used only linking, not embedding, because you decided that both objects were likely to undergo further revision, and you wanted to be able to easily update the document without having to reinsert the objects. As you created the Feedback document, however, you used several different methods to exchange information between documents. As with other aspects of Windows 2000, the focus is on the document, not on the program that created it. You create a document by bringing in tools from other programs without even being aware that you are doing so. Many people see this focus on the document as the future of personal computing.

Session 8.3 QUICK | CHECK

1. What is the difference between linking and embedding?
2. If you want to share a document containing embedded objects with another person, do you need to include the source files? Explain why or why not.
3. When you use the Insert Object method to insert an object into a document, do you first need to open the source file?
4. What's the difference in appearance between tiling and cascading windows?
5. True or False: Media Player plays only video, not audio, clips.
6. Describe these three file types: WAV, MIDI, and AVI.

REVIEW ASSIGNMENTS

1. **Copying and Pasting Text** A friend of yours owns a small tailor shop and wants to advertise his services in the local telephone company's Yellow Pages. He wants feedback from his employees and friends on his advertisement, and wonders if you'd share Maria's feedback process with him. You write him a note and then paste in the steps to your process.
   a. Start WordPad, and then open the **Maria** file on your Data Disk.
   b. Highlight the bulleted list, and then copy it to the Clipboard.
   c. Open the **Tailor** file on your Data Disk, and then scroll to the boldface "Follow this Procedure": heading. Add a few blank lines below the heading, and then paste the copied information. Replace the name "Jan" with your name.
   d. Print and save **Tailor**, and then close WordPad (you can ignore WordPad's warning).
2. **Pasting Text into Paint** In this tutorial, you pasted a Paint graphic into WordPad. Now you'll try pasting in the other direction. You are designing a banner that announces the names of incumbent officers up for reelection for the Jugglers Guild. You have created a Paint graphic called Election. You want to insert the names of the five officers into that graphic.
   a. Start Paint and open the **Election** graphic on your Data Disk.
   b. Start WordPad, open the **Maria** file, and then copy the last five names (not including Maria Arruda) in the Distribution List to the Clipboard. These are the five officers up for reelection.
   c. Close WordPad. Paste the names into the **Election** graphic. Click Yes if Paint asks if you want to enlarge the bitmap.

    d. Drag the pasted names so they are centered below the heading.

    e. Print and save the **Election** graphic, and then close Paint. Now experiment with the pasted information. Are you able to use the source program tools from within Paint?

    f. On your printout, write a paragraph answering the following questions: Is the text you just pasted inserted as an embedded object into the Paint graphic? How can you tell? How does the process you just completed differ from the way you pasted a Paint graphic into a WordPad document in Session 8.2?

3. Linking and Editing a Graphic   You work as a clown named Chester, and you are attending the juggling convention. You want to distribute a flyer at the convention that advertises your clowning services. You have created the flyer in the WordPad document named **Clowning**, and you want to link a graphic file into that document.

    a. Open the WordPad document named **Clowning**.

    b. Use the Insert Object command to insert the graphic named **Chester** into the bottom of the **Clowning** document. Make sure you insert the object with a link.

    c. After you've inserted the **Chester** graphic, open it for editing by right-clicking the object, pointing to Linked Bitmap Image Object, and then clicking Edit. Change Chester's hair color to brown. Close Paint, saving the changes to **Chester**, and then return to the WordPad document.

    d. Update the link, if necessary, and then print and save the **Clowning** document. On the printout, write a paragraph about how editing a linked object from the destination document differs from editing an embedded object.

Explore

4. Using Sound Recorder   If you have a microphone, a sound card, and speakers, you can create your own sound file, using the Sound Recorder accessory that comes with Windows 2000. You want to send a colleague an electronic "Happy Birthday" message, so you decide to sing the Happy Birthday song into the microphone, save it as a sound file, and then embed it into a message.

    a. Click the Start button, point to Programs, point to Accessories, point to Entertainment, and then click Sound Recorder.

    b. Click the Record button on the far right of Sound Recorder.

    c. Sing Happy Birthday into the microphone. (Sing just the first few words to keep the size of the audio clip small.) Click the Stop button when you are finished singing.

    d. Save the document as **Happy Birthday** on a new, blank, formatted disk—not your Data Disk. Label this disk "OLE Disk." (You need a second disk because if you complete all the Review Assignments and Projects, you won't have room on your Data Disk.)

    e. Play the **Happy Birthday** sound file.

    f. Compose a birthday message in WordPad, and embed the **Happy Birthday** sound file into this message.

    g. Print the message and save it as **Birthday Message**. If you have access to e-mail and you know how to send a file, you could send the WordPad file to a friend who's celebrating a birthday.

PROJECTS

1. You work for the Internal Revenue Service and have been using Notepad to draft a brochure to inform taxpayers about online tax filing. Notepad, however, does not offer any text-formatting options, and you'd like to format your document. You decide to move the text into a WordPad document.

    a. Start Notepad, and then open the **IRS** file on your Data Disk.

    b. Start WordPad, and then open the **New** file on your Data Disk.

    c. In Notepad, select and then copy the entire document. Close Notepad.

    d. In the WordPad window, click below the Online Tax Filing heading and then paste the text. Type your name at the top of the document.

    e. Print and save the WordPad document, and then close WordPad.

2. You are a member of the Tokunta Construction Company. You are developing a training manual for new employees. You need to link a graphic that illustrates a construction principle, but you want to display it as an icon.

   a. Open the **House** document in WordPad on your Data Disk.

   b. Use the Insert Object command to insert the **House** graphic at the end of the document. Make sure you link the graphic.

   c. Change the graphic display so that it displays an icon.

   d. Change the icon to the Tools icon on your Data Disk.

   e. Change the caption of the icon to Cantilever.

   f. Print and save the **House** document.

3. Your Data Disk includes a sound file from J. F. Kennedy's inaugural speech. You'd like to link this sound file to a WordPad document that you are creating for a linguistics class, in which you are studying American accents. Kennedy's sound clip exemplifies a Boston accent.

   a. Create a new WordPad document and type "Linguistics, Bostonian accent" at the beginning. Make sure you type your name. Save the document as **Linguistics** on your Data Disk, using WordPad or Microsoft Word.

   b. Use the Insert Object command to insert the Kennedy sound file into your document. Make sure you insert it with a link.

   c. You'll be able to complete this task only if you have a sound card and speakers. Use the linked object's shortcut menu to first play the object and then open it for editing. When you open it for editing, what accessory does Windows 2000 use?

4. You work at CarpetMaster, a company that specializes in residential and commercial carpet cleaning and restoration. A customer wants an estimate for repair costs for an Oriental rug that was damaged in a recent fire. You need to draw a rectangle in Paint that proportionally approximates the carpet size and indicate the area that you'll be repairing. Then you need to embed that graphic into a WordPad document that gives the estimate.

   a. Create a Paint graphic that shows the carpet and the damaged area. Save this graphic as **Carpet** on your OLE Disk (the one you created in Tutorial Assignment 4)—not on your Data Disk. Close Paint. Figure 8-26 shows an example of a graphic with the marked portion of damaged carpet.

Figure 8-26

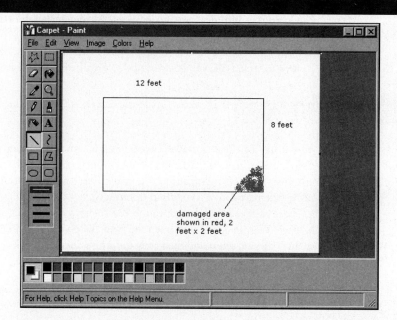

Explore

   b. Create a WordPad document that uses appropriate text for an estimate and includes a description of the necessary repairs. Save the document as **CarpetMaster Estimate**.

   c. Open Calculator and calculate 6.5 hours at $47/hr. Paste this amount into the WordPad document.

   d. Use the Insert Object command to embed the **Paint** graphic in the WordPad document.

   e. Print and save the WordPad document.

5. If you have access to other software programs, such as a word processor, a spreadsheet program, or a database program, experiment with the data transfer operations available in those programs. Create new documents in these programs, add sample data, and then save the documents on your disk. Then try to copy and paste data between the programs. Next try embedding and linking. Write a short essay that answers the following questions:

   a. What programs did you test? In what situations were you able to copy and paste?

   b. In what situations did Paste embed the data? In what situations did Paste simply transfer the data without embedding?

   c. In what situations were you able to do in-place editing?

   d. Were there any situations in which you were unable to link?

   e. Based on your experiments, what conclusions can you draw about whether or not your programs support OLE?

6. You own Circle K Ranch, a working ranch that welcomes families, summer campers, and groups for weekly stays, so they can experience life on a ranch. You are working on a flyer that you will mail to former clients and travel agents.

   a. Create a WordPad document called **Ranch Flyer** on your OLE disk (the one you created in Tutorial Assignment 4—not your Data Disk). Write a brief description of the ranch. Mention that you are working on the summer schedule and that people should make their reservations as soon as possible.

   b. Use Calculator to calculate this year's weekly rate. You need to earn $15,000 this summer from your visitor income, to make an acceptable profit. There are 12 weeks in the summer, and you have room for 8 guests each week. Calculate a room charge per person per week, then click 15000 / 12 / 8 = in the Calculator window. Paste the Calculator results into your document.

   c. Use the Insert Object command to create a new bitmapped image in your advertisement. The Create New option button should be selected, with an object type of Bitmap Image. Create a small Paint graphic that shows a letter K in an interesting font with a circle around it.

   d. Print and save the flyer on your OLE Disk.

LAB ASSIGNMENTS

Multimedia brings together text, graphics, sound, animation, video, and photo images. In this Lab you will learn how to apply multimedia and then have the chance to see what it might be like to design some aspects of multimedia projects. See the Read This Before You Begin page for information on installing and starting the Lab.

1. Click the Steps button to learn about multimedia development. As you work through the Steps, answer all of the Quick Check questions that appear. After you complete the Steps, you will see a Quick Check report. Follow the instructions on the screen to print this report.

2. How many videos are included in the Multimedia Mission Log? The image on the Mission Profile page is a vector drawing. What happens when you enlarge it?

3. Listen to the sound track on Day 4. Is this a WAV file or a MIDI file? Why do you think so? Is this a synthesized or a digitized sound? Listen to the sound track on the first page. Can you tell if this is a WAV file or a MIDI file?

4. Suppose you were hired as a multimedia designer for a multimedia series targeting fourth- and fifth-grade students. Describe the changes you would make to the Multimedia Mission Log so it would be suitable for these students. Also, include a sketch showing a screen from your revised design.

5. The Multimedia Mission Log does not contain any hyperlinks. Suppose that you were hired to revise the design of this product and to add hyperlinks. Provide a list of five specific instances where you would use hyperlinks, and indicate what sort of information each would link to.

6. Multimedia can be effectively applied to projects such as encyclopedias, atlases, and animated storybooks; computer-based training for foreign languages, first aid, or software applications; games and sports simulations; business presentations; personal albums, scrapbooks, and baby books; and product catalogs and Web pages.

7. Suppose you were hired to create one of these projects. Write a one-paragraph description of the project you would be creating. Describe some of the multimedia elements you would include. For each of these elements, indicate its source and whether you would need to obtain permission for its use. Finally, sketch a screen or two showing your completed project.

QUICK CHECK ANSWERS

Session 8.1
1. an area in your computer's memory that stores data you cut or copy
2. When you cut selected text, it is removed from the original document to the Clipboard. When you copy it, a replica of the data is moved to the Clipboard, but the original document remains intact.
3. Ctrl+X to cut, Ctrl+C to copy, Ctrl+V to paste
4. False
5. It is more accurate than typing.

Session 8.2
1. Object linking and embedding—a technology that allows you to transfer data from one program to another and retain the ability to access tools from the original program
2. WordPad is the source program; PowerPoint is the destination program.
3. Paste, Paste Special, or Insert Object. Paste allows you to embed a selected portion of a file, Paste Special allows you to embed a selected portion with more control, and Insert Object allows you to embed an entire file without having to open it first.
4. editing an embedded object using the source program tools without ever leaving the destination document
5. False; older programs might not support Clipboard technology

Session 8.3
1. Linking places a representation of the source file, whereas embedding places a copy of the source file, into the destination document.
2. No. Embedded objects have been copied into the document.
3. No.
4. Tiling arranges open windows so they are all visible. Cascading overlaps open windows so their title bars are visible.
5. False
6. The WAV format records and stores sounds as realistically as possible. The MIDI format uses artificial sounds to mimic real sounds. The AVI format is the Windows video clip format.

In this tutorial you will:

- Get an overview of networks and network terminology

- View your network using My Network Places

- View your network's properties and identify your computer on the network

- Consider network security and access rights issues

- Log on and log off a network account

- Access network resources, including folders and printers

- Map a network folder to a drive letter

- Work with network resources offline

- Share a resource with the network

EXPLORING YOUR NETWORK

Using Network Resources at Millennium Real Estate

CASE

Millennium Real Estate

You are a real estate agent who recently joined Millennium Real Estate Company, a small firm comprised of a real estate division and a land development division. Recently, Millennium connected all their computers together to form a network. A **network** is a collection of computers and other hardware devices linked together so that they can exchange data and share hardware and software.

Networks offer a company such as Millennium many advantages. Groups of computers on the network can use the same printer, so Millennium doesn't have to purchase a printer for each computer. Networks facilitate group projects, because one person can save a document in a folder that other users on other computers can access. A network also improves communication in a company because coworkers can easily share news and information.

Joan Alvarez, the company's owner, wants you to learn to use the Millennium network effectively, and she would like you to spend the next several hours exploring it. She decides to start you off by giving you an overview of the basic concepts of networking. Once you have been introduced to fundamentals, Joan will show you how to use Windows 2000 to be productive on the company's network. You will share an office with Anjali Gregory, one of the Millennium agents, so Joan decides to use the computer in Anjali's office to show you how to use the network.

SESSION 9 .1

In this session, you'll explore some basic network concepts. Then you will learn about some of the Windows 2000 tools that help you understand, view, and work with your network.

Network Concepts

Joan begins her overview by discussing the fundamentals of networks and network terminology. She believes that, armed with these fundamentals, you will be better equipped to use the network effectively.

Each device on a network is called a **node**. A node can be a computer, a printer, or any other kind of hardware that can be accessed over a network. Nodes are typically connected to each other by means of network cabling, although connections can also be established using phone lines, satellites, and infrared signals. If the network nodes are close together, as they would be in a computer lab or the Millennium office suite, the network is called a **local area network**, or **LAN**. Figure 9-1 shows a typical LAN.

| Figure 9-1 | A LOCAL AREA NETWORK |

cable connects nodes on the network

printer can be made available to all computers on the network

each computer on the network is a node

If the nodes are spread out over a wider area, such as across a state or nation, the network is often called a **wide area network**, or **WAN**. For example, an insurance company with offices in many large cities might be on a WAN, so that an office in Detroit can access information about a client whose insurance history is located on a computer in the San Antonio branch of the company. A WAN might use satellite connections to exchange data among the nodes, but it might also use phone lines.

Not only can computers be connected to form networks, but networks can also be connected together to form larger networks. In these situations, each network (sometimes referred to as a subnet) is given a **domain name**, so that other networks on can identify it. Just as information can be shared between nodes in a network, so too can information be shared between computers in different domains. The biggest and most famous example of this is the Internet, which is sometimes referred to as a "network of networks." With Internet access, a computer in one domain can communicate with a computer in a different domain, if a path connects the two networks and these two networks communicate using the same standards and conventions that the Internet uses.

Because Millennium's computers are located in the same building, they are configured as a local area network. There are two models people follow to set up LANs: the hierarchical model and the peer-to-peer model.

Hierarchical Client/Server Network

In a network based on the **hierarchical model** (often called the **client/server model**), computers called **servers** provide access to resources such as files, software, and hardware devices. A computer that uses these resources is called a **workstation** or **client**. Figure 9-2 illustrates the hierarchical model.

Figure 9-2	HIERARCHICAL NETWORK MODEL

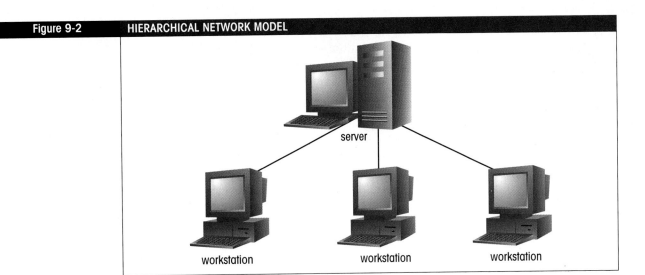

server

workstation   workstation   workstation

Servers offer many resources to the clients on the network. For example, a server might store a database, making it accessible to many workstations. A server might also handle electronic mail, faxes, or printing for a network. If a network is large, it often has several servers, with each server dedicated to the needs of a separate group of users or to a specific task. Most university networks use a hierarchical model, with students, faculty, and staff using workstations to access files and resources stored on servers across campus. A network operating system is usually installed and maintained by an individual called the **network administrator**. The administrator is ultimately responsible for how you interact with the network.

A hierarchical network requires special software on the server. This software, called a **network operating system**, manages the operations of the entire network. In addition, client software must be installed on each workstation so that it can communicate with the server. Windows 2000 comes in several different versions, each of which allows the user different network capabilities. Windows 2000 Server and Windows 2000 Advanced Server provide the network operating system needed to manage medium to large networks. As an end user, and not a network administrator, you will probably work with Windows 2000 Professional, a version of Windows 2000 that allows you to connect to a network and also have some degree of control over the network operations on your workstation. You might also use a third-party network operating system such as Novell NetWare, Windows NT, IBM OS/2 LAN, or Banyan Vines. Windows 2000 is designed to work seamlessly with these products.

Peer-to-Peer Network

A second kind of network model is the peer-to-peer model. In a network based on the **peer-to-peer model**, nodes can act as both clients and servers, with each node sharing specified resources with other nodes on the network. Figure 9-3 shows the layout of a typical peer-to-peer network.

Figure 9-3	PEER-TO-PEER NETWORK MODEL

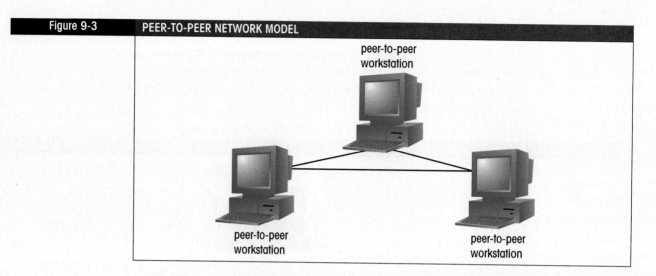

In a large peer-to-peer network, the network administrator often organizes nodes into workgroups. A **workgroup** is a group of computers that performs common tasks or belongs to users who share common duties and interests. A network administrator for a business, for example, might organize computers used by the office staff into an Office workgroup and computers used by upper management into a Management workgroup. Organizing the network in this fashion makes it easier for the network administrator to manage the differing needs of each group.

An advantage of the peer-to-peer model for Windows 2000 users is that the network can be set up without purchasing Windows 2000 Server or a third-party network operating system. Everything needed to create a peer-to-peer network is built into Windows 2000 Professional. One problem with peer-to-peer networks is that performance of individual nodes can deteriorate as they manage tasks for other computers as well as performing their own duties. Moreover, a peer-to-peer network does not have the same extensive network management and security features offered by network operating systems under the hierarchical model. For these reasons, peer-to-peer networks are usually used for smaller networks with just a few nodes. This is the case at Millennium Real Estate.

Each network is different. The network administrator tries to create a network structure that best meets the needs of the users, sometimes including elements from both the hierarchical and peer-to-peer models. How a user interacts with the network can also vary from network to network. In some cases, the network administrator will limit your ability to work on the network, whereas other administrators will give users great flexibility in sharing and accessing network resources. Joan wants you to understand that what you see on the Millennium peer-to-peer network might not necessarily apply to other networks you encounter.

Also, because every network is different, some of the topics in this tutorial will not apply to your network. If this is the case, you should still review those tasks, to further your understanding of the networking capabilities of Windows 2000.

Viewing **Your Network**

To view the contents of your network, you open an icon on the desktop called My Network Places 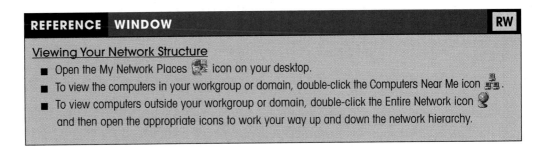. **My Network Places** is a window similar to the My Computer window that allows you to view and access the nodes on the network. It also helps you view your network's structure and see how your computer fits into it.

REFERENCE WINDOW | RW

Viewing Your Network Structure
- Open the My Network Places icon on your desktop.
- To view the computers in your workgroup or domain, double-click the Computers Near Me icon.
- To view computers outside your workgroup or domain, double-click the Entire Network icon and then open the appropriate icons to work your way up and down the network hierarchy.

To view the My Network Places window:

1. Double-click the **My Network Places** icon on your desktop.

   TROUBLE? If there is no My Network Places icon on your desktop, it could be that your computer is not set up to use a network, or that the network administrator has not given you permission to view and access the network. Talk to your instructor or technical support person for assistance.

2. The window shown in Figure 9-4 opens.

Figure 9-4 | MY NETWORK PLACES WINDOW

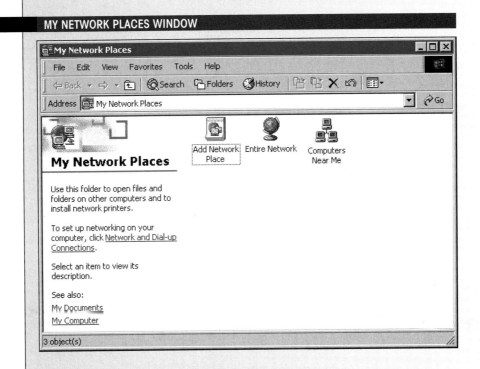

TROUBLE? Depending on how your network is set up, your My Network Places window may appear different from the one shown in Figure 9-4.

The My Network Places window contains three icons (though your window may contain more). See Figure 9-5. Use the **Add Network Place** icon 🔲 to create a shortcut to a folder on your network. You can also create shortcuts to folders on the Internet, such as Web folders or FTP sites. Use the **Entire Network** icon 🌐 to view the entire structure of your network, including any workgroups or domains that you have access to. Finally, you can use the **Computers Near Me** icon 🖧 to view only those computers located in your workgroup or domain.

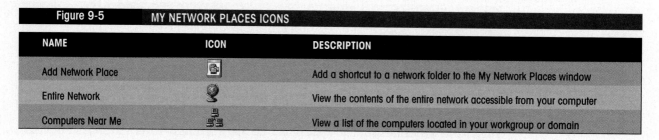

Figure 9-5	MY NETWORK PLACES ICONS	
NAME	**ICON**	**DESCRIPTION**
Add Network Place	🔲	Add a shortcut to a network folder to the My Network Places window
Entire Network	🌐	View the contents of the entire network accessible from your computer
Computers Near Me	🖧	View a list of the computers located in your workgroup or domain

Viewing the Contents of Your Workgroup or Domain

Joan suggests that you open the Computers Near Me icon on Anjali Gregory's computer to view the list of nodes in your workgroup.

> *To view a list of nodes in your workgroup or domain:*
>
> **1.** Double-click the **Computers Near Me** icon 🖧.
>
> Windows 2000 displays a list of workstations and other objects in your workgroup or domain. See Figure 9-6.

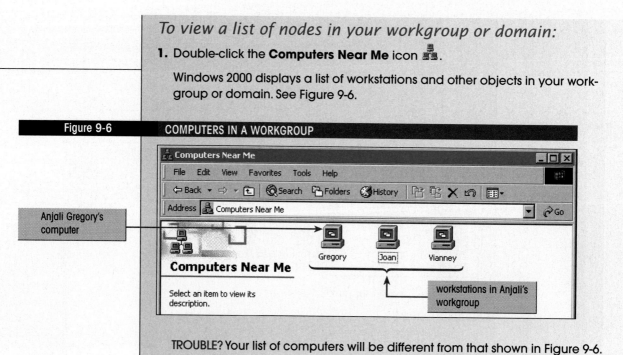

Figure 9-6 — COMPUTERS IN A WORKGROUP

Anjali Gregory's computer

Computers Near Me

workstations in Anjali's workgroup

TROUBLE? Your list of computers will be different from that shown in Figure 9-6.

The three computers in the Anjali's workgroup have the following names:

- Gregory—named for real estate agent Anjali Gregory. This is the computer you and Joan are using to explore Millennium's network.
- Joan—named for the owner of Millennium Real Estate, Joan Alvarez
- Vianney—named for the Millennium office assistant, Jacques Vianney

You can get additional information on each of these workstations by viewing the Properties dialog box for each one.

To view a workstation's properties:

1. Right-click the icon representing one of the workstations in your workgroup or domain.

2. Click **Properties** on the menu.

   Figure 9-7 shows the Properties dialog box for the Joan workstation located on Millennium's network.

Figure 9-7	PROPERTIES OF JOAN'S WORKSTATION

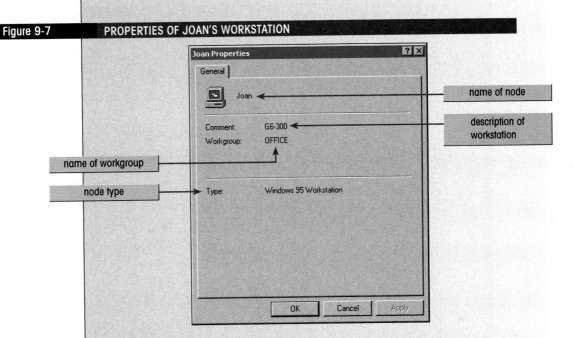

TROUBLE? If there is no Properties command, it might be because your network administrator has not given you access to the Properties dialog box.

3. Click the **OK** button to close the Properties dialog box.

In the Properties dialog box, you can see that Joan's computer uses the Windows 95 operating system. Also you learn that the name of the workgroup she is on is the Office workgroup.

Viewing Your Network's Structure

Joan suggests that you next use My Network Places to explore the structure of Millennium's computer network.

To view the structure of the network:

1. Click the **Up** button to move back up in the My Network Places window.

2. Double-click the **Entire Network** icon .

3. Click the **entire contents** hyperlink on the left side of the Entire Network window.

4. Double-click the **Microsoft Windows Network** icon.

> TROUBLE? Depending on your network's configuration, you may have to click other icons to view the entire structure of your network.

Windows 2000 displays a list of the domains and workgroups available on your network. See Figure 9-8.

Figure 9-8 | WORKGROUPS ON THE MILLENNIUM NETWORK

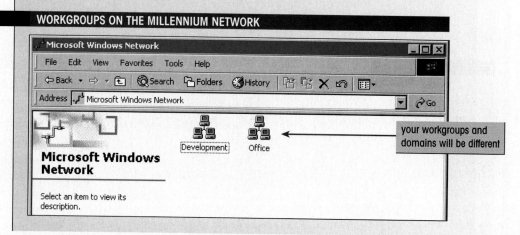

There are two workgroups on the Millennium network: Office and Development. As you saw in Figure 9-7, there are three computers in the Office workgroup—Joan's computer is one of them. What is in the Development workgroup?

To view the contents of a domain or workgroup:

1. Double-click an icon representing a workgroup or domain.

The contents of the domain or network appear. See Figure 9-9.

Figure 9-9 | WORKSTATIONS IN THE DEVELOPMENT WORKGROUP ON THE MILLENNIUM NETWORK

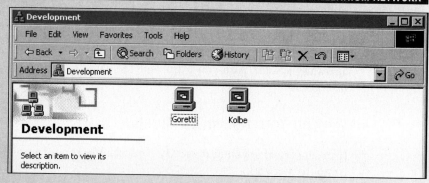

> TROUBLE? On some networks, you will be asked to enter a password before you can access another domain or workgroup. See your instructor or technical support person if this is the case with your network.

2. Close the My Network Places window.

There are two computers in the Development network: Goretti and Kolbe. These computers are used by Tony Goretti and Warren Kolbe, who are part of the development team for Millennium Real Estate.

Network **Protocols and Standards**

You tell Joan you've had some experience using networks because your college computer system was networked. Joan is glad to hear this, but says that there are so many variations in how a network can be set up that you are bound to find differences between what your college network could do and what the Millennium network does. To best understand how to use any network, it's useful to understand how a network operates. Windows 2000 uses four components to provide network access: an adapter, a protocol, a client, and a service component.

A network **adapter** is the hardware device on your computer that enables it to connect to the network. Adapters are usually cards, called **network interface cards**, or **NICs**, inserted into a slot in the back of your computer. The card includes a port into which a network cable is inserted. Figure 9-10 shows an example of such a network interface card.

Figure 9-10	NETWORK INTERFACE CARD

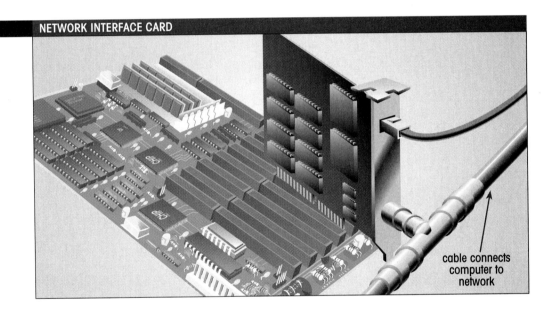

cable connects computer to network

Your computer doesn't have to have a NIC and a network cable to connect to a network—you can also connect using a modem. In these situations, Windows 2000 uses the modem as a **dial-up adapter**, with the phone line acting as a network connection. A phone line does not transmit data nearly as fast as the combination of the NIC and network cable, but for many users phone lines are the only choice. For example, if you have a home PC and you have signed up for access to the Internet using an Internet service provider, you most likely use your phone line to connect to the network. More information about connecting to the Internet over a phone line is included in Appendix A, "Connecting Computers over a Phone Line."

Each NIC uses a **network standard**, which is the manner in which data is handled as it travels over the network cable. Network standards are often compared in terms of how fast they transfer data. The faster a standard can transfer data, the more efficiently the network can share resources among its pool of users. One of the most widely used network standards is the Ethernet standard. The **Ethernet** standard transfers data at 10 megabits per second—much faster than data is transferred over a phone line. Another popular network standard is the **Token Ring** standard. Developed by IBM, the Token Ring standard can transfer data at rates up to 16 megabits per second. As demands on networks increase, so too do demands for new standards that support faster transfer speeds. The newer standards **Fiber Distributed Data Interchange (FDDI)** and **Asynchronous Transfer Mode (ATM)** can transfer data at 100 megabits per second and faster. Another standard, called **Fast Ethernet**, also can transfer data at 100 megabits per second.

The second aspect of network access is the communications protocol. A **communications protocol** determines how computers recognize each other on the network and what rules they use to transfer data. Different network operating systems use different protocols. Computers that connect to the Internet use **TCP/IP** (Transmission Control Protocol/Internet Protocol). With the popularity of the Internet and the World Wide Web, TCP/IP is becoming the protocol of choice. This is the case with the latest releases of NetWare and with Windows 2000. NetWare networks also use **IPX/SPX**, while a Windows NT network often uses the **NetBEUI** protocol. Windows 2000 can handle most of these popular network protocols, but to use Windows 2000 with these networks, you must install support for the appropriate protocol from the Windows 2000 installation CD. Windows 2000 also allows you to work with several different protocols at the same time.

The third component of your network setup is the **client** component, which gives your computer the ability to access shared resources on the network. Each network operating system requires a different client component. Windows 2000 includes client components to support, for example, the Novell NetWare and Microsoft networks.

The final component in your network setup is the **service** component, which enables your computer to share its resources with the network. It also enables a network administrator to manage the software and hardware installed on your machine from a remote location. The service component is used primarily in peer-to-peer networks, in which each user controls how his or her computer shares its resources with the network. On many hierarchical networks, the network administrator will not make this component available to users.

Understanding which components have been installed on your computer helps you understand the capabilities and limitations of your computer on the network.

Viewing **Network Properties**

Now that you have an overview of the different aspects of network setup, you can examine your computer to see which components are installed.

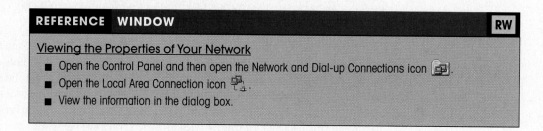

REFERENCE WINDOW RW

Viewing the Properties of Your Network
- Open the Control Panel and then open the Network and Dial-up Connections icon.
- Open the Local Area Connection icon.
- View the information in the dialog box.

To view the properties of your network:

1. Click the **Start** button, click **Settings**, and then click **Control Panel**.

2. Double-click the **Network and Dial-up Connections** icon to display the Network and Dial-up Connections window.

3. Double-click the **Local Area Connection** icon.

   Windows 2000 displays information about the local area network connection. See Figure 9-11.

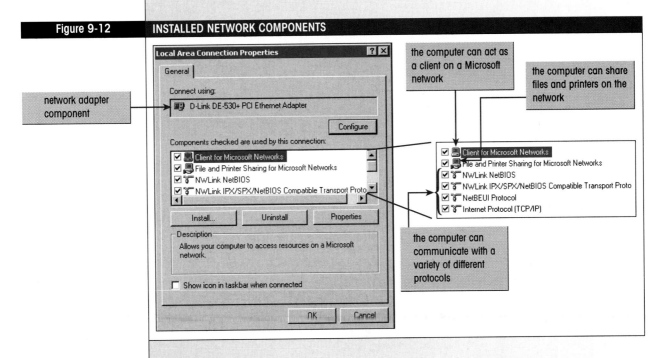

Figure 9-11 | **INFORMATION ABOUT THE CURRENT NETWORK CONNECTION**

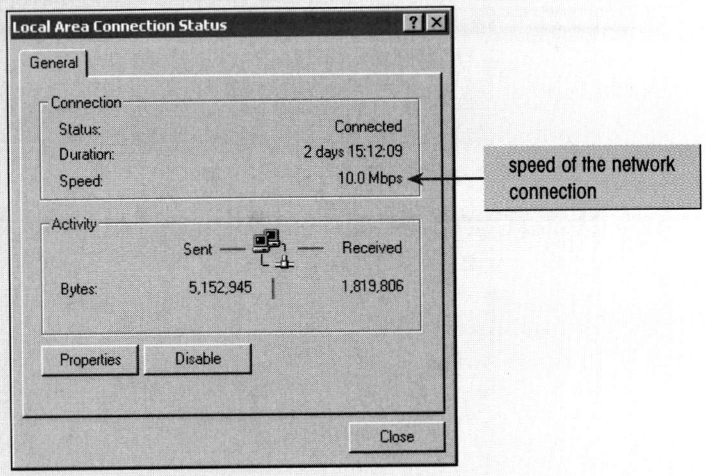

speed of the network connection

From the information shown in Figure 9-11, you can see that this particular connection has been active for about 2 days. The speed of the connection is 10 megabits per second. Now you can check to see which network components have been installed.

To view the list of network components:

1. Click the **Properties** button.

2. The installed components for the network appear, as shown in Figure 9-12.

Figure 9-12 | **INSTALLED NETWORK COMPONENTS**

network adapter component

the computer can act as a client on a Microsoft network

the computer can share files and printers on the network

the computer can communicate with a variety of different protocols

3. Scroll down the list of components, if necessary, to see what is installed on your computer.

TROUBLE? On some networks, you might not have access to this dialog box. If this is the case, read these steps without performing them on your computer.

4. Click the **OK** button to close the dialog box.

5. Click the **Close** button to close the Local Area Connection Status dialog box.

Identifying **Your Computer on the Network**

Recall that the Gregory computer appeared with the name "Gregory" in the My Network Places window. Windows 2000 limits this name to 15 characters and does not allow blank spaces. Depending on the control you have over your computer and how it interacts with the network, you can change this name and the workgroup or domain to which your computer belongs.

To view your network identification:

1. Click **Advanced** on the menu bar and then click **Network Identification**.

2. Click the **Properties** button.

The Identification Changes dialog box opens, as shown in Figure 9-13. From this dialog box you change the computer's name and choose a different domain or workgroup to belong to.

Figure 9-13	IDENTIFYING THE COMPUTER ON THE NETWORK

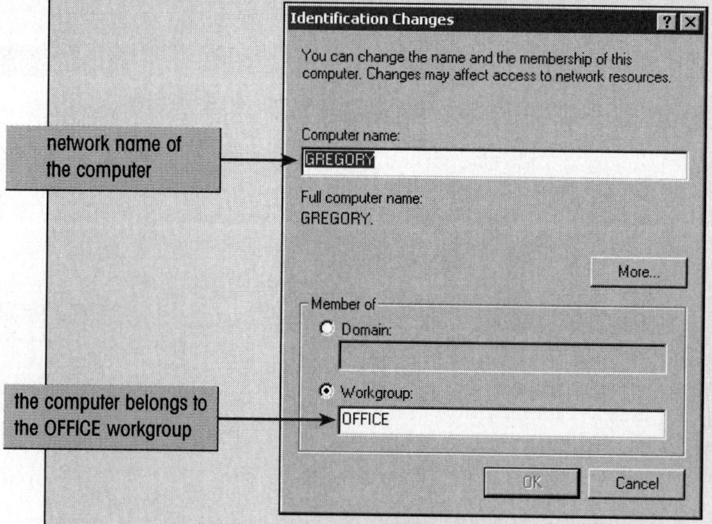

TROUBLE? You might not have access to this dialog box. If not, just read through these steps.

3. Click the **Cancel** button twice to return to the Network and Dial-up Connections dialog box.

4. Close the Network and Dial-up Connections window.

Session 9.1 QUICK CHECK

1. What is a network?

2. Define the following terms:
   a. node
   b. LAN
   c. WAN
   d. server
   e. client

3. Name the two types of network models, and then briefly describe each.

4. Name three tasks a network server might have to perform.

5. What are the four components needed to set up a Windows 2000 machine to work on a network?

6. What is a communications protocol? Give an example of a communications protocol and describe what it is used for.

SESSION 9.2

In this session, you will learn how Windows 2000 manages access to different network resources with user accounts and access rights, and how to log on to your network. You'll learn how to access network resources such as folders and printers. You'll explore how to work with network files when you're no longer connected to the network. Finally, you'll see how to share a folder on your computer with others on your network.

Network Security and Access Rights

You mention to Joan that when you were at the university there were a number of things that, as a student, you were "blocked out" of doing on the network. Joan replies that similar restrictions are in place on the Millennium network. She explains that these restrictions are part of an overall plan for maintaining security on the Millennium network. **Network security** involves the control of two aspects of a network: the people who can access the network and the actions they're allowed to perform on the network once they're connected. At Millennium, Joan explains, the network administrator wants to make sure that the network is used only by Millennium employees and that each employee has access only to those parts of the network that apply to his or her job.

Measures taken to ensure network security vary for different networks. If you have a small network set up in your home, you probably don't need to have a sophisticated security system controlling who has access to the network. You are there to monitor the situation, and you have other means of controlling who gets into your home. However, the network requirements for a small business might be different. A small business might want to have security measures in place to control who gets access to the network; once employees receive authorization, however, they might have free access to all network resources.

A large network with hundreds of people working on different projects involving confidential information is another matter. For example, a university network server that stores, among other things, student grades and records needs tight security over who can access the system and what information they can view once they get access. Likewise, a network at a hospital must have rigorous restrictions in place to limit access to patient data, to ensure the integrity of the doctor-patient relationship.

Network administrators don't just need to restrict access to data; they also need to restrict access to hardware. For example, suppose the graphic arts department on campus has purchased an expensive high-quality color laser printer, and they don't want students from other departments using it. The network administrator might therefore limit access to that printer to students and faculty in the graphic arts department.

Network administrators control who gets on the network—and what users are allowed to do once they are connected—through network accounts and access rights. A **network account** is the collection of information about you and the work that you do on the network. Before you can use the network, the network administrator creates an account for you that identifies you as an authorized user of the network. In a network that has several different servers, you might have several network accounts. For example, a student who is getting an engineering degree but is taking a class in the art department might have two network accounts, one in each department.

Network administrators limit access to network data, software, and hardware through the use of user IDs and passwords. Your **user ID**, or **username**, identifies you to other users on the network. A user ID might be your first name, or a number such as 445228, or a word. On some systems, user IDs are limited to eight characters and exclude spaces or special symbols.

Along with your user ID, you usually must enter your password to log on to a network. Your **password** is a string of symbols, letters, and/or numbers, known only to you and the network administrator, which shows that you are the legitimate user of the account. Passwords are a security device to prevent other people who might know your user ID from using your account. Once you have entered both the user ID and password, the server checks to see if these are valid before allowing you network access.

Once you're connected to the network, your ability to use network resources is controlled by a set of guidelines or **access rights** set up by the network administrator. Access rights can be limited to **read-only access**, which allows you to view the contents of a file but not to edit or delete the file. This might occur if you were a physician who needs to be able to review patient records stored on a hospital network database. Your network administrator might grant you read-only access so that you could view the files without accidentally changing or deleting a record. In other situations you might need **read and write access**, which allows you to view and edit files but not delete them, or **full access**, which gives you the ability to view, edit, and delete a file. Read and write access is often granted on networks where your files are stored in folders located on a network server.

Working with Your Network Account

The process of accessing your account is called **logging on** or **logging in**. If your computer is on a network and network security is in place, you are prompted for your user ID and password in a dialog box called a **logon dialog box** when you first start Windows 2000. You may have to press the Ctrl, Alt, and Del keys simultaneously to display the logon dialog box. Completing this dialog box allows you to access the Windows 2000 operating system and the network on which your computer resides.

The Windows 2000 logon dialog box also can be used in situations where a single workstation is shared by several people. Windows 2000 allows each user to customize the desktop, and stores the desktop settings each user chooses in a file called a **user profile**. Logging on to Windows 2000 accesses your user profile and loads the settings for your customized desktop.

Password Protection

You have already seen how network administrators enforce network security through the use of user IDs and passwords. Joan emphasizes that keeping your password secret helps maintain the security of a network and its resources. If you are allowed to create your own password for your account, you should keep the following principles in mind:

- Do not use fewer than seven characters in your password.
- Do not use your name, birth date, nickname, or any word or number that an unauthorized user might be able to guess.
- Try to include numbers or special symbols (!@#%&*) in your password, because they make it harder for other users to guess your password.
- Never write down your password where others can see it, or share your password with other users.

You also should change your password every few months. On some networks this is a requirement, and the network administrator will set up an automatic prompt that appears when you are supposed to change your password. In the process of changing your password, you will be prompted to enter your old password and then to enter your new password twice. You enter the new password twice to reduce the possibility of a typing error.

Changing Your Password

Joan tells you that password protection is one of Millennium's network security measures, and that you will be required to change your password every two months. Joan suggests that you review the dialog box you will use to do this.

REFERENCE WINDOW	**RW**

Changing Your Windows 2000 Password
- Press the Ctrl, Alt, and Del keys simultaneously.
- Click the Change Password button.
- Type your old password in the Old Password box.
- Type your new password in the New Password box and then again in the Confirm Password box.
- Click the OK button to save the new password.

If you are in a university computer lab, you may not be able to change your password. Your lab may also use a different network operating system, in which case the process of setting up and changing your password could be very different. You should ask your instructor or technical support person about your network's policies for changing passwords. In the next set of steps, you will be directed to click the Cancel button to prevent you from making any changes to your current password.

To change your Windows 2000 password:

1. Press the **Ctrl+Alt+Del** keys simultaneously while in Windows 2000.

   The Windows Security dialog box opens.

2. Click the **Change Password** button.

   The Change Password dialog box opens.

3. Type your current password in the Old Password dialog box.

4. Type a new password in the New Password dialog box.

5. Retype the new password in the Confirm New Password dialog box.

   Because this is just an example, you should close this dialog box without saving your changes.

6. Click the **Cancel** button.

7. Click the **Cancel** button again to return to Windows 2000.

Logging off from Your Account

When you're done using a workstation, you should log off. Logging off is the process of closing your account on the server and preventing others from using your account. It does not necessarily involve turning the computer off. Some servers allow only a limited number of users to be logged on at any given time, and network administrators want to avoid tying up servers with nonactive users. Depending on your network, your network administrator might want you to leave the computer on for those following you to use, so make sure you understand the procedures in your computer lab before you follow any of the instructions here.

There might be several options available to you when you are ready to stop working with Windows 2000 on your workstation. You can:

- **Log off your account**: This option, accessed by the Log Off command on the Start menu, leaves the Windows 2000 operating system loaded and the computer on, but closes any active programs or network accounts. The logon dialog box appears. Network administrators whose workstations are shared among several users often request that you use this option for shutting down your account.

- **Shut down**: This option, accessed by the Shut Down command on the Start menu, closes the Windows 2000 operating system and shuts down the computer. The next user will have to restart the workstation and reload the Windows 2000 operating system. You should check with your instructor to see whether this option is allowed on your network. Many network administrators request users not to shut down individual workstations.

- **Restart**: This option, accessed by the Shut Down command on the Start menu, shuts down and then reloads the Windows 2000 operating system. The next user will have to enter his or her user ID and password in the logon dialog box before using the computer. You might also see the Restart in MS-DOS Mode option, which allows you to restart your computer without loading the Windows 2000 operating system.

If your hardware supports Standby mode, you will also see the Standby option, which is useful for laptops running on batteries that need to go into Standby mode to conserve power.

You should talk to your instructor or network administrator to determine which of these options you should select when you're finished working with Windows 2000. At Millennium, the network administrator prefers the first option: that you log off from your account but keep the Windows 2000 operating system loaded. Joan shows you how to log off from Windows 2000 using this option.

To log off from your account:

1. Click the **Start** button and then click **Shut Down**.

2. Select **Log off (*your account name*)** in the drop-down list box. See Figure 9-14.

| Figure 9-14 | LOGGING OFF YOUR ACCOUNT |

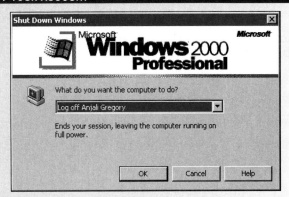

3. Since you don't want to log off just yet, click the **Cancel** button.

Joan emphasizes that you should remember to log off from your account when you're done working. If you leave the workstation running, still connected to your network accounts, other users could access your work.

Using **Network Resources**

Now that you've seen how to work with your user account, Joan wants to show you some of the available resources on the Millennium servers. Currently, you're logged on to the Gregory computer; Joan wants to show you how to access some of the resources on her computer from the Gregory computer.

To access a resource on another workstation:

1. Double-click the **My Network Places** icon on your desktop.

2. Double-click the **Computers Near Me** icon to view the computers in your domain or workgroup.

3. Double-click the icon representing a computer on your network that has a shared resource. Joan has you double-click the icon for the Joan workstation.

A list of resources on the computer appears in the window. See Figure 9-15.

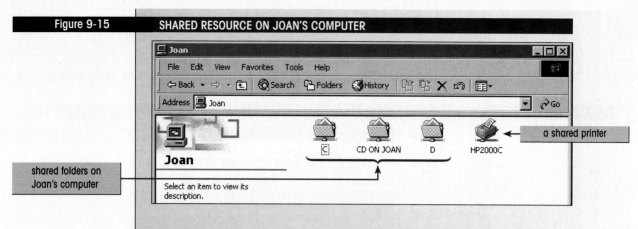

Figure 9-15   SHARED RESOURCE ON JOAN'S COMPUTER

shared folders on Joan's computer

a shared printer

TROUBLE? You can't tell from the icon whether the computer has a shared resource or not. You will have to get help from your instructor or technical support person to locate a workstation that you can access and that has a resource that is being shared with the network.

TROUBLE? You may be asked for a username or password before you can access the resources of the workstation. If that is the case, see your instructor or technical support person about obtaining access privileges.

There are four items shown in Figure 9-15. Folders on the network computer are represented with the 📁 icon. A printer is represented with a 🖨 icon. Folders placed on servers and made available to the network are called **network folders**. Folders on your own computer are called **local folders**. You can work with the files in a network folder using the same techniques you apply to files in your local folders. For example, you could click one of the files, and Windows 2000 would open the file in the appropriate software program. Joan has made three folders on her computer available to other network users. Two of these (labeled C and D) access the contents of her C drive and her D drive respectively, and the third (labeled CD ON JOAN) accesses the contents of her CD-ROM drive. Joan has also made her printer available to the network (labeled HP2000C).

To view the contents of a network folder:

1. Double-click an icon representing a network folder in the window.

2. Windows 2000 opens the contents of the folder. See Figure 9-16.

3. Close the network folder window.

Figure 9-16 **CONTENTS OF JOAN'S C DRIVE**

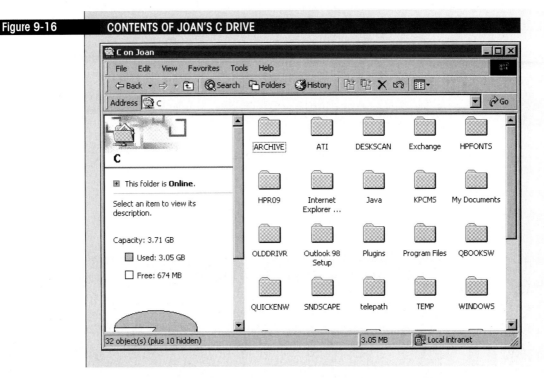

At this point, Joan tells you that you have full access to the files and folders on her C drive—so be careful! You ask Joan whether you have access to all of the resources on Millennium's network. She says no. In some cases, you might not have the same access rights for files on the network server as you do with your own files. You might not be able to move, modify, or delete files. You might not be able to view the contents of a folder. In other cases, you'll have limited access such as the ability to view the contents of a file, but not to delete it.

Windows 2000 manages resource access through usernames and passwords—the same technique it used to control your logon procedure. For example, Warren Kolbe in the Development workgroup shares his hard drive with other members of his workgroup, but he doesn't give the same level of access to people in the Office workgroup. To see how this works, Joan encourages you to try to access the Kolbe workstation using the same method that you used to access her workstation. When you try to do so, you will see the dialog box shown in Figure 9-17.

Figure 9-17 **ATTEMPTING TO ACCESS THE KOLBE WORKSTATION**

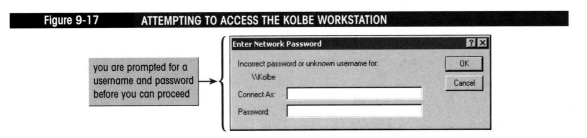

This dialog box prevents users from accessing certain resources unless they can enter a username and password that the workstation containing the resource recognizes. Thus the network keeps you from accessing those resources that you're not allowed to access. Joan reiterates the importance of keeping your own username and password confidential.

Drive Mapping

Newer software programs allow you to access files located on a network through My Network Places. However, to make a network file available to an older software program, you must first "map" the drive or folder that contains the file you want. **Drive mapping** represents a network drive or folder with a single drive letter, just like the drive letters used to identify your hard drive or floppy drive. Your software recognizes the drive letter and gives you direct access to the files it contains (note that you can map a drive only after the user of the computer or the network administrator has given you access to the drive).

Even for newer software programs, drive mapping is useful because it gives you quicker access to network files. The mapped drive letter appears in Windows Explorer and in the Open dialog box on the same level as your own local drives, so you don't need to navigate the network to locate the network drive or folder.

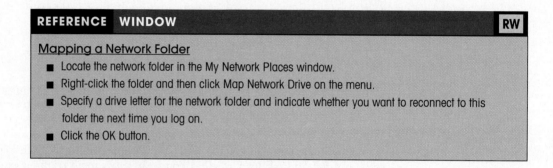

REFERENCE WINDOW   **RW**

Mapping a Network Folder
- Locate the network folder in the My Network Places window.
- Right-click the folder and then click Map Network Drive on the menu.
- Specify a drive letter for the network folder and indicate whether you want to reconnect to this folder the next time you log on.
- Click the OK button.

Mapping a Network Folder

When you map a drive, a letter is assigned to it, which you can change if you want to. The letters A, C, and D are usually used by your floppy drive, your hard drive, and your CD-ROM drive, respectively, so when you map a new drive, Windows 2000 will usually suggest the letter of the alphabet that comes after your last drive letter.

Joan suggests that you map her C drive as the drive letter "E" on your workstation.

To map a network folder:

1. Using My Network Places, view the resources of a workstation on your network.

   Joan directs you to the list of resources on her workstation, shown earlier in Figure 9-15.

2. Right-click a network folder icon 📁 in the window and then click **Map Network Drive** on the menu. See Figure 9-18.

Figure 9-18	MAPPING THE NETWORK FOLDER C ON JOAN'S WORKSTATION

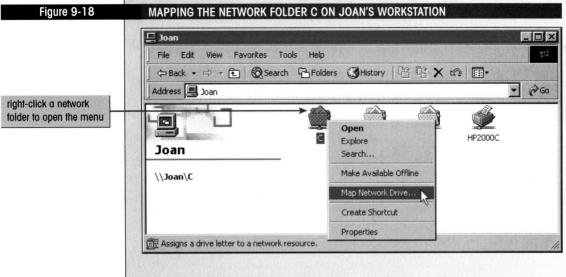

right-click a network folder to open the menu

3. The Map Network Drive dialog box opens, as shown in Figure 9-19.

Figure 9-19	THE MAP NETWORK DRIVE DIALOG BOX

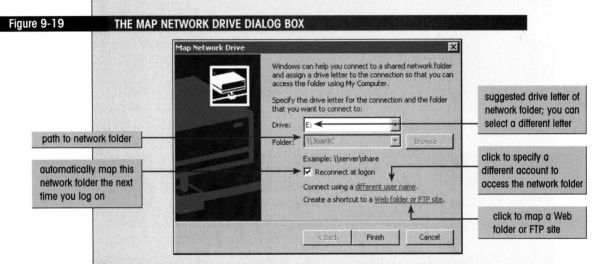

path to network folder

automatically map this network folder the next time you log on

suggested drive letter of network folder; you can select a different letter

click to specify a different account to access the network folder

click to map a Web folder or FTP site

Windows 2000 suggests a drive letter for the network folder. You can choose a different drive letter from the drop-down list box. You can also specify whether or not to remap this drive letter the next time you log on to your account so that the network folder will again be available. Finally, Windows 2000 assumes that you want to connect to this network folder using your username and password. You can specify a different account if you wish (as long as the account exists and has access rights to the network folder).

4. Click the **Finish** button to map the network folder to the drive letter.

Windows 2000 opens the network folder, now mapped with the drive letter.

In this example, you've mapped Joan's C drive to the drive letter E. It appears almost as if you've added a new hard drive (labeled E) to your computer. You can treat it the same way. As you may have noticed in Figure 9-19, you are not limited to mapping network folders; you can also map folders on the Internet, such as Web folders and FTP sites.

When you map a drive, the Map Network Drive dialog box shows the location of the drive you are going to map. This location is called the file's **pathname**. Windows 2000 pathnames follow the **Universal Naming Convention**, or **UNC**, an accepted set of rules for expressing pathnames, including those for network folders. The general form is *server**sharename*, where *sharename* is the name you used when sharing the folder. Thus the pathname to Joan's network folder is \\Joan\C, indicating a shared resource named C located on the server named Joan.

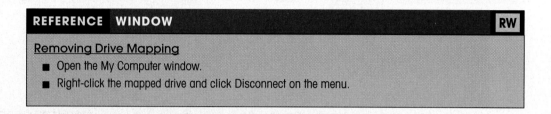

REFERENCE   WINDOW   RW

Removing Drive Mapping
■ Open the My Computer window.
■ Right-click the mapped drive and click Disconnect on the menu.

Removing Drive Mapping

If you want to remove drive mapping, you can do so from the My Computer window.

To remove drive mapping:

1. Click the **Up** button 🔼 in the folder window to move up in the Windows 2000 hierarchy until you get to the My Computer window.

2. Right-click the icon for your mapped drive and click **Disconnect** on the menu. See Figure 9-20.

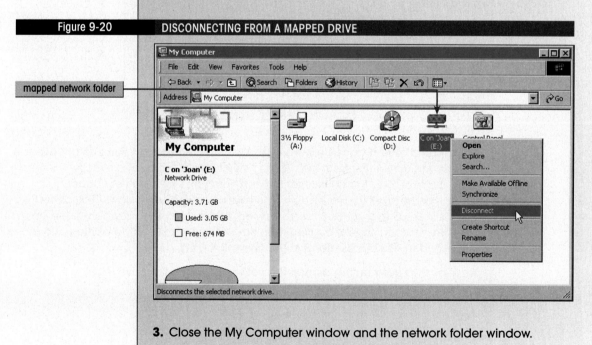

Figure 9-20   DISCONNECTING FROM A MAPPED DRIVE

mapped network folder

3. Close the My Computer window and the network folder window.

The drive letter associated with the network folder is removed from your system.

Creating a Network Place

Another way of quickly accessing a folder on the network is to create a network place. A **network place** is a shortcut to a folder. The icon for the shortcut will appear in the My Network Places window.

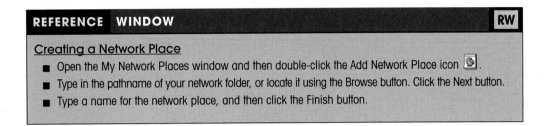

REFERENCE WINDOW RW

Creating a Network Place
- Open the My Network Places window and then double-click the Add Network Place icon 📇.
- Type in the pathname of your network folder, or locate it using the Browse button. Click the Next button.
- Type a name for the network place, and then click the Finish button.

Joan suggests that you create an icon for the C drive on her computer.

To create a network place:

1. Open the My Network Places window.

2. Double-click the **Add Network Place** icon 📇.

Windows 2000 starts the Add Network Place Wizard. At this point you could click the Browse button and locate the network folder by moving through your network's hierarchy. However, if you know the pathname of your network folder, you can also type it in directly.

3. Type in the pathname of the network resource for which you want to create a network place, or click the **Browse** button and locate it in the network hierarchy. See Figure 9-21.

Figure 9-21	ADDING A NETWORK PLACE

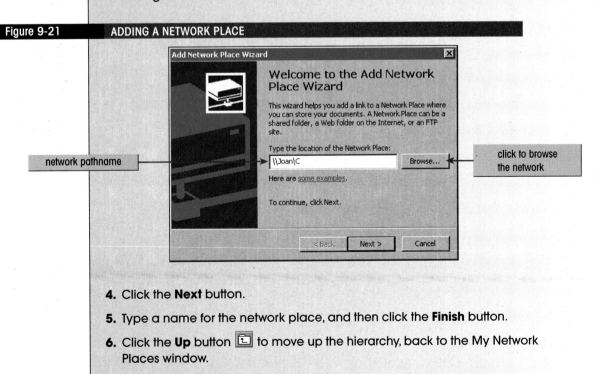

4. Click the **Next** button.

5. Type a name for the network place, and then click the **Finish** button.

6. Click the **Up** button 🔼 to move up the hierarchy, back to the My Network Places window.

Figure 9-22 shows the My Network Places window with the newly created network place—a shortcut pointing to the C drive on Joan's computer.

Figure 9-22	A NEW NETWORK PLACE

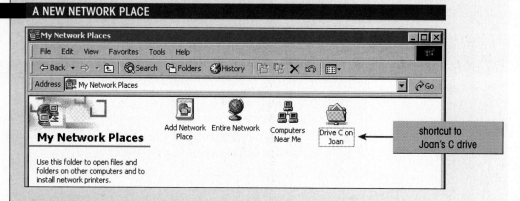

Now that you've seen how to create the shortcut to her folder, Joan asks you to delete it.

7. Click the icon for the network place you created and then press the **Delete** key. Click the **Yes** button to confirm that you want to delete the shortcut.

8. Close all open windows.

Working Offline

So far you've learned from Joan how to access files on her computer, but there will be situations where her workstation will not be available to you (if, for example, her computer is turned off or if you are not logged on). If that is the case, you can still have some access to her files by using offline viewing. **Offline viewing** allows you to store a copy of network files locally on your computer in a folder called the **Offline Files folder**. Even if you're not connected to the network, you can still access the offline (or local) version of her important files. Then, when you are reconnected to the network or her workstation, you can synchronize the Offline Files folder with her files (for a discussion of synchronization, see Chapter 5).

In most cases, Joan tells you, you'll use the offline files feature of Windows 2000 to work with portable computers. For example, your laptop will have a network connection, but once you leave the office with your laptop, the connection is lost and you have to work with offline versions of the network files. In other cases, the workstation storing the network file or folder has been turned off, so that even though you're connected to the network, you still can't access it. Joan suggests that to practice with the offline feature, you should make an offline version of some of her files, and then she'll turn off her computer, allowing you to work with the offline version.

Setting Offline Folder Options

Before you can make a network folder available offline, you have to make sure that Windows 2000 is set up to create and use offline folders.

To set up offline folders on your computer:

1. Open the My Computer window.

2. Click **Tools** on the menu bar and then click **Folder Options**.

3. Click the **Offline Files** tab.

4. Write down which check boxes have been selected in the dialog sheet. You'll want to restore these settings later.

5. If the **Enable Offline Files** check box is not selected, select it. See Figure 9-23.

Figure 9-23	SETTING UP THE OFFLINE FILES FEATURE

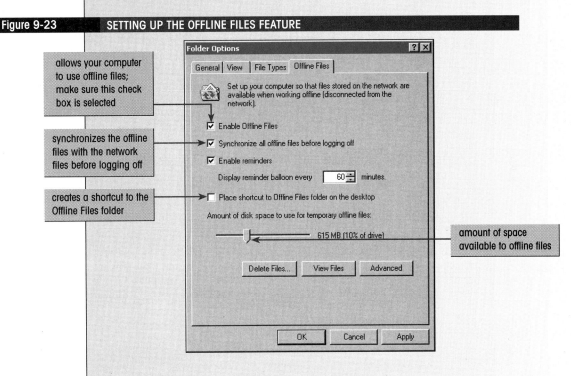

6. Close the Folder Options dialog box and the My Computer window.

Windows 2000 provides various options for managing your offline files. You can have Windows 2000 automatically synchronize all of your offline files before you log off from the computer. You can also have Windows 2000 remind you whenever a computer goes offline, so that you are aware that you no longer have a "live" connection to the network folder. Finally, you can have a shortcut placed on the desktop pointing to all of your offline files and folders.

Since offline files take up space on your computer, Windows 2000 allows you to control how much space these files can occupy. The dialog box in Figure 9-23 shows that a total of 615 MB can be used for offline files. If you try to use more space than this for offline files, Windows 2000 will issue a warning message.

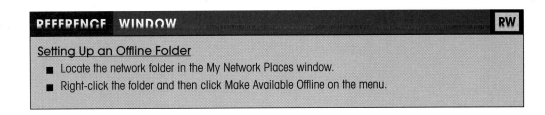

REFERENCE WINDOW	RW

Setting Up an Offline Folder
- Locate the network folder in the My Network Places window.
- Right-click the folder and then click Make Available Offline on the menu.

Setting Up an Offline Folder

Now that you've enabled the offline file viewing, Joan suggests that you create an offline version of the files in her Millennium Documents folder. First you have to locate this folder on the Millennium network.

To make a network folder available offline:

1. Open the My Network Places window and then move through the network hierarchy until you locate the network folder or individual files that you want to make available offline.

   TROUBLE? Talk to your instructor or technical support person before setting up an offline folder. You want to make sure you pick a folder that does not have a lot of files in it. Every file in the folder (and all its subfolders) will be copied to your computer in the form of offline files.

2. Right-click the selected folder or file and then click **Make Available Offline**. See Figure 9-24.

   TROUBLE? If a dialog box opens asking whether you want to make the subfolders available offline, click the Yes option button and then click **OK**.

   The Synchronizing dialog box appears, which transfers the contents of the network file to the offline folder. When the Synchronizing dialog box disappears, the file or folder is now available offline.

| Figure 9-24 | MAKING THE MILLENNIUM DOCUMENTS FOLDER AVAILABLE OFFLINE |

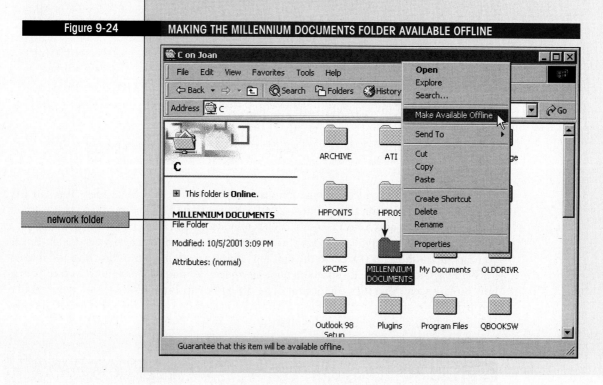

network folder

> TROUBLE? The first time you try to make an item available offline in Windows 2000, the Offline Files Wizard will guide you through the process. Follow the steps of the Wizard and (1) choose to allow Windows 2000 to synchronize the files whenever you log on or log off, (2) choose to place an offline reminder icon on your taskbar, (3) do not choose to create a shortcut to the offline files folder, and (4) choose to make subfolders of the offline folder available to you.
>
> 3. Close the window displaying the contents of the workstation.

REFERENCE   WINDOW   **RW**

Accessing an Offline Folder

- If the network connection is not active: Open the My Network Places window and go to the location where the network folder resides.

  Or, if the network connection is active (and you still want to work with the offline folder): Open the My Computer window.
- Click Tools on the menu bar and then Folder Options.
- Click the Offline Files tab and then click the View Files button.
- Open the desired offline file.

Working with an Offline File

You've created an offline copy of the files from Joan's Millennium Documents folder onto your hard drive. Joan will now turn off her computer, disconnecting from the network, so that you can try to access the offline versions of her files. The offline versions will appear in the same location in the network hierarchy, exactly as if her workstation was still attached to the network. However, each offline folder and file will have a double-arrow symbol, indicating that it is an offline folder (or file), and not the original.

To access the offline files:

1. Turn off the workstation containing the network version of the offline files, or if that is not possible, disconnect the network connection in another way.

   TROUBLE? Don't follow this step without specific directions from your instructor or technical support person. If your instructor or technical support person has not given you this information, read through the rest of the information in this section, but do not attempt to duplicate it on your own computer network.

2. Open the My Network Places window.

3. Wait several minutes, and then navigate through the network hierarchy until you reach the location of your network folder (now available offline).

   TROUBLE? If you get a message saying that the computer wasn't available, try it again a few minutes later. If you still can't get connected to the offline folder, contact your instructor.

Notice that as you navigate the Millennium network, Joan's computer still appears, as if it were still connected to the network (normally if it were turned off, it would not appear). This is because Windows 2000 recognizes that there are some network files that are being accessed offline and includes their network path in the network hierarchy. This gives the appearance that Joan's computer is still connected to the network, though in fact it is not.

Figure 9-25 shows the Millennium Documents offline folder as it appears within Windows 2000.

Figure 9-25	THE OFFLINE MILLENNIUM DOCUMENTS FOLDER

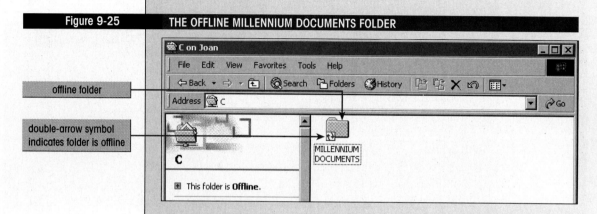

offline folder

double-arrow symbol indicates folder is offline

4. Open the folder containing the offline files.

There are two files (named Financial and Minutes) in the Millennium Documents folder. See Figure 9-26. Note that both file icons have the double-arrow symbol, indicating that they are offline objects.

Figure 9-26	OFFLINE FILES IN THE MILLENNIUM DOCUMENTS FOLDER

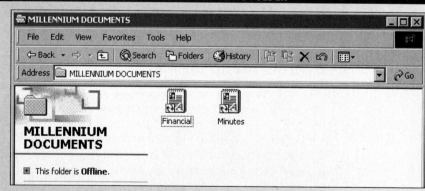

5. Open one of your offline files, make a minor editing change to it, and then close the file, saving your changes.

Under Joan's instruction, you make a change to the Financial file.

TROUBLE? Talk to your instructor or technical support person about which file you should change and the nature of the change you should make to it.

6. Close the window displaying the offline files.

When your folder is available again on the network, Windows 2000 will synchronize the two versions of this file, incorporating your changes into Joan's original files on her workstation.

If you want to work with the offline version of the file even if the network version is available, you can do so by opening the My Computer window and then opening the Folder Options dialog box from the Tools menu. You can access the offline files by clicking the View Files button located in the Offline Files dialog sheet.

Viewing the Status of Offline Objects

After Joan turned off her computer, Windows 2000 detected the fact that the connection between the offline folder and the network folder was lost. An icon appears in the tray of your taskbar to notify you of this. You can open this icon to view the status of your offline objects, such as whether the network connection is active or not, which offline files will be synchronized when the network connection is again active, and so on.

To view the status of your offline files:

1. Click the **Offline Files** icon in your taskbar tray.

The status of your offline files is displayed. See Figure 9-27.

| Figure 9-27 | VIEWING THE STATUS OF YOUR OFFLINE FILES |

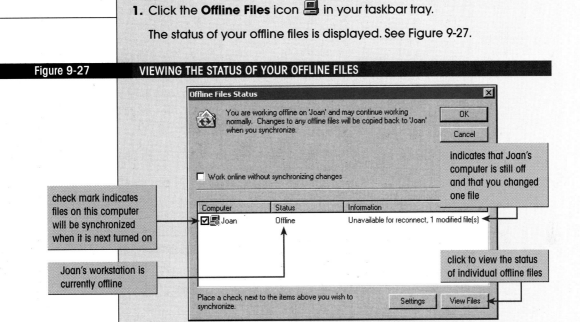

check mark indicates files on this computer will be synchronized when it is next turned on

Joan's workstation is currently offline

indicates that Joan's computer is still off and that you changed one file

click to view the status of individual offline files

TROUBLE? If your dialog box doesn't show the white box as in Figure 9-27, click the Details button.

As shown in Figure 9-27, Joan's workstation is currently offline and unavailable for reconnection. There is one offline file that has been modified. The check box for Joan's workstation is selected, indicating that Windows 2000 will synchronize the offline files and the originals when the connection is restored.

You can also view the current status of individual offline files, determining which files need to be synchronized and which files have not changed since going offline.

To view the status of individual offline files:

1. Click the **View Files** button.

Windows 2000 opens the Offline Files Folder shown in Figure 9-28.

Figure 9-28	THE STATUS OF INDIVIDUAL OFFLINE FILES

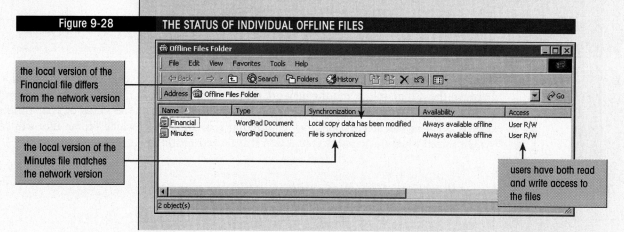

the local version of the Financial file differs from the network version

the local version of the Minutes file matches the network version

users have both read and write access to the files

From Figure 9-28, you can see that the local copy of the Financial file has been changed, while the Minutes file is still synchronized with the network file. You could open the files from this window and make further changes to the local copies; however, in this example, Joan doesn't have any further changes for you to make. You can close the Offline Files Folder window.

To close the Offline Files Folder window:

1. Click the **Close** button ☒.

2. Click the **Cancel** button to close the Offline Files Status dialog box.

TROUBLE? If you click OK, Windows 2000 will attempt to synchronize the offline files. This could result in an error message. If so, ignore the error message and then click the Close button.

Synchronizing Offline Files

Windows 2000 will attempt to synchronize your offline files whenever you log on to or log off from your account. Furthermore, Windows 2000 will notice when your network connection is active again (in this case, when Joan turns her computer back on) and will prompt you to perform a synchronization.

Joan goes back to her office, turns her workstation on, and reconnects to the Millennium network. After a few minutes, Windows 2000 notices that her workstation is back online. The icon in the Taskbar tray changes to a 🗐 to indicate that there is a change in the offline status. When you move the mouse pointer over the icon, a ScreenTip appears reading "Offline Files – Computer(s) available for reconnection". You can now synchronize the local file with the network file.

To synchronize the offline files:

1. If necessary, turn the workstation back on and wait a few minutes for Windows 2000 to note that the workstation is back online.

TROUBLE? Talk to your instructor or technical support person to get directions on how to follow these steps with your network.

2. Open the **Offline Files** icon 🖥 to view the Offline Files Status dialog box.

3. Verify that the check box before the now-reconnected workstation is selected.

4. Click the **OK** button.

Windows 2000 synchronizes the offline files with the network files. The Offline Files icon 🖥 disappears from the taskbar tray since you're no longer working offline.

Removing an Offline Object

When you no longer want to work with a network file offline, you can remove it. This removes the local version of the network file, but does not affect the network version. Joan asks you to remove the local version of her Millennium Documents folder.

To remove an offline file:

1. Reopen the My Network Places window and navigate through your network to the location of the network file or folder.

2. Right-click the network file or folder that you've made available offline, and then click to deselect **Make Available Offline**. See Figure 9-29.

Figure 9-29	REMOVING AN OFFLINE FILE OR FOLDER

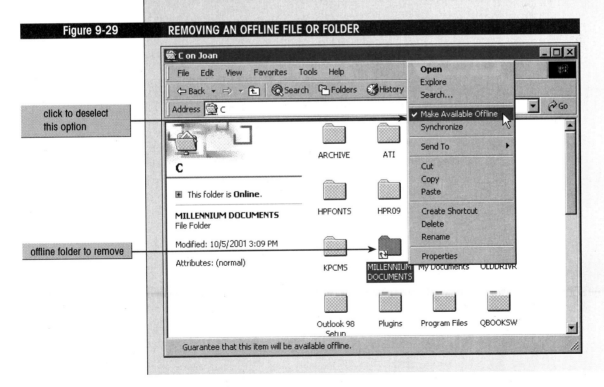

click to deselect this option

offline folder to remove

3. Click the **Yes** option button to indicate that you no longer want the offline folder's subfolders available either and then click the **OK** button.

4. Close the workstation or network forlder.

You ask Joan how Windows 2000 synchronizes files. What sort of rules does it follow? What if she had made changes to the same offline files you had edited? How would Windows 2000 handle the differences? Joan outlines some principles that Windows 2000 follows in performing a synchronization.

- If the original version of the offline file hasn't changed, your changes are copied to the network version.
- If someone else has made changes to the network file, you're given the choice of saving your offline version on the network, keeping the network version and leaving your offline version on your computer, or saving both on the network. If you save both, your version is given a different filename, and both versions will appear in both locations.
- If someone deletes the network version while you are working offline, you are given the option of saving your version to network or deleting it as well.
- If a new file is added to a network folder while you are working offline, the new file will be added to the offline folder.

Sharing a Resource with the Network

Up to now, you've worked with the resources available on other users' workstations. If the network administrator has given you the capability, you can make the resources of your own computer available as well. This is a process called **sharing**, and you can share resources such as individual folders, entire drives, or printers. The process by which you share a resource is the same for any resource.

REFERENCE WINDOW   **RW**

Sharing a Folder with the Network
- Right-click the folder and then click Sharing on the menu.
- Click the New Share button.
- Enter a name for the shared folder and a comment describing the folder.
- Specify the maximum number of users who can access this folder at any one time.
- Click the Permissions button and specify which users or user groups can access this folder, and what privileges they have.

Joan suggests that you try to share your C drive with the Millennium network.

To share a drive:

1. Open the My Computer window.

2. Right-click the icon for the drive you wish to share and then click **Sharing** on the menu. See Figure 9-30.

Figure 9-30	SHARING A DRIVE WITH THE NETWORK

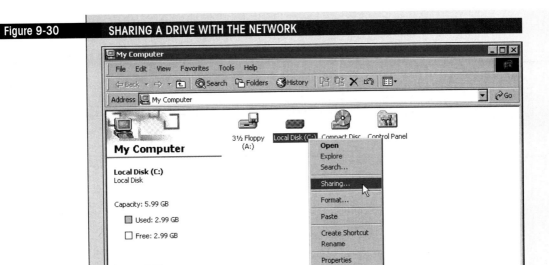

TROUBLE? If the Sharing command does not appear on the menu, you don't have permission to share folders on your computer or the Share feature has not been enabled. Talk to your instructor or technical support person to see if you can share files. If you cannot, continue reading through the following steps without duplicating them on your machine.

The Sharing sheet of the Properties dialog box for your drive appears. See Figure 9-31.

Figure 9-31	THE SHARING DIALOG SHEET

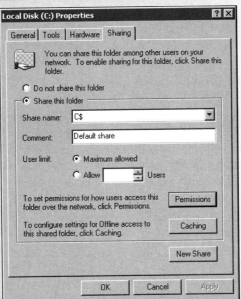

TROUBLE? Depending on how sharing has been set up on your computer, your screen might not match the figure.

When you first attempt to share a drive or folder, you see the dialog box in Figure 9-31. The dialog box seems to indicate that the drive is already shared, and in a sense it is, but only with the network administrator. If you want to share your resource with a wider audience, you have to create a **new share**. In sharing your resource you have to give it a **share name** that network users will see when they browse the network, provide a **share comment** that describes the resource, and indicate the number of users who can access it at one time.

To create a new share:

1. Click the **New Share** button.

2. Click the **Share Name** text box if necessary, enter a name for the shared resource, and then press the **Tab** key.

3. Type a description of the shared resource in the Comment box.

   TROUBLE? If you are sharing a folder on your network, talk to your instructor or technical support person about the names and comments you should enter here.

   You can control how many users can access your drive at one time. The maximum number allowed is 10. Joan suggests that you reduce this number to 5 to avoid having your system overloaded with other users.

4. Click the **Allow** option button and then click the spin arrows to change the number of users to 5. See Figure 9-32.

Figure 9-32	CREATING A NEW SHARE

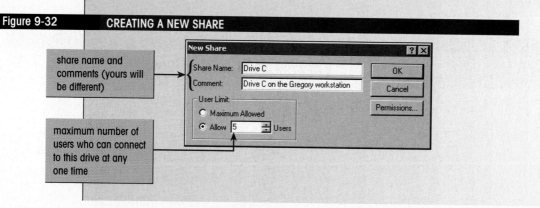

Now that you've given your drive a name and specified how many users can connect to it, you have to specify *which* users can connect to it. You can limit the resource to specific users, or to a specific class of users called a **user group**. For example, Joan tells you that the people in the Development workgroup limit access to only other users in their workgroup and to the network administrator (recall the trouble you had when you tried to access their workstation on the network). You can also control what users can do when they access your drive, such as whether they can edit your files or simply view them.

To set permissions for your resource:

1. Click the **Permissions** button.

   The Permissions dialog box opens, as shown in Figure 9-33.

Figure 9-33	PERMISSIONS DIALOG BOX

users who have access to the resource

your Permissions dialog box may look different

click to add new users

Permissions for Drive C

Share Permissions

Name
Everyone

Add...
Remove

Permissions: Allow   Deny
Full Control   ☑   ☐
Change   ☑   ☐
Read   ☑   ☐

OK   Cancel   Apply

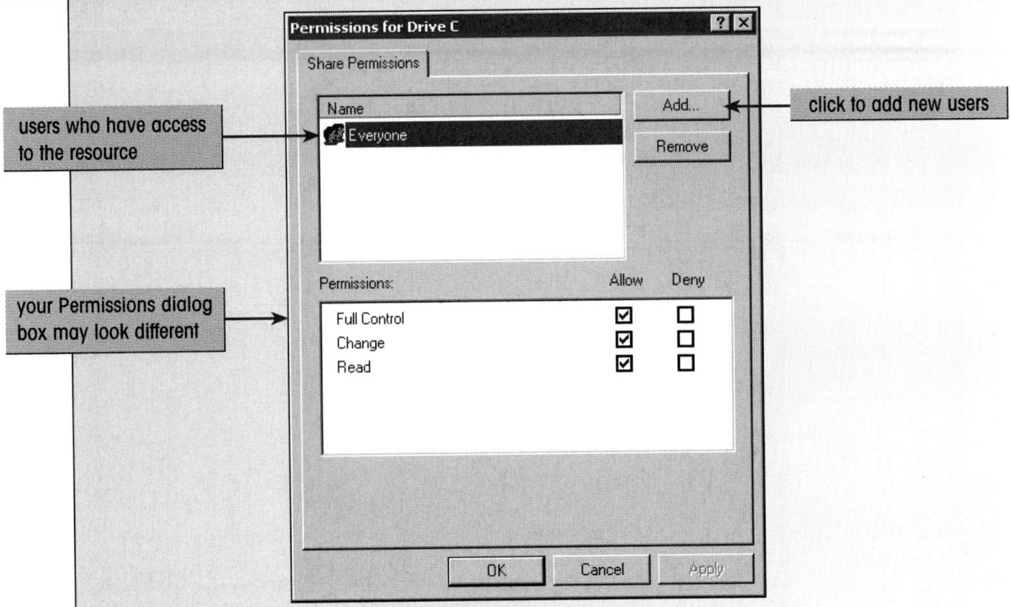

TROUBLE? Talk to your instructor or technical support person about the settings you should use for the permissions on your resource.

The Permissions dialog box in Figure 9-33 opens with the default settings, allowing all users full access to the files. Joan suggests that you change this, giving full access only to Anjali Gregory and no one else. This means that Anjali will be able to access the files on his workstation from other computers on the network, but no one else will be able to do so. To accomplish this, you first have to remove the Everyone user group and then add a new user to the list.

To change the list of approved users:

1. Verify that **Everyone** is selected in the list of users and then click the **Remove** button.

2. Click the **Add** button.

3. Scroll through the list, select the user 🯅 or user group 🯆 that you want to have access to your files, and then click the **Add** button.

   TROUBLE? Ask your instructor or technical support person which user or user group you should add to the list.

   Joan has you select Anjali Gregory from the list, as shown in Figure 9-34.

Figure 9-34 | SELECTING A USER TO ALLOW TO ACCESS A NETWORK RESOURCE

displays only those users and user groups that have an account on the Gregory workstation

list of users and user groups

users and user groups that have access to this network resource

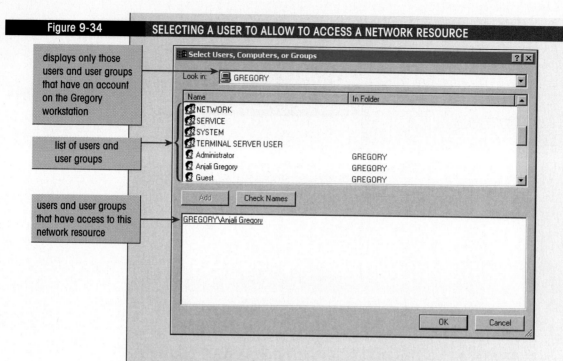

4. Click the **OK** button.

You are returned to the Permissions dialog box.

5. Click the **Full Control** check box under the Allow column.

Anjali Gregory now has full access to the files on drive C. See Figure 9-35.

Figure 9-35 | SETTING PERMISSIONS FOR A SPECIFIC USER

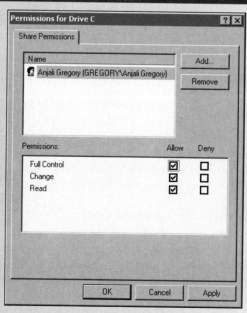

Joan suggests that you complete your work without saving any of your changes. You can redo this later if you need to.

6. Click the **Cancel** button three times to close the dialog boxes without your changes and then close the My Computer window.

Joan tells you that the system administrator will also have access to your workstation and can control the access to your computer's resource. You can always tell when a device such as a drive or printer is shared, since the icon will have a hand added to it. For example, the icon for a shared folder is 🖐 rather than 🗀.

Network Printing

Joan would like to show you one other important resource on Millennium's network: the network printer. A **network printer** is a printer that handles printing jobs for network users. By contrast, a **local printer** is one that is connected directly to your computer. Note that you can have both a local printer and a network printer (or printers) available to any one computer. The operation of a network printer is managed by a server called a **print server**. As shown in Figure 9-36, when a user wants to print a document, Windows 2000 sends the information needed to print the document to the network print queue located on the print server. A network print queue keeps track of the order in which print jobs are received and sends them, in order, to the network printer.

Figure 9-36	PRINT SERVER QUEUES PRINT JOBS

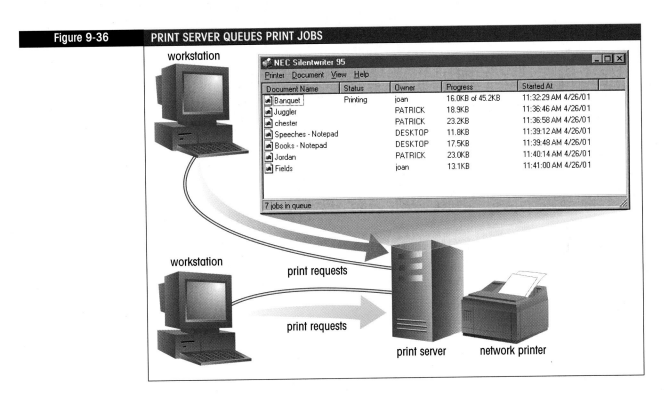

One of the printers available on the Millennium network is a color printer. It is usually reserved for final reports and special projects. Joan tells you that you can access this printer using the same techniques you use to access a local printer. Windows 2000 lists all available printers, both local 🖨 and network 🖨, in the same Print dialog box. To send a print job to a network printer, you simply select the printer name from the list of printers, as shown in Figure 9-37.

Figure 9-37 | SELECTING A NETWORK PRINTER

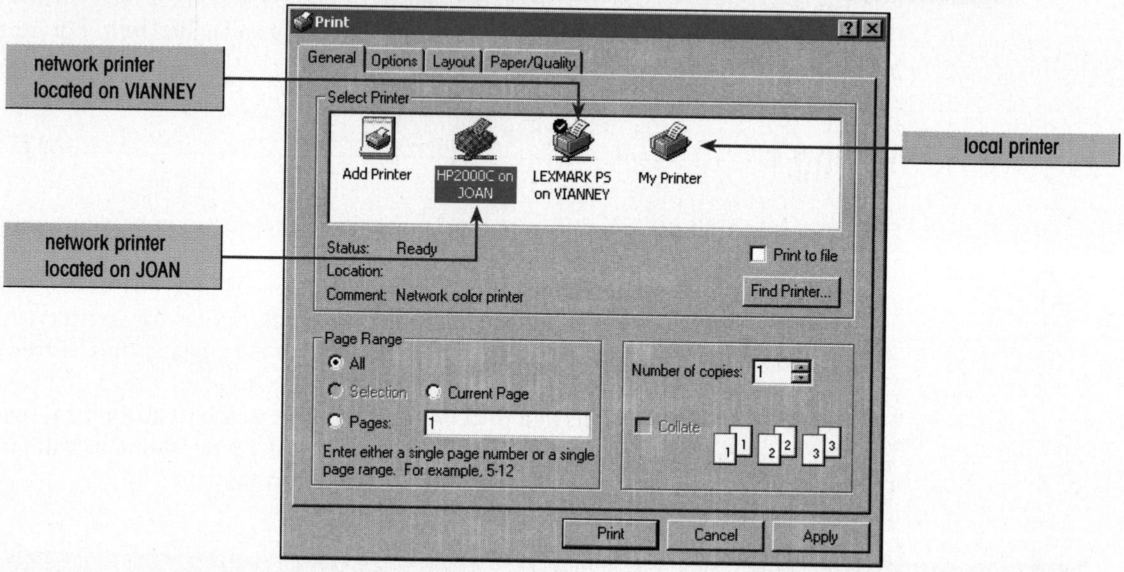

network printer located on VIANNEY

local printer

network printer located on JOAN

Note that the name of the printer gives you an indication of where it is located. For example, the color printer in Figure 9-37 is named "HP2000C" and it's located on the JOAN workstation. If you were to write the network pathname to this particular resource, it would be \\JOAN\HP2000C.

As Joan concludes your training on using the Millennium network with Windows 2000, she explains that in the next few days she'll set up an account for you on your own workstation and will provide you with your own user ID and password. She then reminds you of the importance of keeping your password secret so unauthorized users can't access your account. Once you're set up on your workstation, you should be able to access many of the resources that the network offers you.

Session 9.2 QUICK CHECK

1. Give four guidelines you should follow in choosing a password.
2. What are local folders, network folders, and offline folders?
3. What is drive mapping, and under what circumstances must you use it?
4. What is the pathname for a printer named Work that is located on the GREGORY workstation?
5. Under what circumstances would you create an offline folder?
6. If you edit an offline file, and in the meantime the network file is deleted, what happens when you try to synchronize the offline file?
7. How would you share one of your folders with the network?

REVIEW ASSIGNMENTS

1. **Diagramming Your Network** One way to understand your network is to sketch a diagram of the network layout. Figure 9-38 shows a sample schematic drawing. Create a schematic drawing of the network you use. Identify the servers and the resources they share. If there are a large number of workstations on your network, show only a few of them, identifying them by their node names. Talk to your technical support person or instructor to get the information you need.

Figure 9-38

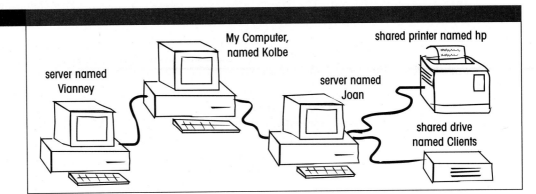

server named
Vianney

My Computer,
named Kolbe

server named
Joan

shared printer named hp

shared drive
named Clients

2. **Reporting Your Network Configuration** Write a description of your network. Include the following information in your report:

   a. The number of nodes on the network
   b. The network model (peer-to-peer, hierarchical, or mixed)
   c. The network operating system
   d. The network standard
   e. The communications protocol used

3. **Password Protection** Part of creating good passwords is understanding how password protection can be overcome by people trying to break into a system. Use the Internet or your library to learn the methods used to bypass password protection. Write a one-page report summarizing these techniques, and include some suggestions for ways to protect yourself against them.

4. **Transferring a File from the Network Folder** (*Note to Instructor: You must place a file onto a network server that your students can retrieve in order to complete Review Assignment 4.*) Your instructor has placed a file in a network folder for you to work with in this assignment. With the filename and name of the folder given to you by your instructor, use My Network Places to copy the file to your Data Disk. Enter your name into the document and then print the file.

5. **Mapping a Network Folder to a Drive Letter** (*Note to Instructor: For students to complete this assignment, you must indicate to which folder they should apply drive mapping.*) You can map network folders from the My Network Places window. Open the My Network Places window and select the network folder indicated by your instructor. Map the folder to the driver letter U. Open the My Computer window on your desktop to verify that the network folder has been mapped to drive U. Print an image of the My Computer window (press the PrintScreeen key, open WordPad, click the Paste button, and then print the WordPad file; close WordPad without saving the file). Remove the drive mapping when you are finished.

PROJECTS

Explore 1. One of the uses of a network server is electronic mail. Servers that handle electronic mail are called "mail servers." Find out which server on your network handles your mail messages, and then investigate the properties of that server to answer the following questions about your mail server:

   a. What is the name of the server that handles your mail messages?
   b. In which network folder are mail messages stored?
   c. Which client program do you use to retrieve your mail messages from the server?

Explore 2. (*Note to Instructor: If the network your students work on is not connected to the Internet, they will not be able to complete parts a and b of Project 2.*) Many university computers are now connected to the Internet. The Internet uses the TCP/IP communications protocol. Try to discover whether your computer has the TCP/IP protocol component installed. Prove your findings by creating a printout of the Local Area Connection Properties dialog box for your computer. Examine the properties for the TCP/IP protocol component and answer the following questions:

a. What is your computer's IP address? (This is the address that other Internet nodes use to identify your computer.)

b. What is the domain for your node? (*Hint:* Look in the DNS Configuration property sheet in the TCP/IP Properties dialog box. The domain is the name for your network.)

Explore

3. (*Note to Instructor: For your students to complete this project, you must give them the name of the server to find.*) You can use the Windows 2000 Search command to find network servers as well as files. To access the Search command, open the My Network Places window, double-click the Entire Network icon 🌐, and click the "Search for computers" hyperlink. Enter the name of the network server given to you by your instructor, and then click the Search Now button. Print a copy of the Search Results window, using the techniques described earlier in Review Assignment 5.

4. (*Note to Instructor: For your students to complete this project, you must make a network folder available to them.*) Use the offline feature of Windows 2000 to create an offline folder of a network folder specified by your instructor. After you've created the folder, use My Computer to open the folder and view the files in it (click Tools, click Folder Options, click the Offline Files tab, and then click the View Files button). Print a copy of the View Files dialog box, using the techniques described in Review Assignment 5. Remove the offline folder when you are finished.

QUICK CHECK ANSWERS

Session 9.1

1. a collection of computers and other hardware devices linked together so that they can exchange data and share hardware and software resources

2. Node: a device on a network; LAN: local area network, a network in which the nodes are located close together; WAN: wide area network, a network in which the nodes are spread out over a wide area such as a state or nation; server: a computer that provides access to its resources to other computers; client: a computer that uses the resources of a server

3. the hierarchical model, in which servers provide resources to the network, and clients use those resources; the peer-to-peer model, in which each computer can act as both client and server

4. store a database, handle electronic mail, manage printing, etc.

5. adapter, client, protocol, and service

6. A communications protocol determines how computers recognize each other on the network and what rules they use to transfer data. TCP/IP is used on the Internet. IPX/SPX is used in NetWare networks. NetBEUI is used in a Windows NT network.

Session 9.2

1. Do not use fewer than seven characters in your password; do not use a word or number that someone might be able to guess; include numbers or special symbols; never write down your password or share it with others.

2. Local folders are the folders on your local computer, network folders are located on network workstations, and offline folders are folders on your local computer that are duplicates of network folders.

3. Drive mapping is the process of assigning a drive letter to a network folder. Drive mapping is used to make it easier (and quicker) to access network folders. Also, many older programs cannot access network folders directly and require a drive letter.

4. \\GREGORY\Work

5. if you were using a portable computer that was only temporarily connected to the network, or if the source of the network file was occasionally unavailable to network users

6. You would be given the option of saving your version to the network or deleting it.

7. Right-click the folder icon and then click Sharing from the menu. Enter a share name and comment for the folder, click the Permission button, and then select a list of users or user groups that have access to the folder.

OBJECTIVES

In this tutorial you will:

- Review hardware device terminology and settings

- Use the Add/Remove Hardware Wizard

- View a list of hardware devices on your system

- Add a printer to your system

- Review the properties of a printer

- Learn to use a print queue

- Learn the principles of disks and disk maintenance

- Schedule hardware maintenance tasks with the Task Scheduler

LABS

Defragmentation and Disk Operations

WORKING WITH HARDWARE

Installing and Troubleshooting Hardware at Chan & Associates

CASE

Chan & Associates

You're a new employee at Chan & Associates, a small desktop publishing company. You work for David Markham, the company's computer systems administrator. Your job is to help David maintain the hardware and software on the company's computers. This involves installing hardware, troubleshooting hardware problems and training the employees in the use of their equipment.

David has a list of assignments for you on your first day. He wants you to install a network card in one of the company's new computers to allow it to share resources with other computers on the company's network. The company has also received a new color printer that has to be installed on a different computer, and then you have to show a new employee how to use the printer.

David also wants you to look at managing hard disks. He wants you to explore some of the tools that Windows 2000 provides to make hard disks operate more efficiently and consistently. These tools provide important protection against data loss and hardware failure.

SESSION 10.1

In this session, you'll learn about how Windows 2000 interacts with the hardware on your computer. You will study some of the basic principles of hardware devices and resources. You'll learn how to use the Device Manager to view the hardware devices installed on your system. You'll also learn how to use Windows 2000 to troubleshoot common hardware problems.

Learning About Hardware

Before you start working with the hardware devices at Chan & Associates, you decide to review some of the principles of hardware devices. **Hardware** is any physical piece of equipment, called a **device**, that is: both connected to your computer and controlled by your computer. These devices include **external** equipment such as keyboards, printers, and scanners, which remain outside the case of the computer, and **internal** equipment, such as disk drives, modems, and network adapter cards, which are placed inside the case of the computer.

External Devices and Ports

An external device is connected to your computer through a **port** (see Figure 10-1). Windows 2000 supports three different types of ports: serial, parallel, and USB.

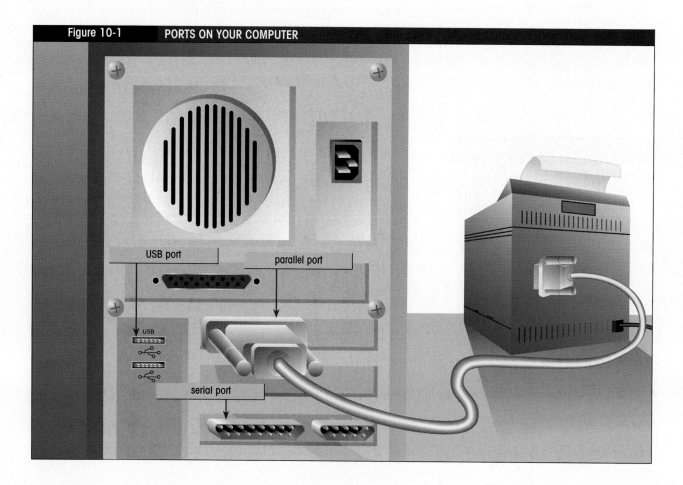

Figure 10-1   PORTS ON YOUR COMPUTER

A **serial port** is one of the older port types, usually used for a mouse or an external modem, although it can be used for some printers. A computer can have up to four different serial ports, although most computers have only two. They are labeled COM1, COM2, COM3, and COM4 (COM stands for "communications"). Serial ports transfer data 1 bit at a time. This is in contrast to a **parallel port**, which transmits data 8 bits at a time. Most computers have only one parallel port, which is usually reserved for a printer. Parallel ports are labeled LPT1, LPT2, and LPT3 (LPT stands for "line print terminal"). Usually, you have only the LPT1 port in use on your computer.

Because of the limitations of serial and parallel ports in terms of speed and the number of connections possible, a new port type called USB has been introduced in the last decade. **USB**, short for **Universal Serial Bus**, provides a high-speed connection to a variety of external devices, such as joysticks, scanners, keyboards, video conferencing cameras, speakers, modems, and printers—and you aren't limited by the number of ports on your computer, as you'll see below. To use USB technology, your computer must have a USB port, and the device you install must have a **USB connector**, a small, rectangular plug. You simply plug the USB connector into the USB port, and the computer will recognize the device and will allow you to use it immediately. USB-compatible computers thus work more like stereo systems, in that you don't have to take apart the computer to add a component.

Owners of computers that take advantage of USB technology no longer have to worry about which ports to use. Any USB device can use any USB port, interchangeably and in any order. You can "daisy chain" up to 127 devices together, plugging one device into another, or you can connect multiple devices to a single inexpensive **USB hub**. Data is transferred through a USB 10 times faster than through a serial port. For many USB devices, power is supplied via the port, so there is no need for extra power cables. Older computers can have a plethora of connectors—a keyboard connector, a mouse port, a parallel port, a joystick port, two audio ports, and two serial ports. USB computers replace this proliferation of ports with one standardized plug-and-port combination.

Internal Devices and Expansion Slots

Internal devices are connected to the **motherboard**, a circuit board inside your computer that contains the **microprocessor** (the "brains" of your computer), the computer memory, and other internal hardware devices. Internal devices are connected either directly to the motherboard (such as the microprocessor and your memory chips) or via a socket in the motherboard called an **expansion slot**. See Figure 10-2. You can insert devices such as network adapter cards, sound cards, or internal modems into expansion slots. Devices that you insert into expansion slots are often called **expansion cards** or **adapter cards**, since they "expand" or "adapt" your computer and they look like large cards. Most computers have about six expansion slots, which limits the number of expansion cards you can plug into your system at any one time.

Expansion cards come in two types: ISA and PCI. **ISA (Industry Standard Architecture)** cards represent the older standard, used primarily for low-speed devices such as internal modems and sound cards. **PCI (Peripheral Component Interconnect)** cards use a newer connection standard, supporting higher connection speeds, and are easier to install and configure. Many computers have a combination of ISA and PCI slots, allowing you to use both types of expansion cards.

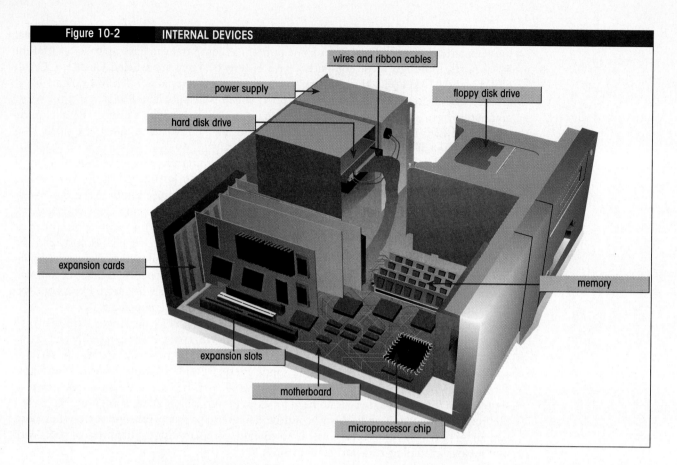

Figure 10-2 INTERNAL DEVICES

Device Resources

Windows 2000 assigns each device a set of system resources to help it work with the computer. There are four resources that can be assigned to a device: an IRQ, a DMA channel, an I/O address, and a memory range. When two devices share a particular resource, a **device conflict** can occur, rendering one or both of the devices unusable. Let's consider each of these resources.

A hardware device often needs to get the attention of the computer when it tries to send or receive information. Sometimes multiple devices will be trying to get the operating system's attention at the same time (for example, you search for a Web page at the same time that you're printing a document, and at the same time you have a sound CD playing). How does the operating system handle these simultaneous requests? It does so by assigning each device an **IRQ (interrupt request line)** that signals the microprocessor that the device is requesting some action. Lower numbers have higher priority and receive attention first. Windows 2000 makes 16 IRQ numbers, numbered from 0 to 15, available to hardware devices. One common hardware headache is to have more devices than available IRQs — this problem was one of the motivations for the creation of USB devices.

If the device does not need to use the microprocessor, information can then be transferred directly between the device and the system's memory. This channel for transferring data is called the **DMA (direct memory access)** channel. Most computers have four DMA channels, numbered from 0 to 3, available for your devices.

When the computer receives information from one of its devices, it needs a place to store that data. It does this by reserving a specific section of the computer's memory for each device. The section of the computer's memory devoted to the different devices on a computer is called the **I/O (input/output) address**. Each device requires a different I/O address.

Finally, some devices, such as video cards, require additional computer memory for their own use (not related to communicating with the microprocessor). This resource is called the **memory address** or **memory range**.

Device Drivers

Each hardware device requires a **driver**, a software file that enables Windows 2000 to communicate with and control the operation of the device. In most cases, the driver comes on a disk with the hardware device and an installation program will automatically install the driver for you. In other cases, Windows 2000 will install the driver for you when you install the operating system. Hardware manufacturers update drivers on a regular basis to improve device performance and speed, so you should periodically check with the manufacturer to confirm that you're using the most current driver version.

Installing a Hardware Device

As far as installation is concerned, hardware devices fall into two categories: legacy and plug and play. A **legacy device** is an older piece of hardware, one whose resources you have to set manually on the hardware device itself. It might also have a special program that you have to run to set it up on your computer. Windows 2000 will support most legacy devices, although it may take extra work to get all of your legacy devices to work together, since they are based on old specifications. You are also more likely to run into device conflicts with legacy devices.

A **plug and play device** uses newer technology that allows Windows 2000 to automatically recognize the new device and set it up, allocating system resources and installing the best driver. In the best case scenario, a plug and play device will require no intervention on your part, although this is not always the case. Most USB devices are plug and play, as are most expansion cards that use a PCI connection. Because Windows 2000 manages the resource allocation, you are less likely to run into problems with device conflicts.

REFERENCE   WINDOW   **RW**

Installing a New Hardware Device
- Turn off your computer.
- Insert the hardware device into your computer, either internally or externally.
- Turn your computer back on and then either follow the steps of the Hardware Installation Wizard or open the Control Panel and then click the Add/Remove Hardware icon.
- Click the Next button, click the Add/Troubleshoot a device option button, and then follow the steps of the Hardware Installation Wizard.

Now that you've reviewed hardware terminology, you're ready to install the new network card David gave you. The network card is plug and play, and it fits into a PCI slot inside your computer. Once you've turned the computer off and inserted the card into the computer, you turn the computer back on. In most cases, your computer will recognize the new plug and play device when it loads Windows 2000, and an installation wizard will start even before you get a chance to work with the operating system. In some cases, however, Windows 2000 won't recognize the new device, and you'll have to tell Windows 2000 to locate it. Let's assume that this is what occurs with the new network card: you have to run the **Hardware Installation Wizard,** a series of dialog boxes in which Windows 2000 prompts you for information about the new device, in order for the device to be set up properly with Windows 2000.

Most likely, you won't be able to actually work with new hardware in your lab, but this tutorial is written so you can complete most of the steps as if you had worked with new hardware. Read through any steps that you can't complete.

To run the Hardware Installation Wizard:

1. Open the Control Panel.

2. Double-click the **Add/Remove Hardware** icon 📦.

3. Click the **Next** button.

4. Click the **Add/Troubleshoot a device** option button if necessary and then click the **Next** button.

Windows 2000 starts searching for the new plug and play device. After a few seconds it indicates that it's found one. See Figure 10-3.

| Figure 10-3 | DETECTING A NEW HARDWARE DEVICE |

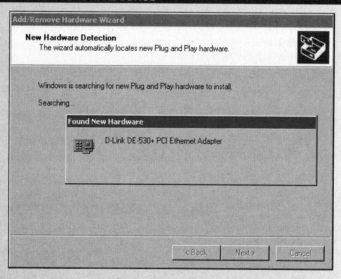

TROUBLE? Since this is an example, your Hardware Wizard will not display a new device. Instead, it will display a list of devices already on your system and give you the choice of installing a new device even if it didn't find one.

5. Click the **Cancel** button since you aren't actually installing a new device. If you were installing one, you would click the Next button and then click the Finish button.

If you are working with a legacy device, or if Windows 2000 doesn't locate your new device, you can still use the Hardware Installation Wizard to do the installation. In this case, you'll have to insert most of the important details yourself. Figure 10-4 summarizes the steps you should follow for a manual installation of a new device after Windows 2000 fails to locate it and install it for you (your screens may look slightly different from those shown in Figure 10-4).

TUTORIAL 10 WORKING WITH HARDWARE **WIN 2000 10.07**

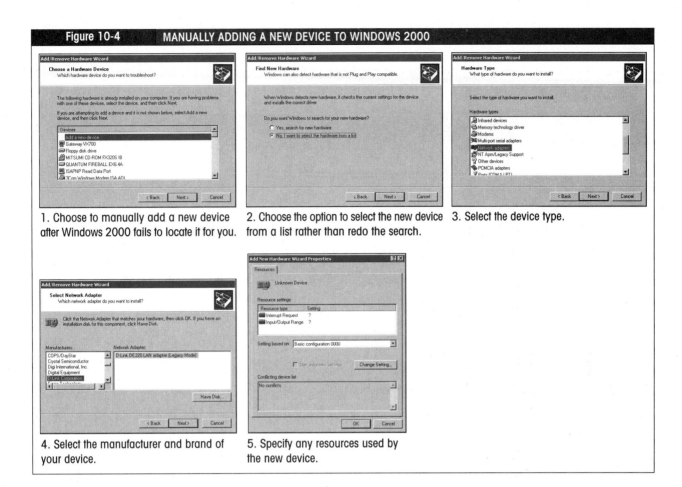

Figure 10-4 | **MANUALLY ADDING A NEW DEVICE TO WINDOWS 2000**

1. Choose to manually add a new device after Windows 2000 fails to locate it for you.

2. Choose the option to select the new device from a list rather than redo the search.

3. Select the device type.

4. Select the manufacturer and brand of your device.

5. Specify any resources used by the new device.

Using the Device Manager

You've installed the network card, but you discover that you can't connect to the company network. One possible source of trouble could be a conflict between the network card and another device on your system. In earlier versions of Windows (and before that, DOS), installing a new hardware device meant juggling all of your system resources and keeping careful written notes about each device's settings. With Windows 2000, however, you can use the **Device Manager**, a tool that makes it easier to manage your devices and the resources they use.

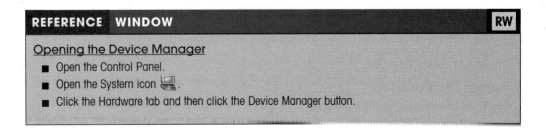

REFERENCE WINDOW | **RW**

Opening the Device Manager

■ Open the Control Panel.

■ Open the System icon 🖳.

■ Click the Hardware tab and then click the Device Manager button.

You decide to open the Device Manager to see whether a resource conflict exists.

To start the Device Manager:

1. Return to the Control Panel.

2. Double-click the **System** icon 🖥.

3. Click the **Hardware** tab in the System Properties dialog box.

4. Click the **Device Manager** button.

The Device Manager window opens, as displayed in Figure 10-5.

| Figure 10-5 | LIST OF DEVICES IN DEVICE MANAGER |

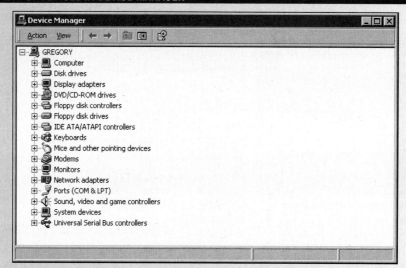

TROUBLE? Since you're working on a different computer, you're Device Manager window will look different from the one shown in Figure 10-5.

By default, the Device Manager shows all of the devices listed by type. You see that this particular computer has a CD-ROM drive, modem, mouse, and sound card, among other devices. You can also view the specific device used within these different categories. You're interested in learning about the state of the network card and whether there is an indication that the card is not working properly.

To display information about a specific hardware device:

1. Click the **plus box** ➕ in front of the **Network adapters** device type.

The brand name of the network card appears in the list. See Figure 10-6 (yours will be different).

Figure 10-6	VIEWING SPECIFIC INFORMATION ABOUT A DEVICE ON YOUR COMPUTER

network adapter card brand name

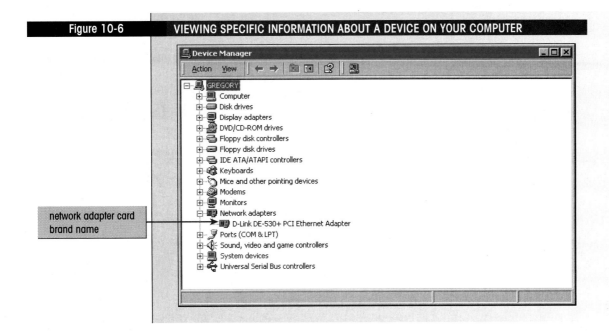

If a device is not working properly, the Device Manager will place an **!** on top of the device's icon. If the device has been disabled, a ✖ will appear on the icon. However, the icon in Figure 10-6 shows neither of these, so there is no indication that the device is not working properly. To find out more, you have to open the Properties dialog box for the device.

Viewing the Properties of a Device

The Properties dialog box for each device on your computer contains additional information about the device, such as the resources and driver file it uses. By viewing the Properties dialog box, you can learn a great deal about the status of your hardware device.

To view the properties of your hardware device:

1. Click the brand name of the device in the Device Manager window to select it.

2. Click the **Properties** button 🖺 on the Device Manager toolbar.

   The Properties dialog box for the network card appears, displaying the General sheet. The General sheet shows information about the network card's brand name and manufacturer. It also displays the status of the device and whether or not it's working properly. As shown in Figure 10-7, there is no indication here that the device is not working.

Figure 10-7 | **GENERAL SHEET IN THE PROPERTIES DIALOG BOX FOR THE NETWORK ADAPTER**

device type and manufacturer

Windows 2000 indicates the current status of the device

click to start the Hardware Troubleshooter

the device is enabled

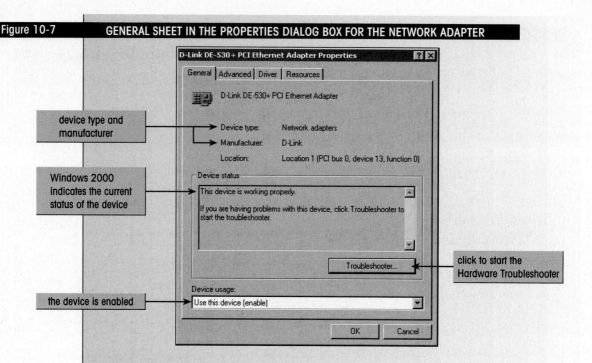

3. Click the **Driver** tab.

The Driver sheet, shown in Figure 10-8, displays information about the driver for the network card. From here you can uninstall the driver for the device, removing it from your system (you would then either remove the device from your computer or try reinstalling the driver). You can also update the driver if you have a more recent version of the driver file.

Figure 10-8 | **INFORMATION ABOUT THE DEVICE DRIVER IN USE**

click to uninstall the device's driver

click to view information about the driver file

click to update the driver file with a newer version

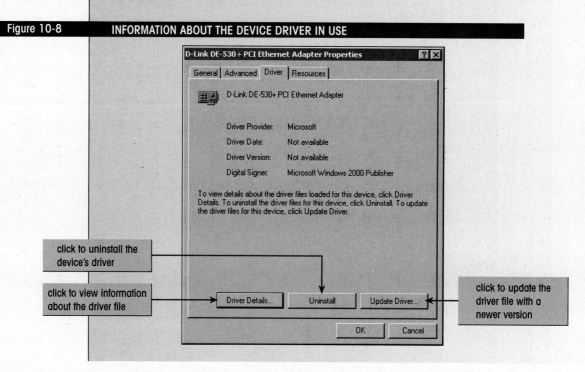

4. Click the **Resources** tab.

The Resources sheet, shown in Figure 10-9, displays the current system resources used by the device. It also indicates whether there are any device conflicts. The network card you just installed uses IRQ 10, an I/O range of 100–107F, and has a memory address of F4000000–F400007F. None of these resources is in conflict with any other device on your system.

5. Leave the Properties dialog box open.

Figure 10-9 | RESOURCES USED BY THE DEVICE

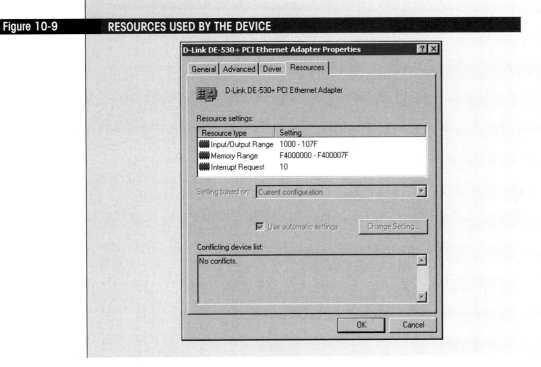

The Properties dialog box for the new network card also contains an Advanced sheet. This sheet contains advanced settings for the network card. Not all devices will have an Advanced sheet.

Troubleshooting a Device

So far you can find no indication that the network card is working improperly, but you are still having problems connecting to the company network. This means that the problem may lie elsewhere. You can try to locate the source of the trouble using the Windows 2000 Troubleshooter. The **Troubleshooter** is a sequence of dialog boxes that contain suggestions and questions about the source of your hardware trouble. By answering a series of questions, you can view tips on solving your problem.

To start the Troubleshooter:

1. Click the **General** tab in the Properties dialog box for your device.

   TROUBLE? If you closed the dialog box for your device, reopen it by repeating Steps 1 and 2 in the last set of steps.

2. Click the **Troubleshooter** button.

3. Select the **My network adapter doesn't work** option button, as shown in Figure 10-10 (you might have to scroll to see it), and then click the **Next** button at the bottom of the Help window.

Figure 10-10 | SELECTING A HARDWARE PROBLEM FROM THE HARDWARE TROUBLESHOOTER

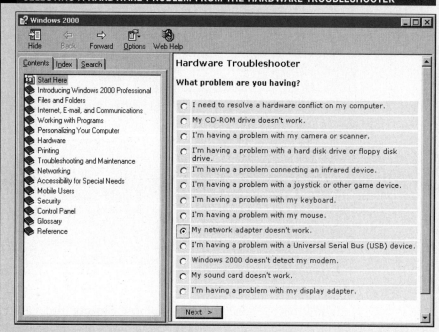

4. The Troubleshooter asks whether your device is on the Hardware Compatibility List (HCL). Since it is, click the **Yes** option button (you might have to scroll to see it) and then click the **Next** button.

5. The Troubleshooter asks you to check the status of your device in the device manager. Since you've already done this, and the adapter still doesn't work, click the **No** option button and then click the **Next** button.

   The next dialog box, shown in Figure 10-11, suggests that you check the network cable, the hub, and the transceiver for faulty connections. You do this and discover that you have a faulty cable. Replacing the cable enables the network connection to start working.

| Figure 10-11 | DETERMINING THE SOURCE OF THE PROBLEM WITH THE HARDWARE TROUBLESHOOTER |

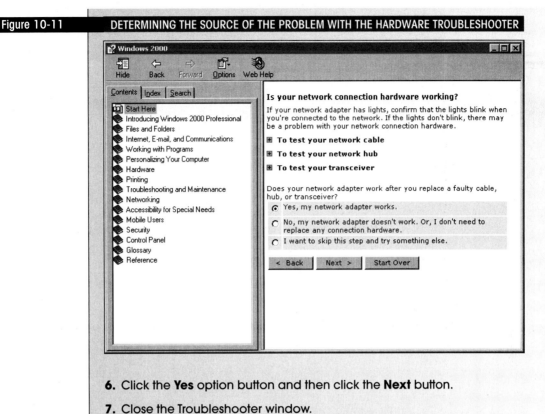

6. Click the **Yes** option button and then click the **Next** button.

7. Close the Troubleshooter window.

8. Click the **Cancel** button to close the Properties dialog box, but leave the Device Manager open.

By using the Troubleshooter, you've located the source of the problem. You decide to explore other functions of the Device Manager.

Changing the Device Manager View

Sometimes you will want to change your view of the devices and resources on your system. For example, you have a limited number of IRQs on the computer. You know that the new network card you inserted uses an IRQ of 10. How many free IRQs do you have left? This information might be important if you intend to add new devices to the computer. You can find out by viewing a list of the IRQs and the devices using them.

To view your device list by resource:

1. Click **View** on the Device Manager menu bar and then click **Resources by type**.

2. Click the **Plus** box ⊞ in front of the Interrupt request (IRQ) icon. See Figure 10-12.

Figure 10-12	VIEWING THE LIST OF USED IRQS

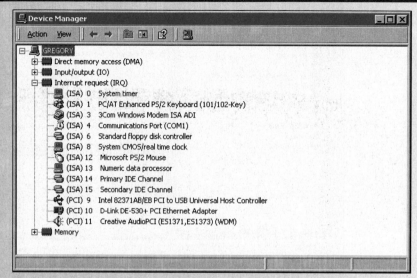

The Device Manager displays all of the used IRQs and the devices using them. Your computer will display different IRQs and devices. In Figure 10-12, note that IRQs 2, 5, and 7 are not in the list, and are therefore free for new devices.

If you want to view how the other resources are used on your computer, you can simply click the plus boxes in front of the DMA, I/O, and Memory icons. However, most of the time you won't have conflicts in these resources, since there is more room for different devices.

Printing a Device List

David wants you to print a hard copy of the device list each time you install new equipment on the company computers. The printout contains information on every device installed on the system and the resources each one uses. If the computer won't start for whatever reason, such a printout might prove useful if these devices have to be reinstalled.

To print out a device list:

1. Click **View** on the Device Manager menu bar and then click **Print**.

2. Click the **All devices and system summary** option button. See Figure 10-13.

Figure 10-13	PRINTING A HARDCOPY OF THE DEVICES AND A SYSTEM SUMMARY

By clicking the All devices and system summary option button, you will create a report detailing each device type on your computer and a summary report of the resources in use.

3. Select a printer and then click the **Print** button.

   The device list report is sent to your printer.

4. Close the Device Manager window.

5. Click the **Cancel** button to close the System Properties dialog box and then close the Control Panel.

You've finished your work inserting the network adapter card into the new computer. Your next task on David's list is to attach a new printer to another computer and then show the user how to use the printer.

Session 10.1 QUICK CHECK

1. List the three types of ports on a standard computer.

2. List two types of cards that can fit into your computer's expansion slots.

3. What is an IRQ? How many IRQs are available on a computer?

4. What is a driver?

5. What is the difference between a legacy device and a plug and play device?

6. Describe how you would view a list of devices installed on your computer.

7. Describe how you would view a list of resources being used on your computer.

SESSION 10.2

In this session, you'll learn how to install a printer. You'll see how to review the properties of your printer and how to change those properties. You'll learn how to print a test page to verify that your printer is working correctly. You'll see how to control who has access to your printer and the permissions they have in working with your printer. Finally, you'll learn how Windows 2000 manages your print jobs and how you can control which documents get printed when.

REFERENCE WINDOW **RW**

Installing a Printer

- Follow the manufacturer's directions to connect the printer to the appropriate port and plug it into a power supply.
- Follow the steps of the wizard that starts. If no wizard starts, click the Start button, point to Settings, and then click Printers; click the Add Printer icon and then press Enter; follow the steps of the Add Printer Wizard.

Installing a Printer

Your next job on David's task list is to install a new printer. To do this, you need to first follow the manufacturer's directions for connecting the printer to the appropriate port on your computer and for plugging the printer into a power supply. After you've done this, you turn the computer back on; most likely, Windows 2000 will recognize the new printer and will start a wizard that will install a driver and choose resource settings for the printer. However, if no wizard starts, you can use the Add Printer Wizard. Although you aren't likely to be able to actually install a new printer in your computer lab, you can still do many of the steps in this session. The steps tell you specifically when you should cancel the procedure. If you were really installing a new printer, you would need to have the manufacturer's disks and the Windows 2000 installation disks handy so Windows 2000 could access installation data.

To start the Add Printer Wizard:

1. Click the **Start** button, point to **Settings**, and then click **Printers**.

2. Click the **Add Printer** icon and then press the **Enter** key.

   The Add Printer Wizard starts.

3. Click the **Next** button.

The first step of the Add Printer Wizard asks you to enter whether you are installing a local printer or a network printer. A **local printer** is one that is connected directly to your computer, usually through the LPT1 parallel port. A **network printer** is connected to another computer on your network, called a **print server**. In this example, you'll be connecting to a local printer, though in working through the tasks, you can also try to connect to a network printer if that is what your instructor wants you to do. If your local printer uses plug and play technology, you can have the Add Printer Wizard search for it and install the drivers and choose resource settings for you. In this example, the local printer does not support plug and play.

To specify the printer type:

1. Click the **Local printer** option button.

TROUBLE? If you're installing a network printer, click the Network printer option button.

2. If necessary, deselect the **Automatically detect and install my Plug and Play printer** check box.

TROUBLE? If you are worried that you haven't actually physically installed a new printer and should therefore not be going through these steps, don't worry. You can go through the steps in the Add Printer Wizard and click the Cancel button at the end to quit the wizard without installing anything.

3. Click the **Next** button.

The Add Printer Wizard prompts you for the port you want the printer to use. For a local printer, you are prompted for the port that the printer is attached to (LPT1, LPT2, COM1, etc.). For a network printer, you have to either enter the network address of the printer (the URL) or browse the network to locate the printer. Figure 10-14 displays dialog boxes for each scenario.

Figure 10-14	SPECIFYING THE LOCATION OF THE PRINTER

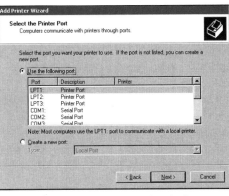 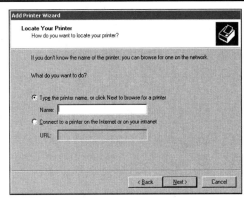

specifying the location of a local printer   specifying the location of a network printer

4. Specify the port for your printer.

- If it's a local printer, click the port name that you've connected the printer to in the list box (usually LPT1) and then click **Next**.

- If it's a network printer, click the **Connect to a printer on the Internet** option button, enter the network address for the printer in the URL text box, and then click **Next**.

- If it's a network printer and you don't know the network address, click the **Type the printer name** option button, leave the Name box blank, and then click **Next**. You can then locate printer on the network by moving through the hierarchy of network objects.

In the next step of the Add Printer Wizard, you specify the printer brand and install the appropriate driver. If you're installing a network printer, Windows 2000 will try to copy the driver files from the print server to your computer, saving you this step. If the print server is using driver files for a previous version of Windows, or if you're installing a local printer, you will have to install the driver files yourself.

To install the printer driver:

1. Select the name of the manufacturer in the Manufacturers list box.

2. Select the printer brand in the Printers list box. See Figure 10-15.

Figure 10-15   SPECIFYING THE PRINTER MANUFACTURER AND BRAND

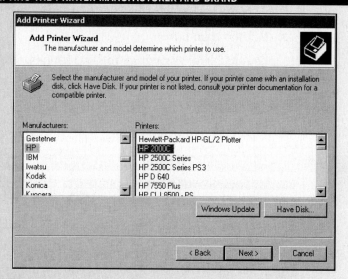

TROUBLE? If you have an installation disk from the printer manufacturer, insert the disk into your computer and then click the Have Disk button to use those driver files. It is usually best to use the drivers supplied by the hardware device's manufacturer rather than those supplied by Windows 2000.

TROUBLE? You may also see a Windows Update button that you can click to connect to the Internet and download the latest driver file.

3. Click the **Next** button.

If you're installing a local printer, you'll now be prompted for the printer name, whether you want to share the printer with the network, and whether or not you want to print a test page. If you're connecting to a network printer, the Add Printer Wizard will skip these steps. If you already have a printer, you will also be prompted to make the new printer the **default printer**, which means that Windows 2000 automatically uses that printer unless you specify one of the others.

To specify the printer name and other properties for your local printer:

1. Enter the printer name in the Printer name text box.

2. If you want this to be the default printer on your computer, click the **Yes** option button (see Figure 10-16) and then click **Next**.

Figure 10-16	SPECIFYING THE NAME OF THE PRINTER

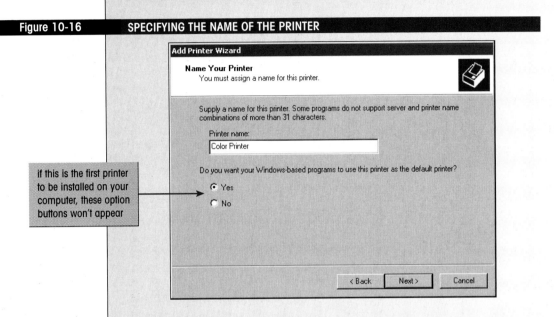

if this is the first printer to be installed on your computer, these option buttons won't appear

TROUBLE? If this is first printer to be installed on your computer, you will not have the option of making the printer the default. Windows 2000 will make it the default printer automatically.

Next you can choose to share this printer with other computers on your network. At this point, you decide not to share the printer.

3. Verify that the **Do not share this printer** option button is selected and then click **Next**.

Finally, you can choose to print a test page. This option allows you to confirm that the printer is up and running and that the connection works. Since this is just an example, you won't create a test page, but in most cases this is a good idea.

4. Click the **No** option button and then click **Next**.

5. You've completed the Add Printer Wizard. If you've been following these steps without intending to add a new printer, click the **Cancel** button. If you've actually added a new printer, click the **Finish** button to add the printer to your printer list.

6. If you installed the printer, an icon for the printer should now appear in the Printers window.

You've completed installation of the new printer. Your next job is to work with the new printer and review the tools that Windows 2000 provides to manage printers.

Managing a Printer

Windows 2000 provides a variety of tools to help you manage your printer. With these tools you can, among other things, update the printer driver, control how documents are sent to the printer, and change printer settings. You access these tools through the printer's Properties dialog box.

To display the printer properties:

1. Right-click the icon for the printer and then click **Properties** on the menu. If you didn't actually install a new printer in the last set of steps, use your regular printer for these steps.

   The Properties dialog box opens, as shown in Figure 10-17.

   TROUBLE? Your Properties dialog box will look different from the one shown in Figure 10-17.

Figure 10-17	THE PRINTER PROPERTIES DIALOG BOX

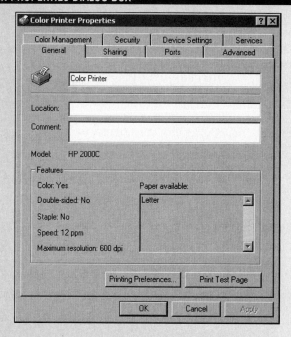

The number of dialog sheets in the Properties dialog box will vary for different printers. There are at least six sheets, though, that appear for every printer.

- **General**: View general information about the printer, such as its name and location.
- **Sharing**: Choose whether or not to share your printer with the network.
- **Ports**: Specify the port that your printer is connected to.
- **Advanced**: Specify the times at which the printer is available, how files are sent to the printer, and other advanced options.

- **Security**: Specify which users can access the printer and what privileges they have in managing the printer and printer documents.
- **Device Settings**: Specify specific settings for the printer (the list will vary between printers).

The General sheet shown in Figure 10-17 indicates that the printer supports color, but not double-sided printing or automatic stapling. The speed of the printer is 12 pages per minute at a maximum resolution of 600 dots per inch. The Properties dialog box in Figure 10-17 displays two additional sheets, Color Management and Services, which apply only to that particular printer.

Printing a Test Page

Sometimes a printer will not be working and you will have to determine whether the problem lies in the program that's using the printer, with Windows 2000, or with the printer hardware itself. One way of locating the source of the trouble is to print a test page.

REFERENCE WINDOW   RW

Printing a Test Page
- Open the Properties dialog box for the printer.
- Click the General tab if necessary.
- Click the Print Test Page button.

If the test page prints correctly, you can eliminate the program as the problem's source. Failure to print a test page may indicate a hardware problem. A test page also provides a hardcopy report on the printer's technical specifications.

To print a test page for your printer:

1. Click the **Print Test Page** button (on the General tab of your printer's Properties dialog box).

   Windows 2000 displays a message telling you that a test page is being sent to your printer..

2. Click the **OK** button when the test page has finished printing and leave the Properties dialog box open.

   TROUBLE? If the test page doesn't print, you can click the Troubleshoot button to access the Print Troubleshooter. You can then use the Troubleshooter to diagnose your problem in the same way that you used the Hardware Troubleshooter in the previous session.

Setting Advanced Options

You have probably printed documents many times in Windows 2000 without giving much thought to what goes on behind the scenes. You might have noticed a dialog box that tells you your document is printing, or you might have seen printer icons appear and then disappear in the taskbar. You might even have heard your hard drive spinning for a second or two when you printed a large document. David suggests that you explore how Windows 2000 manages your print jobs. See Figure 10-18.

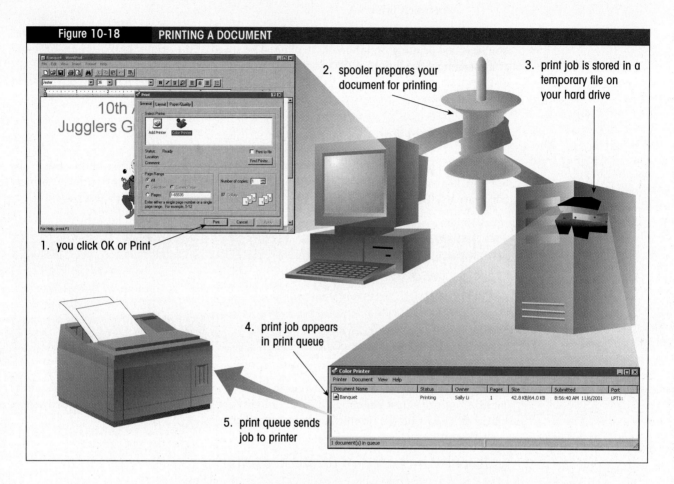

| Figure 10-18 | PRINTING A DOCUMENT |

2. spooler prepares your document for printing

3. print job is stored in a temporary file on your hard drive

1. you click OK or Print

4. print job appears in print queue

5. print queue sends job to printer

When you send a file to your printer, Windows 2000 prepares your document using print spooling. **Print spooling** creates a temporary file on your hard disk containing the electronic codes that control your particular printer, such as the code to move down to the next line or to eject a page. After each page is spooled, Windows 2000 sends the file to the printer to be processed. One of the big advantages of print spooling is that you don't have to wait for the entire document to be printed before you can continue your work at your computer. The printing goes on in the background. You can even have more than one print job being generated at the same time.

You can control how print spooling works on your computer using the Advanced sheet of the Properties dialog box.

To view the advanced properties of your printer:

1. Click the **Advanced** tab in your printer's Properties dialog box. See Figure 10-19.

Figure 10-19	ADVANCED PROPERTIES OF THE PRINTER

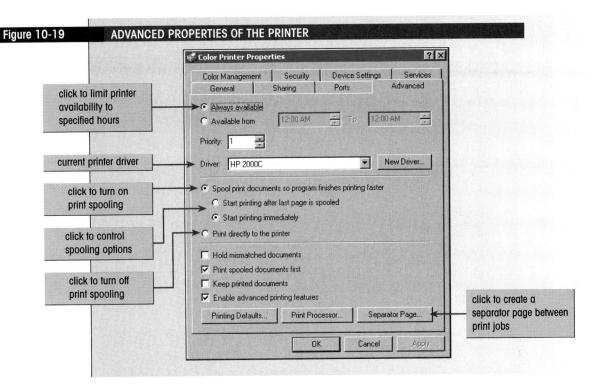

As you can see from Figure 10-19, you can have Windows 2000 either spool your print jobs or send them directly to the printer without spooling. You would only use the second option if your computer lacks the resources to perform spooling. You can also have Windows 2000 send the print job only after all pages have been spooled. This will cause your program to "freeze" until the spooling is completed, but it also provides more system resources, such as memory, to the print job rather than sharing those resources between the program and the spooling process.

Another feature to note in Figure 10-19 is the ability to restrict access to a printer to certain hours. This is useful in a network, when you don't want to have users accessing a printer during hours that the computer attached to that printer is turned off. If someone tries to use the printer during the off hours, the print job is held until the printer is again available. Finally, note that you can also create **separator pages**, pages that separate one print job from another. Once again, this is useful in a network in which several print jobs may be generated from several different users.

Viewing Device Settings

Each printer has its own set of unique device settings, such as the amount of memory installed in the printer, the number and type of paper trays, and whether the printer uses font cartridges. Windows 2000 communicates with your printer to record these device settings. David tells you that sometimes the company's printers are upgraded and these settings need to be changed, so it's important to know how to access these device settings when that occurs.

To view the printer's device settings:

1. Click the **Device Settings** tab in your printer's Properties dialog box. See Figure 10-20.

Figure 10-20 | **DEVICE SETTINGS FOR A SPECIFIC PRINTER**

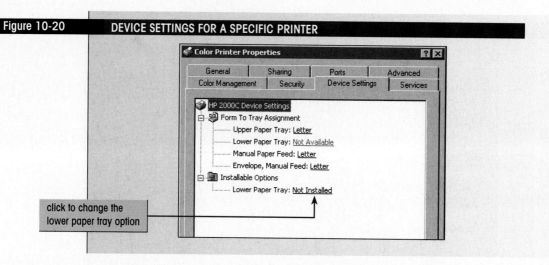

click to change the lower paper tray option

In this case, there is only one upgrade option remaining for the printer, and that is to install a lower paper tray. The company hasn't chosen to install that tray yet.

Viewing Security Settings

Thus far in your job as a technician, you've been working with the settings of the new printer. These commands are not available to every user, nor should they be. It would be an extra headache for you if users could accidentally modify the hardware you just finished installing. To prevent this from happening, Windows 2000 lets you determine which users or user groups can modify the printer you just installed. There are three types of actions that users can perform on the printer:

- **Print**: Users can print documents on the printer.
- **Manage Printer**: Users can change the hardware settings and properties of the printer.
- **Manage Documents**: Users can control the documents printed by the printer, changing the order in which documents are printed or removing print jobs from the printer altogether.

You can allow or deny each of these actions to any user or user group. Windows 2000 sets up defaults for these permissions automatically, but David would like you to review the settings so that you know how to change them if needed.

To review the security settings:

1. Click the **Security** tab in your printer's Properties dialog box. See Figure 10-21.

Figure 10-21   PERMISSIONS FOR THE ADMINISTRATORS GROUP

administrators can print, change printer properties, and manage documents sent to the printer

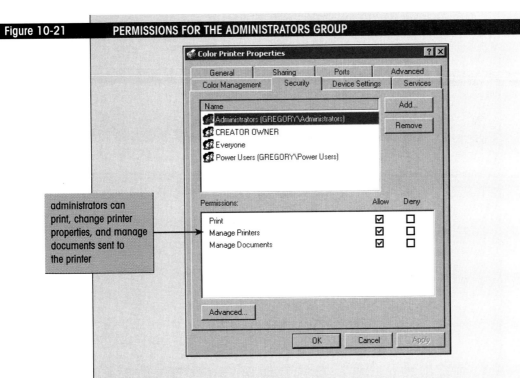

The selected user group in Figure 10-21 is the Administrator group. This is the user group that has complete control of your Windows 2000 computer and all of its hardware. As you can see, users in the Administrator group have the ability to print and manage the printer and documents.

2. Click the **Everyone** user group. See Figure 10-22.

Figure 10-22   PERMISSIONS FOR ALL USERS

all users can print with the printer, but not change printer properties or manage documents sent to the printer

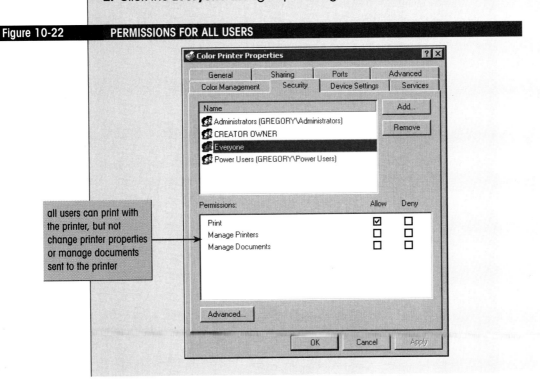

All users on the computer (every user is usually a member of the Everyone group) have the ability to print, but not to manage the printer or documents.

3. Click the **Cancel** button to close the Properties dialog box and avoid saving any changes you may have inadvertently made in the previous steps.

You've completed your work reviewing the properties of the new printer. Your next task is to help a new user operate the printer.

Managing a Print Queue

Sally Li, the user of the new computer, knows all about printing a single document. However, her printer will be shared on the network with other users, and she wants to know how to manage her print jobs in such an environment. You tell her that if there are other print jobs waiting, hers will be put into a **print queue**, a list of jobs being sent to the printer. You can view the print queue by opening the Printers window and then double-clicking the icon for the appropriate printer. The print job listed first in the print queue typically goes to the printer first. Once the entire job is transferred into the printer's temporary memory, it disappears from the print queue.

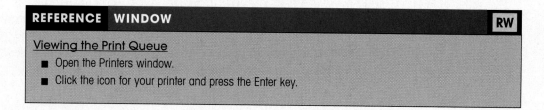

REFERENCE WINDOW   **RW**

Viewing the Print Queue
■ Open the Printers window.
■ Click the icon for your printer and press the Enter key.

The print queue also gives you some control over print jobs waiting to be printed. For example, you can pause or cancel print jobs, or change their order. To do this, you must belong to a user group that has permission to manage the documents on the printer. Sally Li has been given that kind of permission.

Opening the Print Queue Window

To display the print queue for a printer, you open the printer's icon from the Printers window.

To view the print queue:

1. Click the default printer icon 🖨 in the Printers window and then press the **Enter** key.

The print queue window has several columns:

■ **Document Name:** The filename of the document being sent to the printer
■ **Status:** The current status of the print job, such as spooling, paused, or printing
■ **Owner:** The username of the person who sent the print job
■ **Pages:** The number of pages that have printed and the total number of pages in the document

- **Size**: The size of the document in kilobytes
- **Submitted**: The time and date the job was sent to the printer
- **Port**: The port used by the printer

From viewing the print queue, you can see instantly which documents are waiting to be printed, how large they are, who sent them, and other details that might help you manage print jobs.

Sally wants to see how the print queue changes when she sends a document to the printer. You suggest that she print one of the topics in Windows 2000 Help.

To send a job to the printer:

1. Click the **Start** button and then click **Help**.

2. Click **Start Here** from the Contents list if necessary, click the **Options** button on the Help toolbar, and then click **Print**.

3. Click the **Print the selected topic** option button and then click **OK**.

4. Select the default printer icon 🖨 in the Select Printer window and then click the **Print** button.

5. Quickly minimize the Help window so you can see the print queue window you opened earlier and observe the new entry. See Figure 10-23.

| Figure 10-23 | PRINT QUEUE FOR THE COLOR PRINTER |

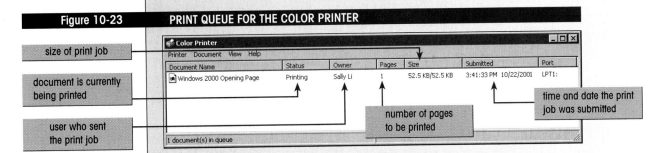

size of print job

document is currently being printed

user who sent the print job

number of pages to be printed

time and date the print job was submitted

TROUBLE? Since you're using a different printer, your print queue will look different from the one shown in Figure 10-23.

TROUBLE? Depending on how fast your printer processes the document, the entry in the print queue might be gone by the time you go back to the print queue window.

The print queue also supports drag and drop. For example, you can drag a document located at the bottom of the queue and drop it at the beginning of the queue. In this way, you can give greater priority to the documents you want printed earlier. Note that you can only do this if you belong to a user group that has permission to manage those print jobs.

Pausing the Print Queue

On occasion you might want to delay your computer from sending jobs to the printer. For example, if you want to use a specific letterhead for a print job, you have to change the paper in the printer before you print a job. Windows 2000 lets you pause one or all documents in the print queue so you can perform such paper changes.

Pausing the Print Queue
- Open the print queue window for your printer.
- Click Printer on the menu bar and then click Pause Printing.

If you want to pause the entire queue, you select the Pause Printing command from the Printer menu. This tells Windows 2000 to stop sending all jobs to the printer. Once you restart printing, the print queue starts sending all print jobs in the order shown in the queue. If you want to pause a specific print job, you select the document you want to pause from the queue, then click the Pause Printing command from the Document menu. Pausing a single print job halts your job while allowing other print jobs in the queue to print. To pause all of the jobs in the print queue, you must have permission to manage documents in the printer. However, you can always pause one or all of your own documents, since you are their owner. Sally asks you to show her how to pause her entire print queue.

To pause the print queue:

1. Click **Printer** on the print queue window's menu bar and then click **Pause Printing**.

   The title bar of the print queue window now has the word "Paused" on it to show that the printer is paused.

2. Return to the Windows 2000 Help window and reprint the Start Here topic.

3. Return to the print queue window. The print queue shows the new print job, but since the queue is paused, the job does not print.

You can now remove this job from the print queue, since you already have a copy of it.

Removing a Job from the Print Queue

Suppose you started to print a document, but then noticed an error in the document that you want to fix before printing. You might want to remove the job from the print queue to prevent it from printing. You can prevent your printer from processing a print job by deleting the job from the print queue.

Removing Print Jobs from the Print Queue
- To remove all jobs, click Printer on the menu bar and then click Purge Print Documents.
- To remove a single job, click the job in the print queue and then either press the Delete key or click Document on the menu bar and then click Cancel Printing.

After you attempt to remove a job, you might discover that all or part of the document prints anyway. If this happens, Windows 2000 had already sent part of the job—maybe even all of it—to the printer before you tried to cancel the print job. Your printer has memory too, and removing print jobs from the Windows 2000 print queue does not affect the parts of a print job already in the printer's memory. You can clear your printer's memory by resetting your printer. How you do this depends on what type of printer you have, but some printers have a Reset button. You decide to show Sally how to remove the print job she just sent.

To remove a job from the print queue:

1. Click **Windows 2000 Opening Page** in the list of document names in the print queue.

2. Click **Document** on the menu bar and then click **Cancel** to remove the document from the queue.

3. Click **Printer** on the menu bar and then click **Pause Printing** to turn off paused printing and restart the print queue.

   Since no documents are in the print queue, turning off paused printing will not cause documents to be printed.

4. Close the print queue window, the Help window, and the Printers window.

Sally thanks you for the help. You're finished with your work on printers and print queues and are ready to start on your next task.

Session 10.2 QUICK | CHECK

1. What is the difference between a local printer and a network printer?

2. How do you print a test page?

3. What is print spooling?

4. What is a print queue?

5. How do you pause the operation of your printer?

6. How do you remove a single print job from the printer?

SESSION 10.3

In this session, you'll learn some of the fundamentals of disks and disk maintenance. You'll see how to clean up your hard disk to remove unnecessary files. You'll learn how to scan your disk, checking for errors and fixing them. You'll learn about fragmentation and how to defragment your disk to improve performance. Finally you'll learn how to schedule disk maintenance tasks to run automatically at specified times.

Windows 2000 Disk Maintenance Accessories

David tells you that disk maintenance is a critical part of your job managing hardware devices at the company. Individuals and businesses are relying more and more on computers and the data they contain. If a computer's hard disk fails, it can be disastrous.

Windows 2000 helps you prevent disk failure from occurring in the first place by providing some valuable disk maintenance accessories. Disk maintenance accessories are available on the

Tools tab of the disk's property sheet (accessible by right-clicking the icon for the disk in the My Computer window and then clicking Properties) or via the System Tools submenu of the Accessories menu.

David suggests that you use these accessories as part of a scheduled comprehensive disk maintenance plan. You should begin your disk maintenance with a "spring cleaning," in which you delete old or unneeded files and scan the disk for **viruses**, programs that run on your computer and disrupt its operations. There are numerous software products on the market designed to protect your computer from viruses by performing regular scans for known viruses. Windows 2000 does not include a virus accessory, so if you own your own computer, you should purchase a virus checker and use it regularly as part of your disk maintenance plan.

Once you have ensured that your computer is free from viruses, you then scan each disk on your computer to locate and repair errors. Then you defragment each disk so that the files it contains are organized most efficiently. If you are responsible for maintaining a computer that is used all day long, you should probably run these maintenance procedures on a weekly or even daily basis. If, on the other hand, you use your computer less frequently—for example, if it is a home computer that you use only for correspondence, games, and maintaining your checkbook—you might only need to run disk maintenance procedures once every month or so.

Removing Unneeded Files

When you work with programs and files in Windows 2000, unnecessary files, such as temporary Web graphics, accumulate on your hard drive. This impairs system performance. The Disk Cleanup accessory helps you free up disk space by getting rid of these files. When you start Disk Cleanup, it displays a list of check boxes corresponding to the types of unnecessary files it located on the disk you are cleaning. See Figure 10-24. When you start Disk Cleanup, you might not see all the options on this list. What you see depends on what files Disk Cleanup finds on your disk.

Figure 10-24	DISK CLEANUP OPTIONS
CATEGORY	**DESCRIPTION**
Temporary Setup files	Temporary files created when you install a program—some programs delete these files when they are no longer needed; others leave them on your hard drive
Temporary Internet files	Web pages stored on your hard disk for quick viewing, stored in the Temporary Internet Files folder
Downloaded program files	Program files downloaded automatically from the Internet when you view certain Web pages
Recycle Bin	Files you deleted from your computer, which are stored in the Recycle Bin until you delete them
Old ScanDisk files	Files created by ScanDisk when it locates corrupted data
Temporary files	Files generated by programs to be used temporarily; usually these are deleted when you close the program, but if the program isn't shut down properly the temporary files remain on your disk
Windows 2000 uninstall information	Files from a previous version of Windows—these appear only if Windows 2000 was installed on a computer that used an older version of Windows; they can be safely deleted if you don't intend to revert to the original version

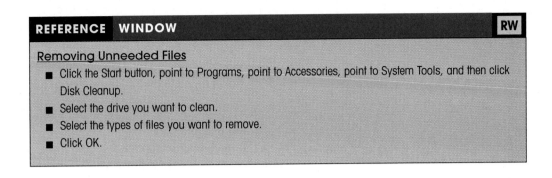

REFERENCE   WINDOW   RW

Removing Unneeded Files
■ Click the Start button, point to Programs, point to Accessories, point to System Tools, and then click Disk Cleanup.
■ Select the drive you want to clean.
■ Select the types of files you want to remove.
■ Click OK.

David provides a computer for you, to see how Disk Cleanup works. At this point, he doesn't want you to change any features on the computer's hard disk, so you'll close Disk Cleanup without actually performing the cleanup.

To start Disk Cleanup:

1. Click the **Start** button, point to **Programs**, point to **Accessories**, point to **System Tools**, and then click **Disk Cleanup**.

2. Click the **Drives** list arrow, click **(C:)** if necessary, and then click the **OK** button. Disk Cleanup calculates how much space you'll be able to clean up and then displays the dialog box shown in Figure 10-25.

   TROUBLE? If drive C doesn't appear or if you receive an error message, you don't have permission to clean up drive C. Click OK to acknowledge the message, close any open windows, and then read through the rest of this section without performing the steps.

Figure 10-25   **CHOOSING FILES TO DELETE**

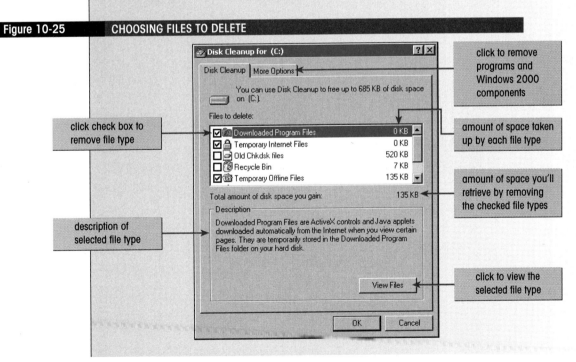

3. Check the boxes corresponding to the files you want to delete and then notice the amount of disk space you can save.

4. Click the **Cancel** button. If you are using your own computer and want to clean up your disk, you can click the OK button and then the Yes button to confirm this.

You can also use the More Options tab of Disk Cleanup to delete optional Windows components or installed programs that you do not use.

Scanning a Disk for Errors

Sections of the magnetic surface of a disk sometimes get damaged. Regularly scanning your disks for errors can be an effective way to head off potential problems that would make data inaccessible. The Windows 2000 Check Disk accessory not only locates errors on a disk, but it also attempts to repair them, or at least to mark the defective portions of the disk so that the operating system won't attempt to store data there.

To understand what errors Check Disk is looking for and how it repairs them, you need to learn a little bit about the structure of a disk. When you format a disk such as a 3½-inch disk (or a hard disk), a formatting program divides the disk into storage compartments. First it creates a series of rings, called **tracks**, around the circumference of the disk. Then it divides the tracks into equal parts, like pieces of pie, to form **sectors**, as shown in Figure 10-26.

Figure 10-26	A FORMATTED DISK

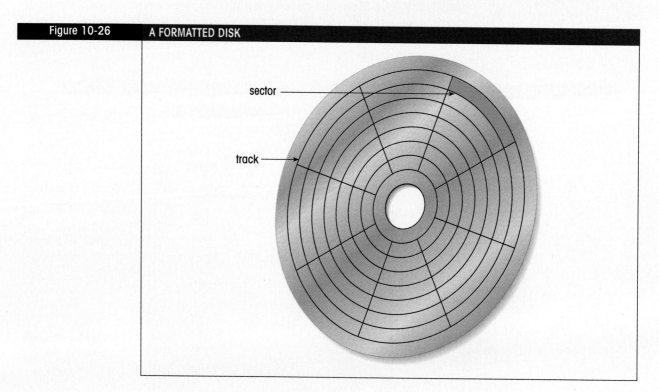

The number of sectors and tracks depends on the size of the disk. A high-density disk, such as your Data Disk, stores data on both sides of the disk. Each side has 80 tracks, and each track is divided into 18 sectors. Each sector can hold 512 bytes, for a total of 1,474,560 bytes or 1.44 MB (a megabyte is 1024 bytes).

Although the physical surface of a disk is made up of tracks and sectors, a file is stored in clusters. A **cluster**, also called an **allocation unit**, is one or more sectors of storage space—it represents the minimum amount of space that an operating system reserves when saving the contents of a file to a disk. Most files are larger than 512 bytes (the size of one sector). Therefore, a file might be stored in more than one cluster. Figure 10-27 shows a file that takes up four clusters on an otherwise empty disk.

Figure 10-27	FILE STORED IN CLUSTERS

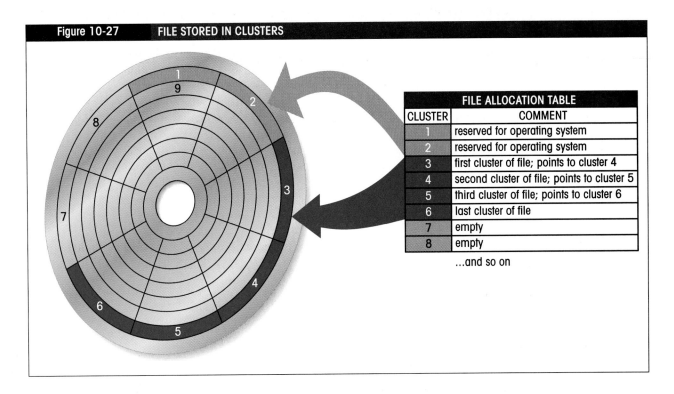

FILE ALLOCATION TABLE	
CLUSTER	COMMENT
1	reserved for operating system
2	reserved for operating system
3	first cluster of file; points to cluster 4
4	second cluster of file; points to cluster 5
5	third cluster of file; points to cluster 6
6	last cluster of file
7	empty
8	empty

...and so on

A unique number identifies each cluster; the first two clusters, shown in yellow, are reserved by the operating system.

Types of File Systems

Windows 2000 maintains a **file allocation table** (or **FAT**) for each disk, which lists the clusters on the disk and records the status of each cluster: whether it is occupied (and by which file), available, or defective. Each cluster in a given file "remembers" its order in the chain of clusters—and each cluster points to the next one until the last cluster, which marks the end of that file.

Another type of file system supported by Windows 2000 is **FAT32**. Previous versions of Windows used FAT (now referred to as FAT16) to manage the data on a disk, but FAT16 could work only with hard drives smaller than 2 GB in size. FAT32 improves on FAT16 by using disk space much more efficiently than FAT16 and accessing hard drives up to 2 terabytes in size (a terabyte is 1,000,000,000,000 bytes). Older computers that upgraded to Windows 2000 might still use FAT16, but if Windows 2000 was installed on a new computer, it probably uses FAT32. David explains that if you are using an older computer, you can convert a FAT16 drive to FAT32 using the Drive Converter accessory on the System Tools submenu of the Accessories menu, but that once you convert a drive to FAT32 you can't convert it back without reformatting it. Hence Drive Converter won't be covered in this tutorial.

The final type of file system supported by Windows 2000 is NTFS. **NTFS** is a file system used by Windows NT. NTFS supports file system recovery (in the case of a hard disk failure) and can access disk drives up to 2 terabytes in size. Generally, NTFS provides higher performance than both FAT16 and FAT32. NTFS is the preferred file system if your disk drive is larger than 32 gigabytes in size. Be aware that some older disk maintenance tools will not work with NTFS. So carefully consider your decision before converting your disk to NTFS.

Running Check Disk

When you use Check Disk to check your disk for errors, you can specify whether you want it to check the physical surface of the disk, the files, or both the surface and the files. Check Disk checks the disk surface by looking for damaged sectors. If it finds any, it marks those sectors and prevents data from being stored there. A damaged sector is called a **bad sector**.

Check Disk checks the files on a disk by comparing the clusters on the disk to the file allocation table. It looks specifically for lost clusters and cross-linked files. A **lost cluster** is a cluster that contains data that the file allocation table can't match to a file. If your computer suffers a power surge, a power failure, or any problem that locks it up, the operating system might lose one or more clusters from a file that was open when the problem occurred, and you might lose the data stored in those clusters. The presence of lost clusters on a disk is not damaging, but lost clusters do take up valuable space, and if there are too many of them, the disorder of clusters on your disk might lead to further errors. Check Disk identifies lost clusters and either deletes them or saves them to a new file. Although sometimes you recover lost data from such a file, more often you won't be able to do much with the file and should simply delete it. Figure 10-28 shows how Check Disk repairs lost cluster problems on a 3½-inch disk.

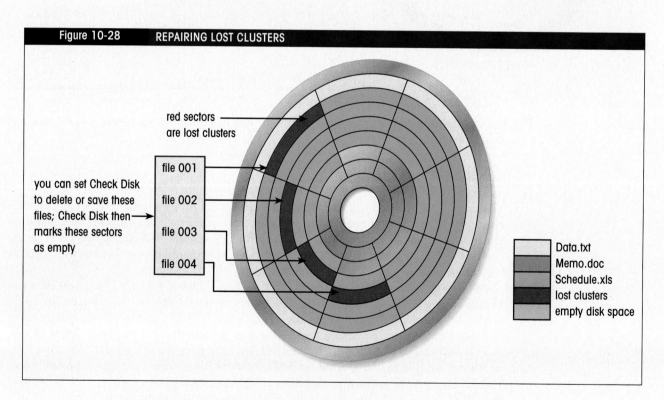

Figure 10-28   REPAIRING LOST CLUSTERS

red sectors are lost clusters

you can set Check Disk to delete or save these files; Check Disk then marks these sectors as empty

file 001
file 002
file 003
file 004

Data.txt
Memo.doc
Schedule.xls
lost clusters
empty disk space

Check Disk also checks for cross-linked files. A **cross-linked file** contains at least one cluster that has been allocated to more than one file in the file allocation table. Like lost clusters, cross-linked files can result from an abrupt termination of a program. Because a cluster should be occupied by data coming from only one file, the file allocation table becomes confused about which clusters belong to which files. You can tell Check Disk how you want it to handle such a file—by deleting it, copying it, or ignoring it. If you want to maintain the integrity of your files, it's best to allow Check Disk to copy each file to a new location on the disk and remove the original files so they are no longer cross-linked. This procedure often saves both files, although you might lose a portion of one of the files where the cross-link occurred. In most cases, the saved files can be deleted.

REFERENCE WINDOW | RW

Running Check Disk
- Open the My Computer window.
- Right-click the drive you want to check and then click Properties on the menu.
- Click the Tools tab.
- Click the Check Now button.

David says that the first thing he wants you to do is scan your disk for errors. Note that although you'll be performing the scan on a 3½-inch disk, this procedure is most useful for maintaining a hard disk.

To start Check Disk:

1. Close all open programs—if a program is in use while a disk is being scanned, you could lose data.

2. Place your Data Disk in the appropriate drive. Use the Data Disk you used for Tutorial 8.

3. Open the **My Computer** window and then right-click the **3½ Floppy (A:)** icon.

4. Click **Properties** on the menu and then click the **Tools** tab.

5. Click the **Check Now** button.

   As shown in Figure 10-29, Windows 2000 allows you to automatically fix file system errors. All files must be closed for this to happen. If the drive is already in use, Windows 2000 will ask you if you want to reschedule the operation for the next time you restart the computer. You can also have Windows 2000 scan for, and attempt the recovery of, bad sectors. If you choose this option, you do not need to select the check box to automatically fix file system errors, since this will happen when Windows 2000 recovers the bad sectors.

Figure 10-29 | **SELECTING CHECK DISK OPTIONS**

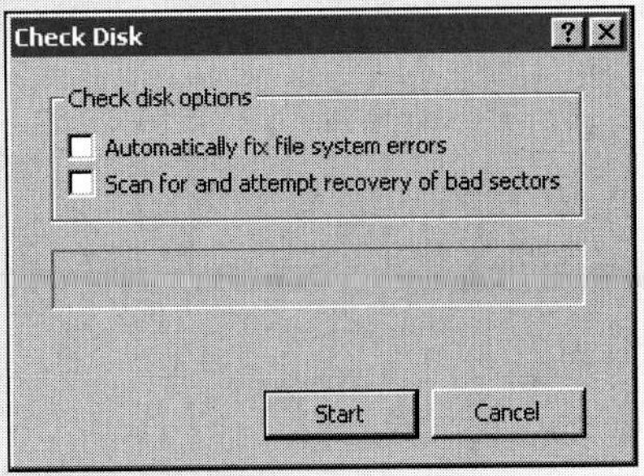

6. Click the **Scan for and attempt recovery of bad sectors** check box.

7. Click the **Start** button in the Check Disk dialog box.

   Windows 2000 takes a few minutes to scan the floppy disk, checking for errors. When it's finished it reports any errors that it finds on your disk.

8. Click the **OK** button twice to close the two dialog boxes, and then close the My Computer window.

Your computer might be set up to run Check Disk automatically in situations where Windows 2000 has been improperly shut down (such as a power failure during operation). When you next launch Windows 2000 after such a shutdown you might be asked if you want to run Check Disk.

Defragmenting **Your Disk**

Now that you've corrected any errors on your disk, you can use Disk Defragmenter to improve the disk's performance so that programs start and files open more quickly. When you save a file, Windows 2000 puts as much of the file as it can into the first available cluster. If the file won't fit into one cluster, Windows 2000 locates the next available cluster and puts more of the file in it. Windows 2000 attempts to place files in contiguous clusters whenever possible. The file is saved once Windows 2000 has placed all the file data into clusters. In Figure 10-30, you have just saved two files to a new 3½-inch disk: Address and Recipes.

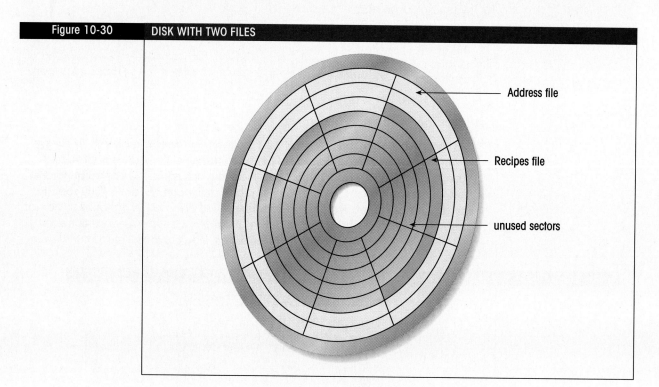

| Figure 10-30 | DISK WITH TWO FILES |

Address file

Recipes file

unused sectors

As you create and save new files, more clusters are used. If you delete a file or two, those clusters are freed. In Figure 10-31, you have saved a new file, Memo, and then deleted Recipes.

Figure 10-31	ADDING A FILE, THEN DELETING A FILE

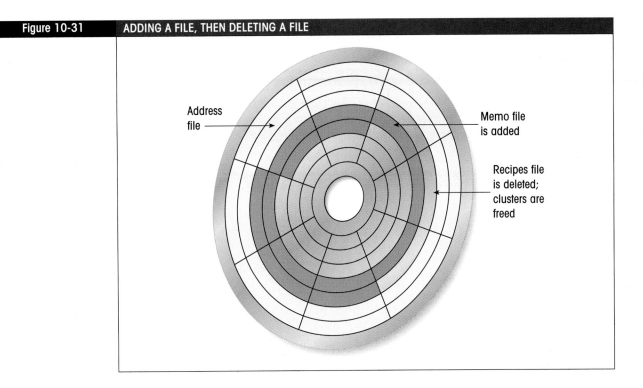

The next time you save a file, Windows 2000 searches for the first available cluster, which is now between two files. Figure 10-32, shows what happens when you save a fourth file, Schedule. It is saved to clusters that are not adjacent.

Figure 10-32	ADDING A NEW FILE IN FRAGMENTED CLUSTERS

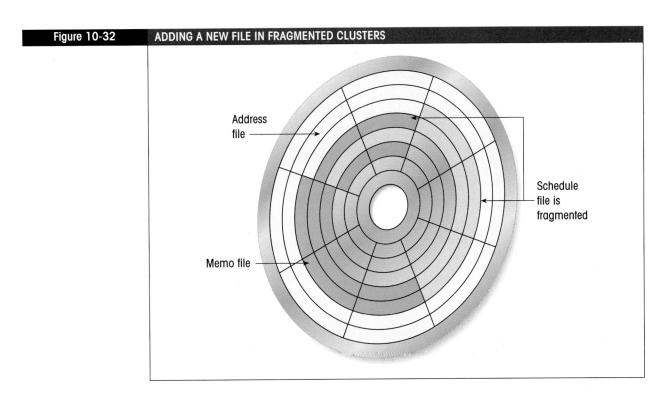

The more files you save and delete, the more scattered the clusters for a file become. A disk that contains files whose clusters are not next to each other is said to be **fragmented**. The more fragmented the disk, the longer Windows 2000 takes to retrieve the file, and the more likely you are to have problems with the file. Whenever a disk has been used for a long time, it's a good idea to defragment it. Defragmenting rearranges the clusters on the disk so each file's clusters are adjacent to one another. Figure 10-33 shows a fragmented disk. When a program tries to access a file on this disk, file retrieval takes longer than necessary because the program must locate clusters that aren't adjacent.

| Figure 10-33 | FRAGMENTED FILES |

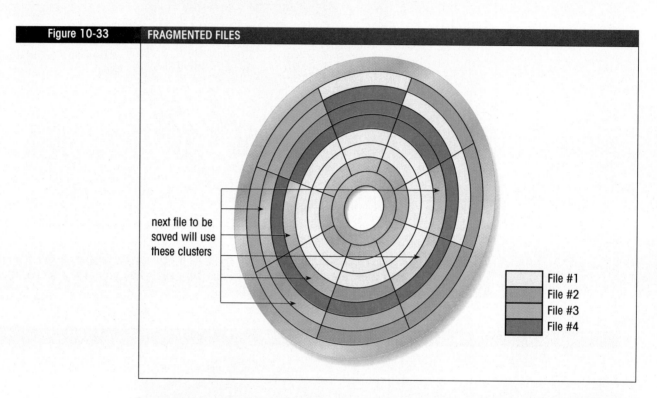

next file to be saved will use these clusters

File #1
File #2
File #3
File #4

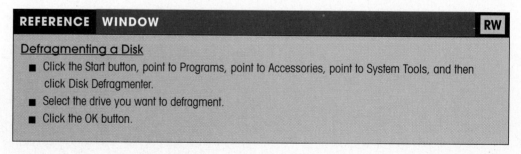

REFERENCE WINDOW   **RW**

<u>Defragmenting a Disk</u>
- Click the Start button, point to Programs, point to Accessories, point to System Tools, and then click Disk Defragmenter.
- Select the drive you want to defragment.
- Click the OK button.

You're ready to defragment your disk. David tells you that he can't guarantee that your disk needs defragmenting. It's possible that you'll go through the defragment procedure but Windows 2000 won't have to make any changes because your disk is not fragmented. If this is the case with your disk, you might not be able to perform all the steps in this section.

To start Disk Defragmenter:

1. Close all open programs to prevent loss of data.

2. Click the **Start** button, point to **Programs**, point to **Accessories**, point to **System Tools**, and then click **Disk Defragmenter**.

The Disk Defragmenter window opens, as shown in Figure 10-34.

Figure 10-34	THE DISK DEFRAGMENTER DIALOG BOX

drive size and the amount of free space on the drive

drive name

file system used by the drive

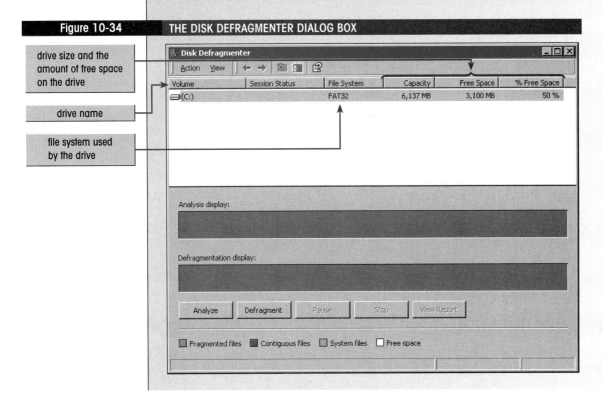

Before attempting to defragment a hard disk, you should analyze the current state of the disk. The report that's generated will tell you how badly fragmented the disk is, and whether Windows 2000 recommends that you proceed to defragment the disk. Defragmenting can be a time-consuming process, so you will not always want to start a defragmentation.

To analyze your disk:

1. Select a disk on your computer.

2. Click the **Analyze** button at the bottom of the window.

The analyzing process will take several minutes. After the analysis is finished, Windows 2000 presents its recommendation about whether or not you should defragment the drive.

3. Click the **View Report** button.

The Analysis Report dialog box in Figure 10-35 shows information about the drive, including the file fragmentation and a list of fragmented files. At the top of the dialog box is the recommendation to defragment the drive.

Figure 10-35   FRAGMENTATION ANALYSIS REPORT DIALOG BOX

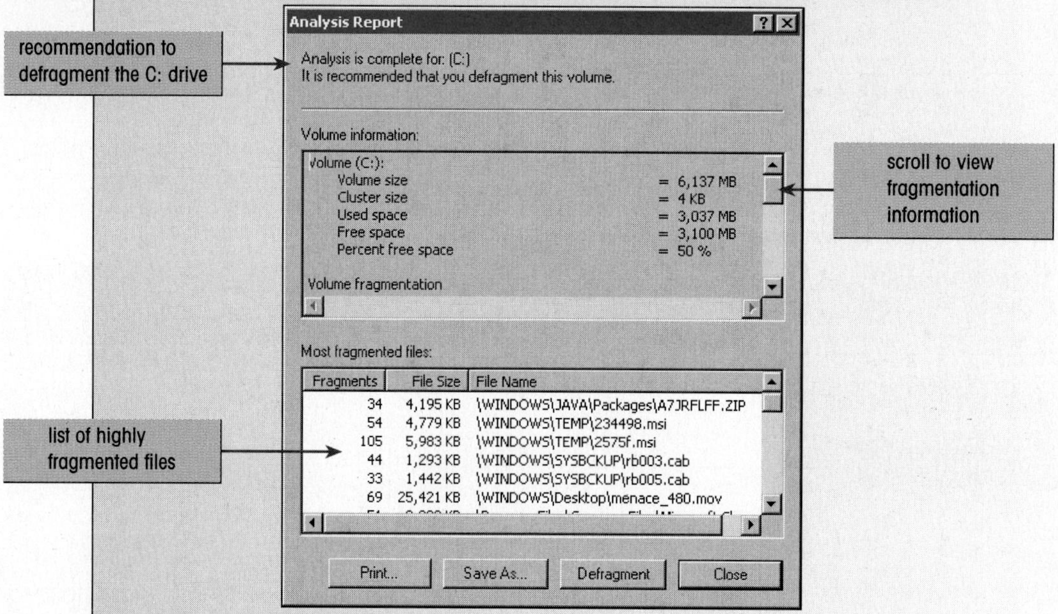

recommendation to
defragment the C: drive

scroll to view
fragmentation
information

list of highly
fragmented files

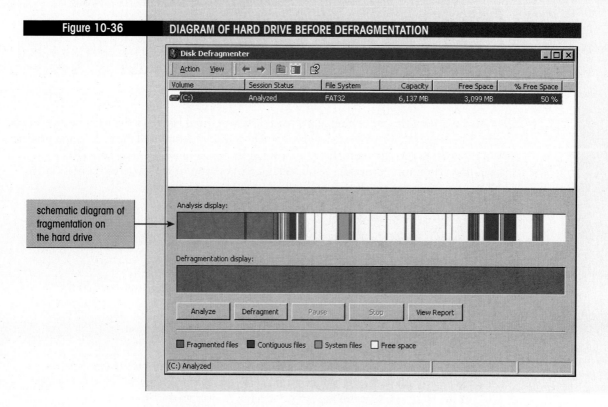

4. Click the **Close** button.

Disk Defragmenter shows a schematic diagram (see Figure 10-36) of the
current state of the drive.

Figure 10-36   DIAGRAM OF HARD DRIVE BEFORE DEFRAGMENTATION

schematic diagram of
fragmentation on
the hard drive

> You could click the Defragment button now to start defragmenting the hard disk. However, since this could take an hour or longer, you'll simply close the window without doing the defragmentation.
>
> **5.** Close the Disk Defragmenter window.

If you own your own computer, you can run Disk Defragmenter at a time when you won't need to use the computer for other tasks.

Scheduling Disk Maintenance Tasks

Performing disk maintenance tasks regularly will help your computer run efficiently. You can schedule Windows 2000 to take care of the tasks automatically using the Windows 2000 Task Scheduler. The Task Scheduler schedules and then runs programs according to your computer's clock (if your computer is on). You'll use the Task Scheduler to schedule a weekly cleanup of the hard disk.

> *To start the Task Scheduler:*
>
> **1.** Click the **Start** button, point to **Programs**, point to **Accessories**, point to **System Tools**, and then click **Scheduled Tasks**.
>
> **2.** Click the **Add Scheduled Task** icon and then press the **Enter** key. The Scheduled Task Wizard starts.
>
> **3.** Click the **Next** button.
>
> **4.** Click **Disk Cleanup** in the applications list (you may need to scroll to see it) and then click **Next**.

When you create a scheduled task, you give that task a name and specify when and how often the task should be performed.

> *To create a scheduled task:*
>
> **1.** Type **Clean the Hard Drive** in the task name box.
>
> **2.** Click the **Weekly** option button, as shown in Figure 10-37, and then click the **Next** button.

Figure 10-37	CREATING A WEEKLY SCHEDULE TO CLEAN THE HARD DRIVE

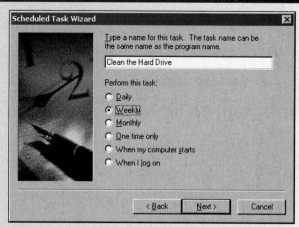

You decide to clean the hard drive every Friday night at 6 p.m.

3. Enter **6:00 PM** in the Start Time box.

4. Verify that 1 is entered in the Every weeks box and then click the **Friday** check box. See Figure 10-38.

Figure 10-38	SETTING THE SCHEDULE FOR EVERY FRIDAY AT 6 P.M.

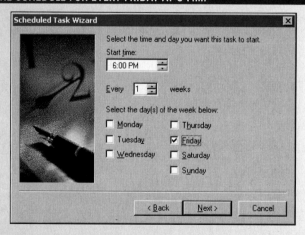

5. Click the **Next** button.

Finally, you specify the user who will be credited for running the task. Since you're working on Sally Li's computer, you'll enter her name in the User Name box. On your own computer, you can enter your own username.

6. Enter (*your user name*) in the Enter the user name box if necessary and then click the **Next** button. No password is necessary.

7. Click the **Finish** button.

The Clean the Hard Drive icon now appears in the Scheduled Tasks window. If you close the window now, your computer will automatically run the CleanDisk program at 6 p.m. on Friday (or, if the computer is off then, Windows 2000 will ask if you want to run CleanDisk the next time you turn on your computer). David suggests that you delete the task from the list until you can confer with Sally Li to make sure that running this task at that time won't interfere with her work.

To delete a task:

1. Click the **Clean the Hard Drive** icon in the Task Scheduler.

2. Press the **Delete** key and click **Yes** when Windows 2000 asks you to confirm the file deletion.

3. Close the Scheduled Tasks window.

You've completed your work with hardware and Windows 2000. With the tools you've learned, you can manage most of the hardware problems that you might encounter in your job at Chan & Associates.

Session 10.3 QUICK CHECK

1. A destructive program that runs on your computer and disrupts its operations is called what?

2. Why should you regularly defragment your disks?

3. What is a cluster?

4. What is the purpose of the file allocation table?

5. True or False: Windows 2000 always stores a file in adjacent clusters.

6. How does a disk become fragmented?

REVIEW ASSIGNMENTS

1. Exploring Your Computer Open the Device Manager on your computer. Using the information in the Device Manager, answer the following questions:

Explore
    a. What type of display adapter is your computer using? What resources is the display adapter using? How old is the driver for the display adapter? If there is no date for the driver, make a note of this.

Explore
    b. What DMA numbers are being used and by which devices?

    c. What IRQ numbers are being used and by which devices?

2. Exploring Your Printer Open the Print dialog box (you can open it from WordPad or Paint), and then answer the following questions on a piece of paper. When you are finished, close the Print dialog box.

    a. What is the name of your printer?

    b. What is your printer's manufacturer and brand name?

    c. Through what kind of port is your printer connected?

    d. Is the printer a local printer or a network printer?

    e. What driver does your printer use?

    f. Describe how your computer is set up to handle spooling.

Explore

3. Troubleshooting a Hardware Problem You are providing hardware support for some Windows 2000 users at your work. A user contacts you because of a problem he or she is having playing audio CDs on the CD-ROM player. The CD-ROM player is listed on the Windows 2000 Hardware Compatibility List, and you learn that the MCI CD audio driver is installed. Use the Hardware Troubleshooter to determine what you should have the user do next to determine the source of the trouble.

4. Cleaning up a Hard Disk Upon returning from a business trip to Chan & Associates, you decide to apply some of the disk maintenance procedures you learned. You decide to use the Disk Cleanup accessory to explore the different types of files that are likely to be cluttering up your disks.

    a. First start the Disk Cleanup accessory and select your Data Disk (the same disk you used in this tutorial). What check box options appear in the cleanup list? Are there fewer than in the list that was shown in Figure 10-25?

    b. Close and then restart Disk Cleanup, and this time select drive C. What appears in the cleanup list when you select drive C? Are there more or fewer options than those listed in Figure 10-25? If there are any differences, can you account for them?

    c. Select all of the check boxes available for drive C, and record the amount of disk space you could save by running the Disk Cleanup accessory.

    d. If you are using a lab computer, close Disk Cleanup without cleaning up any disks. If you are using your own computer, proceed with the Disk Cleanup procedure to clean up your hard disk.

Explore

5. Defragmenting a Hard Drive If you have your own computer or have permission from the computer lab's staff, work on defragmenting your computer's hard drive.

    a. Analyze your hard drive and then print the defragmentation analysis report.

    b. Print the screen shot of the schematic diagram of your hard disk (press the PrintScreen key, open Paint, paste the image, print the image from Paint, and then close Paint without saving changes).

    c. Start the defragmentation.

    d. After the defragmentation is finished, print a screen shot of the schematic diagram. Compare the two diagrams (before and after defragmentation).

Explore

6. Scheduling Tasks You've learned how to schedule maintenance tasks using the Task Scheduler. You can use the Task Scheduler to schedule additional programs. Now you'd like to schedule a virus checker on your computer. If you have access to a computer with a virus checker, schedule the virus checker so that it runs whenever you start Windows 2000. If you don't have a virus checker, choose a different program to schedule.

    a. Open the Task Scheduler and add a new task for your virus checker (or a different program if you prefer). Using the techniques listed in Exercise 5 above, print a screen shot of each dialog box in the Add Task wizard.

    b. Restart your computer and verify that the task starts as planned.

    c. If you are working in a lab, remove the task you added from the Task Scheduler.

PROJECTS

Explore

1. You can learn a lot about your system from the System Information tool.
   a. To open the System Information window, click the Start button, point to Programs, point to Accessories, point to System Tools, and then click System Information.
   b. Print the System Summary information.
   c. Print the component information for the Display component.

Explore

2. You can customize your hardware settings on your computer through hardware profiles. Using Windows 2000 Help, read up on hardware profiles and write a report describing what hardware profiles are, when you would typically use them, and how to set up a hardware profile on your computer.

Explore

3. Another way of checking on the performance of your hardware is to use the System Monitor. The System Monitor displays real-time information on system usage. One of the things you may want to monitor is **% Processor Time**, which is the percentage of time that the processor is executing. It's used as a measure of the load on the system's processor.
   a. To open the System Monitor, open the Control Panel, open Administrative Tools, click Performance, and then press the Enter key.
   b. Click the Add button ⊞ and add the processor time to the list of items being monitored.
   c. Using the techniques listed in Review Assignment 5 above, create a screen shot of the system monitor showing the % Processor Time being graphed.
   d. Stop and remove the process from the System Monitor.

4. Another type of port that your computer might be using is a SCSI port. Research the topic of SCSI ports and SCSI devices and write a report based on your research. In your report, write out what the acronym "SCSI" stands for, describe the differences between these ports and the ports described in this tutorial, and describe the advantages and disadvantages of SCSI ports and devices.

LAB ASSIGNMENTS

Defragmentation and Disk Operations In this Lab, you will format a simulated disk, save files, delete files, and undelete files to see how the computer updates the FAT. You will also find out how the files on your disk become fragmented and what a defragmentation utility does to reorganize the clusters on your disk. See the Read This Before You Begin page for instructions on installing and starting the Lab.

1. Click the Steps button to learn how the computer updates the FAT when you format a disk and save, delete, and undelete files. As you proceed through the Steps, answer all of the Quick Check questions that appear. After you complete the Steps, you will see a Quick Check Summary Report. Follow the instructions on the screen to print this report.

2. Click the Explore button. Click the Format button to format the simulated disk. Try to save files 1, 2, 3, 4, and 6. Do they all fit on the disk?

3. In Explore, format the simulated disk. Try to save all the files on the disk. What happens?

4. In Explore, format the simulated disk. Save FILE-3, FILE-4, and FILE-6. Next, delete FILE-6. Now, save FILE-5. Try to undelete FILE-6. What happens, and why?

5. In Explore, format the simulated disk. Save and erase files until the files become fragmented. Draw a picture of the disk to show the fragmented files. Indicate which files are in each cluster by using color, crosshatching, or labels. List which files in your drawing are fragmented. Finally, defragment the disk and draw a new picture showing the unfragmented files.

QUICK CHECK ANSWERS

Session 10.1

1. parallel, serial and USB
2. PCI and ISA
3. IRQ stands for interrupt request line and is used by the computer to handle simultaneous requests for action from hardware. There are 16 IRQs available to use.
4. A driver is a file on your computer that enables Windows 2000 to communicate with and control the operation of a hardware device.
5. A legacy device is an older hardware device on your system whose settings you have to enter manually. A plug and play device is a hardware device that can be configured automatically by Windows 2000.
6. Open the Control Panel, open the System icon, and click the Device Manager button to open the Device Manager window.
7. Open the Device Manager window and then click View and Resources by type or Resources by connection.

Session 10.2

1. A local printer is connected directly to your computer through a parallel or serial cable. A network printer is a printer connected via the network.
2. Open the Properties dialog box for the printer and then click the Print Test Page button on the General sheet.
3. Print spooling is the process of creating a file on your hard disk containing the codes to control the operation of your printer. The file is then sent to the printer to create the printed document.
4. The print queue is a list of documents waiting to be printed on the printer.
5. Open the print queue window and then click Pause Printing from the Printer menu.
6. Right-click the document in the print queue window and press the Delete key.

Session 10.3

1. virus
2. to prevent files from being stored inefficiently on the disk
3. one or more sectors of storage space—the minimum amount of space that an operating system reserves when saving the contents of a file to a disk
4. The FAT keeps track of the clusters on a disk and the status of each cluster.
5. False
6. A disk becomes fragmented when it contains files whose clusters are not next to each other.

MANAGING WINDOWS 2000

Using Administrative Tools at Copy City

CASE

Copy City Copiers

You've just been hired at Copy City Copiers, a copy shop in Springdale, Illinois. Copy City Copiers provides a wide range of desktop publishing, printing, and copying services to its customers. Part of your job is to manage the computers at Copy City. Some of the computers are used to control large print jobs, while other computers are available to customers for their own printing and copying needs. Another group of computers is used for administrative tasks, such as payroll, scheduling and accounting.

Anyone should be able to use the customer computers, but only a few select individuals should be able to configure them. Customers, for example, should not be able to change any of the computer settings or install their own programs. The computers used for the large print jobs should be available to all of the Copy City employees, but not to the customers. Finally, the computers used for administrative tasks should be available only to a few select employees who are responsible for managing the payroll and accounting software.

Another part of your job will be to perform periodic backups of the data on these computers. The copy shop needs to be able to recover data quickly and easily in the case of computer failure. A backup tape drive has been purchased for this purpose.

Your supervisor, Bruce Clemons, has recently installed Windows 2000 on all of these machines. He has heard that Windows 2000 has several features that allow one to create and manage user groups as well as to perform periodic backups. Bruce asks you to explore how to use Windows 2000 to perform these tasks on the computers at Copy City Copiers.

SESSION 11.1

In this session, you'll learn how to create and manage user accounts and user groups. You'll study the different kinds of user groups on your system and how those groups relate to system security. You'll learn how to control access to your system using security policies. Finally, you'll see how to lock your computer to prevent unauthorized access.

Introducing Users and User Groups

In your work with Windows 2000, you've probably seen the terms "user" and "user groups." For example, you work with user groups in controlling who has access to your computer in a local area network, and you can also specify which users have the ability to manage the printer on your computer. How did these users and user groups get set up on the computer? Let's look at user groups first, to understand the process.

A **user group** is a group of users who share the same rights and privileges on a computer or computer network. These privileges could include the ability to install and remove programs, to perform system backups, or to change hardware settings.

There are two types of user groups: global and local. A **global** or **domain group** is a user group that is managed by a network administrator. Global groups allow users to access their accounts from any computer on the network. A **local group** is a user group created for a specific computer. You can add global users and global groups to a local group. Since managing a global group requires special software and training, we'll confine our interest to local groups, but many of the principles and techniques you learn can be applied to global groups as well.

Windows 2000 has a set of predefined user groups that cover most of the different kinds of users who will work on your computer. Figure 11-1 describes these user groups.

Figure 11-1	WINDOWS 2000 BUILT-IN USER GROUPS
USER GROUP	**DESCRIPTION**
Administrators	Users have full control over all computer operations and security settings.
Backup Operators	Users can back up and restore files on the computer. They can also log on to the computer and shut it down, but they cannot change security settings.
Guests	Users can log on to and off the computer and save files, but they cannot install programs or change system files or security settings.
Power Users	Users can create and modify user accounts (except for administrators and backup operators), but they can't take control of files owned by other users.
Replicator	Users can replicate files within a domain (used by specialized programs, not actual users).
Users	Users can perform most common tasks, such as running programs, using local and network printers, and shutting down the system. Users can create their own user groups, but can't modify other user groups, nor can they run programs installed by other users.

When you first install Windows 2000, the operating system creates these user groups along with two users: Administrator and Guest. **Administrator** is a member of the Administrators user group. This is the first user account set up on your computer. The Administrator account can never be deleted or disabled, ensuring that the computer's owner will never lose the ability to configure the computer's settings. You can, however, rename the Administrator account. Like changing a password, renaming the account prevents unauthorized users from accessing the account, since both the password and the account name are required to access the account.

The **Guest** user is a part of the Guest user group, and shares the limited capabilities given to members of that group. This account is disabled by default.

A third account has probably been set up on your computer—your account. If you are working on your own computer, you are, in most cases, the sole user on your computer and thus, by default, the Administrator. If you are in a lab, an account has been set up for you in which your permissions are limited. To perform the steps in this tutorial, your instructor or technical support person will need to ensure that you have extended permissions.

Adding a New User

Copy City Copiers has a new employee, Joyce Tallent, who will be working as an assistant in the payroll department. She will be sharing a computer with Wai Chen and needs to have her own account set up on the computer. Bruce wants you to set up an account for her. She should have the same permissions as Wai: she should be able to run programs and create files, but she shouldn't be able to modify the settings of the computer. Bruce wants you to assign her to the Users group, which will give her these limited privileges.

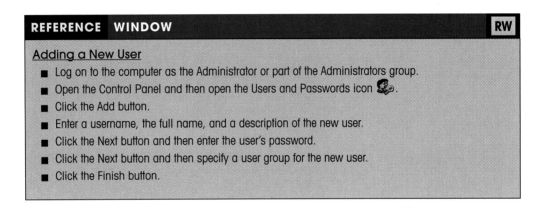

REFERENCE   WINDOW   RW

Adding a New User
- Log on to the computer as the Administrator or part of the Administrators group.
- Open the Control Panel and then open the Users and Passwords icon.
- Click the Add button.
- Enter a username, the full name, and a description of the new user.
- Click the Next button and then enter the user's password.
- Click the Next button and then specify a user group for the new user.
- Click the Finish button.

To create a new user:

1. Log on to your computer as the Administrator or as a member of the Administrators group.

   TROUBLE? If you don't know how to log on with administrative privileges, talk to your instructor. If you *can't* get administrative privileges, review the material in this session without performing the steps.

2. Click the **Start** button [Start], point to **Settings**, and then click **Control Panel**.

3. Open the **Users and Passwords** icon.

   The Users and Passwords dialog box lists the user accounts installed on the computer. See Figure 11-2.

Figure 11-2 | THE USERS AND PASSWORDS DIALOG BOX

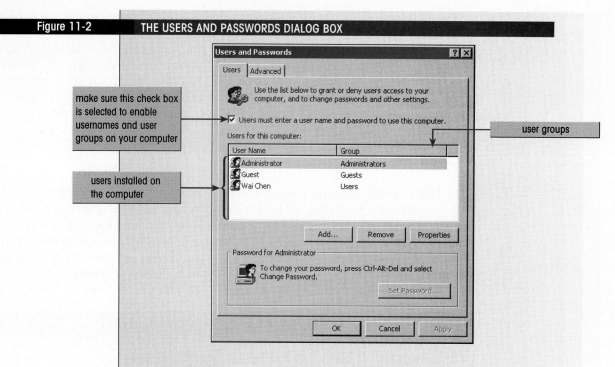

make sure this check box is selected to enable usernames and user groups on your computer

users installed on the computer

user groups

4. Click the **Add** button.

TROUBLE? If the Add button is grayed out, click the Users must enter a user name ... check box located above the user name list, to enable usernames and groups for your computer. If you don't have the Users must enter a user name...check box talk to your instructor to learn the specific step for adding new users to your computer system.

5. Type **JTallent** in the User Name box, **Joyce Tallent** in the Full Name box and **Payroll Assistant** in the Description box. See Figure 11-3.

Figure 11-3 | SPECIFYING A NAME AND DESCRIPTION FOR A NEW USER

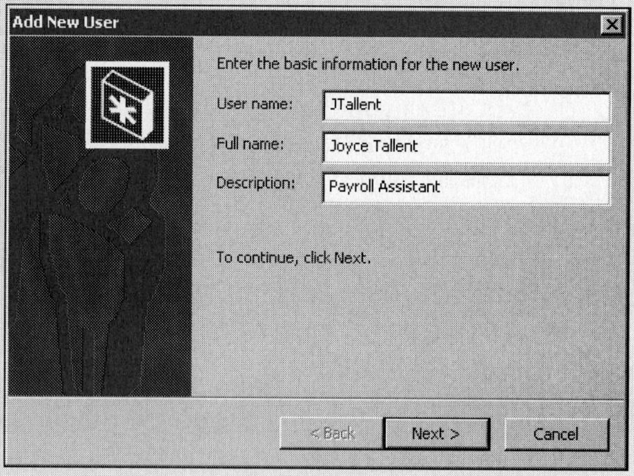

Add New User

Enter the basic information for the new user.

User name: JTallent

Full name: Joyce Tallent

Description: Payroll Assistant

To continue, click Next.

< Back | Next > | Cancel

6. Click the **Next** button.

Now you could enter a password for Joyce Tallent, but you'll leave these boxes blank so that no password is required.

7. Click the **Next** button.

The final step is to specify a user group for the new user. You can either specify a standard user (a member of the Power Users group), a restricted user (from the Users group) or select from the drop-down list containing all user groups installed on the computer. You'll place Joyce Tallent in the Users group.

8. Click the **Restricted user** option button. See Figure 11-4.

Figure 11-4	SPECIFYING THE USER GROUP FOR A NEW USER

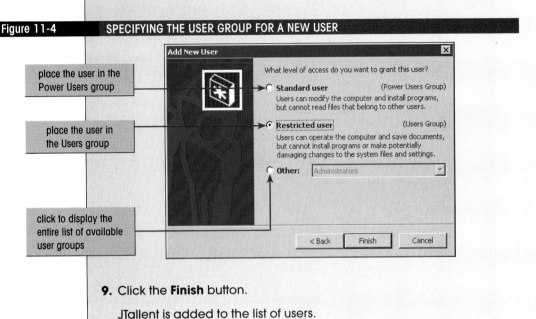

9. Click the **Finish** button.

   JTallent is added to the list of users.

Setting Advanced User Properties

Once you create a new user, you can further define properties for that user. For example, on some systems users are required to change their passwords every few months to improve security. You set a particular user's password so that it never expires. In the same vein, on some systems several people will share the same user account. Rather than allow one person to change the password (potentially locking out the other persons) you can set up the user account so that the user *cannot* change the password. Without making any changes, you decide to view the list of properties for Joyce Tallent's account.

To access a list of advanced properties:

1. Click the **Advanced** tab in the Users and Passwords dialog box.

2. Click the **Advanced** button.

   The Local Users and Groups window opens. This window shows the current properties for all of the local groups and users set up on your computer.

   TROUBLE? Your system may also be set up to display global users and groups, in addition to the local users and groups.

3. Click the **Users** folder icon in the left pane 📁 to view a list of local users.

4. Click **JTallent** in the list of users and then click the **Properties** button 🔧.

The Properties dialog box opens, as shown in Figure 11-5. Note that you can select or deselect several check boxes related to the properties that you want to set for this user.

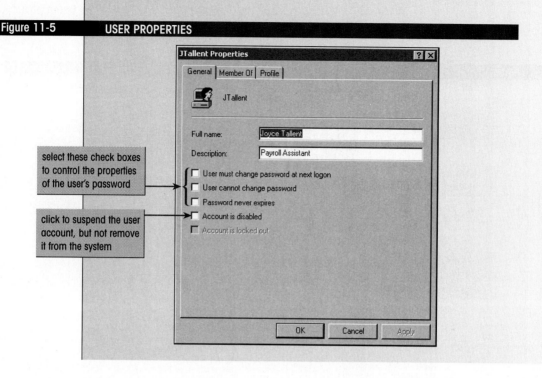

select these check boxes to control the properties of the user's password

click to suspend the user account, but not remove it from the system

Note that you can also disable a user account. A disabled account remains on the system but is no longer usable. Often when an employee leaves a company, the employee's account is disabled rather than deleted, allowing the system administrator to determine all of the settings for the next user of the account.

Working with User Profiles, Home Folders, and Logon Scripts

Another aspect of configuring a user account is using user profiles, home folders, and logon scripts. A **user profile** is a file loaded when the user logs on, and it defines the properties of the Windows 2000 environment—aspects such as the desktop appearance, network connections, printer settings, and screen colors. User profiles can be **roaming profiles**, which are downloaded from a network server whenever the user logs on to a computer anywhere on the network. Roaming profiles are automatically updated whenever the user changes desktop settings. Thus the user will see the same desktop whenever he or she logs on to the network. Another type of profile, the **mandatory profile**, is created by the system administrator and is not updatable by the user. This fact ensures that the same desktop is presented to each user.

Each user can access a folder called the **home folder**, which contains files and folders accessible to that user. Some programs use the home folder as the default folder for the Open and Save As dialog boxes. The home directory can be placed on your computer or on a network server so that the user will automatically connect to the home directory no matter what computer he or she logs on to.

Finally, a logon script can be assigned to each user account. A **logon script** is a file that contains commands and that is run automatically whenever the user logs on to Windows 2000. The logon script is typically used to configure the Windows 2000 settings that are not covered by the user profile.

To take advantage of these three features, you usually have to be the administrator of a local area network, since most of these files and folders will reside on the network server.

To see how to set up the user profiles, logon scripts, and home directories:

1. Click the **Profile** tab.

   The Profile sheet appears, as shown in Figure 11-6.

Figure 11-6	USER PROFILE INFORMATION

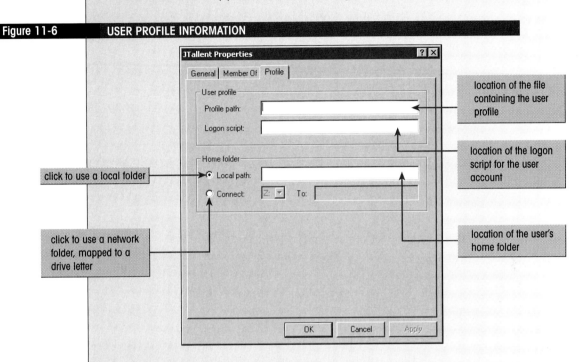

2. Within each text box, you could enter the name and location of the files and folders that you might want to use for user profiles, logon scripts, and home directories.

3. Click the **Cancel** button to close the dialog box.

Creating a User Group

You can create your own user groups to organize your user accounts. User groups can be used to organize different types of employees at a company, or students within a course. Bruce has asked you to create a user group for the office staff. You can then add Joyce Tallent to that group.

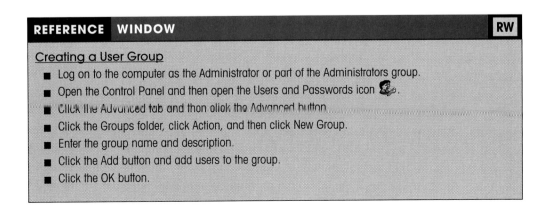

REFERENCE WINDOW   **RW**

<u>Creating a User Group</u>
- Log on to the computer as the Administrator or part of the Administrators group.
- Open the Control Panel and then open the Users and Passwords icon 🖳.
- Click the Advanced tab and then click the Advanced button.
- Click the Groups folder, click Action, and then click New Group.
- Enter the group name and description.
- Click the Add button and add users to the group.
- Click the OK button.

To create a new user group:

1. Click the **Groups** folder icon 📁.

2. Click **Action** on the menu bar and then click **New Group**. The New Group dialog box opens.

3. Type **Office Staff** in the Group name text box and then type **Office staff at Copy City Copiers** in the Description text box.

4. Click the **Add** button.

5. Click **JTallent** in the list of users and then click the **Add** button.

6. Click the **OK** button.

   Figure 11-7 shows the completed New Group dialog box.

Figure 11-7   ADDING THE JTALLENT ACCOUNT TO THE OFFICE STAFF USER GROUP

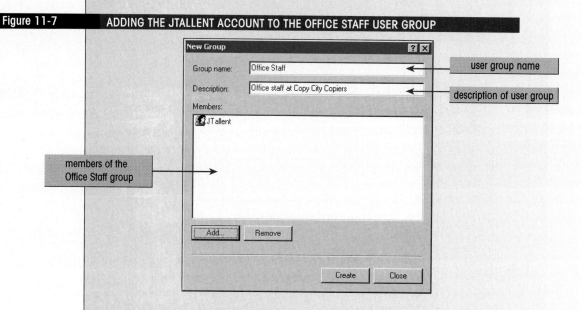

7. Click the **Create** button and then click the **Close** button.

   The Office Staff group is now listed in the Local Users and Groups window along with the other local groups on your computer.

8. Close the Local Users and Groups window.

9. Click the **OK** button to close the Users and Passwords dialog box.

Managing Local Security Policies

How do the various privileges given to users and user groups get assigned? One way is on a case-by-case basis. For example, you determine which user or user group has access to a shared network folder. You can also control the properties of a printer, determining who has the right to manage the print queue or change the settings of the printer.

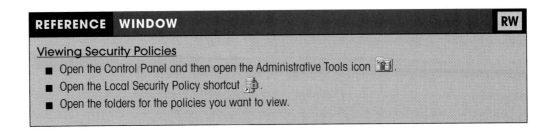

More generally, you can manage the security on your computer with one of the Windows 2000 administrative tools. The **Local Security Policy** applet allows you to set rules, or **policies**, that control some of the basic operations of your computer. To access these policies you need to have administrative access to your computer. Since changing these policies can have a great (and possibly negative) impact on your computer, Bruce doesn't want you modifying any of the settings. Instead, he wants you to confine yourself to viewing the current settings and seeing how you *could* change the policies if you needed to.

To open the Local Security Policy applet:

1. Open the **Administrative Tools** icon 🗂 in the Control Panel.

TROUBLE? If you receive an error message when you attempt to open this icon, you might not be logged on as an account that has administrative privileges. See your instructor or technical support person for assistance.

2. Open the shortcut to your **Local Security Policy** 🗐.

The Security Settings window opens, as shown in Figure 11-8.

Figure 11-8	SECURITY SETTINGS WINDOW

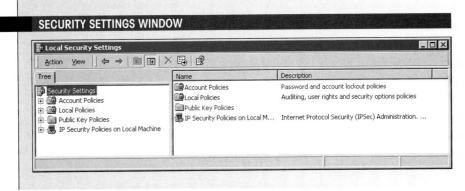

In this dialog box, the various policies on your computer are organized into four categories: Account, Local, Public Key, and IP Security. We'll look first at the Local Policies and then the Account Policies.

Local Policies

You'll first look at the **local policies**, which are rules that apply to your computer and are not set from a network administrator. You can make some of the policies accessible to specific users or user groups.

To view local policy settings:

1. Click the **plus box** ⊞ in front of the Local Policies folder.

2. Click the **User Rights Assignment** folder icon 📖.

3. A list of policies that can be assigned to specific users or user groups appears. See Figure 11-9.

Figure 11-9	SECURITY SETTINGS WINDOW

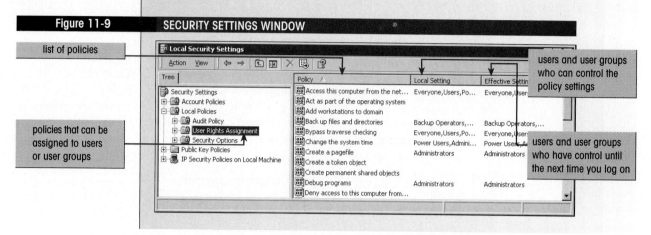

Many of the policies in this list are extremely technical in nature. One relatively simple policy is the ability to shut down the computer. Bruce suggests that you open this policy to see who has access to it.

To open a policy:

1. Scroll to and double-click the **Shut down the system** policy in the Policy list.

   A list of user groups who have the ability to shut down the system is shown in Figure 11-10.

Figure 11-10	CONTROLLING THE SYSTEM SHUTDOWN POLICY

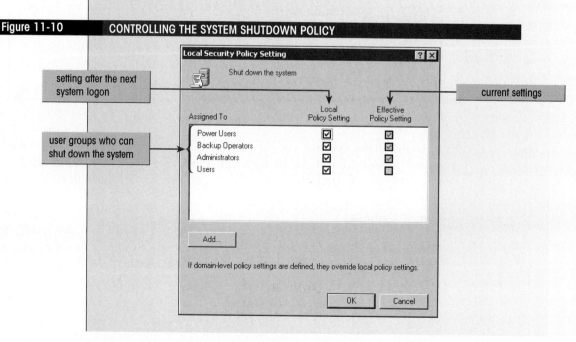

> Bruce points out that the Guest user group is missing from the list of user groups. This is because Copy City Copiers doesn't want customers (the ones who usually log on using the Guest account) to shut down the computers on the self-service floor. When Guest users complete their work on the computer, they can click the Shut Down command from the Start menu, but the only option they'll see is the Log Off option, and not the option to shut down the computer.
>
> **2.** Click the **Cancel** button to close the dialog box without saving any inadvertent changes.

Other policies that you can control are security options, such as whether CD-ROM drives can be accessed over the network or whether users can install printer drivers on the computer. These policies can be enabled or disabled for all users.

Account Policies

The other types of policies that affect users are the **account policies**. These are policies that affect all of the local accounts on the system. There are two types of account policies: password policies and account lockout policies. The password policies determine how passwords are managed on your computer. For example, you can specify the minimum number of characters a password must have before it is accepted by the system or how long a password can stay on your system before it expires and must be replaced by a new password.

Lockout policies specify the conditions under which a user account is locked out. Locking out an account prevents the account from being accessed until the system administrator unlocks it. This is an added security feature that helps prevent an outsider from hacking his or her way into the system. One policy might lock out the account if someone tries to access it using a wrong password 10 times in a row (indicating that there may be an unauthorized user trying to "fish around" for the correct password).

Bruce suggests that you review how these policies can be accessed on your computer.

> *To view the password policies:*
>
> **1.** Click the **plus box** ☐ in front of the Account Policies folder icon.
>
> **2.** Click the **Password Policy** folder icon ▩.
>
> **3.** Double-click the **Maximum password age** policy in the Policy list.
>
> **4.** The Local Security Policy Setting dialog box shown in Figure 11-11 indicates that passwords expire in 42 days on this system (your setting may be different).

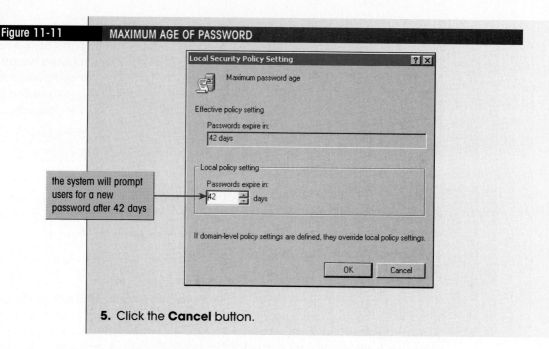

Figure 11-11 MAXIMUM AGE OF PASSWORD

the system will prompt users for a new password after 42 days

5. Click the **Cancel** button.

Now view the account lockout policy on your computer.

To view the account lockout policy:

1. Click the **Account Lockout Policy** folder icon.

2. Double-click the **Account lockout threshold** policy in the Policy list.

The dialog box shown in Figure 11-12 shows that accounts will be locked out after 10 failed logon attempts—this discourages unauthorized users from trying to guess your username and password. If you want to change this value, you can click the spin box arrows to increase or decrease the value.

Figure 11-12 SETTING THE ACCOUNT LOCKOUT POLICY

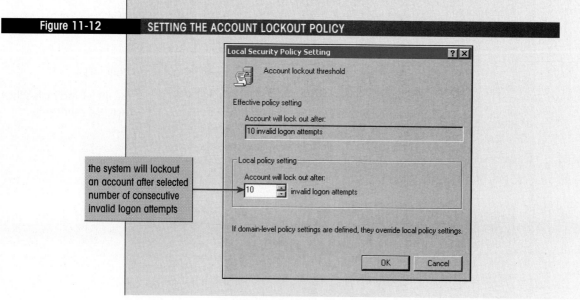

the system will lockout an account after selected number of consecutive invalid logon attempts

> TROUBLE? Your dialog box may show a value of 0, which has the effect of disabling the account lockout policy.
>
> **3.** Click the **Cancel** button and then close the Local Security Settings window.
>
> **4.** Click the **Up** button 🔼 in the Administrative Tools window to return to the Control Panel window.

Having viewed the Security Settings window, you can see how you can control many of the features of the computers at Copy City Copiers. Bruce cautions you that you should not make any changes to these settings without discussing the changes with him.

REFERENCE WINDOW   RW

Removing a User
- Log on to the computer as the administrator or part of the Administrators group.
- Open the Control Panel and then open the Users and Passwords applet 🐾.
- Select the user account you want to remove and click Remove.

Removing **Users and User Groups**

When an employee leaves Copy City Copiers, the user account must be either disabled or removed. Bruce suggests that you practice removing user accounts and user groups by deleting the JTallent account you created earlier, as well as the Office Staff group.

> *To remove a user account:*
>
> **1.** Open the **Users and Passwords** icon 🐾.
>
> **2.** Select **JTallent** in the list of user names, click the **Remove** button, and then click the **Yes** button to confirm the deletion.

Now remove the Office Staff user group.

> *To remove a user group:*
>
> **1.** Click the **Advanced** tab, click the **Advanced** button, and then click the **Groups** folder in the left pane.
>
> **2.** Click **Office Staff** in the list of user groups, click the **Delete** button ❎, and then click the **Yes** button to confirm the deletion.
>
> **3.** Close the Local Users and Groups window, the Users and Passwords dialog box, and the Control Panel.

Locking Your Computer

Bruce tells you that you should be careful when working as the administrator. If you leave your desk with the account still open, anyone can sit down at your workstation and make fundamental changes to the system. Bruce instructs you to make sure that you lock the computer down whenever you leave your desk. Before you perform these steps, make sure that you know your username and password.

To lock your computer:

1. Press the **Ctrl**, **Alt**, and **Del** keys simultaneously.

The Windows Security dialog box appears.

2. Click the **Lock Computer** button.

A dialog box appears indicating that the computer is in use and has been locked. The computer will not be unlocked until you enter your password into the dialog box.

TROUBLE? If you get a message indicating that you need to press Ctrl+Alt+Del, do so and then continue to Step 3.

3. Type your password into the Password text box and then click the **OK** button.

You are returned to the Windows 2000 desktop.

Bruce is finished showing you the security features and user account tools that Windows 2000 provides. In the next session, you'll learn about some of the tools you can use to monitor your computer's performance and control its behavior.

Session 11.1 QUICK CHECK

1. What are the two different types of user groups supported by Windows 2000?

2. What user group gives you complete control over all aspects of your computer?

3. If you want a user to always access the same folder and files whenever he or she logs on to a computer, you must create a _____.

4. A file that defines the Windows 2000 environment when the user logs on to the computer is called the _____.

5. What is a policy?

6. How would you set up your computer to help lock out hackers?

SESSION 11.2

In this session you'll look at some of the tools that Windows 2000 provides to help you manage system performance. You'll see how to track the performance of key components of your computer using the Performance Monitor and log files. You'll see how to set up an alert to warn of certain behavior on your computer. Finally, you'll learn about the various services that are being constantly run on your computer. You'll see how to access those services and control them.
Note: You will need a blank, formatted floppy disk for some of the steps described in this session.

Monitoring System Performance

One aspect of your job at Copy City Copiers is to make sure that the computers are running at peak efficiency and to help resolve any hardware and software difficulties. One user is complaining that his computer has been slow lately. There are a number of things that could cause this. The user may have too many programs running at the same time. The computer may be low on memory. Or the computer may need to have its processor upgraded to a faster one. You need to have some way of measuring the performance of the system in numerical terms.

One way of accomplishing this task is to use the Windows 2000 Performance Monitor, which can display the amount of system resources that your computer is using at any given time. Bruce suggests that you run the Performance Monitor on the user's computer.

To start the Performance Monitor:

1. Open the Control Panel and then open the **Administrative Tools** icon.

2. Open the **Performance** shortcut.

   The Performance window opens, as shown in Figure 11-13.

Figure 11-13 | THE PERFORMANCE MONITOR

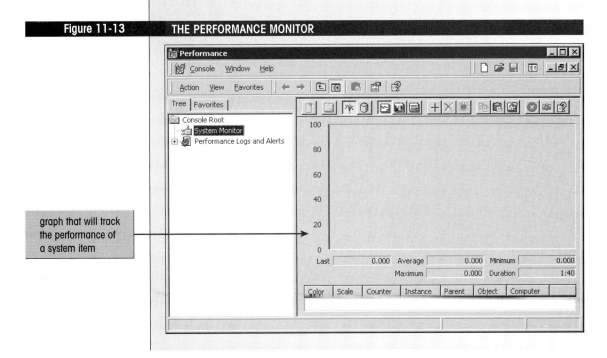

graph that will track the performance of a system item

Graphing System Performance

Before you can use the Performance Monitor, you must add an item, called a **counter**, to track the aspect of interest. Once you do, the values of the counter are shown in the graph, displayed in Figure 11-13. The counter is updated at intervals you specify—usually every few seconds. You can track such things as the amount of time your processor is not idle (a measure of how busy your system is) and the speed of the computer in retrieving data from your hard drive. If your computer is acting as a print server for a network, you can track how many print requests it's receiving and the number of pages it has printed.

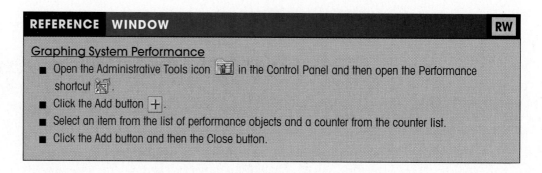

REFERENCE WINDOW   **RW**

Graphing System Performance

- Open the Administrative Tools icon   in the Control Panel and then open the Performance shortcut .
- Click the Add button ⊞.
- Select an item from the list of performance objects and a counter from the counter list.
- Click the Add button and then the Close button.

Tracking this type of information can locate the source of trouble in a slow system, and may help you determine what needs to be done to speed up the system. Bruce suggests that you track the amount of time the processor on the computer is in use.

To track processor time:

1. Click the **Add** button ⊞, located on the toolbar above the graph area. The Add Counters dialog box opens.

2. Select **Processor** in the Performance object list box if it's not already selected.

3. Verify that the **Select counters from list** option button is selected.

4. Click **%Processor Time** in the list of counters if it's not already selected.

5. Click the **Explain** button. See Figure 11-14.

Figure 11-14	SELECTING AN ITEM TO TRACK

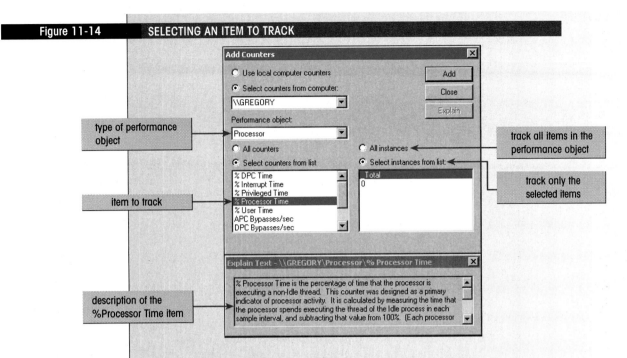

type of performance object

item to track

description of the %Processor Time item

track all items in the performance object

track only the selected items

A short description of the item you're about to track appears at the bottom of the Add Counters dialog box. In this case, you'll be measuring the percentage of time that the processor is not idle. A value near 100% will suggest that the processor is almost never idle.

6. Click the **Add** button and then click the **Close** button.

The Performance Monitor starts tracking the percentage of time that the processor is in use each second. See Figure 11-15.

Figure 11-15	TRACKING THE %PROCESSOR TIME

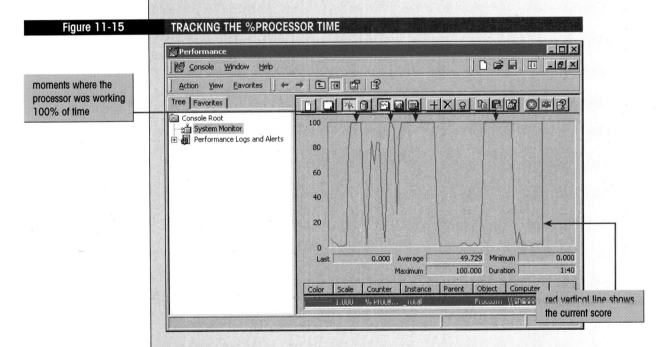

moments where the processor was working 100% of time

red vertical line shows the current score

TROUBLE? Your Performance Monitor will show different results from the one shown in Figure 11-15.

From the results shown in Figure 11-15, you note there are several periods of time when the processor use jumped to 100%. If this were the case on your computer, you would want to examine the types of programs that the computer is running. It's possible that one of these programs is causing a heavy load on the system, slowing it down.

Bruce has enough information on the performance of the processor, so you can turn off the Performance Monitor.

To turn off the performance graph:

1. Click the **Delete** button ⊠, located just above the graph area.

   The Performance Monitor stops tracking the performance of the processor.

Logging System Performance

Sometimes you will find it useful to have a permanent record of the results from the System Monitor. For example, you can create a **baseline chart**, a chart of the computer's performance when it's running at a normal level. When there are problems, administrators can create another performance chart to compare to the baseline one. Using baseline charts, administrators can anticipate and then prevent problems.

You create a baseline chart by first creating a **log file**, a file that will be saved on your computer and that will contain all of the performance values shown in the graph. Bruce asks you to do this with the processor score, storing the log files on a floppy disk that you can give to him later.

To create a log file of the performance values:

1. Place a blank, formatted floppy disk in your floppy disk drive.

2. Click the **plus** box ⊞ in front of the Performance Logs and Alerts icon 🗐.

3. Click the **Counter Logs** icon 📝.

4. Click **Action** on the menu bar and then click **New Log Settings**. The New Log Settings dialog box opens, and you can type a name for the log file there.

5. Type **Processor Performance** in the New Log Settings dialog box and then click the **OK** button.

   A dialog box appears in which you can specify which items you want to track in the log file.

6. Click the **Add** button.

7. Verify that the **%Processor Time** counter is selected from the list box in the Select Counters dialog box, click the **Add** button, and then click the **Close** button.

   You can determine how often the system will monitor the performance of the processor. You decide to sample the performance every five seconds.

8. Click the **Interval** spin arrows, decreasing the interval value to **5** seconds. See Figure 11-16.

Figure 11-16	SPECIFYING DATA TO SAVE IN A LOG FILE

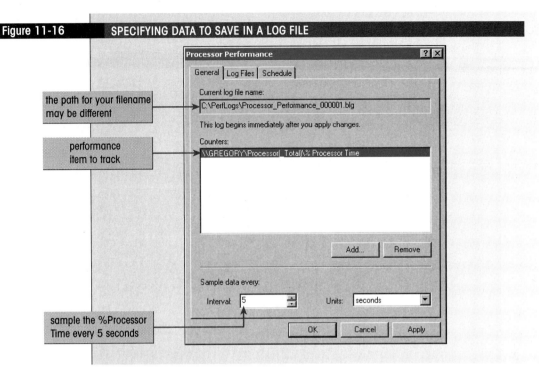

the path for your filename may be different

performance item to track

sample the %Processor Time every 5 seconds

Now, you'll specify where you want the log file saved. In this case, you'll save the log file to your floppy disk.

To save the log file:

1. Click the **Log Files** tab.

2. Click the **Location** text box, if necessary, and then type **A:** (or the drive letter of your floppy drive).

   Each filename can have appended a series of numbers or dates so that you can create several performance log files, with the files distinguished by either the date on which they were created or the order in which they were created. In this case, since you are creating only one log file, you'll remove that feature from the log filename.

3. Deselect the **End file names with** check box.

   The log file will be stored under the name, "Processor _Performance.blg" on your floppy disk (the underscore and file extension are added by Windows 2000). See Figure 11-17.

Figure 11-17   SPECIFYING A FILENAME AND LOCATION FOR THE PERFORMANCE LOG

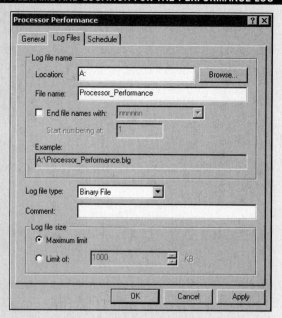

4. Click the **OK** button.

5. Click the **Processor Performance** icon 🗄.

Once you click the icon, Windows 2000 starts tracking performance data and changes the Processor Performance icon from 🗄 to 🗄, an indication that the log file has gone from inactive to active. Every five seconds after that, new performance data will be sampled and then stored on the log file on your floppy disk. This will continue until you manually stop the sampling or the floppy disk is filled up.

To stop sampling:

1. Wait about half a minute to obtain a good sample.

2. Right-click the **Processor Performance** icon 🗄 and then click **Stop**. The icon returns to red, indicating that it is again inactive.

If you were to look at the contents of your floppy disk, you would see a file named "Processor_Performance.blg". You could take this file to Bruce for him to examine or you could file it away as a permanent record of the processor performance of this particular computer.

To view the contents of the log file, you open it within the Performance Monitor. Try this now.

To view the contents of the Processor_Performance log file:

1. Click the **System Monitor** icon 🖳.

2. Click the **View Log File Data** button 🗄, located above the graph area.

3. In the Select Log File dialog box, open the **Processor_Performance.blg** file located on your floppy disk.

A log file can contain several different items, so you have to select which item you want to display on the monitor.

4. Click the **Add** button [+].

5. Verify that **Processor** is the selected performance object (it will have to be since that is the only item you've logged), click the **Add** button, and then click the **Close** button.

The Performance Monitor shows the contents of the log file, as displayed in Figure 11-18, (your graph will be different).

| Figure 11-18 | VIEWING THE PROCESSOR PERFORMANCE LOG FILE |

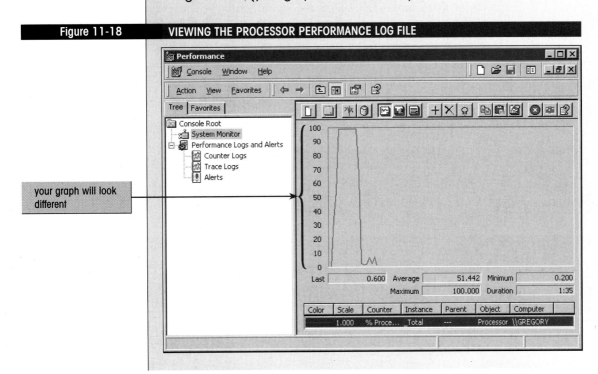

your graph will look different

Now that you've created the log file, you should delete the Processor Performance item from the list of counter logs. Deleting the Processor Performance item does not affect the log file you just created.

To delete the Processor Performance icon:

1. Click the **Counter Logs** icon.

2. Click the **Processor Performance** icon.

3. Click the **Delete** button [X].

4. Remove your floppy disk from the drive.

Bruce can store this log file in his office, to be used in the future as a baseline against which other performance charts can be compared.

Creating a Performance Alert

Often you will not want to monitor your system's performance every second; instead, you will want the monitoring to be done in the background, with the system alerting you if certain conditions are met. Bruce suggests that you create an alert to let you know when the percentage of non-idle processor time exceeds 75%.

To create an alert:

1. Click the **Alerts** icon.

2. Click **Action** on the menu bar and then click **New Alert Settings**.

3. Type **Processor Alert** in the New Alert Settings dialog box and then click the **OK** button.

4. Type **Alert when processor usage exceeds 75%** in the Comment box.

5. Click the **Add** button.

6. Verify that **Processor** is selected in the Performance object list box and that **%Processor Time** is selected in the list of counters.

7. Click the **Add** button and then click the **Close** button.

8. Click the **Alert when the value is** list arrow and then click **Over**.

9. Type **75** in the limit text box.

   Figure 11-19 shows the completed dialog box.

Figure 11-19 | **SETTING AN ALERT WHEN THE %PROCESSOR TIME RISES ABOVE 75%**

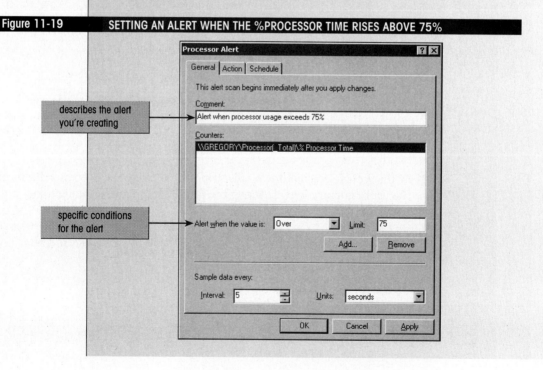

describes the alert you're creating

specific conditions for the alert

Now that you've defined the conditions under which an alert will occur, you next have to specify the action that the operating system will take. There are four possibilities (you can choose any or all of the four):

■ Place an entry in the application event log

■ Send a message to a specific user on the system

■ Start logging the performance of the item in a log file

■ Run a specific program

You'll choose the first option, to place an entry in the system's application event log (you'll learn what this log does shortly).

To specify an action for the event:

1. Click the **Action** tab.

2. Verify that the **Log an entry in the application event log** check box is selected, and that no other check box is selected.

3. Click the **OK** button.

4. Click the **Processor Alert** icon .

The performance alert log is now started. When the conditions of the alert are met, this fact will be noted in the application event log.

Note that logging events does not do anything to address the reason that the events are occurring—it merely records the fact that the events did occur. Many system administrators choose to run a program (the last option in the bulleted list above) when the conditions of an alert are met, since this is the only way a problem can be fixed.

Tracking Events on Your System

As you work on your computer, Windows 2000 is constantly tracking the events that occur and recording them in a file called an **event log**. You can use these event logs to help you diagnose problems that your system may be having. Figure 11-20 shows three types of event logs created by Windows 2000.

Figure 11-20	TYPES OF EVENT LOGS
EVENT LOG	**DESCRIPTION**
Application	Contains events logged by applications or programs.
System	Contains events logged by the Windows 2000 operating system, such as the failure of a hardware driver to load upon startup.
Security	Records events related to system security, such as valid and invalid logons and account lockouts.

Managing the computers at Copy City Copiers, you'll occasionally have to search through event logs, especially in situations where a system has crashed and you need to track down the reason for it. What sorts of things were happening before the system failed? An event log might provide valuable information.

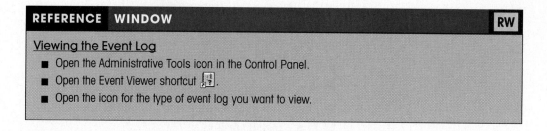

REFERENCE WINDOW **RW**

Viewing the Event Log
- Open the Administrative Tools icon in the Control Panel.
- Open the Event Viewer shortcut.
- Open the icon for the type of event log you want to view.

In this case, you've created an alert condition in the performance monitor, and you're using the application event log to store the times when and situations in which the alert is triggered. You decide to open the application event log to see if this has occurred.

To view the application event log:

1. Return to the Administrative Tools window.

   TROUBLE? If the Administrative Tools window is not open, reopen the Control Panel and then reopen the Administrative Tools icon.

2. Open the **Event Viewer** shortcut.

3. Click the **Application Log** icon.

   A list of events that have been generated by applications is shown in the panel on the right. See Figure 11-21.

Figure 11-21   **EVENT VIEWER WINDOW**

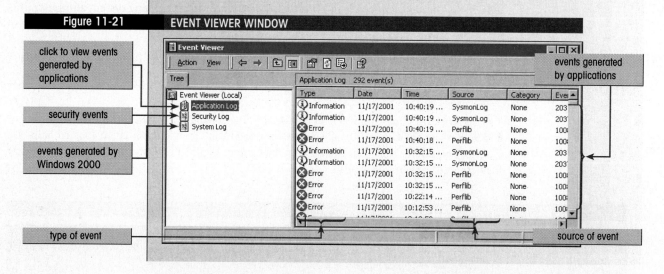

Depending on your computer, you may or may not have activated the alert for percent processor time above 75%. However, one event that is sure to be logged is the event that started the alert monitor in the first place. This will be one of the more recent alerts in the list, identified with the Information icon, indicating that the event is logged for your information only. A Warning icon indicates that the event may cause problems in the future, for example, low disk space. On the other hand, an Error icon indicates a significant problem, possibly resulting in lost data or the failure of an application.

To view information on an event:

1. Double-click one of the **Information** events (i) at the top of the list of events.

   Figure 11-22 shows the event in which the conditions of the processor alert have been met (your event dialog box will probably show something else).

Figure 11-22	PROPERTIES OF AN EVENT

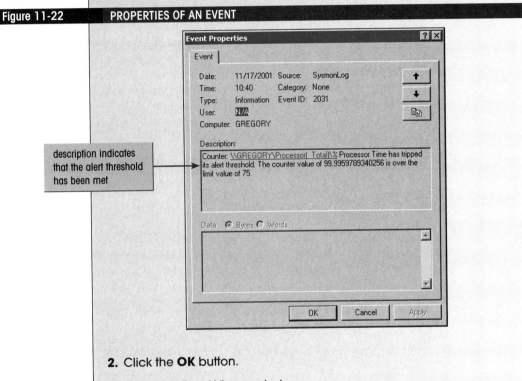

description indicates that the alert threshold has been met

2. Click the **OK** button.
3. Close the Event Viewer window.

Now that you've seen how the event log works, you should remove the processor alert that you created earlier.

To remove the processor alert:

1. Return to the Performance window, click the plus box [+] next to Performance Logs and Alerts if necessary, and then click **Alerts**.

   TROUBLE? If you've closed the Performance window, return to the Administrative Tools and open the Performance shortcut icon.

2. Select the **Processor Alert** icon in the list of alerts and then click the **Delete** button [X].

3. Click **OK** if you are asked to confirm the deletion.

4. Close the Performance window.

Viewing the Service List

The event log is working in the background constantly checking for events and then entering them into a log, thus the list can get quite long. You might wonder how the event log gets started. The event log is an example of a **service**, a small program controlled by Windows 2000, designed to manage one or more aspects of the computer. Event logs, the print spooler, and the ability to detect a plug and play device are all examples of services.

Services are either started automatically (as in the case of the event log) when Windows 2000 starts, or they are started manually in response to an application or command. Sometimes the administrator of the system will want to have control over the services on the computer in order to shut down an active service or manually start one up.

Bruce suggests that you "take a look under the hood" of Windows 2000 to see how this process works. To do this, you can open another one of the Windows 2000 administrative tools; this one controls the operation of the various services on your computer.

To access the list of services:

1. Return to the Administrative Tools window.

2. Open the **Services** shortcut 🐾.

   The Service window opens, displaying the list of services in the right-hand pane. See Figure 11-23. Notice that one of the services in the list is "Event Log," the service that you've seen that automatically logs all events.

| Figure 11-23 | LIST OF SERVICES |

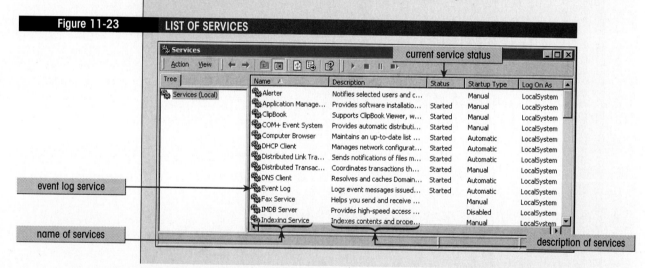

event log service

name of services

description of services

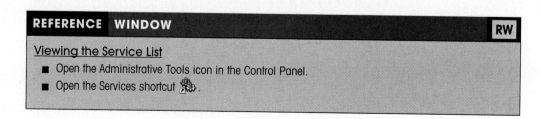

REFERENCE WINDOW   **RW**

Viewing the Service List
- Open the Administrative Tools icon in the Control Panel.
- Open the Services shortcut 🐾.

From the Status column, you can see which services have already started. To get more detailed information about a service, you can open its icon in the list. Bruce suggests that you do this with the Event Log service. Bruce asks that you be sure not to change any of the settings however.

To view information about a service:

1. Double-click the **Event Log** service in the Service list.

   The Event Log Properties dialog box opens, as shown in Figure 11-24.

Figure 11-24	PROPERTIES OF THE EVENT LOG SERVICE

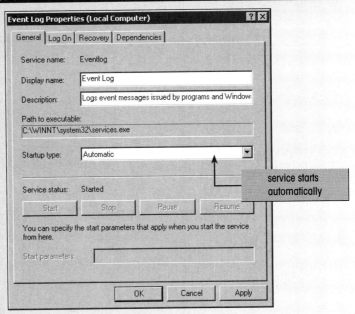

The Startup type drop-down list box in Figure 11-24 controls how the Event Log is run. Currently it starts automatically when Windows 2000 starts. You can click this drop-down list box to change the startup to manual or to disable the service entirely.

2. Click the **Recovery** tab.

   From this dialog sheet you can control what happens when a service fails to start. In this case no action is taken, but in some situations you will want Windows 2000 to try to restart the service or reboot the computer.

3. Click the **Cancel** button.

4. Close the Services window.

Running the Computer Management Tool

Bruce tells you that many of the tools you've been using to administer your system and manage the computer's hardware and software have been brought together in the **Computer Management** tool. From a single window, you can manage user accounts and user groups, monitor your system's performance, view the list of devices on your system, and manage your computer's hard disks.

To open the Computer Management tool:

1. Return to the Administrative Tools window, if necessary.

2. Open the **Computer Management** shortcut 🖳.

The Computer Management window opens, as shown in Figure 11-25.

| Figure 11-25 | CONTENTS OF THE COMPUTER MANAGEMENT WINDOW |

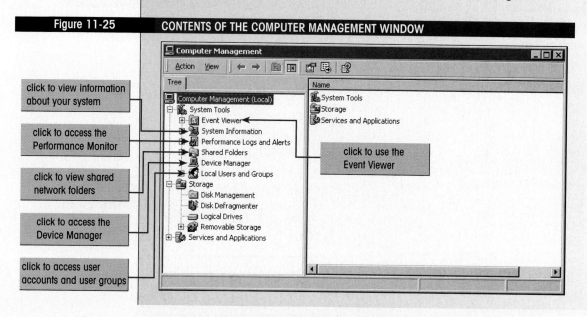

As you can see from Figure 11-25, many of tools you've used in this tutorial and others are shown in the window. The event viewer and performance logs and alerts are displayed as part of the system tools. You can also manage your shared network folders, hardware devices, and user groups. From the list of storage tools, you can defragment a hard disk and view information about the various drives on your system. There are also some tools that you haven't seen yet. Let's open one of these, the Disk Management tool, to explore the state of the various drives on your system.

REFERENCE WINDOW   **RW**

Opening the Computer Management Window
- Open the Administrative Tools in the Control Panel.
- Open the Computer Management icon 🖳.

To use the Disk Management tool:

1. Click the **Disk Management** folder in the left pane.

A graphical display of your storage devices opens in the right pane (see Figure 11-26).

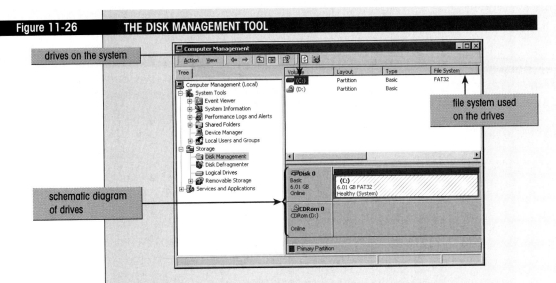

| Figure 11-26 | THE DISK MANAGEMENT TOOL |

drives on the system

file system used on the drives

schematic diagram of drives

From this tool you can reformat your disks, create disk partitions, and assign different drive letters. Since most of these changes would fundamentally affect your system, you'll close the window without making any changes.

2. Close the Computer Management window.

3. Close the Administrative Tools window and, if necessary, the Control Panel window.

You're finished with the administrative tools that allow you to monitor and alter the behavior of your computer. In the next session, Bruce will show you how to back up the files on Copy City Copier computers.

Session 11.2 QUICK CHECK

1. What would you use the Performance Monitor for?

2. What does the %Processor Time counter measure?

3. How would you set up your computer to alert you when the %Processor Time counter rises above 95%?

4. What are three types of events that are tracked by your system?

5. What is a service?

6. How would you turn off a service?

SESSION 11.3

In this session, you'll learn about the principles of backing up files on your computer. You'll learn about different types of backups and when to apply them. You will use the Backup program supplied by Windows 2000 to back up files from your hard drive to a floppy disk. You'll then restore the files from the floppy disk to the hard drive. *Note*: You will need a blank floppy disk for this session.

Computer Backups

No one is safe from computer problems that result in data loss. A power surge, a power loss, a failed section of a hard disk, or a computer virus—these problems can strike at any time. Rather than risk disaster, you should make copies of your important files regularly. You have already learned how to copy data from one 3½-inch disk to another and how to copy a file from one disk to another. Making a copy of a disk or a file is one way to protect data. Copying a disk or a file is your only choice when you store your data on a 3½-inch disk, as is usually the case in a computer lab, where you usually don't have access to a hard disk.

To protect data on a hard drive, however, you will almost certainly want to use a backup program instead of a copy or disk-copy procedure. A **backup program** copies and then automatically compresses files and folders from a hard disk into a single file, called a **backup file**. The backup program stores this file on a **backup medium** such as a 3½-inch disk, tape cartridge, or ZIP disk. Bruce explains that such a software program, called Backup, comes with Windows 2000.

When you back up a set of files with the Windows 2000 Backup program, you go through the following steps.

1. You designate the folders and files you want to back up.

2. The Backup program creates a **backup job,** which lists the files you want to back up and tells your computer how, when, and where to perform the backup.

3. The Backup program copies the files and folders listed in the backup job, compresses them, and stores them in a backup file.

4. The Backup program stores the backup file on the backup medium you specify.

5. Information about the backup, including a list of the files and folders that have been saved, is stored in a file called a **catalog**.

Suppose you store all of your important files in three folders on drive C, named Projects, Accounts, and Clients. Figure 11-27 shows how Backup backs up the files in these folders.

Figure 11-27	BACKING UP DATA

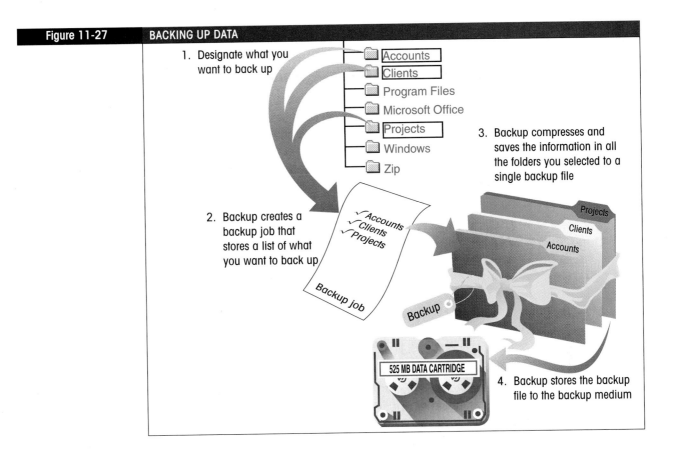

This process is different from simply copying files, because Backup copies files into a single, compressed file, whereas a copy simply duplicates the files. Figure 11-28 points out the differences between copying and backing up, showing why backing up files is a better data-protection method than simply copying files.

Figure 11-28	COPYING VS. BACKING UP FILES

COPY	BACKUP
A copy of a file occupies the same amount of space as the original file. For this reason, making a copy of all the files on a hard disk is impractical.	Because it is compressed, a backup of a file is usually much smaller than the original file, depending on the file type.
It would take a lot of time and effort to copy all the files on a hard disk to 3½-inch disks—not least because of the time it would take to swap disks in and out of the floppy drive. Copying 800 MB of data would require more than 560 3½-inch disks.	Backups are much quicker. If you have a tape drive, you can back up 800 MB of data to a single tape in a matter of minutes.
Because you can't split a large file over two 3½-inch disks, you must manually break up the file into smaller parts and then copy them to separate 3½-inch disks.	Backup is designed to split files across disks.
Every time you want to back up your data, you must either copy all the files on your disk again or you must painstakingly locate and then copy only those files that have changed.	Backup can automatically detect and back up only those files that have changed since your last backup.
If you do lose data because of a computer failure, there is no easy way to locate a file you need.	The Backup program keeps track of the files you have backed up, and it's very easy to find and recover a file.

Placing Files on the Hard Disk to Back Up

Bruce explains that the simplest way of saving data is to use a 3½-inch disk. To protect data on a 3½-inch disk, you simply copy the disk from My Computer or Windows Explorer, because the Backup accessory is designed to back up the contents of a hard drive (or several hard drives). Because Bruce wants you to learn how to perform a real backup, you must first place some data on the hard disk, which you can then back up onto the blank disk you brought to the store.

Although in this example you will simulate backing up files to a 3½-inch disk, in reality using 3½-inch disks as your backup medium is impractical if you have more than just a few files to back up. A more practical solution, if you can afford it, is to purchase a drive such as a tape, Zip, or CD rewriteable drive that lets you back up your data to larger storage devices.

You will place three new files in a new folder you'll create in a moment. You will then back up the files to your blank disk, which you will name "Backup Disk."

To create new files on your hard disk:

1. Right-click an empty spot on your desktop, point to **New**, and then click **Folder**. Remember that any folders and files on the Desktop are actually stored on the hard drive.

   TROUBLE? If you are in a computer lab and are not permitted to save files to your computer's hard disk, ask your instructor or technical support person where you should create files to back up.

2. Type **Copy City Copiers** and then press the **Enter** key.

3. Open the Copy City Copiers folder.

4. Click **File**, point to **New**, and then click **Text Document**. Type **Test1.txt** for the name of the text file and then press the **Enter** key.

5. Repeat Step 4, creating two additional empty text documents named **Test2.txt** and **Test3.txt**.

6. Close the Copy City Copiers folder window.

Backup Strategies

You start the backup process by designating which files and folders you want to back up. In this simulation, the designation is easy: you just tell your backup program to use the Copy City Copiers folder. However, Bruce explains that in reality, choosing which files you want to back up is a little more complicated because it is part of a larger backup strategy.

A **backup strategy** is a plan you develop to ensure that you have a backup of all the files on your computer in their most current version. The foundation of a backup strategy is a **full backup**, a backup of all the files on your computer. A full backup can contain the Windows 2000 program, all your system files, all your program files, and all the data files that existed on the day you performed the backup. Some people don't include their operating system or other software programs in a full backup because they feel they can simply reinstall the software from the original disks. Once you have a full backup, you can perform **partial backups**, which back up only the files that have changed since the last time you backed up your data. There are two kinds of partial backups: differential and incremental. In a **differential backup**, the backup program searches for and backs up only those files that have changed since the last full backup. In an **incremental backup**, the backup program searches for and backs up only those files that have changed since the last backup, regardless of whether it was a full or partial backup. Figure 11-29 will help you understand the difference.

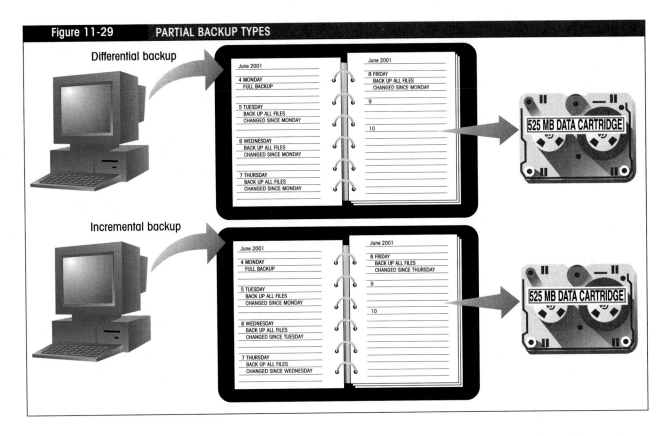

Figure 11-29   PARTIAL BACKUP TYPES

Differential backup

June 2001
4 MONDAY
FULL BACKUP

5 TUESDAY
BACK UP ALL FILES
CHANGED SINCE MONDAY

6 WEDNESDAY
BACK UP ALL FILES
CHANGED SINCE MONDAY

7 THURSDAY
BACK UP ALL FILES
CHANGED SINCE MONDAY

June 2001
8 FRIDAY
BACK UP ALL FILES
CHANGED SINCE MONDAY

9

10

525 MB DATA CARTRIDGE

Incremental backup

June 2001
4 MONDAY
FULL BACKUP

5 TUESDAY
BACK UP ALL FILES
CHANGED SINCE MONDAY

6 WEDNESDAY
BACK UP ALL FILES
CHANGED SINCE TUESDAY

7 THURSDAY
BACK UP ALL FILES
CHANGED SINCE WEDNESDAY

June 2001
8 FRIDAY
BACK UP ALL FILES
CHANGED SINCE THURSDAY

9

10

525 MB DATA CARTRIDGE

Incremental backups are generally faster and take less space, but restoring from an incremental backup can be slow. Differential backups, on the other hand, are generally slower and require more space, but restoring is quicker.

You might think that to be on the safe side, you should simply perform a full backup every time you back up your data. However, a full backup can take several hours, depending on how many hard disks you have and how big they are. For this reason, most users perform a full backup only once a week or once a month, depending on how substantially their files change from day to day. Many of your files don't change at all over the course of weeks or months. Your program files, for example, change only when you install a new version of software. Some users choose not to back up program files because those files are preserved on the original installation disks.

How often should you perform full and partial backups? It's best to develop a backup strategy based on a schedule. For the user in Figure 11-29, a backup strategy begins with a full backup at the beginning of the week. Then this user performs a partial backup on a daily basis. Perhaps the last thing he or she does before leaving the computer for the evening is run the backup software to back up any files changed during the day.

Some users might want to perform more frequent backups—especially those who can't afford to lose even a few hours' work. They might perform a partial backup more than once a day—at lunch time, after work, and then at midnight, for example. You don't want to overdo it, however. Even a partial backup can slow your productivity, because, even if the backup program is running in the background, it uses system resources. If you can structure it so that your computer runs backups while you are busy doing something else, that's best.

The important thing is that you back up your data often enough so that if your computer fails, your backup will contain enough of your data that it won't take you too long to reconstruct the rest.

Backing Up Files

In this simulation, you are not going to perform a full backup. Instead, you are going to perform a backup of only one folder: the Copy City Copiers folder. There are circumstances in which you might want to back up only the contents of one or several folders. For example, suppose you habitually store all the files you work with on a daily basis in the Copy City Copiers folder or the My Documents folder. You might want to back up just that folder. It will speed up the daily backup process considerably if Backup doesn't have to search your entire computer for changed files. Users who perform more than one backup a day might especially profit from searching just a few folders.

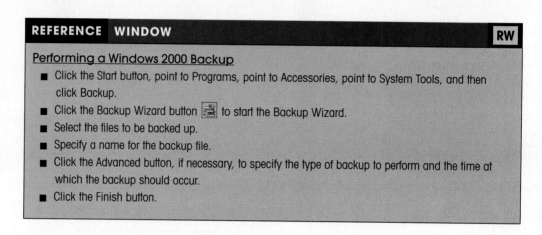

REFERENCE WINDOW **RW**

<u>Performing a Windows 2000 Backup</u>
- Click the Start button, point to Programs, point to Accessories, point to System Tools, and then click Backup.
- Click the Backup Wizard button ⊞ to start the Backup Wizard.
- Select the files to be backed up.
- Specify a name for the backup file.
- Click the Advanced button, if necessary, to specify the type of backup to perform and the time at which the backup should occur.
- Click the Finish button.

Now you're ready to start Backup.

To start Backup:

1. Click the **Start** button, point to **Programs**, point to **Accessories**, point to **System Tools**, and then click **Backup**. The Backup window opens, as shown in Figure 11-30.

   TROUBLE? If a message appears warning you that there is no backup device (other than the floppy drive), click No to acknowledge the message and continue with the steps. This message appears the first time you start Backup if you don't have a backup device such as a tape or optical drive installed.

   TROUBLE? If Backup does not appear as an option on the menu, then you cannot complete this session until the Backup program is installed. Check with your instructor or technical support person for directions.

Figure 11-30   **STARTING THE BACKUP PROGRAM**

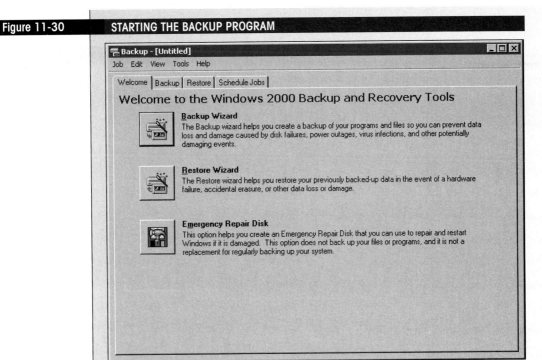

2. Click the **Backup Wizard** button 🖳 and then click the **Next** button.

3. Click the **Back up selected files, drives, or network data** option button and then click the **Next** button. The next Backup Wizard dialog box allows you to choose the items you want to back up.

Selecting Files and Folders to Back Up

To select the files or folders you want to back up, you navigate through the hierarchy of objects and folders on your computer. To include a folder in the backup job, you click the empty box ☐ next to the folder, to place a check mark in it. A blue check mark ☑ indicates that the entire folder or file will be backed up. A gray check mark ☑ indicates that only part of the contents of that folder or drive will be backed up. If you want to include only selected files in a folder, you click the folder's icon in the Folders list and then click the empty boxes for just those files.

You want to select the Copy City Copiers folder on your desktop to back up.

To select the Copy City Copiers folder:

1. Click the empty box ☐ to the left of the Copy City Copiers folder. A blue check mark appears in the box, indicating that all contents of the folder have been selected for backup. See Figure 11-31.

Figure 11-31 SELECTING THE COPY CITY COPIERS FOLDER TO BACK UP

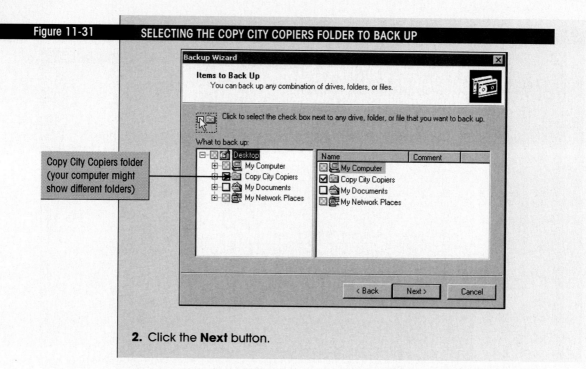

Copy City Copiers folder
(your computer might
show different folders)

2. Click the **Next** button.

The next step of the Wizard will determine where you want the backup file to be stored. Depending on the hardware devices on your system, you may see different dialog boxes. If you have a backup tape drive, you will see an option to use that device. In this case, you'll write the backup to a file on your floppy disk.

To continue with the Backup wizard:

1. If necessary, select **File** in the Backup media type drop-down list box and type **A:\Backup.bkf** in the Backup media or filename text box if necessary. See Figure 11-32.

TROUBLE? If you don't have a backup medium such as a tape, Zip, or CD rewriteable drive, the Backup media type drop-down list box will be grayed out.

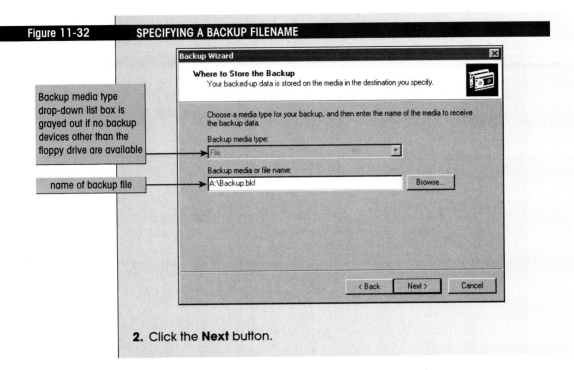

Figure 11-32   **SPECIFYING A BACKUP FILENAME**

Backup media type drop-down list box is grayed out if no backup devices other than the floppy drive are available

name of backup file

2. Click the **Next** button.

Setting Advanced Backup Options

You've reached the end of the Backup Wizard. At this point you can finish the Wizard, accepting the backup defaults that the Wizard has chosen for you. You can also specify some of the advanced options. This includes specifying whether you are performing a full, differential, or incremental backup. You can also have the backup program verify the backup, this involves comparing the files on the backup medium to the source files on the hard disk. Verification takes longer, but ensures that the files you've backed up are stored correctly on the medium. Bruce suggests that you review the advanced backup options.

To specify the advanced options:

1. Click the **Advanced** button.

The first dialog box allows you to specify the type of backup you want to perform. Normal is the default value, which is equivalent to a full backup.

2. Click the **Next** button.

The next step allows you to verify the backup. Bruce suggests that this is a good idea, as long as time is not a concern, which it isn't with such a small backup.

3. Click the **Verify data after backup** check box and then click the **Next** button.

Next, you can specify whether to append the backup file to the backup medium, or to overwrite previous backup files with this one. This option only really applies to backup tapes, in which the backup files are laid down in a sequential order. When you're backing up to a floppy disk, the issue of appending or replacing the file is not relevant. The default option is to append to the backup medium.

4. Click the **Next** button.

In the next step, you can enter a label for you backup. This isn't a filename, but a description of the backup file, which the backup program displays.

5. Type **Test Backup** in the Backup label text box and then press the **Tab** key.

6. Type **CCC Backups** in the Media label text box and then click the **Next** button.

Finally, you can specify whether to backup now or at a scheduled time. The default is to backup immediately.

7. Verify that the **Now** option button is selected and click the **Next** button.

8. Place a blank formatted disk in your floppy disk drive and then click the **Finish** button.

The Backup program starts. After a few seconds, the backup job is complete, and the dialog box shown in Figure 11-33 appears.

Figure 11-33   COMPLETION OF BACKUP JOB

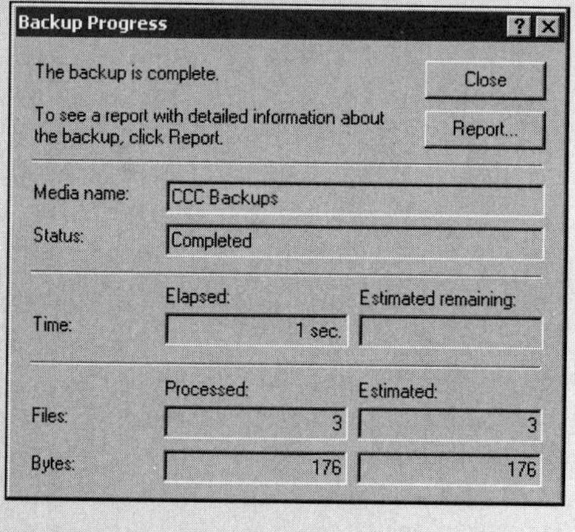

9. Click the **Close** button. You return to the Backup window.

Once you have the backup, what should you do with it? Or more appropriately, what should you not do with it? You should not store it near your computer. A fire that destroys your computer will probably destroy your backup as well. If a thief wants your data, it's quicker to steal your backups than your computer. Many computer owners rent safe deposit boxes at banks and store their backups there. Business owners sometimes store their backups off-site at their own homes. Backup storage is part of your overall backup strategy. You need to decide how often you will put your backup media into storage. Many users maintain two backup tapes or disks: They store the backups for a single week, and then at the end of the week they put the backups into storage. They use the other tape or disk for the following week, and then at the end of the week they swap the backups.

Restoring Files

Bruce asks you to imagine that disaster has just struck. Your hard disk has failed, and your computer maintenance person believes data recovery is hopeless—you're going to have to reformat your hard disk. "I hope," says your maintenance person, "you made a backup." If you did, then your problem is solved. You simply take the backup out of storage and run the Restore procedure on the backup containing the files you lost.

Bruce says that to simulate a file restoration, you'll first delete the Copy City Copiers folder from your desktop. In a real-life situation, these files might have been ruined in a power failure, by a disk defect, by a virus, or by some other misfortune.

To delete the Copy City Copiers folder from the desktop:

1. Minimize the Backup window.

2. Right-click the **Copy City Copiers** folder icon and then click **Delete**.

3. Click the **Yes** button to confirm the deletion.

Bruce points out that at this point you could recover the folder and its contents from the Recycle Bin, but he asks you to imagine that you emptied the Recycle Bin after deleting the Copy City Copier folder, to free up disk space.

You are ready to use Backup to restore the folder to your hard disk. You must first identify the backup that contains the Seminar folder. In this simulation, there will be only one backup on your disk: the Copy City Copier folder Backup you created earlier. In real life, there could be multiple backups on your backup disk—especially if you run backup jobs regularly. How you restore data depends on what kind of loss you suffered. If you lost only a single file, you can choose the backup that you made after you changed the file. If the file or folder you want to restore is not in that backup, that means you haven't worked with it since the last backup, in which case you'll have to check another backup. If you have lost all the data on your disk, how you recover it depends on what kind of partial backups you use. If you use incremental backups, you will need to use all the backups you've created since your most recent full backup. You would start by restoring the full backup, and then restoring each backup, one at a time, beginning with the oldest. If you use differential backups, you restore the full backup and then the most recent differential backup.

You are ready to restore the Copy City Copier folder.

To select the files to restore from the backup media:

1. Return to the Backup window.

2. Click the **Restore Wizard** button 🖳 and then click the **Next** button.

The Restore Wizard displays the backup file on the floppy disk. This is the CCC Backups file—the catalog you created earlier. From this file you have to select the files and folders that you want to restore. To do so you have to work down through the hierarchy of objects in the backup media.

3. Click the **plus** box ⊞ in front of the **File** icon 🖬.

4. Click the **plus** box ⊞ in front of the **CCC Backups** icon 🖳.

At this point you can select the C folder (or whichever folder contains the original files) to restore the files (you don't have to navigate through the rest of the folder hierarchy).

5. Click the box ☐ in front of the **C** drive icon. See Figure 11-34.

Figure 11-34   **SELECTING THE FILES TO RESTORE**

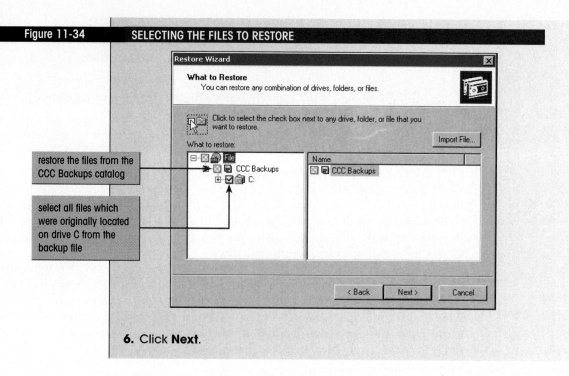

restore the files from the CCC Backups catalog

select all files which were originally located on drive C from the backup file

6. Click **Next**.

At this point you can restore the files to the original locations. If you want to select a different location for the files, you can use the advanced restore options. The advanced options also allow you to specify whether you want files from the backup media to overwrite files on the hard disk. Bruce suggests that you examine the advanced restore options.

To view the advanced restore options:

1. Click the **Advanced** button.

The first dialog box lets you specify a location for the restored files. If you select Alternate Location from the Restore files to drop-down list box, you will be prompted for the new location. The default is to restore the files to the original location, which you'll accept.

2. Click the **Next** button.

If you're restoring files that currently exist on the hard drive, you can either (1) leave the files on the hard drive untouched, (2) overwrite the files on the hard drive if the file on the backup medium is a newer version, or (3) always replace the hard drive files. In this case, you won't be restoring over any existing files, so you can safely continue on with the Restore Wizard.

3. Click the **Next** button.

The last advanced option allows you to restore special system files or security files. None of these options apply to the files you created in the Copy City Copiers folder.

4. Click the **Next** button.

You've finished reviewing the advanced options. Now you can complete restoring the backed up files.

To restore the files:

1. Make sure your floppy disk is in the drive and click the **Finish** button.

   The backup program examines the floppy disk. Since there may be more than one backup file on the disk, it prompts you for which file to restore from.

2. Verify that A:\Backup.bkf is displayed in the Restore from backup file text box.

3. Click the **OK** button.

   After a few seconds the files are restored. Windows 2000 displays the dialog box shown in Figure 11-35.

Figure 11-35	COMPLETION OF THE FILE RESTORE

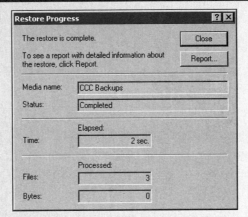

4. Click the **Close** button.

5. Minimize the Backup window and verify that the Copy City Copiers folder has been restored to the desktop (the icon may be in a different location than it was before).

6. Delete the Copy City Copiers folder to return the Desktop to its original state.

7. Close the Backup program.

Bruce tells you that if you're lucky, you'll never have to use Restore to recover lost data. Then he tells you that Backup is probably one of the most important topics he's discussed with you. Practically everyone who has been using computers for very long has a data-loss story to tell. Many computer owners who now have backup drives, such as tape drives or optical disc drives, learned the hard way how important it is to protect data. If you are a computer owner, put a backup strategy planning session at the top of your list, and then stick to your strategy scrupulously. You won't be sorry.

Session 11.3 QUICK CHECK

1. How does copying a disk differ from backing up a disk?

2. What is the difference between a backup job and a backup?

3. What is a partial backup? Identify and differentiate between two kinds of partial backups.

4. Why would you use a partial backup rather than perform a full backup?

5. When you select the folders and files to back up, Backup uses colored check marks to indicate which files and folders will be backed up. If a folder has a blue check mark in front of it, will the entire folder be backed up?

REVIEW ASSIGNMENTS

1. Creating a New User Bruce has a new user account for you to create. The user's name is David Clemons, and his username will be DClemons. He works in the copier maintenance department and will belong to the Power Users group. His password should never expire.

   a. Create this user on your computer. When you're finished, print screen images of the properties for DClemons, showing both the General sheet and the Group Membership sheet. (To print images of the screen, press the PrintScreen key, start WordPad, click the Paste button, print the document, and then close WordPad without saving the file.)

   b. Open the advanced properties for DClemons, and set his password never to expire. Print a screen image of the appropriate dialog box (see Step a).

   c. Remove DClemons from your system when you're finished.

2. Creating a New User Group Bruce wants you to create a new user group for employees in the maintenance department. The name of this user group should be "Maintenance Department."

   a. Create the Maintenance Department user group on your system. Add your own user account to the group.

   b. Print an image of the screen, displaying the properties of the Maintenance Department group (see Review Assignment 1a).

   c. Delete the Maintenance Department group from your system when you're finished.

3. Changing a Password Policy Some of the employees at Copy City Copiers have been complaining that it seems as if they constantly have to change their passwords. It's been decided to change the expiration age for passwords from 42 days to 66 days. In exchange for relaxing this requirement, users will be required to have at least eight characters in their passwords. Accounts with longer passwords are more difficult for hackers to break into. Bruce asks you to change the password policy on your computer to reflect this decision.

a. Open the Local Security Policy window on your computer. Note the current password policies in place on your system.

b. Change the expiration date of passwords to 66 days.

Explore

c. Change the length of password characters to 8 characters.

d. Print an image of the screen displaying the changed password policies (see Review Assignment 1a).

e. Restore the policies back to the original values.

4. Monitoring Hardware Interrupts Bruce has asked you to create a baseline report on the number of hardware interrupts on your computer. The more hardware you have on your system, the more times per second the processor will be interrupted to deal with a hardware request.

Explore

a. Open the Performance Monitor and track the total number of hardware interrupts per second experienced by the Processor performance object. Print an image of the screen showing the real-time results from the performance graph (see Review Assignment 1a).

b. Create a log file containing the interrupts per second, sampling the data every five seconds. Sample the data for about a minute. Save the log to a file named "Interrupt.blg" on your floppy disk.

c. Delete the log file you created in Step b.

Explore

d. Write a short description of the interrupts/second value. What does it signify and how is it calculated?

5. Printing an Event from the System Log One of the computers at Copy City Copiers has been crashing a lot lately. Bruce has asked you to examine the problem. He wants you to work on the computer and print some of the entries from the event log. He wants you to pay close attention to any warning messages that have been generated by either the system or applications on the system.

a. Open the log for system events on your computer.

b. Open the latest warning event in the log. If there are no warning events listed, open the latest event of any kind in the list.

c. Copy the description of the event from the event properties dialog box (you can use the Copy button) and paste the description into a Notepad file. Print the Notepad file.

d. Repeat these steps for items in the log of application events.

6. Working with the Plug and Play Service One of the computers at Copy City Copiers has just had a new video card installed. Although the card is a plug and play device, Windows 2000 did not automatically recognize the new card. Bruce wants you to track down the problem. The card may be defective, but he also wonders whether the Plug and Play service on that computer is working. Bruce asks you to examine this.

a. Open the Services window on your computer.

b. Open the properties for the Plug and Play service. Does the service start automatically or must it be manually started? How does the system recover if the Plug and Play service fails?

c. Print a screen shot of the properties of the Plug and Play service, including images of the General dialog sheet and the Recovery dialog sheet (see Review Assignment 1a).

7. Performing a Backup You would like to back up some of the Copy City Copier files on your hard disk to your Backup Disk. You'll need to create a folder on your hard disk, create some files in the folder, and then back them up.

a. Open Windows Explorer and create a folder named CCC on your hard drive. Create one new Bitmap Image file named CCCLogo and two new Text Document files named CopyList and EmpList. You don't need to enter any data in these files.

b. Place your backup disk in the appropriate drive. Start Backup and create a new backup job to back up the CCC folder and its files.

c. Select your backup disk as the backup device. Name the backup "CCC Backup" and name the backup job "CCC Files".

d. Delete the CCC folder from your hard disk. Hand in your backup disk.

PROJECTS

1. Examine your own user account on your computer and answer the following questions. Print the appropriate screen shots proving the answers you give.

a. What is your username?

b. What user group do you belong to?

c. If you have one, where is your home folder located? What is your user profile?

d. Can you change your password?

2. Examine the security policies on your computer and answer the following questions. Again, print the appropriate screen shots to prove your answers.

a. What is the maximum age of passwords? What is the minimum password length?

b. Are accounts locked out after a certain number of invalid logons? If so, how many invalid logons are allowed?

Explore

c. Which users or user groups have the right to increase disk quotas?

Explore

d. Can users install printer drivers on the computer?

Explore

e. How many days before the password expires, will the system start prompting users to change their password?

Explore

3. You can use the Computer Management tool to print out summary information about your computer. Open the Computer Management window, and then open the System Summary folder (found under the System Information icon). Print the summary information.

4. If you have your own computer and it has a tape drive, you can do this project. Otherwise, just read this assignment so you can see how you would back up an entire system. Backing up your full system is an important part of a comprehensive backup strategy, but it can take an hour or more, depending on the speed of your backup drive and the size of your hard disk or disks.

   a. Start Backup and choose the Backup Wizard.

   b. Choose the Back up everything on my computer option button and the New and changed files option.

   c. When you choose the backup device, make sure you select the backup device on your computer, not a file on a 3½-inch disk.

   d. Name the backup job "My Computer Backup."

   e. Follow the prompts that appear on the screen. Be prepared to wait an hour or more for the backup to finish. Print an image of the Backup summary dialog box before you close Backup, and then hand this printout in to your instructor.

5. Ask your instructor for the names of businesses whose systems managers might take a few minutes with you on the phone to be interviewed. You could also ask your employer. You might ask the systems managers the following questions:

   a. What training did you receive to get this job?

   b. How many computers do you manage? Are they on a network?

   c. What backup media do you use?

   d. How often do you back up the entire system?

   e. How often do you perform partial backups?

   f. Do you perform incremental or differential backups? Explain why you chose to perform this type of partial backup.

   g. Are individual employees responsible for their own backups?

   h. If an employee has a problem with a computer, who is expected to fix the problem?

6. You work at Hal's Food Warehouse in inventory management. You are responsible for backing up the computer system. You performed a full backup on Friday, and then on Monday you worked with a database file named Orders. You performed an incremental backup on Monday evening. On Tuesday you worked with the Orders file again, and on Tuesday evening you performed an incremental backup. When you attempt to open the Orders file Wednesday morning, you receive an error message that says the file cannot be found. How would you restore the file?

7. If you have your own computer, do you use a disk maintenance strategy? If not, now's your chance to implement one. Ask yourself the following questions, and then write a disk maintenance strategy and schedule:

   a. How often do I install different software on my computer?

   b. How often do I work with important files, and how much are they worth to me?

   c. What would I lose if the hard disk drive failed?

8. Research the different types of backup media available, such as tape drives, CD write-able drives, and Zip drives. You can use the Internet or computing trade magazines as sources. Make a chart with four columns: backup medium name (such as tape drive), description of the backup medium (describe tape drives), brand names, and price. (Include both the price of the drive and the disks the drive uses, if applicable.) Then write a paragraph below the chart describing which device you would purchase for your own computer, and why.

LAB ASSIGNMENTS

Data Backup   The Data Backup Lab gives you an opportunity to make tape backups on a simulated computer system. Periodically, the hard disk on the simulated computer will fail, which gives you a chance to assess the convenience and efficiency of different backup procedures. See the Read This Before You Begin page for instructions on installing and starting the lab.

1. Click the Steps button to learn how to use the simulation. As you work through the Steps, answer all of the Quick Check questions that appear. After you complete the Steps, you will see a Summary Report of your Quick Check answers. Follow the directions on the screen to print this report.

2. Click the Explore button. Create a full backup every Friday using only Tape 1. At some point in the simulation, an event will cause data loss on the simulated computer system. Use the simulation to restore as much data as you can. After you restore the data, print the Backup Audit Report.

3. In Explore, create a full backup every Friday on Tape 1, and a differential backup every Wednesday on Tape 2. At some point in the simulation, an event will cause data loss on the simulated computer system. Use the simulation to restore as much data as you can. Print the Backup Audit Report.

4. In Explore, create a full backup on Tape 1 every Monday. Make incremental backups on Tapes 2, 3, 4, and 5 each day for the rest of the week. Continue this cycle, reusing the same tapes each week. At some point in the simulation, an event will cause data loss on the simulated computer system. Use the simulation, to restore as much data as you can. Print the Backup Audit Report.

5. Photocopy a calendar for next month. On the calendar, indicate your best plan for backing up data. In Explore, implement your plan. Print out the Backup Audit Report. Write a paragraph or two discussing the effectiveness of your plan.

QUICK | CHECK ANSWERS

Session 11.1

1. local groups and global or domain groups

2. administrators

3. Home folder

4. user profile

5. A policy is a set of rules that governs an operation on your computer.

6. Set up an accounting policy that will count the number of invalid logons. If a certain number of invalid logons occur within a certain space of time for an account, the account is locked out and must be manually unlocked by the administrator.

Session 11.2

1. to track the performance of various tasks on the system in order to discover the source of any problems, such as a slow computer

2. It measures the percentage of time that the processor is not idle.

3. Open the Performance shortcut in the Administrative Tools window and then open the Performance and Log Alerts icon. Create a new Alerts log, recording the %Processor Time value, specifying that values over 95 should result in an alert message sent to the application event log.

4. application, security and system

5. A service is a small program that is run by your computer, designed to manage one or more aspects of the computer.

6. Open the Services icon in the Administrative Tools window, open the service from the list of services, and then click the Stop button.

Session 11.3

1. Copying a disk duplicates the disk contents, whereas backing up a disk compresses the files on the disk into a single, smaller file.

2. A backup job contains the list of files and folders you are backing up and the settings you are using; the backup itself is the compressed file that contains the data you backed up.

3. A partial backup is a backup of files that have changed since your last backup. An incremental backup backs up the files since the last backup, regardless of whether it was full or partial. A differential backup backs up the files since the last full backup.

4. It takes less time.

5. yes

CONNECTING COMPUTERS OVER A PHONE LINE

Windows 2000 **Dial-up Accessories**

Windows 2000 makes communicating with computers easier than ever because it provides accessories that allow you to connect your computer to other computers and to the Internet. If you are using a computer on a university or institutional network, you are probably already connected to the Internet, and you can skip this appendix. This appendix is useful for people who are not connected to the Internet but who have their own computer with a modem and access to a phone line.

Computers at universities or large companies are likely to be connected to the Internet via expensive, high-speed wiring that transmits data very quickly. Home computer owners, however, usually can't afford to run similar cables and wires to their homes, and instead rely on phone lines that are already in place, as shown in Figure A-1.

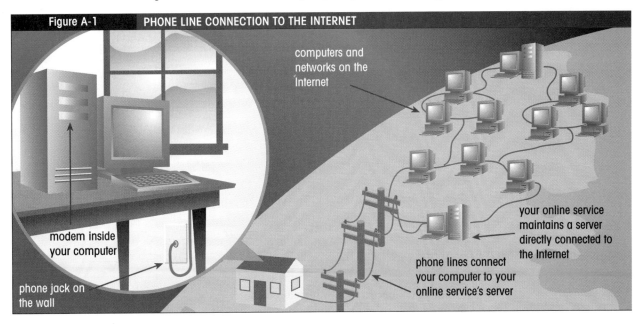

Figure A-1   PHONE LINE CONNECTION TO THE INTERNET

computers and networks on the Internet

your online service maintains a server directly connected to the Internet

phone lines connect your computer to your online service's server

modem inside your computer

phone jack on the wall

When a modem uses an ordinary voice phone line, which uses analog signals, it converts the modem's digital signals to analog, as shown in Figure A-2.

Figure A-2	DATA TRAVELING OVER A PHONE LINE

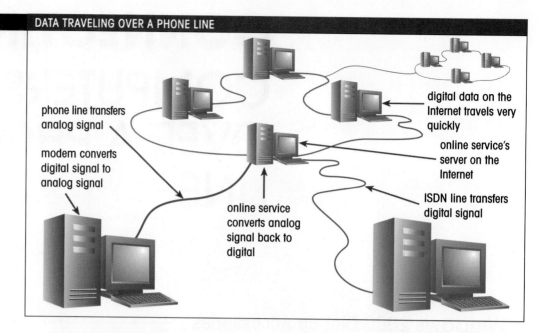

phone line transfers analog signal

modem converts digital signal to analog signal

online service converts analog signal back to digital

digital data on the Internet travels very quickly

online service's server on the Internet

ISDN line transfers digital signal

The receiving computer converts the analog signal back to digital. Data usually travels more slowly over phone wires than over the networking infrastructure of the Internet. If there are any problems with the phone connection, data can be lost. But regular phone lines are often the only practical choice for homes and small businesses. In some areas, **ISDN lines**, wires that provide a completely digital path from one computer to another, are dropping in price so that small businesses and homeowners can afford them. Whether you use a regular phone line or a faster ISDN line, Windows 2000 can help you establish a connection to the Internet. You will need to select an Internet service provider (ISP), a company that provides Internet access. ISPs maintain servers that are directly connected to the Internet 24 hours a day. You dial into your ISP's server over your phone line to use its Internet connection. You pay a fee for this service, most often with a flat monthly rate.

Once you've selected an ISP, you can use Windows 2000 to set up your connection. Figure A-3 shows the accessories Windows 2000 includes to help you.

Figure A-3	WINDOWS 2000 CONNECTION ACCESSORIES	
ACCESSORY	**DESCRIPTION**	
Dial-up Networking	Some computer users have one Internet account for home use and a different one for business use. The Dial-up Networking accessory helps you manage the accounts that you use to connect to the Internet.	
Connection Wizard	The Connection Wizard makes it easy to create an Internet account for the first time by prompting you for information through a series of dialog boxes.	

You can also use the Internet Connection Wizard to locate an ISP in your area. There are probably more ISPs in your area than are listed by the Internet Connection Wizard.

Setting Up Dial-up Networking

If you want to connect to the Internet and other networks with your home computer, you can set up a dial-up connection using the Internet Connection Wizard. The Internet Connection Wizard is a series of dialog boxes that prompt you for information your computer needs to connect to the Internet.

Starting the Internet Connection Wizard

If your ISP has provided you with an installation program to set up the connection, install and run that program instead of using the Windows 2000 Internet Connection Wizard. To see how the Internet Connection Wizard works, you'll use it to create a dial-up account. These steps assume you have signed up for an account with an ISP and haven't set up the account yet. Before you perform the steps, you should gather any documentation from your ISP, such as phone numbers, passwords, and special settings.

To begin setting up a dial-up connection:

1. Click the **Start** button, point to **Programs**, point to **Accessories**, point to **Communications**, and then click **Internet Connection Wizard**.

2. Click the **I want to set up my Internet connection manually** option button.

   Choose the first option to connect to a referral service that helps you select an ISP (you use that option only if you haven't already purchased an account). Choose the second option to transfer your account from one of the ISPs listed by the Internet Connection Wizard. Choose the third option when you have an ISP account, but that account is *not* supported by the Internet Connection Wizard referral service, or if you want to set up your account manually.

3. Click the **Next** button and then click the **I connect through a phone line and a modem** option button.

   Choose this option when you are not on a local area network, which you are not if you are connecting your home computer to an ISP.

4. Type the area code and telephone number of your ISP in the appropriate boxes. See Figure A-4. Your numbers will be different.

Figure A-4	ENTERING ISP PHONE INFORMATION

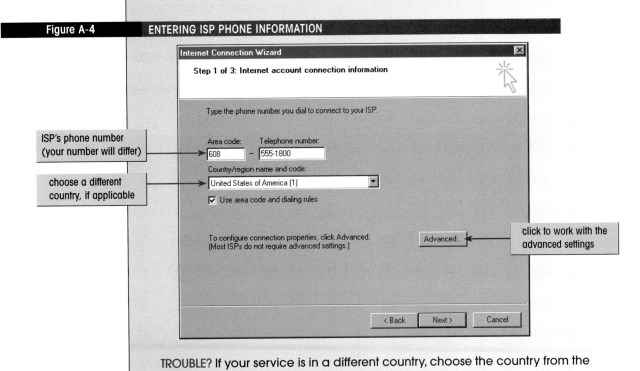

ISP's phone number (your number will differ)

choose a different country, if applicable

click to work with the advanced settings

TROUBLE? If your service is in a different country, choose the country from the Country name and code list.

At this point in the Internet Connection Wizard, you have the choice of setting some of the Advanced options in your Internet connection.

Entering Advanced Settings

The advanced settings control the technical aspect of how your computer communicates with your ISP. If you choose not to change advanced settings, you might encounter problems with your connection, if the Windows 2000 default settings don't match those of your ISP.

To enter advanced settings:

1. Click the **Advanced** button to open the Advanced Connection Properties dialog box.

    TROUBLE? If you are sure you can proceed using the default settings, do not click the Advanced button and instead read through the rest of these steps without performing them.

2. Click the **PPP**, **SLIP** or **C-SLIP** option button, depending on what your ISP's documentation specifies.

    A **connection type** is the kind of connection between your computer and your ISP's server. Windows 2000 offers three connection types: PPP, SLIP and C-SLIP. The preferred and more common connection type today is **Point-to-Point Protocol**, or **PPP**, which provides error checking and can cope with noisy phone lines. **Serial Line Internet Protocol**, or **SLIP**, is a basic connection type that runs well on most systems but has no error-checking or security features. **Compressed Serial Line Internet Protocol** or **C-SLIP** is similar to SLIP but compresses some of the data in order to speed up the connection. Most ISPs use a PPP connection, but some require SLIP or C-SLIP; check your ISP documentation to see which one to use.

3. Click the appropriate **Logon Procedure** option button.

    Some ISPs require you to log on before you can use the service. In some cases, you must log on manually, providing the information required by your ISP when you attempt to connect. In other cases, you can use a **logon script**, a program that runs on your computer and logs you on to the service automatically.

4. If you need to use a logon script, click the **Use this logon script** option button, click the **Browse** button, locate and select the logon script specified by your ISP's documentation, and then click the **Open** button. See Figure A-5.

Figure A-5	CHOOSING A CONNECTION TYPE AND LOGON PROCEDURE

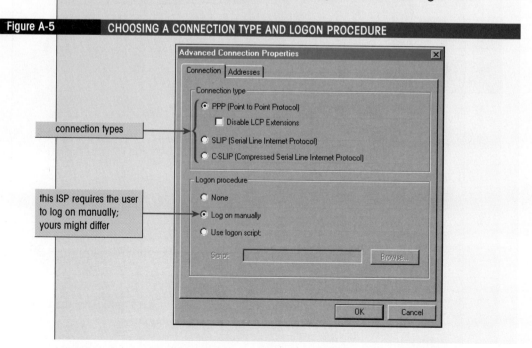

connection types

this ISP requires the user to log on manually; yours might differ

5. Click the **Addresses** tab.

6. Choose the appropriate **IP address** option button, and then, if you selected the second option, enter the IP address. An **Internet Protocol**, or **IP address**, is a unique address that identifies a server on the Internet. Usually your ISP automatically assigns you one when you log on, because you are only a temporary user of the address (only during the period of time that you are logged on).

7. Choose the appropriate **DNS server address** option button, and then, if you selected the second option, enter the DNS numbers. The **Domain Name System**, or **DNS**, is a database service that helps computers look up the names of other computers and locate their corresponding IP addresses. If your ISP documentation provides you with primary and secondary DNS server addresses, enter them here, as shown in Figure A-6.

Figure A-6	CHOOSING AN IP ADDRESS AND DNS SERVER ADDRESS

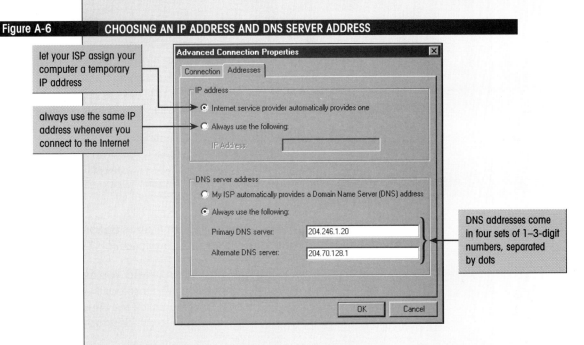

let your ISP assign your computer a temporary IP address

always use the same IP address whenever you connect to the Internet

DNS addresses come in four sets of 1–3-digit numbers, separated by dots

8. Click the **OK** button to close the Advanced Connection Properties dialog box and save your settings.

Entering Account Information

After working with the advanced settings, you are returned to the first step of the Internet Connection Wizard. At this point in the process, you enter information about your account, such as your username and password. You'll also enter a name for your ISP.

To enter your account information:

1. Click the **Next** button to move to Step 2 of the Internet Connection Wizard.

2. Type your username in the User name box, and then press the **Tab** key. Your ISP documentation will provide you with the username and password you should use.

TROUBLE? If you can't find your username in your documentation, it might be called User ID, Member ID, Login Name, or something similar.

3. Type your password in the Password box. As you type the password, asterisks appear instead of the letters you type, as shown in Figure A-7. This protects your password from the eyes of people who might be walking by your computer. You should keep your password secret, so that unauthorized users cannot access your account.

Figure A-7	ENTERING A USERNAME AND PASSWORD

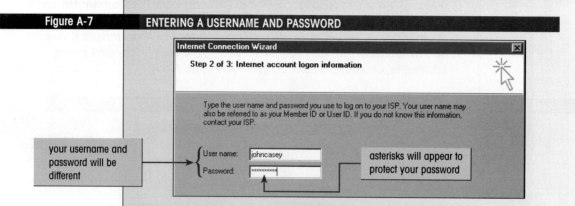

your username and password will be different

asterisks will appear to protect your password

4. Click the **Next** button, type a name for your connection (such as your ISP's name), and then click the **Next** button. Since you are setting up only your dial-up connection, not your mail and news options, proceed by clicking **No** and then clicking **Next**.

TROUBLE? If you want to set up your mail and news options now on your own computer, you can do so by clicking Yes and following the prompts.

5. You've completed the Internet Connection Wizard. You could connect to the Internet right now, but you don't need to yet. Deselect the **Connect to the Internet Immediately** check box, and then click the **Finish** button. The Internet Connection Wizard closes, and you return to the desktop.

Although the steps didn't direct you to set up your mail and news options, you can do that from within Outlook Express, Outlook (if you have Microsoft Office), or whatever mail and news software you are using.

Using the Network and Dial-up Connection Window

Once you have established a dial-up connection, you are ready to use it to connect to the Internet or another network or computer. Windows 2000 will try to connect to the Internet automatically whenever you start a program that requires Internet access, such as your Web browser. If you have more than one ISP, you will be prompted to select which one you want to use to establish the Internet connection.

Another way of establishing your Internet connection is to open the Network and Dial-up Connections window and then to double-click the icon for your ISP. This window also provides tools to change your dial-up settings or any of your network connections (through your modem or local area network).

To view your Network and Dial-up Connections window:

1. Click the **Start** button ![Start], point to **Settings**, and then click **Network and Dial-up Connections**.

   The window opens as shown in Figure A-8.

| Figure A-8 | NETWORK AND DIAL-UP CONNECTIONS WINDOW |

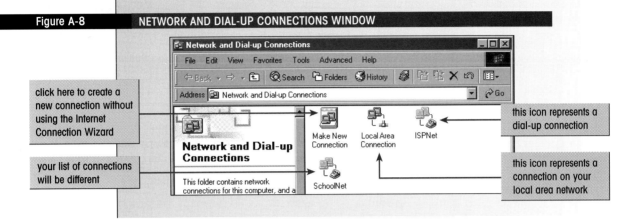

click here to create a new connection without using the Internet Connection Wizard

your list of connections will be different

this icon represents a dial-up connection

this icon represents a connection on your local area network

You can have more than network service, in which case multiple icons appear in the Network and Dial-up Connections window. One connection might provide your business Internet service, another might be for home or family use, and another might access your local area network.

To connect to your dial-up service through the Network and Dial-up Connections window:

1. Connect your phone line to your computer's modem.

2. Double-click the icon for your ISP.

3. The Connect dialog box opens.

4. Click the **Dial** button and then wait as your modem connects.

5. The Connecting dialog box appears and identifies the steps of establishing a connection. First it uses your modem to dial the number, then it verifies your username and password, and finally it establishes a connection. A Connection Complete dialog box (or something similar) may open, indicating that you are connected to your ISP.

6. If necessary, click **OK** to close the Connection Complete dialog box.

7. An icon ![icon] appears on your taskbar that indicates you are connected. You can now start your Internet browser to view Web pages, check your e-mail, or use any of the other Windows 2000 communications features.

Your dial-up account will remain connected until you leave your computer idle for several minutes, in which case your ISP may automatically disconnect you, or until you disconnect from your account yourself.

To disconnect your dial-up account:

1. Right-click the **Connection** icon 📇 on the taskbar. A pop-up menu appears, shown in Figure A-9.

| Figure A-9 | DISCONNECTING FROM YOUR ISP |

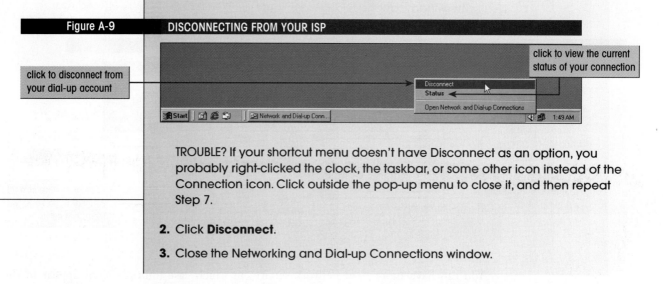

click to disconnect from your dial-up account

click to view the current status of your connection

TROUBLE? If your shortcut menu doesn't have Disconnect as an option, you probably right-clicked the clock, the taskbar, or some other icon instead of the Connection icon. Click outside the pop-up menu to close it, and then repeat Step 7.

2. Click **Disconnect**.

3. Close the Networking and Dial-up Connections window.

The Internet service provider market is changing very rapidly, so make sure you compare prices and features before choosing the ISP you want.

EXPLORING ADDITIONAL WINDOWS 2000 TOOLS

Using Power Management Features

The Windows 2000 **power management features** allow you to control the amount of power your computer and its devices require when you don't need them to be running at full capacity. If you're taking a short break, you might not want to turn your system off completely, because shutting down and then restarting the computer is time-consuming. Instead, you can place the computer on **standby**, a mode that reduces the amount of power consumed by your drives and monitor, but still allows you to return to work quickly because the computer is not actually turned off. Some users leave their computers on 24 hours a day to perform resource-intensive tasks in the middle of the night, or to use their computers to receive faxes or download files when they are not sitting at their computer. Standby mode is useful for such users. Standby is also useful for conserving battery power in portable computers. You can specify one standby setting for battery power and a different setting for AC power.

These features conserve both energy and money, but your computer will be able to use the Windows 2000 power management features only if its hardware is designed for that purpose.

Working with Power Management Schemes

You change power management settings via the Control Panel by working with **power schemes**, groups of preset power management options. A power scheme controls, for example, the amount of time you want to elapse before the system turns off the monitor. Windows 2000 comes with the power schemes shown in Figure B-1, although you can create additional ones for your own needs.

| Figure B-1 | POWER MANAGEMENT SCHEMES |

WINDOWS 2000 POWER SCHEME	TURNS OFF MONITOR	TURNS OFF HARD DISKS
Home/Office Desk	After 20 minutes	Never
Portable/Laptop	After 15 minutes	After 30 minutes
Presentation	Never	Never
Always on	After 20 minutes	Never
Minimal Power Management	After 15 minutes	Never
Max Battery	After 15 minutes	Never

To view your computer's power management settings:
1. Click the **Start** button, click **Settings**, and then click **Control Panel**.
2. Click the **Power Options** icon and then press the **Enter** key.
   The Power Options Properties dialog box opens as shown in Figure B-2.

Figure B-2 **POWER MANAGEMENT SCHEMES**

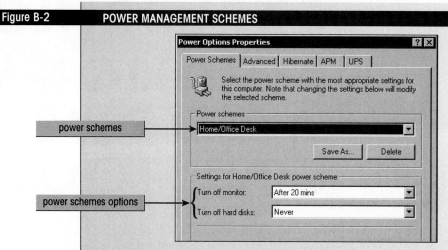

power schemes

power schemes options

3. On the Power Schemes tab, click the **Power schemes** list arrow. Note the schemes available to your computer. The Settings pane below the Power schemes list box shows the options for the currently selected scheme.

TROUBLE? If you don't see the Power Schemes tab or the Power schemes list arrow, you might not have administrative control over your computer. Ask your instructor or technical support person for assistance. If you can't get administrative control, review this material without performing the steps.

4. Click outside the list to close it.

Using Hibernation

You can also save power by putting your computer in **hibernation** mode, which turns off your monitor and hard disk, but saves your work to your hard disk before your computer shuts down. When you restart your computer and log on, your desktop will appear just as you left it, with all the programs and files you left open already available.

To enable hibernation on your computer:

1. Click the **Hibernate** tab in the Power Options Properties dialog box.
2. Click the **Enable hibernate support** check box as shown in Figure B-3.

Figure B-3 **ENABLING HIBERNATION**

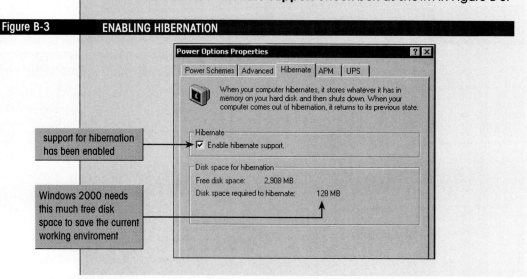

support for hibernation has been enabled

Windows 2000 needs this much free disk space to save the current working enviroment

Once this feature has been enabled, you can go into hibernation mode by clicking the Shut Down command on the Start menu and then selecting the Hibernate option in the Shut Down Windows dialog box. You can set up Windows 2000 either to lock out all users until you return to your account, or to allow other users to log on while your account is hibernating. This feature is available on the Advanced sheet of the Power Options Properties dialog box, once hibernation has been enabled.

Using an Uninterruptible Power Supply

The safest way to guard your computer against the possibility of power failure (and the associated loss of data) is with an **uninterruptible power supply**, or **UPS**. When your computer experiences a power failure, the UPS immediately detects it and supplies emergency power from a battery to the computer through a COM port. Then you can safely shut down your computer without the loss of critical data.

You can install support for a UPS from the Power Options Properties dialog box. Note that if you were actually adding a UPS device to your system, you would perform these steps after connecting the device to your computer.

To enable support for a UPS:

1. Click the **UPS** tab in the Power Options Properties dialog box. Figure B-4 shows the UPS dialog sheet.

Figure B-4	SELECTING AND CONFIGURING A UPS DEVICE

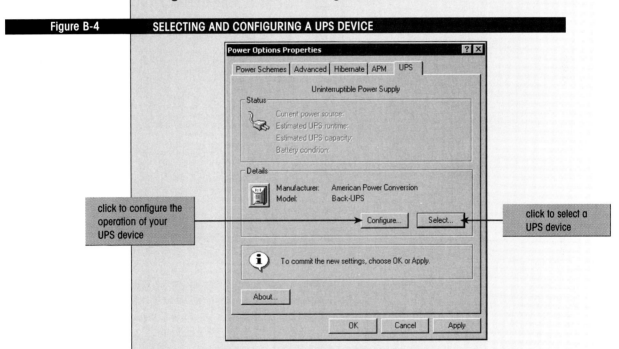

click to configure the operation of your UPS device

click to select a UPS device

If you have a UPS, you can click the Select button and select your model from a list of UPS devices. Once you've installed the UPS, you can click the Configure button to control how the UPS interfaces with Windows 2000. You can have Windows 2000 shut down automatically after running on the UPS's battery after a period of time, or have the computer sound an alarm to notify you of the power failure so you can decide whether to shut down the computer.

2. Click the **Cancel** button to close the Power Options Properties dialog box without saving any changes to your power configuration. Leave the Control Panel open.

Customizing the Mouse

The Mouse Properties dialog box, available through the Control Panel, lets you customize the mouse settings. You can configure the mouse for the right or left hand, adjust the double-click speed, choose different pointer shapes, turn on pointer trails, and adjust the pointer speed. If you have a Microsoft IntelliPoint mouse or some other pointing device, you might see additional features in the Mouse Properties dialog box that are specific to that pointing device.

Configuring the Mouse for the Right or Left Hand

You can configure the mouse for either right-handed or left-handed users. If you select the left-handed setting, the operations of the left and right mouse buttons are reversed.

To configure the mouse for right-handed or left-handed users:

1. Double-click the **Mouse** icon 🖱 in the Control Panel to display the Mouse Properties dialog box. You can set the mouse for right-handed users or left-handed users by clicking the appropriate option button. See Figure B-5.

Figure B-5	THE MOUSE PROPERTIES DIALOG BOX

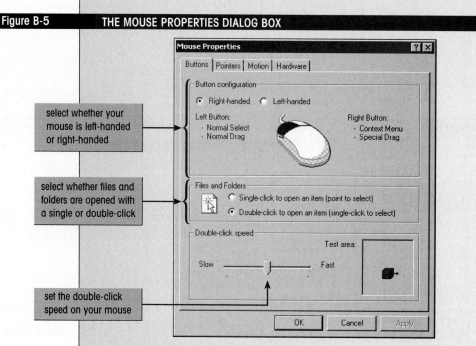

select whether your mouse is left-handed or right-handed

select whether files and folders are opened with a single or double-click

set the double-click speed on your mouse

2. Click the **Right-handed** option button if you are right-handed, or click the **Left-handed** option button if you are left-handed. As you change this setting, the description and picture of mouse operations change.
3. If you are working on your own computer, click the **Apply** button to apply your changes, and then test the new mouse setting by dragging the Mouse Properties dialog box with the appropriate mouse button.
4. Return this setting to its original state and then click the **Apply** button.

    TROUBLE? If Step 4 doesn't seem to reset your mouse, try using the other mouse button!

Adjusting Double-Click Speed

Many Windows programs allow you to use **double-clicking**, or clicking the mouse twice quickly, to select or open objects. Some new users have difficulty double-clicking, so Microsoft designed Windows 2000 to work without double-clicking. Other users find double-clicking the quickest way to work.

To test the current double-click speed:

1. Position the pointer over the purple box in the Test area of the Mouse Properties dialog box.
2. Place your hand on the mouse and quickly press and release the left mouse button twice.

TROUBLE? If you changed the mouse to left-handed operation, you will need to double-click by quickly pressing and releasing the right mouse button twice.

3. If you double-click successfully, the jack-in-the-box pops out of the box.

4. Double-click the purple box again to close it.

TROUBLE? Don't worry if you can't open the jack-in-the-box. In the next series of steps you'll learn how to adjust the double-click speed for your convenience. If you have trouble double-clicking, you can slow down the double-click speed by using the Double-click speed slider.

To slow down the double-click speed:

1. Drag the **Double-click speed** slider toward Slow.

2. Double-click the **jack-in-the-box** to see if you can make it pop up.

3. If you still cannot successfully double-click, drag the **Double-click speed** slider even farther toward Slow and then repeat Step 2.

4. Once you can successfully double-click, try increasing or decreasing the double-click speed to find the most comfortable speed for you.

5. If you are using your own computer, click the **Apply** button to change the double-click speed to the new setting. If you are in a lab, make sure to restore this setting to its original status.

Adjusting Pointer Speed

You can also adjust the pointer speed or the relative distance the pointer moves on the screen when you move the mouse. It can be easier to use a slower speed when you need more control. Likewise, you might need faster speed if you have limited desktop space.

To adjust the pointer speed:

1. Click the **Motion** tab in the Mouse Properties dialog box to display the Motion property sheet. See Figure B-6.

Figure B-6 **MOTION SETTINGS FOR THE MOUSE**

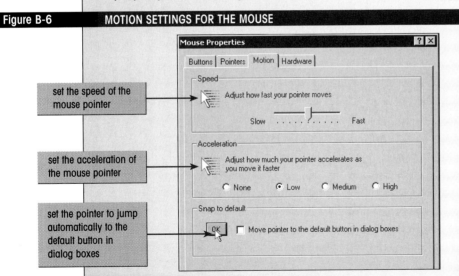

set the speed of the mouse pointer

set the acceleration of the mouse pointer

set the pointer to jump automatically to the default button in dialog boxes

2. To decrease the pointer speed, drag the **Speed** slider toward Slow and then practice moving the mouse with the new setting.

3. To increase the pointer speed, drag the **Speed** slider toward Fast and then practice moving the mouse with the new setting.

4. If you are using your own computer, choose the pointer speed setting that is most comfortable for you and then click the **Apply** button. If you are using a lab computer, return the slider to its original position.

Changing Your Mouse Pointer

Windows 2000 uses a default set of pointer icons, called a **pointer scheme**, to represent the actions of your mouse on the computer screen. There are other schemes available with Windows 2000. Some pointer schemes are comic in nature; others supply large pointer icons for users with vision problems. You can also download pointer icons from the Internet.

To view the list of Windows 2000 pointer schemes:

1. Click the **Pointers** tab in the Mouse Properties dialog box to display the Pointers property sheet.
2. Click the **Scheme** drop-down list arrow to display the list of pointer schemes available on your computer and then click **Hands 1**.

   The Customize list box displays each of the pointer icons for the various states of the pointer (Normal Select, Help Select, and so on). See Figure B-7.

Figure B-7	SELECTING A POINTER SCHEME

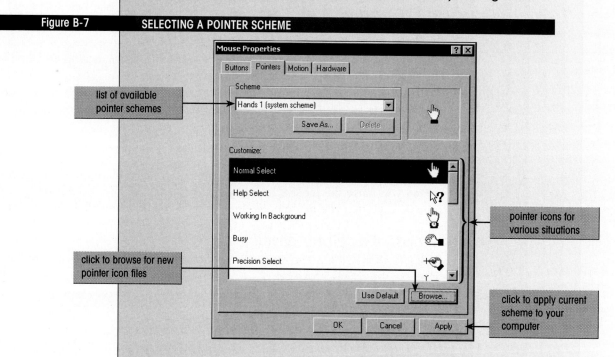

list of available pointer schemes

pointer icons for various situations

click to browse for new pointer icon files

click to apply current scheme to your computer

3. Scroll through the Customize list to view the icons for the various activities of the pointer.

   If you want to install a third-party pointer icon, you can select the state that you want to replace in the Customize list box and then click the Browse button. Pointer icon files will have either a .cur file extension for normal pointers, or the .ani file extension for animated pointers.
4. Click the **Cancel** button to close the Mouse Properties dialog box. Leave the Control Panel open.

You can adjust additional mouse settings using the Accessibility Options feature, as you'll see in the next section.

Using Accessibility Options

Accessibility options are Windows 2000 settings that you can change to make it easier to interact with your computer. Although designed primarily for users with special vision, hearing, and mobility needs, users without special needs also find it helpful to adjust accessibility settings for when they are working with drawing software and need more control over mouse and keyboard settings, using a portable computer with a small screen, or working in a poorly lit room.

There are two ways to change accessibility settings. You can open the Accessibility Properties dialog box from the Control Panel to access individual accessibility settings, or you can use the Accessibility Settings Wizard to determine what settings you should change to work most effectively. First, you'll examine some of the individual accessibility settings, and then you'll walk through part of the Accessibility Settings Wizard.

To open the Accessibility Properties dialog box:

1. Double-click the **Accessibility Options** icon 🔲 in the Control Panel. The Accessibility Options dialog box opens. See Figure B-8.

Figure B-8	ACCESSIBILITY OPTIONS DIALOG BOX

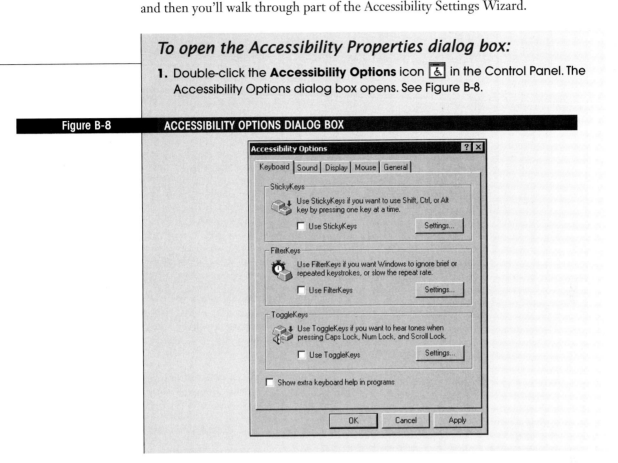

The Accessibility Options dialog box has five tabs: Keyboard, Sound, Display, Mouse, and General. First you'll explore some of the most commonly used accessibility options.

Using MouseKeys to Control the Pointer

All users occasionally have trouble using the mouse to control the pointer when using drawing or graphics programs. You can turn on MouseKeys to control the pointer with the numeric keypad as well as with the mouse. This is also a useful feature if you have a hand injury.

To turn on MouseKeys:

1. Click the **Mouse** tab in the Accessibility Options dialog box.

2. Click the **Use MouseKeys** check box to place a check mark in it.

3. If number lock is not on, press the **NumLock** key on your keyboard.

4. Click the **Apply** button to activate MouseKeys. After a short time, the MouseKeys icon 🖱 appears in the taskbar tray. See Figure B-9.

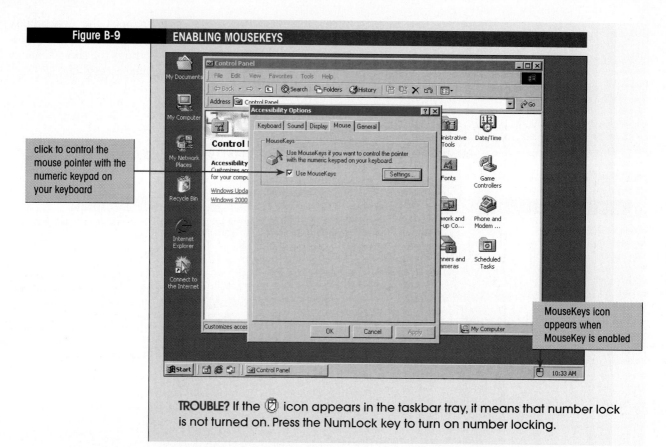

Figure B-9   ENABLING MOUSEKEYS

click to control the mouse pointer with the numeric keypad on your keyboard

MouseKeys icon appears when MouseKey is enabled

TROUBLE? If the icon appears in the taskbar tray, it means that number lock is not turned on. Press the NumLock key to turn on number locking.

Before you try working with MouseKeys, study Figure B-10, which describes some of the mouse actions you can duplicate using keys on the numeric keypad.

Figure B-10   MOUSEKEYS AND CORRESPONDING KEYS

MOUSE ACTION	CORRESPONDING NUMERIC KEYPAD KEY
Move pointer horizontally	Press 4 to move left, 6 to move right
Move pointer vertically	Press 8 to move up, 2 to move down
Move pointer diagonally	Press 7, 1, 9, and 3
Click	Press 5
Double-click	Press + (plus)
Right-click	Press − (minus), then press 5 (pressing − assigns the right-click function to 5; when you are done right-clicking, press / to restore 5 to clicking)
Begin dragging after pointing to object	Press Insert and then press arrow keys
End dragging	Press Delete to release mouse button
Move a single pixel at a time	Press and hold Shift, then use directional keys

To practice using MouseKeys:

1. Use the numeric keypad to move the pointer over the Start button. The 1 (End) key moves the pointer to the lower left.

   TROUBLE? Most keyboards have two keypads: one with only arrows and one with numbers and arrows. Make sure you are using the keypad with arrows and numbers.

TROUBLE? If MouseKeys isn't working, it's possible that Windows 2000 is set to reset accessibility options after a specified amount of time. Return to the Mouse property sheet and then reset MouseKeys by clicking the Apply button. Then click the General tab and see if the Automatic reset check box is selected. If it is, click the check box to turn it off for now and then click the Apply button.

2. Press the **5** key once the pointer is over the Start button.
3. Hold down the **8** key to move the pointer to **Programs**.
4. Use the **9** and **6** keys as necessary to move the pointer to **Accessories**.
5. Move the pointer to **Paint**, and then press the **5** key to start the Paint program.
6. Practice moving the pointer by pressing the number keys (all except 5, which is used for clicking) on the numeric keypad.
7. Press the **Insert** key on the numeric keypad to start drawing. Press the number keys to move the pointer and draw precise vertical, horizontal, and diagonal lines.
8. Press the **Delete** key on the numeric keypad to stop drawing.

If you've used Paint before, you might notice that this is a much slower method of drawing, but it is more precise. Now close Paint and deactivate MouseKeys.

To use MouseKeys to close the Paint window:

1. Use the keys on the numeric keypad to move the pointer over the **Close** button ☒ in the Paint window.
2. Press the **5** key to click ☒.
3. Use the keys on the numeric keypad to move the pointer over the **No** button on the Paint dialog box, and then press the **5** key to close Paint.
4. Click the **Use MouseKeys** check box to turn this feature off and then click the **Apply** button.

Simplifying Key Operation with StickyKeys

Many actions performed with the mouse can also be performed by holding down one key while pressing another key. For example, instead of clicking the Start button to open the Start menu, you can use Ctrl+Esc. Key combinations like this one are often called **keyboard shortcuts**. Some users have trouble pressing two keys at once; StickyKeys is a feature that makes it easier. Three keys typically used in conjunction with other keys to perform keyboard shortcuts are the Shift key, the Ctrl key, and the Alt key. These keys are also known as **modifier keys**—you hold them down while pressing another key, to modify the action of the second key.

To more clearly show the effect of StickyKeys, you'll start by using a keyboard shortcut without StickyKeys enabled.

To test the normal behavior of a modifier key:

1. Click the **Control Panel** button on the taskbar to bring the Control Panel window to the foreground if the Accessibility Properties dialog box hides it.

   TROUBLE? If the Control Panel window minimizes instead of coming to the foreground, click the Control Panel button a second time.

2. Press the **Alt** key and then notice the underlined character in each word on the Control Panel menu bar. For example, notice the underlined F in File and the underlined V in View. You can use the underlined character with a modifier key to open the menu.
3. Press and hold the **Alt** key while you press the **F** key. The File menu opens.
4. Press the **Esc** key to close the File menu.
5. Click the Minimize button ▬ to minimize the Control Panel window.

Now try enabling StickyKeys to see how it affects the way you use key combinations.

To turn on StickyKeys:

1. Click the **Keyboard** tab in the Accessibility Properties dialog box to display the keyboard properties.
2. Click the **Use StickyKeys** check box to place a check mark in it.
3. Click the **Apply** button to activate StickyKeys. After a few moments the StickyKeys icon ⌨ appears in the taskbar tray.

Once StickyKeys is enabled, you can press *and release* the modifier key and then press the action key instead of having to hold down the modifier key.

To test the effect of StickyKeys:

1. Click the **Control Panel** button on the taskbar to bring the Control Panel window to the foreground.
2. Press and release the **Alt** key. A sound indicates that a StickyKey has been pressed. The sound and the icon indicate that the next key you press will be combined with the Alt key.

   TROUBLE? If you didn't hear a sound, sounds might not be enabled on your StickyKeys settings or on your computer. To enable sounds, click the Settings button in the Keyboard property sheet and select the sound settings you want.

3. Press the **F** key. The File menu opens again. Because StickyKeys was activated, you did not have to hold down the Alt key while you pressed the F.
4. Press the **Esc** key to close the File menu.
5. Click the **Minimize** button 🗕 to minimize the Control Panel window.
6. In the Accessibility Properties dialog box, click the **Use StickyKeys** check box to remove the check mark, and then click the **Apply** button to deactivate StickyKeys. The StickyKeys icon disappears from the taskbar.

Note that you can also start StickyKeys by pressing the Shift key on your keyboard five times in succession.

Enabling High Contrast

The Display property sheet in the Accessibility Options dialog box lets you set the screen display to high contrast. **High contrast** uses large white letters on a black background and increases the size of the title bar and window control buttons, making objects and text stand out more. If you have limited vision or if you're in a dark office, high-contrast mode can make it easier to see what's on your screen.

To turn on high contrast:

1. Click the **Display** tab in the Accessibility Options dialog box to see the display properties.
2. Click the **Use High Contrast** check box to place a check mark in it.
3. Click the **Apply** button to activate the high-contrast settings. After a short time, the screen changes to the high-contrast display. See Figure B-11. On screens set to a lower resolution, high contrast can make the desktop appear crowded.

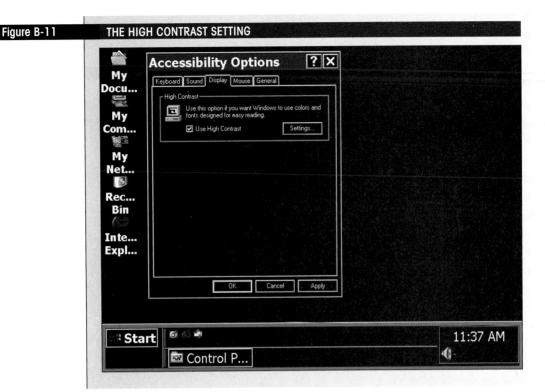

The high-contrast setting affects all programs, but it does not affect the contents of the document window in a program. Now you should return the setting to its original state.

To turn off the high-contrast setting:

1. Click the **Use High Contrast** check box to remove the check mark.
2. Click the **Apply** button to apply the new setting. After a short time the screen returns to the normal display.
   TROUBLE? If the Apply button is hidden behind the taskbar, drag the title bar of the Accessibility window up until you can see the Apply button.
   TROUBLE? If clicking Apply does not return the screen to its normal display, right-click a blank area of the screen, click Properties, click the Appearance tab, click the Scheme list arrow, and then click Windows Standard.
3. To return the taskbar to its normal height, position the pointer over the top edge of the taskbar, then drag the top edge of the taskbar down to the normal height and release the mouse button.

Turning off Accessibility Options Automatically

You can set accessibility features to turn off automatically after the computer sits idle for a period of time. This is ideal for situations such as computer labs, where you want to use accessibility options but other users don't. Windows 2000 automatically turns off an accessibility option if the computer sits idle for a period of time.

To make sure that the accessibility options turn off after a specified period of time:

1. Click the **General** tab in the Accessibility Options dialog box.
2. If the **Turn off accessibility features after idle for:** check box is not checked, click it to activate this feature.
3. You can click the minutes list arrow to select a period of time from 5 to 30 minutes, after which the accessibility features automatically turn off. Study Figure B-12 to see

how you would make sure that the accessibility features turn off after a specified period of time. Don't make this change, however, if you are using a lab computer.

| Figure B-12 | SETTING ACCESSIBILITY OPTIONS TO AUTOMATICALLY TURN OFF |

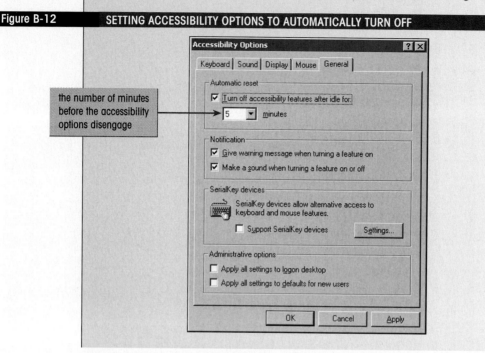

the number of minutes before the accessibility options disengage

Other Accessibility Options

There are other commands in the Accessibility Options dialog box to allow you to set up your computer for users with special needs. Figure B-13 summarizes other Accessibility features.

| Figure B-13 | ADDITIONAL ACCESSIBILITY FEATURES |

ACCESSIBILITY FEATURE	DESCRIPTION	FOUND IN
FilterKeys	Used to ignore brief or repeated keystrokes, or to slow the rate at which keystrokes are repeated	The Keyboard sheet of the Accessibility Options dialog box
ToggleKeys	Used to hear tones when pressing the Caps Lock, Num Lock and Scroll Lock keys	The Keyboard sheet of the Accessibility Options dialog box
SoundSentry	Used to generate a visual warning when your system makes a sound	The Sound sheet of the Accessibility Options dialog box
ShowSounds	Used to tell your programs to display captions for the speech and sounds they make	The Sound sheet of the Accessibility Options dialog box
SerialKey Devices	Used to connect to input devices taking the place of keyboards and mice	The General sheet of the Accessibility Options dialog box

If you want to further refine your accessibility settings, you can use the Accessibility Wizard found by clicking the Start button, pointing to Programs, Accessories and then clicking Accessibility.

Working with Fonts

From the Control Panel you can open the Fonts window, which you use to manage the fonts on your computer. You can open fonts to look at their style and print a test page. You can also install or delete fonts.

The Fonts window shows many more fonts than appear in a program's Font list because there are many fonts that Windows 2000 needs but that are not available to programs.

To view the fonts installed on your computer:

1. Return to the Control Panel window.

2. Click the **Fonts** icon 🄰 and then press the **Enter** key. The Fonts window opens as displayed in Figure B-14.

| Figure B-14 | FONTS WINDOW |

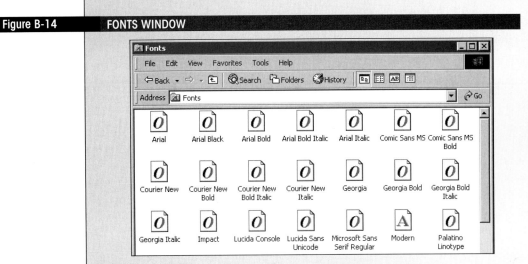

3. To display more details about your fonts, click **View** on the Fonts window menu bar and then click **Details**.

4. Scroll down the list of fonts to see which fonts are installed on your computer.

| Figure B-15 | VIEWING FONTS DETAILS |

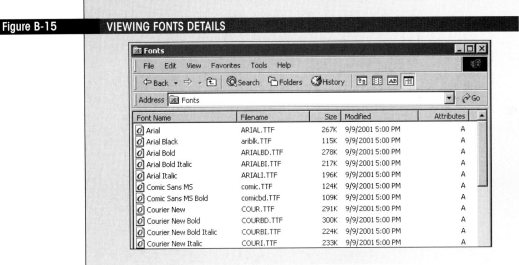

Font Types

In Details view, the Control Panel Fonts window shows you the name of the font and its filename. A **font file** contains the information Windows 2000 needs to display the font or print the font. A font file's name is not necessarily the same as the name of the font itself, as you can see in Figure B-15. The Arial Bold font, for example, is stored in a file named ARIALBD.ttf. To understand what fonts are available in the Fonts window and how you can use these fonts, you need to know about what font types you can use with Windows 2000. Figure B-16 describes the font types.

Figure B-16	FONT TYPES
FONT TYPE	**DESCRIPTION**
Printer fonts	Fonts built into your printer. These are not stored in files on your computer and therefore do not appear in the Fonts window.
Screen fonts	Fonts used by your computer monitor to display the text that appears in dialog boxes, menus, buttons, and icons. Screen fonts are also used when you preview how your document will look when printed. When you create a document in a Windows 2000 program, you choose a font and Windows 2000 tries to match a screen font to it. Screen fonts do not always perfectly match up with the fonts your printer uses. This can cause your documents to print in ways slightly different from what you expect.
TrueType fonts	Fonts capable of both being displayed on your monitor and being printed on your printer with minimal change in appearance. Windows 2000 includes many of these fonts, and you will probably prefer to use them because there is no guesswork involved in how the printout will compare with what you see on the monitor. You can also **scale** a TrueType font—you can enlarge or shrink it without its losing its shape and appearance. You can also rotate a TrueType font.
Postscript fonts	Fonts developed by a company called Adobe that are described by a special language called **Postscript**. You can scale and rotate Postscript fonts, but they require an extra software utility called the **Adobe Type Manager** to be converted into a form that can be displayed on a computer monitor.

You probably noticed as you scrolled through the Fonts window that there are two different kinds of icons that represent fonts. One icon represents TrueType fonts, whereas the other icon represents screen fonts. The filenames for TrueType fonts end with the .ttf file extension, whereas screen font filenames end with .fon, as you can see if your computer's view options are set to display file extensions.

Some fonts use more than one file. For example, Times New Roman uses four files: Times.ttf, Timesbd.ttf, Timesbi.ttf, and Timesi.ttf—Times New Roman, Times New Roman Bold, Times New Roman Bold Italic, and Times New Roman Italic, respectively. When you choose an attribute such as bold or italic from within a program you are actually choosing an alternate file. If you're interested in viewing only the font names, you can use the Hide Variations command on the View menu. The Fonts window hides the font variations, reducing the number of fonts you have to scroll through to find a font.

Font files are widely available. Windows 2000 is shipped with several different TrueType fonts. Many programs, such as Microsoft Office, include fonts, and you can also find them on the Internet or in font collections on disk or CD-ROM.

Opening a Font

You can open a font in the Fonts window to see its characteristics and how it will look in a variety of sizes. One of the fonts that comes with Windows 2000 is Comic Sans MS.

To open the Comic Sans MS font:

1. Right-click the **Comic Sans MS** font icon.

   TROUBLE? If the Comic Sans MS font does not appear in your Fonts window, choose a different font to complete these steps.

2. Click **Open**. A window displays the font in different sizes, along with information about the font and its creator at the top of the window. See Figure B-17.

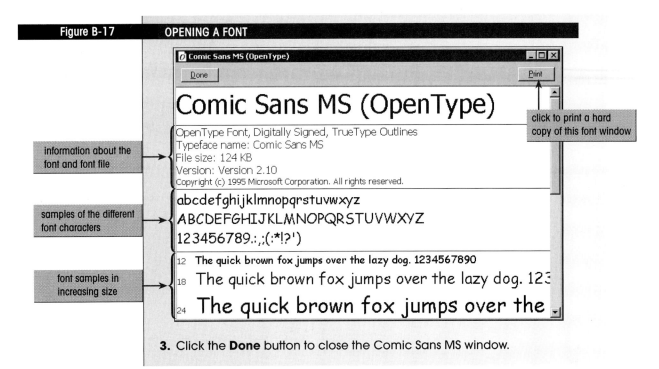

information about the font and font file

samples of the different font characters

font samples in increasing size

click to print a hard copy of this font window

3. Click the **Done** button to close the Comic Sans MS window.

Installing a Font

You can find font files on the Web to use for special documents. All font files must be placed in the Fonts folder on your hard disk. You can install a font using the Install New Font command in the Fonts window.

To install a new font:
1. Click **File** then click **Install New Font**. The Add Fonts dialog box opens. See Figure B-18.

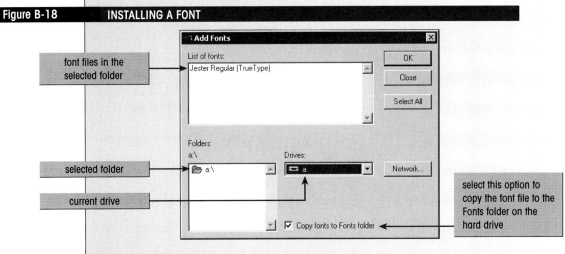

font files in the selected folder

selected folder

current drive

select this option to copy the font file to the Fonts folder on the hard drive

If you needed to install a font, you would select the drive and folder containing the font. It would then appear in the List of fonts box. You would click it and then click the OK button.
2. Click the **Close** button to close the Add Fonts dialog box without installing a font and then close all open windows.

Deleting a Font

Many users collect fonts to give their documents variety. Once you start adding fonts, though, you might find you have many that you don't use often. Fonts take up valuable disk space, so you should periodically delete those you don't need. You can delete a font by clicking the font icon in the Fonts window and then pressing the Delete key.

You need to be careful when you delete fonts, however. A document might use a font you deleted, and then that document would no longer print correctly. You also should not delete fonts with the $\boxed{A}$ icon, because you might inadvertently delete a font that Windows 2000 needs to display objects on the screen. If you are working in a computer lab, it is unlikely that you will be able to delete fonts.

You've completed your work with the Control Panel.

To close the Font window and the Control Panel:

1. Click the **Cancel** button ☒.

Working with the Recycle Bin

Deleting a file is a two-step process. First, you delete the file using an application such as Windows Explorer. The file no longer appears in the contents of the folder or device from which you deleted it. However, Windows 2000 has not actually removed it from the disk. It remains on the disk, and the information about its original location is stored in the Recycle Bin. To delete a file completely from your hard drive, you must empty the Recycle Bin by right-clicking its icon 🗑 in Windows Explorer or the desktop and then clicking Empty Recycle Bin. Emptying the Recycle Bin frees disk space, but do not choose this option unless you are absolutely sure you will no longer need the files.

You can restore a deleted file to its original location by opening the Recycle Bin, selecting the file, and choosing the Restore command. Note however, that you cannot restore files you deleted from a floppy disk or from a network drive, because these are not stored in the local drive's Recycle Bin. Once you empty the Recycle Bin, it is almost impossible to recover the file.

To restore a file from the Recycle Bin:

1. Right-click the **Recycle Bin** 🗑 on your desktop and click **Open**.
The Recycle Bin window opens as shown in Figure B-19.

Figure B-19	THE RECYCLE BIN WINDOW

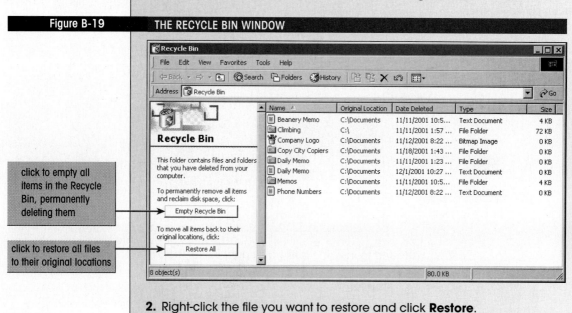

click to empty all items in the Recycle Bin, permanently deleting them

click to restore all files to their original locations

2. Right-click the file you want to restore and click **Restore**.
The file is restored to its original location in your computer.
3. Click the **Close** button ☒ to close the Recycle Bin window.

INDEX

F

**Fast Ethernet standard,
WIN 2000 9.10**

**Fast Forward button, AVI file
format, WIN 2000 8.26**

FAT32, WIN 2000 10.33

**FAT (file allocation table),
WIN 2000 2.03, WIN 2000 3.02,
WIN 2000 10.33**

Favorites folder, WIN 2000 5.16–19

    adding items, WIN 2000 5.17–18

    displaying, WIN 2000 5.16–17

    organizing, WIN 2000 5.18–19

**Favorites pane, Windows Explorer,
WIN 2000 3.04**

**Favorites tab, Help window,
WIN 2000 1.26**

**FDDI (Fiber Distributed Data
Interchange) standard,
WIN 2000 9.10**

file(s), WIN 2000 2.01. *See also*
document(s)

    backing up. *See* backup(s)

    copying, WIN 2000 2.24–25,
      WIN 2000 2.26–27

    cross-linked, WIN 2000 10.34–35

    deleting. *See* deleting files

    destination, WIN 2000 8.08

    displaying, WIN 2000 2.16–17,
      WIN 2000 2.19–20

    downloading, WIN 2000 5.20–21

    embedding portions,
      WIN 2000 8.17–18

    finding. *See* finding files

    finding text strings,
      WIN 2000 6.10–11

    font, WIN 2000 B.13

    fragmented, WIN 2000 10.36–38

    graphic. *See* graphics

    icons, WIN 2000 2.19

    .LOG, creating, WIN 2000 4.05–06

    moving, WIN 2000 2.24,
      WIN 2000 2.25,
      WIN 2000 2.26–27

    names. *See* filenames

    offline. *See* working offline

    opening, WIN 2000 2.11–12,
      WIN 2000 6.08

    previewing, WIN 2000 2.13

    printing. *See* printing

    related, moving to new folder,
      WIN 2000 3.23

    renaming, WIN 2000 2.25–26

    restoring, WIN 2000 11.38–41

    saving, WIN 2000 2.07–10

    selecting. *See* selecting files in
      Windows Explorer

    source, WIN 2000 8.08

    specifying type, WIN 2000 2.09–10

**file allocation table (FAT),
WIN 2000 2.03, WIN 2000 3.02,
WIN 2000 10.33**

file history. *See* **History pane,
Internet Explorer; History pane,
Windows Explorer**

**filenames, WIN 2000 2.07,
WIN 2000 6.06**

    extensions, WIN 2000 2.07

    renaming files, WIN 2000 2.25–26

    specifying, WIN 2000 2.09–10

**file systems, WIN 2000 2.03,
WIN 2000 10.33–34**

file types

    bitmapped graphics,
      WIN 2000 7.12

**file types, finding files by,
WIN 2000 6.16–17**

**Fill With Color tool, Paint,
WIN 2000 7.06,
WIN 2000 7.30–31**

FilterKeys, WIN 2000 B.12

finding. *See* **finding files; Search
Explorer bar; searching; searching for Web pages; Search tool**

finding files, WIN 2000 6.12–18

    by date, WIN 2000 6.15–16

    recent documents,
      WIN 2000 6.18–19

    by size, WIN 2000 6.17

    in specific folders,
      WIN 2000 6.12–13

    by type, WIN 2000 6.16–17

**flipping graphics,
WIN 2000 7.24–25**

floppy disks

    copying, WIN 2000 2.27–28

    formatting. *See* formatting disks

**floppy drives, moving and copying
files, WIN 2000 3.24–27**

folder(s), WIN 2000 2.21–24

    active, WIN 2000 3.08

    creating. *See* creating folders

    displaying in Folders pane,
      WIN 2000 3.06–07

    finding files, WIN 2000 6.12–13

    hierarchy, WIN 2000 2.22–24

    icons, WIN 2000 2.19

    local, WIN 2000 9.18

    moving files between. *See* moving
      files in Explorer window

    navigating through hierarchy,
      WIN 2000 2.22–24

    network. *See* network folders

    offline. *See* working offline

    Outlook Express, viewing,
      WIN 2000 5.42–43

    parent, WIN 2000 2.21

    renaming, WIN 2000 3.10

    selecting. *See* selecting folders

    subfolders, WIN 2000 2.21

    viewing contents, WIN 2000 2.23

**Folder bar, Outlook Express
window, WIN 2000 5.36**

folder icons, WIN 2000 3.06

**Folder Options icon,
WIN 2000 4.41**

TASK	PAGE #	RECOMMENDED METHOD
Accessibility options, set	WIN 2000 B.07	Open the Control Panel, open the Accessibility Option icon [&]
Active Desktop, enable	WIN 2000 5.23	Right-click a blank area of the desktop, point to Active Desktop, click View As Web Page
Active Desktop item, add	WIN 2000 5.23	Right-click a blank area of the desktop, point to Active Desktop, click Customize My Desktop, click Show Web content on my Active desktop, click New, click Yes, click item you want to add, click Add to Active Desktop, click Yes, click OK
Active Desktop item, close	WIN 2000 5.27	Point to item and wait for a title bar to appear, then click [x]
Active Desktop item, move	WIN 2000 5.25	Point to item and wait for a title bar to appear, then drag title bar
Active Desktop item, remove	WIN 2000 5.27	Right-click a blank area of the desktop, point to Active Desktop, click Customize My Desktop, click item, click Delete, click Yes, click OK
Active Desktop item, remove	WIN 2000 5.31	Open the Display Properties dialog box, click the Web tab, deselect the checkbox for the active desktop item
Active Desktop item, resize	WIN 2000 5.26	Point to item and wait for a border to appear, then drag border or border corner
Active Desktop item, schedule an update for	WIN 2000 5.31	See Reference Window: Scheduling an Update
Active Desktop item, synchronize	WIN 2000 5.28	See Reference Window: Synchronizing an Active Desktop Item
Active Desktop item, view an update schedule	WIN 2000 5.28	Move over the top of the item to show the title bar, click the down arrow button in upper-left corner of the title bar, click Properties, click the Schedule tab
Backup, restore files from	WIN 2000 11.39	Open Microsoft Backup, click the Restore Wizard button [icon], and follow the steps of the wizard
Backup wizard, start	WIN 2000 11.34	See Reference Window: Performing a Windows 2000 Backup
Calculator, start	WIN 2000 8.05	Click [Start], point to Programs, point to Accessories, click Calculator
Character, insert	WIN 2000 2.07	Click where you want to insert the text, type the text
Computer, identify on a network	WIN 2000 9.12	Open the Network and Dial-up Connections icon [icon] in the Control Panel, click Advanced on the menu bar, click Network Identification
Computer, lock	WIN 2000 11.14	Press the Ctrl, Alt and Del keys simultaneously, click the Lock Computer button
Computer Management window, open	WIN 2000 11.28	See Reference Window: Opening the Computer Management Window
Control Panel, open	WIN 2000 4.40	Click the Start button [Start], click Settings, click Control Panel

TASK	PAGE #	RECOMMENDED METHOD
Data, transfer using Cut, Copy, and Paste	WIN 2000 8.03	*See* Reference Window: Using Paste to Transfer Data from One Document to Another
Data Disk, create	WIN 2000 2.15	Click **Start** point to Programs, point to NP on Microsoft Windows 2000 – Level I, click Disk 1, click OK
Desktop, access	WIN 2000 1.14	Click the icon on the Quick Launch toolbar
Desktop, change appearance	WIN 2000 4.22	Right-click a blank area of the desktop, click Properties, click Appearance tab, choose a different scheme, or click Item list arrow, change size or color, click OK
Desktop background, change	WIN 2000 4.16	Right-click a blank area of the desktop, click Properties, click Background tab, select pattern or wallpaper you want, click OK
Desktop background, use HTML file for	WIN 2000 5.33	Open the Display Properties dialog box, click the Background tab, click the Browse button, select the HTML file
Desktop color palette, change	WIN 2000 4.29	Right-click a blank area of the desktop, click Properties, click Settings tab, click Colors list arrow, click palette you want, click OK
Desktop document, create	WIN 2000 4.02	*See* Reference Window: Creating a New Document Icon on the Desktop
Desktop document, open	WIN 2000 4.04	Click the document icon
Desktop properties, view	WIN 2000 4.15	Right-click a blank area of the desktop and click Properties
Desktop resolution, change	WIN 2000 4.25	Right-click a blank area of the desktop, click Properties, click Settings tab, drag Screen area slider, click OK
Device, select	WIN 2000 3.08	Click the device icon on the Explorer bar of Windows Explorer
Device Manager, open	WIN 2000 10.07	*See* Reference Window: Opening the Device Manager
Disk, format a	WIN 2000 2.03	Right-click the 3½ Floppy icon, click Format on the shortcut menu, specify the capacity and file system of the disk, click Start
Disk, quick format	WIN 2000 3.02	In My Computer, right-click disk icon, click Format, click Quick Format, click Start
Event log, view	WIN 2000 11.24	*See* Reference Window: Viewing the Event Log
Explorer bar, view	WIN 2000 3.04	In Windows Explorer, or the My Computer window, click View, point to Explorer Bar, click Explorer bar you want
Favorites folder, add a Web page to	WIN 2000 5.17	*See* Reference Window: Adding a Web Page to the Favorites Folder
Favorites folder, organize	WIN 2000 5.19	*See* Reference Window: Organizing the Favorites Folder
Favorites folder, view	WIN 2000 5.16	Click View in Windows Explorer, point to the Explorer Bar, click Favorites
File on the Web, locate by query	WIN 2000 6.24	*See* Reference Window: Searching by Query
File on the Web, locate by subject	WIN 2000 6.26	*See* Reference Window: Searching by Subject

TASK REFERENCE

TASK	PAGE #	RECOMMENDED METHOD
File, copy	WIN 2000 2.24	*See* Reference Window: Moving and Copying a File
File, copy from one floppy disk to another	WIN 2000 3.26	*See* Reference Window: Copying a File from One Floppy Disk to Another
File, delete	WIN 2000 2.26	*See* Reference Window: Deleting a File
File, download from Web	WIN 2000 5.20	In Internet Explorer, right-click file you want to download, click Save As (or Save Picture As, or something similar), enter a location, click OK
File, locate by contents	WIN 2000 6.10	In Search, click the Containing text box, type the text you want to search for, click Search Now
File, locate by date	WIN 2000 6.15	Click the Search Options link, click the Date checkbox, enter the date criteria
File, locate in a specific folder	WIN 2000 6.12	*See* Reference Window: Searching for File in a Specific Folder
File, locate one you were working with recently using the Documents menu	WIN 2000 6.19	Click **Start**, point to Documents
File, move	WIN 2000 2.24	*See* Reference Window: Moving and Copying a File
File, move or copy from floppy disk to hard disk	WIN 2000 3.24	In Windows Explorer, select files on floppy disk you want to move, right-click selection, click Cut or Copy, right-click folder on hard drive, click Paste
File, move or copy with Cut and Paste	WIN 2000 3.21	*See* Reference Window: Moving or Copying Files with Cut, Copy, and Paste
File, move or copy with the Move To and Copy To Folder commands	WIN 2000 3.22	*See* Reference Window: Moving or Copying Files with the Move To Folder and Copy To Folder commands
File, open from My Computer	WIN 2000 2.11	Open My Computer, open the window containing the file, click the file, press Enter
File, open from Search	WIN 2000 6.08	Locate the file using Search, right-click the file in the Results list, click Open
File, open from within a program	WIN 2000 2.12	Start the application, click Open on the File menu, select the file in the Open File dialog box, click Open
File, print	WIN 2000 2.13	Within a program, click 🖨
File, rename	WIN 2000 2.25	*See* Reference Window: Renaming a File
File, save	WIN 2000 2.07	Within a program, click 💾
File, select	WIN 2000 3.14	*See* Reference Window: Selecting Files
File, select all but a certain one	WIN 2000 3.15	*See* Reference Window: Selecting All Files Except Certain Ones

TASK	PAGE #	RECOMMENDED METHOD
File, select in Web style	WIN 2000 3.16	In Windows Explorer or the My Computer window, hover the mouse pointer over the file icon until the icon is selected
File or folder, delete	WIN 2000 3.27	Click the file or folder icon, then press the Delete key
Files, locate by type or size	WIN 2000 6.16	Click the Search Options link, click the Type box or the Size box, enter the search criteria
Files, view as large icons	WIN 2000 2.18	Click View, click Large Icons
Files, view as small icons	WIN 2000 2.18	Click View, click Small Icons
Files, view details	WIN 2000 2.18	Click View, click Details
Files, view in list	WIN 2000 2.18	Click View, click List
Files, view thumbnails	WIN 2000 2.18	Click View, click Thumbnails (Windows Explorer only)
Floppy disk, copy a	WIN 2000 2.28	*See* Reference Window: Copying a Disk
Folder hierarchy, move back in the	WIN 2000 2.23	Click the Back button ⇐
Folder hierarchy, move forward in the	WIN 2000 2.23	Click the Forward button ⇒
Folder hierarchy, move up the	WIN 2000 2.23	Click the Up button 🔼
Folder options, restore default settings	WIN 2000 2.21	Click Tools, click Folder Options, click the General tab, click the Restore Defaults button, click the View tab, click the Restore Defaults button, click OK
Folder or device, share on a network	WIN 2000 9.32	*See* Reference Window: Sharing a Folder with the Network
Folder, create	WIN 2000 2.22	*See* Reference Window: Creating a Folder
Folder, create	WIN 2000 3.09	*See* Reference Window: Creating a Folder in Windows Explorer
Folder, rename	WIN 2000 3.10	Right-click the folder icon, click Rename, type the new folder name
Folder, select	WIN 2000 3.09	Click the folder icon on the Explorer Bar of Windows Explorer
Font, delete	WIN 2000 B.16	Select a font in the Fonts window and then press the Delete key
Font, install	WIN 2000 B.15	In the Fonts window, click File, click Install New Font, locate and install the font file
Font, open	WIN 2000 B.14	In the Fonts window, right-click the font you want and then click Open
Fonts window, open	WIN 2000 B.13	Click 🏁Start, point to Settings, point to Control Panel, right-click Fonts, click Open
Graphic, add text	WIN 2000 7.34	*See* Reference Window: Adding Text to a Graphic
Graphic, change foreground or background color	WIN 2000 7.33	In Paint, click color in color box with left mouse button to change foreground color or with right mouse button to change background color

TASK REFERENCE

TASK	PAGE #	RECOMMENDED METHOD
Graphic, color	WIN 2000 7.30	*See* Reference Window: Filling an Area with Color
Graphic, copy, paste, and move portions	WIN 2000 7.23	*See* Reference Window: Copying, Cutting, and Pasting Graphics
Graphic, crop	WIN 2000 7.07	*See* Reference Window: Cropping a Graphic
Graphic, erase	WIN 2000 7.09	In Paint, click ⟨⟩, drag area you want to erase
Graphic, flip	WIN 2000 7.24	In Paint, click Image, click Flip/Rotate, click option button you want, click OK
Graphic, magnify	WIN 2000 7.16	*See* Reference Window: Magnifying a Graphic
Graphic, save in a different format	WIN 2000 7.13	Click File, click Save As, click Save as type list arrow, click the file type you want, type file name, click Save
Graphic, stretch	WIN 2000 7.26	In Paint, click Image, click Stretch/Skew, enter a stretch or skew percentage, click OK
Grid, show in magnified view	WIN 2000 7.16	In Paint, click View, point to Zoom, click Show Grid
Hard disk, check	WIN 2000 10.35	*See* Reference Window: Running Check Disk
Hard disk, defrag	WIN 2000 10.38	*See* Reference Window: Defragmenting a Disk
Hard disk, schedule maintenance	WIN 2000 10.41	Click ⟦Start⟧, point to Programs, Accessories, System Tools and Schedule Tasks; click Button ⟦◌⟧, select one of the disk maintenance tasks from the wizard
Hardware device list, print	WIN 2000 10.14	Open the Device Manager, click View, click Print
Hardware device properties, view	WIN 2000 10.09	Open the Device Manager, right-click the device's icon, click Properties
Hardware device, install	WIN 2000 10.05	*See* Reference Window: Installing a New Hardware Device
Hardware device, troubleshoot	WIN 2000 10.11	Open the hardware device's properties dialog box, click the General tab, click the Troubleshoot button
Help, display topic from Contents tab	WIN 2000 1.26	From Help, click the Contents tab, click ⟦◆⟧ until you see the topic you want, click ⟦?⟧ to display topicx
Help, display topic from Index tab	WIN 2000 1.27	From Help, click the Index tab, scroll to locate topic, click topic, click Display
Help, return to previous Help topic	WIN 2000 1.28	Click ⟦⇐⟧
Help, start	WIN 2000 1.25	*See* Reference Window: Starting Windows 2000 Help
History pane, display	WIN 2000 3.28	Click View, point to Explorer Bar, click History
History pane, display by most visits	WIN 2000 3.30	Click View in the History pane and click By Most Visited
History pane, display recently opened files in the	WIN 2000 3.31	Click View in the History pane and click By Order Visited Today
History pane, search the	WIN 2000 3.32	Click the Search button in the History pane, enter the search parameters

TASK	PAGE #	RECOMMENDED METHOD
Hibernation, use	WIN 2000 B.02	Open the Power Options Properties dialog box from the Control Panel, click the Hibernate tab, click the Enable hibernate support check box
High Contrast, use	WIN 2000 B.10	Open the Accessibility Options dialog box from the Control Panel, click the Display tab, click the Use High Contrast check box
Icon, change	WIN 2000 8.16	*See* Reference Window: Changing an Icon
Insertion point, move	WIN 2000 2.05	Click the location in the document to which you want to move
Internet Connection, set advanced settings for your	WIN 2000 A.04	Start the Internet Connection Wizard and set up the connection manually, click the Advanced button in Step 3 of the wizard
Internet Connection wizard, start	WIN 2000 A.03	Click ⊞Start, point to Programs, point to Accessories, point to Communications, click Internet Connection Wizard
Internet Explorer, start	WIN 2000 5.06	*See* Reference Window: Starting Internet Explorer
Links, manage and update	WIN 2000 8.22	*See* Reference Window: Managing Links
List box, scroll	WIN 2000 1.23	Click ▼ to scroll down the list box
LOG file, create	WIN 2000 4.05	In Notepad, type .LOG
Menu option, select	WIN 2000 1.08	Click the menu option, or if it is a submenu, point to it
Menu option, select	WIN 2000 1.21	Click the menu option
Mouse double-click speed, set	WIN 2000 B.05	Open the Mouse Properties dialog box from the Control Panel, click the Buttons tab, set the double-click speed, click OK
Mouse pointer speed, set	WIN 2000 B.05	Open the Mouse Properties dialog box from the Control Panel, click the Motion tab, set the pointer speed, click OK
Mouse pointer, change	WIN 2000 B.06	Open the Mouse Properties dialog box from the Control Panel, click the Pointers tab, select a mouse pointer, click OK
Mouse properties, view	WIN 2000 B.04	Open the Control Panel, open the Mouse icon 🖰
MouseKeys, use	WIN 2000 B.07	Open the Accessibility Options dialog box from the Control Panel, click the Mouse tab, click the Use MouseKeys check box
My Computer, open	WIN 2000 2.16	Click My Computer on the desktop, press Enter
Network folder, map to a drive letter	WIN 2000 9.20	*See* Reference Window: Mapping a Network Folder
Network folder, remove drive mapping	WIN 2000 9.22	*See* Reference Window: Removing Drive Mapping
Network folder, view	WIN 2000 9.18	Open the My Network Places icon 🖥️, open a network workstation, open a folder on that workstation
Network place, create	WIN 2000 9.23	*See* Reference Window: Creating a Network Place
Network properties, view	WIN 2000 9.10	*See* Reference Window: Viewing the Properties of Your Network
Network, log off	WIN 2000 9.17	Click ⊞Start, click Shut Down, select Log off [your account name] in the drop-down list box

TASK	PAGE #	RECOMMENDED METHOD
Network, view	WIN 2000 9.05	*See* Reference Window: Viewing your Network Structure
Object, display as icon	WIN 2000 8.14	Right-click object, click Object Properties, click View tab, click Display as icon, click OK
Object, edit in-place	WIN 2000 8.11	*See* Reference Window: In-place Editing
Object, embed using Insert Object	WIN 2000 8.13	*See* Reference Window: Embedding an Object with Insert Object
Object, embed using Paste	WIN 2000 8.09	Select object, cut or copy to the Clipboard, click desired location in destination document, click 📋
Object, embed with different methods	WIN 2000 8.18	*See* Reference Window: Methods of Embedding
Object, link	WIN 2000 8.20	*See* Reference Window: Linking an Object
Object, resize	WIN 2000 8.10	*See* Reference Window: Resizing an Embedded Object
Objects, display or hide in the Folders pane	WIN 2000 3.06	*See* Reference Window: Displaying or Hiding Objects in the Folders Pane
Offline folder, access	WIN 2000 9.27	*See* Reference Window: Accessing an Offline Folder
Offline folder, remove	WIN 2000 9.31	Locate the offline folder in the My Network Places window, right-click the offline folder, deselect Make Available Offline
Offline folder, set up	WIN 2000 9.25	*See* Reference Window: Setting Up an Offline Folder
Outlook Express, receive e-mail from	WIN 2000 5.47	Click the Send/Recv button 📧
Outlook Express, reply to e-mail from	WIN 2000 5.59	Click the Reply button 📧
Outlook Express, send e-mail from	WIN 2000 5.43	*See* Reference Window: Sending an E-mail Message
Outlook Express, set up an e-mail account for	WIN 2000 5.39	*See* Reference Window: Setting up an E-mail Account
Outlook Express, start	WIN 2000 5.36	Click the Start button 🏁 Start , point to Programs, click Outlook Express
Paint, start	WIN 2000 7.05	Click 🏁 Start , point to Programs, point to Accessories, click Paint
Paint tools, use	WIN 2000 7.06	*See* Figure 7-2
Panes, adjust width	WIN 2000 3.10	*See* Reference Window: Adjusting the Width of the Exploring Window Panes
Password, change	WIN 2000 9.15	*See* Reference Window: Changing Your Windows 2000 Password
Pattern, apply to desktop	WIN 2000 4.20	Right-click a blank area of the desktop, click Properties, click Background tab, click Pattern, click pattern you want, click OK, click OK

TASK	PAGE #	RECOMMENDED METHOD
People, locate on the Web	WIN 2000 6.28	Click ▓Start point to Search, click For People, choose the service you want, type the name you want to search for, click Find Now
Power options properties, view	WIN 2000 B.01	Open the Control Panel, open the Power Options icon 🔌
Print queue, pause	WIN 2000 10.28	*See* Reference Window: Pausing the Print Queue
Print queue, remove jobs from	WIN 2000 10.28	*See* Reference Window: Removing Print Jobs from the Print Queue
Print queue, view	WIN 2000 10.26	*See* Reference Window: Viewing the Print Queue
Printer, install	WIN 2000 10.16	*See* Reference Window: Installing a Printer
Printer properties, view	WIN 2000 10.20	Right-click the icon for the printer and then click Properties
Program, close	WIN 2000 1.12	Click ✕
Program, close inactive	WIN 2000 1.14	Right-click program button, click Close
Program, start	WIN 2000 1.10	*See* Reference Window: Starting a Program
Program, switch to another	WIN 2000 1.13	*See* Reference Window: Switching Between Programs
Properties, view	WIN 2000 4.15	Right-click the object, click Properties
Recycle Bin, open	WIN 2000 B.16	Open the Recycle Bin icon 🗑 on the desktop
Recycle Bin, restore file from	WIN 2000 B.16	Open the Recycle Bin, right-click the file you want to restore, click Restore
Results list, sort	WIN 2000 6.14	Display the file list in Details view, click the title buttons on the top of the search results list
Screen, print	WIN 2000 3.18	Press PrintScreen, start WordPad, click 📋, click 🖨
Screen saver, activate	WIN 2000 4.23	Right-click a blank area of the desktop, click Properties, click Screen Saver tab, click Screen Saver list arrow, click OK
ScreenTips, view	WIN 2000 1.07	Position the pointer over the item
Search, clear	WIN 2000 6.13	In Search, click the New button near the top of the left pane
Search, locate by name	WIN 2000 6.05	*See* Reference Window: Searching for a File by Name
Search, start	WIN 2000 6.04	Click ▓Start point to Search, click the option you want
Search page, view on the Internet	WIN 2000 6.20	Click ▓Start point to Search, click On the Internet
Security policy, view	WIN 2000 11.09	*See* Reference Window: Viewing Security Policies
Send To command, copy files with the	WIN 2000 3.25	Right-click the file icon, point to Send To, select the destination of the file
Service list, view	WIN 2000 11.26	*See* Reference Window: Viewing the Service List
Shortcut, create	WIN 2000 4.07	*See* Reference Window: Creating a Shortcut on the Desktop
Shortcut icon, delete	WIN 2000 4.14	Select the shortcut icon, press Delete, click Yes

TASK REFERENCE

TASK	PAGE #	RECOMMENDED METHOD
Start Menu, add an item to	WIN 2000 4.36	*See* Reference Window: Adding an Item to the Start Menu
Start menu, open	WIN 2000 1.07	Click **Start**
Start Menu, remove an item from	WIN 2000 4.38	*See* Reference Window: Removing a Start Menu Item
StickyKeys, use	WIN 2000 B.10	Open the Accessibility Options dialog box from the Control Panel, click the Keyboard tab, click the Use StickyKeys check box
Subfolders, view or hide	WIN 2000 3.07	Click + or −
System performance, graph	WIN 2000 11.16	*See* Reference Window: Graphing System Performance
System performance alert, create	WIN 2000 11.22	Open the Performance window from the Control Panel, double-click Performance Logs and Alerts , click Alerts , enter the name and settings of the alert
System performance log, create	WIN 2000 11.18	Open the Performance window from the Control Panel, double-click Performance Logs and Alerts , click Counter Logs , add an item to track, click the Log Files tab, enter a name for the log file, click OK
Taskbar, moving and resize	WIN 2000 4.29	*See* Reference Window: Moving and Resizing the Taskbar
Taskbar, set properties	WIN 2000 4.30	Right-click the taskbar, click Properties
Taskbar toolbar, create	WIN 2000 4.34	Right-click a blank area on the taskbar, point to Toolbars, click New Toolbar, select the new toolbar
Taskbar toolbar, display	WIN 2000 4.32	*See* Reference Window: Displaying a Taskbar Toolbar
Taskbar toolbar, modify the appearance of	WIN 2000 4.33	Right-click the taskbar, click Properties, modify the properties that apply to the taskbar's appearance
Taskbar toolbar, remove	WIN 2000 4.34	Right-click a blank area on the taskbar, point to Toolbars, deselect the toolbar from the list
Test page, print	WIN 2000 10.21	*See* Reference Window: Printing a Test Page
Text, select	WIN 2000 2.06	Click and drag the pointer over the text
Toolbar button, select	WIN 2000 1.22	Click the toolbar button
Toolbars, control display	WIN 2000 2.17	Click View, point to Toolbars, select the toolbar options you want
Thumbnail, show in magnified view	WIN 2000 7.17	In Paint, click View, point to Zoom, click Show Thumbnail
Thumbnails, view your graphic files as	WIN 2000 7.38	In Windows Explorer, click View, click Thumbnails
Unneeded files, delete	WIN 2000 10.31	*See* Reference Window: Removing Unneeded Files
UPS device, configure	WIN 2000 B.03	Open the Power Options Properties dialog box from the Control Panel, click the UPS tab, set the UPS options, click OK
User group, create	WIN 2000 11.07	*See* Reference Window: Creating a User Group

TASK	PAGE #	RECOMMENDED METHOD
User properties, set	WIN 2000 11.05	Open the Users and Passwords dialog box from the Control Panel, click the icon for the user, click Properties, change the desired settings, click OK
User, create	WIN 2000 11.03	*See* Reference Window: Adding a New User
User, remove	WIN 2000 11.13	*See* Reference Window: Removing a User
Video clip, change settings	WIN 2000 8.27	Right-click video clip, click Linked Video Clip Object if an OLE object, click Edit (or just click Edit), change the desired settings, click OK
Video clip, play	WIN 2000 8.24	Right-click video clip object or file, click Linked Video Clip Object if an OLE object, click Play, or just click Play
Wallpaper, use graphic image	WIN 2000 4.21	Right-click a blank area of the desktop, click Properties, click Background tab, click Browse, locate and select file, click Open, click OK
Web page, activate link	WIN 2000 5.09	In Internet Explorer, click link on Web page
Web page, open with URL	WIN 2000 5.08	*See* Reference Window: Opening a Page with a URL
Web page, print	WIN 2000 5.20	In Internet Explorer, view page, click File, click Print, click OK
Web page, return to previous	WIN 2000 5.13	In Internet Explorer, click the Back button
Wildcards, use to find files by name	WIN 2000 6.09	Start Search, type search string in the "Search for files or folders named" box, using ? in place of single characters and * in place of multiple characters
Window, close	WIN 2000 1.18	Click ☒
Window, maximize	WIN 2000 1.18	Click ☐
Window, minimize	WIN 2000 1.18	Click ▬
Window, move	WIN 2000 1.20	Click and drag the title bar
Window, resize	WIN 2000 1.20	Click and drag ↖
Window, restore	WIN 2000 1.18	Click ❐
Windows 2000, shut down	WIN 2000 1.15	Click Start, click Shut Down, click the Shut Down option button, click OK
Windows 2000, start	WIN 2000 1.04	Turn on the computer
Windows Explorer, start	WIN 2000 3.03	Click Start, point to Programs, point to Accessories, click Windows Explorer
Workstation properties, view	WIN 2000 9.07	Right-click the icon representing the workstation, click Properties

File Finder

Location in Tutorial	Name and Location of Data File	Student Saves File As...	Student Creates New File
WINDOWS 2000 LEVEL I, DISK 1 & 2 **Tutorial 1**	No Data Files needed.		
Tutorial 2 Session 2.1			Practice Text.doc
Session 2.2 *Note:* Students copy the contents of Disk 1 onto Disk 2 in this session.	Agenda.doc Budget2001.xls Budget2001.xls Budget2002.xls Exterior.bmp Interior.bmp Logo.bmp Members.wdb Minutes.wps Newlogo.bmp Opus27.mid Parkcost.wks Proposal.doc Resume.doc Sales.wks Sample Text.doc Tools.wks Travel.wps Practice Text.doc *(Saved from Session 2.1)*		
Review Assigments & Projects	*Note:* Students continue to use the Data Disks they used in the Tutorial. For certain Assignments, they will need a third blank disk.	Woods Resume .doc *(Saved from Resume.doc)*	Letter.doc Song.doc Poem.doc
WINDOWS 2000 LEVEL II, DISK 3 **Tutorial 3** Session 3.1	[16 files] Clients(folder) Advanced (folder) [4 files] Alpine (folder) [3 files] Ice (folder) [2 files] Sport (folder) [2 files] Basic (folder) [4 files] Gear (folder) [3 files] Guides (folder) [3 files]	[16 files] Clients(folder) Advanced (folder) [4 files] Alpine (folder) [3 files] Ice (folder) [2 files] Sport (folder) [2 files] Basic (folder) [4 files] Gear (folder) [3 files] Hardware (folder) Ropes and Harnesses (folder) Guides (folder) [3 files]	Gear (folder) Hardware (folder) Ropes and Harnesses (folder)

File Finder

Location in Tutorial	Name and Location of Data File	Student Saves File As...	Student Creates New File

Session 3.2	(Continued from Session 3.1)	[4 files]
		Clients(folder)
		    Advanced (folder)
		      [4 files]
		    Alpine (folder)
		      [5 files]
		    Ice (folder)
		      [2 files]
		    Sport (folder)
		      [2 files]
		    Basic (folder)
		      [13 files]
		Gear (folder)
		    Hardware (folder)
		    Ropes and Harnesses (folder)
		      [5 files]
		Guides (folder)
		    [3 files]	

Session 3.3	No Data Files needed.		
Review Assignments and Projects			C:/Advertise A:/All Clients
Tutorial 4 Session 4.1	Same files used as in Session 3.2.		Phone Log.txt
Session 4.2	Logo.bmp		
Session 4.3	No Data Files needed.		

Review Assignments and Projects			Classes.txt
			A:/Sally (folder)
			    Smith.txt
			    Arruga.txt
			    Kosta.txt
			A:/My Signature.bmp

Tutorial 5 Session 5.1	No Data Files needed.		lake.jpg
Session 5.2	Highland.htm [15 supporting files]		
Session 5.3			Highland.htm [15 supporting files]

Tutorial 6
Session 6.1
	Alphabet (folder)
	    [25 files]
	Authors (folder)
	    [25 files]
	Comedy (folder)
	    [18 files]
	Images (folder)
	    [2 files]
	Social (folder)
	    [16 files]
	Topics (folder)
	    [19 files]		

Session 6.2	No Data Files needed.		
Review Assignments and Projects	Same as Session 6.1		

File Finder

Location in Tutorial	Name and Location of Data File	Student Saves File As...	Student Creates New File
WINDOWS 2000 LEVEL II, DISK 5, 6			
Tutorial 7			
Session 7.1	Sports.bmp		Skis.bmp Skis256.bmp
Session 7.2	Skis2.bmp Brush.bmp Mountain.bmp	Skis.bmp Kiana.bmp Mountain and Sun.bmp	
Session 7.3	(Continued from Session 7.2)		
Review Assignments	Sports.bmp Kiana.bmp	Kiana2.bmp	Bowling Ball.bmp Tennis Rackets.bmp Rings.bmp Skier.bmp
Projects	Sports.bmp		Letter J.bmp Fonts.bmp Sailboat.bmp Chess.bmp Chess with Text.bmp
Tutorial 8			
Session 8.1	Maria.doc		Feedback.rtf
Session 8.2	Pins.bmp Pins10.bmp Icon.bmp		
Session 8.3	Pins2.bmp Video.avi		
Review Assignments	Maria.doc Tailor.doc Election.bmp Clowning.doc Chester.bmp		Happy Birthday.wav Birthday Message..rtf
Projects	IRS.txt New.doc House.doc House.bmp Kennedy.wav Paint.bmp		Linguistics.rtf Carpet.bmp CarpetMaster Estimate.rtf Ranch Flyer.rtf
Tutorial 9			
Session 9.1	No Data Files needed.		
Session 9.2	No Data Files needed.		
Review Assignments & Projects	The instructor will supply Data Files.		
Tutorial 10			
Session 10.1	No Data Files needed.		
Session 10.2	No Data Files needed.		
Session 10.3	(Use the Data Disk used for Tutorial 8.)		
Review Assignments & Projects	No Data Files needed.		
Tutorial 11			
Session 11.1	No Data Files needed.		
Session 11.2	Need blank, formatted disk		
Session 11.3			Test1.txt Test2.txt Test3.txt Backup.bkf

File Finder

Location in Tutorial	Name and Location of Data File	Student Saves File As...	Student Creates New File
Review Assignments & Projects			Interrupt.blg
Appendix A	No Data Files needed.		
Appendix B	No Data Files needed.		